Fifth Edition

Criminology

A Canadian Perspective

Rick Linden
University of Manitoba

THOMSON

NELSON

D1275246

Australia   Canada   Mexico   Singapore   Spain   United Kingdom   United States

THOMSON

NELSON

Criminology: A Canadian Perspective
Fifth Edition

by Rick Linden

Editorial Director and Publisher:
Evelyn Veitch

Executive Editor:
Joanna Cotton

Marketing Manager:
Lenore Taylor

Senior Developmental Editor:
Edward Ikeda

Permissions Coordinator:
Patricia Buckley

Production Editor:
Wendy Yano

Copy Editor:
Wendy Thomas

Proofreader:
Matthew Kudelka

Indexer:
Elizabeth Bell

Production Coordinator:
Hedy Sellers

Creative Director:
Angela Cluer

Interior Design:
Peter Papayanakis

Cover Design:
Angela Cluer

Cover Image:
Photonica

Compositor:
Carol J. Anderson

Printer:
Transcontinental

National Library of Canada Cataloguing in Publication Data

Criminology: a Canadian perspective / [edited by] Rick Linden.—5th ed.

Includes bibliographical references and index.
ISBN 0-17-622479-3

1. Criminology—Canada I. Linden, Rick.

HV6807.C76 2003   364.971
C2003-904434-3

To Christopher, who gave so much and asked so little
and
Dan Koenig, a wonderful colleague and friend

Brief Contents

Contents

PART 3: PATTERNS OF CRIMINAL BEHAVIOUR   407

CHAPTER 14 Conventional or "Street" Crime   408
Daniel J. Koenig, Formerly of University of Victoria
Rick Linden, University of Manitoba

CHAPTER 15 Organized Crime   444
Rodney T. Stamler, Assistant Commissioner RCMP (Rtd)

CHAPTER 16 Corporate and White-Collar Crime   480
John Hagan, University of Toronto

Preface

Since it was first published in 1987, *Criminology: A Canadian Perspective* has been used to introduce this field to more than 50 000 students across the country. At that time, most criminology courses in Canada were taught using American texts. It was our intention to provide a text that was written *by* Canadians, *for* Canadians. Over the past three decades, the discipline of criminology has grown from a few widely scattered faculty members to a large community of academics, researchers, practitioners, and students. The fifth edition of *Criminology: A Canadian Perspective* continues to reflect their work. That said, criminology remains a small and underfunded discipline in Canada. As a result, much of the new theoretical and empirical work in the field continues to come from the United States and Europe. This fifth edition represents our continued effort to provide you with the best Canadian scholarship in combination with the most relevant research from other countries.

Advantages of a Multiauthored Text

The many different theories proposed to explain criminality are continually being revived and revised. Often the popularity of a particular theory owes as much to ideological commitment and academic fashion as it does to the explanatory power of the theory. As a result of this unresolved diversity, the pages of many texts are littered with the bodies of straw men, set up only to be sacrificed to the author's favourite approach. The authors of this text are among Canada's leading criminologists. The advantage of having such a multiauthored text is that the diverse perspectives of criminology can be fairly represented. In this book, each chapter is written by someone who has used the perspective in his or her own research and who understands its strengths and weaknesses.

Organization of the Text

This book is intended as a text for a one-term course in introductory criminology. While the book deals extensively with theories about the causes of crime (which have largely been developed elsewhere), its purpose is to provide students with information about crime in Canada.

The chapters of this text have been organized into three parts. Part 1, "Crime and Society," provides some of the basic information about crime: the sources of criminal law; the legal elements of crime; the sources of information about crime; the social correlates of criminal behaviour; and a discussion of women and crime. This part provides the student with the background necessary to assess the theories of crime causation presented in Part 2. In this part, entitled "Explanations of Crime," all the major theories are covered, including biological, psychological, and sociological explanations. In Part 3, "Patterns of Criminal Behaviour," many of the most serious and frequent types of crime are discussed. The way we have arranged the chapters is our suggestion for presenting the material, but instructors are encouraged to assign these chapters in whatever order best suits their course needs.

Features of the Text

Each chapter begins with a brief *Introduction* and a list of *Learning Objectives* and concludes with a *Summary, Questions for Critical Thinking, Net Work* (an Internet activity), a list of *Key Terms, Suggested Readings*, and a *Bibliography*. This text also features *Web Links* to interesting related websites, a *Running Glossary*, which defines the key terms in the margin next to the paragraph in which they first appear, and a full *Glossary* at the end of the text.

The following ancillary products are also available to augment teaching and learning inside and outside the classroom and to facilitate testing: a printed and computerized test bank, a study guide, PowerPoint slides, and a website (www.lindencriminology5e.nelson.com).

New to the Fifth Edition

This edition of *Criminology: A Canadian Perspective* provides us with the opportunity to update crime statistics, to add new research material, and to make some major revisions that have been suggested by reviewers. These major revisions include two new chapters and significant changes to several others.

The book begins with a new chapter that introduces students to the discipline of criminology and discusses the regulation of behaviour, the definition of crime, and the conflict and consensus theories of law. Chapter 3 is a new chapter on criminal law written by Simon Verdun-Jones. This chapter highlights the impact of the *Charter of Rights and Freedoms* on the law and on legal procedure.

Major revisions have been made to Chapter 6 ("Women and Crime"), Chapter 14 ("Conventional or 'Street' Crime"), and Chapter 16 ("White-Collar and Corporate Crime"). Chapter 6 has been reorganized and includes new material dealing with the connections between a woman's law violations and her history of abuse and with the claim that women are as likely as men to commit domestic violence. Chapter 14 has been extensively revised. The chapter now includes an expanded section outlining the routine activities approach and new discussions of the dynamics of several offences, including homicide and robbery. There is a new section on auto theft and several new boxes. Chapter 16 includes new material documenting the extent of corporate and white-collar crime and discussing the recent Enron and WorldCom frauds. Chapter 16 ends with an extensive discussion of different types of occupational crimes.

ACKNOWLEDGEMENTS

It has become traditional for authors to thank families for not making demands, and spouses, or close friends, both for moral support and for those unspecified but essential services that writing seems to require. Since my wife and children had already reached their tolerance limit with my work schedule, I decided that I couldn't just disappear into my office and reappear two years later with a book. Thus it is to them that I owed my wise decision to get help from the friends and colleagues who co-authored the text. For the time I did spend writing, I thank for their support Olive, Brad, Chris, Robin, Shawn, T.J., and Amanda. By the time of the fourth edition, all my children were old enough that they no longer cared about my working hours. However, their place at my work table has been taken by pets, and I thank Nicholas, Morris, Annie, and Edward for ensuring that each page in this manuscript has been stepped on or slept on by an orange cat.

Working with the people at Nelson has been a delightful experience. For significant improvements in this fifth edition, I thank Joanna Cotton, Edward Ikeda, and Wendy Yano.

Special thanks to the reviewers who have given us good advice over the various editions: Bill Avison, Marilyn Belle-McQuillan, Thomas Bernard, Augustine Brannigan, David Brownfield, Tullio Caputo, Elaine DeCunha-Bath, Sange de Silva, Robert Drislaine, Karlene Faith, Thomas Gabor, Colin Goff, Jim Hackler, Sheilagh Hodgins, Carl Keane, Gail Kellough, John Martin, Robynne Neugebauer, Gary Parkinson, Michael Petrunik, Karen Richter, Vincent F. Sacco, Les Samuelson, Bernard Schissel, Alfredo Schulte-Bockholt, Phillip C. Stenning, Lee Stuesser, Diane Symbaluk, and Austin T. Turk.

I would also like to thank each of the authors who contributed to the book. I appreciate your enthusiastic responses to revision suggestions and your efforts to meet deadlines. I continue to enjoy and to learn from your work.

Individual authors wished to make the following acknowledgements: J. Evans and A. Himelfarb (Chapter 4)—"The authors wish to thank the Canadian Centre for Justice Statistics for providing much of the data presented in this chapter. Tim Foran, Gordon MacKay, and Peter Morrison were particularly helpful." T.F. Hartnagel (Chapter 5)—"I wish to thank Kerri Calvert of the Sociology Information Centre, University of Alberta, for her help in locating references and generally keeping me informed of recent material. I also wish to acknowledge the research assistance of Marianne Nielson, Hannah Scott, Cora Voyageur, and Xavier Cattarinich, who helped me with the various editions of this text."

Rick Linden
University of Manitoba

Crime and Society

This part provides some basic information about crime: the origins of our criminal law, the legal elements of crime, the sources of information about crime, and the social correlates of criminal behaviour.

Chapter 1 introduces you to the discipline of criminology, which is the scientific study of crime and criminals. This chapter explores the role played by rules and shows how these rules are sometimes formalized in laws. The chapter also looks at several different ways of defining crime and points out that because crime is socially defined, the definition of crime can change over time.

In Chapter 2, we learn how our system of law has developed as we have evolved from simple hunting and gathering societies to modern industrial ones. With the increased complexity and growth of modern societies comes the need for a formal legal system to maintain order. We also learn why some social harms are defined as illegal, while others are not.

The legal elements of a crime are *actus reus* (the physical element) and *mens rea* (the mental element). These are discussed in Chapter 3, along with defences available to an accused, a history of criminal procedure, and an outline of the social factors affecting the definition of specific types of crime.

We cannot study crime systematically unless we can measure it. Chapter 4 details some of the ways we count crime, such as official government statistics, victimization surveys, and self-report surveys. None of these methods is completely adequate; you will learn the strengths and weaknesses of each.

Before we can explain a phenomenon such as crime, we must know something about the way it is distributed demographically. In Chapter 5, a number of correlates of crime are discussed, including age, sex, race, and social class. In recent years, there has been an increased recognition of the importance of looking at the issue of women and crime. Because of this, Chapter 6 considers the correlate in more depth. The explanations of crime discussed in Part 2 may be judged according to how well they account for these regularities.

Crime, Criminals, and Criminology

RICK LINDEN
University of Manitoba

Canadians seem to have an endless fascination with crime. Our daily newspapers and television news programs are saturated with stories about crime and criminals. Movies, television shows, and video games are often filled with depictions of violence and other criminal behaviour. While crime is a matter of public concern and a favourite form of entertainment, it is also the subject of serious academic study. This chapter will introduce you to the discipline of criminology, which is the scientific study of crime and criminals.

LEARNING OBJECTIVES

After reading this chapter, you should be able to

- Define the term *criminology.*
- Understand the different subject areas studied by criminologists.
- Explain the role played by rules in our daily lives and understand how these rules can become formalized in law.
- Understand the different ways of defining crime. These are a strict legal definition, an expanded legal definition that goes beyond just considering the criminal law, a definition based on the protection of people's human rights, and a definition that places acts of deviance and crime on a continuum ranging from minor acts of deviance to serious offences that almost everyone agrees are wrong.
- Explain how crime is socially defined and how people's ideas about crime can change over time.
- Understand the two main theoretical perspectives on how some acts get defined as criminal and others do not. These are the conflict and consensus perspectives.

Robert and Danny Sand grew up in an Alberta family with their father, Dennis, and their mother, Elaine. Robert was born in 1978 and Danny was born in 1980. Dennis Sand, who had served time in jail in his youth for a variety of crimes including armed robbery, gave up crime when he was 20 and later supported his family by doing a variety of jobs. Now in his late 40s, he lives in Westlock, Alberta, where Elaine runs a karaoke business, and both are well thought of by other members of the community (Staples, 2002). As youngsters, Robert and Danny had lots of energy and were constantly in trouble along with several of their closest friends who made up a group composed of the only mixed-race boys in their town. The boys had difficulty in school and often refused to do any work. Their misbehaviour couldn't be controlled by their parents and the boys were frequently suspended from school. By junior high they began to get into more serious trouble and often tried to intimidate other students. The boys' behaviour came to the attention of the police, and at age 15 Danny was sent to a youth centre for beating up another student. They began to steal cars and to use a variety of drugs, including crack cocaine. Newspaper reporter David Staples described the situation of the brothers and their friends:

> Their contact with adults was minimal. No teachers, because the teens had all dropped out. No parents, because most didn't live at home. They relied on each other to figure out the world, believing their friends were closer and wiser than any adult. They're all there to protect each other, and they can't see past that, says [one of the mothers]. The teens suffered from the moral blindness of those who have achieved nothing in life and have nothing to lose. But they weren't entirely lacking in vision. They had an inkling of the difference between right and wrong. They certainly understood when someone did wrong to them, or to one of their closest friends. They just didn't see it as a problem to rob or injure someone outside of their group. It was us vs. them, with them being teachers, the RCMP, car owners, property owners, anyone with something they wanted to grab. (Staples, 2002, D2)

In 1998, after several armed robberies and a lengthy police chase, Robert received a seven-year jail sentence. He became a model inmate, though counsellors said he could never explain why he had behaved the way he did. Danny also ended up in jail for a number of crimes, including attacking a police officer. After his release, Danny got involved in another incident that foretold the crime that would end in his death. An Edmonton police officer used his cruiser car to block an alley where Danny Sand was suspiciously parked in a stolen truck. Instead of giving up, Danny sped toward the cruiser and seemed to swerve toward the police officer. After this incident, he joined Robert in Drumheller Penitentiary, where he continued to get into trouble and where he acquired a stomach tattoo saying "Fearless, Painless, Senseless." After his release Danny told people that he would never go back to jail.

In October of 2001, Robert was released to an Edmonton halfway house. He could find only menial work and began to fear that he had cancer. He reunited with Laurie Bell, a former girlfriend who was a very heavy drug user. He left the halfway house, which meant that he had broken his parole and would be pursued by the police. On December 18, Robert and Laurie, along with Danny, who was also violating his parole, headed for the Maritimes where they had vague plans for making a new life. They never made it past Manitoba.

In the midst of a crime spree that included robbing a bank, breaking into homes, and stealing several vehicles, the three made it to the town of Russell, Manitoba. Shortly after midnight on December 21, Danny drove onto the main highway without first stopping at a stop sign. When RCMP constables Brian Auger and Dennis Strongquill tried to stop the vehicle because of this violation, Robert fired several shotgun blasts at the police. When the police drove away, Danny chased the police SUV into town. He rammed the SUV after it stopped at the Russell RCMP Detachment. Robert jumped out of their truck and fired several shotgun blasts at Constable Strongquill, who was trapped in the damaged police vehicle. Four of the shots hit Constable Strongquill and he died almost immediately.

After an extensive manhunt, the RCMP found the trio at a motel near Wolseley, Saskatchewan. A police sniper fatally wounded Danny Sand, and Robert Sand and Laurie Bell were captured and charged with first-degree murder. While in prison awaiting trial, Robert kept a diary in which he reflected on the shooting:

> I was in one of my moods so I asked to see the pictures again of my case. There are pics of trucks burnt, crashed shot up etc. Homes broken into, property of ours and others and of course pics of the dead cop, shot up cop cars and Dan. Now I've seen them before and without emotion, I've no more tears to shed. But I was looking at this man, on a table. And I started to think, he's just a man, and shouldn't be dead. He had a family and friends, and now he's a body on a table. I realized it's not the man I hated, but the uniform he wore. His flag, colours of war. But seeing him without his uniform I felt bad for the loss of his life. But then I flipped to the pics of Dan, and my thoughts changed. Cause now I felt that the other man is right where he should be. And losses on both sides are to be expected, only Dan took my place. And when I looked upon the cop car I felt pride, and remembered the battle, I remembered how these enemy soldiers fled in fear and cowardess. I saw how much damage I'd caused to their unit and smiled, from the knowledge that the enemy isn't as strong as they want us to believe. But they should beware that the moment they fly their flag, wear their uniform. That they're at war and people die in war, everyone has their enemies.

Robert Sand, who physically attacked his own lawyer in court at the end of his trial, is now serving a life sentence after being convicted of first-degree murder; Laurie Bell was convicted of manslaughter.

One of the challenges of the discipline of criminology is to make sense of cases such as this one. Why did the Sand brothers live such wild and undisciplined lives? Why did they aggressively pursue Constable Strongquill and his partner? Why did Robert see the world as a war zone? Is there anything we can do to prevent tragedies like this in the future?

More specifically, criminologists have considered a wide range of theories to explain crime, and you will learn about many of these theories in this text. Some focus on biology—could Robert and Danny have inherited traits from their parents that made their criminality more likely? Others look at an individual's psychological make-up—were the Sand brothers psychopaths or could other mental conditions have caused their behaviour? Other theories are sociological—what role did their family and friends play in their violence? Could the schools have done a better job motivating the brothers to study and to become involved in legitimate outlets for their energy? What role did racism and the brothers' poor economic prospects play in their lives?

These questions are very complex and we may never be able to adequately explain individual cases such as this one. However, even if we could explain the factors that led Robert Sands to kill Constable Strongquill, would the same explanation apply to another homicide case that was being dealt with at the same time as Robert Sands was facing the court on murder charges? Diego Zepeda-Cordera, a Toronto barber, was a member of the Missionary Church of Christ (Galloway, 2003). His 19-year-old son, Walter, began to behave in a way that troubled Zepeda-Cordera, who was very devoted to his religious beliefs. Walter began to go out to bars, he smoked, and he wouldn't help out around the house. His parents found a satanic magazine in his room. His father became extremely concerned when Walter began to speak in gibberish at a religious meeting. Believing his son was possessed by the devil, Mr. Zepeda-Cordero and a friend tied Walter to two metal chairs in their apartment building. Their minister and many church members came to the home to pray over Walter in order to exorcise the devil they believed was inside him. Walter remained tied to the chairs, often with duct tape over his mouth, for seven days before he died of dehydration. Although the judge in the case believed that the men genuinely thought Walter was possessed and sought to help him, he sentenced them to four years in jail after they pleaded guilty to manslaughter.

As these two examples suggest, there are many different patterns of homicide that have little in common other than the death of a victim. Some involve intoxicated people who stab friends during drinking parties; others involve a settling of accounts among organized criminals; some abusive men kill their wives and children; some corporate executives kill their customers by selling defective products in order to enhance their profits, while others kill their employees by providing unsafe working conditions; and some predators kill children after having sex with them. In your criminology course, you will learn about these and many other patterns of criminal behaviour.

WHAT IS CRIMINOLOGY?

The term **criminology** is used in a number of different ways. Detectives in mystery novels and forensic scientists and crime analysts on television shows are sometimes referred to as criminologists. The term is also sometimes applied to physicists and chemists who specialize in studying the trajectories of bullets or the characteristics of the ink used in counterfeit money. Most commonly, the term is applied to academics who study and teach about crime and the criminal justice system. In this text, we will follow the definition of the discipline given by two famous American criminologists, Edwin Sutherland and Donald Cressey: "Criminology is the body of knowledge regarding crime as a social

criminology
The body of knowledge regarding crime as a social phenomenon. It includes the processes of making laws, breaking laws, and reacting to the breaking of laws. Its objective is the development of a body of general and verified principles and of other types of knowledge regarding this process of law, crime, and treatment.

phenomenon. It includes within its scope the processes of making laws, of breaking laws, and of reacting to the breaking of laws.... The objective of criminology is the development of a body of general and verified principles and of other types of knowledge regarding this process of law, crime, and treatment" (1960, 3). This definition implies that criminologists take a scientific approach to the study of crime.

Why Should We Study Crime?

There are three reasons why it is important for us to know more about crime. First, social scientists feel that it is intrinsically worthwhile to understand more about all aspects of our social lives, including criminal behaviour and society's response to this behaviour. Learning about crime can tell us a great deal about our society. For example, the United States has a much higher rate of violent crime, particularly firearms crime, than Canada. The United States also has a much harsher justice system than Canada (see Box 12.1). These differences highlight important value differences between the two countries. Similarly, changes in the patterns of crime over time can help us to identify and to understand changes in our society. Second, if we wish to reduce crime we need to understand it. Just as an understanding of a disease helps medical scientists to develop cures, we must understand crime in order to prevent it. For example, criminologist Richard Tremblay conducted several studies tracking the behaviour of children in Montreal as they grew up. One of his more interesting findings was that boys whose violent behaviour had not followed the normal pattern of declining by age 16 were more likely than other boys to be the sons of young mothers with low levels of education. Based on this research, he has worked with the Quebec government to develop support programs for mothers who fit these risk profiles to see if this support will help to reduce the criminality of their children (Blumstein, 2003). Finally, crime directly or indirectly affects all of us. Many of us have been victims of crime and all of us pay for the costs of crime and the crime control system. Also, many Canadians are employed in the justice system or in security-related businesses.

The Discipline of Criminology

The discipline of criminology includes six major areas: the definition of crime and criminals; the origins and role of law; the social distribution of crime; the causation of crime; patterns of criminal behaviour; and societal reactions to crime.

The Definition of Crime and Criminals

Not all social harms are criminal nor are all criminal acts harmful. Thus it is necessary to specify what kinds of acts are defined as crimes. Also, while it might at first seem obvious, there is also some question concerning who should be defined as criminals for purposes of criminological research. For example, should we include someone who has been charged with a criminal offence but has not been convicted? What about the person who has committed a criminal offence but not been charged? And how about the person who has been convicted

Criminal Code of Canada
laws.justice.gc.ca/en/C-46/index.html

Crime and the Media

Most Canadians learn about serious crime through the media rather than from first-hand experience. Stories on television and radio and in newspapers, magazines, and books shape our views about crime and criminals. However, the media provide a highly distorted picture of crime. Writers of television series and movies use violence to attract viewers and to sell tickets. Newspaper editors and television reporters also select the crime news we hear about and construct the way in which this news is presented to us in order to attract an audience.

Unfortunately, the picture of crime we receive from the media is very inaccurate. For example, while most crime is property crime, most stories in the media deal with violent crime. Typical of research in this area was a review of all the crime-related stories reported over two months in an Ottawa newspaper (Gabor, 1994). Over half the stories focused on violent crimes, particularly murders. However, violent crimes made up only 7 percent of reported crimes in Ottawa, and the city averaged just six murders per year. While violent crimes were over-reported, property crimes rarely received much attention, and white-collar and political crimes were almost never discussed. Between 1990 and 1996, the homicide rate in Canada declined by almost 20 percent while the murder coverage on CBC and CTV national television news programs increased by 300 percent. Calgary had 12 murders in 1996, a year in which the *Calgary Herald* published 1667 murder-related stories (National Media Archive, 1997).

The portrayal of crime in the fictional media is even more distorted. Consider the partial list of the 221 violent acts depicted in *South Park: Bigger, Longer & Uncut*, the recent R-rated movie based on the animated series *South Park*, and ask whether the list reflects the reality of the lives of today's young people:

130 weapons fire (with multiple killings), 18 electric shocks, 10 blows to the body, 8 blood spatterings, 3 burnings, 3 hanging-body scenes, 1 breaking of body in half, 1 assault

with chain saw, 1 attempted electrocution, and 1 dog attack. (Media Index, 1999)

Why do the media misrepresent crime? The primary goal of the media is to make profits by selling advertising. Stories that attract viewers or readers will boost ratings and circulation even if these stories do not represent the reality of crime. The informal news media rule "If it bleeds, it leads" reflects the fact that the public is fascinated by sensationalized, bloody stories such as mass murders or attacks against helpless senior citizens. Commenting on his experience with the media, the executive director of the Nova Scotia Bar Society said, "If there's no blood and gore, or there's no sex, it's not newsworthy. And if it falls into the category of being newsworthy, then they have to show the dead body. They've got to show the corpse" (McCormick, 1995, 182).

The media's misrepresentation of crime has several consequences. First, Canadians greatly over-estimate the amount of violent crime and have a fear of crime that is higher than the actual risk of victimization. Crime stories lead us to see Canada as a violent and dangerous place although it is in reality a very safe country. Second, the media provide us with a distorted stereotype of offenders. Violent crimes are most often committed by relatives, friends, and acquaintances, not by the anonymous stranger so many of us fear. Consider even our image of the mass murderer. Everybody in Canada knows about Clifford Olson and Paul Bernardo. However, few recognize the names of mining executives Clifford Frame, Gerald Phillips, and Roger Parry, who may have been responsible for the deaths of 26 miners in the 1992 Westray Mine disaster in Stellarton, Nova Scotia. Our fear of crime and our image of the criminal have an impact on government policy toward crime. Actual crime trends are irrelevant—if the public feels crime is out of control, it demands that government do something about it. Although crime rates are declining, a combination of increasing media coverage of crime and pressure from a variety of interest groups has led the federal

(continued)

government to tighten several laws, including those dealing with immigration, young offenders, and firearms.

The media may also contribute to crime. There is some evidence that children who are exposed to a great deal of television violence are more likely to be violent themselves, but this linkage is complex and people disagree about the degree to which television influences behaviour rather than simply reflecting an interest in violence. However, there is some anecdotal evidence that the media do play a role in individual cases. For example, Virginia teenager Josh Cooke was a fan of the movie *The Matrix*. He had a large poster from the film in his room and had a trench coat like the one worn by Neo, the character Keanu Reeves played in the movie. He also bought a shotgun similar to one used by Reeves in his movie fight against the "agents." In 2003, Cooke used the shotgun to kill his father and mother and then turned himself in to the police. His defence is that he was attempting to escape the matrix. Several other killers across the United States have also claimed to be affected by *The Matrix*, and two of these accused have been found not guilty by reason of insanity (Jackman, 2003). Lee Boyd Malvo, the young man accused of being one of the Washington snipers, has written,

> Wake up! Free your mind, you are a slave to matrix "control"... The outside force has arrived. Free yourself of the matrix "control". Free first your mind. Trust me!! The body will follow. Remove fear, doubt, distrust, watch the change then. (Jackman, 2003, 3)

While it is obvious that most people who see movies such as *The Matrix* do not commit murders, many researchers believe that media exposure can influence people who are already vulnerable or predisposed to commit violence.

of violations of laws governing a safe workplace after an employee was killed on the job, when these laws are not part of the Criminal Code?

The Origins and Role of the Law

It is important to understand the social origins of our laws as well as the role that law plays in society. Why do some acts get defined as criminal, while others are dealt with under other types of legislation or are not sanctioned at all?

The Social Distribution of Crime

In order to understand crime we must know such things as the characteristics of people who commit crimes; trends in the occurrence of crime over time; and differences between cities, provinces, and countries in the rates and types of crime. These and other dimensions of the social distribution of crime help criminologists to understand the causes of crime.

The Causation of Crime

One of the most important questions for criminologists is why some people commit crimes, while others live more law-abiding lives. In this text you will learn about a wide variety of explanations of criminal behaviour ranging from the biological to the individual to the social.

Patterns of Criminal Behaviour

Criminal acts are defined by law in particular categories such as homicide, theft, and sexual assault. Criminologists have conducted a great deal of research analyzing the patterns of these offences. Among the questions asked by criminologists are these: Who are the offenders? Who are the victims? Under what social circumstances are offences most likely to take place? What are the consequences for the victims of crime? How can particular types of crime be prevented?

Societal Reactions to Crime

Historically, societies have responded to crime in many different ways, and the issue of how best to deal with offenders is an important one. In our society we normally process law violators through a criminal justice system that includes the police, the courts, and the corrections system. Criminologists have studied each of these institutions very extensively.

Overview of the Book

In the first three chapters of this text you will learn about the definition of crime and criminals and about the origins of law and the legal system. Chapter 4 describes how we obtain data about crime and criminals and Chapter 5 outlines the social distribution of crime in Canada. Chapter 6 deals with issues involving women and crime and introduces you to some of the theories that criminologists have developed to explain crime. Chapters 7 to 13 deal with early theories of crime and its causation, and with biological, psychological, and sociological explanations of criminality. The last section of the book deals with patterns of crime, including conventional or "street" crime (Chapter 14), organized crime (Chapter 15), and corporate and white-collar crime (Chapter 16). This text will not discuss the police, courts, and corrections because at most colleges and universities the operation of the criminal justice system is usually covered in a separate course.

RULES AND LAWS

The Regulation of Behaviour

All groups have rules that guide their members' behaviour. Society cannot function without them—if we are to live and to work with others, rules are necessary. We must also have a reasonable expectation that other people will obey the rules. Think of the chaos that would result if each driver decided which side of the road she would drive on each day, or which stop sign he would decide to obey. Most of the time most of us conform to the **norms** our group prescribes. Of course, not all members of the group obey all the time. All of you have broken many rules, perhaps some of them important ones. In this text, we shall consider the topic of crime—behaviour that breaks the rules. How do rules get established? Why do people break them? How do groups respond to this violation?

norms

Established rules of behaviour or standards of conduct.

We learn most rules so well that we follow them without thinking about them. Following accepted ways of walking and talking is almost automatic as these norms have been internalized. Often we cannot even specify all the rules that govern a particular behaviour, we just follow them. For example, when you try to learn a foreign language you suddenly become aware of all sorts of rules, such as those governing verb tenses, that you aren't consciously aware of when you are using English. Other rules are not followed in this routine fashion. Many of us may wish to drive above the speed limit, park illegally, or use marijuana but refrain from doing so because of our fear of penalties. Others may break these rules whenever they get a chance.

Think of some of the informal rules (or folkways) that govern your conduct. When you were younger, your parents probably tried to persuade you to eliminate some of your favourite habits such as eating with your fingers, dipping food in your milk, and banging your toys on the furniture. These are very basic rules—others can be more complex. For example, how do you address the Queen or the Lieutenant-Governor if you meet them? Whose name do you mention first when you introduce your 22-year-old spouse to your 60-year-old employer? What are we to make of these rules that seem, on their face, to be trivial or silly? Rules help us to select from the vast numbers of potential behaviours of which we are capable. Do we bow, kiss, or shake hands as a greeting? Which of two persons holds a door for the other? Who gets served first and last at dinner? How do we handle the important milestones in life such as marriage and death? While the way each society solves these little problems may vary widely, each society has provided solutions. Not only do these solutions avert potential chaos, but following the rules enhances our sense of belonging. The penalties for not following these rules are normally informal ones—the disapproval of family, friends, or colleagues or perhaps a reprimand from an organization to which the violator belongs. However, we normally don't think of the penalties, but continue to obey these rules because we have been taught to obey them and because they are part of belonging to the group.

In our society, not all actions are governed only by these informal means of social control. Why do some informal rules become more formal regulations or laws? Consider the early days of the automobile. Driving was not regulated and the only rules of the road were those that applied to horse-drawn carriages. When automobiles were open and speeds slow, drivers gave right of way to other drivers who had higher social status, just as was done when walking down the street. However, as speeds became higher and as drivers ranged farther from their homes, this became impractical, and the state had to establish more formal regulations. In this and in many other cases, we might say that the law exists when order can no longer be maintained through informal rules. The law also deals with behaviour that is too serious to be left to informal mechanisms.

What Is a Crime?

As you will read in Chapter 2 (The Origins and Role of Law in Society), the concept of crime has been developed relatively recently. That does not mean that people didn't do harmful things to one another in earlier times, but this harmful behaviour was handled quite differently than it is now. Prior to the 18th century, in most societies offences were handled privately by the wronged individual and his or her family. The early courts in Europe and North America dealt with religious and civil law rather than with criminal law.

The Legal Definition of Crime

The most common **definition of crime** is a *legalistic* one that defines a crime as an act that violates the criminal law and is punishable with jail terms, fines, and other sanctions. This legal definition is satisfactory for most purposes and will fit most of the crimes discussed in this text. However, some criminologists have argued for a sociological definition of crime that encompasses a broader range of harmful behaviour than this strict legal definition provides. Among the strongest advocates of this broader approach have been Edwin Sutherland, Herman and Julia Schwendinger, and John Hagan.

Is White-collar Crime Really Crime?

Edwin Sutherland was one of the most important figures in the development of the discipline of criminology and you will read about his work on crime causation later in this text. In his famous presidential address to the American Sociological Association in 1939, Sutherland (1940) argued that focusing only on violations of the criminal law had led criminologists to present a misleading picture of crime. Limiting criminological research to offences that were dealt with in the criminal courts, such as burglary, assault, and theft, led to the conclusion that crime was primarily a lower-class phenomenon. However, Sutherland pointed out that many **white-collar crimes** were committed by middle- and upper-class people in the course of their business activities. Criminologists neglected these crimes because they were not dealt with by the criminal courts:

> The crimes of the lower class are handled by policemen, prosecutors, and judges, with penal sanctions in the form of fines, imprisonment, and death. The crimes of the upper class either result in no official action at all, or result in suits for damages in civil courts, or are handled by inspectors, and by administrative boards or commissions, with penal sanctions in the form of warnings, orders to cease and desist, occasionally the loss of a license, and only in extreme cases by fines or prison sentences. (Sutherland, 1940, 8)

Sutherland argued that even though they may not be dealt with in criminal court, the great harm caused by white-collar criminals made it imperative that criminologists study them. Thus he was suggesting that the legal definition of crime be expanded to encompass the violation of other types of laws.

Human Rights Violations as Crime

Another attempt to expand the definition of crime was made by Herman and Julia Schwendinger (1970), who advocated a definition of crime based on **human rights** rather than on legal statutes. If an action violated the basic rights of humans to obtain the necessities of life and to be treated with respect and dignity, criminologists should consider it a crime. Thus government policies that create poverty and homelessness should be studied as crimes along with other practices that cause social harm, including imperialism, sexism, and

legal definition of crime
Crime is an act that violates the criminal law and is punishable with jail terms, fines, and other sanctions.

white-collar crime
Crime that is committed by middle- and upper-class people in the course of their legitimate business activities.

human rights
The minimum conditions required for a person to live a dignified life. Among the rights set out by the Universal Declaration of Human Rights are the right to life, liberty, and security of the person; the right to be free of torture and other forms of cruel and degrading punishment; the right to equality before the law; and the right to the basic necessities of life.

Universal Declaration of
Human Rights
www.un.org/Overview/rights.html

racism. Advocates of this critical or humanistic approach feel that the criminal law has been established by those who control the power in society so that acts committed by powerful people are not criminalized and the law is biased against the poor. The Schwendingers' proposal explicitly places criminology on the side of the poor and powerless. While this approach has not received a great deal of support from other criminologists, it does play a useful role in drawing attention to the way in which we view social harms.

A Continuum of Crime and Deviance

While few criminologists today would limit their work to the strict legal definition of crime, most would also not make the definition as broad as the human rights approach would suggest. John Hagan (1985) has proposed another approach to defining crime that reflects the way most criminologists view their discipline. Hagan says that a definition of crime must encompass not only violations of the criminal law, but also "a range of behaviors that for all practical purposes are treated as crimes (e.g., Sutherland's white-collar crimes), as well as those behaviors that across time and place vary in their location in and outside the boundaries of criminal law. In other words, we need a definition that considers behaviors that are both actually and potentially liable to criminal law" (1985, 49). Hagan proposed that deviance and crime be considered as a continuum ranging from the least serious to most serious acts. Seriousness can be assessed on three dimensions:

- *The degree of consensus that an act is wrong.* Most people feel that mass murder is wrong, but there is much less agreement over the issue of using marijuana.

- *The severity of the society's response to the act.* Murder is punishable by death in some societies and life imprisonment in others. On the other hand, possession of small amounts of marijuana may be ignored by the police, and in 2003 the government proposed to decriminalize this behaviour.

- *The assessment of the degree of harm of the act.* Drug use, illegal gambling, and prostitution are often considered to be "victimless" crimes that harm only the offender, while crimes of violence are considered to be very harmful.

Although these three dimensions are normally closely related, this is not always the case. For example, the operators of the Westray mine, whose unsafe practices resulted in the death of 26 miners in Nova Scotia, caused a great deal of harm (see Box 16.1). However, even though most Canadians would probably agree that this negligence was wrong, none of the people responsible for the mine were penalized for their actions. This approach recognizes that "the separation of crime from other kinds of deviance is a social and political phenomenon" (Hagan, 1985, 49) and allows criminologists to consider a broad range of behaviours, including some types of deviance that may not be against the law. Hagan's approach is illustrated in Figure 1.1, which shows four major categories of crime and deviance: consensus crimes; conflict crimes; social deviations; and social diversions. Although this text will not specifically consider social devia-

FIGURE 1.1 Hagan's Varieties of Deviance

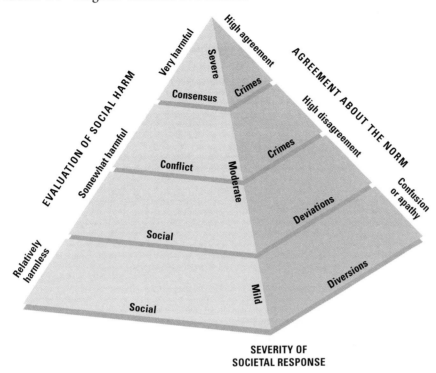

Source: John Hagan. (1991). *The Disreputable Pleasures: Crime and Deviance in Canada,* 3rd ed. Toronto: McGraw-Hill Ryerson, p. 13. Reprinted by permission.

tions and social diversions, the distinction between consensus and conflict crimes is an important one that will be discussed in several chapters of this text.

Crime Is Socially Defined

Can you think of any type of behaviour that everybody condemns? Most people might consider killing another person to be an act that is always evil, but this is not the case. Soldiers are considered heroes for killing the enemy during time of war. Society allows police officers to kill under some circumstances, and all of us have the right to kill a person who is threatening us with lethal force. Even those who commit what most of us would call murder are not always classified as murderers by the courts. For example, a man may kill his neighbour and be found not guilty by reason of insanity. If the same man were sane but intoxicated at the time of the offence, he might be found guilty only of manslaughter. Even for an act as serious as killing another person, we must understand the social context of the act before we can determine whether it is deviant and how it should be classified.

Just as murder is socially defined, so are other types of crime and other forms of deviance. An act is deviant only from the point of view of a set of rules and regulations, and these vary widely from society to society and from group to group. There are some broad similarities in acts that are defined as deviant.

For example, most societies, most of the time, frown upon members killing one another or plotting the violent overthrow of the government. However, there are also great differences between societies and within societies over time. Some societies consider as unlawful many acts that are tolerated or even encouraged in Canada while others permit practices that we restrict. For example, in Saudi Arabia women are not permitted to drive cars or wear short skirts, in Singapore it is unlawful to possess chewing gum (it creates messy streets and transit vehicles), and on some French beaches it is unlawful to wear clothes. All these practices are quite acceptable here. On the other hand, Canada and most western countries have laws against helping a terminally ill person to commit suicide (see Box 3.2), while in Holland doctor-assisted suicide is common.

Thus there is nothing inherent in any act that makes it unlawful. We can define deviance as behaviour that violates the rules, whatever those rules may be. However, this definition leaves us with problems. Whose rules are to be followed? Consider the case of the Muslim father living in Winnipeg who went to court because he wanted his 14-year-old daughter to marry her 27-year-old fiancé. However, such a marriage is not permitted by Manitoba law, which sets the minimum age for marriage at 16 (*Winnipeg Free Press*, 1993). Thus, behaviour that is normative from the father's perspective is considered deviant from the province's perspective. What about a person who belongs to an outlaw motorcycle gang? Behaviour that conforms to the standards of the group will often violate the rules of the broader society. The same is true of those who use terrorism to fight what they feel is an unjust political system. If the revolution is successful, they will be heroes. Many political leaders, including Menachem Begin of Israel, Fidel Castro of Cuba, and China's Mao Tse-tung, began their political careers by using violence to achieve power. However, if the revolution fails, the leaders will be killed or imprisoned. This important question of "Who sets the rules?" will be discussed more fully later in this chapter.

The Relativity of Crime

Another implication of the fact that crime is socially defined is that the rules can change. A situation in the United States a few years ago highlighted just how relative the law can be. Because of pressure from the federal government, a number of states raised their legal drinking age from 18 to 21. At least one state did this in stages, with the drinking age rising one year each January 1. In a television interview, one university student whose 18th birthday was in late November described what he was facing for the next three years. Each year, he would be able to legally drink alcohol from his November birthday until midnight on December 31. Since the drinking age changed with the new year, he had to return to soft drinks until the following November when he turned 19. This would go on every year until he was 21, which meant that he could legally drink for less than 6 months out of the 36 months between his 18th and 21st birthdays.

A more important example is the fact that only a few decades ago, the sexual acts of gays and lesbians were prohibited by the Criminal Code and subject to maximum penalties ranging from five to fourteen years, depending on the specific act (Rodgers, 1962). When former prime minister Pierre Trudeau was the

Minister of Justice, he declared that the "state has no place in the bedrooms of the nation" and removed these sections from the Criminal Code. Since that time there have been dramatic changes. Gays and lesbians now have most of the rights of married couples and as this chapter is being written, the federal government is preparing legislation to legalize same-sex marriages following an Ontario court decision that made such marriages legal in that province.

These examples point out the fact that criminal and non-criminal are not two distinct categories. There is an overlap between the two, and the line between them can be very ambiguous. We often speak as if the world were divided between criminals and noncriminals. However, we have all broken the law at times—does this mean we are "criminals"? In fact, phrases like "everybody does it" are used to justify crimes that are committed by "respectable" people, including stealing from employers, not reporting tips and other income on tax forms, downloading music and movies, and copying software (Gabor, 1994). How do people draw the line between respectable citizens who occasionally do bad things and those they consider "criminals"? What are the consequences of thinking of crime as being a matter of degree?

WHO MAKES THE RULES? CONFLICT VERSUS CONSENSUS THEORIES OF LAW

Of course the law is not completely subjective. Many criminal laws reflect serious social harms that are illegal in most societies and that most people condemn. However, as you have learned, the exact form of the laws and the specific behaviour prohibited vary greatly in different places and at different times. Why do some acts become subject to criminal sanctions while others do not?

One of the most important questions in the study of criminology is "Who sets the rules?" Who decided that selling marijuana is illegal, while selling cigarettes is a respectable business? Who determines that an impaired driver who causes the death of a pedestrian is severely sanctioned, while an employer whose violation of workplace safety rules causes death may receive only a small fine? We have seen that rules can take many different forms, so the issue of how rules come to have a specific content is an important one. There have been two distinct approaches to this question, the consensus and conflict perspectives.

The Consensus Approach

Following the work of the famous 19th-century French sociologist Émile Durkheim, **consensus theorists** believe that law represents the consensus of the people. That is, the law is simply a codification of the **values** shared by most members of a society. For example, several Muslim countries have institutionalized sharia law, which is explicitly based on the Koran, so the law reflects those societies' religious values. Similarly, many of the early European settlers in the United States were Puritans who left England for the colony of Massachusetts so that they would be free to practise their religious beliefs. Not surprisingly, the legal code of the new colony reflected these beliefs. Much of their legal code of

Department of the Solicitor General of Canada
www.sgc.gc.ca

Department of Justice Canada
canada.justice.gc.ca

consensus theory

Laws represent the agreement of most of the people in society that certain acts should be prohibited by the criminal law.

value

A collective idea about what is right or wrong, good or bad, and desirable or undesirable in a particular culture.

1648 was taken directly from the Bible, and many crimes were punishable by death. These capital crimes included "idolatry, witchcraft, blasphemy, bestiality, sodomy, adultery, rape, man stealing, treason, ... cursing or smiting of a parent, stubbornness or rebelliousness on the part of a son against his parents, and homicide committed with malice prepense, by guile or poisoning" (Haskins, 1969, 37). Of course, religious values are not the only ones enshrined in law, but they do illustrate how values become codified in law.

Support for the consensus view is also found in the fact that there is a broad agreement regarding many laws, particularly those that deal with street crimes such as robbery, burglary, and murder. Several studies have asked people to rate the seriousness of a broad range of criminal offences. These studies have demonstrated that there is considerable agreement among people from Canada and the United States concerning the rankings of these offences (Normandeau, 1966, Akman et al., 1967).

The Conflict Approach

class conflict theory

Laws are passed by members of the ruling class in order to maintain their privileged position by keeping the common people under control.

Conflict theorists do not share the view that our laws reflect a consensus of members of society. This is particularly apparent in the work of **class conflict theorists**, who take the view that laws are passed by members of the ruling class in order to maintain their privileged position by keeping the common people under control. Activities that threaten those with power are defined as illegal, and the legal mechanism of the state is used to enforce the laws. One example from Canada's early history shows how the law can be used to further the aims of the politically powerful at the expense of the common people. After the Riel Rebellion in 1885, Hayter Reed, the assistant commissioner of Indian Affairs, used his powers under the Indian Act to control the Aboriginal population. He deposed many of the chiefs he felt were disloyal and undermined the authority of other chiefs and headmen by instructing his staff to deal directly with individuals and families rather than with the bands. He also confined Indians to their reserves by ordering the implementation of a pass system that had no justification in law:

> Officials of the [North West Mounted Police] were never comfortable with the absence of any legal foundation for the pass system. The lack of a legal basis in this case undermined the validity of all NWMP operations: they were trying to demonstrate to the Indians that the police enforced a rational system of laws that operated to the benefit of all.... In 1893 a circular letter was issued directing all police officers to refrain from ordering Indians without passes back to their reserves.
>
> Hayter Reed would have none of these weak-kneed, legalistic concerns. He urged the police to continue enforcing the pass system on the grounds that the "moral responsibilities of the Indian Department transcended treaty obligations." Reed's views triumphed. By at least 1896 the police had reversed their position. In that year Commissioner Herchmer issued a circular letter instructing police who encountered any Indian without a pass to "use all possible pressure to persuade him to return to his reserve."(Carter, 1990, 153–54)

The pass system was eventually ended, but it did restrict the movement of Indians for 20 years. In this case, the law was used to restrict the movement of those who represented a threat to those holding power—the government and the white settlers who were moving onto the Prairies.

Consensus and conflict theories each provide explanations of the formation and persistence of some laws. However, as Hagan's definition of crime suggests, neither provides a complete explanation. While the majority of the populace does support many laws, some do benefit the powerful at the expense of the rest of us. Others fit in neither category. For example, there is no consensus in our society about the propriety of abortion, gambling, prostitution, or marijuana use, but laws regulating these behaviours do not reflect any particular class interest. Thus some feel that the most accurate way of describing the process of law formation is group conflict theory. This perspective recognizes that all laws are the result of a political process, and that this process typically involves a conflict or a debate between different interest groups. You will learn more about these theories later in this text.

SUMMARY

- The term *criminology* is used in a number of ways. In this text it will refer to the body of knowledge regarding crime as a social phenomenon. It includes within its scope the processes of making laws, breaking laws, and reacting to the breaking of laws. The objective of criminology is the development of a body of general and verified principles and of other types of knowledge regarding this process of law, crime, and treatment.

- The discipline of criminology includes six major areas. These are the definition of crime and criminals; the origins and role of law; the social distribution of crime; the causation of crime; patterns of criminal behaviour; and societal reactions to crime.

- Our behaviour is strongly influenced by norms, many of which we have internalized. Much of the time we don't even consciously think about the rules that govern our behaviour. Most of the time, rules are enforced through informal means such as the disapproval of our family and friends. However, in some cases the rules are formalized into laws.

- The strict legal definition of crime is an act that violates the criminal law and is punishable with jail terms, fines, and other sanctions. Sociologists have expanded this definition in a number of different ways. In his discussion of white-collar crime, Sutherland said that criminologists should also include violations of other types of laws in addition to criminal law. The Schwendingers proposed that crime be defined as a violation of human rights. Hagan felt that criminologists should consider deviance and crime as a continuum ranging from the minor acts of deviance to serious crimes.

- Crime is socially defined. No behaviour is inherently good or evil, and we must understand the social context of an act before we can determine whether it is deviant and how it should be classified. Also, the form of laws and the specific behaviour that is prohibited vary greatly in different places and at different times.

■ Consensus theorists believe that laws represent the will of most of the people in a particular society. On the other hand, conflict theorists feel that law reflects power relationships in society, as those with power use to the law to help maintain their position. Some laws fit each of these perspectives.

QUESTIONS FOR CRITICAL THINKING

1. Look at Figure 1.1 (see page 13), which shows different types of crime and deviance. Can you think of examples of behaviours that fit into each of the four categories (consensus crimes, conflict crimes, social deviations, and social diversions)? How can particular behaviours move from one category to another? Can you think of examples of behaviours that have moved from one category to another?

2. Look at the way your local newspaper handles crime stories. What picture of crime in your community is provided by the newspaper? If you have a tabloid paper (such as the *Toronto Sun*, the *Winnipeg Sun*, or the *Vancouver Province*) in your community, does it handle crime stories in a different manner from other newspapers?

3. Think of a law people are currently lobbying to change. What kind of changes to the law are being advocated? Why do some people want to change the law? If anyone is resisting the legal change, why are they offering this resistance? What do you think will be the outcome of this attempt at legal change?

4. Discuss some of the advantages and disadvantages of the Schwendingers' suggestion that crime be broadly defined as a violation of human rights.

5. Many college and university students have used drugs, and some who work as restaurant servers do not declare all of their income on their tax forms. Should these students be called criminals? Why do you feel they should or should not be called criminals?

NET WORK

A group led by criminologist Delbert Elliott has established a website dedicated to the prevention of violence. The groups has assessed over 600 violence prevention programs and has selected a small number that have a demonstrated ability to reduce violence. Go to the website for Blueprints for Violence Prevention at **www.colorado.edu/cspv/blueprints/model/overview.html**. Look at three of the model programs that have been selected by the project. For each of these programs, can you determine what aspect of the child's social environment the program planners are trying to change? What does the success of the three programs you have selected tell you about the causes of crime?

KEY TERMS

class conflict theory   legal definition of crime
consensus theory   norms
criminology   value
human rights   white-collar crime

BIBLIOGRAPHY

Akman, D.D., A. Normandeau, and S. Turner. (1967). "The Measurement of Delinquency in Canada." *Journal of Criminal Law, Criminology and Police Science* 58:330–37.

Blumstein, Alfred. (2003). "The Kid Whiz: Richard Tremblay." *Time* May 26:54.

Carter, Sarah. (1990). *Lost Harvests.* Montreal: McGill-Queen's University Press.

Gabor, Thomas. (1994). *Everybody Does It: Crime by the Public.* Toronto: University of Toronto Press.

Galloway, Gloria. (2003). "Parents Sentenced for Exorcism Gone Wrong." globeandmail.com. www.theglobeandmail.com/servlet/story/RTGAM.20030522.ue. Accessed May 28.

Hagan, John. (1985). *Modern Criminology: Crime, Criminal Behaviour, and Its Control.* New York: McGraw-Hill.

Haskins, George Lee. (1969). "A Rule to Walk By." In Richard Quinney (ed.), *Crime and Justice in Society* (pp. 33–54). Boston: Little, Brown and Company.

Jackman, Tom. (2003). "Murder Defendants Claim Connection with Hit Movie." HoustonChronicle.Com.   www.chron.com/cs/CDA/printstory.hts/nation/1923147. Accessed May 28.

McCormick, Chris. (1995). *Constructing Danger: The Misrepresentation of Crime in the News.* Halifax: Fernwood Publishing.

Media Index. (1999). "South Park Gets Nasty at Record-Setting Pace." *Austin American-Statesman,* July 16:E1.

National Media Archive. (1997). "T.V. Coverage Down: Murder Rate Up Slightly." *On Balance* 10(7). Vancouver: The Fraser Institute.

Normandeau, Andre. (1966). "The Measurement of Delinquency in Montreal." *Journal of Criminal Law, Criminology, and Police Science* 57:172–77.

Rodgers, R.S. (1962). *Sex and Law in Canada: Text, Cases and Comment.* Ottawa: Policy Press.

Schwendinger, Herman, and Julia Schwendinger. (1970). "Defenders of Order or Guardians of Human Rights." *Issues in Criminology* 5:123–57.

Staples, David. (2002). "Fearless, Painless, Senseless: The Sand Brothers." *Edmonton Journal,* March 31: D1.

Sutherland, Edwin. (1940). "White-Collar Criminality." *American Sociological Review* 5:1–12.

Sutherland, Edwin, and Donald Cressey. (1960). *Principles of Criminology,* 6th ed. Philadelphia: J.B. Lippincott.

Winnipeg Free Press. (1993). "Law, Religion Clash over Child Marriage." (September 24).

2

The Origins and Role of Law in Society

RODNEY KUENEMAN
University of Manitoba

People in all forms of human society have disputes, and every human group has developed mechanisms for restoring social order. Today the law plays a prominent role in the restoration process, but not all communities have relied on formally enacted laws that are enforced by the power of a state. In small-scale societies, victims or their relatives were responsible for settling disputes, and the major goal of dispute settlement processes was to restore harmonious relationships between the conflicting parties. In this chapter, you will learn how our system of formal laws has developed.

After reading this chapter, you should be able to

LEARNING OBJECTIVES

- Trace the changes from community-based dispute resolution processes in small-scale societies to state-controlled processes in more complex societies.
- Explain why knowledge of social context is important in understanding the existence and the operation of different dispute settlement systems.
- Understand the emergence and consolidation of social and economic power in human societies and how the consolidation has made it difficult to control the actions of those who have power.
- Explain why the rule of law has become a primary force in modern societies and understand the limitations of law as a means of controlling behaviour.
- Understand the importance of restorative dispute settlement processes in small-scale societies and explain why they are once again becoming popular.

Throughout most of human existence, we lived in small hunting and gathering communities. Cooperation, mutual aid, and kinship within these communities were the essential means of preserving harmony and restoring order. The absence of a centralized power structure meant that these communities had to rely on these different mechanisms to keep the peace. One of the tasks of this chapter is to show how different dispute settlement mechanisms can be understood only within their social context. As patterns of societal organization changed, different forms of dispute settlement emerged. The general role of dispute settlement processes in all societies is the restoration of order; however, the nature of these different social orders and the groups who have received the most benefit from order within them have changed significantly. As we shall see, dispute settlement processes are intimately involved in the structuring of social relationships.

This textbook is about crime. It is important to realize that crime does not exist in all societies. In a technical sense, a crime is a violation of a law, and not all societies have had formulated laws. While each society has had to develop a moral order complete with stated expectations for acceptable behaviour, not all societies have developed laws to restrain their members. The formulation of law requires the existence of a central body such as a **state** that develops law and enforces compliance with it. This is not only a matter of semantics. For much of human history, social order was maintained by other means. It is equally important to note that criminal law, as we know it, has not been part of the social fabric for most of human history. Harms between individuals were resolved by various forms of redress in societies without a state. Even in societies with a state apparatus, many disputes are regulated by civil law. Under civil law, the state adjudicates between the parties to the dispute in an effort to repair the damage. Criminal law comes into existence at the point when the state declares itself to be the injured party for certain types of infractions. In its narrowest sense, criminology is concerned with this limited subset of laws and social infractions. But in order to understand the broad question of social order, it is important to see criminal law within a historical and social context that considers the full spectrum of dispute settlement practices.

Finally, it is important to reflect on the human condition. The human animal does not rely on the use of instincts. In place of the instincts that order so much of the lives of other animals, human beings must fashion their collective stability by way of culture. While humans share common emotional, intellectual, and motivational attributes, they have produced an amazing variety of solutions to the problems they have faced. Equipped with a powerful imagination, members of our species have introduced both inspiring and terrifying innovations to their communities. This human imagination has contributed to the development of human culture. But it is also a principal source of instability that has threatened to erode, weaken, and destroy the social fabric it has created. Humans have the ability to create disputes and to upset social arrangements. Law and other forms of dispute settlement are at the heart of our efforts to limit and to recover from the harm that is inflicted. Although there are many differences between societies, each social order must be recognized as a response to the need to construct a moral, or at least a legal, order.

It will not be possible here to provide a detailed description and analysis of the vast array of human cultures. Instead, our inquiry will examine two patterns of social organization.

state

As defined by Max Weber (1864–1920), the state is an institution that claims the exclusive right to the legitimate exercise of force in a given territory through the use of police to enforce laws or the army to maintain civil stability. While there have been stateless societies, most complex societies have state systems of formal government and administrative bureaucracies.

PATTERNS OF HUMAN SOCIAL ORGANIZATION

mode of production

The dominant form of social and technical organization of economic production in a society. Historically, a variety of modes of production can be distinguished based on both technology and the structure of social relationships.

Cultures have been classified in many different ways. Lenski (1966) emphasized the **mode of production** used by societies. He developed the following classification: hunting and gathering, pastoral, horticultural, agricultural, and industrial societies. This chapter will focus primarily on the hunting and gathering and the industrial forms because they provide the greatest contrast with respect to dispute settlement practices.

The **hunting and gathering society** has been a dominant form of social order in the history of the human species. For example, Michalowski (1985) argues that humans have lived in small-scale societies for the vast majority of the time that we have been in existence:

> Acephalous [headless, leaderless] societies were the only type of human community for 30 000 of the 40 000 years since the evolution of modern humans. It is also highly probable that archaic humans had been living in acephalous social arrangements for the preceding 200 000 years. Acephalous societies are small, economically cooperative and relatively egalitarian societies with simple technology and division of labor based mainly upon age and sex. Stratification in terms of differential access to material goods and political power does not exist. While these societies lack rulers or governments with the power to command, direct and correct the behavior of others, acephalous societies are generally characterized more by order and cooperation than by chaos and competition.

Some of these **acephalous societies** did change their mode of production and were transformed into pastoral and horticultural forms. Under certain conditions, some of them were further transformed into agricultural and industrial societies. The hunting and gathering form, however, persisted in many parts of the world into this century. It has been virtually eliminated by contact with the Western world.

The change in the mode of production to the pastoral or horticultural form created new possibilities for patterns of social organization. These new patterns slowly and inexorably transformed some human cultures and are now visible in modern industrial society. The emergence of surplus, **stratification**, technological innovations, social power, and large populations has made possible the growth of the industrially based social system (Newman, 1983).

The rest of this chapter will outline the basic characteristics of the dominant social forms and will show how the dispute settlement processes used in these different settings were a part of the social fabric. It will become clear that the discussion of custom, law, and dispute settlements must be placed within a social context in order to understand how each settles the troubles that spring up in all human societies.

Small-Scale Society

In this section, the general characteristics of small-scale societies will be described as a prelude to a discussion of their typical practices for settling disputes. Although such attributes are not present in all small-scale societies, they do appear in virtually all hunting and gathering societies and hence are useful as "**ideal types**" for the purposes of analysis.

Without underestimating the often harsh realities of the small-scale society or succumbing to the propensity to romanticize it, there is no question that

hunting and gathering society
Probably the earliest form of human society that still persists in remote regions of the world, to some extent. These societies have an economic base that rests on the use of the naturally occurring animal and plant resources of the environment. They do not practise agriculture or raise animals.

acephalous society
Literally "headless," meaning that the society is without any formalized or institutionalized system of power and authority. Collective decisions are made in a variety of ways, including informal community gatherings, that will change according to circumstances.

stratification
A social division of individuals into various hierarchies of wealth, status, and power. There is disagreement about how to describe stratification systems; some sociologists favour the concept of class and others discuss status differentiations.

ideal type
An abstract model of a classic, pure form of social phenomenon. It is a model concept and does not necessarily exist in exact form in reality. An example is Ferdinand Tönnies's (1855–1936) dichotomy *Gemeinschaft* and *Gesellschaft*.

such communities were characterized by a strong **collective solidarity**. Whether living in the High Arctic, on the plains, or in the tropical rainforests, hunters and gatherers were well aware that they were part of a natural ecosystem that had forces they could not control. They were aware of their individual vulnerability and realized that their collective life was an exercise in mutual survival. The cooperative, mutual-aid character of these societies was not accidental. The near certainty of death for those who lacked the assistance of the group strengthened the group's solidarity.

collective solidarity
Similar in meaning to Émile Durkheim's term mechanical solidarity, this refers to a state of social bonding or interdependency that rests on similarity of beliefs and values, shared activities, and ties of kinship and cooperation among members of a community.

The Need for Self-Restraint

Hunting and gathering groups were small communities of approximately 50 members who had closely related kin ties. In these small, face-to-face communities, social networks were dense and were characterized by a high degree of social visibility. The mutual-aid character of such social relationships meant that there was an expectation of continuity of relationships over time. The absence of a complex division of labour made it necessary for each individual in the group to fulfil a number of roles with other members. This **diffuseness of roles** placed a premium on cooperation since each member was intimately involved with other members. Continuous interaction with other members of the group provided each member with feedback from others concerning the acceptability of certain types of behaviour and created a climate for the development of common norms and the cultivation of a consensus.

diffuseness of roles
A characteristic of relatively simple societies in which people encounter one another in a variety of overlapping roles—there is little occupational specialization and no clear separation of private and public spheres of life. People are continuously reminded of their extensive bonds with others.

In such close and intimate quarters, members were reluctant to offend one another because of their mutual interdependence. Each member learned to cultivate personal restraint and the control of impulse in order to prevent the breakdown of a working order. Colson (1974) shows how these social circumstances fostered the development of forbearance, the avoidance of disputes, the sharing of resources, and the tolerance of human foibles. She relates how the Tonga of Zambia attempted to sidestep controversial issues and were reluctant to allow others to drag them into disputes. The Tongas' social structure worked against the outbreak of violence, the fear of attack by sorcerers, or other forms of retaliation. This contributed to the development of self-restraint.

Colson also reminds us that it is not that these people lacked "occasion for quarrels and hostility but they learn that they must control their hostility, their greed, and their envy if they are to survive" (61). Such communities could easily punish any individual who consistently went his or her own way. The self-restraint that members exercised stemmed not only from the close, intimate, and friendly ties that are a product of common life, but also out of the fear of reprisal and the desire to keep hostilities from surfacing and disturbing the business of living. Ross (1989), a Crown attorney in northern Ontario, relates how the principle of emotional restraint still operates in some remote Ojibway communities (see Box 2.1). The practice of "burying" old disputes and declining to revisit the emotions that they evoke was an exercise in individual restraint that kept these disruptions of the past from damaging current social relations.

BOX 2.1

FOCUS

The Principle of Emotional Restraint in the Ojibway Community

Grief, anger and sorrow [should] be quickly buried. They should not be expressed, for that only serves to burden the person who hears. They should not be explored or indulged privately, for doing so results in a lessened capacity to contribute the fullest energy, attention and skills which the hunter-gatherer society needed to maintain survival. Expressions of anger or criticism would serve only to create friction, a dangerous luxury to a people who required the maximum cooperation of all. Even the *thinking* of critical thoughts about others was to be avoided. Quite simply, the past was the past, and its negative parts were to be buried and forgotten as quickly as possible....

While such overt observances of these rules are declining, it remains a central tenet of life in many communities that it is wrong to speak of your hurts and angers and criticisms, wrong to indulge your private emotions. Instead, you bury and you carry on, resisting the backwards glance. I recall one teenage rape victim who refused to testify when her assailant finally came to trial more than a year after the event; her reason was simply that he should have paid his penalty by now and be getting on with his life. For her, it was simply too late to put him through it. The past was the past.

Asking a Native accused to explain what it was that aggravated him to such a degree that he attacked his victim is the subject of a special constraint, already referred to, which forbids the criticism of others.

Source: Rupert Ross. "Leaving Our White Eyes Behind: The Sentencing of Native Accused." [1989] 3 *Canadian Native Law Reporter* 1 at 4.

Mutual Dependence

Living in a subsistence economy, where little or no surplus could be generated, created the necessity for the group to share the fruits of a day's hunting or foraging. Typically, the spoils were distributed in such a way as to ensure that everyone received an equal and adequate share, regardless of the extent and nature of each one's contribution. In such a distribution system, there may have been collective scarcity if food was not found, but there was never poverty in the sense that some ate while others went hungry. Though a member was not expected to love everyone else, each one was expected to care for all members of the community. This ensured that all members would be cared for in the nonproductive times of their life such as childhood and old age, and during times of sickness. This bond of mutual dependence helped to keep greed and the desire for advantage in check.

A Community of Belief

The structure of small-scale society fostered both moderation and compassion, which acted as powerful curbs to selfishness. A shared system of customs and patterns of behaviour in domestic, economic, and political life grew out of the personal and interpersonal accommodations that were required of such intimate social actors. There is no question that this type of society was coercive;

there was virtually no freedom of belief. One's location in the kinship system established basic duties, obligations, rights, and privileges. Failure to meet obligations jeopardized one's relationship with many members of this primary group and, especially, the face-to-face interaction with one's immediate kin. The notion of collective responsibility, which was prevalent in such communities, made kin groups accountable for the behaviour of their members. The positive dimension of community membership was that throughout the life cycle, the customary ways provided meaning for members. This sense of purpose helped foster commitment to community beliefs and practices.

The Absence of Surplus, Stratification, and the State

The life of the hunters and gatherers was an exercise in cooperative living. The inability to produce or to keep large amounts of food on hand meant that food gathering was a regular activity that included all able-bodied members. The division and distribution of foodstuffs to all community members underscored the understanding that everyone had a right to the fruits of this collective activity; they were a group possession to be shared by all. The need to move regularly acted to limit the amount of personal belongings a person could accumulate, and since each member had access to the same raw materials, there was little difference in the individuals' limited possessions. The possibility of generating any significant **surplus** under these conditions was limited. Small-scale society, then, acted as a brake on the human tendency to secure an advantageous individual position. By identifying one's "self" with the interests of the entire group, the individual self so familiar to our society was superseded by a social or collective self-concept.

The absence of surplus was a strong force that suppressed the emergence of economic stratification and any form of statelike structure or political institution. Small-scale societies have been characterized as acephalous (without a head) because there was no distinct source of social power or authority independent of the collective will. The only form of power available to special individuals in such societies was influence. Influence was based on status derived from hunting skill, sex, wisdom, or generosity, and not on differential access to, and accumulation of, material resources. Social status was a group property, not a personal attribute. The members of the group could give it and take it away. Hoebel (1973) comments on the position of the Inuit headman:

> The headman possesses no fixed authority; neither does he enter into formal office. He is not elected, nor is he chosen by any formal process. When other men accept his judgement and opinions, he is headman. When they ignore him, he is not.

Thus, if an esteemed individual became arrogant or tried to force others to comply in ways that were deemed inappropriate, the special status was removable. All aspects of group life worked in a systematic fashion to control and limit the will of the individual in the best interests of the group. This is the type of society to which Tönnies (1887) applied the term *Gemeinschaft*, where human beings "remain essentially united in spite of all separating factors."

surplus

The excess of production over the human and material resources used up in the process of production. In simple societies, there was often little if any surplus since the production from hunting and gathering was entirely used up in subsistence. With the development of animal herding and settled agriculture, production exceeds immediate subsistence needs, and social inequality and class division become possible when particular individuals or groups are able to take control of this surplus.

Gemeinschaft

A German word, translated as "community," used by sociologist Ferdinand Tönnies (1855–1936) to define an *ideal type* or model of a society in which social bonds are personal and direct and there are strong shared values and beliefs. Characteristic of small-scale, localized societies, it is in contrast to *Gesellschaft*, which refers to complex, impersonal societies.

Dispute Settlement in Small-Scale Society

The major goal of dispute settlement in small-scale societies was to restore harmonious relations between parties that could not interact because of some conflict. It was essential that problems be settled as quickly as possible in mutually agreeable ways for all involved parties so as not to impede group life. The absence of an independent political institution meant that disputants typically had to resolve their differences without the assistance of an adjudicator (Gulliver, 1979). Community pressure was applied to the parties in a dispute to meet and to bring an end to the discord. Each party had to give and to receive information from the other in order to learn of the other party's needs and expectations. In a series of such educational exchanges, an attempt was made to move toward a mutually agreeable outcome and the restoration of harmonious interaction.

This type of approach to discord led to a general airing of all the issues that created friction between the parties. This ensured that an effort was made to keep the conflict from escalating and to lead the discordant parties to a mutually satisfying conclusion to their problem. Potential troublemakers had to recognize that at some point they would have to confront those whom they had directly harmed, rather than some abstract system of justice and a victim who was a stranger. Inside this general framework, there was some variation in the types of disputes and the form of the settlement practices.

Types of Disputes and Their Settlement

Newman (1983) provides rich detail concerning the types of disputes that arose in hunting and gathering societies. Many disputes among hunting and gathering peoples concerned women. Because women were valuable producers, adultery, failure to honour marriage agreements, and the taking of a woman by an enemy caused serious disruptions. While women were not necessarily considered the property of their fathers or husbands, there was an interest in controlling them as valuable resources to the kin system. Other causes of conflict involved such acts as improper food distribution, asymmetrical gift exchange, laziness, stinginess, theft, and murder. Theft was an infrequent offence among nomadic foragers because of the relative absence of property. Murders were relatively infrequent and almost always resulted from disputes concerning women. Because of the emergence of the notion of property among sedentary food collectors, however, there was a greater incidence of theft and disputes over the use of land in those societies.

The primary method of redress in small-scale society itself was self- or kin-based redress. Other methods, used less frequently, were advisor or mediator systems.

Self- or Kin-Based Redress The range of responses available in self- or kin-based redress included public criticism, shaming rituals, temporary ostracism, expulsion from the group, blood feuds, and reprisal killings. Some sedentary food gatherers also developed a scale of fines for certain types of infractions. This list in no way exhausts the full range of responses that were employed, but it does encompass those used most frequently. Less harsh methods were often employed initially, and only when they failed were more punitive responses called forth. In some instances, a disputant may simply have chosen to leave the group and join another on a temporary or permanent basis.

The injured party had to initiate the dispute process because there was no centralized authority. This does not mean that the victim was free to do to an offender whatever the victim chose. The society had customary expectations about the appropriateness of different reprisals. Too harsh a response could evoke group disapproval and sanctions. For example, among the Aranda of Australia, the socially defined punishment for adultery included cuts around the shoulder blades of the offending man inflicted by the cuckolded husband during hot pursuit of the offender. If the cuts were too deep and exceeded the standard of acceptable punishment, however, the husband stood to forfeit his wife. Among the Mataco of South America, if the reprisal was considered to be more serious than the original offence, the initial offence was expunged and the offender became the injured party. An individual could lose the support of his or her family by retaliating too vigorously. It is important to emphasize here that self-redress is a regulated social process. The image of small-scale societies as violent and constantly feuding is inaccurate. The ordered independence, which was the hallmark of such social formations, did not allow for anarchy when wrongs were redressed. While it is true that disputes did escalate into blood feuds and cycles of revenge killings, even these proceeded in an orderly fashion. Furthermore, small-scale society had a body of custom that was coupled with the fear of reprisal and that acted as a brake on such escalation by defining an appropriate level of redress for various offences.

Clearly defined notions of right and wrong behaviour existed in spite of the absence of third-party authority figures. It should be noted that formalized civil or criminal law was not present or necessary for these small, kin-based communities to restore order. If an individual violated a custom, he or she suffered the consequences. His or her kin did not provide protection from legitimate retaliation. If the punishment was too harsh or unfairly exacted, a retaliation was initiated, and conflict continued until both sides were satisfied with the resolution of the situation. An exchange of gifts often signalled the end to hostilities.

Advisor Systems The advisor system was really only an extension of the self-redress method of dispute settlement because it was once again ultimately the victim or kin who would enforce any retaliation. Disputants approached advisors, who tended to be men who were distinguished warriors, hunters, or speakers. They were mature, although not always the oldest men of the community, and were regarded as public repositories of wisdom about customs and rituals. In general, they were not selected because of birth right.

The process of dispute settlement was activated when one or both parties sought out one of these high-status figures. They were not required to turn to this third party, but it was expected that they would do so. Each party presented its case, and after considering the facts, the advisor recommended what should be done. He interpreted the case with respect to custom, and it was his role to ensure that the social group's conception of appropriate behaviour was protected.

He was a moral authority, but he could not enforce compliance. He could, however, attempt to influence disputants with shaming rituals and his ability to make compelling arguments. Among some groups, the advisor could take a more active role by indicating which side his own kin group would back in the event of a reprisal. Here, too, the advisor could not direct his kin group, but only report its position with reference to the dispute. The advisor was, essentially, a communication link between parties and attempted to coordinate a settlement without violence. An advisor gained status by being able to settle disputes without the outbreak of revenge activity. A demonstrated ability to resolve disputes peacefully strengthened his moral authority. If the advisor overstepped his bounds and tried to make his authority too exacting, the community would stop using him in his capacity of advisor. Thus, the advisor system was still firmly controlled by the community.

Most hunting and gathering societies relied on self-redress; a smaller proportion developed an advisor system.

In general, the dispute settlement processes used by small-scale societies were designed to restore social integration and harmony. These societies tried to surround and contain problems involving members of the community and sought to resolve them through compromise and reconciliation. Each member was tied to other members for a variety of social purposes. The discord created by disputants interfered with these other positive and necessary ties. These people simply could not afford to have long-standing anger and discord. As Ross (1989) points out, traditional Inuit and Ojibway dispute settlement mechanisms provide a poignant contrast to the assumptions of the Canadian criminal justice system (see Box 2.2).

On the whole, small-scale society had considerable success in avoiding the outbreak of serious trouble. Each member of the community was able to exercise some measure of control over others, so power remained diffuse. As a community, members were able to deal with discord in such a way that victim and offender could once again enter into harmonious interaction after a mutually agreeable settlement of a dispute had been made.

THE TRANSFORMATION FROM SMALL-SCALE SOCIETY TO THE STATE

Within the last 6000 to 8000 years, most hunting and gathering societies have been transformed into pastoral, horticultural, agricultural, and industrial societies, as a result either of their own development or the invasion of an outside culture. The transformation of some small-scale societies to state societies will be outlined in this section, along with a discussion of the way in which this transformation affects the dispute settlement process.

BOX 2.2

FOCUS

Traditional Inuit and Ojibway Dispute Settlement

The practice in one Inuit village was to call the entire village together, and to put the actual event forward as a *hypothetical* event which might happen some time in the future. All people, including the miscreant and his victim, were required to put forward their views as to how things might be handled peacefully and properly were the situation ever to arise. There was no blaming, no pointing of fingers, no requirement of explanation; nor was there ever any discussion, much less imposition, of either punitive or restitutionary response. At an Ojibway Reserve in my district similar dynamics governed. While the miscreant and his victim were summoned before an Elders Panel, there was never any discussion of what had happened and why, of how each party felt about the other or of what might be done by way of compensation. Nor was there any imposition of punishment. Each party was instead provided with a counselling Elder who worked privately to "cleanse his spirit." When both counselling Elders so signified by touching the peace pipe, it would be lit and passed to all. It was a signal that both had been "restored to themselves and to the community." If they privately arranged recompense of some sort, that was their affair. As far as the community was concerned, the matter was over. While I have not learned what the private counselling did consist of, I have been told that it did not involve retrieval and re-examination of the past in either its factual or emotional facets. It concentrated upon the future, and its spiritual component was central.

As a footnote, such ethics also cast the behavior of native victims in a very different light. Refusal or reluctance to testify or, when testifying, to give anything but the barest and most emotionless recital of events, may of course have been prompted by fear of the accused, by fear of the court, by love for and forgiveness of the accused or by any other such "sensible" reason (including the possibility, of extreme rarity in my experience, that they are uncomfortable because they are lying). Another reason, culturally foreign to us, could be that giving testimony face to face with the accused is simply considered wrong. It was not part of the traditional processes described above, where in fact every effort seems to have been made to *avoid* such direct confrontation. I recall one Indian woman who repeated her entire story of abuse to me in vivid detail before going into court and then asked me to do whatever I could to have the court send her very dangerous assailant to jail for as long as possible. Ten minutes later she took the witness stand and absolutely refused to say anything of an accusatory nature. When such witnesses regularly ask why they have to repeat their stories in court when they have already told "us" (meaning the police and the Crown), I have come to suspect that it is more than fear or embarrassment at work. I suspect instead that it is perceived as ethically wrong to say hostile, critical, implicitly angry things about someone *in their presence*, precisely what our adversarial trial rules have required.... In fact, we have taken this legal challenge into our daily lives, exhorting each person to open up with the other, to be honest and up front, to get things off our chests, etc., all of which are, to traditional native eyes, offensive in the extreme. When they refuse to follow the exhortations of our rules, we judge them as deficient in rule-obedience or, worse still, rule-less. In our ignorance we have failed to admit the possibility that there might be rules other than ours to which they regularly display allegiance, an allegiance all the more striking because it is exercised in defiance of our insistent pressures to the contrary.

Source: Rupert Ross. "Leaving Our White Eyes Behind: The Sentencing of Native Accused." [1989] 3 *Canadian Native Law Reporter* 1 at 5–6.

The Slow Emergence of Social Power

Hunting and gathering communities were long able to resist any aspirations to autonomy and power by their members. While positions of influence did exist for those who made special contributions to the group, this status was not consolidated by greater access to material resources. Influential members still had to be responsive to the opinions, expectations, and judgements of the rest of their community in order to retain their special status.

At some point, the mutuality of **tribalism** was ruptured. The emergence of the concept of property slowly and progressively created social power for families and individuals. Privately owned land and livestock meant that the more fortunate members of the community were in a position to generate a surplus (Newman, 1983). This surplus increasingly gave them and their progeny the ability to rely less on the community for their survival. Under such circumstances, some of the ancient patriarchs began to define women as property, to secure not only control of their labour, but also their reproductive capacities "in order to ensure that there would be determinate heirs to function as the designatable future owners of individually held accumulations of private property" (Clark and Lewis, 1977).

tribalism

Where social bonds are based primarily on people's real or assumed common descent from an ancestor or group of ancestors, and this shared identification distinguishes the group from outsiders. In such societies, all social relationships tend to be direct and quasi-familial.

The Evolution of Inequality

The power constellation of small-scale society was that of the community as a whole, which moved against the interests of individuals or factions when their undertakings were viewed as a serious threat to the good of the group. New forms of power inaugurated important changes. The emergence of surplus, stratification, and the basis for factional power gave rise to the development of the state in rudimentary form. The role of mediators, elders' councils, restricted councils, and then chieftainships shows the slow, yet progressive, development and consolidation of a social form of power independent of the community as a whole.

In small-scale society, each individual was expected to discharge his or her obligations directly to other community members. Slowly, the social elites were able to redirect this exchange to consolidate and to enhance their position in the changing social order. The goods that had been readily available to all members in a simple economy of sharing became distributed in patterns that reflected the stratified nature of pastoral, horticultural, agricultural, and industrial orders. These new modes of production made it increasingly possible for powerful groups and individuals to extract surplus value from those who turned to them in order to make a living. The ability to have other people help generate their personal wealth greatly accelerated the formation of stratified inequality. Less powerful segments in society found it increasingly difficult to resist those social forces that were compromising their interests.

Ultimately, the state would emerge in agricultural society, and it would champion and represent the interests of the powerful. The growing size, technological sophistication, and complexity of social systems gave rise to the need for large bureaucracies and a class of officials whose personal interests would become fused with those of the state. Human history was firmly established on a course that would generate hitherto unseen levels of surplus, poverty, and social inequality. The interests of whole groups of individuals were devalued and subordinated to the interests of powerful factions and the state. The equality of condition in small-scale society had been replaced by a class system rife with disparities.

The dispute settlement practices that emerged with these different social forms and the types of offences committed in such societies reflected the basic changes in social structure that have been outlined in this section. Attention will now be focused on the dispute process and the changes that took place that created law as it exists today.

Transformation in the Forms of Dispute Settlement

As societies changed their form, social relationships became complex and the types of disputes that arose in these societies changed. For example, with the emergence of private property, theft became possible. The concepts of rent and the violation of contracts became grounds for disagreement. When individuals began writing wills, problems emerged concerning appropriate or disputed inheritance. The emergence of contracts and wills contributed to the need for more codified conventions and a body of civil law. Finally, the emergence of surplus meant that disputes could be settled by the payment of various types of fines to compensate the party who had been wronged. For example, under Anglo-Saxon law, if a woman was raped, a compensatory fee was paid to either her husband or her father, depending on who exercised the rights of ownership over her at the time of the offence. The fee was not paid directly to the woman herself as she was not considered to be the person who had been wronged by the act (Clark and Lewis, 1977).

Increased productive capacity resulted in disputes concerning property, accompanied by increasingly complex legal codifications to deal with them. The creation of chiefdoms, and eventually states, was accompanied by the emergence of offences such as treason, slander, and libel, and, in general, the possibility for criminal law as defined as offences against the Crown. Failure to pay taxes or to work on public projects became offences and sources of litigation. In this section, some of the basic features of elders' councils, chieftainships, and paramount chieftainships will be examined. These are the dominant structural elements in dispute settlement that distinguish societies lying between small-scale societies and state systems.

Elders' Councils

Elders' councils performed legal, political, economic, and administrative functions. Disputants were required to submit their dispute to these councils, whose verdicts were binding. There were often several levels of councils, including local and regional councils with different powers; for example, one level would hear appeals. The membership in these councils was representative of the influential segments of the society. The members of the council may have included all married males or the oldest male in each family. In all instances, each family was represented, and hence membership was basically democratic. Participation was not contingent upon wealth, although there was a clear sex bias. Eventually, most men in the community would have occasion to sit on the elders' councils.

Council procedures were marked by a high degree of formality. This is uncharacteristic of the forms of dispute settlement discussed so far. Formal language, recourse to precedents, and rules of conduct all marked the seriousness of the occasion. The conclusions of these councils carried considerable weight because they were made by a representative group of elders who were charged with the duty of determining a dispute in the best interests of the community. Community pressure dictated the obligation to accept the judgement of the council. If an individual was recalcitrant, the council could enlist local men to threaten the offender and deprive him or her of property, or direct the kinsmen of the victim to retaliate. This was the only type of self-redress that was available in these systems.

Chieftainships

A chief was the highest political authority in the community and was recognized as having the ultimate power in settling disputes. The chief's decisions were binding, although others may have been required to enforce them. Chieftainships tended to be based on heredity or supernatural knowledge. Chiefs were primarily rich men from influential families. They also were expected to display oratorical skills, wisdom, and knowledge of customary ways. Chiefs usually served on a permanent basis and held office through their productive years, either voluntarily relinquishing it when they judged themselves incapable of continuing or being overthrown by rebellions when they fell from popularity. Chiefs often had the right to select their successor, although this was contingent upon community approval.

Chieftainships made possible a formalization and institutionalization of the legal system. The chief was able to intervene in a dispute without being requested to do so and heard appeals if more informal attempts to settle a dispute failed. Chiefs had the power to order executions, beatings, public reprimands, and economic sanctions such as fines and destruction or confiscation of property. No form of self-redress was allowed unless the approval of the chief had been secured. Considerable power was placed in the hands of the chief, although he often consulted community members prior to making a decision.

Paramount Chieftainships

paramount chieftainship

A political system similar to a kingdom that brings together a number of partly autonomous villages or communities under the hierarchical rule of a grand chief.

The **paramount chieftainship** was a form of social order that took a significant step away from the participatory and democratic features of other models. Paramount chieftainships were much like kingdoms. They were based on hereditary aristocracies and drew together a large number of communities or villages that retained some level of local autonomy. Paramount chieftainships were complex, hierarchical structures. The chief was surrounded with retainers and nobles who performed judicial and administrative tasks. Many such chieftainships had a "civil service" recruited from the ranks of royalty to handle daily affairs. This apparatus allowed a more formal and structured legal system to develop. In this way, the paramount chief was able to extend control over a large geographical region and a sizable population.

The paramount chief held court in a capital city, and the paramount chief's court served as the highest court of justice. District or circuit courts were used as a first resort to settle disputes, but more serious cases came under the jurisdiction of the paramount chief, who had the final authority to make binding decisions. In many societies, the chief had an advisory council made up of royalty. However, the final decision in settling cases rested with the chief, who had a full range of options available. From the structure of paramount chieftainship, it was a small step to the creation of the state.

The transformation of the hunting and gathering social form and the attendant dispute-settling processes are dramatic when considered in this comparative framework. But the changes occurred so gradually that the historical actors barely noticed them. Once the checks on the accumulation of wealth and power that bound small-scale society together were undercut, there seemed to be an inevitable chain of events that led to the emergence of a state system. Some of the reasons for this steady and cumulative development have been discussed in general terms. In the next section of this chapter, the modern state system will be examined in greater detail. Implicit in this analysis will be a comparison of modern social and legal structures with those of small-scale society.

MODERN STATE SYSTEMS

The full emergence of the state in the past 3000 or 4000 years has created a rich and complex social tapestry. We will outline the essential changes in social-power constellations that transformed land-based **feudalism** into the modern capitalist state. This historical outline will be somewhat detailed in order to provide an adequate basis for a sophisticated analysis of the key structural changes that would ultimately result in the emergence of modern commercial, industrial society. The case of England provides the basis for the analysis of the emergence of law in Western democratic states. This focus is clearly appropriate when seeking to understand the legal system in Canada and the United States of America. The analysis of law in state systems in other historical circumstances is beyond the scope of this chapter.

From Tribalism to Feudalism

The primary basis for social order prior to feudalism was tribal kinship. In this social order, military leaders had already begun to emerge in a class system where conquered individuals became followers tied to their leaders with reciprocal obligations (Jeffery, 1969; Kennedy, 1976). A patchwork of local fiefdoms under the control of local lords began to develop. The invasions of England, especially the Norman Invasion, accelerated the full development of a feudal order. In essence, feudalism was a social system based on the tenure of land, which was the dominant form of capital in an agrarian mode of production. The use of land was granted to the vassal in return for military service or, in later years, for rent. Those who held land had obligations to protect and to provide food for their serfs in hard times. These serfs were typically tied to the land and were required to deliver labour service, tribute, and the like. This relationship, while based on subjection, had a quasi-familial tone. Land was not a commodity that was for

feudalism

A system of economic and social organization found historically in several areas of the world including Japan and other parts of Asia and many countries of eastern and western Europe. In western Europe, feudalism was at its height between about 1000 and 1500. The usual economic foundation of the system was the feudal manor, an agricultural organization that included a central farm owned by the landlord and small land holdings for a class of bonded farm labourers (serfs). The serfs were required to work the central manorial farm and to provide the lord with produce and money payments in return for their right to use the land. The system gradually declined as cities and towns grew and power became centralized in nation-states under monarchies.

sale. The right to use the land was controlled by the lord. A serf could lose the right to land use only for neglect of the land or failure to meet obligations.

No central power existed in the early period of feudalism. Social order was maintained through the kinship system as well as the developing land tenure system in which the vast majority of individuals were eventually required to have a lord. In tribal times, blood feuds were the primary dispute settlement mechanism. In medieval England, the secure emergence of local fiefdoms resulted in intervention by the local lord, who had the authority to administer a variety of different sanctions. As feudalism developed and the notion of collective responsibility was replaced with that of individual responsibility, money settlements and fines were used to settle serious disputes, with the exception of those committed by outlaws, who were slain without fear of reprisal. By the year 871, feuds could be resorted to only if other forms of compensation had been requested and denied. Compliance with such standards was through local custom since no centralized source of power had emerged to enforce them. Local lords were not willing or able to become involved in all disputes. For example, only the rape of wealthy, propertied virgins would typically secure the involvement of the powerful lords who protected them (Brownmiller, 1975).

Once these Anglo-Saxon lords were able to consolidate some power in England, they began to develop a body of law to deal with disputes. Under this system, trial by ordeal (using such methods as walking on hot coals or reaching into boiling water to pick up a pebble) was the means to establish guilt or innocence for those disputants who could not find some other way to settle a dispute. The pattern is clear; kin-based dispute settlement practices were being continuously undermined and replaced by feudal lords and their laws.

The Emergence of the Centralized State

With the success of the Norman Invasion in 1066, William the Conqueror declared himself the "supreme landlord" of all England, so that all individuals who held land held his land. Over the succeeding centuries, the English kings slowly expanded and consolidated their power over the feudal landscape. Harms committed in disputes between individuals increasingly were seen to harm the *mund*, or the king's region. As a result, compensation was paid to kings, lords, and bishops, rather than to kinship groups. Originally, the King's Peace referred to his ability to protect his own person, but, as Jeffery argues, the development of the central state meant that "gradually it was extended to include the king's court, army, servants, hundred-court, and finally the four main highways of England." The Norman kings saw themselves as the injured party when a crime was committed since the harm was against their peace. Since some crimes were now against the Crown, criminal law became a reality. The Crown replaced the victim as the injured party, and compensation to the victim's family was replaced by punitive fines that were payable to the Crown.

This trend continued, as the king could enforce his increased claims to **sovereignty** with force. A central authority had emerged in England to replace the authority of feudal lords. By 1180, Henry II had introduced a system of

"Historical Origins of Government's Monopoly on Criminal Justice"
National Center for Policy Analysis (USA)
www.ncpa.org/studies/s181/s181c.html

sovereignty

The authority possessed by the governing individual or institution of a society. Sovereign authority is distinct in that it is unrestricted by legal regulation since the sovereign authority is itself the source of all law.

royal courts and a system of royal writs. Thus, **common law** came into existence as the law of the Crown available to all individuals. As Jeffery (1969) has stated, "The family was no longer involved in law and justice. The State was the offended unit, and the State was the proper prosecutor in every case of crime." The pivotal role that law and the courts played in this undertaking to consolidate centralized political and economic power is of primary significance. Another major factor was the growth of trade and the rise of the merchant class. These developments led to the decline of the feudal system and to the rise of towns and cities at the expense of the rural manors. Cities began to arise during the reign of King John (1199–1216) and, although they were situated on land controlled by feudal lords, they fell under the jurisdiction of the Crown. A new system of social relationships developed that was based on commerce instead of on feudal obligations.

> **common law**
>
> The common law tradition found in English Canada derives from feudal England, where it had become the practice for the king to resolve disputes in accordance with local custom. Customs that were recognized throughout the country were called common custom, and decisions made by the king and by subsequent courts set up to settle disputes became known as common law. Common law is considered a source of law.

The Coalition of Merchants and Monarchs

William the Conqueror had established a state apparatus when he made all nobles take an oath to establish him as their feudal overlord. With this came the power to create laws to govern the kingdom, royal officials to protect the king's interests, and royal courts to dispense the king's justice. This state apparatus was superimposed on feudalism. While feudalism was dominant, the king used the state apparatus to defend the common interests of feudal lords. However, the breakdown of feudal obligations and the feudal tax system also meant a loss of revenue for the Crown, which needed to find new ways to finance war and the state. This was accomplished by going outside the feudal system to negotiate loans with merchants, using land as collateral. The king wanted his power consolidated and needed political support and financial assistance, while the merchants wanted a unified and safe trading area (Chambliss, 1969; Hall, 1969a). The state was to become the vehicle that the Crown and its merchant allies would use to defeat the resistance impeding the development of the new social order. In return for their support, Henry VIII conceded that Parliament would have control over tax revenues and the legislative function. Thus, the state, which was staffed with the **bourgeois class**, would become the mechanism for change by statute. Laws would be passed by Parliament.

> **bourgeois class**
>
> The term bourgeois class, or bourgeoisie, was used by Marx to refer to the capitalist or ruling class in modern societies.

The merchants benefited from this new arrangement because they were able to gain greater access to land. The feudal lords' losses in war brought the merchants the land that the lords had put up as collateral for loans. When Henry VIII expropriated church land, over one-sixth of the land in England was removed from its connection to feudalism. Henry sold this land to friends and allies, for whom he created peerages with seats in the House of Lords. This action more than doubled his revenue, placed a large block of land outside feudal control, and made this land available for the money market. As the feudal system declined, many lords were tied into feudal land arrangements of rent, which were driving them into financial ruin. Eventually, their lands also were freed of feudal ties and became part of the commodity market to be bought and sold as private property in the interest of profit. In 1540, Henry VIII also gave his support to the Statute of Wills, which made most land in England transmittable by will. The role of the Crown had changed from that of shared owner of land under feudalism to that of land regulator via the state, which was becoming a separate and sovereign entity.

The labour of serfs, which had been tied to the land under feudalism, was freed from the land, as were the lords. In addition, much of the land that had been controlled by the church was also made available as commons for serfs to graze their animals. However, the new owners enclosed a great deal of this land for wool production and thoroughly disrupted the lives of the commoners. The right of commoners to hunt, fish, and gather wood on their lord's manor was extinguished under the new property relations. The Black Act of 1723 increased the number of offences for which the courts could impose the death penalty. These harsh measures were seen as necessary to encourage the common people to abandon these feudal practices (Thompson, 1976). The new land regulations displaced the rural workforce, which then became the new workforce of the factories made possible by technological innovation.

These fundamental changes contributed to the increased importance of commerce and money. The close and personal ties of fealty and its reciprocal duties and obligations were being eclipsed by the abstract and anonymous transactions of money in commercial enterprise. The growth of banking institutions, the use of paper currency, and other instruments of credit created new occasions for theft by trusted third parties. The famous Carrier's Case of 1473 made it clear that the law of theft would need to be refined in order to prevent intermediaries from keeping goods put in their possession for transport (Hall, 1952). International trade, which was spurred by Britain's colonial empire, also necessitated an expansion and refinement of the concept of theft. Hall (1969b) recounts how the law governing embezzlement was enacted to make theft of paper money and commercial bonds a crime. If a business was run by members of a household, behaviour was regulated by custom and by family ties. However, when businesses grew they needed to hire employees from the larger communities who had no other ties to the owners. Transactions between anonymous parties would henceforth be regulated by law because of the absence of customary ties between them.

The role of law and the place of lawyers would figure prominently in the regulation of the new social relationships. In order to chart the consolidation of state power within the context of law, it is essential to study the activities of various interest groups with respect to commerce and contract law. The consolidation of a new form of social life based on contract was achieved within the context of commerce and the rise of the bourgeois class.

Commerce, Contracts, and the Primary Role of Law

The growth of commerce, spurred by the Industrial Revolution and the expansion of trade, required greater uniformity and enforceability of trading arrangements. Towns, cities, and even nation-states realized that a system of law, and a court system to apply it, would be essential if trade was to stabilize and grow. The volume of trade, its growing impersonality, the practice of joint ventures, and the long distances involved in international trade created the need for a mechanism to secure the interests of traders. Legal contracts, which had existed since Roman times, became the dominant mechanism that would tie social relationships together in the new social order. Tönnies (1887) argued that the *Gesellschaft* (i.e., the modern society) came to exist as a superior power to enforce the terms set out in the contracts of the merchants and capitalists. Lawyers grew in number and importance as new contract forms were developed to meet the increasingly complex trade arrangements of the time. Contracts, which had been private agreements, now became widely used to bind together individuals in the new social order. This new reliance on contract required changes in the court structure. In the feudal era, common law had developed to settle disputes. This law was applied in church courts, as well as in the King's Court.

During the mid-1500s, the king sought to consolidate power, and he found that great inroads could be made into common law by throwing his support behind merchant law in support of the merchant class. In return for taxes and loans, the Crown placed the power of the state behind the laws of commerce and enforced these laws. The merchant class supported the legislative and judicial power of the Crown in exchange for the development of legal mechanisms that would further strengthen their class position, increase their fortunes, and consolidate their power. The law and lawyers had been guaranteed a primary role in the new industrial, capitalist mode of production. The bourgeois had helped to strengthen the power of the monarch in order to be protected by his state apparatus. The king's support of merchant law as the law of the land helped to stabilize the necessary social and legal conditions for commerce.

The power of the nation-state was solidified around the interests of commerce, and the role of custom and kinship was eroded. The basis for the new social order was predicated on law, in the realm of both commercial and criminal activity. While the primary interest of this chapter is criminal law, it is important to track the rise of the institution of law in the modern state—and this was primarily within the context of merchant interests.

The merchant class had supported the aspirations of the Crown because they needed a stable and modified system in order to conduct their affairs. However, once the land had been redistributed and feudal village life had been disrupted, the bourgeois became interested in forming a new alliance so as to curb the Crown's ability to restrict trade. Tigar and Levy (1977) document the new alliance with common-law lawyers.

The Consolidation of Bourgeois Ascendance

Contracts under merchant law were enforced in merchant courts, as well as in chancery and admiralty courts. Common-law lawyers realized that the portion of law that they administered was shrinking with the decline of the landed nobility. Some of them were eager to have merchant law enforced in their courts. The bourgeois were supportive of such a development, as it would make them less dependent on the king and his special courts. Common-law lawyers made a concerted effort to make their courts more receptive to bourgeois legal principles. By 1600, an alliance between the common-law lawyers and the bourgeois was finding success in introducing the bourgeois theory of contract into

Gesellschaft

A German word, translated as "society-association," used by Ferdinand Tönnies (1855–1936) to refer to an *ideal type* or model of a society in which social bonds are primarily impersonal, instrumental, and narrow. Characteristic of large-scale, complex societies, with a strict division between private and public spheres of life, it contrasts to the community-oriented life of the *Gemeinschaft*.

common-law courts. A conflict between the Crown and the merchant class ensued because the Crown wanted to control merchant activity through the monarch's court, and the bourgeois wanted to evade the Crown's attempts at controlling trade by having matters handled through the common-law courts.

The merchant class gained a strong hold on the Parliament as the landed aristocracy's power waned. Parliament used its control over tax revenues in its efforts to limit the king's control of trade. This conflict was resolved in the English Civil War of 1642–48 by a reduction in the power of the monarchy and the establishment of the bourgeois-controlled Parliament as the sole source of political control.

Peasants and workers were not represented in this early Parliament, and the modern state developed under the influence of the bourgeois. The rise of the labour movement would come later, but as Miliband (1969) has convincingly displayed in his book *The State in Capitalist Society*, the power of organized labour has never managed to match that of organized business. Whatever advances have been made in democratizing the state apparatus, it remains a political and legal structure to protect the interests of property. In the arena of modern political life, various interest groups bring pressure on the state to protect their interests under the rule of law.

State, Law, and Interest Groups

As the structures of feudalism declined, the state became the dominant institution regulating social order and settling disputes. State decisions were backed up by military and police organizations. The state stood as the superior force behind the contractual arrangements of business and property in order to ensure that the terms of these agreements were observed.

In this context, the law has become the dominant means to regulate human affairs: legislation and administrative directives are the legal apparatus that creates the bases of modern nation-states; property, commerce, real estate, labour, and contractual agreements are all regulated by law; municipalities and corporations are governed by law; the protection of the environment is regulated by law; and disputes over person and property are handled through family, civil, and criminal law. In short, the law is the principal means whereby human activity is prohibited, permitted, or required, and the state and the law are intimately meshed in the creation of the modern social order.

As shown in earlier sections, the merchant class was quite successful in promoting and protecting its interests as it helped shape the nature of the state and the law. But business interest groups are not the only ones that approach the state to promote their interests. A variety of cultural, ethnic, minority, class, economic, and political interest groups lobby the state in order to promote their own interests. The modern state has become a vehicle sought after by a variety of groups, each seeking certain guarantees and protections. The heterogeneous nature of modern societies and the antagonistic relationships between various groups ensure that the state cannot promote the interests of all groups. Choices need to be made. Given the nature of electoral politics, the state is under some pressure to promote the values and interests of the majority and of powerful minorities in order to maintain legitimacy and popularity. In the remainder of this chapter, several examples will be reviewed to provide some insight into the range of interest groups seeking to influence the content and role of law in modern society. Given the sheer volume of law and the complexity of modern society, this review is meant to be only illustrative of the role of law in modern society.

Regulation by Law

Some authors argue that the law reflects the values of the majority of the population, while others analyze various laws to show that powerful minority interests have shaped the content of the law. There is no reason to conclude that only one of these positions is correct. It is clear that some legal enactments reflect the values of the majority and it is also clear that other laws clearly do not reflect the values of the majority, but instead reflect the values of powerful minorities. The significant impact of powerful interests on the content of law is a topic that is subject to much debate. In this section, examples that demonstrate both points of view will be discussed.

Consensus and the Law

Under some circumstances, there is broadly based consensus about limiting certain forms of behaviour. There is general consensus regarding laws that seek to protect individuals from common assault in public places, from breaking and entering, and from theft of property from their residence. There is also considerable agreement about what constitutes serious crime. Rossi and Waite (1974) replicated the earlier work of Sellin and Wolfgang (1964) on the ranking of seriousness of crimes and came to the following conclusion: "The norms defining how serious various criminal acts are considered to be, are quite widely distributed among blacks and whites, males and females, high and low socio-economic levels, and among levels of educational attainment" (237). This basic consensus about what constitutes crime against person and property should not be understated.

Interest Groups and the Law

Most of the research on law, however, shows the operation of interest groups. Chambliss demonstrates how various interest groups have been able to influence the content and the use of vagrancy laws (see Box 2.3).

Hagan and Leon (1977) and Platt (1969) show the operation of various "moral entrepreneurs" who were part of a child-saving movement, and the responsiveness of the state in creating legislation and a separate juvenile court. West and Snider (1985) have also documented the operation of interest groups here, but they expand the argument by suggesting that their motives were not only to save children, but also to deal with an excess labour supply.

Research on drug legislation also shows the state responding to various forms of pressure. Becker (1963) attempts to demonstrate that drug legislation in the United States was the result of the efforts of a civil servant, Harry Anslinger, who was primarily a moral entrepreneur. Dickson (1968) further argues that this bureaucrat was able to use his access to government services not only to foster particular moral objectives, but possibly also to save his organization and help it expand. The research of Shirley Small (1978) into Canadian

BOX 2.3

The Origin and Evolution of Vagrancy Law

In sum, the vagrancy laws constituted a legislative innovation designed to provide an abundance of cheap labor to England's ruling class during a period when serfdom was breaking down and the pool of available labor was depleting. They hit at the "idle" and "those refusing to labour." With the breakup of feudalism, the utility of these laws disappeared. The increased dependence of the economy upon commerce and trade made the former use of the vagrancy statutes irrelevant. In the early 17th century, the emphasis turned to "rogues," "vagabonds," and others suspected of criminal activities. During this period, the statutes embraced "roadmen" who preyed upon citizens transporting goods from one place to another. The increased importance of commerce to England during this period brought forth protective laws. The vagrancy statutes originally aimed at providing serfs for feudal landlords became a weapon in this new enterprise.

In the United States during the late 19th and early 20th centuries, vagrancy statutes were used, much as they had been in England, to create a labor force. The end of the Civil War left Southern plantation owners and Northern industrialists wishing to industrialize the South without an adequate work force. The Emancipation Proclamation and the passage of the 13th and 14th Amendments freed the slaves, but a system of wage labor did not exist. Also, there was unwillingness on the part of the plantation owners or industrialists to pay wages where slavery had previously provided cheap labor. A solution to the dilemma posed by the abolition of slavery was to arrest "free Negroes" for vagrancy and then force them to labor by leasing them to landowners, mining companies, or industrialists.

The use of vagrancy statutes to create and control the labor force in the United States is not limited to the South or to the period immediately following the Civil War. Until very recently, during times of harvest people were arrested for vagrancy and given the option of either working as a farm laborer or being sent to jail. These statutes were also used to control "undesirables." California used them to limit the immigration of unemployed persons during the depression. Vagrancy statutes also came to serve the police as a catch-all to permit them to arrest, harass, or jail persons whom they found to be a nuisance or suspected of being potential criminals.

The very nature of vagrancy statutes as catch-all categories pinpointing a status rather than an act makes them swim in vagueness.... Because of the vagueness of the statutes and the unbridled discretion granted law enforcers, the enforcement of these statutes has culminated in a large body of appellate court decisions. In 1972, a group of people arrested under the Jacksonville, Florida, statute appealed to the U.S. Supreme Court arguing that their arrest [was] unconstitutional because the statute was too vague.... The Supreme Court [supported] the defendants' appeal.... As a practical matter, the long, disreputable history of vagrancy statutes in the United States ended with this decision.

Source: William Chambliss. (1988). *Exploring Criminology.* New York: Macmillan, pp. 109–11. Reprinted by permission of the author.

narcotics legislation suggests that strong racist sentiments against Asians were a motivating force in the push for drug laws. Comack (1985) suggests that these anti-Asian sentiments were grounded in labour disputes that were being handled in racial terms instead of in class terms.

Graham's (1976) analysis of amphetamine legislation clearly demonstrates the operation of special interests. In spite of strong support from the American public and the president, attempts to change the Federal Drug Administration's

(FDA) control of amphetamine production failed because of pressure from the powerful drug companies. A legislative remedy would have gone a long way in promoting the common good with regard to this significant problem, but the power of a sizable lobby stifled the attempted changes. This fact was hidden from public view.

The analysis of the history of rape legislation (Brownmiller, 1975; Clark and Lewis, 1977; Kinnon, 1981) shows that such laws were enacted to protect the transmission of property in the male line of descent. Fathers used rape laws to avoid transferring property to men of whom they disapproved but who had taken their daughters by bride capture. They also sought compensation for the reduction of bride price that they suffered because their daughters had lost virginal status. Husbands wanted to secure control over their wives' reproductive capacity to ensure that they transferred their property to their own sons. Therefore, women and children became the property of the man of the household, and the act of rape became an offence against the husband. Over time, and as the result of concerted feminist activity, the act of sexual assault has been reconceptualized as a crime against the woman who has been victimized, and in some jurisdictions, including Canada, the husband can now be prosecuted for the rape of his wife (Chapter 5). This, of course, means that women have succeeded in having themselves redefined as persons and not merely as the property of their fathers or husbands.

Research conducted on anticombines legislation in Canada also provides the kind of evidence that demonstrates the operation of class-based interest groups in the framing of the law. Smandych (1985) outlines the confrontation that was brewing in the 1880s between labour and capital. The Knights of Labour movement specifically focused on the monopolistic nature of industrial capitalism and demanded the elimination of combines. A royal commission was established, and it submitted its report in the same year that the first anticombines legislation was enacted. But as Goff and Reasons (1978) point out, the wording of the statute was weakened in comparison with proposals in preliminary drafts. So the statue appeared to constrain capital interests when, in fact, it hardly did so. More changes to this statute in the 1970s further liberalized the circumstances under which mergers were permissible. Thus not only was the state unwilling to champion the interests of organized labour in the legislation, but as Goff and Reasons, and Snider (1980), have shown, the act has been applied only to small firms in Canada. In spite of the evidence of higher prices under conditions of oligopoly and in spite of protests by organized labour, the Canadian government has been unwilling to regulate the larger corporations in order to make Canada competitive in the international market. The government appears to be afraid of the loss of investor confidence and the flight of capital.

The history of occupational health and safety legislation is also very instructive. Friedman and Ladinsky (1980) trace the changes in the law governing industrial accidents and relate that, initially, employers were held responsible for injuries to workers under tort law, even if such injury resulted from the negligence of another employee. But this doctrine of *respondeat superior* was

The Canadian Centre for
Occupational Health and Safety
www.ccohs.ca

slowly replaced by the fellow-servant rule, which did not allow an employee to sue the employer in the case of injury unless harm was caused by the employer's personal misconduct. This move effectively prevented thousands of lawsuits in the United States, but the large number of accidents generated a continuing series of cases. Pressure was exerted by workers and their unions, and, in some jurisdictions, legislation was introduced to exclude the application of the fellow-servant rule. Workers' compensation schemes were proposed, but employers showed little interest in them until judges began awarding damages to employees. The compensation legislation that was finally enacted was based on a compromise position. Employers and employees would both contribute to the cost of the program, which would guarantee the injured employee compensation based on statutory schedules. However, the employer would be protected from the bulk of civil liability litigation because employee claims would be handled by an administrative agency instead of by the courts.

While this compensation program has been more or less acceptable to workers and owners, Walters (1983) shows how the Ontario government has undertaken changes in occupational health and safety legislation in an effort to reduce the cost of running its health-care system. It has been estimated that $1.4 billion is added to the health-care system's bill every year because of industrial accidents. Here is an interesting case of the state enacting legislation not to promote or protect the interests of any specific interest group, but rather to reduce its own deficit. It is interesting to note that Snider (1994) found that the greatest gains in the regulation of dangerous corporate behaviour have been in the realm of occupational health and safety.

These examples demonstrate that the process of law creation is heavily influenced by various interest groups and the pressure that they bring to bear on the state. It seems quite clear that the state often does find itself in situations in which it can make decisions based on the wishes and interests of the majority. At other times, it finds itself hard pressed to regulate effectively some of the special interest groups.

The Failure to Regulate: The Eclipse of the State?

There is growing concern among some analysts that transnational corporations operating in countries all over the globe have amassed so much economic power that they are getting beyond the control of nation-states. These corporations are expanding at two to three times the rates of growth of national economies, and the scale of such organizations gives them considerable power to resist the efforts of nation-states to regulate them. These corporations can, and do, bring considerable pressure to bear on national governments. If a government is too restrictive in its regulatory policies, a **transnational corporation** can relocate operations to another country with laws more to its liking. It is clear that corporations are responsible for behaviour that is harmful to various other interest groups and that these harms are not being effectively controlled by the state and the rule of law. The following examples help make the point.

transnational corporation

A corporation that has sales and production in many different nations. As a result of their multinational reach, these corporations are often thought to be beyond the political control of any individual nation-states.

Victims of Avoidable Harms

Reasons et al. (1981) recount numerous instances in which Canadian workers were needlessly exposed in the workplace to risks that resulted in injury and death. Many of these dangers are known to employers and are avoidable, leading Reasons et al. to suggest that these casualties are "victims without crimes," and that such injuries should be conceptualized as "assaults" on the worker. Stone (1975) recounts cases of corporate actions involving injury that would have resulted in criminal trials and possibly death sentences had they been committed by individuals. Dowie (1977) reports that the design problems of the Ford Pinto that resulted in passenger injury and death were known by the auto manufacturer, that these problems could have been addressed by cost-effective measures, and that the corporation chose not to make the improvements. Internal Ford memos reveal that the costs of design changes were compared to the costs of potential litigation for death, dismemberment, and injury, and that the company decided to put Pinto passengers at risk. It is hard to conceive of the death and injury created by the Pinto as accidental when such injury and death were anticipated and could have been avoided. It could be argued that these deaths were homicides and that such harmful behaviour ought to come under the control of the Criminal Code. Ford was, in fact, charged with homicide for one of the Pinto accidents, but was acquitted by an Indiana jury. These cases are common and make it clear that the modern consumer-citizen is not being protected under the rule of law from dangerous corporate misbehaviour.

The courts could move in the direction of holding corporations and their managers accountable for harms such as the one that took place in Cook County, Illinois. On July 1, 1985, three former executives of a silver-recycling plant were convicted of murder, and each received a sentence of 25 years in prison and a fine of $10 000 for the death of an employee. The company had exposed workers to cyanide gas by intentionally concealing warnings of hazards from immigrant workers. These murder convictions are believed to be the first in the United States of corporate officials in a job-related death. But to date, governments have not pursued a vigorous policy of bringing such corporate harms under the appropriate sections of the Criminal Code. This case turned out to be a rarity and not a harbinger of greater corporate accountability.

Finally, Brodeur (1985) has provided a detailed analysis of problems associated with the asbestos industry in the United States and Canada. It has come to light that the industry had been aware of the health hazards related to the inhalation of asbestos particles since the 1930s, but that it withheld this information from workers and did not take steps to improve the safety of the workplace. *Facts on File* has kept track of the significant developments related to the claims against asbestos companies. It is estimated by a U.S. Federal Appeals Court "that the number of current and future claimants [is] expected to reach several million" (*Facts on File*, 1997). Asbestos firms have been flooded with lawsuits in which courts have been finding them responsible for the resultant illnesses and deaths and have awarded victims sizable punitive damages. In

The Asbestos Institute Online
www.asbestos-institute.ca

1982, the Johns-Manville Corporation, with assets of more than $2 billion, filed for bankruptcy in the United States in an effort to escape paying the damages assessed for its harmful business practices. The U.S. government was put under considerable corporate pressure to grant this request. However, it was also faced with pressure to hold corporate citizens accountable to the same laws that ordinary citizens are bound to obey. It is increasingly clear that the government's response to this situation is to make use of *civil* rather than *criminal* courts. Reasons, Ross, and Paterson (1981) make a compelling case in arguing that many "accidents" in the workplace are not unforeseen and therefore not accidents. They argue that they should properly be conceptualized as "assaults on the workers" and handled by way of the Criminal Code rather than by occupational health and safety legislation, offering the following example: "It has been revealed that asbestos companies continued to expose workers to that substance in spite of the fact that they had had evidence concerning its fatal effects for some thirty years. Such conscious, premeditated, and rational behaviour undoubtedly led to thousands of deaths and disabilities. Nonetheless, asbestos companies are only liable to civil lawsuits" (6).

The court system initially declined to allow victims to bring forward class action suits, but finally, in 1991, the judicial panel on Multidistrict Litigation allowed more than 26 000 personal injury cases involving asbestos to be consolidated "in order to reduce delays and rising costs in asbestos litigation, which many lawyers said had reached a crisis level, with plaintiffs dying or depleting their resources before a verdict was handed down" (*Facts on File*, 1991). Since then, other courts have also consolidated asbestos cases because they are the largest number of civil cases in U.S. federal courts. This decision has made it easier for victims to gain access to damage awards. (Similar class action, or "mass tort," cases are also being used or contemplated in actions against tobacco companies as well as the manufacturers of the Dalkon Shield, Agent Orange, and silicone breast implants.) In an effort to limit their liability in future claims, large asbestos companies proposed a settlement under which "220 companies and their insurers would resolve outside of court as many as 100,000 new asbestos-injury claims for $1 billion over the next decade" (*Facts on File*, 1993). This settlement was an attempt by the companies to set a limit on monetary damages that they would be liable to pay to claimants after the number of claims and the size of settlements being awarded threatened to bankrupt many of them. An appeals court struck down the settlement package in May 1996. The appeals court ruled "that the agreement, which would bar individuals from pursuing future claims against the manufacturers, could compromise the rights of people who were currently unaware that they had been exposed to asbestos" (*Facts on File*, 1997). This decision was upheld by the Supreme Court on June 25, 1997. So the outcome of this episode of corporate deviance is far from settled. The state finds itself in the middle between the rights of individuals to damages and the needs of the corporations to limit damages so that they can remain in business. The state clearly has an interest in keeping corporations in business because they are the major employers in an industrial economy. Many jurisdictions are considering legislation that could limit the amount of damages for which corporations could be sued. It remains to be seen whether the United States is prepared to hold major corporations responsible under the law for their reckless and harmful behaviour.

Transnational corporations exist to make profits for investors, but the pursuit of profit has often been maximized by reckless and dangerous behaviour. The growing evidence of the serious harm to employees, customers, and the environment that has resulted suggests that a very powerful set of human actors is currently operating beyond the control of law. For example, Marchak (1991) describes some of the serious harms that stem from the creation of free trade zones within Third World countries. **Free trade zones** are created by countries within their borders to attract corporations to set up businesses. The corporations that work within these zones have often been able to negotiate very favourable terms, including freedom from taxation, exemptions from labour and environmental legislation, and very favourable labour regulations that allow them to hire workers very cheaply. One of the more harmful practices discussed by Marchak is the use of noncitizen, female workers from neighbouring states in microchip production and the garment industry. For example, "Singapore has imported Malaysian, Thai, Filipina, and Indonesian women as guest workers. These women have no citizen rights and no civil rights, and are deported if their eyesight or productivity fails to please, or if markets slow down" (Marchak, 1991, 147). When they are sent back home, they receive no compensation or benefits and typically face severe financial difficulties.

At present, many such harms cannot be brought to the courts for remedy because the state has not defined them as disputes or crimes. It may be asked whether the modern state has truly established the rule of law when serious sources of harm escape regulation and control. In some important ways, the legal power of the state has been superseded by the economic power of the modern corporation. The law cannot function to restore order in areas of social life where the state does not establish its jurisdiction. The absence of protection from the raw economic power of corporations places individuals, and perhaps even humanity, in harm's way.

Snider (1999, 2000) carefully illustrates many of the acts of corporate impropriety in Canada and documents the steps taken by the Canadian government to "make corporate crime disappear." She recounts how, in 1986, the House of Commons passed legislation that abolished the Combines Investigation Act and replaced it with the Competition Act. Among other things, this change removed criminal sanctions from the merger and monopoly sections and removed the public interest criterion that had previously been used when evaluating proposed mergers. She documents how these changes have further eroded the weak record of Canadian government scrutiny and intervention in corporate mergers that have been harmful to other groups in Canadian society. She notes that "the significance of the disappearance of corporate crime speaks volumes about the potential of state law to harness capital. The corporate counter-revolution illustrates how profoundly dependent the promulgation and enforcement of nation-state law is on the balance of powers operating within a society" (Snider, 1999, 204). She notes that when unions or social movements are strong, such as in Europe or Scandinavia, corporate "downsizing and decriminalization will be resisted longer and more effectively"

free trade zone

A specially designated geographical area within a nation that is exempt from the regulations and taxation normally imposed on business. These zones are intended to facilitate cross-border production and trade. Examples of these zones are found along the United States–Mexico border, where they are referred to as *maquilladora*.

(204). When they are weak, as in Canada and the United States, corporate wrongdoing is increasingly decriminalized and subject to decreasing scrutiny. Further, she stresses that progressive social movements have a vital role to play in developing and applying pressure on the state to use law as a mechanism for controlling harmful corporate behaviour.

CONCLUSION

In this chapter, the changing forms of social order have been traced from early small-scale societies to the complex arrangements of the modern era. Small communities based on self-restraint and mutual dependence were transformed into large industrial states in which social life is controlled by political and economic power. Societies that based their order on customary beliefs have been eclipsed by those that are organized according to differential access to surplus and the resultant stratification. These changing patterns of organization did not always happen as a result of historical developments within a single society. Often important external forces played an essential role in shaping the form and content of law. This is well illustrated by the case of Canada's legal inheritances in Box 2.4.

BOX 2.4

FOCUS

Canada's Legal Inheritances

Canada's Legal Inheritances is a collection of scholarly research reports that trace some of the key "threads in the tapestry that is Canada's current law. The weave is created from a complex of colonial, federal, provincial and local jurisdictions, ancient and recent, patterned from a multiplicity of statutes, judgments, behavioural rules and by-laws, some written and many oral, each coloured by religious values, private interests, moral maxims, public needs, and raw power."

While many people live out their lives close to the place of their birth and are guided by the culture of that place, many others move great distances, take their birth-culture with them and yet must learn the cultural expectations of their new residence. This phenomenon is part of the experience of many people in "an immigrant constructed country like Canada."

Canadian law is the product of several legal inheritances that include "indigenous laws and imported laws" reaching back to the 1620s when "the French were settling the northern St. Lawrence River valley and the English annually visiting Newfoundland, importing their respective legal inheritances; but, at least for that century, they applied their laws almost exclusively to themselves, as the Hudson's Bay Company would later in Rupert's Land. Aboriginal peoples, whether Algonquin or Huron, were repeatedly described ... by the Jesuits as having and applying their own legal inheritances to themselves.... The French had their indigenous laws, now transplanted, and the First Nations had theirs with neither importing the other into their indigenous laws. Likewise for Newfoundland, so long as the fishing fleet English remained seasonal visitors, the Beothuk legal inheritance did not connect with English admiralty law, any more than it did with the laws of other regular fishing fleets from Spain and Portugal.

(continued)

"By the end of the eighteenth century, approximately nine generations of imported European laws, in Lower Canada (Quebec), the Maritimes, Newfoundland and Rupert's Land had begun a more deliberate extension westward. The French led as coureurs de bois, soon followed by the English and Scots for the fledgling Hudson's Bay Company after 1670 and its later Montreal-based competitors. Then came an even larger group, the Loyalist immigrants fleeing the thirteen southerly secessionist New England colonies after 1774, mainly into Upper Canada (Ontario).... The Loyalists imported after 1774 an English common law shaped by their New England experiences. By then, there was little European sensitivity left for recognition of Canada's first indigenous Aboriginal law, a century and a half after the first European settlements. By mid-century, French and English laws had become the indigenous laws in their respective territories, awaiting the next wave of immigrants, largely from the newly formed United States. Nevertheless, Canada's three legal inheritances were in place: Aboriginal, French and English."

Significant changes came in 1763 when the "Treaty of Paris (3 September 1763) vested France's Lower Canada (Quebec), and lands east of the Mississippi River, in Great Britain's empire. Then Britain's Royal Proclamation of 1763 (7 October) played a double role in Canada's legal inheritances. It imposed the complete replacement of French civil law with the English common law in Lower Canada: '... as near as may be agreeable to the Laws of England.' The Proclamation had grown alongside events beginning with Quebec's capture in 1759 and become an instrument to neutralise Britain's expanded array of Aboriginal peoples. It did so by recognising their use of reserved lands, without mention of any rights, and only according to the English law based on royal prerogative, not on parliamentary or judge-made law, and not on any formal recognition of Aboriginal law. Defeating Old France had not translated into winning New France, and Britain soon had to restore French civil laws and procedures to Lower Canada (1774), albeit retaining the English criminal law." The British then set out to pacify "Aboriginal peoples without acknowledging their laws."

"Lord Durham's Report (1839), in the wake of Quebec's *patriote* rebellion, effectively imposed an English transplanted stability on the two territorial legal inheritances, which was institutionalised in the confederation created by the British North America Act (1867). Shortly thereafter the need to people the vast continent, at the expense of the Aboriginal birth and residence cultures, became too great to be limited to more English and French immigrants. The gates opened to Icelanders and Mennonites on the prairies, Irish in Newfoundland, Chinese in British Columbia." Each immigrant group brought its own "birth-culture laws and most kept them as their new residence-culture laws" to the extent possible. And so Canadian law emerged and continues to reemerge from a multitude of local and imported legal inheritances that have continued to refashion the codes of conduct in the many locales of Canadian life.

Source: Guth, DeLloyd J. "Prologue to Law in Canada: Dynamics and Roots" in DeLloyd J. Guth and W. Wesley Pue, eds. (2001). *Canada's Legal Inheritances*, Canadian Legal History Project, Faculty of Law, The University of Manitoba, Winnipeg, pp. xxx–xxxv. Reprinted with permission of the author.

The nature of dispute settlement has undergone a dramatic transformation from the small-scale society in which every member had direct access to the process of redress, to the present era in which not everyone can afford the costs of seeking a remedy through the courts. Furthermore, some serious harms are not currently subsumed under the law and, without a crime, there are few alternatives available for victims to seek redress. The concentration of social power has seen the state come to play a central role in the dispute settlement process.

"Overview of Dispute Resolution" Hill and Associates, Technical Arbitration and Conflict Resolution
www.batnet.com/oikoumene/tacr.html

Tudor

Refers to the period of English history from 1485 to 1603, when the nation's monarchs were descended from Owen Tudor and Catherine (1401–1437), widow of Henry V.

Since **Tudor** times, the administration and control of the legal process have been the prerogative of the state. While the interests of all members formed the basis of customary practice in small-scale communities, the interests of the merchant class have been given a special place in law in Western industrial societies. The modern state has not extended protection to all interest groups under the law since the heterogeneous nature of contemporary society and inherent conflicts of interest of various groups make this impossible. Nevertheless, there is growing pressure on the state to regulate the business practices of transnational corporations when they cause serious harm to human beings and the natural environment. However, some argue convincingly that nation-states lack the ability, or the will, to regulate such powerful organizations, which have come to dominate the social landscape in the past 50 years. It remains very much an open question whether the state and its legal system are up to the task of bringing these behemoths back under the rule of law.

While controlling modern corporations will require new and innovative legal methods, developments on other fronts bring this discussion of the evolution of law back to where we began. Many critics of the present justice system have advocated returning to a fundamentally different way of approaching criminal justice, to a system that is intended to restore social relationships rather than simply to punish. Advocates of restorative justice seek to return the focus of the justice system to repairing the harm that has been done to the victim and the community. A key element of restorative justice is the involvement of the victim and other members of the community as active participants in the process. The focus of the restorative justice approach is to reconcile offenders with those they have harmed and to help communities to *reintegrate* victims and offenders. The source of peace and order lies in a strong, active, and caring community, and proponents of restorative justice feel that a more humane and satisfying justice system can help to rebuild communities that may have been weakened by crime and other social ills.

Canada and New Zealand have led the way in the field of restorative justice. This is due at least in part to the influence of Aboriginal people in these two countries. Rupert Ross (1996) discusses some of the steps being undertaken in Aboriginal communities to place a renewed emphasis on healing as the community response to individual wrongdoing. Many community leaders view the restorative justice approach as a way to restore harmonious relationships and to foster the development of healthy communities.

The restorative approach is not just limited to Aboriginal communities. The Young Offenders Act and its successor, the Youth Criminal Justice Act, mandated youth courts to look for alternative measures to traditional punishment, and options such as restitution, alternative dispute resolution, victim–offender reconciliation, community group conferences, and sentencing panels are being used much more frequently for both juvenile and adult offenders. Braithwaite and Mugford (1994) have discussed some of the ways in which the traditional practices of shame, reintegration, and healing might be introduced into modern urban settings. The restorative approach helps to empower the victims of crime and to increase their participation in the dispute resolution process. While it is too soon to know the degree to which these prac-

Center for Restorative Justice and Mediation, University of Minnesota
ssw.che.umn.edu/ctr4rjm

"Aboriginal Corrections Publications"
Solicitor General Canada
www.sgc.gc.ca/abor_corrections/publications_e.asp

tices will replace more punitive methods of justice, it is clear that these traditional ideas are worth reconsidering.

SUMMARY

- For most of human history, we lived in small groups. Because individuals lacked the resources to live independently, such societies were coercive in their enforcement of codes of conduct.

- In small-scale societies, disputes were primarily settled by the parties to the dispute or by their kinship groups. The individual was expected to show a considerable degree of self-restraint because the survival of the group depended upon the cooperation of all its members.

- While people in small-scale societies were relatively equal to one another, changes in methods of production led to new social formations in which some families and individuals gained greater access to material surplus. This resulted in the growth of social power, the stratification of society, and the emergence of rulers. This process eventually gave rise to the development of the state.

- The rise of the central authority of the state undermined local kinship-based methods of resolving disputes. The harm was seen to be done to the ruler, who displaced the real victim of harm.

- As the merchant class grew, social life became increasingly regulated by contracts that were regulated and enforced by a strong central state. The interests of the capitalist class became central to the modern state, and the rule of law became the dominant means of regulating all aspects of human affairs.

- In democratic political structures, some laws reflect a broadly based consensus that certain behaviours need to be discouraged; however, other laws are passed because of the influence of groups with the power to have their interests reflected in legislation.

- In recent years, we have seen a return to restorative justice practices that are similar to those used in small-scale societies.

QUESTIONS FOR CRITICAL THINKING

1. Proponents of restorative justice are advocating that we move away from legalistic, punishment-oriented ways of dealing with social conflict. Do you think this will work in our contemporary society? Can you think of examples of restorative justice programs in your own community?

2. This chapter has discussed the role played by special interest groups in the passage and enforcement of particular laws. What are some of the laws that reflect the interests of some groups at the expense of others? What are some examples of laws that reflect the consensus of most members of society?

3. Assume you live in a small city. A local chemical company has been found to be improperly disposing of hazardous wastes by burying them underground. The wastes have leached into local wells and contaminated the water supply. Some say the company should be prosecuted and its operations shut down; however, the company is the largest employer in the community. Describe several ways in which the community might approach this problem. What sort of outcome is most likely?

4. Read the discussion of the history of vagrancy laws in Canada. What is the current Canadian law dealing with vagrancy? (Note: You can find the Criminal Code on the Internet at **canada.justice.gc.ca/STABLE/EN/Laws/Chap/C/C-46.html**.) Why do you think the police can no longer arrest someone who has no place to live and no money?

5. One of the problems with dispute resolution systems based on intervention by the victims or their kinship groups is that such a system can lead to feuds or vendettas among groups that do not agree with the manner in which a conflict was resolved. How did small-scale societies avoid prolonging these disputes?

NET WORK

You have learned in this chapter that one of the major trends in criminal justice is the return to methods of restorative justice. To learn more about methods of restorative justice, go to the Correctional Service of Canada website at **www.csc-scc.gc.ca**. About halfway down the page, click on "Satisfying Justice." This will give you access to a report written by the Church Council on Justice and Corrections. Using this report, answer the following questions:

1. What do the authors mean by "satisfying justice"? How can you use this concept to understand the dissatisfaction most Canadians seem to have with our present criminal justice system?

2. Describe four different types of restorative justice programs, and give an example of each.

KEY TERMS

acephalous society
bourgeois class
collective solidarity
common law
diffuseness of roles
feudalism
free trade zone
Gemeinschaft
Gesellschaft
hunting and gathering society

ideal type
mode of production
paramount chieftainship
sovereignty
state
stratification
surplus
transnational corporation
tribalism
Tudor

SUGGESTED READING

Braithwaite, John. (1989). *Crime, Shame, and Reintegration.* Cambridge: Cambridge University Press. The author reviews the dominant traditions in criminological theory and then suggests that we should seriously consider using the "family model of the criminal process: reintegrative shaming." His suggestion is that shaming is a powerful mechanism that should be used more deliberately to respond to deviance from core values in any good society. The intent should be to abhor the crime and not the person who commits it. The community should work to help the offender understand that harm has been caused, to feel shame, and then to seek and be granted reintegration into the community.

Chambliss, William, and Robert Seidman. (1982). *Law, Order, and Power.* (2nd ed.). Reading, Mass.: Addison-Wesley. Using a critical conflict perspective, the authors compare state and stateless societies with respect to dispute settlement. Primary emphasis is placed on the state system, the rule of law, and the role of social power in modern class-based social systems.

Friedman, Wolfgang. (1972). *Law in a Changing Society.* (2nd ed.). New York: Columbia University Press. This text traces legal change in a number of types of law, including contract, tort, insurance, criminal, family, and public law. The state, economic power, and corporate power are all examined for the part they have played in legal change. The changing place of the individual within modern law receives attention, as does the changing scope of international law.

Marchak, Patricia. (1991). *The Integrated Circus: The New Right and Restructuring of Global Markets.* Montreal and Kingston: McGill-Queen's University Press. The author reviews the international market economy from World War II up to the present. She shows the various manoeuvres that transnational corporations employ in the global arena to promote their interests. It becomes very evident why nation-states are increasingly unable to regulate these corporations and to protect their citizens from the negative consequences of profitable but damaging business practices.

Ross, Rupert. (1992). *Dancing with a Ghost: Exploring Indian Reality.* Markham, Ont.: Octopus Publishing Group. Some of the author's work is featured in Box 2.1 and Box 2.2 in this chapter. This book compares Aboriginal and white culture within the framework of the justice system. The reader is provided a standpoint from which to appreciate the problems that members of these two cultures have in understanding the actions of others as they interact within the modern dispute settlement process in Canada.

Ross, Rupert. (1996). *Returning to the Teachings: Exploring Aboriginal Justice.* Toronto: Penguin. Ross continues his efforts to sensitize non-Aboriginal readers to the traditional Aboriginal values and processes that were used to settle disputes. This thought-provoking text discusses how the Hollow Water community has worked to revitalize the traditional healing approach, which was seriously undermined and eroded in the last 50 years, in order to help this Aboriginal community deal with the devastating effects of sexual abuse. Clearly, there are challenges in accommodating this approach within a judicial system that is based on a different set of organizing principles.

Synder, Francis. (1981). "Anthropology, Dispute Processes and Law: A Critical Introduction." *British Journal of Law and Society* 8(2) (Winter). This review article examines current anthropological studies of law and dispute processes. It provides an excellent overview of major work and attempts to assess the value of these contributions for the development of social theories of law. It is an excellent article that will help a newcomer get his or her bearings.

BIBLIOGRAPHY

Anderson, Sarah, and John Cavanagh. (1996). "Corporate Empires." *Multinational Monitor* (December): 26–27. Washington D.C.: Essential Information, Inc.

Becker, Howard. (1963). "Moral Entrepreneurs." In Becker, *The Outsiders*. New York: Free Press.

Braithwaite, John, and S. Mugford. (1994). "Conditions of Successful Reintegration Ceremonies." *British Journal of Criminology* 34(2):139–71.

Brodeur, Paul. (1985). "The Asbestos Industry on Trial." In *The New Yorker* (June 10, June 17, June 24, July 1).

Brownmiller, Susan. (1975). *Against Our Will: Men, Women and Rape*. New York: Simon and Schuster.

Chambliss, William. (1969). "The Law of Vagrancy." In Chambliss (ed.), *Crime and the Legal Process* (pp. 51–63). New York: McGraw-Hill.

Clark, Lorenne, and Debra Lewis. (1977). *Rape: The Price of Coercive Sexuality*. Toronto: The Women's Press.

Colson, Elizabeth. (1974). *Tradition and Contract: The Problem of Order*. Chicago: Aldine Publishing.

Comack, Elizabeth. (1985). "The Origins of Canadian Drug Legislation: Labelling versus Class Analysis." In Thomas Fleming (ed.), *The New Criminologies in Canada: State, Crime and Control* (pp. 65–86). Toronto: Oxford University Press.

Dickson, Donald. (1968). "Bureaucracy and Morality: An Organizational Perspective on a Moral Crusade." *Social Problems* 16(2) (Fall):143–56.

Dowie, Mark. (1977). "Pinto Madness." *Mother Jones* 2(8) (Sept./Oct.).

Facts on File. (1991). 51 (August 8):2646.

———. (1993). 53 (March 25):2718.

———. (1997). 57 (June 26):2951.

Friedman, Lawrence, and Jack Ladinsky. (1980). "Social Change and the Law of Industrial Accidents." In William Evan (ed.), *The Sociology of Law* (pp. 395–414). New York: Free Press.

Goff, Colin, and Charles Reasons. (1978). *Corporate Crime in Canada*. Scarborough: Prentice Hall.

Graham, James. (1976). "Amphetamine Politics on Capital Hill." In William Chambliss (ed.), *Whose Law, What Order?* (pp. 107–22). New York: Wiley.

Gulliver, P.H. (1979). *Disputes and Negotiations: A Cross-Cultural Perspective*. New York: Academic Press.

Guth, DeLloyd J., and W. Wesley Pue (eds.). (2001). *Canada's Legal Inheritances*, Canadian Legal History Project, Faculty of Law, The University of Manitoba, Winnipeg.

Hagan, John, and Jeffrey Leon. (1977). "Rediscovering Delinquency: Social History, Political Ideology and the Sociology of Law." *American Sociological Review* 42 (August):587–98.

Hall, Jerome. (1952). *Theft, Law, and Society*. (2nd ed.). Indianapolis: Bobbs-Merrill.

———. (1969a). "Theft, Law and Society: The Carrier's Case." In William Chambliss (ed.), *Crime and the Legal Process* (pp. 32–51). New York: McGraw-Hill.

———. (1969b). "Crime and the Commercial Revolution." In Donald Cressey and David Ward (eds.), *Delinquency, Crime and Social Process* (pp. 100–10). New York: Harper and Row.

Hoebel, E. Adamson. (1973). *The Law of Primitive Man.* New York: Atheneum Press.

Jeffery, Clarence Ray. (1969). "The Development of Crime in Early English Society." In William Chambliss (ed.), *Crime and the Legal Process* (pp. 12–32). New York: McGraw-Hill.

Kennedy, Mark. (1976). "Beyond Incrimination: Some Neglected Facets of the Theory of Punishment." In William Chambliss (ed.), *Whose Law, What Order?* (pp. 34–65). New York: Wiley.

Kinnon, Dianne. (1981). *Report on Sexual Assault in Canada.* Report to the Canadian Advisory Council on the Status of Women.

Lenski, Gerhard. (1966). *Power and Privilege: A Theory of Social Stratification.* New York: McGraw-Hill.

Marchak, Patricia. (1991). *The Integrated Circus: The New Right and the Restructuring of Global Markets.* Montreal: McGill-Queen's University Press.

Michalowski, Raymond. (1985). *Law, Order and Crime.* New York: Random House.

Miliband, Ralph. (1969). *The State in Capitalist Society.* London: Quarter Books.

Newman, Katherine. (1983). *Law and Economic Organization: A Comparative Study of Preindustrial Societies.* London: Cambridge University Press.

Nielsen, Marianne. (1992). "Criminal Justice and Native Self-Government." In Robert Silverman and Marianne Nielsen (eds.), *Aboriginal Peoples and Canadian Criminal Justice.* Toronto: Penguin.

Platt, Anthony. (1969). *The Child Savers: The Invention of Delinquency.* Chicago: University of Chicago Press.

Reasons, Charles, Lois Ross, and Craig Paterson. (1981). *Assault on the Worker.* Toronto: Butterworths.

Ross, Rupert. (1989). "Leaving Our White Eyes Behind: The Sentencing of Native Accused." 3 *Canadian Native Law Reporter* 1 at 4.

———. (1996). *Return to the Teachings: Exploring Aboriginal Justice.* Toronto: Penguin.

Rossi, Peter, and Emily Waite. (1974). "The Seriousness of Crimes: Normative Structure and Individual Differences." *American Sociological Review* 39 (April):224–37.

Sellin, Thorsten, and Marvin Wolfgang. (1964). *The Measurement of Delinquency.* New York: Wiley.

Small, Shirley. (1978). "Canadian Narcotics Legislation, 1908–1923: A Conflict Model Interpretation." In W. Greenaway and S. Brickey (eds.), *Law and Social Control in Canada* (pp. 28–42). Scarborough: Prentice Hall.

Smandych, Russell. (1985). "Marxism and the Creation of Law: Re-examining the Origins of Canadian Anti-Combines Legislation 1890–1910." In Thomas Fleming (ed.), *The New Criminologies in Canada: State, Crime and Control* (pp. 87–99). Toronto: Oxford University Press.

Snider, Laureen. (1980). "Corporate Crime in Canada." In Robert Silverman and James Teevan (eds.), *Crime in Canadian Society* (pp. 348–68). (2nd ed.). Toronto: Butterworths.

———. (1994). "The Regulatory Dance: Understanding Processes in Corporate Crime." In Ronald Hinch (ed.), *Readings in Critical Criminology* (pp. 276–305). Scarborough: Prentice Hall.

———. (1999). "Relocating Law: Making Corporate Crime Disappear." In Elizabeth Comack (ed.), *Locating Law: Race, Class/Gender Connections* (pp. 183–207). Halifax: Fernwood Publishing.

———. (2000). "The Sociology of Corporate Crime: An Obituary." *Theoretical Criminology* 4(2):169–206.

Stone, Christopher. (1975). *Where the Law Ends: Social Control of Corporate Behavior*. New York: Harper and Row.

Thompson, Edward P. (1976). *Whigs and Hunters: The Origin of the Black Act*. New York: Pantheon Books.

Tigar, Michael, and Madeleine Levy. (1977). *Law and the Rise of Capitalism*. New York: Monthly Review Press.

Tönnies, Ferdinand. (1887). *Community and Society*. New York: Harper Books.

Walters, Vivienne. (1983). "Occupational Health and Safety Legislation in Ontario: An Analysis of Its Origins and Content." *Canadian Review of Sociology and Anthropology* 20(4) (November):138–69.

West, Gordon, and Laureen Snider. (1985). "A Critical Perspective on Law in the Canadian State: Delinquency and Corporate Crime." In Thomas Fleming (eds.), *The New Criminologies in Canada: State, Crime and Control*. Toronto: Oxford University Press.

Criminal Law

3

SIMON VERDUN-JONES
Simon Fraser University

Criminology is concerned with crimes and those individuals who commit them. It is necessary for criminologists to acquire a basic understanding of the criminal law because it is this body of legal rules and principles that designates which types of behaviour should be prohibited and punished and also determines whether those persons who are accused of committing crimes should be convicted and officially labelled as criminals.

After reading this chapter, you should be able to

- Define a crime.
- Identify the sources of Canadian criminal law.
- Distinguish between regulatory offences and "true crimes."
- Analyze criminal offences in terms of the *actus reus* (physical) and *mens rea* (mental) elements.
- Understand the differences between subjective and objective *mens rea* requirements.
- Describe the different ways in which a person may become a party to a criminal offence.
- Identify the basic components of the inchoate crimes of counselling, attempt, and conspiracy.
- Describe the major defences that may be raised in response to a criminal charge: not criminally responsible on account of mental disorder; mistake of fact; mistake of law; intoxication; necessity; duress; provocation; and self-defence.

LEARNING
OBJECTIVES

WHAT IS A CRIME?

For a lawyer, the definition of a **crime** is remarkably simple: namely, the coupling of a *prohibition* against certain conduct with a *penal sanction* (such as imprisonment or a fine). In Canada, all crimes are the creatures of a legislative process and are contained in statutes such as the Criminal Code. Some crimes may reflect an almost universal social consensus that certain conduct is wrong and should be punished (for example, murder and sexual assault). Other crimes may not be based on such a general consensus and a significant proportion of Canadians may not consider them to be inherently wrong and deserving of punishment (for example, assisting a terminally ill patient to commit suicide

crime
Conduct that is prohibited by law and that is subject to a penal sanction (such as imprisonment or a fine).

when he or she is in great pain). While legislators need to wrestle with the ongoing task of trying to bring the criminal law into line with emerging community notions of crime and justice, the police and the judiciary are required to enforce the existing criminal law, regardless of their own private views as to whether particular conduct should or should not be defined as a crime (see Box 3.1). Therefore, while it is important to be aware of the intensely political nature of the process that results in the enactment of legislation dealing with crime and punishment, such considerations fall outside the scope of a chapter dealing with the contents of the existing criminal law.

BOX 3.1

FOCUS

Conflict of Values: The Case of Euthanasia

If a person is suffering from a terminal illness, is in great pain, and wishes to end his or her life, should a physician be able to grant that wish by, for example, administering a lethal injection? In Canada, the Criminal Code (section 14) clearly prohibits anyone, including a physician, from killing another human being—even if that person has given an unequivocal consent to the taking of his or her life. As a consequence, in Canada, a so-called mercy killing constitutes murder under the Criminal Code. However, in both the Netherlands and Belgium, recent legislation has been passed that permits physicians to perform euthanasia on their patients in certain, strictly defined, circumstances. Does the existing criminal law in Canada reflect current values? What should the Parliament of Canada do if Canadians are profoundly divided on this issue?

In October 1993, Robert Latimer, a Saskatchewan farmer, killed his severely disabled daughter, Tracy. Although the 12-year-old Tracy was not capable of giving consent, the homicide was portrayed by many as a "mercy killing." Ultimately, Latimer was convicted of second-degree murder. Under the Criminal Code [section 745(c)], the minimum sentence that may be imposed for second-degree murder is life imprisonment with no possibility of parole for a period of 10 years. Some Canadians argued that this sentence should not apply to a father who had killed his daughter in order to spare her further pain

and suffering. In fact, polls consistently indicated that most Canadians believed that the sentence was excessively harsh. On the other hand, other Canadians asserted that, if the courts were to impose a more lenient sentence on Latimer because his motive was that of compassion, they would be implicitly diminishing the value of the lives of persons with disabilities. After all, Tracy was not consulted as to her fate: her father made the decision for himself that her life was not worth living. In 2001, the Supreme Court of Canada ruled that the mandatory sentence in the Criminal Code did not contravene the Canadian Charter of Rights and Freedoms and that Latimer was not entitled to receive a so-called constitutional exemption that would relieve him of the penalty of life imprisonment. However, the Court did point out that the government of Canada has the power to exercise the "Royal Prerogative of Mercy" [Criminal Code, section 748(1)] and grant Latimer an early release. Was Latimer's sentence too harsh? Should Latimer be released before the ten-year period of ineligibility for parole has expired?

For further reading, see *R. v. Latimer*, [2001] 1 S.C.R. 3, available online at www.lexum.umontreal.ca/csc-scc and R. Malhotra. (2001). "Tracy Latimer, Disability Rights and the Left." *Canadian Dimension* (July/August 2001), available online at www.canadiandimension. mb.ca/v35/344rm.htm.

WHAT IS CRIMINAL LAW?

The body of jurisprudence known as **criminal law** includes not only the definitions of the various crimes and the specification of the respective penalties but also a set of general principles concerning criminal responsibility and a series of defences to a criminal charge. In this chapter, the main focus will be on the general principles underlying Canadian criminal law and the major defences that have been developed both by the Parliament of Canada and by judges in the course of deciding specific cases that have come before them.

criminal law

A body of jurisprudence that includes the definition of various crimes, the specification of various penalties, a set of general principles concerning criminal responsibility, and a series of defences to a criminal charge.

THE SOURCES OF CRIMINAL LAW

One of the most basic questions that might be asked about criminal law is "Where does it come from?" There are two primary sources of Canadian criminal law: (i) legislation and (ii) judicial decisions that either interpret such legislation or state the "common law."

Federal Legislation and Criminal Law

Since Canada is a federal state, legislation may be enacted both by the Parliament of Canada and by the legislatures of the various provinces and territories. However, under the terms of the Canadian Constitution, there is a distribution of specific legislative powers between the federal and provincial or territorial levels of government. Under the terms of the Constitution Act, 1867, the federal Parliament has the exclusive jurisdiction to enact "criminal law and the procedures relating to criminal matters." One might well think that it is relatively simple to define the term "criminal law" for the purpose of interpreting the scope of the federal criminal law power under the Constitution Act, 1867. However, this task is not quite as straightforward as it may appear at first glance. It was noted above that, for most purposes, a crime can be defined in terms of two basic elements: (i) a *prohibition* against certain conduct and (ii) a *penalty* for violating that prohibition. However, when the courts are required to decide whether Parliament has enacted legislation that legitimately falls within the scope of its criminal law power, a third element must be added to the definition of a crime. More specifically, the Supreme Court of Canada has ruled that the prohibition and penalty must be directed against a "public evil" or some form of behaviour that is having an injurious effect on the Canadian public. If any of these three elements are missing, the legislation concerned may not be considered to fall within the legitimate scope of the federal criminal law power; indeed, it may be ruled invalid insofar as it intrudes into areas of legislative authority that have been specifically allocated to the provincial and territorial legislatures. Consider the problem of environmental pollution. In the case of *Hydro-Québec* (1997), the Supreme Court of Canada held that the Parliament of Canada could use its criminal law power to enact legislation that imposes penalties on those individuals who engage in serious acts of pollution. The particular legislation in question in this case was the Canadian Environmental Protection Act, R.S.C. 1985, c. 16. In the words of Justice La Forest, "pollution is an 'evil' that Parliament can legitimately seek to suppress." Therefore, the Canadian Environmental Protection Act was considered to constitute "criminal law" because the Parliament of Canada was unequivocally concerned with the need to safeguard public health from the devastating consequences of toxic pollution. If the Supreme Court had ruled that this statute was not a genuine exercise of the Parliament of Canada's criminal law power, then the Court would have ruled that the Act was invalid.

What important pieces of legislation has the Canadian Parliament enacted in the field of criminal law? Undoubtedly, the most significant federal statute, dealing with both the *substantive criminal law* and the *procedural* law relating to criminal matters, is the Criminal Code, R.S.C. 1985, c. C-46 (first enacted in 1892). "Substantive criminal law" refers to legislation that defines the nature of various criminal offences (such as murder, manslaughter, and theft) and specifies the various legal elements that must be present before a conviction can be entered against an accused person. The term also refers to the legislation that defines the nature and scope of such defences as provocation, duress, and self-defence.

criminal procedure

A body of legislation that specifies the procedures to be followed in the prosecution of a criminal case and defines the nature and scope of the powers of criminal justice officials.

The term **criminal procedure** refers to legislation that specifies the procedures to be followed in the prosecution of a criminal case and defines the nature and scope of the powers of criminal justice officials. For example, the procedural provisions of the Criminal Code classify offences into three categories: (i) *indictable* offences; (ii) offences punishable on *summary conviction*; and (iii) *"mixed" or "hybrid" offences* that may be tried either as indictable or as summary conviction offences. These provisions then specify the manner in which these different categories of offences may be tried within the system of criminal courts. For example, they spell out whether these offences may be tried by a judge sitting alone or by a judge and jury, and indicate whether they may be tried before a judge of the Superior Court or a judge of the Provincial (or Territorial) Court. Indictable offences carry the most serious penalties upon conviction of the accused. The procedural provisions of the Criminal Code are also concerned with defining the nature and scope of the powers of such officials as police officers. For example, these provisions stipulate the nature and scope of the powers of the police in relation to the arrest and detention of suspects. Likewise, the Criminal Code articulates the powers of judges in relation to the important task of sentencing convicted offenders.

In addition to the Criminal Code, a number of other federal statutes unquestionably create "criminal law." These include the Controlled Drugs and Substances Act, S.C. 1996, c. 19, and the Youth Criminal Justice Act, S.C. 2002, c. 1.

Federal and Provincial or Territorial Regulatory Legislation: Quasi-Criminal Law

Under the Constitution Act, 1867, the provincial and territorial legislatures have been granted exclusive jurisdiction to enact legislation in relation to such issues as health, education, highways, liquor control, and hunting and fishing. This legislation may be enforced through the imposition of "a fine, penalty or impris-onment." At first blush, it may seem that the use of punishments of these types would persuade the courts to treat such legislation as criminal law—an area of legislative authority that is reserved exclusively for the Parliament of Canada. However, such regulatory legislation does not constitute "real" criminal law for the purpose of the distribution of powers under the Constitution because such legislation lacks the necessary element of "public evil" that was discussed earlier. Indeed, regulatory legislation is concerned with the orderly regulation of activi-ties that are inherently legitimate (such as driving a vehicle or operating a busi-ness). Criminal law is directed toward the control of behaviour that is considered to be inherently wrong (namely, **"true crimes"** such as theft, assault, sexual assault, and wilful damage to property). **Regulatory offences**, therefore, are quite distinct from the "true crimes" that arise under the Criminal Code or the Controlled Drugs and Substances Act, and they are, therefore, classified as quasi-criminal law ("quasi" means seeming, not real, or halfway).

Regulatory offences are generally far less serious in nature than "true crimes." Indeed, the maximum penalties that may be imposed for violation of regulatory offences are generally no more than a fine or a maximum term of imprisonment of six months or both. Under the Criminal Code or the Controlled Drugs and Substances Act, however, the penalties may range as high as a life term of imprisonment.

Regulatory offences are also to be found in a broad range of federal statutes that regulate activities that fall within the jurisdiction of the Parliament of Canada: for example, the Competition Act, R.S.C. 1985, C. c-34; the Food and Drugs Act, R.S.C. 1985, F-27; The Fisheries Act, R.S.C. 1985, c. F-14; and the Trade-Marks Act, R.S.C. 1985, c. T-13. Taken together with the quasi-criminal offences created under provincial and territorial legislation, these federal regu-latory offences contribute to a vast pool of quasi-criminal law that has become increasingly complex as modern society has developed. Even the average lawyer is acquainted with only a fraction of the hundreds of thousands of regulatory offences that currently exist under both federal and provincial or territorial leg-islation. However, ignorance of the law is no excuse for those who commit reg-ulatory offences.

Judge-Made Criminal Law

The second major source of criminal law in Canada is the large body of judicial decisions that either interpret criminal legislation or expound the "**common law**"—a term that refers to that body of judge-made law that evolved in areas that were not covered by legislation. Parliament cannot possibly provide for every possibility or provide comprehensive definitions of every term used in the legislation that it enacts; therefore, there is always great scope for judicial inter-pretation of the Criminal Code. For example, in section 380 of the Code, Parliament has created the offence of fraud. According to section 380, fraud may be committed by "deceit, falsehood, or other fraudulent means." However, the term "other fraudulent means" was left undefined and it was left to the Supreme Court of Canada to provide a working definition in the case of *R. v.*

"true crime"
A "true crime" occurs when an individual engages in conduct that is not only prohibited but also constitutes a serious breach of community values; as such, it is perceived by Canadians as being inherently wrong and deserving of punishment. Only the Parliament of Canada, using its criminal law power under the Constitution Act, 1867, may enact a "true crime."

regulatory offences
Regulatory offences arise under legislation (either federal, provin-cial, or territorial) that regulates inherently legitimate activities connected with trade, commerce, and industry or with everyday living (driving, fishing, etc.). These offences are not considered to be serious in nature and usually carry only a relatively minor penalty upon conviction.

common law
The body of judge-made law that has evolved in areas not covered by legislation.

Olan, Hudson and Hartnett (1978), namely, "all other means which can properly be stigmatized as dishonest."

As far as the common law is concerned, it is important to recognize that, historically, much of the English criminal law, upon which the Criminal Code of 1892 was loosely based, was developed by judges who were required to deal with new situations and challenges that were not dealt with by the legislation of the day. In Canada, there is one common law offence that still exists—namely, contempt of court. However, with the exception of contempt of court, the Criminal Code (section 9) has, since 1954, made it clear that judges cannot create any new common law crimes. On the other hand, the judges have developed a number of common law defences that were not dealt with by legislation. For example, Canadian courts have developed a defence of necessity even though it is not mentioned in the Criminal Code; hence, necessity is known as a common law defence. Section 8(3) of the Criminal Code preserves any common law "justification," "excuse," or "defence" to a criminal charge "except in so far as they are altered by or are inconsistent with this act or any other act of the Parliament of Canada." This provision is particularly significant because it means that common law defences, such as necessity, may still be developed by Canadian judges.

IMPACT OF THE CANADIAN CHARTER OF RIGHTS AND FREEDOMS ON CRIMINAL LAW

Charter

The Canadian Charter of Rights and Freedoms, enacted by the Canada Act 1982 (UK) c. 11 (see glossary for extended definition).

The enactment of the Canadian Charter of Rights and Freedoms as part of the Constitution Act, 1982, heralded a dramatic new era in the relationship between judges and the elected members of the Parliament of Canada and the legislative assemblies of the various provinces and territories. As an entrenched bill of rights, the **Charter** empowers judges to declare any piece of legislation to be invalid—and of no force or effect—if the latter infringes on an individual's Charter rights (such as the presumption of innocence [section 11(d)] or the right not to be deprived of the right to life, liberty, and security of the person except in accordance with the principles of fundamental justice [section 7]). Canadian judges have demonstrated a willingness to use this awesome power where they believe it is necessary to do so. For example, in *R. v. Morgentaler, Smolig and Scott* (1988), the Supreme Court of Canada declared the controversial abortion provisions of the Criminal Code (section 287) to be invalid because they unjustifiably infringed the right of Canadian women to "security of the person" (protected by section 7 of the Charter). However, the courts are bound to take into account the provisions of section 1 of the Charter, which permit Parliament or the provincial or territorial legislatures to impose "such reasonable limits [on Charter rights] as can be demonstrably justified in a free and democratic society." This provision requires Canadian courts to engage in an elaborate balancing act in which they must decide whether the infringement of an individual's Charter rights can be justified in the name of some "higher good." For example, in *R. v. Sharpe* (2001), the Supreme Court of Canada ruled that certain aspects of the child pornography provisions of the Criminal Code (section 163.1) infringed the accused person's right to "freedom of thought, belief, opinion and expression"—a right that is guaranteed by section 2(b) of the Charter. However, the Court also ruled that the child pornography provisions constituted a "reasonable limitation" on the accused's section 2(b) right and were, therefore, justified under section 1 of the Charter (see also Box 3.2).

BOX 3.2

FOCUS

Giving the Dying a Helping Hand: Physician-Assisted Suicide

Canada no longer treats those who attempt to commit suicide as criminals. However, section 241(b) of the Criminal Code makes it an offence, punishable by up to 14 years' imprisonment, to assist another person to commit suicide. Suppose that an adult who is competent to make important life decisions for him or herself is suffering from a terminal illness, is suffering considerable pain, and wishes to die at a time of his or her own choosing. Should this person be able to seek the assistance of a physician to end his or her life? Section 241(b) currently renders it a crime for a physician (or anyone else) to provide such a helping hand. Unlike euthanasia, where a physician deliberately causes the death of a patient through the administration of a lethal dose of a drug, physician-assisted suicide occurs when a physician provides the patient with the means to bring about his or her own death (by providing the necessary drugs).

Sue Rodriguez, a middle-aged woman, was dying from amyotrophic lateral sclerosis (a degenerative disease of the muscles). Ms. Rodriguez wished to terminate her own life before she became incapable of independent movement, and she wished to obtain the assistance of a physician to provide her with the means to bring about her own death. She went to court to seek a declaration that section 241(b) was invalid because it infringed her rights under sections 7 and 15 of the Canadian Charter of Rights and Freedoms. However, by a slim 5–4 majority, the Supreme Court of Canada upheld the validity of section 241(b), thereby denying Sue Rodriguez the right to a physician-assisted suicide. For the majority of the justices of the Supreme Court, the prohibition of physician-assisted suicide was necessary in

order to affirm the fundamental principle of the sanctity of human life; to permit a doctor to "lawfully participate in taking life would send a signal that there are circumstances in which the state approves of suicide."

In *Nancy B. v. Hôtel-Dieu de Québec* (1992), a 25-year-old woman had been suffering for two years from Guillan-Barré syndrome, an incurable neurological disorder. She was totally paralyzed and needed a respirator to keep her alive. Nancy B. wished to die rather than continue her life "literally tied to her hospital bed." She asked a judge to declare that she had a right to refuse any further treatment and to have the respirator disconnected. The judge declared that a competent adult has the right to refuse any further treatment, even if that decision brings about her death. Since Nancy B. could not do so herself, her physician disconnected the respirator and death ensued. Did Nancy B. commit suicide? If so, how is her case different from that of Sue Rodriguez? Are the different results in the two cases justifiable with regard to sound policy or logic?

Should the Parliament of Canada legalize physician-assisted suicides? In Europe, both Belgium and the Netherlands have enacted such legislation and have incorporated a strict regime of regulation of physicians' conduct in this context. In the American state of Oregon, physician-assisted suicide was legalized by the Death with Dignity Act, which became effective in 1997. Between 1997 and 2002, 129 patients in Oregon were given prescriptions for lethal medications by their physicians. However, in April 2002, the European Court of Human Rights ruled, in the case of Mrs. Diane Pretty, that the United Kingdom's criminal prohibition of assisted suicide

(continued)

did not infringe her rights under the European Convention of Human Rights—a decision that closely parallels the ruling of the Supreme Court of Canada in the case of Sue Rodriguez. What are the arguments for and against making assisted suicide a criminal act? Does the state have any legitimate reason to interfere in the relationship between doctor and patient? Would legalization of assisted suicide send Canadians down the "slippery slope" toward acceptance of suicide as a normal response to a painful process of dying? Should society place greater emphasis on providing effective "palliative care" (pain-relieving treatment administered by doctors and nurses to those patients who are terminally ill) rather than approving physician-assisted suicides? Why do you think the Supreme Court of Canada was so deeply split over the Charter challenge in the *Rodriguez* case?

See *Rodriguez v. British Columbia (Attorney General)*, [1993] 3 S.C.R. 519, available online at www.lexum.umontreal.ca./csc-scc/, and *Nancy B. v. Hôtel-Dieu de Québec* (1992), 69 C.C.C. (3d) 450 (Québec Superior Ct.), available online through Quicklaw, [1992] Q.J. No 1.

THE BASIC ELEMENTS OF A CRIME: *ACTUS REUS* AND *MENS REA*

The study of criminal law invariably commences with the statement that every criminal offence can be analyzed in terms of two major elements: namely, *actus reus* and *mens rea*. These terms are derived from the Latin maxim, *actus non facit reum nisi mens sit rea* (which, translated literally, means that an act does not render a person guilty unless his or her mind is also guilty). Based on this principle, it can be stated that an accused person may not be convicted of a criminal offence unless the prosecution can prove the following beyond a reasonable doubt:

(a) that a particular event or state of affairs was "caused" by the accused person's conduct (*actus reus*); and

(b) that this conduct was simultaneously accompanied by a certain state of mind (*mens rea*).

In essence, the concept of *mens rea* refers to the mental elements of an offence while the term *actus reus* refers to all the other elements that must be proved by the Crown. However, there is an important gloss that must be placed on this seemingly simple formulation: namely, that the *actus reus* of a criminal offence includes an element of voluntariness. As Justice McLachlin said, in delivering the judgment of the majority of the justices of the Supreme Court of Canada in the case of *Théroux* (1993),

> The term *mens rea*, properly understood, does not encompass all of the mental elements of crime. The *actus reus* has its own mental element; the act must be the voluntary act of the accused for the *actus reus* to exist.

actus reus

All the elements contained in the definition of a criminal offence—other than the mental elements (*mens rea*).

The *Actus Reus* Elements of a Crime

In general, it is possible to divide the **actus reus** into three separate components:

(i) conduct (a voluntary act or omission constituting the central feature of the crime);

(ii) the surrounding or "material" circumstances;

(iii) the consequences of the voluntary conduct.

For example, in order to prove that an accused person is guilty of the offence of assault causing bodily harm (section 267 of the Criminal Code), the Crown must establish that the accused applied force to the body of the victim (conduct); that the force was applied without the consent of the victim (circumstances); and that the application of force caused bodily harm (consequences). Bodily harm is defined in section 2 of the Criminal Code as meaning "any hurt or injury to a person that interferes with the health or comfort of the person and is more than merely transient or trifling in nature." For example, a swollen face and bleeding nose have been considered to constitute "bodily harm" and Canadian courts have also ruled that the term even includes psychological harm.

There are some significant exceptions to the division of the *actus reus* into three elements. For example, perjury (section 131 of the Criminal Code) is an offence that does not require proof of any consequences. Provided the accused person knowingly makes a false statement with intent to mislead a court, he or she will be guilty of perjury even though not a single person believed the false statement. However, consequences do constitute a crucial element of the *actus reus* of most criminal offences. Consider, by way of illustration, the offences of dangerous driving causing death or dangerous driving causing bodily harm (section 249 of the Criminal Code): these carry maximum penalties of 14 and 10 years respectively. In contrast, the "simple" offence of dangerous driving (where the Crown does not have to prove the consequences of death or bodily harm) carries a maximum penalty of only five years. Occasionally, the *actus reus* of an offence does not contain the requirement that the accused engage in conduct of any kind; instead, the Crown must prove that the accused was found in a particular "condition" or "state." For example, it is an offence [section 351(1) of the Criminal Code] to be in possession of housebreaking instruments without a lawful excuse for having them. It is not necessary for the prosecution to establish that the accused person actually used the housebreaking instruments; it is enough that the accused person was found in possession of the instruments concerned. The rationale for this type of offence is that it is often necessary to use the criminal law in a preventative manner; it is undoubtedly preferable to stop the break-in before it occurs and it is only "guilty" possession that is the target of section 351(1) of the Criminal Code.

An important question that must be addressed is whether a mere failure to act (an omission) can qualify as the conduct element of the *actus reus* of an offence. The answer is that a failure to act can constitute a crime only if the accused was under a pre-existing legal duty to act. A good illustration is the duty owed by a parent to a small child to provide the latter with the "necessaries of life"—for example, by feeding the child and providing him or her with necessary medical care (section 215 of the Criminal Code). Under Canadian criminal law, there is no duty to rescue a stranger who is in serious danger. However, there is a duty to rescue when the person in danger is a child or spouse of the accused person or is in some other relationship that imposes a duty to act (for example, a prisoner is owed such a duty by the officer in charge of the jail in which the prisoner is being held). It has been argued that the criminal law is seriously deficient insofar as it does not require every adult citizen to take active steps to rescue a person who is in danger—provided, of course, that the rescue may be undertaken without an unreasonable degree of danger to the rescuer. However, it may be very difficult to enforce such a duty in practice. For example, suppose a radio message is broadcast that informs listeners that volunteers are needed to help rescue children in a collapsed school building. Should everyone who hears that message be legally required to forsake what they are doing and rush to the scene of the disaster?

A final point that needs to be made about the *actus reus* component of an offence concerns the requirement that the accused's conduct be voluntary. If a driver is repeatedly stung by a swarm of bees and crashes his or her vehicle, the accident would be considered the consequence of a series of reflex actions that were beyond the driver's control; clearly, they did not flow from the free exercise of his or her will. Similarly, if an accused person's consciousness is impaired to such an extent that he or she is unable to control his or her actions, it may be concluded that there was no *actus reus* of any criminal offence because the accused acted involuntarily; when this situation occurs, the accused may raise the defence of automatism. In fact, automatism is a rare—and somewhat exotic—defence and may be successfully raised only in a very limited number of situations. For example, if an individual is hit on the head and immediately thereafter enters a state of impaired consciousness and assaults another person, he or she may claim the benefit of the defence of automatism—provided it is established that the assault constituted an involuntary action. In practice, automatism is a difficult defence to claim successfully because, in the *Stone* case (1999), the Supreme Court of Canada ruled that the burden of proving the defence is placed on the accused person who raises it (normally, the Crown is required to prove every element of the *actus reus* and *mens rea* components of an offence). Stone had been charged with the murder of his wife, following a series of provocative statements that she had directed at him. The accused had stabbed his wife 47 times but claimed that, at the time, he was in a state of dissociation following the shock of the "psychological blow" that had been inflicted on him by his spouse's hurtful words: more specifically, he stated that a "whoosh" sensation had swept over him and that he was unaware of what he was doing. Ultimately, the jury concluded that the claim of automatism had not been proved by Stone. However, Stone was convicted of manslaughter rather than murder because the jury concluded that there had been provocation (within the meaning of section 232 of the Criminal Code). Stone's conviction of manslaughter was later affirmed by the Supreme Court of Canada, where Justice Bastarache stated that the plausibility of a claim of automatism in such cases is significantly reduced if the victim is alleged to be the "trigger" of the violence directed at him or her. A successful defence of automatism presupposes that accused persons are plunged into such a state of impaired consciousness that they are barely aware of what is happening around them. In Stone's case, the accused responded directly to what he perceived to be insults and the jury evidently believed that his actions were those of a man who knew where he was and what he was doing.

The *Mens Rea* Elements of a Crime

Basically, **mens rea** refers to all the mental elements (other than voluntariness) that the Crown must prove (beyond a reasonable doubt) in order to obtain a conviction of a criminal offence. *Mens rea* is rather like a chameleon insofar as it changes its nature from one offence to another. Obviously, the *mens rea* for murder is very different from that required for theft. Furthermore, *mens rea* is not one mental state but rather a combination of mental states; indeed, it is necessary to analyze the *mens rea* required in relation to each of the three elements of the *actus reus* of any particular crime—that is, conduct, circumstances, and consequences.

> **mens rea**
> The mental elements (other than voluntariness) contained in the definition of a criminal offence.

The requirement that the prosecution prove *mens rea* reflects basic values that Canadians hold in relation to civil liberties. In essence, the *mens rea* requirement ensures that only those defendants who are morally blameworthy are convicted of "true crimes" under the Criminal Code. As Justice McLachlin said in the Supreme Court of Canada's decision in *Théroux* (1993),

> *Mens rea* ... refers to the guilty mind, the wrongful intention, of the accused. Its function in the criminal law is to prevent the conviction of the morally innocent—those who do not understand or intend the consequences of their acts.

Subjective and Objective *Mens Rea*

There are two very distinct types of *mens rea* requirements in Canadian criminal law: (i) subjective and (ii) objective.

Subjective *mens rea* is based on the notion that accused persons may not be convicted of a criminal offence unless (a) they *deliberately intended* to bring about the consequences prohibited by the law; (b) *subjectively realized* that their conduct might bring about such prohibited consequences but recklessly continued with that conduct in spite of their knowledge of the risks involved; or (c) were *wilfully blind* in that they deliberately closed their minds to the obvious criminality of their actions. As Justice McLachlin explained in the Supreme Court of Canada's decision in *Creighton* (1993),

> **subjective *mens rea***
> The *mens rea* elements of a criminal offence are considered to be subjective if they are based on a determination of "what actually went on in the accused person's mind." The forms of subjective *mens rea* are intention and knowledge; recklessness; and wilful blindness.

> The requisite intention or knowledge may be inferred from the act and its circumstances. Even in the latter case, however, it is concerned with "what was actually going on in the mind of this particular accused at the time in question."

Subjective *mens rea*, therefore, constitutes a requirement that the accused *deliberately choose to do something wrong*.

Objective *mens rea* is predicated on the principle that accused persons should be convicted of certain offences, not because they intended to bring about the prohibited consequences or acted recklessly, but rather because

> **objective *mens rea***
> The *mens rea* elements of a criminal offence are considered to be objective if they are based on a determination of whether a reasonable person, in the same circumstances and with the same knowledge as the accused, would have appreciated the risk involved in the accused's conduct and would have taken steps to avoid the commission of the *actus reus* elements of the crime in question.

reasonable people, in the same situation, would have appreciated that their conduct created a risk of causing harm and would have taken action to avoid doing so. Here the fault of the accused does not lie in deliberately choosing to do something wrong; instead, the culpability lies in the fact that the accused person had the capacity to live up to the standard of care expected of a reasonable person and failed to do so. As Justice McLachlin said in *Creighton* (1993), "Objective *mens rea* is not concerned with what was actually in the accused's mind, but what should have been there if the accused proceeded reasonably." Who is the "reasonable person"? The answer to this question is simply that it is up to the judge or jury (if there is one) to decide what is reasonable in all the circumstances of the case and, no doubt, they call upon their own reservoir of life experience to determine what they think is reasonable. Nevertheless, this means that it is always difficult to predict whether a judge or jury will determine that a specific defendant in a criminal trial acted reasonably.

In the *Creighton* case (1993), Justice McLachlin emphasized that the "moral fault of the offence must be proportionate to its gravity and penalty": in other words, the most serious crimes, carrying the most severe penalties, should generally be based on a subjective *mens rea* requirement. Significantly, in the case of *Martineau* (1990), the Supreme Court of Canada ruled that the crime of murder is so serious and carries such a high degree of stigma that criminal responsibility for this offence must be based on subjective *mens rea*; indeed, the Court stated that the Charter requires that the Crown prove either that the accused deliberately intended to kill or, at the very least, subjectively foresaw that his or her conduct was likely to cause death. However, in *Creighton* (1993), the Supreme Court held that responsibility for manslaughter could be based on an objective *mens rea* requirement because the degree of stigma and the penalties attached to it were considerably less severe than is the case for murder. In Creighton's case, the accused had injected a quantity of cocaine into the arm of the victim. In order to convict Creighton of manslaughter, the Crown first had to prove that he had intentionally committed an unlawful act that had resulted in death. The unlawful act was the offence of trafficking in narcotics (trafficking includes the act of administering a drug) and there was no doubt that the victim died as a direct consequence of the injection. The *mens rea* for so-called "unlawful act manslaughter" is objective in nature. Therefore, the second task confronting the Crown was to prove that any reasonable person would have foreseen the risk of non-trivial bodily harm as a consequence of committing the unlawful act. The Supreme Court of Canada had no doubt that Creighton was correctly convicted of manslaughter because any reasonable person who administered a dangerous drug intravenously would foresee the risk of some degree of bodily harm.

There are three forms of subjective *mens rea* that the Crown may be required to prove in a criminal prosecution: intention and knowledge; recklessness; and wilful blindness.

Section 155(1) of the Criminal Code provides a typical example of the subjective *mens rea* requirement of intention and knowledge; indeed, it provides that an individual commits incest if, knowing that another person is "by blood relationship his or her parent, child, brother, sister, grandparent or grandchild," he or she intentionally has sexual intercourse with that person. Usually, the Criminal Code will require the Crown to prove a specific mental element in addition to intention and knowledge. Take, for example, the offence of first-degree murder. Section 231(2) of the Code states that this offence is committed when murder is "planned and deliberate." In order to convict an accused person of murder, the Crown must establish that this person either intended to kill or intended to inflict bodily harm that he or she knew was likely to cause death and was reckless (did not care) whether death ensued or not [section 229(a)]. However, if the offender is to be convicted of first- as opposed to second-degree murder, then normally the Crown must also prove that the killing was planned and deliberate in the sense that the accused did not act impulsively and was following some pre-existing plan to kill someone. Intoxicated defendants who are found to have the necessary *mens rea* for murder will often be acquitted of first-degree murder because they acted on impulse or without thinking about what they were going to do ahead of time; these accused persons will instead be convicted of second-degree murder.

Recklessness is a form of subjective *mens rea* where the accused knows that his or her conduct could cause certain prohibited consequences but deliberately proceeds with that conduct because he or she does not care one way or the other. Take the case of arson. Section 434 of the Criminal Code states that a person who "intentionally or recklessly causes damage by fire or explosion to property that is not wholly owned by that person" is guilty of an indictable offence and may be sentenced to a maximum of 14 years in prison. If Nero throws a lighted cigarette onto a haystack, realizing that there is a good chance the haystack will catch fire, he will be convicted of arson even if he can demonstrate that he did not start the fire deliberately and that, in fact, he hoped very sincerely that there would not be any blaze as a consequence of his actions. Nero is guilty of arson because his recklessness constitutes one of the forms of *mens rea* that is necessary for conviction under the terms of section 434.

Wilful blindness is the final form of subjective *mens rea*. It exists where accused persons have every reason to make some kind of inquiry as to whether there are circumstances that would render their conduct criminal but deliberately choose to shut their eyes to the obvious because they wish to avoid being convicted of an offence. The most common example of wilful blindness occurs in relation to the crime of being in possession of stolen property [section 354(1) of the Criminal Code]. Suppose that an accused person pays for goods at a relatively small fraction of their known value but deliberately refrains from asking whether they are stolen because he or she wants to deny actual knowledge when subsequently confronted by the police. Such a person would be considered to have been wilfully blind as to the criminality of his or her actions and would be treated as though there had been actual knowledge that the goods were stolen.

Objective *mens rea* has been applied to a significant number of offences under the Criminal Code. For example, the following offences have all been characterized by the courts as requiring proof only of objective, rather than subjective, *mens rea*: manslaughter, dangerous driving, assault causing bodily harm, and criminal negligence causing death or bodily harm. However, it is important to bear in mind that the courts have consistently stated that accused persons may not be convicted of "true crimes" under the Criminal Code merely because they were "careless" in the sense that their conduct fell below the standard of care expected of a reasonable person acting prudently in the same circumstances as the accused. As Justice McLachlin said, in the *Creighton* case (1993), "The law does not lightly brand a person as criminal." Therefore, for crimes that are based on objective *mens rea*, the Crown must prove that there was a *marked departure* from the standard of care expected of the reasonable person acting prudently. Furthermore, the Supreme Court of Canada has repeatedly stated that the courts should apply a "modified objective test" in such cases. This means that a judge or jury (if there is one) must ask what the accused person in the case before them actually knew about the circumstances surrounding their actions. The judge or jury must then decide whether the accused's behaviour constituted a marked departure from the standard of care expected of a reasonable person who faces the identical circumstances as the accused and who is armed with exactly the same knowledge of those circumstances. Suppose, for example, an accused person suffers an epileptic fit while driving a vehicle and he or she crosses over the centre of the road and causes a fatal collision with a car that is travelling in the opposite direction. On the face of it, straying over the centre line and causing a collision constitutes a marked departure from the standard of care expected of a reasonable person. However, if the accused did not know that he or she was likely to suffer from an epileptic fit, there would be no conviction on a charge of dangerous driving causing death [section 249(4) of the Criminal Code]. A reasonable driver, with no knowledge of the likelihood that he or she might suffer an epileptic fit, would have behaved in the same way as the accused. However, the situation would be very different if the accused person knew that he or she was suffering from epilepsy or subject to sudden fainting spells and, without first obtaining medical clearance, continued to drive a motor vehicle. Clearly, a reasonable person armed with this knowledge would never attempt to take a vehicle on the road; therefore, the accused's conduct would almost certainly be considered a marked departure from the standard of care expected of the reasonable person.

Although it may appear somewhat harsh to convict individuals of serious crimes on the basis of objective *mens rea*, it is clear that the courts have watered down the objective test of liability by requiring that the judge or jury take into account the subjective knowledge accused people have of the relevant circumstances surrounding their actions. Furthermore, if an accused person lacks the normal capacity of the reasonable person to appreciate that his or her conduct might create a risk of harm, that person may not be convicted of a crime, even if it is based on proof of objective *mens rea*. For example, suppose a 20-year-old man has a mental age of 10 and he hits a neighbour with a metal bar. Tragically, the neighbour dies from his injuries. In the case of an ordinary person who does not suffer from a severe disability, it would be relatively easy for the Crown to prove a charge of manslaughter. The *mens rea* requirements are objective in nature. The accused must be proved to have intentionally applied force to the victim and the Crown must then proceed to establish that a reasonable person would have foreseen the risk of non-trivial bodily harm. Any reasonable person would foresee the risk of fairly serious bodily harm if an attack is carried out with a metal bar; therefore, most accused persons would be routinely convicted of manslaughter in such circumstances. However, if the accused is so developmentally disabled that he cannot foresee that his actions may cause non-trivial bodily harm, he may not be convicted of manslaughter. The essence of culpability in objective *mens rea* is the notion that the accused had the capacity to foresee—and avoid—the risk of physical harm but did not do so. If the accused lacks this basic capacity, to convict him of manslaughter would amount to punishing someone who lacks any blame-worthiness. In *Creighton* (1993), the Supreme Court of Canada ruled that such an outcome would infringe the fundamental principles of justice that are enshrined in the Charter (section 7).

Mens Rea and Regulatory Offences

Earlier in this chapter, a distinction was drawn between regulatory offences ("quasi-criminal law") and "true crimes." Where "true crimes" are concerned, the Crown usually has to prove the required *mens rea* of the offence beyond a reasonable doubt. However, most regulatory offences are considered to be offences of strict liability. This means that the Crown only has to prove the *actus reus* elements of the offence; the onus is then on the accused to prove, on the balance of probabilities, that he or she was not negligent (or that he or she "acted with due diligence"). The rationale for strict liability is that it would be extremely difficult to conduct effective prosecutions of regulatory offences if the Crown were required to prove that accused persons were negligent. Usually, it is the accused person who has the best knowledge of the steps that he or she has taken to comply with the regulations that apply to his or her field of manufacturing or business activities, and so on; therefore, it is not unfair to require the accused to present this evidence and prove that he or she acted with the due diligence expected of a reasonable person in the same circumstances. Furthermore, the penalties for regulatory offences are comparatively lenient, since they rarely include imprisonment as a realistic sentencing alternative. In any event, strict liability is infinitely preferable to a régime of absolute liability, in which the accused is not permitted to claim a lack of *mens rea* as a defence. Prior to the decision of the Supreme Court of Canada in the case of *Sault Ste. Marie (City of)* in 1978, the majority of regulatory offences imposed absolute liability and accused persons were prevented from asserting that their actions were not blameworthy. However, since the *Sault Ste. Marie* case, by far the greatest proportion of regulatory offences have been considered to impose a regime of strict liability, leaving the accused with the opportunity to prove that he or she has done all that reasonably could be expected to be done in order to comply with the relevant regulations that apply to his or her business, occupation, industry, and so on.

In the *Wholesale Travel Group Inc.* case (1991), the accused had been charged with the regulatory offence of false or misleading advertising, under the federal Competition Act, R.S.C. 1970, c. C–23. The Act clearly imposed strict liability insofar as it permitted the accused to raise a defence of having acted "with due diligence." Essentially, the defence would be available where the accused proved that the "act or omission giving rise to the offence" was the "result of error" and that he or she "took reasonable precautions and exercised due diligence to prevent the occurrence of such error." It was contended before the Supreme Court of Canada that, because strict liability requires accused persons to prove their innocence, it infringed the presumption of innocence, enshrined in section 11(d) of the Charter, and was, therefore, invalid. However, the Supreme Court of Canada ultimately held that strict liability was not invalid under the provisions of the Charter. The *Wholesale Travel Group Inc.* case is, therefore, a decision of great importance since it has affirmed the legitimacy of the basic principles of liability that are at the heart of the vast network of regulatory legislation that governs the everyday lives of all Canadians.

BECOMING A PARTY TO A CRIMINAL OFFENCE

Individuals can be convicted of criminal offences even if they are not the persons who actually commit them. For example, section 21(1) of the Criminal Code provides that anyone is a party to an offence who (i) actually commits it; (ii) aids another person to commit it; or (iii) abets (encourages) any person to commit it. In a homicide case, the person who actually commits the offence would be the individual who, for example, actually stabs a victim to death. However, the person who intentionally provides assistance and/or encouragement is liable to be convicted of murder on the same basis as the actual killer. In the *Thatcher* case (1987), which received wide publicity because the accused, Colin Thatcher, was the former leader of the Saskatchewan Liberal Party and the son of a former premier, the Crown contended that the accused either committed the murder of his ex-wife himself or aided and/or abetted another person to do it. The Supreme Court of Canada ruled that it was not necessary for the jury to be unanimous in its verdict as to whether Thatcher himself was the killer or he aided and/or abetted another party to do it on his behalf. As Justice Dickson noted, section 21 of the Code "has been designed to alleviate the necessity of choosing between the two different forms of participation in a criminal offence." Each form of participation in the murder was equally culpable and section 21 established "one single mode of incurring criminal liability." Similarly, a person who counsels ("procures," "solicits," or "incites") another to commit a crime becomes a **party to that crime** even if "the offence was committed in a way different from that which was counselled" (section 22 of the Criminal Code).

An individual may also become a party to a criminal offence that has been committed by other people when he or she had previously formed a common intention with them to commit a crime. Section 21(2) of the Criminal Code

party to a crime

The Criminal Code specifies that one is a party to—and liable to conviction of—a criminal offence if one actually commits it; aids and/or abets it; becomes a party to it by virtue of having formed a common intention with others to commit a crime; or counsels the commission of an offence that is actually committed by another person.

deals with the situation in which two or more persons have agreed to commit a crime and to assist one another in carrying out this "common purpose." Each of these individuals is considered a party to any offence committed by the other person(s) who entered the original agreement provided (i) that this other offence was committed in order to carry out the "common purpose" and (ii) that these individuals either knew or ought to have known that the commission of this other offence "would be a probable consequence of carrying out the common purpose." Suppose that Arthur, Benedict, and Cassio agree to commit a robbery and to help one another in carrying out this "common intention." Cassio—without consulting his colleagues in crime—kills one of the robbery victims. In these circumstances, Arthur and Benedict would be convicted of manslaughter if they either knew or ought to have known that inflicting nontrivial bodily harm on the intended victim(s) would be a probable consequence of implementing their common intention to commit robbery. Since robbery necessarily involves an element of violence or threatened violence, any reasonable person would foresee the probability that someone may be seriously hurt; therefore, Arthur and Benedict would almost certainly be found guilty of manslaughter. The use of the phrase "or ought to have known" indicates that the *mens rea* elements are objective in nature and this means that the scope of potential liability under section 21(2) is remarkably broad. The only exception to this form of objective liability arises where the offence of murder is concerned. Since the Supreme Court of Canada has ruled [in *Martineau* (1990)] that an accused person may be convicted of murder only where there was an actual intention to kill or subjective foresight of the likelihood of death, Arthur and Benedict would be convicted of murder only if they subjectively realized that death was a probable consequence of carrying out their common intention to commit robbery.

One question that immediately springs to mind when discussing section 21(2) is whether an individual who agreed with others to commit a crime and to provide the necessary assistance to achieve his goal should be entitled to change his or her mind and withdraw from the common intention. The answer is that an individual may withdraw from the common intention, but may do so effectively only when he or she gives unequivocal notice to the other party or parties of his or her wish to abandon the criminal enterprise. Once effective notice has been given, the individual is no longer liable for any subsequent crimes committed by the other party or parties in pursuit of the common intention.

THE USE OF CRIMINAL LAW AS A PREVENTATIVE TOOL: INCHOATE OFFENCES

Any system of criminal law will permit the police to intervene and arrest those who, in some way, demonstrate that they are about to embark upon the commission of a serious crime. If members of a gang of professional kidnappers agree to abduct a particular victim and to hold him or her to ransom, the police do not have to wait until the abduction is actually carried out before they intervene. Even though the kidnapping may exist only in the intentions of the members of the gang, it is undoubtedly legitimate for the state to punish them for having participated in a conspiracy to commit kidnapping. Conspiracy is an **inchoate crime** (literally, a crime "in embryo"); once their agreement to commit a crime has been reached, the accused may be convicted of the crime of conspiracy even though the offence that they originally planned to commit is never brought to fruition. Other inchoate crimes are criminal attempt and counselling an offence that is not committed.

Inchoate crimes raise serious questions about the civil liberties of those who are charged with having committed them. In general, it is accepted that the criminal law should not punish people simply for entertaining evil thoughts. However, society does have the right to prevent individuals from translating their evil thoughts into criminal acts. The problem lies in defining the point at which the state is justified in laying a charge against someone who has not yet committed the crime that he or she has in mind. Basically, accused persons must take some form of action that manifests their intention to commit a crime; in counselling, the accused must importune another person to commit a crime; in attempt, the accused must take a substantial step toward completion of a crime; and, in conspiracy, the accused must enter into an agreement to commit a crime.

Counselling an Offence That Is Not Committed

According to section 22 of the Criminal Code, it is a crime to **counsel** another person to commit an offence that is not ultimately brought to fruition. Since the main focus of the offence is on the accused person's intentions, it does not matter that no one is actually influenced by the accused person's efforts to procure, solicit, or incite someone to commit a crime. Furthermore, once their counselling action is completed, accused persons cannot escape criminal conviction merely because they change their minds and renounce their criminal intent.

Criminal Attempt

The offence of **criminal attempt** is focused on an accused person's intention to commit a crime that is never realized. Section 24(1) of the Criminal Code provides that "everyone who, having an intent to commit a crime, does or omits to do anything for the purpose of carrying out his intention is guilty of an attempt to commit the offence whether or not it was possible under the circumstances to commit the offence." Clearly, the *mens rea* of criminal attempt is nothing short of an actual intent to commit an offence. The *actus reus* of attempt is any step taken by the accused toward the completion of the offence, provided that this step goes beyond "mere preparation" and is not considered to be "too remote" from the completed offence. For example, buying a train ticket with a view to travelling to another city in order to rob a bank would be considered "mere preparation" and "too remote" from the completed robbery to justify convicting the accused of a criminal attempt. However, if the accused person actually reaches the front doors of the bank before being arrested by the police,

inchoate crime
A criminal offence that is committed when the accused person seeks to bring about the commission of a particular crime but is not successful in doing so. The three inchoate offences in the Criminal Code are attempt, conspiracy, and counselling.

counselling
Procuring, soliciting, or inciting another person to commit a crime.

criminal attempt
A criminal attempt occurs when an individual does—or omits to do—anything for the purpose of carrying out a previously formed intention to commit a crime. The conduct in question must constitute a substantial step toward the completion of the crime that is intended.

it is clear that the *actus reus* of the offence of attempted robbery has been established. Unfortunately, it is often very difficult to predict exactly where the court will draw the line between mere preparation and an act that warrants conviction for a criminal attempt. It should also be emphasized that a criminal attempt may be committed even though it would be impossible for the accused to commit the complete offence that he or she has in mind. For example, if someone tries to steal a motor vehicle that has been totally disabled by its owner, this person would be guilty of attempted theft even though it would have been impossible for that person to take the vehicle from the spot where it had been parked. Similarly, if an accused person mistakenly shoots a wax dummy, believing it is an enemy, that person will be guilty of attempted murder. What is important to recognize is that the accused person seriously intended to commit murder and that there is a very real likelihood that, having failed on this particular occasion, the accused will try again and, perhaps, be more successful on that subsequent occasion.

Conspiracy

The crime of **conspiracy** is established when two or more individuals form a common intention to commit a crime. In addition, the Crown must prove that each individual who is charged with conspiracy actually intended to put the common design into effect. The *actus reus* of conspiracy is the agreement to engage in criminal conduct, while the *mens rea* component consists of the intent not only to enter into this agreement but also to implement it. Suppose two individuals apparently agree to kidnap a third party. However, it later turns out that one of these individuals was actually an undercover police officer who never had any intention to act on this supposed agreement. In this case, neither of the individuals may be convicted of conspiracy. The police officer lacks the necessary *mens rea* for conspiracy and the other individual cannot be convicted of this offence because the Crown must prove that there are at least two persons who seriously intended to implement the plan to commit murder. On the other hand, if there are two or more individuals who agree to commit murder and who fully intend to carry out their homicidal plans, they would be convicted of conspiracy even if an undercover officer is also part of this group. As long as there is a minimum number of two individuals who intend to carry out an agreement to commit a crime, there is a conspiracy. Conspiracy is a crime that provides the Crown with a number of distinct advantages. For example, certain types of evidence may be accepted at the joint trial of a group of alleged co-conspirators that would never be admitted against specific members of that group, had they been tried separately. In effect, there is always the danger of "guilt by association" in conspiracy trials.

conspiracy

An agreement by two or more persons to commit a criminal offence.

DEFENCES TO A CRIMINAL CHARGE

Conviction of a "true crime" should not occur unless the accused person is considered blameworthy. Merely because individuals engage in conduct that, from an objective point of view, is either actually or potentially harmful does not mean that they should be punished under the provisions of the criminal law. Indeed, the requirement of *mens rea* ensures that the Crown must first prove a culpable mental state or the prosecution will fail. However, in addition to the *mens rea* requirement, there are a number of distinct defences that may be raised by an accused person in a criminal trial. When analyzed carefully, some of these defences, such as mistake of fact, basically amount to a denial that the Crown has proved the necessary *mens rea,* but there are other defences, such as duress, that may be raised successfully even though the accused possessed the necessary *mens rea* for the offence that has been charged. Essentially, the patchwork of defences has evolved as a means of ensuring that those individuals who have a justification or excuse for their conduct are either acquitted of criminal charges or treated more leniently (for example, by conviction of a less serious offence).

Mental Disorder as a Defence to a Criminal Charge

In the Supreme Court of Canada's decision in the case of *Winko* (1999), Justice McLachlin said:

> In every society, there are those who commit criminal acts because of mental illness. The criminal law must find a way to deal with these people fairly, while protecting the public against further harms. The task is not an easy one.

In Canada, this difficult task is undertaken through the application by the courts of the special defence of **not criminally responsible on account of mental disorder (NCRMD)**. The current test that must be used in deciding whether an accused should be found NCRMD is articulated in section 16(1) of the Criminal Code:

> No person is criminally responsible for an act committed or an omission made while suffering from a mental disorder that renders the person incapable of appreciating the nature and quality of the act or omission or of knowing that it was wrong.

NCRMD

The special verdict of "not criminally responsible on account of mental disorder." In order to be found NCRMD, it must be proved on the balance of probabilities that, because of mental disorder, the accused lacked the capacity to appreciate the nature and quality of the act or omission in question or of knowing that it would be considered morally wrong by the average Canadian.

The first requirement of the NCRMD defence is that the accused was suffering from a "mental disorder" at the time of the alleged offence(s). In fact, the Supreme Court of Canada has adopted an extremely broad definition of mental disorder but it is only those individuals who are suffering from very serious forms of mental disorder (such as schizophrenia) who will meet the other criteria specified in section 16(1), namely, that the accused has been rendered incapable either of appreciating the physical nature and quality of the act or omission in question or of knowing that the act or omission is considered morally wrong by the everyday standards of the ordinary Canadian. Most mentally disordered people understand the physical nature of their conduct (for example, do they realize stabbing someone in the heart will cause death?). Similarly, the majority of mentally disordered persons are capable of knowing that their conduct would be "morally condemned by reasonable members of society" [as Justice Arbour of the Supreme Court of Canada put it in the *Molodowic* case (2000)]. Significantly, section 16(1) does not extend the benefit of the NCRMD defence to mentally disordered persons who claim that—as a consequence of mental disorder—they succumbed to an irresistible impulse to commit a crime; provided such individuals were capable of understanding what they were doing and that it was wrong, they are not considered to be NCRMD in Canadian criminal law.

The very narrow scope of the NCRMD defence ensures that relatively few accused persons may raise it successfully at their trials (see Box 3.3). In addition, it is significant that section 16 places the burden of proving the NCRMD defence on the shoulders of the accused person if he or she raises it at trial; in this situation, the accused person has to prove the defence on the balance of probabilities. Although this provision infringes the presumption of innocence, enshrined in section 11(d) of the Charter, the Supreme Court of Canada ruled, in the *Chaulk* case (1990), that this infringement of the accused person's right was justified as a reasonable limitation under section 1. The Court took the view that it would be impractical to require the Crown to prove beyond a reasonable doubt that the accused was not mentally disordered—particularly, in light of the fact that an accused person may refuse to cooperate with a psychiatrist nominated by the Crown to report to the court on the accused's mental condition.

Accused persons who are found NCRMD are not acquitted in the technical sense of that word. Indeed, section 672.1 of the Criminal Code states that a verdict of NCRMD constitutes a finding that "the accused committed the act or omission that formed the basis of the offence with which the accused is charged but is not criminally responsible on account of mental disorder." NCR accused may be granted (i) an absolute discharge; (ii) a conditional discharge; (iii) an order holding them in custody in a psychiatric facility. Section 672.54(a) of the Criminal Code provides that, unless a court or review board determines that an NCR accused person constitutes a "significant threat to the safety of the public," then it *must* order an absolute discharge. In *Winko* (1999), the Supreme Court of Canada ruled that the threshold for justifying the imposition of restrictions on the liberty of a person who has been found NCRMD is very high:

> A "significant threat to the safety of the public" means a real risk of physical or psychological harm to members of the public that is serious in the sense of going beyond the merely trivial or annoying. The conduct giving rise to the harm must be criminal in nature.

General Defences to a Criminal Charge

Mistake of fact may constitute a defence to a criminal charge if it causes the accused to erroneously believe that the circumstances facing him or her did not render his or her actions criminal. For example, if a woman participates in a marriage ceremony with a man erroneously believing that her first husband is dead, she would not be guilty of the crime of bigamy. The central element of the *actus reus* of bigamy is that one of the parties to a marriage ceremony is already married. If the accused honestly believed that she was a widow, then—in the circumstances as she perceived them to be—she was not committing a prohibited act because she was no longer married to her first spouse. When the

mistake of fact

Mistake of fact may be a defence where the accused person acts under the influence of an honest mistake in relation to any of the elements of the *actus reus* of the offence charged.

BOX 3.3

FOCUS

Should We Punish Mentally Disordered Persons Who Commit Criminal Acts?

It is difficult for a mentally disordered person to prove that he or she was "incapable of appreciating the nature and quality of the act or omission" that led to the laying of a criminal charge or that "of knowing that it was wrong" [section 16(1) of the Criminal Code]. As we have seen, the legal criteria for a finding that an accused person is not criminally responsible on account of mental disorder are extremely limited in their scope. Generally, only the most severely mentally disordered defendants will be able to benefit from the NCRMD defence. However, whenever a trial judge has discretion to do so, he or she will consider the existence of a mental disorder at the time of the offence to be a mitigating factor in sentencing.

Take, for example, the case of Christian McEachern, a former Canadian soldier who had been a peacekeeper in both Africa and Yugoslavia. In March 2001, he drove his vehicle into the wall of a military garrison in Edmonton, Alberta. At his trial in December 2002, defence counsel argued that McEachern was suffering from post-traumatic stress disorder (PTSD)—a condition that has been experienced by a number of members of the armed forces who have been on active duty. It was alleged that this disorder caused McEachern to act in a robotic state. While the trial judge found that McEachern was suffering from a "disease of the mind," she nevertheless ruled that his actions were voluntary; therefore, McEachern was considered to be capable of appreciating the nature and quality of the act that he had committed and of knowing that it was wrong. McEachern was convicted of driving "over 80" [over the blood-alcohol limit in section 253(b) of the Criminal Code]; assaulting a peace officer; mischief; and dangerous driving. Although these were serious offences, Madam Justice Sulyma imposed a sentence that undoubtedly reflected the influence that McEachern's mental disorder had exerted on his behaviour: she sentenced him, in February 2003, to a conditional sentence of 14 months and a fine of $2000 and placed restrictions on his owning a gun (for ten years) and on his driving (for one year).

Do you think that this outcome was just in all the circumstances of the case? Should Canadian criminal law recognize a special defence of diminished responsibility for mentally disordered persons? Such a defence would permit a court to convict a mentally disordered accused person of a less serious charge (for example, manslaughter instead of murder) and, therefore, ensure that a more lenient sentence is imposed. At present, Canadian criminal law does not recognize such a defence for mentally disordered accused who cannot prove that they were not criminally responsible within the meaning of section 16 of the Criminal Code. Should mentally disordered persons always obtain a "discount" in their sentences when they are convicted of criminal offences? Would you impose a less severe sentence on an offender who was diagnosed as a psychopath?

See: *R. v. McEachern*, 2003 ABQB 87, available online at www.albertacourts.ab.ca.

accused operates under a mistake of fact, he or she is really stating that the Crown has failed to prove the necessary *mens rea* of the offence. One of the most controversial uses of the defence of mistake of fact used to occur when an accused person who was charged with sexual assault claimed that he honestly believed in the complainant's consent, even though he was mistaken. However, section 273.2(b) of the Criminal Code (enacted in 1992) states that mistaken belief in consent will not be a valid defence to a charge of sexual assault unless the accused took "reasonable steps, in the circumstances known to the accused at the time, to ascertain that the complainant was consenting." By requiring the accused person to act reasonably, this amendment to the Code has considerably reduced the opportunities for abuse of the defence of honest belief in consent.

While honest mistake of fact constitutes a valid defence to a criminal charge, a mistake concerning the nature or scope of the criminal law does not absolve an accused person of criminal liability. Indeed, section 19 of the Criminal Code makes it very clear that ignorance of the law is no excuse. This is a harsh rule but an inevitable one since it would be impossible for the Crown to prove actual knowledge of the relevant legal principles. There are some exceptions to this rule. One of the more important exceptions arises when an official who is charged with the administration of certain types of regulatory legislation gives erroneous legal advice. If the accused person reasonably relies on this advice, he or she may take advantage of the defence of "officially induced error." For example, if a factory inspector tells a manufacturer that it is acceptable to modify a certain safety device, it would clearly be unfair to convict that manufacturer of a violation of the relevant occupational safety legislation. If the manufacturer reasonably relied on the advice of the factory inspector and committed what a court later concludes is a regulatory offence, then the defence of officially induced error will come to the rescue of the manufacturer.

Intoxication is a complex, and highly problematic, defence. A high proportion of violent crimes are committed by individuals who have abused alcohol and/or other drugs and the great majority of the inmates in Canada's prisons have been diagnosed as having suffered from a substance abuse disorder. If the scope of a defence of intoxication were drawn too broadly, many violent offenders would escape criminal liability even though they were considered to have ingested alcohol and/or other drugs voluntarily. One of the main effects of alcohol (and some other drugs) is to cause disinhibition—a condition in which the accused may be rendered less able to control his or her conduct. However, the courts have consistently ruled that intoxication may not be raised as a valid defence by accused persons who simply claim that alcohol and/or other drugs impaired their ability to control their conduct. Instead, the intoxication defence focuses on whether the accused's state of intoxication (from alcohol and/or other drugs) prevented him or her from forming the necessary *mens rea* for the crime in question.

The defence of intoxication is primarily a "common law" defence in the sense that it was developed by the courts in the absence of any legislation that defined its nature and scope. Traditionally, the defence has applied only to those offences that required proof of a complex form of *mens rea* known as "specific intent." Therefore, the defence of intoxication may reduce the severity of a charge (for example, from murder to manslaughter or from robbery to assault). On the other hand, it has been a longstanding principle that intoxication is not a valid defence to a charge of such "basic intent" offences as assault, sexual assault, or damage to property (mischief). The legal rationale for maintaining the distinction between crimes of specific and basic intent is that intoxication does not normally impair people to the extent that they do not even have the minimal degree of *mens rea* required to assault someone or to damage property.

intoxication

Intoxication caused by alcohol and/or other drugs may be a defence if it prevents the accused from forming the intent required for a specific intent offence, such as murder or robbery.

Even extremely intoxicated people have some degree of awareness of what they are doing and the acts of committing an assault or damaging property require only a very minimal degree of intent. On the other hand, assaulting someone with the specific intent to kill (murder) or forcefully taking something from another individual with the specific intent to steal (robbery) are acts that require a considerably more complex pattern of thought, and intoxication may well prevent the accused from forming the necessary specific intent that is required for conviction of these serious crimes.

In the case of *Daviault* (1994), the Supreme Court of Canada changed the traditional approach to the defence of intoxication. Daviault had been charged with sexual assault, a basic intent crime. He claimed that he had consumed seven or eight beers during the daytime and some 35 ounces of brandy on the evening of the alleged sexual assault. A pharmacologist who had been called by the defence to testify at the trial stated that Daviault's blood-alcohol content would have been in the region of 400 to 600 mg per 100 mL of blood. For most individuals, such a blood-alcohol level would cause a coma or death but, since Daviault was an alcoholic, he was "less susceptible to the effects of alcohol" and, according to the expert witness, the accused may have been suffering from a blackout during which he would not have been aware of his actions. Under the traditional approach, even such an extreme degree of intoxication as was claimed by Daviault could not be raised as a successful defence to a crime of basic intent such as sexual assault. However, in *Daviault*, the Supreme Court ruled that it would constitute an unjustifiable infringement of sections 7 and 11(d) of the Charter to convict accused persons of basic intent crimes if these persons were so severely intoxicated that they were in a "state akin to automatism or insanity." The Court ordered a new trial in Daviault's case and held that he would have to prove the defence of extreme intoxication on the balance of probabilities. Tragically, the complainant in this case died and a new trial could not be held. Although the Supreme Court had taken great care to emphasize that a "Daviault defence" could be raised successfully only in the most extreme—and rare—cases, there was nevertheless considerable public concern that the *Daviault* decision would be used by certain men to escape responsibility for the commission of crimes of violence against women and children. Parliament responded to this concern by enacting section 33.1 of the Criminal Code. Section 33.1 essentially states that accused persons who commit a basic intent offence that involves "an assault or any other interference with the bodily integrity of another person" will not be entitled to raise the defence of intoxication—even if they were "unaware of, or incapable of consciously controlling, (their) behaviour." Whether the Supreme Court of Canada will rule that section 33.1 of the Code should be ruled invalid, as an unjustified breach of an accused person's Charter rights, remains to be seen.

The defences of **necessity** and **duress** are based on the notion that it would be unfair to convict individuals of a criminal offence if they did not have a genuine choice at the time that they committed it. These defences are conceptualized by the courts as being "excuses"; as Justice Dickson said, in the Supreme Court of Canada's decision in *Perka* (1984), "an 'excuse' concedes the wrong-

necessity

Necessity may be a defence to a criminal charge when the accused person commits the lesser evil of a crime in order to avoid the occurrence of a greater evil.

duress

Duress may be a defence to a criminal charge when the accused was forced to commit a crime as a consequence of threats of death or serious bodily harm made by another person.

fulness of the action but asserts that the circumstances under which it was done are such that it ought not to be attributed to the actor." Necessity is a common law defence that arises when the accused person can avoid some disaster or calamity only by breaking the law. In these circumstances, the accused person is considered to act involuntarily from a "moral or normative" point of view. As Justice Dickson stated in the *Perka* case (1984),

> The lost Alpinist who, on the point of freezing to death, breaks open an isolated mountain cabin is not literally behaving in an involuntary fashion. He has control over his actions to the extent of being physically capable of abstaining from the act. Realistically, however, his act is not a "voluntary" one. His "choice" to break the law is not true choice at all; it is remorselessly compelled by normal human instincts.

The "evil" that the accused person seeks to avoid must be greater than the "evil" involved in the breaking of the law, and the accused must have no reasonable legal alternative but to break the law. Take the case of a surgeon who is contemplating the surgical separation of conjoined twins who share vital organs, such as the heart or the lungs. Without an operation to separate the babies, both of them will ultimately die. However, the operation will save one of the twins, while inevitably killing the other. Is the surgeon justified in killing one twin in order to save the other? In these particular circumstances, one can assume that the defence of necessity would be available to the surgeon should he or she ever be charged with murder.

When claiming the defence of necessity, defendants may point to any circumstances that constitute a threat to life or limb; however, where the defence of **duress** is raised, defendants are really asserting that their power of choice is being overborne by another human being. In the *Hibbert* case (1995), the Supreme Court of Canada ruled that duress, like necessity, was a defence that was based on the concept of "normative involuntariness." Section 17 of the Criminal Code sets out the requirements for the defence of duress but, in the case of *Ruzic* (2001), the Supreme Court of Canada ruled that these requirements were so restrictive that they could result in the denial of the defence to an individual who was not blameworthy; therefore, the court struck down these requirements as being invalid under the Charter. The Supreme Court then held that the courts should apply the "common law" defence of duress. The main elements of this defence are that the accused had been subjected to a threat of death or serious bodily harm that is directed either toward the accused or toward another person (such as a child or spouse). The threat must be so serious that the accused believes it will be carried out and the court must also be satisfied that it would have caused a reasonable person, placed in exactly the same position as the accused, to act as he or she did. Finally, it should be established that the accused had no obvious "safe avenue of escape." After all, if the accused had the option to escape from the person who was making threats, he or she cannot now claim that he or she was acting involuntarily.

In the *Ruzic* case, for example, the accused was charged with importing a narcotic and use of a false passport. Two kilograms of heroin had been found strapped to her body when she arrived at Pearson Airport in Toronto. Ruzic admitted the offences but asserted that she had acted under duress. Her story was that she lived with her mother in Belgrade (in the former Yugoslavia) and that she had been persistently threatened by a "paramilitary" man who physically assaulted and sexually harassed her. The man had a reputation for extreme violence and he informed Ruzic that she must take a consignment of heroin to Toronto. When the accused protested, the man threatened to harm her mother. At the time of these threats, law and order had largely broken down in Belgrade and Ruzic said that she did not inform the Belgrade police of the threats against her mother because they were "corrupt and would do nothing to assist her." The jury acquitted Ruzic on both charges and the Supreme Court of Canada ultimately upheld the acquittal. Ruzic had met all the requirements contained in the common law defence of duress. She clearly believed that she had absolutely no alternative to bringing the heroin into Canada; if she had not done so, her mother might have been seriously harmed or killed, and seeking the assistance of the local police would have been a futile gesture given the particular circumstances that existed in Belgrade at that time.

Other important defences are provocation and self-defence. **Provocation** is only a partial defence; it may be raised only when the accused is charged with murder. If provocation is raised successfully by the accused, he or she is convicted of manslaughter rather than murder. The defence is available even though the accused undoubtedly possessed the *mens rea* for murder. Under the terms of section 232 of the Criminal Code, murder may be reduced to manslaughter if the accused killed "in the heat of passion caused by sudden provocation." Before the defence may be raised successfully, it must be established that the provocation was of a kind that would be "sufficient to deprive an ordinary person of the power of self-control." This would appear to establish an objective test; however, the Supreme Court of Canada has effectively watered down the objective requirements of the defence by ruling that the issue is whether an ordinary person with the particular characteristics associated with the accused would have lost the power of self-control if confronted with the specific situation that confronted him or her. As Justice Cory stated in the *Thibert* case (1996), "If the test is to be applied sensibly and with sensitivity, then the ordinary person must be taken to be of the same age, and sex, and must share with the accused such other factors as would give the act or insult in question a particular significance." It also has to be established that the accused acted in the heat of the moment "before there was time for his or her passion to cool." The *Stone* case (1999), discussed earlier in connection with automatism, constitutes a typical case of provocation insofar as the accused killed the victim immediately following a series of hurtful insults (that included raising doubts about the paternity of his children and denigrating his sexual prowess). Clearly, the jury believed that an ordinary husband would be likely to lose the power of self-control in such circumstances and that Stone must be considered to have responded to sudden provocation before there had been time for his passion to cool.

The **self-defence** provisions of the Criminal Code are extraordinarily complex and, in certain respects, contradictory. However, the central provision is

provocation

Provocation may be a partial defence to a charge of murder (if successful, it reduces the offence from murder to manslaughter). The required elements of provocation are (i) that the accused responded to a wrongful act or insult that was of such a nature that an ordinary person would have been likely to lose the power of self-control and (ii) that the accused acted "on the sudden and before there was time for his (or her) passion to cool."

self-defence

The Criminal Code permits the use of force in self-defence in certain circumstances where the individual concerned becomes the object of an unlawful assault. Where the individual acted in self-defence without intending to inflict death or grievous bodily harm on the assailant, it must be shown that no more force was used than was necessary in the circumstances. Where the individual concerned inflicted death or grievous bodily harm, then it must be shown that he or she acted under a reasonable apprehension of death or grievous bodily harm and under a reasonable belief that he or she had no alternative but to employ lethal force.

section 34 of the Criminal Code. Section 34(1) applies where an accused person has used force in self-defence but did not do so with the intent to inflict death or grievous bodily harm. The accused must demonstrate that he or she was unlawfully assaulted and did not provoke the assault. In addition, it must be shown that the force used was "no more than is necessary to defend him(her)self"; this requirement is significant because it means that there must be a degree of objective proportionality between the force used by the assailant and the force used in self-defence in response to the assailant. This principle has been encapsulated in the phrase "One cannot use a tank against a chariot."

When an accused who has acted in self-defence has either killed the assailant or inflicted grievous bodily harm, he or she will rely on section 34(2) of the Criminal Code. Under this provision, an accused person who is unlawfully assaulted is justified in using lethal or potentially lethal force if

(a) he causes it under reasonable apprehension of death or grievous bodily harm from the violence with which the assault was originally made or with which the assailant pursues his purposes, and

(b) he believes, on reasonable grounds, that he cannot otherwise preserve himself from death or grievous bodily harm.

It would appear that Parliament intended to impose an objective test for self-defence in these circumstances; indeed, section 34(2) clearly refers to "reasonable apprehension" and belief "on reasonable grounds." However, the Supreme Court of Canada has consistently softened the objective nature of the requirements for self-defence under section 34(2) by emphasizing that the real question is whether the particular accused acted reasonably in the specific circumstances that faced him or her at the time of the assault upon him or her. For example, the Supreme Court of Canada has emphasized the need to ensure that women who are the victims of domestic violence are judged by the standards of "reasonable women" who face the same circumstances of ongoing abuse and not by the standards of "reasonable men" brawling in a bar. In the *Lavallee* case (1990), the accused had shot her abusive male partner (Rust) in the back of the head. Rust was leaving Lavallee's room just after he had physically assaulted her and threatened her with death. At Lavallee's trial for murder, a psychiatrist gave expert testimony concerning the so-called battered wife syndrome in order to help the members of the jury to determine whether the accused woman's beliefs and actions were reasonable in light of her experience of chronic abuse at the hands of her partner. The psychiatrist asserted that Lavallee "had been terrorized by Rust to the point of feeling trapped, vulnerable, worthless and unable to escape the relationship despite the violence." This witness concluded that Lavallee's shooting of Rust should be viewed as "a final desperate act by a woman who sincerely believed that she would be killed that night." The jury acquitted Lavallee. The Supreme Court of Canada later upheld the acquittal and ruled that the trial judge had acted appropriately in permitting an expert witness to testify about the "battered woman syndrome" as a means of assisting the members of the jury to assess the reasonableness of Lavallee's beliefs and actions.

In a later case, *Malott* (1998), the Supreme Court of Canada suggested that this type of evidence should be presented to the jury in order to assist them in understanding at least four separate issues: (i) why an abused woman might remain in an abusive relationship; (ii) the nature and extent of the violence that may exist in an abusive relationship; (iii) the woman's ability to perceive when her partner was dangerous; and (iv) whether she believed on reasonable grounds that she could not otherwise preserve herself from death or grievous bodily harm. Furthermore, the Supreme Court has held that there is no requirement in section 34(2) that the accused person must actually be under attack or even that the accused must be in imminent danger of such an assault. Indeed, in the *Pétel* case (1994), the Supreme Court held that imminence is "only one of the factors which the jury should weigh in determining whether the accused had a reasonable apprehension of danger and a reasonable belief that she could not extricate herself otherwise than by killing the attacker." This means that a woman who is in acute fear for her life does not have to wait until she is actually being attacked or until such an assault is imminent, before she uses lethal force in self-defence. In *McConnell* (1996), the Supreme Court of Canada extended this notion to an entirely different context—namely, the highly charged atmosphere of a penitentiary. In this case, the Court indicated that it is possible to draw an analogy between the battered wife syndrome and the so-called prison environment syndrome. It was suggested by an expert witness, at the trial of two inmates for the murder of another prisoner, that—in an environment in which inmates had to "kill or be killed"—it might be reasonable for an inmate to believe that he or she was being assaulted (because of credible threats) even though the threatened violence was not imminent. Using section 34(2), it was argued that attacking another inmate from behind might constitute a reasonable action, from the point of view of the accused, if he believed that there was no other way of protecting himself from death or grievous bodily harm. It has certainly been suggested that the *McConnell* case has, perhaps, expanded self-defence far beyond the boundaries of the original defence that was envisaged by the legislators when Parliament first enacted section 34(2) of the Criminal Code. Does this case suggest that the "law of the jungle" might operate in certain penitentiaries?

While this concludes our brief survey of Canadian criminal law, it is important to recognize that one of the most significant developments in recent years has been the evolution of a body of international criminal law. The establishment in 2003 of the permanent International Criminal Court in The Hague, the Netherlands, heralds an age in which certain horrendous crimes may be tried outside of the courts and tribunals of individual nation-states (see Box 3.4). Significantly, Canada has been one of the foremost supporters and promoters of the International Criminal Court. The recent experience of "ethnic cleansing" in parts of the former Yugoslavia and of genocide in Rwanda suggests that the International Criminal Court is an institution that is sorely needed in the modern age.

BOX 3.4

FOCUS

The International Criminal Court

Crimes are committed not only under the laws of individual states, such as Canada. Indeed, serious crimes, such as genocide, crimes against humanity (including all forms of sexual violence and exploitation), and war crimes, may also be prosecuted under international law. On March 11, 2003, the International Criminal Court (I.C.C.) was officially opened at The Hague, in the Netherlands. This Court is the first permanent tribunal to try cases under international criminal law, and it has the power to order that reparations be paid to the victims of crimes that fall within its jurisdiction. Eighteen judges have been sworn in and will constitute the Judges' Chamber of the I.C.C. A Canadian, Philippe Kirsch, has been elected the first president of the Court.

The establishment of the I.C.C. was made possible when 60 nations ratified the Rome Statute, which was signed at the Rome Diplomatic Conference in 1998. To date, 89 countries (including Canada) have ratified the Rome Statute. The I.C.C. will try cases involving grave crimes only when national courts are unable or unwilling to do so. For example, a country's court system may have collapsed following an armed conflict or a state may refuse to prosecute an individual who has the power or influence to escape justice within his or her own country. Canada has played a major role in implementing the Rome Statute. However, the United States has refused to ratify the Rome Statute and has indicated that it will not permit the Court to try an American citizen for a crime under international law. Do you think that there is a need for a permanent international criminal court? In what circumstances should an individual be brought before the I.C.C.?

For further information, see the websites of the Rome Statute of the International Criminal Court: www.un.org/law/icc/ and the International Criminal Tribunals for the Former Yugoslavia and Rwanda: www.un.org/icty/ and www.ictr.org.

SUMMARY

- A crime consists of a prohibition against certain conduct and a penal sanction (such as imprisonment or a fine).
- The sources of criminal law are (i) legislation and (ii) judicial decisions.
- Under the terms of the Canadian Constitution, the Parliament of Canada has the exclusive authority to enact "criminal law and the procedures relating to criminal matters."
- There is a significant difference between "true crimes" that arise under the Criminal Code and regulatory offences that arise under regulatory legislation enacted both by the various provinces and territories and by the Parliament of Canada.
- The enactment of the Canadian Charter of Rights and Freedoms has given judges the power to invalidate criminal law that unjustifiably infringes on an accused person's Charter rights.
- Each criminal offence can be analyzed in terms of its *actus reus* and *mens rea* elements.

- The *actus reus* generally consists of three components: conduct, circumstances, and consequences.
- *Mens rea* may be subjective or objective.
- Subjective *mens rea* may consist of intention and knowledge; recklessness; or wilful blindness.
- Objective *mens rea* is based on the requirement that there be a marked departure from the standard expected of the reasonable person acting prudently.
- An individual may become a party to a criminal offence in a number of different ways: actually committing an offence; aiding and/or abetting an offence; becoming a party to an offence by way of common intention; and counselling an offence that is committed.
- There are three inchoate offences that permit the police to intervene before a particular crime is committed: counselling an offence that is not committed; criminal attempt; and conspiracy.
- A successful defence of not criminally responsible on account of mental disorder (NCRMD) is not an acquittal; instead, it is a finding that the accused person has committed the act or omission in question but may not be held criminally responsible on account of mental disorder.
- The most important defences to a criminal charge include mistake of fact; intoxication; necessity; duress; provocation; and self-defence.

QUESTIONS FOR CRITICAL THINKING

1. Why does Canadian criminal law place such importance on the requirement that the Crown prove the relevant *mens rea* elements of a criminal offence? Would it not make more sense for the state to intervene and deal with offenders solely on the basis of the fact that they have committed the *actus reus* of an offence (a harmful or potentially harmful act or omission)?
2. Bill is driving his car down a steep hill in a large Canadian city. He discovers that his brakes are not functioning properly and the vehicle starts to gain speed. In the near distance, Bill notices that there is a group of schoolchildren who are crossing the road. Worried that he may collide with these children, Bill decides to steer his speeding car onto the sidewalk. Bill is aware that there is an elderly man on the sidewalk but he is confident that he can avoid hitting him. Tragically, at that moment, Bill suffers a fainting spell and, while he is unconscious, his car not only strikes and kills the man on the sidewalk but also returns to the road and injures five of the schoolchildren who are on the clearly marked crossing. There is some evidence that Bill had experienced brief fainting spells before but he did not consider them to be serious. After the accident, it is discovered that Bill probably suffers from a mild epileptic condition. Is Bill guilty of dangerous driving causing death and dangerous driving causing bodily harm?

3. Should the criminal law be used as a preventative tool? Should the police be able to intervene and bring individuals to the criminal courts before those individuals have actually committed the crime(s) that they are planning to carry out? Do the existing inchoate offences in the Criminal Code strike an acceptable balance between the demands of public security and the civil rights of accused persons?

4. It has been suggested that the defence of provocation should be abolished because it is frequently raised in the context of family violence [see, for example, the *Stone* case (1999) in this chapter]. Do you think that there is any place for a defence of provocation in a modern Criminal Code?

5. Do you think self-induced intoxication should ever be a defence to a crime of violence? What are the arguments for and against permitting defendants to raise a defence of intoxication? For example, is it fair that an intoxicated person may kill someone and be sentenced to two years' imprisonment while a sober person who deliberately kills another will be convicted of first- or second-degree murder and be sentenced automatically to life imprisonment?

NET WORK

Increasingly, basic legal research is being conducted online. The federal government and the governments of the various provinces and territories in Canada operate websites that offer swift access via the Internet to the full text of legislation and the decisions of the courts. In addition, a number of commercial electronic database services, such as Quicklaw, provide information concerning legislation, cases, and legal literature (journal articles and textbooks). You should be able to gain access to Quicklaw through your university or college. If you have access to Quicklaw, find Canadian cases in which the courts have discussed the defence of duress.

You may start to explore the powerful electronic tools that are available for research into Canadian criminal law by visiting the website of the Access to Justice Network, which supplies links to many other websites that are relevant to the field of criminal law: **www.acjnet.org**.

Another valuable website is operated by the Department of Justice Canada. This site not only provides detailed information about the activities of the Department of Justice and federal legislation concerning criminal law but also includes convenient links to provincial and territorial websites that offer direct access to legislation and court cases: **www.canada.justice.gc.ca**.

Using either the Access to Justice Network or the Department of Justice websites, see what information is available concerning the Youth Criminal Justice Act, which came into effect in April 2003.

You may access the text of all Supreme Court of Canada cases since 1985 by visiting the following website: **www.lexum.umontreal.ca/csc-scc/en/**. See if you can find the case of *R. v. Ruzic*, [2001] 1 S.C.R. 687 by accessing the Lexum website.

Find the relevant website for the courts in your own province or territory (for example, in Ontario, log on to www.ontariocourts.on.ca). You can find the relevant link at the websites of the Access to Justice Network and the Department of Justice Canada (see above). As an exercise, find out if your provincial or territorial court of appeal has decided any cases concerning the offence of fraud (section 380 of the Criminal Code).

KEY TERMS

actus reus	*mens rea*
Charter	mistake of fact
common law	necessity
conspiracy	not criminally responsible on account
counselling	of mental disorder (NCRMD)
crime	objective *mens rea*
criminal attempt	party to a crime
criminal law	provocation
criminal procedure	regulatory offence
duress	self-defence
inchoate crime	subjective *mens rea*
intoxication	"true crime"

SUGGESTED READING

The following texts provide an introduction to Canadian criminal law:

Roach, Kent. (2000). *Criminal Law*. (2nd ed.). Toronto: Irwin Law. Available online, through Quicklaw.

Verdun-Jones, Simon. (2002). *Criminal Law in Canada: Cases, Questions and the Code*. (3rd ed.). Toronto: Harcourt Canada.

The following text is the leading authority on Canadian criminal law and is frequently cited by the courts:

Stuart, Don. (2001). *Canadian Criminal Law*. (4th ed.). Toronto: Carswell.

The following books offer a selection of various cases, source materials, and commentaries in the field of Canadian criminal law:

Abell, Jennie, and Elizabeth Sheehy. (2002). *Criminal Law and Procedure: Cases, Context, Critique*. Concord, Ont.: Captus Press.

Stuart, Don, and Ronald Deslisle. (2001). *Learning Canadian Criminal Law*. (8th ed.). Toronto: Carswell.

The following Canadian texts cover issues that are closely related to criminal law:

Delisle, Ronald, and Don Stuart. (2000*). Learning Canadian Criminal Procedure*. (6th ed.). Toronto: Carswell.

Quigley, Tim. (1997). *Procedure in Canadian Criminal Law*. Toronto: Carswell.

Manson, Allan. (2001). *The Law of Sentencing*. Toronto: Irwin Law. Available, online, through Quicklaw.

Salhany, Roger. (2002). *The Practical Guide to Evidence in Criminal Cases*. (6th ed.). Toronto: Carswell.

Stuart, Don. (2001). *Charter Justice in Canadian Criminal Law*. (3rd ed.). Toronto: Carswell.

CASES CITED

R. v. Chaulk, [1990], 3 S.C.R. 13031. Available, online, at www.lexum.umontreal.ca/csc-scc/en/

R. v. Creighton, [1993] 3 S.C.R. 3. Available, online, at www.lexum.umontreal.ca/csc-scc/en/

R. v. Daviault, [1994] 3 S.C.R. 63. Available, online, at www.lexum.umontreal.ca/csc-scc/en/

R. v. Hibbert, [1995] 2 S.C.R. 973. Available, online, at www.lexum.umontreal.ca/csc-scc/en/

R. v. Hydro-Québec, [1997] 3 S.C.R. 213. Available, online, at www.lexum.umontreal.ca/csc-scc/en/

R. v. Lavallee, [1990] 1 S.C.R. 852, Available, online, at www.lexum.umontreal.ca/csc-scc/en/

R. v. Malott, [1998] 1 S.C.R. 123. Available, online, at www.lexum.umontreal.ca/csc-scc/en/

R. v. Martineau, [1990] 2 S.C.R. 633. Available, online, at www.lexum.umontreal.ca/csc-scc/en/

R. v. McConnell, [1996] 1 S.C.R. 1075. Available, online, at www.lexum.umontreal.ca/csc-scc/en/

R. v. Molodowic, [2000] 1 S.C.R. 420. Available, online, at www.lexum.umontreal.ca/csc-scc/en/

R. v. Morgentaler, Smolig and Scott, [1988] 1 S.C.R. 30. Available, online, at www.lexum.umontreal.ca/csc-scc/en/

R. v. Olan, Hudson and Hartnett, [1978] 2 S.C.R. 1175. Available, online, through Quicklaw.

R. v. Perka, [1984] 2 S.C.R. 232. Available, online, at www.lexum.umontreal.ca/csc-scc/en/

R. v. Pétel, [1994] 1 S.C.R. 3. Available, online, at www.lexum.umontreal.ca/csc-scc/en/

R. v. Ruzic, [2001] 1 S.C.R. 687. Available, online, at www.lexum.umontreal.ca/csc-scc/en/

R. Sault Ste. Marie (City of), [1978] 2 S.C.R. 1299. Available, online, through Quicklaw.

R. v. Sharpe, [2001] 1 S.C.R. 45. Available, online, at www.lexum.umontreal.ca/csc-scc/en/

R. v. Stone, [1999] 2 S.C.R. 290. Available, online, at www.lexum.umontreal.ca/csc-scc/en/

R. v. Thatcher, [1987] 1 S.C.R. 652. Available, online, at www.lexum.umontreal.ca/csc-scc/en/

R. v. Théroux, [1993] 2 S.C.R. 5. Available, online, at www.lexum.umontreal.ca/csc-scc/en/

R. v. Thibert, [1996] 1 S.C.R. 37. Available, online, at www.lexum.umontreal.ca/csc-scc/en/

R. v. Wholesale Travel Group Inc., [1991] 3 S.C.R. 154. Available, online, at www.lexum.umontreal.ca/csc-scc/en/

Winko v. British Columbia (Forensic Psychiatric Institute), [1999] 2 S.C.R. 625. Available, online, at www.lexum.umontreal.ca/csc-scc/en/

4

Counting Crime

JOHN EVANS
President, Management and Policy International, Inc.

ALEXANDER HIMELFARB
Privy Council Office

This chapter is about statistics on crime and criminal justice. Those who have tried to understand crime have, over the past century, relied heavily on statistical descriptions of criminal behaviour, criminals, and the criminal justice response. What we know about crime, then, depends on the quality, coverage, reliability, and validity of our measures of crime.

This chapter describes how social scientists count crime. After discussing the problems of the validity and reliability of our measures of crime, we introduce the long-standing debate over whether crime statistics reflect accurately the amount of crime in Canada or whether they merely reflect the activities of the criminal justice system. To help you to understand the strengths and weaknesses of Canadian crime statistics, we describe how the administrative records of the police, courts, and prisons are turned into measures describing the amount of crime and the characteristics of offenders and victims. This process involves developing clear procedures concerning units of count, levels of data aggregation, definitions, data elements, and counting procedures. Particular attention will be paid to the most commonly used measure of crime: the Uniform Crime Report system (UCR). The UCR is based on crimes reported to the police across the country. Finally, the chapter describes victimization surveys and self-report studies. These provide data that are complementary to those produced by the UCR system.

LEARNING OBJECTIVES

After reading this chapter, you should be able to

- Describe how the administrative records collected in the criminal justice system are turned into statistics about crime and the characteristics of offenders and victims.

- Understand the problems of the reliability and validity of our measures of crime and criminals.

- Understand the system that produces Canadian crime and criminal justice statistics.

- Describe the trends in Canadian crime rates over the past four decades.

- Describe the strengths and weaknesses of victimization and self-reported criminality surveys and understand how these two methods enhance our understanding of the problem of crime in Canada.

CONTROVERSIES OVER COUNTING CRIME

The first concern of those who sought to measure crime was coverage—how can one obtain data about the amount and nature of crime in a society? As the official sources of statistics have increased, and as creative **methodologies** for data collection have advanced, the questions of **reliability** and **validity** have become the most pressing. In simple terms, are the methods and techniques involved in gathering statistics strong enough that anyone following the procedures would produce the same counts (reliability)? And do the statistics collected count what they purport to count (validity)?

Imagine a situation in which you wished to test a theory of crime causation. For example, what aspects of communities create pressures to greater criminality? Further, let us say that your theory predicts higher **crime rates** in big cities than in small towns. You are then going to need statistical data on the amount of crime in these two types of settings. How do you get these counts? You could consult police statistics. Police gather vast amounts of information on suspects, incidents, arrests, and charges. These are the data most often used by criminologists to test their ideas. However, there have always been problems with police statistics. When police officers are dispatched to a call, each officer must use his or her own judgement to decide whether a crime has been committed or whether the call is unfounded. If the officer determines that there has been an offence, a report will be filled out by the officer and processed by police department staff. Most police departments then send the data from each incident to the Canadian Centre for Justice Statistics (CCJS), which is part of Statistics Canada. Police are supposed to follow a uniform set of rules (the Uniform Crime Reporting Rules) in recording criminal incidents or calls for service. Yet it has been discovered that different police departments often use different rules for recording their information. In fact, individual police officers exercise a good deal of discretion in what they decide to record and how they record it. There may be doubts, then, about the reliability of the statistics derived from police records. However, there is perhaps an even more fundamental problem. Are suspects criminals? Are those arrested and charged criminals? Are all incidents that are recorded actual crimes, and are these incidents a complete count of crimes? Do the data provide a valid count of crime?

A particular difficulty arises in crime counts because as the reliability of a statistical measure increases, its validity as a count of crime frequently decreases. Thus, while the police certainly never detect or become aware of all crimes, and despite enormous problems of reliability, their counts of crime are likely to be a far more valid reflection of the amount of criminal behaviour than are counts of convictions or counts of prisoners. The criminal justice system operates as a funnel: only some fraction of incidents result in a police record of a criminal incident; only a portion of recorded incidents result in suspects identified; only a portion of suspects are arrested or charged; only a portion of charges result in conviction; and only a portion of convictions result in incarceration (see Figure 4.1). The further you go into the system, the more confident you can be that the count is accurate and reliable and that it is a decreasingly valid representation of all criminal behaviour. Also, there are built-in biases

methodology

The study or critique of methods. There are many philosophical issues about the use of a particular method or about positivism or measurement itself.

reliability

Identifies one of the standards (another being *validity*) against which the tools used to measure concepts are judged. Reliability refers to consistency of results over time. If a bathroom scale is used to measure the concept of weight, one must ask, Is this tool (the bathroom scale) reliable? Does it provide consistent results? Notice that the bathroom scale or any other measure may be reliable and yet be inaccurate.

validity

The extent to which a tool or instrument (questionnaire, experiment) actually measures the concept the researcher claims to be interested in and not something else. For example, measuring people's feet to learn about the concept of intelligence, on the surface at least, does not seem valid.

crime rate

When studying crime, if a researcher wishes to compare the amount of crime over time or between communities of different sizes, it is not enough to just do a gross count of the amount of crime. To get around the problems involved with this, criminologists calculate crime rates (or rates of incarceration, conviction, or recidivism). This is done by dividing the amount of crime by the population size and multiplying by 100 000. This produces the standard rate per 100 000, but occasionally it is useful to calculate a rate per million or some other figure.

FIGURE 4.1   The Crime Funnel: Break-and-Enter Offences Processed through the Canadian Criminal Justice System

Note: This diagram illustrates the processing of break-and-enter offences through various stages in the criminal justice system. Data are approximations.

ALL BREAK AND ENTER: Offences reported and not reported to the police.

REPORTED: About 2 out of 3 break and enters are thought to be reported to the police.

ACTUAL: The police assess slightly over 9 out of 10 offences as actual.

CHARGED: For about every 8 offences that occur, 1 person is charged.

PROSECUTED: For about every 20 offences that occur, 1 person is prosecuted.

CONVICTED: For about every 23 offences that occur, 1 person is convicted.

SENTENCED: For about every 43 offences that occur, 1 person is sentenced to either a prison or penitentiary.

Source: Solicitor General Canada. (1984). *Reported and Unreported Crimes.* Canadian Urban Victimization Survey, Bulletin No. 2; Solicitor General Canada. (1981). *Selected Trends in Canadian Criminal Justice.* Reproduced with the permission of the Minister of Public Works and Government Services Canada, 1999.

in that some crimes (and some criminals) are more likely than others to be reported and to result in arrest, charge, conviction, and a sentence to incarceration. For example, murderers are more likely to be arrested and to go to jail than are corporate criminals or shoplifters. The further you go into the system, the more obvious it becomes that you are counting something about how the system itself operates; you are counting official decisions about crime and criminals. To put this another way, statistical descriptions of the prison

population may provide valid indicators of one way that a society and its criminal justice system respond to crime. These descriptions, however, do not provide a valid measure of the amount and the nature of crime.

How have criminologists handled these problems? For a long time, they acknowledged the problems and then, when they needed data, they pretended the problems away. Kaplan's "law of the hammer" holds that if you give a small child a hammer, he or she discovers that everything needs pounding. Similarly, social scientists have often been accused of letting their methods, or statistics that were most readily available, dictate their theories. Social scientists will often find out what they are able to discover most easily and build their theories around this limited information. Many of the early theories of criminology discussed elsewhere in this text were built upon a rather uncritical acceptance of official sources of statistics. Many early criminologists used prisoners to study the differences between criminals and noncriminals. Some used police records of arrest or charge; some used court records. These criminologists rarely asked the following questions: Are all criminals equally likely to get arrested? To be charged? To be put in prison? Even when criminologists recognized the limits of the available information, they used these unreliable and often invalid measures because this was all they had.

In the 1960s and the 1970s, a number of sociologists and criminologists focused their attention on the systematic biases of past theories built on official records. New theories suggested that official records showed us how the criminal justice system operated to create crime and criminals. The statistics revealed information about the police, about the courts, and about whom they selected for their attention and worst punishments. Arrest, charge, and conviction were parts of a formal labelling process, a ceremony of degradation in which a person was formally stigmatized. These labelling or social reaction theories asked why certain people were more often selected for this process and studied the consequences for these people of being labelled and stigmatized. The same bodies of "crime statistics" that had been used to describe the behaviour of criminals were now being used to describe the official agents of social control. More recently, criminologists are increasingly becoming polarized. Many seem to be returning to the conservative criminology of the past, to the acceptance of official records as a reasonable indicator of crime, and focusing on explaining crime for the purpose of controlling it. Others, influenced by some variant of "critical" criminology, see crime statistics as simply part of the government's control mechanism, a way of characterizing the crime problem, a means of self-justification, and a reflection of more fundamental structural inequalities.

Are crime statistics whatever one makes of them? Are statistics simply a resource to tell lies or support one's own favoured position? Yes, sometimes. But they need not be. **Theories** about crime and facts about crime are built simultaneously, are mutually dependent, and shape one another. Theory without facts is indistinguishable from **ideology**; facts without theory are often implicit ideology; statistical facts without theory are numerology, often bent to ideological ends. Theorists and policy-makers have often been guilty of using statistics to

population

All members of a given class or set. For example, adult Canadians, teenagers, Canadian inmates, or criminal offenders can each be thought of as populations. Populations are difficult to study because we cannot find all the members (heroin addicts) or because of the expense (teenagers). Social scientists avoid this problem by gathering a *sample* from the population and then generalizing from the sample to the population.

theory

All sciences use theory as a tool to explain. It is useful to think of theory as a conceptual model of some aspect of life. We may have a theory of mate selection, of the emergence of capitalist societies, of criminal behaviour, or of the content of dreams. In each case, the theory consists of a set of concepts and their nominal definition or assertions about the relationships between these concepts, assumptions, and knowledge claims.

ideology

A linked set of ideas and beliefs that act to uphold and justify an existing or desired situation in society. Ideologies offer explanations and justifications of features of society such as the distribution of wealth, status, and power.

their own ideological ends, using crime counts to show that we are going through a crime wave, or using the same counts to show how we are living through a wave of repression. We live in an age when numerical values have a certain magic and a power to convince us, to make arguments seem true. Statistics can be dangerous if we do not have the tools to consider them critically.

For example, imagine that you read, in some credible source, that violence in Canadian society has risen by 100 percent over the past decade. Before you set off to explain this "fact," before you turn your home into a fortress, you should ask, Just what is being counted as violence? Crimes? Some crimes? Political dissent? Violence by the state? Domestic violence? What theory or ideological assumptions have guided this choice of "fact"? And how good are the facts? How well and consistently have they been counted? Are they reliable and valid?

What have social scientists and policy-makers done about the lack of good crime information? Over 30 years ago, the American sociologist Ned Polsky (1967) argued that our understanding of crime would never be significantly advanced if we relied on statistical data. He was concerned that sociologists and criminologists relied too heavily on remote sources of information. They remained too distant from the criminals they wished to understand. He advocated field research through which social scientists live among, and learn from, the criminals themselves. Not surprisingly, few have followed Polsky's lead. Rather, most have worked to improve the quality of statistics based on official sources, to specify the valid uses of these statistics, and to develop innovative methodologies to complement official data and to fill gaps. Despite the problems, criminological theory and criminal justice policy remain heavily dependent on statistics about crime and the criminal justice system.

One might distinguish three broad types of criminal justice statistics: statistics about crime and criminals, statistics about the criminal justice system and its response to crime, and statistics about perceptions of crime and criminal justice. Theory and policy require statistics about the decisions of those who break the law, about the decisions of those who maintain it, and about what people think of all of this. For the most part, statistics on the criminal justice system are the most developed.

STATISTICS ON THE CRIMINAL JUSTICE SYSTEM

administrative record

Collection of information about individual cases, such as statistics concerning what is common among individual cases. An administrative record contains information that can be the basis of statistics, provided that clear procedures are developed for handling the data and generating statistical descriptions.

The criminal justice system produces an enormous amount of raw data in the form of police reports and records, the recorded decisions of prosecutors and judges, the **administrative records** of prisons and penitentiaries, and the recorded decisions of parole boards and probation and parole services. One might then assume that Canada has a sophisticated system of statistics on the criminal justice system. However, this is not entirely the case.

From Records to Statistics

Administrative records are not statistics. Records are about individual cases and are intended primarily to help practitioners make decisions about these individual cases. Statistics are aggregated; they are about what is common among individual cases. Statistics are meant to provide information about larger questions: planning and evaluation, policy and program development, and theory building and testing. While good records are the base, the conversion of records into statistics requires a number of conceptual decisions. The potential clients or users of the statistics must decide what it is they want to know and how they plan to use the information. Statistical systems should be built to address the enduring theoretical and policy concerns.

Specifically, the following issues must be addressed before records can be converted into statistics: unit of count, **levels of aggregation**, definitions, **data elements**, and **counting procedures**.

(A) Unit of count—consensus about what it is that we are counting.

In the course of their everyday activities, the police, for example, may count many different things: suspects, offences, charges, or calls for service. Typically, they work with occurrences. An occurrence may involve several offenders, several victims, and several offences. The unit we wish to count in a statistical system will depend on whether we are trying to learn something about police workload or productivity, or whether we are seeking to learn something about crime or victims. Recently, for example, there has been a growing awareness among policy-makers and criminologists that victims have been an ignored unit of count, and we know little about their characteristics. Some units of count are specific to a particular sector. For example, the prison sector can count inmates; the court sector, convictions; and the police, suspects.

(B) Levels of aggregation—consensus about how to combine data.

A crucial decision is the level at which we want our statistics. For example, do we want to combine police records for a city? Do we want to combine statistics for an entire province? Or region? Or the nation? To the extent that we want to generalize our theories or develop or evaluate national policies, we are likely to want national statistics. But several criminologists have warned that the further you move from those who produce the data and the more you try to combine data from different sources, the more questionable is the result. They prefer the richer and more detailed information available from local police to the abstracted, less complete data available about national policing.

(C) Definitions—consensus about how to define what is being counted.

While the Criminal Code provides a common set of definitions for counting crime, there remains a good deal of discretion about when an incident of crime is truly an incident, or even what, for example, constitutes "inmate." If one wishes to count inmates, should one count those who are temporarily absent, or those on remand, or those in community correctional facilities, or those assigned to mental institutions? Common definitions are essential. This is not merely a technical issue. Depending on how the terms are defined, you can inflate or deflate the statistics; you can make it appear that crime is higher or lower, or that there are more or fewer prisoners.

levels of aggregation
This refers to how data are to be combined. Do we want city-level, provincial, or national data? Among other things, data aggregation requires common rules, allowing confidence in the *reliability* and *validity* of the measures used.

data element
What, specifically, is to be collected. Operational issues may require more detail than the statistical system does. Also, statistical needs may require that operational agencies collect data that they do not need (or do not think that they need) for operational purposes. In any statistical system, there must be detailed agreements on exactly what is to be collected.

counting procedure
In any statistical system, there must be consensus on how to count units and data elements. This is not as easy an issue as it appears. For example, if an offender goes on a break-and-enter spree and steals from a half dozen houses, is this to be counted as one incident or six?

(D) Data elements—consensus about what specific information should be collected.

While the police will need certain kinds of information to help them in their investigative activities, this information will be far more detailed than, and sometimes quite different from, what is needed as aggregated statistics. Similarly, the police in one jurisdiction may, for their own good reasons, maintain records quite different from those of other police departments. As understandable as this is, it is extremely difficult to build aggregated statistics out of different types of records that may be incompatible.

(E) Counting procedures—consensus on how to count units and elements.

If an offender goes on a break-and-enter spree and hits a half-dozen houses in an evening, how many offences should be counted—six or one? Or, if, during a break and enter, an offender is confronted by the home-owner and assaults him or her, is this one or two offences? If one, which offence should be counted? If we agree that the most serious should be counted, how do we determine seriousness?

Canadian Criminal Justice Statistics

The questions or issues of unit of count, levels of aggregation, definitions, data elements, and counting procedures are at the base of much of the technical and critical literature on criminal justice statistics. Within Canada, attempts to answer these questions have traditionally been the responsibility of our national statistical service, Statistics Canada. More recently, the federal and provincial governments have created a national institute, the **Canadian Centre for Justice Statistics (CCJS)**, a satellite of Statistics Canada, governed by a board of directors of senior officials responsible for justice.

The major difficulty confronting the centre is getting agreement on priorities such as whose needs should be met. Crime statistics are used by different people and for different purposes: criminologists and researchers want to build and test theories; policy-makers and analysts want to identify problems and develop and test solutions; and administrators and program managers want to plan and run their operations and to monitor and evaluate their programs. Most important, statistics serve the public interest by keeping people informed and by providing some measure of public accountability. Good statistics are important, but they are important in different ways for different users.

At the present time, Canada has reasonably good national data on criminal justice inputs such as resources and expenditures. The data are far weaker when it comes to outputs such as incidents, arrests, charges, convictions, and dispositions. In fact, there have been no national statistics on court decisions since 1973. The CCJS does have the Adult Criminal Survey under development, intended to be a census of courts in Canada. As of 2002, the survey collects data from jurisdictions that represent about 80 percent of the national criminal court caseload. Correctional statistics are the most accurate since we can give a fairly accurate count of the number of prisoners in Canada and provide some information on their social characteristics. Despite some difference in counting from province to province, Canada can produce a reasonably accurate descrip-

Canadian Centre for Justice Statistics

A division of Statistics Canada, formed in 1981, with a mandate to collect national data on crime and justice.

"Justice and Crime"
Statistics Canada
www.statcan.ca/english/Pgdb/
justic.htm

tion of its inmate population. This can be quite useful for projecting future inmate populations and for planning future facilities and services. When linked to other data, it can also be useful for developing correctional policy. For example, how much are we using incarceration and are we doing so in the most useful and appropriate ways?

Data on prisoners, however, do not tell us much about crime and criminal behaviours. They tell us about the criminal justice system. The confusion comes when people equate "criminal" with "prisoner." Some people are more likely to be caught; some people are more likely to be charged; some people are more likely to be convicted; and some people are more likely to be sentenced to prison or to a penitentiary. We know too much about how people get selected for incarceration to assume that prison statistics tell us very much about crime.

But what can such data show? Figure 4.2 shows the growth in number of those incarcerated in Canada between 1950 and 2001. In this period, the inmate population increased approximately 2.5 times. Obviously, these figures are important for administrative and planning purposes. But do these figures tell us something about growing crime in Canada? No. Do they tell us something about harsher or more punitive sentencing practices? No. In fact, if we look at the rate of incarceration (per 100 000 adult Canadians), we see that much of the growth in penitentiary population can be accounted for by the growth of the Canadian population (Figure 4.3). That is, the number of people incarcerated per 100 000 Canadians has remained relatively constant since 1950.

International comparisons are difficult and problematic, but they show Canada to be a nation that incarcerates at a much higher rate than most western

FIGURE 4.2 Average Inmate Count, 1950–2001

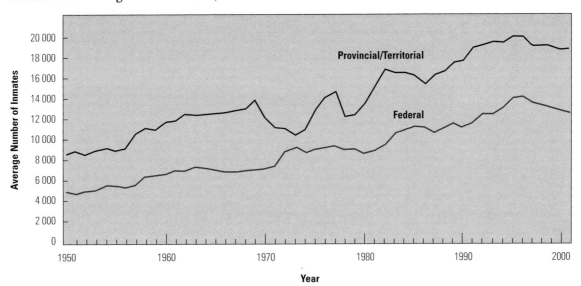

Source: Statistics Canada. Canadian Centre for Crime Statistics. Data derived from *Average Offender Counts for Canada, Fiscal Years 1950–51 to 1993–94, Corrections Key Indicator Report for Adults and Young Offenders*, 1996/97, Catalogue No. 85-222-XPE, and *Adult Correctional Services in Canada 2000/01*, Catalogue No. 85-002-XIE, Vol. 22, No. 11.

FIGURE 4.3   Incarceration Rate per 100 000 Adult Population, 1950–2001

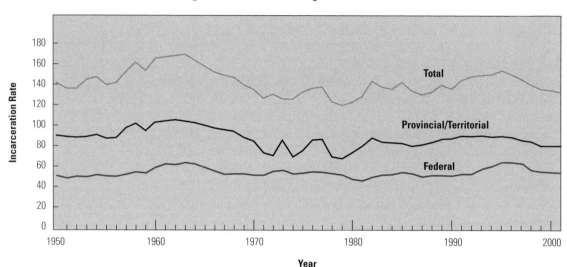

Source: Statistics Canada. Canadian Centre for Crime Statistics. Data derived from *Average Offender Counts for Canada, Fiscal Years 1950–51 to 1993–94, Corrections Key Indicators Report for Adults and Young Offenders*, 1996/97, Catalogue No. 85-222-XPE, and *Adult Correctional Services in Canada 2000/01*, Catalogue No. 85-002-XIE, Vol. 22, No. 11.

European nations but a much lower rate than the United States, where, in 2002, over 2 million people were incarcerated. Some have argued that this is proof that Canada is too punitive, that too many people are being put behind bars and put there for too long. Others have argued that it simply means that Canada has more serious crime than many other nations. The debates flourish. Canadian statistics do not provide the answers; they only indicate where problems may exist.

HOW MUCH CRIME?

dark figure of crime

The amount of crime that is unreported or unknown. The total amount of crime in a community consists of crimes that are known or recorded and the dark figure of crime. Criminologists have used differing methods (such as victimization surveys) to try to decrease the amount of unknown or unrecorded crime.

It should come as no surprise that criminologists have had difficulty counting crime. By its very nature, crime is typically a secretive activity. When people commit crimes, they try to avoid becoming part of the count of criminals. (They do not want to become a statistic!) The "best" crime is one that no one knows about, and no criminal justice system will ever be able to ferret out all the crimes and criminals. Some crimes are harder to detect than others, and some criminals are harder to apprehend and convict. Criminologists have long recognized that the major problem of counting crime is the so-called **dark figure of crime** that remains unreported, unrecorded, and largely unknown. In response to the problem, criminologists have developed a variety of ways of counting crime, or at least to describe crime patterns and trends. They have tried to rationalize and improve official statistics, but they have also developed approaches that do not depend on official counts of crime. In the next section, we look at official records, victimization surveys, and self-report studies as sources of data about crime.

OFFICIAL STATISTICS: CANADIAN UNIFORM CRIME REPORTS

Despite their problems, we rely heavily on official counts of the amount of crime. Until 40 years ago, we were dependent on local police records collected for police purposes and handled differently in each locale. For over four decades now, Canada has had in place a system called the Canadian **Uniform Crime Reports (UCR)**, designed to provide uniform, comparable, and national statistics. However, just what this system counts has been the subject of an almost endless debate within criminology.

While the Canadian Uniform Crime Reports drew heavily from a similar system in the United States, it is an improvement over the American system. First, common crime classifications and definitions are easier to arrive at in Canada than in the United States since Canada operates under a common criminal code while each American state has a separate code. Second, the coverage of police departments is far more complete in Canada than in the United States. But both systems share some fundamental problems. Some of these problems can be corrected by further improvements to the Uniform Crime Report system; however, some of the problems are more fundamental because they are built into all official statistics.

Let us first look at the problems that could be corrected, indeed are being corrected in both Canada and the United States. A number of studies (Nettler, 1974; Silverman and Teevan, 1975; Silverman, 1980; de Silva and Silverman, 1985) have documented some of the problems in the recording and scoring rules and how these rules are applied. Specifically, the studies have examined the implications of the "**seriousness rule**," which holds that only the most serious crime is scored in an incident involving multiple crimes. The concerns are threefold: first, this rule deflates the total crime count since less serious crimes are not counted separately; second, it inflates serious crimes as a proportion of the total; and third, the way in which seriousness is scored is problematic because not enough qualitative data about the crimes are recorded to use a sophisticated scale of seriousness. See Box 4.1 for a discussion of the main UCR categories and the most serious offence rule.

Concerns have also been expressed that the crime categories used are too general, allowing too many different kinds of acts to be recorded in the same way. For example, thefts and attempted thefts are recorded under the same category.

Furthermore, as previously indicated, it is not always entirely clear just what it is we want to count. In Canada, the count of crimes includes violations of the Criminal Code, violations of other federal and provincial statutes, and violations of some municipal by-laws. Many of these criminal and quasi-criminal laws are not what most Canadians think of as crime. When most people think of crime, when they worry about or fear crime, they are thinking about particular offences. They are not thinking about the Criminal Code and the full

Uniform Crime Reports (UCR)

Since 1961, Canada has had the Uniform Crime Reporting system developed by Statistics Canada and the Canadian Association of Chiefs of Police. This system is designed to provide a measure of reliability for crime statistics through providing police agencies with a standardized set of procedures for collecting and reporting crime information.

seriousness rule

If there are multiple crimes committed in one incident, only the most serious crime is counted.

BOX 4.1

FOCUS

UCR Categories and the Most Serious Offence Rule

Violent incidents involve offences that deal with the application, or threat of application, of force to a person. These include homicide, attempted murder, various forms of sexual and non-sexual assault, robbery, and abduction. Traffic incidents that result in death or bodily harm are included under Criminal Code traffic incidents.

Property incidents involve unlawful acts with the intent of gaining property but do not involve the use or threat of violence against an individual. Theft, breaking and entering, fraud, and possession of stolen goods are examples of property crimes.

Other Criminal Code incidents involve the remaining Criminal Code offences that are not classified as violent or property incidents (excluding traffic). Examples are mischief, bail violations, disturbing the peace, arson, prostitution, and offensive weapons.

Total Criminal Code incidents is the tabulation of all violent, property, and other Criminal Code incidents reported for a given year.

Most Serious Offence

The UCR Survey classifies incidents according to the most serious offence (MSO) in the incident. In categorizing incidents, violent offences always take precedence over non-violent offences. Within violent and non-violent, offences are then sorted according to the maximum sentence under the Criminal Code. The UCR Survey scores violent incidents differently from other types of crime. For violent crimes, a separate incident is recorded for each victim (categorized according to the most serious offence against the victim). If, for example, one person assaults three people, then three incidents are recorded. If three people assault one person, only one incident is recorded. For non-violent crimes, one incident (categorized

according to the most serious offence in the incident) is counted for every distinct or separate occurrence. Robbery is one exception to the above scoring rule. Robbery is categorized as a violent offence. Unlike all other violent offences, one occurrence of robbery is equal to one incident, regardless of the number of victims. The reason for this exception is that robbery can involve many people who could all be considered victims. In a bank robbery with 5 tellers and 20 customers present, 25 incidents of robbery would be counted if the normal scoring rule for violent incidents were applied. This would seriously overstate the occurrence of robbery. Thus, the total number of incidents recorded by the UCR Survey is not a census of all violations of the law that come to the attention of police. Rather, it is equal to the number of victims of violent (other than robbery) plus the number of separate occurrences of non-violent crimes (and robberies).

Actual Incidents

When a crime is reported to the police, the incident is recorded as a "reported" incident. Police then conduct a preliminary investigation to determine the validity of the report. Occasionally, crimes reported to the police prove to be unfounded. Unfounded incidents are subtracted from the number of reported incidents to produce the number of "actual incidents." Numbers and rates of crime are calculated on the basis of "actual incidents" categorized according to the most serious offence.

Source: Adapted from the Statistics Canada publication, "Canadian Crime Statistics," Catalogue No. 85-205-XIE, Canadian Centre for Justice Statistics, Ch. 6. Reprinted with permission of the Minister of Industry, 2003.

gross counts of crime
A count of the total amount of crime in a given community, making no distinction between crime categories.

range of behaviours legally defined as criminal. When we seek to count crime, we are invariably struck with a complex mix of these two sets of definitions. For this reason, **gross counts of crime** may be very misleading. For example, in 1969 the Ouimet report pointed out that total convictions for all criminal offences in Canada increased by an alarming 2500 percent between 1901 and

1965. The report added, however, that 98 percent of the increase was accounted for by summary convictions—less serious crime—particularly traffic offences. Thus much of the apparent increase in crime actually reflected the increased use of automobiles in Canada during this period. With the report of the gross crime counts alone, most people would no doubt have had horrific visions of violent predators preying on innocent victims, rather than the more accurate vision of careless motorists abusing one another and pedestrians. For these reasons, UCR programs count offences within particular offence categories so that each offence can be examined separately.

Another often-cited problem is that the Canadian UCR treats property crimes and personal crimes differently. Several property crimes, even if they involve different victims, may be recorded as a single offence if they are considered to be part of the same incident. This is not the case for personal offences. However, even for personal offences, the UCR program collects very little information about victims and offenders. The CCJS has sought to rectify this by developing a richer incident-based UCR, the UCR2. This new form of the UCR collects data on characteristics of the victim and the accused as well as characteristics of the incident itself. Canadian police agencies are now in the process of converting to the UCR2. The question remains, however, whether the new and improved Canadian UCR will provide us with an accurate count of crime or even a reasonable indicator of crime and crime trends. Can official statistics ever tell us about total crime? Are official statistics useful only for understanding the criminal justice system?

We might have discussed the Canadian UCR under the heading of criminal justice statistics because these official data may tell us more about police activities than about crime. "Official violations" statistics are, in part, a product of policy decisions within the criminal justice system, that is, decisions about which criminal infractions deserve the most police attention and resources. Furthermore, crime statistics are the product of individual police decisions made in the exercise of police discretion about what crimes are serious enough to attend to, record, and pursue. In fact, the ways in which police and police departments apply crime recording and scoring procedures reflect, to some extent, the policing style and policy of the particular police department. Combining or comparing statistics from different departments is highly problematic (Silverman, 1980).

Police statistics are also shaped by public perceptions, concerns, and fears. The police are very much dependent on the accounts of victims and witnesses. In other words, victims and witnesses must recognize an act as a criminal justice matter, must believe it to be of sufficient seriousness to warrant a report to the police, and must believe that reporting the act is worthwhile—all this before the police make their decisions about how to respond to and record an act. (See, for example, Shearing, 1984.)

Official crime statistics, then, are shaped by both common-sense and legal definitions of what constitutes crime. These statistics reflect the decisions of many people, not simply the behaviours of criminals. Official counts of crime will change as legal definitions change, as common-sense definitions change, and as the priorities of agents of law enforcement change. For example, if

Parliament made premarital sex illegal, we could well expect a rather sharp increase in crime. Would this be reflected in official crime counts? To the extent that there are no direct victims to bring these offences to police attention, the answer is probably no. Much would depend on the priority attached to enforcement of this offence.

Consider two less hypothetical examples. As official statistics reveal to us increasing rates of family violence, theoretical explanations of the crisis in the nuclear family abound. But has the incidence truly increased, or have Canadians, within and outside the criminal justice system, become increasingly intolerant of such behaviour and more willing to bring such incidents to police attention? Have police become more sensitive to the seriousness of the problem and more likely to record the incidents as crimes? In other words, has the incidence increased, or have the definitions and reporting and recording behaviours changed?

Similarly, recorded cannabis offences increased during the 1990s while cocaine and heroin offences declined. In 1997, cannabis offences accounted for 72 percent of all drug crimes, compared with 58 percent in 1991. In contrast, cocaine accounted for 17 percent of all cases in 1997, down from 28 percent in 1991, and heroin accounted for about 2 percent of all cases, down marginally from 1991. Nearly half of all drug offences were for possession of cannabis (Statistics Canada, 1999). Total recorded drug offences increased by 15 percent during this period, while most other crimes were declining.

Drug offence statistics may change significantly in the future, not so much as a result of changes in behaviour but rather because of changes to the law. Both a Senate committee and a House of Commons committee issued reports in 2002 urging dramatic changes to the law, particularly to those laws governing cannabis.

Why has there been such an increase in cannabis-related offences? Has its use really increased or have the priorities of law enforcement agencies shifted over time? Has a decline in the use of harder drugs led police to focus on cannabis users? One factor contributing to the increase has been the effort to shut down marijuana-growing operations across the country as hydroponic growing techniques have enabled Canadian growers to supply an increasing share of the domestic market. Cultivation charges have increased dramatically, though they still make up only 14 percent of all marijuana offences (Statistics Canada, 1999). Because statistics for victimless crimes such as drug use are as much a result of police priorities and budgets as they are of the amount of criminal behaviour, official statistics tell us little about the actual prevalence of these behaviours.

What, then, can the Canadian UCR tell us? From the inception of the Uniform Crime Reports in 1962, the total Criminal Code offence rate nearly tripled from 2771 offences per 100 000 Canadians to 7590 in 2002. Figure 4.4 shows the trend line during this period.

During this period, both violent and property crime rates increased steadily until 1992. They continued to decline until 2002, though there was a slight increase in 2001. Violent crimes, however, were consistently a small proportion of total crimes—about 13 percent as opposed to the more frequent property crimes, 50 percent of the total (see Figure 4.5A and Figure 4.5B). Those who

FIGURE 4.4 Total Criminal Code Offences Reported to Police by Most Serious Offence, Rate per 100 000 Canadians, 1962–2002

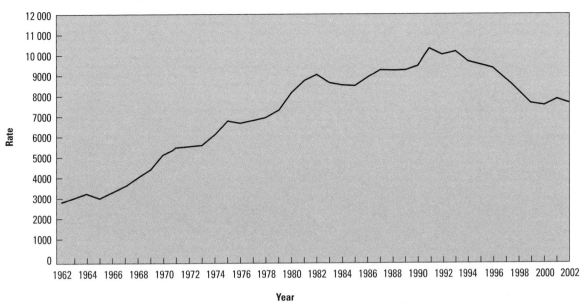

Source: Statistics Canada. Adapted from *Crime and Traffic Enforcement Statistics*, Annual Catalogue No. 85-205; *Juristat* 18(11), Catalogue No. 85-002-XPE; *Juristat* 22(6), Catalogue No. 85-002-XIE; and *Juristat* 23(5), Catalogue No. 85-002-XIE. Reproduced with the permission of the Minister of Industry, 2003.

FIGURE 4.5A Violent Crimes Reported to Police by Most Serious Offence, Rate per 100 000 Canadians, 1962–2002

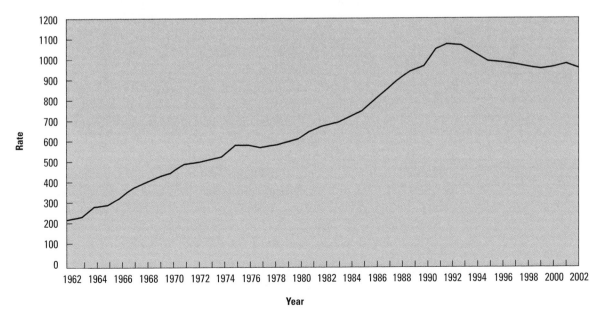

Source: Statistics Canada. Adapted from *Crime and Traffic Enforcement Statistics*, Annual Catalogue No. 85-205; *Juristat* 18(11), Catalogue No. 85-002-XPE; *Juristat* 22(6), Catalogue No. 85-002-XIE; and *Juristat* 23(5), Catalogue No. 85-002-XIE. Reproduced with the permission of the Minister of Industry, 2003.

FIGURE 4.5B   **Property Crimes Reported to Police by Most Serious Offence, Rate per 100 000 Canadians, 1962–2002**

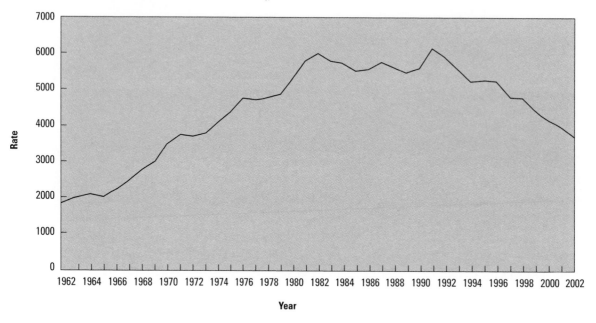

Source: Statistics Canada. Adapted from *Crime and Traffic Enforcement Statistics*, Annual Catalogue No. 85-205; *Juristat* 18(11), Catalogue No. 85-002-XPE; *Juristat* 22(6), Catalogue No. 85-002-XIE; and *Juristat* 23(5) Catalogue No. 85-002-XIE. Reproduced with the permission of the Minister of Industry, 2003.

work with crime statistics generally refer to crime rates when they wish to take into account the size of the population. The crime rate is simply the number of incidents for every 100 000 Canadians. Reference to rate, then, rather incidence, makes sure that comparisons from jurisdiction to jurisdiction, or over time, do not reflect differences in population size rather than differences in criminal behaviour.

Violent crimes are relatively rare. In 2002, Canada had 582 homicides (first- and second-degree murder, manslaughter, and infanticide) and 682 attempted murders. Together these crimes account for less than half of 1 percent of reported violent incidents. If we exclude 15 homicides allegedly committed in B.C. by Robert Pickton that were reported in 2002, but committed in earlier years, the homicide rate remained stable in 2002 for the fourth consecutive year. The 2002 rate (1.9 homicides per 100 000 population) is about the same as during the late 1960s. The rate for attempted murder decreased 7 percent in 2002, following a similar decline in 2001. Violent crimes continue to be about 13 percent of total offences. In fact, the category "violent offences" includes robberies, which are judged to have had the potential for violence even if no violence occurred. The presence of a weapon, even if the weapon was not used, and even if no injury occurred, would include the incident in the violent crime count.

Things seem to be getting better. Although the crime rate rose from 1962 to 1991, it has generally declined since then. (See Table 4.1.)

The crime rate is now at the 1979 level. The property crime rate decreased slightly (−1 percent), continuing the downward trend in these offences seen

"Crime Statistics, 2002"
Statistics Canada
**www.statcan.ca/Daily/English/
030724/d030724a.htm**

since the early 1990s. A 3 percent decline in break-ins contributed to this decrease, along with a decline in motor vehicle thefts. The 2002 property crime rate was the lowest in nearly 30 years.

Remember that all these data are based on reports to the police. The UCR yields additional data on victims of these reported crimes and those charged. Table 4.1 illustrates the kinds of data available from the UCR on criminal justice reporting.

But what can we say about crime rates given all the cautions with which we began this chapter? How much crime remains hidden to the police? Which crimes? How much do police recording practices shape the UCR figures? How much do these practices change over time? Are these data useless? The answer to the last question is no. For example, the homicide statistics collected by the Canadian Centre for Justice Statistics probably reflect the actual number of homicides fairly accurately. It is also probable that certain other offences that are of high priority within the criminal justice system, and which victims are likely to report, are relatively well captured by the UCR program. Motor vehicle theft is probably the best example of this type of offence. In sum, we can learn something about the incidence of crime from these data, but we are not sure how much.

We can be more confident that if police departments across Canada are recording and reporting crimes relatively consistently, then the UCR data give us a picture of what crimes the police are processing. For example, recent changes in police policy limit police discretion in laying charges when handling domestic violence incidents. This policy has produced more official incidents of such assaults, reflecting changes in police practice if not changes in criminal behaviour. Some optimists would argue that the UCR gives an indication of trends in crime. The less optimistic say no, there is too much we do not know about victim reporting behaviour, about the exercise of police discretion in deciding what is criminal and what is not, about police recording and reporting practices, and about the nature and seriousness of the offences captured by the UCR. Out of these concerns have emerged attempts to develop other ways of counting crime. The most important of these is the victimization survey.

VICTIMIZATION SURVEYS

Victimization surveys are based on the idea of going directly to the people to ask them to indicate whether they have been victims of acts that the Criminal Code defines as criminal; to describe the nature and consequences of their victimization experiences; to describe the criminal justice response; to indicate whether victims or others brought the incidents to official attention, and, if not, why not; and to indicate their perceptions and attitudes about crime and criminal justice in Canada. The first large-scale victimization survey in Canada was carried out in 1982 by the Ministry of the Solicitor General of Canada and Statistics Canada. Beginning in 1998, Statistics Canada has conducted a victimization survey every five years as part of the General Social Survey.

victimization survey

A survey of a random *sample* of the population in which people are asked to recall and describe their own experience of being a victim of crime.

TABLE 4.1 Federal Statute Incidents Reported to Police, by Most Serious Offence, Canada, 1998–2002[1]

	1998 Number	1998 Rate	1999 Number	1999 Rate	2000[y,2] Number	2000[y,2] Rate	2001 Number	2001 Rate	2002 Number	2002 Rate	%change in rate* 2001–2002	%change in rate* 1992–2002
Population	30 248 412		30 509 323		30 790 834		31 110 565		31 413 990			
Homicides[3]	558	2	538	2	546	2	553	2	582	2	4.2	-28.2
Attempted murder	745	2	687	2	767	2	725	2	682	2	-6.8	-41.6
Assaults—												
Total (levels 1, 2, 3)	**223 926**	**740**	**221 348**	**726**	**233 719**	**759**	**239 957**	**762**	**235 270**	**749**	**-1.7**	**-2.0**
Level 1	183 999	608	181 330	594	190 467	619	191 147	614	189 158	602	-2.0	-2.8
Level 2—Weapon	37 302	123	37 501	123	40 686	132	43 094	139	43 427	138	-0.2	4.7
Level 3—Aggravated	2 625	9	2 517	8	2 566	8	2 716	9	2 685	9	-2.1	-31.7
Other assaults	12 147	40	12 126	40	12 164	40	12 260	39	12 357	39	-0.2	-30.9
Sexual assaults—Total	**25 553**	**84**	**23 859**	**78**	**24 001**	**78**	**24 044**	**77**	**24 350**	**78**	**0.3**	**-36.0**
Level 1	24 805	82	23 185	76	23 428	76	25 563	76	23 813	76	0.1	-34.9
Level 2—Weapon	529	2	461	2	391	1	320	1	381	1	17.9	-63.2
Level 3—Aggravated	219	1	213	1	182	1	161	1	156	0	-4.0	-64.6
Other sexual offences	3 445	11	3 300	11	3 114	10	2 689	9	2 744	9	1.1	-38.6
Abduction	829	3	729	2	750	2	674	2	609	2	-10.5	-54.9
Robbery—Total	**28 963**	**96**	**28 740**	**94**	**27 037**	**88**	**27 284**	**88**	**26 700**	**85**	**-3.1**	**-27.4**
Firearms	5 324	18	5 122	17	4 323	14	3 818	12	3 472	11	-9.9	-64.1
Other Weapons	10 326	34	10 500	34	9 901	32	10 280	33	10 095	32	-2.7	-15.5
No Weapons	13 313	44	13 118	43	12 813	42	13 186	42	13 133	42	-1.4	-13.2
Violent crime—Total	*296 166*	*979*	*291 327*	*955*	*302 098*	*981*	*305 186*	*981*	*303 294*	*965*	*-1.6*	*-10.9*
Break & enter—Total	**350 774**	**1 160**	**318 054**	**1 042**	**293 357**	**953**	**279 461**	**898**	**274 894**	**875**	**-2.6**	**-41.9**
Business	92 590	306	83 971	275	82 074	267	80 264	258	79 724	254	-1.6	-44.0
Residential	221 366	732	197 022	646	175 804	571	166 500	535	162 851	518	-3.1	-40.1
Other	36 818	122	37 061	121	35 479	115	32 697	105	32 319	103	-2.1	-45.1
Motor vehicle theft	165 920	549	161 388	529	160 315	521	168 595	542	161 506	514	-5.1	-0.6
Theft over $5000[4]	23 600	78	22 493	74	21 354	69	20 845	67	19 885	63	-5.5	-85.0
Theft $5000 and under[4]	713 632	2 359	678 367	2 223	663 040	2 153	669 589	2 120	668 589	2 128	0.4	-26.7
Possession of stolen goods	29 156	96	29 308	96	28 530	93	26 960	87	27 836	89	2.3	-20.3
Fraud	94 819	313	90 371	296	85 791	279	86 486	278	91 235	290	4.5	-34.5
Property crime—Total	*1 377 901*	*4 555*	*1 299 981*	*4 261*	*1 252 387*	*4 067*	*1 241 939*	*3 992*	*1 243 945*	*3 960*	*-0.8*	*-32.9*
Mischief	326 918	1 081	312 266	1 024	326 374	1 060	333 136	1 071	332 723	1 059	-1.1	-33.7
Counterfeiting currency	39 830	132	36 265	119	35 937	117	38 674	124	50 498	161	29.3	500.2
Bail violation	73 034	241	72 192	237	78 105	254	90 545	291	93 873	299	2.7	29.5
Disturbing the peace	65 513	217	69 570	228	80 085	260	89 971	289	92 592	295	1.9	48.5

	1998		1999		2000[2]		2001		2002		%change in rate* 2001–2002	%change in rate* 1992–2002
	Number	Rate	Number	Rate	Number	Rate	Number	Rate	Number	Rate		
Offensive weapons	16 766	55	16 007	52	15 324	50	15 876	51	15 834	50	-1.2	-19.2
Prostitution	5 969	20	5 255	17	5 051	16	5 087	16	5 773	18	12.4	-48.6
Arson	12 947	43	12 756	42	13 733	45	14 484	47	13 192	42	-9.8	-9.4
Other	246 112	814	241 212	791	243 674	791	239 916	771	232 523	740	-4.0	-13.1
Other Criminal Code—Total	787 089	2 602	765 523	2 509	798 283	2 593	827 689	2 660	837 008	2 664	0.1	-12.7
CRIMINAL CODE WITHOUT TRAFFIC—TOTAL	2 461 156	8 136	2 356 831	7 725	2 352 768	7 641	2 374 811	7 633	2 284 247	7 590	-0.6	-24.4
Impaired driving[5,6]	87 660	290	85 997	282	79 225	257	82 718	266	80 789	257	-3.3	-44.9
Fail to stop/remain[7]	39 087	129	17 972	59	19 522	63	22 538	72	21 974	70	-3.4	-70.4
Other Criminal Code Traffic	14 406	48	13 681	45	13 698	44	14 978	48	14 870	47	-1.7	-33.6
Criminal Code Traffic—Total	141 153	467	117 650	386	112 445	365	120 334	386	117 633	374	-3.1	-51.6
CRIMINAL CODE—TOTAL	2 602 309	8 603	2 474 481	8 111	2 465 213	8 006	2 495 045	8 020	2 501 880	7 964	-0.7	-26.3
DRUGS	70 922	234	80 142	263	88 091	286	89 395	287	92 590	295	2.6	42.0
Cannabis	50 917	168	60 011	197	66 274	215	67 921	218	69 989	223	2.0	80.7
Cocaine	12 183	40	11 963	39	12 829	42	12 145	39	12 431	40	1.4	-20.6
Heroin	1 323	4	1 323	4	1 226	4	951	3	787	3	-18.0	-50.9
Other drugs	6 499	21	6 845	22	7 762	25	8 378	27	9 383	30	10.9	2.1
OTHER FEDERAL STATUTES	35 816	118	38 942	128	34 587	112	38 013	122	40 081	128	4.4	-19.0
TOTAL FEDERAL STATUTES	2 709 047	8 956	2 593 565	8 501	2 587 891	8 405	2 622 453	8 429	2 634 551	8 387	-0.5	-25.0

* Percent change based on unrounded rates.
r revised

1 Rates are calculated on the basis of 100 000 population. The population estimates come from the Annual Demographic Statistics, 2002 report, produced by Statistics Canada, Demography Division. Populations as of July 1st: final postcensal estimates 1998 and 1999, updated postcensal estimates for 2000 and 2001, and preliminary postcensal estimates for 2002.

2 Data for 2001 have been revised for Ontario and Canada due to reporting changes for the OPP and most of the 41 police services reporting to the Ontario OMMPAC system.

For further information on the impact of this change, refer to the text box entitled 'Reporting Changes to Ontario Data.'

3 Homicide investigations undertaken by the Missing Women's Task Force in Port Coquitlam, B.C resulted in 15 homicides being reported by police in 2002. Homicide counts reflect the year in which police file the report.

4 Prior to 1995, theft offences were categorized as Theft $1 000 and Under and Theft Over $1 000. In 1995 the dollar value was increased.

5 Include impaired operation of a vehicle causing death, causing bodily harm, alcohol rate over 80mg, failure/refusal to provide a breath/blood sample.

6 Revisions have been made to the number of "actual" impaired driving incidents for the RCMP in 2000 and 2001 and estimates have been provided for these two years. These revisions resulted in a 6% reduction in actual incidents at the Canada level for 2000 and 9% for 2001. These changes did not affect the national impaired driving trend. The number of persons "charged" with impaired driving offences did not require revision.

7 Beginning in 1999, "fail to stop or remain" incidents for Toronto are now included under "provincial statutes" instead of Criminal Code.

Source: Statistics Canada. Adapted from the Statistics Canada publication, *Crime Statistics in Canada, 2002*, Catalogue No. 85-002, Vol. 23, No. 5, Reproduced with permission of the Minister of Industry, 2003.

sample

A group of elements (people, offenders, inmates) selected in a systematic manner from the population of interest.

For the 1999 survey, interviews were conducted by telephone with a random **sample** of approximately 26 000 people, aged 15 and older, living in the ten provinces. Those interviewed were asked for their opinions concerning the level of crime in their neighbourhood, their fear of crime, and their views concerning the performance of the justice system. They were also asked about their experiences with criminal victimization. Respondents who had been victims of a crime in the previous 12 months were asked for detailed information on each incident, including when and where it occurred; whether the incident was reported to the police; and how they were affected by the experience.

Not all crimes can be captured through this survey method. One need not be a methodologist to recognize that murder cannot be included in such a survey. Nor can consensual crimes for which there are no direct victims—drug use, gambling, and the like. These consensual crimes are not captured very well through official data nor through victimization surveys. Similarly, those crimes designed to keep victims unaware that they have been victimized cannot be captured accurately in victimization surveys (or official data sources). Fraud, embezzlement, employee pilferage, price fixing, and the wide range of consumer, corporate, and white-collar crimes were not included in the survey. The eight categories of crime included were sexual assault, robbery, assault, break and enter, motor vehicle theft, theft of household property, theft of personal property, and vandalism. A full account of the methodology of the 1982 survey can be found in Catlin and Murray (1979), Solicitor General Canada (1983; 1984a; 1984b; 1985a; 1985b; 1985c; 1986), Evans and Leger (1978), and Skogan (1981).The major findings of the 1999 survey are set out below.

Highlights

- Canada's victimization rate was virtually unchanged in 1999. According to the 1999 General Social Survey (GSS) conducted by Statistics Canada, 25 percent of Canadians aged 15 and older were victims of at least one crime in the previous year, compared to a figure of 23 percent in 1993, when the victimization survey was last conducted. Of the eight crimes measured by the GSS, the rates for sexual assault, robbery, assault, break and enter, motor vehicle/parts theft, and vandalism did not change significantly between 1993 and 1999. However, increased rates were observed for theft of personal property and theft of household property.

- Reporting to the police declined in 1999. For the eight GSS crime types, fewer than four in ten incidents (37 percent) were reported to the police. This was down from 42 percent in 1993. The main reason that victims cited in 1999 for not reporting their incident was because it was "not important enough" (36 percent of unreported incidents). This same reason was given for 25 percent of unreported incidents in 1993.

- In all, 8.3 million victimization incidents were reported to the GSS in 1999. About one-half of these incidents involved a personal crime (sexual assault, robbery, assault, or theft of personal property), while about one-third involved a household crime (break and enter, motor vehicle/parts theft, theft of household property, or vandalism). The remaining 15 percent of incidents could not be classified into one of these eight crime types.

■ Overall, for the four personal crimes that were examined, the rates for men and women were very similar. Higher rates of victimization were reported by young people (15 to 24 years), urban dwellers, and those with household incomes under $15 000.

■ For the four household crimes, the rate of victimization was once again higher for urban residents. However, households with higher incomes ($60 000+) had a higher rate than households with lower incomes. As well, the rate of household crime was highest for people living in a semi-detached, row house, or duplex compared with an apartment or single home. Rates were higher for those who rented rather than owned their home.

■ Victimization rates tended to be higher in western Canada. Among the ten provinces, British Columbia had the highest rates of both personal and household victimization in 1999, due partly to higher rates for theft of personal and household property. Newfoundland, New Brunswick, and Nova Scotia had the lowest rates of personal victimization, while Prince Edward Island, Newfoundland, and New Brunswick had the lowest household victimization rates.

■ The majority of Canadians believe that crime levels are stable. In 1999, 54 percent of the population believed that crime in their neighbourhood had stayed the same in the last five years. This was up considerably from the figure of 43 percent recorded by the 1993 GSS.

■ The GSS results indicate that a large proportion of the population is satisfied with their personal safety and that this percentage is growing. In particular, 91 percent of Canadians reported being very or somewhat satisfied with their personal safety in 1999, an improvement from 86 percent in 1993. Additionally, people felt safer in a variety of situations, such as when home alone, walking alone, or using public transportation alone after dark.

■ Canadians are quite satisfied with the job being done by their local police. They are far less satisfied with the performance of the criminal courts, the prison and the parole systems. (Statistics Canada, 2000; reprinted with permission of the Minister of Industry, 2003)

Note that of the incidents identified, fewer than four of ten (37 percent) had been reported to the police or had otherwise come to police attention. Recognizing that the victimization survey cannot capture all of that "dark" figure missed by the UCR, the survey data do reveal that many more Canadians are victimized by crime than is revealed by official statistics.

As most would guess, a large proportion of the unreported crime is relatively trivial, the kinds of incidents that most of us would not expect the police to devote time or resources to. For example, a few dollars stolen by somebody within the household, a toy stolen from the porch, or an umbrella stolen from a restaurant are the kinds of common incidents that are rarely reported.

Nonetheless, as Figure 4.6 shows, more serious incidents may often go unreported. For example, in the 1982 Victimization Survey (with a sample size of 65 000) about two-thirds of the women who had been sexually assaulted did not report the incident to the police. In explaining their decision, many of the women indicated concern about the attitudes of those within the criminal justice system as being an inhibiting factor. Women assaulted by people they knew indicated that fear of revenge was one of the reasons they failed to report. Figure 4.7 presents the major reasons for failing to report to the police in the 1999 survey.

Where incidents produced great financial loss to the victim, reporting was far more likely, even more likely than for those incidents that resulted in pain or injury but no loss. As concluded by the Solicitor General Canada (1984b) study: "For many, it would seem, reporting crimes is less an act of justice (or even revenge) than a far more utilitarian act—seeking redress, recompense or recovery." Figure 4.8 displays the data on reasons for reporting from the 1999 survey. The survey data confirm many of the concerns about official sources of crime data. Some crimes are more likely to come to police attention than others. Some categories of victims are more likely to report their victimizations, and

FIGURE 4.6 Incidents Reported to Police, 1988, 1993, and 1999

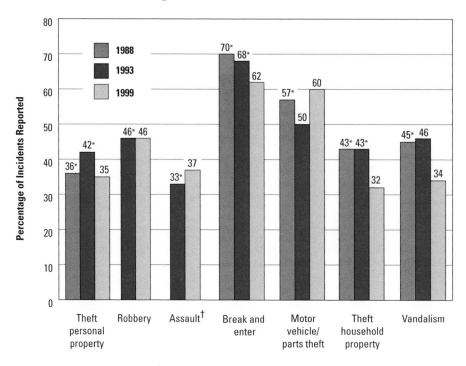

* The difference between this figure and the one for 1999 is not statistically significant.
† Excludes incidents of spousal sexual and physical assault. The 1993 data use the revised definition of assault. Figures for sexual assault are too small to be expressed. There are no comparable 1988 data for violent crimes.

Source: Statistics Canada. Adapted from the Statistics Canada publication, *Criminal Victimization in Canada*, Catalogue 85-002, Vol. 20, no. 10, p. 12. Reprinted with permission of the Minister of Industry, 2003.

FIGURE 4.7   Reasons Given for Failure to Report to Police

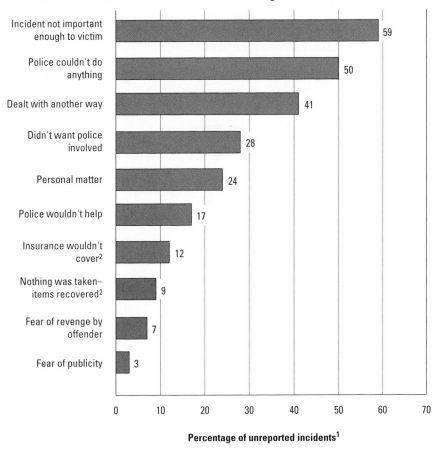

1   Total exceeds 100% due to multiple responses. Excludes incidents that were not
    classified by crime type and incidents of spousal sexual and physical assault.
2   Excludes incidents involving sexual assault or a physical attack.

Source: Statistics Canada. Adapted from the Statistics Canada publication, *Criminal Victimization in Canada*. Catalogue No. 85-002 Vol. 20, no. 10, p. 12. Reprinted with permission of the Minister of Industry, 2003.

some categories of offenders (for example, family members) are less likely to be reported. In general, it is only through such knowledge that we can begin to understand the UCR data and the dark figure of crime. Because victimization surveys are based on victims' perceptions and experiences, and because they collect information about the victims of crime, they are useful in identifying those categories of people most at risk of criminal victimization. For example, the Highlights (above) of the 1999 survey show that, contrary to the conventional wisdom, the risk of victimization is lowest for older Canadians, especially those 65 years of age or older. In fact, the victimization data provide a profile of the victim of crime that explodes many popular myths. The typical victim of crime is young, single, male, not employed full-time, and living an active social life. In particular, the number of evenings spent outside the home is one of the best predictors of whether one will have been victimized or not. Some of the reasons for

FIGURE 4.8   Reasons Given for Reporting to Police

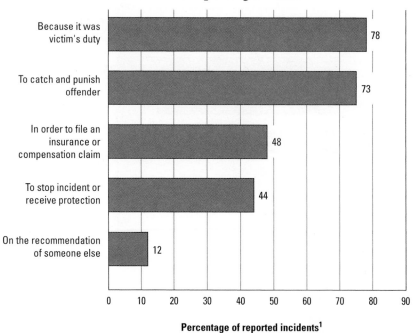

Percentage of reported incidents[1]

*1 Total exceeds 100% due to multiple responses. Excludes incidents that were not
classified by crime type and incidents of spousal sexual and physical assault.*

Source: Statistics Canada. Adapted from the Statistics Canada publication, *Criminal
Victimization in Canada*. Catalogue No. 85-002 Vol. 20, no. 10, p. 12. Reprinted with
permission of the Minister of Industry, 2003.

these patterns of victimization are discussed in Chapter 14. Perhaps most important, victimization surveys allow us to go beyond merely counting incidents. They
provide data on the costs of victimization, the financial losses, the physical injuries,
and the concern and fear victimization may produce. In addition, these data allow
the exploration of various dimensions of seriousness. Clearly, victimization hits
some harder than others. When victimized, women and elderly people suffer most,
and their fear is greatest. There is little wonder that women and the elderly fear
crime in a way that might be described as disproportionate to their risk of victimization. Even those women and elderly people who had not been victimized were
likely to express fear of crime—an expression of their vulnerability and perhaps a
realistic understanding of the consequences of crimes for them when they do
occur. Victimization surveys try to gauge the kinds of activities people engage in to
avoid victimization. As Figure 4.9 shows, about 3 in 10 people changed activities
or avoided certain places, and about one-fifth installed security hardware. This and
similar studies have shown that fear does not lead to constructive action, and it
may in itself be a problem to be addressed by the criminal justice system. An accurate portrayal of crime in Canada through better methods of counting crime and
better crime statistics can help to minimize fears based on myth and media.

Victimization surveys cannot measure all crimes. They are dependent on the
vagaries of human memory and are subject to the kinds of criticisms levelled

FIGURE 4.9   Crime Prevention Measures

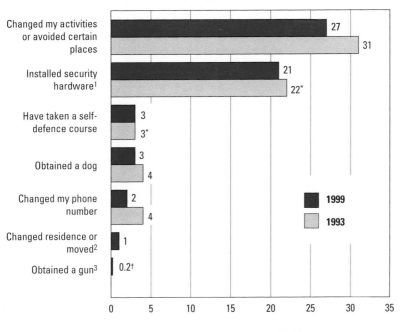

Percentage of population 15+

† *Coefficient of variation between 16.6% and 33.3%.*
* *The difference between this figure and the one for 1999 is not statistically significant.*
1 *Includes new locks and burglar alarms.*
2 *Not asked in 1993.*
3 *Figure for 1993 is too small to be expressed.*

Source: Statistics Canada. Adapted from the Statistics Canada publication, *Criminal Victimization in Canada*. Catalogue No. 85-002 Vol. 20, no. 10, p. 12. Reprinted with permission of the Minister of Industry, 2003.

against any survey, including the fact that some people may not tell interviewers the truth. Victimization surveys are dependent on respondents' ability not only to recall incidents and their details, but also to place the incidents correctly in time. We know that respondents are fallible. And, as Skogan (1978) suggests, well-educated, articulate respondents are more likely than others to talk to interviewers and to give rich and full accounts of their victimization experiences, thus perhaps biasing the data. There is reason as well to be cautious about interpreting data on domestic and sexual assaults that have been collected through surveys. Respondents may well be reluctant to discuss such experiences with an interviewer. Also, the methodology is still relatively young. Special methods will be needed to get data about rural victimization and victimization of Aboriginal Canadians. Special methodologies are also required to measure white-collar crime, consensual crime, and what has come to be called enterprise crime—organized crime and the crimes of organizations and the state. More information is required on the psychological and emotional impact of victimization.

Despite the limitations, these data provide us with the opportunity to go beyond counting incidents and to gain some understanding of what it is we are

BOX 4.2

FOCUS

"If It Bleeds, It Leads": The Media and Public Perceptions of Crime

Most Canadians learn about crime through the media rather than from first-hand experience. As a result, the stories portrayed on television and radio, and in newspapers, magazines, and books, shape our views about crime and criminals. But the media do not always simply "report" the news. In fact, editors and reporters select the crime news that they wish to run and construct the ways in which that news is presented to us. Unfortunately, the picture of crime we receive from the media is not always accurate. For example, while most actual crime consists of property crime, most of the stories about crime in the media deal with violent crime. Thomas Gabor reviewed all the crime-related stories reported over two months in an Ottawa newspaper (Gabor, 1994). Over half the stories focused on violent crimes, particularly murders; however, violent crimes made up only 7 percent of reported crimes in Ottawa, and the city averaged just six murders per year. While violent crimes were over-reported, property crimes received little attention, and white-collar and political crimes were almost never discussed.

Why do the media misrepresent crime? The truth is that stories that attract viewers or readers boost ratings and circulation. The informal media rule "if it bleeds, it leads" reflects the fact that the public is fascinated by sensationalized, bloody stories. Commenting on his experience with the media, the executive director of the Nova Scotia Bar Society said, "If there's no blood and gore, or there's no sex, it's not newsworthy. And if it falls into the category of being newsworthy, then they have to show the dead body. They've got to show the corpse" (McCormick, 1995, 182).

The media's misrepresentation of crime has several consequences. First, Canadians greatly over-estimate the prevalence of violent crime and have a fear of crime that is disproportionate to the real risk of victimization. One survey found that the vast majority of Canadians (75 percent) felt that more than half of all crimes are accompanied by violence. The true figure is less than 10 percent (Doob and Roberts, 1983). Crime stories lead us to see Canada as a violent and dangerous place.

The media also provide us with a distorted stereotype of offenders. Violent crimes are most often committed by relatives, friends, and acquaintances, and not by the anonymous stranger that so many of us fear. The trouble is that our fear of crime and our image of the criminal have an impact on government policy toward crime. Actual crime trends are irrelevant—if the public feels crime is out of control, it will demand that government do something about it. While crime rates are in reality on the decline, a combination of increasing media coverage of crime and pressure from a variety of interest groups has led the federal government to tighten several laws, including those concerning immigration, young offenders, and firearms.

self-report study

A method for measuring crime involving the distribution of a detailed questionnaire to a sample of people, asking them whether they have committed a crime in a particular period of time. This has been a good method for criminologists to determine the social characteristics of offenders.

counting. The data are an important, perhaps essential, complement to other sources of crime statistics.

SELF-REPORT STUDIES

Yet another approach to generating data on the nature and distribution of crime is the **self-report study**. The people who know the most about crime are those who break the law. Rather than relying on police data that will inevitably be incomplete or on the knowledge of victims, why not just ask criminals what they do and how often they do it? Many sociologists have done this, most commonly through questionnaires given to students in junior and senior high schools. A study done by Travis Hirschi (1969) in the San Francisco area is typical of self-report studies (you will read about some of the results of this study in Chapter 13, "Social Control Theory"). Hirschi took a random sample of all the junior and senior high school students in Richmond, California, and administered questionnaires to 5545 students. The survey was a very lengthy one, and we will consider here only the questions measuring delinquent behaviour. The students were asked six questions about their illegal conduct and for each were asked to check off one of the following responses: A. No, never; B. More than a year ago; C. During the last year; and D. During the last year *and* more than a year ago. The delinquency questions were the following:

- Have you ever taken little things (worth less than $2) that did not belong to you?
- Have you ever taken things of some value (between $2 and $50) that did not belong to you?
- Have you ever taken things of large value (worth over $50) that did not belong to you?
- Have you ever taken a car for a ride without the owner's permission?
- Have you ever banged up something that did not belong to you on purpose?
- Not counting fights that you may have had with a brother or sister, have you ever beaten up on anyone or hurt someone on purpose?

Hirschi looked at responses to these delinquency questions and compared them with other measures, including such things as students' reports of their friends' behaviour, and their family and school relationships, in order to try to shed some light on what caused some students to become delinquent while others did not. Like victimization surveys, self-report studies were used to try to overcome some of the weaknesses of police data. In most cases the results have supported the view that there are systematic biases.

Because self-report studies supposedly avoid these biases, they have been particularly important in research and theory on the causes of crime and delinquency, especially the relationship between social class and crime. For a long time, these studies were not very carefully scrutinized. They were perceived as such a significant breakthrough that few questions were asked. A major work to determine the reliability of self-report studies was carried out by Hindelang, Hirschi, and Weis (1981). They concluded that the self-report method does demonstrate that people are willing to report crimes, both those known and not known to officials, and that respondents' reports are internally consistent. A difficulty arises in that it appears that different populations answer self-report questions in different ways. Lower-class males and black males, in the United States study, are more likely to underreport their own criminal behaviour than are middle-class white males. Similarly, in Canada, Fréchette and LeBlanc (1979; 1980) confirm that while self-report studies do uncover much hidden delinquency and raise questions about the biases in official statistics that show the preponderance of lower-class crime, previous self-report studies have also masked the fact that lower-class crime is typically more serious and persistent.

There are two related problems here. First, it would appear that those who are typically law abiding are more likely to report completely their occasional infractions than are the more committed delinquents to report their more serious and frequent infractions. Second, differences between official statistics of delinquent behaviour and self-report data may reflect not simply biases in official data, but biases in the self-report method as well. The official data are likely to include more serious offences, and self-report data are more likely to include more minor infractions, as you can see from the items used in Hirschi's studies.

A number of other more technical problems regarding, for example, sampling—the difficulty in getting "hard-core criminals" in a sample, disagreements about which offences to select and which produce the most reliable and valid data, and which scoring procedures best suit the uses of the data—are given full discussion in Hindelang, Hirschi, and Weis (1981), and in Thornberry and Krohn (2000). Although self-report studies are never likely to be an instrument for counting crimes, recent methodological refinements have enhanced their potential for addressing fundamental questions about crime and the correlates of crime.

Self-report data can be used for other purposes as well. By using formal self-report surveys such as Hirschi's or by interviewing criminals in prison or in other, less restrictive situations we can learn a great deal about their motivations for committing crimes and the techniques they use to commit crimes. This information is invaluable for understanding the causes of crime and for helping to prevent it. Since this chapter is about counting crime, these issues will not be considered here, but in later chapters of the book you will read about many of the lessons that criminologists have learned from talking to criminals.

THE FUTURE OF CRIME AND CRIMINAL JUSTICE STATISTICS

The importance of good statistics for planning, policy-making, and administration has long been recognized within the criminal justice system. Out of this recognition and concern emerged, in 1981, the Canadian Centre for Justice Statistics, with a mandate to collect national statistics. The existence of the Canadian Centre is a recognition—in a country with shared jurisdiction for criminal justice—of the importance of developing national commitment and national strategies for producing and sharing criminal statistics.

The new information technology holds great promise for improving the official records that form the basis of most criminal justice statistics on prisons, courts, and police. Canada is virtually alone among Western nations in its lack of national court data on convictions and sentences, so crucial for understanding how our criminal justice system is working. However, as noted above, progress is being made and the adult court survey now covers approximately 80 percent of criminal cases. Perhaps the new commitment and the new technology will allow us to fill these gaps. It is only through a nationally coordinated effort that we can avoid the danger of developing incompatible systems in each province (or worse, municipality) that feed many different criminal justice systems and inhibit the continued development of a coordinated national system of justice.

The methods for counting crimes are still in their formative stages. Some, like the UCR, will be derived from official records (designed in accordance with UCR rules) and will, therefore, suffer the limitations of all such official statistics. Nevertheless, recent advances in police management information systems and crime classification systems hold great promise for providing us with a measure of calls for police service, police caseloads, and police activity. Other methods, like victimization surveys, will draw on people's experiences and will, therefore, suffer the limitations of all such surveys. Significant progress has been achieved in Canada in the development and refinement of victimization surveys and self-report studies.

How much crime is there in Canada, and what are the trends? Is it bad and getting worse? Do we have cause for alarm? Are things good and getting better? Do we have cause for complacency? Depending on your bias and prejudices, the state of the art allows you to find some evidence and numbers to justify either extreme. But, with the improvements in our knowledge about crime and the development of new methods, we are coming to recognize the complexity of the questions. When taken together, the UCR and the victimization surveys encourage neither alarm nor complacency. Overall, there is certainly less serious crime than most Canadians assume based on media accounts and the high visibility of sensational incidents. At the same time, we are starting to uncover some particular kinds of serious incidents which have, for too long, remained hidden. Sexual assault and family violence are two important examples. Much more work is needed. Only through an integrated program of criminal justice statistics, recognizing the limits of any one source of information, will we be able to build powerful theories of crime and sound policies and programs for crime prevention and control.

SUMMARY

- Statistics can help us to better understand the nature and extent of crime in Canada. However, in order to interpret these crime statistics properly, we must understand their strengths and weaknesses.

- The quality of official statistics varies depending on their sources. Corrections data are the most reliable and valid because the task of counting prisoners can be done accurately. On the other hand, crimes known to the police, the most commonly used statistics, will always be biased by inconsistencies in reporting and recording.

- Administrative records can be the basis of statistics if clear procedures are developed about units of count, levels of data aggregation, definitions, data elements, and counting procedures.

- The Canadian Uniform Crime Report (UCR) system is designed to provide uniform and compatible national statistics. There is much debate about just what is counted. Some hold that the UCR provides a reasonable estimate of crime rates. Others hold that what is being measured is criminal justice processing.

- The crime rates provided by the UCR, based on crimes reported to the police, have declined since the peak year of 1991. Both violent and property crimes have declined. The overall decline from 1991 to 2002 is about 26 percent.

- Victimization surveys provide an alternative and complementary method of measuring crime. These surveys ask random samples of the population about their victimization experiences. They also provide data on such important issues as reasons for not reporting crimes to the police.

- Self-report studies are not serious rivals of either the UCR or victimization surveys as a method of measuring crime. However, they do have a useful place in answering specific questions related to understanding the causes and correlates of crime.

- Developing Canada's national statistics will take continued effort and commitment from all the actors in the system. A good start has been made, but Canada still lacks crucial data. For example, national sentencing data are limited.

QUESTIONS FOR CRITICAL THINKING

1. Crime rates in Canada declined between 1992 and 2002. How would you account for this decline? You might wish to read ahead in Chapter 5 to help you find some possible answers to this question.
2. The media do not provide an accurate portrayal of the nature and extent of crime in Canada. Can you find examples in your own community of media distortions of crime? Why do the media behave in this way? What are the consequences of these distortions?
3. Victimization surveys reveal that many crimes, including serious violent crimes, are not reported to the police. Why not? What is the significance of this for society?
4. To what extent do official statistics measure the amount of crime in society? What are the major biases in official statistics?
5. How are self-report studies used in criminology? Can you find examples of the use of self-report data in later chapters of this book?

NET WORK

Canadian crime statistics are compiled by the Canadian Centre for Justice Statistics, which reports the annual number of crimes reported to the police. Go to the Statistics Canada website at **www.statcan.ca/english/Pgdb/justic.htm.**

Using the information on "Crimes, by type of offence," identify the trends in the crimes reported in Figures 4.4, 4.5A, and 4.5B of this text. Look at the information on "Homicide offences, number and rate." Have homicide rates gone up or down in the past five years? Which provinces and territories have the highest rate of homicide? Do the actual crime figures reported by Statistics Canada correspond with your perception of crime rates reported by the mass media?

KEY TERMS

administrative record

Canadian Centre for Justice Statistics

counting procedure

crime rate

dark figure of crime

data element

gross counts of crime

ideology

levels of aggregation

methodology

population

reliability

sample

self-report study

seriousness rule

theory

Uniform Crime Reports (UCR)

validity

victimization survey

SUGGESTED READING

Alvazzi del Frate, Anna, Ugljesa Zvekic, and Jan J.M. van Dijk (eds.). (1993). *Understanding Crime: Experiences of Crime and Crime Control.* Rome: United Nations Interregional Crime and Justice Research Institute. This is a good source for international insights and comparisons.

Fréchette, M., and Marc LeBlanc. (1980). "Pour une pratique de la criminologie: configurations de conduites délinquantes et portraits de délinquants." *Inadaptation juvénile* Cahier 5. Montréal: Université de Montréal. Fréchette and LeBlanc's monograph provides not only rich data and insights on delinquency but also a good illustration of the use of self-report studies.

Miller, Jerome G. (1996). *Search and Destroy: African-American Males in the Criminal Justice System.* Cambridge, UK: Cambridge University Press. This book examines the vast over-representation of African Americans in the United States justice system. It is an object lesson for those who think that accurate counts are not important.

Skogan, W. (1981). "Issues in the Measurement of Victimization." Washington, DC: U.S. Department of Justice, Bureau of Justice Statistics. Skogan's monograph on victimization surveys, one of many he has written in this area, is the most readable and exhaustive account of the potential and limits of this approach to counting crime. His discussion is based largely on the American experience.

Solicitor General Canada. (1983). "Victims of Crime." Canadian Urban Victimization Survey. Ottawa: Solicitor General Canada. This, the first in a series of bulletins, provides a brief overview of the major findings and methodology of the first large-scale Canadian victimization survey, conducted in 1982.

Statistics Canada. (1997). "An Overview of the Differences between Police-Reported and Victim-Reported Crime." Ottawa. This report reduces the level of confusion arising from the use of crime data originating from two very different sources—the Uniform Crime Report (UCR) system and the General Social Survey (GSS)—and informs discussions about which is the better measure of crime. It explains why the findings based on these data sources diverge and summarizes the major differences between the two sources.

Statistics Canada. (1998). "Family Violence in Canada: A Statistical Profile." Ottawa. This series provides the most up-to-date data on the nature and extent of family violence in Canada and monitors trends over time. Each year, the report has a special focus or theme.

Statistics Canada. (2002). "National Trends in Intimate Partner Homicides, 1974–2000." *Juristat* 22(5). Catalogue no. 85-002-XIE. This *Juristat* documents trends in spousal homicides as well as subgroup variations (e.g., common-law, separated and divorced partners, age group variations), and it identifies factors that may be associated with the decline in spousal homicide over the past 25 years.

Statistics Canada. (2002). "Criminal Victimization: An International Perspective—Results of the 2000 International Crime Victimization Survey." *Juristat* 22(4). Catalogue no. 85-002-XPE. This *Juristat* presents results from the 2000 victimization survey of 17 industrialized countries.

Statistics Canada. *Juristat.* Ottawa. The Canadian Centre for Justice Statistics at Statistics Canada produces Canadian Crime Statistics. The *Juristat* series of reports provides detailed statistics and analysis on a variety of topics and issues concerning Canada's justice system. Annual *Juristats* are produced in the following areas: crime statistics, homicide, impaired driving, justice system resources and expenditures, youth court statistics, youth custody and probation, and corrections statistics. Additional *Juristats* are also produced each year on current topics of interest to the justice community. This is a unique periodical, of great interest to those who have to plan, establish, administer, and evaluate justice programs and projects, or anyone who has an interest in Canada's justice system. These publications are available from Statistics Canada in print.

BIBLIOGRAPHY

Besserer, S., and C. Trainor. (1999). "Criminal Victimization in Canada, 1999." Statistics Canada. Catalogue No. 85-002-XIE Vol. 20, no. 10.

Catlin, G., and S. Murray. (1979). "Report on Canadian Victimization Survey Methodological Pretests." Ottawa: Statistics Canada.

de Silva, S., and R.A. Silverman. (1985). "New Approaches to Uniform Crime Reporting in Canada." Paper presented at the annual meeting of the American Society of Criminology, San Diego (November).

Doob, A., and J.V. Roberts. (1983). *An Analysis of the Public's View of Sentence.* Ottawa: Department of Justice Canada.

Evans, J., and G. Leger. (1978). "The Development of Victimization Surveys in Canada." *Public Data Use* 6 (November).

Fréchette, M., and Marc LeBlanc. (1979). "La délinquance cachée à l'adolescence." *Inadaptation juvénile* Cahier 1. Montreal: Université de Montréal.

———. (1980). "Pour une pratique de la criminologie: configurations de conduites délinquantes et portraits de délinquants." *Inadaptation juvénile* Cahier 5. Montreal: Université de Montréal.

Gabor, T. (1994). *Everybody Does It: Crime by the Public.* Toronto: University of Toronto Press.

Hindelang, M.J., T. Hirschi, and J.G. Weis. (1981). *Measuring Delinquency.* Beverly Hills: Sage.

Hirschi, Travis. (1969). *Causes of Delinquency.* Berkeley: University of California Press.

McCormick, C. (1995). *Constructing Danger: The Misrepresentation of Crime in the News.* Halifax: Fernwood Publishing.

Nettler, G. (1974). *Explaining Crime.* New York: McGraw-Hill.

Polsky, Ned. (1967). *Hustlers, Beats, and Others.* Chicago: Aldine.

Shearing, Clifford D. (1984). "Dial-A-Cop: A Study of Police Mobilization." Report for the Centre of Criminology, University of Toronto.

Silverman, R.A. (1980). "Measuring Crime: More Problems." *Journal of Police Science and Administration* 8(3):265–74.

Silverman, R.A., and J. Teevan. (1975). *Crime in Canadian Society.* Toronto: Butterworths.

Skogan, W. (1978). "Review of Surveying Crime." *Journal of Criminal Law and Criminology* 69: 139–40.

———. (1981). "Issues in the Measurement of Victimization." Washington, D.C.: U.S. Department of Justice, Bureau of Justice Statistics.

Solicitor General Canada. (1983). "Victims of Crime." Canadian Urban Victimization Survey. Ottawa: Solicitor General Canada.

———. (1984a). "Reported and Unreported Crimes." Canadian Urban Victimization Survey. Ottawa: Solicitor General Canada.

———. (1984b). "Crime Prevention: Awareness and Practice." Canadian Urban Victimization Survey. Ottawa: Solicitor General Canada.

———. (1985a). "Female Victims of Crime." Canadian Urban Victimization Survey. Ottawa: Solicitor General Canada.

———. (1985b). "Cost of Crime to Victims." Canadian Urban Victimization Survey. Ottawa: Solicitor General Canada.

———. (1985c). "Criminal Victimizations of Elderly Canadians." Canadian Urban Victimization Survey. Ottawa: Solicitor General Canada.

———. (1986). "Household Property Crimes." Canadian Urban Victimization Survey. Ottawa: Solicitor General Canada.

Statistics Canada. (1999). "Illicit Drugs and Crime in Canada." *Juristat* 19(1). Catalogue No. 85-002-XPE.

———. (2000). "Criminal Victimization in Canada, 1999." *Juristat* 20(10). Catalogue No. 85-002-XIE.

———. (2001). "Canadian Crime Statistics, 2000." Catalogue No. 85-002-XIE.

———. (2002a). "Adult Correctional Services in Canada, 2000/01." *Juristat* 22(10). Catalogue No. 85-002-XIE.

———. (2002b). "Canadian Crime Statistics, 2001." *Juristat* 22(6). Catalogue No. 85-002.

Thornberry, Terence P., and Marvin D. Krohn (2000). "The Self-Report Method for Measuring Delinquency and Crime." *Criminal Justice 2000,* Vol. 4. National Institute of Justice, Washington, D.C.

van Dijk, Jan J.M. (1999). "The Experience of Crime and Justice." In Graeme Newman (ed.), *Global Report on Crime and Justice.* United National Office for Drug Control and Crime Prevention, Centre for International Crime Prevention. New York: Oxford University Press.

Waller, I., and N. Okihiro. (1978). *Burglary: The Victim and the Public.* Toronto: University of Toronto Press.

Correlates of Criminal Behaviour

TIMOTHY F. HARTNAGEL
University of Alberta

Which Canadians are most likely to commit crimes? Are older people more likely to commit crimes than younger people? Are men more likely to commit crimes than women? Are upper-class people more or less likely to break the law than their lower-class counterparts? Which provinces have the highest rate of crime? Each of these questions asks about a correlate of crime. A correlate is a phenomenon that accompanies another phenomenon and is related in some way to it. **Correlates** of crime are those phenomena that are associated with criminal activity. While a list of such phenomena would include any number of conditions, the discussion in this chapter will be limited to some of the social conditions that are correlated with crime. We will describe and discuss the relationship between criminal behaviour and age, sex, race, social class, and region.

correlate

Any variable that is related to another variable. Age and sex are the two strongest correlates of crime.

LEARNING OBJECTIVES

After reading this chapter, you should be able to

- Distinguish between correlates and causes of criminal behaviour.
- Identify and describe the major social correlates of criminal behaviour in Canada.
- Describe and explain trends in the age and sex distribution of criminal behaviour.
- Describe and explain the over-representation of Aboriginal people in the Canadian criminal justice system.
- Discuss and reconcile the apparently conflicting evidence regarding the correlation between social class and criminal behaviour.
- Describe how crime rates vary by geographic region.

CORRELATES DEFINED

Before turning to the details of these specific correlates, the concept of correlation itself should be considered briefly. **Correlation** refers to a relationship between at least two phenomena that are related, or occur, or vary together. For example, some criminologists have claimed that delinquent behaviour is

correlation

A relationship that exists when two or more variables are associated.

correlated with physique or body type. They claim that adolescent males with an athletic, muscular body build commit more delinquent acts than those whose physique is lean and fragile. Other criminologists have shown that some types of crime occur more frequently in larger cities than in smaller towns and rural areas. They argue that city size and crime vary together. These examples give measurements on two variables (for example, city size and crime) for a number of individuals or aggregates (for example, cities). The task is to determine whether and how these two sets of measurements go together—that is, whether and how they're correlated. When we analyze the relationship between two variables, we may find that they are positively correlated, negatively correlated, or unrelated to each other. A positive relationship means that as one variable increases, the other also increases. For example, the more deviant friends we have, the more likely we are to be deviant ourselves. A negative relationship means that as one variable increases, the other decreases. For example, as we get older, we are less likely to be involved in criminal behaviour. Discovering such correlations or relationships is an important first step for any scientific discipline such as criminology. Thus, a good deal of the early work in criminology was devoted to the task of identifying and describing the correlates of crime.

Having identified and described a correlate of crime—a relationship—it is natural to want to know why it exists. How might this relationship be explained? What might have produced it?

One explanation for a correlation or relationship between two variables is causal. The concept of causation has been debated by philosophers and social scientists. At the very least, the idea of causation has proven to be a useful way of thinking about the natural and social world. A causal explanation refers to the inference that a change in one variable results from or is produced by change in another variable. A common mistake is to confuse correlation with causation and so to infer that one variable causes another from the fact that they are correlated. However, correlation means only that two variables are related. They are associated or go together, but change in one does not necessarily produce a change in the other. Criminologists are frequently interested in establishing causal explanations. They are not usually satisfied, for example, with knowing that poverty and crime are correlated; they want to know if crime results from poverty, and if it does, how? However, it would be a mistake to conclude from their correlation alone that poverty causes crime. So correlation between two variables is a necessary first step toward causal explanation but is not in itself sufficient for inferring such an explanation.

The second element of a causal explanation is a *theory* linking the variables. Events may occur together, but one will not be viewed as causing the other unless we have some explanation of how they are linked. We look for correlates of crime to help us to explain criminal behaviour, and our explanatory theories must be tested against what we know about crime. For example, we may have a theory that the movement of the planets causes criminality. However, when we test this explanation, we find that there is no correlation between planetary movements and crime rates. Thus, we will reject the theory, at least until some evidence supporting it can be found. Much of the attention of criminologists has been devoted to developing and testing theories of crime, and these theories must explain the facts about crime. Therefore, the correlates discussed in this chapter set the stage for the theories that follow.

Human beings have a tendency to simplify their perceptions of the world. This tendency can lead to a distortion of the understanding of correlates and causes. There is a temptation to assume that an effect can have only one cause that is both necessary and sufficient. There is also the temptation to assume that causes must be perfectly correlated with their effects and that no other variables are necessary for interpreting how the cause operates or for specifying the particular conditions or circumstances under which it has its effect(s) (Hirschi and Selvin, 1966). But reality is substantially more complicated than this, and it would be wise to develop the habit of thinking of crime as the consequence of multiple causes that combine in complicated ways to produce their effects. Nettler (1982) uses the image of a dense web to communicate the meaning of this view of causation. He describes this as a multiplicity of tightly packed causes that interact strongly and nonuniformly. As selected correlates of crime are examined, then, the urge to reach hasty conclusions concerning the causal character and significance of these correlations should be resisted.

AGE

Peak Ages for Crime

"Youth Crime in Canada: Public Perception vs. Statistical Information"
John Howard Society of Alberta
To find this and other interesting research papers, go to
www.acjnet.org

Without much exaggeration, crime can be said to be a young man's game. To put this into more technical terms, age and sex are strong correlates of criminal behaviour. Any number of criminologists have singled out these two variables for their strong relationship with crime. For example, Sutherland and Cressey (1978) state that sex status is of greater importance in differentiating criminals from noncriminals than any other trait, and that statistics from a variety of years and jurisdictions uniformly indicate a higher prevalence of crime among young persons compared with other age groups.

Figures 5.1A and 5.1B show the distribution of persons accused of property and violent crimes by age for 1997. While the percentage of persons accused of crime increases from early adolescence to young adulthood and then generally declines, this pattern is much stronger for property crimes. While persons accused of property crimes are particularly likely to be young, the age range of persons accused of violent crimes is much wider (Kong, 1998). Thus, more than 40 percent of persons accused of property crimes were between 13 and 20 years old, while this age group accounted for less than 25 percent of persons accused of violent crimes. While youths aged 12 to 17 account for a disproportionate share of accused persons compared to their proportion in the total population (8.1 percent), this over-representation is greatest for property crimes.

In 2001, the peak age of offending among all offenders for both violent and property crimes was 16. Those aged 15 to 24 represented 14 percent of the total

FIGURE 5.1A   Persons Accused of Property Crimes by Age, 1997

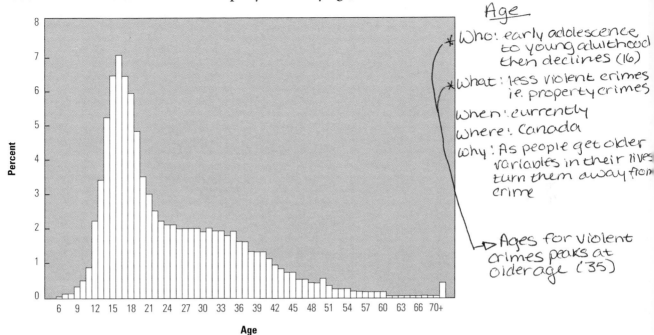

Handwritten annotations:

Age

* Who: early adolescence to young adulthood then declines (16)

* What: less violent crimes ie. property crimes

When: currently

Where: Canada

Why: As people get older variables in their lives turn them away from crime

▷ Ages for violent crimes peaks at older age (~35)

Source: Statistics Canada. Adapted from the Statistics Canada publication, "Canadian Crime Statistics, 1997." *Juristat*, Catalogue 85-002, Vol. 18, No. 11, June 1998, p. 12. Reproduced with the permission of the Minister of Industry, 2003. Based on a random sample of 179 police agencies.

population while accounting for 46 percent of those charged with property crimes and 31 percent of persons charged with violent crimes. Those 25 to 34 years of age also accounted for 14 percent of the population, but only 18 percent and 24 percent of property and violent offenders, respectively (Savoie, 2002).

Data for 2000–01 from the Adult Criminal Court Survey (Thomas, 2002) also show that younger adults are over-represented among accused persons when comparing the age distribution of offenders to the age distribution of the general adult population. For example, 18-to-24-year-olds made up 12 percent of the adult population but accounted for 31 percent of all cases in adult criminal court in 2000–01. In contrast, persons 55 or older represented 28 percent of the adult population but only 5 percent of the adult criminal court cases. This age distribution is stronger for property crimes (38 percent of accused were 18 to 24) than for violent crimes (25 percent were 18 to 24).

Different crimes peak at different ages, and rates of some types of crime decline much more slowly with increasing age (Steffensmeier et al., 1989). Some crimes, including embezzlement, fraud, and gambling, do not conform to the general pattern and peak later in the life cycle (Steffensmeier and Allan, 1995). Braithwaite (1989) has pointed out that white-collar crimes, which are committed by persons of respectability and high status in the course of their occupation, peak later in life because these crimes require the opportunities provided by occupations that most people under 25 have yet to attain.

FIGURE 5.1B   Persons Accused of Violent Crimes by Age, 1997

Source: Statistics Canada. Adapted from the Statistics Canada publication, "Canadian Crime Statistics, 1997." *Juristat*, Catalogue 85-002, Vol 18, No. 11, June 1998, p. 12. Reproduced with the permission of the Minister of Industry, 2003. Based on a random sample of 179 police agencies.

Self-report data also support the age–crime relationship, though such research has generally limited its attention to juveniles and is, therefore, of only limited usefulness for examining the full range of the age–crime relationship. Empey (1982) concludes that the self-report results from a national survey of adolescents in the United States by Ageton and Elliott only partially agree with the official data concerning age and crime. Ageton and Elliott's results suggest that the peak ages for youthful crime are somewhat younger than the official data indicate, with the highest incidence for many property and violent offences occurring between the ages of 13 and 15. Juvenile diversion programs and a hesitancy to formally process adolescents through the criminal justice system may play some role in explaining the higher peak ages in official data on arrests and convictions. Osgood et al. (1989) compared offence rates based on arrests and on self-reports and found that both methods show substantial declines from ages 17 through 23 for virtually all offences, with the major exception of arrests for assault.

Canadian self-report research in Montreal by LeBlanc (1983) found that in a sample of adolescents aged 12 to 18, self-reported delinquency increased progressively until age 16 or 17 and then diminished, though this pattern varied with the nature of the delinquency. Serious delinquency tended to diminish with increasing age, while drug and status offences increased. Similarly, Fréchette (1983) found delinquency to be closely linked with age in his sample of male wards of the Montreal Social Welfare Court. Seventy-five to 80 percent of his respondents reduced or stopped their delinquency during the second half of their adolescence. However, he found an abrupt and substantial rise in criminal activity with the onset of adulthood. Fifteen to 20 percent of his initial sample of respondents had an adult record for serious crime.

Since younger age categories are over-represented among criminal offenders, it's quite likely that changes over time in the crime rate reflect, at least in part, changes in the age composition of the total population. Several researchers have shown that a significant amount of the rise and fall of U.S. crime rates can be explained by the changing age composition of the American population, primarily the aging of the "baby boomers" (Cohen and Land, 1987; Sagi and Wellford, 1968; Steffensmeier and Harer, 1991; Wellford, 1973). Overall crime rates rose as this group reached their late teens in the 1960s and then fell as they began to reach their 30s a decade later (Carrington, 2001). Similarly in Canada, baby boomers—those born between 1947 and 1966—reached 15 years of age in the 1960s and 1970s, a time when violent and property crime rates were rising. Figure 5.2 shows the trend in overall crime and in the number of 15-to-24-year-olds and 25-to-34-year-olds as rates per 100 000 population. The rate of 15-to-24-year-olds began dropping in the early 1980s, and the 25-to-34-year-old age group declined in the early 1990s. The general decline in crime rates since the early 1990s coincided with a decrease in the proportion of persons aged 15 to 24 and 25 to 34 during the same time period (Savoie, 2002). Ouimet (2002) examined the drop in crime in the 1990s in both the United States and Canada and attributed it primarily to these shifts in the age composition of the population, as well as improved employment opportunities. Carrington (2001) has forecast that all types of crime in Canada should decline to the year 2041 because of the continuing aging of the population, ignoring all other factors that might affect crime rates.

Maturational Reform

To conclude this discussion on age and its relation to crime, the ways in which criminologists have attempted to explain this correlation should be briefly noted. Factors such as bias in the criminal justice system in favour of the very young or the much older offender, increased skill in avoiding detection with advancing age, and the decline in physical strength and agility associated with aging have all been mentioned as possible causes. However, the social position of youth in urban, industrial society has been seen as the major contributor to "**maturational reform**," or the rapid decline in crime as adolescents move into young adulthood. Various authors have argued that adolescence is a time of transition, a period between childhood and adulthood, and that the ambiguities and marginality of the social position of youth in modern societies create a variety of tensions and problems, of which crime is but one example (Nettler, 1984). Adolescents tend to be excluded from participation in adult roles such as marriage, work, and adult leisure activities. At the same time, they experience emancipation from the constraints and demands of childhood and are encouraged to aspire to adult status (Bloch and Niederhoffer, 1958; West, 1984). As

maturational reform

The observation that involvement in crime tends to decrease as people age.

FIGURE 5.2   Crime Rate and Selected Demographics Canada 1962–2002[1]

Rate per 100 000 total population

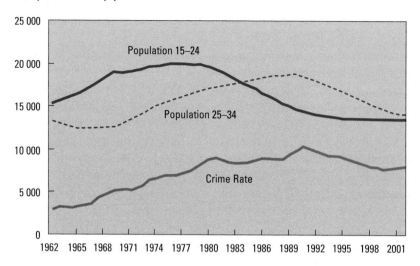

[1] Note that the population 15–24 and population 25–34 refer to changes in the population for these age groups and not changes in crime rates.

Source: Statistics Canada. Adapted from the Statistics Canada publication, "Crime Statistics in Canada, 2002." *Juristat*, Catalogue 85-002, Vol. 23, no. 5. Reproduced with permission of the Minister of Industry, 2003.

Nettler (1984, 217) remarks, "[S]tructures of modern states encourage crime and delinquency. They lack institutional procedures for moving people smoothly from protected childhood to autonomous adulthood." But, as youth move into the adult ages and their social status and integration increase, the personal costs of crime to the individual also increase—they now have more to lose—while at the same time, crime becomes somewhat redundant to their improved social position. Youth acquire added stakes in conforming behaviour (see Chapter 13) as they occupy social roles and acquire material goods that would be jeopardized by criminal behaviour. They become more socially integrated into relationships, groups, and organizations and, therefore, more dependent on the social rewards of conformity (Rowe and Tittle, 1977). New rewards and costs associated with their new adult status replace those that sustained delinquency in adolescence; new satisfactions replace those previously provided by delinquency (Trasler, 1980).

Greenberg (1979) has offered the most elaborate version of this type of explanation. He argues that adolescents in North American society are particularly vulnerable to the expectations and evaluations of their peers because of the increased age segregation resulting from the exclusion of young people from adult work and leisure activity. At the same time, money is necessary for participation in this youth culture, but the deterioration of the teenage labour market has resulted in adolescents being less able to finance their costly social life. Greenberg regards theft as a way of financing participation in activities with peers in the absence of legitimate sources of income. With increasing age, both the dependence on peers and the lack of legitimate sources of funds are reduced for many of these young people; consequently, theft declines. Greenberg also discusses how the extended requirements for schooling restrict adolescent autonomy and how public humiliation of some students by teachers undermines self-esteem and produces embarrassment before peers. This can result in nonutilitarian crime, such as vandalism and violence, as an attempt to assert independence and enhance self-esteem before a sympathetic audience of peers. These motivations to crime are removed when young people leave the restrictive and sometimes degrading school setting. Greenberg also claims that the cost of crime for youth through legal penalties increases as they progress from early to later adolescence, as do opportunities for establishing stakes in conforming behaviour, particularly employment. These social controls, or costs, increase with age and, therefore, also contribute to the decline in crime.

Hirschi and Gottfredson (1983) present evidence that the relationship of age to crime has been similar in earlier historical times and in other types of society, thus challenging the premise that the nature of modern, urban, industrialized society is crucial for explaining this age–crime correlation. Hirschi and Gottfredson cite research suggesting that the effects of age on crime do not depend on such life-course events as leaving school, finding gainful employment, getting married, and so forth: "Age affects crime whether or not these events occur" (1983, 580). Some recent research (Tittle and Ward, 1993) also supports the Hirschi–Gottfredson hypothesis that the correlates and causes of crime do not significantly vary by age. Furthermore, Tanner and Krahn (1991) report a small *positive* effect of part-time work on illegal behaviour among Canadian high school seniors, although other variables were more strongly linked to this self-reported delinquency. Teenagers with part-time jobs while in school were more likely than those not working to report illegal behaviour, a finding somewhat at odds with Greenberg's (1979) argument. These findings undermine the maturational reform type of explanation, though other research questions this interpretation.

Recent research examining crime over the life course suggests that such salient life events as leaving school, entering the labour market, and getting married influence the likelihood of criminal behaviour (Loeber and LeBlanc, 1990; Sampson and Laub, 1990; 1992). Maturational reform among males may be accelerated by such events as completion of education, marriage, and parenthood, and delayed by events such as joining a gang or experiencing unemployment (Rand, 1987). A longitudinal study of Canadian high school graduates, which followed them during the transition into young adulthood, found that those who had delinquent friends reported more criminal behaviour (Hartnagel, 1998). Furthermore, the combination of longer amounts of unemployment and having delinquent peers during this time of transition also led to increased crime. So, despite evidence of continuity in deviant behaviour over the life course, certain social transitions help explain the decline in crime in young adulthood. Finally, Warr (1993) has recently shown that the age–crime relationship is modified by the amount of exposure to delinquent peers, casting additional doubt on Hirschi and Gottfredson's claim that the age distribution of crime cannot be explained by social variables. Although the correlation of age with crime is one of the most undisputed facts of criminology, its interpretation and explanation still remain open to a good deal of debate.

SEX

"Correlates of Delinquency: A Look at Gender Differences" Linda Simourd and D.A. Andrews, Correctional Service of Canada **www.csc-scc.gc.ca/text/pblct/forum/ e061g_e.shtml**

Sex

Who: Male criminals out-scores female criminals

What: Mostly for crimes of violence, except females are found to have their highest % in property crimes

When: over time gap is converging

Where: Canada

Why: Women's equality, place in the domestic role, increase in workforce → more pressure

Sex Differences and Crime Trends

As has already been indicated, sex is strongly correlated with crime. The crime rate for men greatly exceeds the rate for women. In Canada, in 2002, adult males constituted 82 percent of adults charged with Criminal Code offences, while 75 percent of youths charged with Criminal Code offences were male (Wallace, 2003).

This sex difference in crime varies somewhat by type of crime. Figure 5.3 shows that males made up 84 percent of the adults charged with violent crimes in 2002, 77 percent of those charged for property crime, and 82 percent of those charged with other crimes. Females, in contrast, constituted only 16 percent, 23 percent, and 18 percent of those charged for violent, property, and other crimes, respectively. Violent crime, in particular, then, is correlated with being male.

Data from victim surveys parallel arrest statistics in demonstrating that offenders are disproportionately male (Bureau of Justice Statistics, 1993). Victimization data from the 1999 General Social Survey in Canada (Besserer and Trainor, 2000) estimated that males represented 92 percent of the perpetrators of sexual assault, 84 percent of robbery, and 60 percent of assault—figures reasonably similar to those provided by the official data on males charged with these offences in 1999 (except for assault, which equalled 82 percent).

FIGURE 5.3 **Ratio of Persons Reported Charged by Sex and Offence Group, Canada, 2002**

Source: Statistics Canada. Adapted from the Statistics Canada publication, *Canadian Crime Statistics*. Catalogue No. 85-205, 2003. Reproduced with the permission of the Minister of Industry, 2003.

Self-report research with juveniles has generally substantiated this sex difference in delinquency, though the gap is not as great as in the official data on adults. Hagan (1985) noted that the sex ratio in a number of self-report surveys conducted in the United States in the 1970s showed males exceeding females in self-reported delinquency by more than 2 to 1, compared to the 1975 official arrest ratio of 3.72 to 1 for those younger than 18. From a study in the Toronto metropolitan area conducted in 1979, Hagan et al. (1985) reported strong gender effects on self-reported "common" delinquent behaviour such as minor theft and aggression. On average, males scored 2.28 points higher on their delinquency scale than did females, with the greatest differences occurring for the offences of stealing cars and fighting. Yet LeBlanc's (1983) research in Montreal showed a much smaller gap between male and female delinquency (3 to 1) than the official statistics indicated (8 or 10 to 1). This may, at least in part, reflect differences in police handling of juvenile offenders. Gomme et al. (1984) carried out a self-report study among senior elementary and junior high school students in a small rural-urban school district in southern Ontario and found that for all offences except for running away from home, the mean frequencies on self-reported delinquencies were significantly higher for males. The mean sex ratio for the respondents reporting any delinquency involvement was 1.19 to 1 for juvenile status offences, but 1.34 to 1 for serious criminal offences. In particular, males exhibited a greater propensity for damaging property and engaging in interpersonal aggression. However, females were fairly frequently involved in theft offences, with a sex ratio of about 1.1 to 1, though less than 2 percent of females reported ever being involved in major thefts (compared with 10 percent of males), and only 9 percent reported involvement in even medium-serious thefts (compared with 20 percent of males). Compared with official data, then, these self-report results demonstrate a somewhat greater similarity in the types of delinquent acts committed by males and females. But Hindelang et al. (1979) have argued that sex differences found in self-report studies are highly contingent upon the content of the specific items asked. They concluded that once the typically limited seriousness of these items is taken into account, apparent discrepancies between self-report and official data prove to be illusory; they don't measure the same domain of behaviour.

These official statistics and self-report studies are static and don't give any indication of historical trends. For instance, it is *possible* that sex differences in crime have varied over the years such that at certain times, females may have approached equality with males in a broad spectrum of offences. In fact, some criminologists have argued that a new female criminal has arisen in the past few years (Adler, 1975). She argues that not only has the participation of women in crime increased, but they have moved into areas of lawbreaking that were formerly the exclusive domain of men. The data on trends through time in the criminality of men and women should be considered, then, to see whether the gap between them has expanded and/or narrowed over the years.

Table 5.1 presents the rate of adults charged in Canada, by sex, for the years 1968 and 2000. Over the 32 years, the rate for all Criminal Code offences for

TABLE 5.1   Rate of Adults Charged[1] by Sex per 100 000 Population[2] for Selected Criminal Code Offences, Canada, 1968, 2000

	1968		2000	
	Males	*Females*	*Males*	*Females*
Homicide	2.4	0.3	2.7	0.3
Robbery	26.6	1.6	38.3	3.5
Crimes of violence	270.5	15.0	652.7	112.7
Break and enter	157.6	3.4	130.0	9.8
Theft over[3]	82.4	8.5	9.7	2.9
Theft under[4]	175.0	49.7	253.4	100.7
Frauds	105.0	12.8	103.9	43.9
Property crimes	639.7	79.2	636.1	176.7
Criminal Code	1443.4	152.0	2059.7	432.4

[1]   Source: Statistics Canada. (1968). *Crime Statistics, 1968*, Catalogue No. 85-205; Canadian Centre for Justice Statistics. (2001). *Canadian Crime Statistics, 2000*, Catalogue No. 85-205.

[2]   Sources of population estimates: Statistics Canada. (1970). *Estimates of Population by Marital Status, Age and Sex, Canada and Provinces, 1968*. Catalogue No. 91-203; Statistics Canada. (2002). E-STAT, Table 051-0001, Estimates of population, by age group and sex, Canada, provinces and territories, annual (persons). 1968 males = 10 409 900; females = 10 334 100; 2000 males = 15 234 321; females = 15 535 348.

[3]   1968—Theft over $50; 2000—Theft over $5000.

[4]   1968—Theft $50 and under; 2000—Theft $5000 and under.

males increased by 43 percent, while for females, the increase was 184 percent. The percentage of females increased from 9 percent to 18 percent of adults charged with Criminal Code offences. For violent crime, the rate at which males were charged increased by 141 percent and for females, 652 percent. For property crime, the male rate declined slightly (–5 percent) while the female rate increased by 123 percent. So the increases for females have greatly exceeded those for males over this 32-year period. However, a quick glance down the two columns of rates for 2000 will reveal that large absolute differences remain, with the male rates greatly exceeding those for females, particularly for crimes of violence. In 1968, only 10 percent of all women charged were charged for violent crimes, while 52 percent were charged for property crimes. By 2000, the number of women charged for violence had increased to 26 percent of all women charged, but 41 percent were charged with property crime. However, the highest rates for women charged continue to be for less serious thefts of property.

A number of researchers have examined and attempted to interpret trends in male and female contributions to crime in the United States (Simon, 1975; Hagan, 1985; Steffensmeier, 1978; Steffensmeier et al., 1979; Austin, 1993). The general consensus of this research is that the gender gap in crime, particularly serious and violent crime, remains substantial. O'Brien (1999) examined the trends in selected arrest rates for males and females in the United States over a longer time period (1960 to 1995). He reported that the rates appeared to be converging for robbery, burglary, and auto theft and diverging for homicide, with no significant overall trends in either direction for aggravated assaults or larceny. This shows the importance of examining male and female trends in specific crimes, some of which appear to be converging. In Canada there has been a definite narrowing of the gender gap in crime overall, and for both violent and property offences (Campbell, 1990). But the speed of convergence has not been constant, depending upon the time period examined, and most Canadian female crime still consists of petty property offences such as shoplifting (Boritch, 1997).

Fisher (1986) replicated Steffensmeier's U.S. research with Canadian data on trends in persons charged by sex between 1962 and 1978. Like Steffensmeier, she found a narrowing of the relative gap between males and females in property crime charge rates, with the greatest increases in the rate at which females are charged with petty property crime—the crimes with which women have traditionally been associated. However, the absolute gap widened for all property crimes except for theft over $200, such that female property crime levels continue to lag behind those of males despite large increases in the rate at which females are charged for property crime. The relative gap between the sexes in violent crime remained about the same, while the absolute gap widened. Violent crime remained predominantly the domain of males. Fisher also documented the much lower base rates from 1962 for females. Therefore, large percentage increases resulted from relatively small absolute increases in female crime. Fisher's Canadian results are generally quite comparable to those of Steffensmeier for the United States, though the Canadian crime rates for both men and women are lower, particularly for violent crime.

Conclusions about trends in female crime that are based on official data sources, such as arrest rates or charge rates, are vulnerable to the claim that such official data reflect changes in the response to female crime by the criminal justice system as much as or more than they do real changes in criminal behaviour. Therefore, it would be desirable to have trend data from alternative sources such as self-report research. But self-report data are generally very time-bound, having been conducted in a particular location at a given point in time, and they are, therefore, limited in their usefulness for examining trends in crime. However, Smith and Visher (1980) analyzed 44 different self-report and official data studies that reported on the relationship between sex and deviance and found that the year the data were gathered was an important factor in explaining the magnitude of the sex-deviant behaviour correlation. They found that this correlation has been decreasing in size over time—meaning less gender disparity in deviant behaviour—and has declined more rapidly according to self-report studies than to research based on official sources of data. This narrowing of the gap is mainly for minor acts of deviance rather than for serious criminal behaviour and more for youths than for adults. There was also some indication of increased rates of female delinquency in Canada in the 1970s in the previously discussed self-report research of Gomme et al. (1984) since the sex ratio for comparable offences was 1.34 to 1, smaller than the ratio of 1.67 to 1 reported by Linden and Fillmore (1981) for Edmonton in 1965.

These various data on sex differences and crime trends lead to the conclusion that sex, like age, remains strongly correlated with criminal behaviour. Males are much more involved in criminal acts than females. Women have increased their participation in crime, including violent crime, although the increase has been greatest for minor property crimes such as theft and fraud. These two categories include offences such as shoplifting, credit card fraud, and passing bad cheques that women have commonly committed in the past. While the gender gap in crime has narrowed somewhat, it remains substantial, particularly for the most serious offences.

Role Convergence?

Criminologists have offered various explanations for the sex difference in criminal involvement, as well as for the changes in female participation in crime through time. Early theories of female criminality emphasized biological and psychological factors (Smart, 1976). Some claimed that sex differences in criminality were illusory and resulted from the greater cunning and deceitfulness of women, as well as from their preferential treatment by the police and the courts (Pollak, 1950). More recently, greater emphasis has been placed on the importance of socially structured differences in gender roles. This line of reasoning argues that males and females are subjected to differing expectations and demands regarding appropriate behaviour, as well as being subject to different mechanisms of social control. Boys are socialized to greater independence and risk taking and are, therefore, freer to experiment with deviant conduct (Hagan et al., 1979). Girls, on the other hand, are rewarded for compliance and dependence and so have fewer opportunities to experiment with delinquency. The traditional division of labour between the sexes, with women facing greater restriction to the private sphere in the domestic roles of wife and mother, further limited women's opportunities to engage in many forms of criminal conduct. The more public role of men, on the other hand, not only provided more opportunities for certain crimes, it also exposed them, to a much greater extent, to the formal social controls of the criminal justice system (Hagan et al., 1979).

Changes in gender role expectations should have consequences on the actual behaviour of males and females, including their criminal behaviour. More specifically, the convergence hypothesis suggests that as the social roles of the sexes become more equal or begin to converge, differences in their criminal behaviour should diminish (Nettler, 1984; Fox and Hartnagel, 1979). In one version of this thesis, Simon (1975) suggested that increases in property crimes committed by women could be attributed to the expansion of employment opportunities for women. This apparent emancipation of women from domestic roles may bring with it increased opportunities to commit property crime as well as subjecting women to greater pressures for achievement, which may create pressures or strains toward crime (Merton, 1938). Fox and Hartnagel (1979) tested the **role convergence** hypothesis by examining the relationship between changes in the Canadian conviction rate for females from 1931 to 1968 and three measures

role convergence

Explanation for the rising crime rate among women has been that their roles have become similar to (converged with) those of men.

of women's changing gender role. Women's participation in the labour force over these same years and the rate at which females were granted post-secondary degrees were used as measures of the convergence of gender roles, while the total fertility rate indicated the degree of persistence of women's domestic role. The convergence hypothesis was generally supported by this analysis, particularly for the female conviction rate for theft. As the female labour force participation rate and the rate at which females were granted post-secondary degrees increased and the fertility rate declined, the female conviction rate for theft increased. However, the authors note that they were unable to introduce measures to control for an alternative hypothesis. Changes in the treatment of females by the police or courts may better account for any changes in the female conviction rate. Less preferential treatment for women by the criminal justice system could explain rising female crime rates.

Other criminologists have questioned the role convergence hypothesis. Steffensmeier (1980), for example, has argued that most of the increase in female property crime is for the traditional female crimes of petty theft and fraud. These crimes are more related to the traditional female domestic roles of shopper and consumer. He questioned the degree to which gender roles have really changed by pointing to women's restricted labour market participation. Most women work in jobs with limited access to illegitimate opportunities. Furthermore, women still have primary responsibility for home and child care. "Female experiences are not moving beyond traditional roles, either legitimate or illegitimate" (1980, 1102). As Holly Johnson (1987) has reminded us, the high proportion of women offenders charged with theft or fraud (54 percent of all Criminal Code charges against women in 1988) is consistent with women's traditional role as consumers and, increasingly, as low-income, semi-skilled, single parents. Female offenders tend to be young, poor, undereducated and unskilled, suggesting that female crime is at least partly the product of women's subordinate socio-economic position (Boritch, 1997; Johnson, 1987). The typical crimes of women may be symptomatic of their economic deprivation and marginality. Box and Hale (1984) found some limited evidence in their British data that deteriorating economic conditions experienced by women, rather than female emancipation, were related to increases in female crime. Steffensmeier and Streifel (1992) tested alternative explanations for changes in the female share of property crime arrests in the United States. Their findings did not support the gender equality–role convergence argument. Instead, increases in the female share of property crime were largely a function of more formal, bureaucratic policing and, to a lesser extent, the greater economic marginality of women. Finally, the historical research of Boritch and Hagan (1990) suggests that common structural forces may be operating to affect both male and female crime over the long term and that changes in the forms of social control on women contributed to the decline in female arrest rates during the late 19th and early 20th centuries. Further research on this topic should include attention to the relation between gender roles and patterns of social control.

Race and Crime

While not as strongly related to crime and delinquency as age and sex, race has been found to be a good predictor of criminality, at least in the United States (Tonry, 1995). However, Canadian research on race and crime is much more limited since such information is generally not collected by the criminal justice system. The question of whether race and crime data should be routinely collected in Canada has been the subject of some debate (Johnston, 1994; Roberts, 1994). In 1990, Statistics Canada decided to collect police data on the race of crime suspects on a trial basis but had to reverse this decision when only a minority of police forces were willing or able to provide such data and because of criticism from various minority organizations and academics (Roberts and Doob, 1997). Thus, our information on the relationship between race and crime in Canada is very limited.

The information that is available suggests that certain racial minorities are over-represented in the Canadian correctional system. Specifically, these data reveal that while Aboriginal Canadians represented approximately 4 percent of the population in 1996, they accounted for 14 percent of federal prison inmates in 1997; and while black people were only 2 percent of the population, they represented over 6 percent of those in federal penitentiaries. However, Asians were under-represented in prison (Wortley, 1999). Using 1991 census data from Ontario and 1992–93 prison admissions data from Ontario provincial correctional facilities, Roberts and Doob (1997) calculated prison admission rates of 705 per 100 000 for whites compared to 1993 for Aboriginals and 3686 for blacks. When the male data were analyzed separately, the black admission rates rose to 6796, compared to 3600 for Aboriginals and 1326 for whites. Despite apparent increased attention on the "problem" of crime committed by immigrants, Thomas (1993) concluded that the foreign-born were highly under-represented among those incarcerated for violent crimes. While the circumstances of Aboriginal Canadians in the criminal justice system—particularly in correctional institutions—have received a fair amount of attention, this is much less so in the case of the black population and other visible minorities. Therefore, the remainder of this section will focus on Aboriginal over-representation in the criminal justice system.

Over-representation of Canadian Aboriginal People in the Criminal Justice System

over-representation
A group that has a number of its members in some condition in greater numbers than their population would suggest. If a group makes up 20 percent of the population, then a researcher might predict, other things being equal, that they would represent 20 percent of offenders.

As early as 1967, the report *Indians and the Law* (Canadian Corrections Association, 1967) showed the disproportionate presence of Aboriginal people in the Canadian criminal justice system (Nielsen, 1992). Subsequently, a number of commissions and task forces have recognized this **over-representation** and made numerous recommendations to respond to it (see, for example, LaPrairie, 1996; Manitoba Public Inquiry into the Administration of Justice and Aboriginal People, 1991; Task Force on the Criminal Justice System and Its

Impact on the Indian and Métis People of Alberta, 1991). Although the over-representation of Aboriginal people is widely recognized (LaPrairie, 1983), implementation of recommendations to change this situation has been slow (Blackburn, 1993), and the over-representation persists.

Currently, the only available data on offenders in the Canadian criminal justice system are in correctional statistics. Additional data concerning Aboriginal offenders can be found in various reports and special studies and in the homicide database. These data sources document various aspects of the disproportionate involvement of Aboriginal offenders in the criminal justice system. For example, while Statistics Canada projected the Aboriginal population at 2.7 percent of the total Canadian population in 1996 (Royal Commission on Aboriginal Peoples, 1996), Aboriginal offenders accounted for 16 percent of all sentenced admissions to provincial custody in 1996–97, 12 percent of all intakes to provincial probation, and 15 percent of admissions to federal prisons (Reed and Roberts, 1998). These incarceration data probably even underestimate the extent of Aboriginal over-representation (Task Force on Aboriginal Peoples in Federal Corrections, 1989). Aboriginal offenders in the Prairie provinces and the Yukon are particularly at risk for incarceration and probation. When these provincial custody data are averaged over the years 1989 to 1994 and compared to the provincial Aboriginal population, Saskatchewan (6.8 times), Alberta (5.5 times), and Manitoba (4.9 times) have the greatest over-representation (LaPrairie, 1996).

A survey of all on-register inmates on October 5, 1996, revealed an even greater over-representation of Aboriginal offenders than that found in the admission data above (Robinson et al., 1998). On that date, 18 percent of provincial and territorial inmates were Aboriginal and 14 percent of all federal prisoners were Aboriginal, for an overall average of 17 percent. Figure 5.4 shows that while the Aboriginal proportion of inmates varied considerably, in all jurisdictions their proportion was substantially larger than the proportion of Aboriginal persons in the population. They were particularly over-represented in the prisons of Saskatchewan, Alberta, and Manitoba. In federal institutions, the largest percentage of Aboriginal inmates were serving sentences for homicide/attempted murder (23 percent), followed closely by robbery (21 percent), and sexual assault (20 percent); the largest percentage of non-Aboriginal inmates were doing time for robbery (25 percent), homicide/attempted murder (24 percent), sexual assault (12 percent), and break and enter (12 percent). Break and enter was the most frequently sentenced offence for both Aboriginal (18 percent) and non-Aboriginal (18 percent) inmates of provincial and territorial institutions.

In 2000–01 Aboriginal people accounted for 19 percent of provincial and territorial admissions to sentenced custody, and 17 percent of federal sentenced custody. Since 1992–93, the proportion of sentenced Aboriginal offenders beginning provincial or territorial incarceration has fluctuated between 15 and 19 percent; while the proportion in sentenced federal custody has increased from 12 percent in 1990–91 to 18 percent in 1997–98, stabilizing at 17 percent in recent years (Hendrick and Farmer, 2002).

Indian and Northern Affairs Canada
www.ainc-inac.gc.ca

FIGURE 5.4   Aboriginal Persons—Proportion of Adult Population and Inmates by Jurisdiction

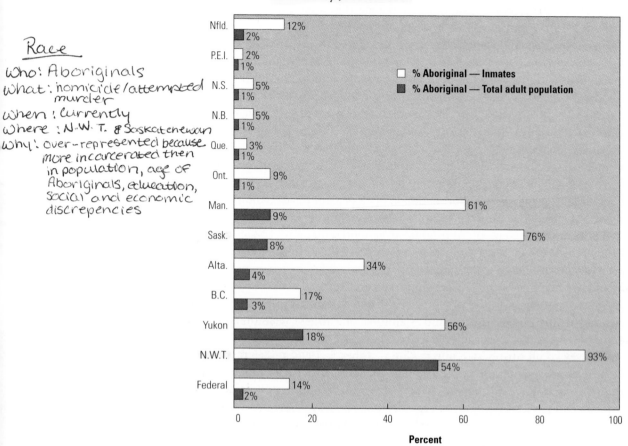

Handwritten notes in left margin:

Race

Who: Aboriginals
What: homicide/attempted murder
When: Currently
Where: N.W.T. & Saskatchewan
Why: over-represented because more incarcerated then in population, age of Aboriginals, education, social and economic discrepencies

Source: Statistics Canada. Adapted from the Statistics Canada publication, "A One-Day Snapshot of Inmates in Canada's Adult Correctional Facilities," Catalogue 85-601, March 1999, 1–14. Reproduced with the permission of the Minister of Industry, 2003.

Previous research indicates that this prison over-representation has persisted for some time (Indian and Northern Affairs Canada, 1980). The report of the Task Force on Aboriginal Peoples in Federal Corrections (1989) concluded that the rate of growth of the Aboriginal offender population has exceeded that of the general inmate population since at least 1982–83.

LaPrairie's (1996) review of various surveys and research studies dealing with Aboriginal inmates also indicates that they are generally younger, have more prior contact with the criminal justice and correctional systems, and come from more dysfunctional backgrounds than non-Aboriginal offenders. Proportionately, more Aboriginal than non-Aboriginal offenders are serving time for fine defaults, and Aboriginal women are particularly over-represented in correctional institutions. While use of incarceration as a sentence is greater for federal Aboriginal offenders after controlling for type of offence (but without information on prior record), they also receive shorter sentences on average than non-Aboriginal offenders in both federal and provincial institutions (LaPrairie, 1996).

There is only limited evidence concerning the over-representation of Aboriginal peoples at earlier stages of the criminal justice system. Two studies of urban Aboriginal crime (in Calgary, Regina, Saskatoon, and Vancouver) concluded that for those offences with an identified accused, Aboriginal persons were more likely than non-Aboriginals to be accused of a property or violent offence or to have been the victim of a violent crime (Griffiths et al., 1994; Trevethan, 1993). In these four cities, Aboriginals constituted from 2 to 6 percent of the population but represented from 9 to 43 percent of those accused of a crime, depending on the type of crime and on the city.

Homicide data for 2000 show that Aboriginal persons represented 24 percent of all homicide suspects and 15 percent of all homicide victims. Thus about one in four people accused of committing homicide and approximately one in six people killed in a homicide incident were of Aboriginal background. One factor that may contribute to this over-representation is the age composition of the Aboriginal population. The high-risk age group for homicide and other violent crime is 15 to 34, and this age group accounted for 36 percent of the Aboriginal population in 2000 compared to 28 percent for the rest of the population (Fedorowycz, 2001). A detailed analysis of homicides involving Aboriginal people in Ontario between 1980 and 1990 revealed that the rate of homicides among Aboriginal people on reserves was approximately the same as the rate off reserve, although in both settings, the suspect and victim rates were considerably higher than the rates for non-Aboriginal people (Doob et al., 1994). On most comparisons, on- and off-reserve Aboriginal homicides and homicides involving Aboriginal victims were more likely to have occurred after a nonviolent social encounter, a verbal argument, or a fight that escalated. This pattern of results suggests that the causes of Aboriginal homicides are likely to be different from those of non-Aboriginal homicides (Doob et al., 1994).

Similarly, research by the Canadian Centre for Justice Statistics (1991) showed that crime committed on Saskatchewan reserves differed markedly from that of other rural and urban areas. Not only were offence rates considerably higher on reserves, but violent offences accounted for about 25 percent of all Criminal Code offences, compared with less than 10 percent in other areas. The reserve violent crime rate was about five times higher than would be expected on the basis of the proportion of the population resident on reserves. However, property crimes were not disproportionately committed on reserves.

Although the level of crime among Aboriginal people, particularly violent crime, is considerably higher than that for non-Aboriginals, there is still a great deal of variation in the rates of both violent and property crimes among Aboriginal communities and Aboriginal populations across Canada (Wood and Griffiths, 1996). This variation in recorded crime is probably at least partly due to differences in the nature of policing in these communities and jurisdictions, as well as differences in the likelihood of the police recording incidents reported to them (Roberts and Doob, 1997). A comparison of several research studies conducted in different jurisdictions revealed that the mean of the rates for violent crimes varied between 19 and 70 per 1000 population, while for property crime the rates ranged from 22 to 108 per 1000 population (Wood and Griffiths, 1996). This means that at least some Aboriginal communities have rates of crime below the average for Canada.

Explanations of Aboriginal Over-representation

There are a number of potential explanations for this over-representation of Aboriginal people in the Canadian criminal justice system. These include the following: conflict between the values of Aboriginal culture and the dominant Canadian culture; the social and economic deprivation experienced by many Aboriginal peoples stemming from their colonization and oppression and resulting in higher Aboriginal offending rates and/or their discriminatory treatment by the criminal justice system; the commission by Aboriginals of types of offences more likely to result in a justice system response; and a decline in interdependency in Aboriginal communities, resulting in cultural dislocation and the decline of informal mechanisms of social control (see, for example, LaPrairie, 1983; 1996).

Verdun-Jones and Muirhead (1979/80) distinguish between cultural and structural explanations. **Cultural explanations** emphasize the lack of certain traits in Aboriginal culture that are valued by the dominant white culture. James (1979), while claiming that the core values of Aboriginal and white cultures may be essentially the same, argues that there is conflict in the ways in which these values are expressed behaviourally in society. "Native values are placed under stress by the pressures of expressing them acceptably in a complex urban society" (1979, 455). For example, James suggests that the sharing of material possessions among Aboriginal people implies a potentially reciprocal action rather than a permanent transfer of ownership. However, when such sharing of belongings is practised without permission in the dominant culture, it is called theft. The Native Counselling Services of Alberta (1982) has identified a number of areas of conflict between Aboriginal and non-Aboriginal cultures related to the legal system and has suggested that many Aboriginal people have only a limited understanding of the dominant Canadian legal and justice system. Similarly, Dumont (1993) describes a number of conflicts between Aboriginal responses to the law and the expectations of the Canadian legal system. For example, while Aboriginal culture emphasizes mediation and negotiation to resolve disputes and reconcile offenders with victims, the Canadian legal system is based on retributive justice with punishment set by legislation. Furthermore, Aboriginal defendants are reluctant to testify and often plead guilty on the basis of honesty or the avoidance of confrontation; in contrast, the Canadian system is adversarial and assumes innocence until proven guilty. So cultural explanations emphasize conflicting values. The over-representation of Aboriginals results from the imposition of a somewhat alien set of values and rules on Aboriginal culture, as well as from the higher rate of commission by Aboriginals of acts called crime by Canadian law but regarded as normative or expected behaviour in the context of Aboriginal culture.

cultural explanation

An explanation for crime that is phrased in terms of the culture of the subgroup or the culture of that nation.

Structural explanations of Aboriginal over-representation emphasize the economically and socially dependent position of Aboriginals in Canadian society. Thus, Hylton (1982) claims that the over-representation of Aboriginal people is a symptom of the underlying social and economic inequality of Canadian society, while LaPrairie (1983) states that the suggestion of a link between the living conditions of Aboriginals and their over-representation in the criminal justice system is compelling. She views over-representation as an effect of structural disadvantage. She documents examples of such disadvantage with comparisons between Aboriginals and non-Aboriginals in federal penitentiaries. Only 12 percent of Aboriginal inmates compared to 26 percent of non-Aboriginal inmates had more than a Grade 9 education; 31 percent of Aboriginal inmates but only 19 percent of non-Aboriginal inmates had either no education or education of only Grade 6 or less. The Métis and Non-Status Indian Crime and Justice Commission (1978) report also attributed the high rate of Aboriginal imprisonment to their deprived social situation, illustrated by the report's findings from a survey of Aboriginal inmates in federal penitentiaries. Fifty-seven percent of the inmates said they were unemployed at the time of their offence; 49 percent had spent time in skid row areas of cities; and 49 percent had less than a Grade 9 education. More recently, the final report of the Task Force on Aboriginal Peoples in Federal Corrections (1989) concluded that any reduction in Aboriginal crime must address the correlated socioeconomic conditions among Aboriginals—conditions that, compared to those of other Canadians, are discouraging. Generally, Aboriginals continue to have a lower average level of education, fewer marketable skills, a higher rate of unemployment, an infant mortality rate twice the national rate, a higher degree of family instability, and a rate of violent death three times the national average. Aboriginal inmates, then, are even more disadvantaged in some respects than other inmates.

Trevethan (1993) attributed at least some of the Aboriginal over-representation among urban accused persons to the fact that Aboriginal persons in Calgary, Regina, and Saskatoon tended to be younger, have lower educational levels, have higher levels of unemployment, and have substantially lower average incomes than non-Aboriginals. Similarly, a study of Aboriginal residents of the inner-city areas of four Canadian cities (Edmonton, Regina, Toronto, and Montreal) explained the over-representation of Aboriginal people by their marginalization and alienation resulting from unstable and violent childhoods, as well as their lack of opportunity and dependency on alcohol (LaPrairie, 1995).

Verdun-Jones and Muirhead (1979/80), moreover, argue that the structurally deprived position of Aboriginals in contemporary Canadian society is rooted in a history of exploitation by the dominant white society through what was, in essence, a colonial system based on the fur trade. From this perspective, the criminal justice system functions today primarily to control subjugated groups such as Aboriginals—to keep them in their dominated, powerless position—in order to protect the interests of the dominant, powerful segment of society. This dominant segment of society is made up of the white majority generally and, more particularly, its leading, economically powerful segments.

structural explanation

An explanation for crime that focuses on *social structure* (usually this refers to inequality, poverty, or power differentials). For example, the patriarchal structure of the family might help explain the abuse of women and children within the family.

The criminal justice system, and the state generally, are seen by these authors as agents of the economically powerful who control the underclasses. The criminal justice system mirrors the socio-economic organization and operation of society. Hence, over-representation of Aboriginals within the criminal justice system is merely a reproduction of the basic socio-economic inequalities present in the surrounding society. Furthermore, the criminal justice system functions to support and maintain that structure of inequality. Thus, the Canadian justice system has been seen as the central institution that reinforces colonial relationships against Aboriginal people, with over-representation a systemic problem of a society structured on discriminatory values, beliefs, and practices (Monture-Angus, 1996).

LaPrairie (1996) has argued recently that a decline in traditional interdependency in Aboriginal communities has resulted from their colonization and the creation of the reserve system, as well as their cultural dislocation and the decline of informal mechanisms of social control. "The end result is socially stratified communities where limited resources and resource distribution create large groups of disadvantaged people, a growing youth sub-culture with few legitimate outlets or opportunities, decontextualized exposure to the mass media, and the lack of cultural and social resources to assist in identity formation which support pro-social values" (LaPrairie, 1996, 63). The result is a large group of marginalized and nonintegrated people in many Aboriginal communities who have few tools for survival or integration into mainstream society when they leave reserves for urban areas. Their lack of skills, coupled with substance abuse problems and dysfunctional family life, leads to negative peer associations and the adoption of pro-criminal attitudes. Structural explanations, then, regard higher Aboriginal crime rates as a product of the social and economic oppression of Aboriginals by the dominant white society. The majority of Aboriginals are kept poor and dependent, and this breeds crime, violence, and other social disorders to which the criminal justice system responds, thereby furthering Aboriginals' exploitation by the existing system of inequality.

Discriminatory treatment of Aboriginal people by the criminal justice system has also been offered as an explanation of over-representation by several task forces (Manitoba Public Inquiry, 1991; Task Force on the Criminal Justice System, 1991) and some criminologists (Havemann et al., 1985; Monture-Angus, 1996). The Manitoba Inquiry, for example, pointed out that Aboriginal people were more likely to face multiple charges, to be held in jail before their court appearance, to spend a longer time in custody before their trials, to see their lawyers less frequently and for less time, to enter guilty pleas, to be sentenced to jail terms, to receive longer sentences, and to receive absolute or conditional discharges less frequently.

Several Canadian research studies that investigated this hypothesis of differential treatment by the criminal justice system included race as a variable in their analysis. The most relevant of these studies for the present discussion is no doubt Hagan's (1974) research in five Alberta correctional institutions. He examined the sentences received by Indian and Métis inmates, who were represented at least four times as often among newly incarcerated offenders as among the general population. Hagan discovered that Aboriginals were primarily charged with minor offences and, as a result, received shorter sentences. Incarceration resulting from failure to pay a fine was nearly twice as common for Aboriginals as for non-Aboriginals. Almost two-thirds of Aboriginal inmates were serving sentences resulting from such default. Race, therefore, played no *direct* role in influencing the over-representation of Aboriginals in these institutions. The sentences imposed conformed to legal requirements and reflected the disproportionate involvement of Aboriginals in minor offences, particularly involving alcohol abuse, for which they received a fine. However, because of their poverty, many were unable to pay these fines and ended up serving time in jail for minor offences. In a subsequent analysis, Hagan (1977) found that Aboriginals were more likely to be sent to jail in default of fine payments in rural than in urban Alberta communities, a finding he attributed to the trend toward greater uniformity of treatment in the more bureaucratic urban criminal justice system. Other research has suggested that limited sentencing options in remote Aboriginal communities may explain some of the disproportionate use of incarceration for convicted Aboriginals (LaPrairie, 1990).

Several other studies have examined the hypothesis of selective enforcement against Aboriginal people in different parts of the criminal justice system. Hagan (1977), for example, found that probation officers in rural jurisdictions in Alberta were more likely to recommend more severe sentences for Aboriginal offenders in their presentence reports, without the justification of legally relevant considerations such as prior record, seriousness of offence, or number of charges. But Boldt et al. (1983) found no racial effect on presentence recommendations in the Yukon. In general, Hagan (1975a; 1975b) failed to discover evidence of differential treatment due to race itself in presentence recommendations or sentencing, though probation officers took a dimmer view of Aboriginal defendants' prospects for success on probation, which in turn affected their sentence recommendations and the final disposition of the case by the judge. But judges characterized by Hagan as less concerned about the maintenance of a conservative notion of "law and order" used part of their discretion to sentence Aboriginal defendants more *leniently* (Hagan, 1975c). Since there is evidence that Aboriginal offenders sentenced to incarceration receive shorter sentences for certain offences than comparable non-Aboriginal offenders, over-representation of Aboriginals in prisons cannot be simply explained by racial discrimination (LaPrairie, 1990). Research on parole decision making by Demers (1978) supported Hagan's conclusion that Aboriginal candidates were less likely to receive favourable recommendations from parole officers. This was probably due to a variety of factors, but indirectly produced racial inequality in parole release decisions made by the Parole Board, which is dependent on parole officers for information and advice. Wynne and Hartnagel (1975) found evidence from a study of Crown prosecutors' files that Aboriginals were less likely than whites to successfully engage in plea bargaining, though this depended on certain conditions, such as being represented by defence counsel and the presence of repetitious counts and/or multiple charges in the indictment.

Unfortunately, there is little evidence on how the police exercise their discretion with respect to Aboriginal people. It has been suggested that in cities, Aboriginal people may tend to attract police attention by their physical appearance and/or location in run-down, skid row areas (Canadian Corrections Association, 1967). Aboriginals may have a greater public visibility, particularly when drinking, and this may result in more frequent arrests (Bienvenue and Latif, 1974). Some criminologists (Giffen, 1966; Greenaway, 1980; Frideres, 1988) have even argued that the police "find" crime where they look for it, at least with respect to public-order offences such as public drunkenness. Therefore, police initiative and discretion in seeking out the poor and disadvantaged may be implicated to some extent in the higher frequency of Aboriginal arrests for certain types of crime. But there is also some evidence that the police may be called by Aboriginal people in some communities to deal with problems that would not be seen as police business in non-Aboriginal communities, due in part to the fact that the police may be the only service available in the community to deal with such problems (Roberts and Doob, 1997).

The Role of Alcohol

There is strong evidence for an association between alcohol use and crime, although it is unclear whether this correlation also implies a causal relationship (Mosher and Jernigan, 2001; Parker and Auerhahn, 1998). Fagan's (1990) review of a large amount of research shows that people who become aggressive after consumption of intoxicants often have a long history of aggression; there is only limited evidence that ingestion of intoxicants is a direct pharmacological cause of aggression. A survey by the Correctional Service of Canada (1991) revealed that 52 percent of a sample of federal inmates reported that they were under the influence of alcohol or other drugs when they committed at least one of the crimes on their current sentences; 44 percent had consumed alcohol and 27 percent had consumed alcohol and other drugs. Alcohol consumption was more frequent than other drugs among offenders involved in violent crimes other than robbery. Eighty-one percent of those who had consumed alcohol claimed that consumption was a precipitating factor in their crime. Data from the 1997 Homicide Survey show that of the 581 homicides in Canada that year, one in three victims and one in two accused had been drinking alcohol and/or using drugs at the time of the crime (Tremblay, 1999). So the ingestion of drugs, particularly alcohol, is common among those involved in crime, although the relationship between substance use and crime is complex and affected by a variety of other factors. Although intoxication may not directly cause aggression, there is evidence that in situations that become violent, substance use may increase the severity of the violence (Wolff and Reingold, 1994).

Alcohol abuse has had a severe impact on Aboriginal people. The survey *Indian Conditions* (Indian and Northern Affairs Canada, 1980) estimated that between 50 and 60 percent of Indian illnesses and deaths were alcohol related. Alcohol also plays a major role in Native American criminal behaviour (Lester, 1999). Havemann et al. (1985) have reviewed a number of Canadian studies that identify alcohol as a major contributor to the crimes Aboriginal people commit. This contribution can be direct, through the violation of liquor laws, as well as indirect, as when other crimes are committed under the influence of alcohol. Bienvenue and Latif (1974) showed that Aboriginals were most over-represented in arrests for liquor violations. A survey of Aboriginal inmates in Ontario (Irvine, 1978) found that 38 percent had been convicted of specific alcohol offences, while 86 percent admitted that alcohol was involved in the crimes for which they were incarcerated. The survey of federal penitentiary inmates by the Métis and Non-Status Indian Crime and Justice Commission (1978) found that only 10 percent of the Aboriginals committed the major charge resulting in their imprisonment with no alcohol or drug involvement. Thirty percent had been taking both alcohol and drugs, while the greatest pro-portion (48 percent) committed their offence under the influence of alcohol alone. Hagan's (1974) study in Alberta correctional institutions discovered that 48 percent of the Aboriginal offenders had drinking problems, compared to 25 percent of non-Aboriginal offenders.

However, the link between alcohol abuse and Aboriginal criminality is not well understood or agreed upon. Some have suggested that heavy drinking has become a regular, normal occurrence within some Aboriginal communities, associated with family and group activities and, therefore, accorded a good deal of tolerance (Brody, 1971; Jensen et al., 1977). Highly visible group drinking may be socially accepted and expected, without the development of corresponding informal social controls to regulate or limit the extent of such drinking. An addi-tional possibility is that alcohol abuse and its associated criminal consequences may be a response to, or reaction against, the poverty and deprivation experi-enced by so many Aboriginal people. Alcohol may provide some respite, how-ever temporary, from their oppressive life circumstances, whether on reserves, in impoverished rural areas, or in the city slums. Havemann et al. (1985) expand on this argument by linking alcohol and involvement with the criminal justice system with the social impact of the underdevelopment of Aboriginal communi-ties. They argue that alcohol is used as a means to modify moods and escape real-life situations; that it is a way for Aboriginal people to manage the alienation created by the destruction of their culture and economic exploitation of their land resources for the benefit of southern Canada and the corporate structure. Thus, these authors locate the use of alcohol by Aboriginal people and their con-sequent over-representation in the criminal justice system in the structure of socio-economic relations between Aboriginal people and the dominant white society, rather than in some disease model or other individualistic-type expla-nation that ends up blaming the victim.

This short review of what is currently known concerning the relationship of Canadian Aboriginal people to crime and the criminal justice system sug-gests that Canadian criminology needs to devote more of its research effort to this topic (LaPrairie, 1990). While it is clear that Aboriginal people are over-represented in the criminal justice system, the reasons for such over-represen-tation remain in doubt. Furthermore, little research has been done in Canada on the ways in which crime may be produced by the relations between indige-nous Aboriginal society and culture and the dominant white society and its culture. However, the disproportionately high rates of Aboriginal crime and violence suggest "a serious rupture of traditional control mechanisms in contemporary aboriginal communities" (LaPrairie, 1992, 285).

SOCIAL CLASS

Conflicting Evidence?

Few issues have been in greater dispute among criminologists in recent years than the correlation between social class and criminal behaviour. Thus, Gordon (1976), for example, regards the crime or delinquency relationship with social class status as one of the most thoroughly documented, while Tittle and Villemez (1977) conclude that the purported relationship between class and criminality is problematic; Tittle et al. (1978) refer to such a relationship as a myth. Hindelang et al. (1979) state that illusions of discrepancies in the research evidence abound, while Braithwaite (1981) concludes from his review of over 100 studies that class is one of the very few correlates of criminality, which is persuasively supported by a large body of empirical evidence. Clearly, this is a controversial question among criminologists, and there are disagreements over what the research literature reveals.

Official data appear to support an inverse or negative relationship. Those arrested, convicted, and/or incarcerated are more likely to come from lower socio-economic categories of the population as indexed by such variables as income, education, and occupational status. Tittle and Villemez (1977) report that of the 23 studies on this relationship they could locate that used official police or court data, 65 percent found a negative relationship, while another 8 percent detected class variation in crime but only for some subcategories of individuals. Twenty-six percent of these studies found no consistent class variation. Of course, these official records may underestimate the amount of crime committed by those in the higher socio-economic positions. Nettler (1984) states that official statistics on serious crimes from a variety of countries show that people with less money, lower occupational status, and less schooling are disproportionately represented. But it could be immediately asked: what qualifies as a serious crime? Some would argue that bank embezzlement, for example, is at least as serious as bank robbery or that corporate crimes are more seriously harmful than many of the crimes typically committed by lower-class individuals.

Additional evidence, using official crime statistics, on the class–crime relationship comes from the long history of research on poverty, economic inequality, and crime. While the argument that crime is one of a number of undesirable consequences of poverty can be traced far back into antiquity, the first empirical research examining the relationship between poverty and crime can be found in the mid-19th-century work of Guerry and of Quetelet in Europe (Vold and Bernard, 1986). Anticipating later developments, this early work showed that wealthier provinces had higher property crime rates and suggested that the greater opportunities for theft and other property offences offered by these wealthier regions might explain this unexpected pattern. Quetelet also suggested that great inequality between wealth and poverty in the same place, rather than absolute poverty, might be a critical factor. While poverty refers to the lack of that level of income necessary for mere survival, economic inequality signifies the size of the income gap between those who have the least income and those who have the most income (Vold and Bernard, 1986).

Since this early research, criminologists have continued to analyze and interpret various data relating economic conditions and crime at different levels of ecological aggregation ranging from city neighbourhoods to nation-states. Summarizing this large body of research is complicated by this variation in units of analysis, as well as by such factors as varying measurement of poverty and inequality, the inclusion of a variety of crime types, and the use of differing sets of control variables. However, there appears to be some consensus that the degree of economic inequality rather than the amount of poverty is the more important variable (Braithwaite, 1979; Box, 1987; Vold and Bernard, 1986). More specifically, nations with greater economic inequality have higher homicide rates, particularly under conditions of political democracy (Krahn et al., 1986). Cross-national comparisons of property crime rates are more inconsistent, perhaps as a result of the effect of varying opportunities for property crime in different nations (Stack, 1984). Economic inequality and crime rates, with the possible exception of homicide, are fairly strongly and consistently related in studies of U.S. cities and Standard Metropolitan Statistical Areas, but less so at the level of states. Daly et al. (2001) reported a strong, positive relationship between the income inequality and homicide rates of the ten Canadian provinces, averaged across a period of 15 years, a relationship that persisted when controlling for provincial median household income levels. So this body of work suggests that the degree of contrast between economic classes—poverty amid affluence—is more strongly correlated with rates of crime than the proportion of the population in the poorest class. The limited Canadian research on this topic also supports this interpretation (Kennedy et al., 1991).

Evidence from self-report research seems to challenge this conclusion of a negative relationship between class and criminal behaviour. It was Short and Nye's (1957) use of the self-report measurement of delinquency that stimulated much of the later debate concerning the class and delinquency correlation, since they reported no relationship between self-reports of delinquency and parental socio-economic status. However, they did find a moderately strong relation between social class and incarceration in a training school. Fifty percent of the institutionalized boys studied came from the lowest socio-economic status category, compared to only 13 percent of the high school boys. But Hindelang et al. (1979) have shown how Short and Nye overestimated the strength of the relationship between official delinquency and socio-economic status, since the institutionalized boys did not constitute a representative sample. Tittle and Villemez's (1977) review of 26 studies using the self-report technique to investigate the class and crime relationship found that 50 percent reported no significant relationship.

Their own self-report study among adults showed social class to be largely unrelated to criminality, though this conclusion is limited by the fact that they inquired about only six criminal acts with a restricted range of seriousness. Tittle et al. (1978) examined 35 studies in which the relationship between a measure of individual class position and a measure of crime or delinquency was reported and found, on average, only a very slight, negative correlation (−.09). Moreover, this conclusion didn't appear to vary in the presence of different conditions such as type of offence, age, sex, or race, the specific indicator of socio-economic status used, and so forth. The two exceptions to this, however, were type of data (official or self-report) and the decade in which the study was conducted. Tittle et al. (1978) claim that studies using official data show a more marked negative correlation (average of −.25) than do those based on self-report data (−.06). They argue that the average correlation between class and crime or delinquency showed a steady decline in strength from the 1940s (−.73) to the 1970s (−.03), a trend they believe is largely the result of a decline in the relationship between class and official measures of crime, since the correlation for self-report measures remained relatively constant and low. However, others (Clelland and Carter, 1980) have pointed out that none of the 1970s research reviewed by Tittle et al. (1978) involved adults. In fact, prior to the 1970s, only six studies of adult crime and social class were included in their review. In any event, Tittle et al. interpret these findings as a reflection of changes in the way in which criminal justice agencies deal with members of the various social classes. Their interpretation implies that the true correlation between class and crime "has remained consistently near zero and has only appeared to be greater because official data reflected biases in the law enforcement process which have now been ameliorated" (1978, 652). Of course, any number of researchers have attempted to account for the apparent discrepancy between self-report versus official measures of delinquency in their relationship to socio-economic status by examining the hypothesis of official discrimination against lower-class adolescents in the enforcement of the law (see Nettler, 1984, for a review of many of these studies). However, once legally relevant factors such as seriousness of the offence and prior record of the suspect or accused are taken into account, the evidence for such class bias in law enforcement is weak and is, therefore, unlikely to substantially affect the official statistics.

Two more recent studies that used the self-report technique found a negative relationship between class and crime once certain refinements in measurement and analysis were introduced. Elliott and Ageton's (1980) research, which involved a national sample with a fairly large number of respondents and a self-report measure covering the full range of delinquent and criminal acts with a true measure of frequency, discovered class differences on an overall delinquency scale as well as for predatory crimes against persons, but not for other types of offences. Lower-class respondents reported close to four times as many predatory crimes against persons (for example, assault and robbery) as did middle-class respondents. But these differences were largely the result of the high-frequency offenders. Lower-class youth were found disproportionately among high-frequency offenders; they reported more than one and a half times as many offences overall as middle-class youth in the high-frequency category, and nearly three times as many predatory crimes against persons. So Elliott and Ageton seem to have demonstrated a behavioural basis for the class differences observed in the official data since the more frequent and serious offenders are more likely to be arrested and the class differences in self-reported delinquency are greater at the high end of the frequency continuum and for serious, predatory crimes.

In the second study, Farnworth et al. (1994) argued that criminological theories imply that it is the sustained experience of deprivation and poverty among the underclass that creates a greater risk of crime and delinquency. Furthermore, these authors claimed that most theories that incorporate class as an important predictor of delinquency are concerned with explaining a serious, frequent, and persistent pattern of offending. Therefore, measures of class and crime should be consistent with these theoretical concerns. In this study, the strongest and most consistent class–crime relationships were found between measures of continuing underclass membership and sustained involvement in street crimes.

These two studies, then, support the conclusion of a negative correlation between social class and crime under certain conditions, specifically for more serious offences and among more frequent and adult offenders, particularly those most disadvantaged educationally, racially (blacks), and in employment status.

There is comparatively little Canadian research on the class and crime relationship. The studies that do exist illustrate some of the same problems and apparently conflicting conclusions as discussed. Bell-Rowbotham and Boydell (1972) looked at the official data concerning the characteristics of persons convicted of indictable offences and found both educational and occupational status were related to such convictions. Those with no schooling had much higher rates of conviction for virtually all of the more serious offences, while those with some education beyond high school had the lowest rates, except for homicide. However, there were some crimes—fraud is an example (Giffen, 1965)—for which those with more education had the highest rates, probably as a result of the opportunities available to those with white-collar occupations. But to the extent that educational attainment can be taken as a measure of socio-economic status, these data generally support the negative correlation between class and crime. West (1984) has noted that a study by Byles in Toronto found that working-class juveniles were five times more likely to be arrested than middle-class juveniles and that about 90 percent of Ontario training school inmates were from working-class backgrounds. West goes on to argue that, although official delinquency is largely a working-class phenomenon, officially defined delinquents are not representative of all those who commit delinquencies.

Canadian self-report studies raise the same issues as the U.S. studies discussed. LeBlanc (1975) found no difference in the self-reported delinquency of adolescents from working-class areas compared to those from upper-class neighbourhoods, using a standard set of self-report delinquency items, even though adolescents from the working-class neighbourhoods were more likely to be officially labelled as delinquent by the police. Gomme's (1985) analysis of self-reported delinquency among younger adolescents (Grades 7 to 10) in a small urban centre in southern Ontario found no direct relationship between socio-economic status, measured by father's occupation, and participation in delinquent behaviour. But in a study in New Brunswick, Tribble (1972) concluded that the higher the status of the father's occupation, the lower was the probability that the son would be involved in delinquency. Furthermore, among the delinquents, the higher the status, the fewer the number of offences reported.

Several studies have reported an inverse relationship between level of family income and wife abuse in Canadian households (Lupri, 1989; Kennedy and Dutton, 1989; and Smith, 1990). But the results from a national study attributed this to the confounding effect of age: young men are more likely to be associated with both higher rates of severe abuse and low income (Lupri et al., 1994). However, a much larger study, Statistics Canada's Violence Against Women Survey, supported the view that domestic violence is greatest in the lower class (Johnson, 1996). The study found that men who were out of work committed assaults at twice the rate of men who were employed and that men who earned less than $15 000 per year assaulted their wives at twice the rate of men with higher incomes. Above this $15 000 level, there was no relationship between income and wife assault. This again suggests that the highest crime rates can be found at the very bottom of the economic ladder.

Reconciling the Apparent Conflicts

There are several methodological and substantive issues in the research on class and crime which, once understood, should help clarify and, one hopes, reconcile the apparently conflicting conclusions of different studies. First, most of these studies of the relationship between class and crime are not very representative of the population at large, and this severely limits the degree to which one can generalize from them. Almost all of this research has focused on juveniles rather than adults and, more specifically, on white male adolescents in small towns to medium-sized cities (Elliott and Ageton, 1980; Tittle et al., 1978). Poor adults in large cities—precisely those whom many criminologists would expect to have higher crime rates—have been very under-represented in the research on socio-economic status and crime (Clelland and Carter, 1980). Recent research by Hagan and McCarthy (1990) has suggested that the use of self-report surveys administered for convenience to school populations has diverted attention from street youth who experience current class conditions that are more likely to cause serious delinquency. Baron (1994) has shown that living on the street detaches youth from conventional society as they come to blame society for their predicament and immerses them in a lifestyle centred on drugs, alcohol, and criminal behaviour. Street youth develop the view that the legitimate labour market is closed to them and turn to crime since it pays them better than conventional jobs, provides structure to their day, brings excitement to their lives, and funds drug habits. Their illegal behaviour also offers them a sense of being in control of their lives, which the experience of unemployment and poverty tends to strip away. Baron interviewed 200 western Canadian street youth and found that they reported committing an average of 1673 crimes in a year, 72 percent of which were drug offences. Many of the remaining offences were serious crimes such as robbery, break and enter, and assault, showing that these lower-class youth represented a major source of crime in that community. Because these youth were not in school, their offences would not be represented in typical self-reported delinquency surveys.

Second, serious crime is a relatively rare event, so rare that the victimization surveys in the United States spend a large amount of money to draw a sample of the general population large enough to identify sufficient numbers of crime victims to make comparisons with the official data. The typically small sample sizes, restricted time frame, and crude measurement of frequency of crime commission in self-report studies make it extremely difficult to identify class differences in serious crime, given its low prevalence in the general or adolescent population (Hindelang et al., 1979).

Third, it is inappropriate to compare most self-reports with official data on crime since they only rarely refer to the same domain of conduct (Hindelang et al., 1979). The usual set of self-report items is weighted in favour of less serious acts, particularly those trivial acts for which middle-class adolescents report higher prevalence (Elliott and Ageton, 1980). So the typical self-report delinquency scale overlaps only in part with the crimes in official statistics, particularly those predatory, interpersonal crimes most often officially reported. Therefore, one should be cautious about generalizing from the failure to find class differences in the self-reports of the less serious forms of delinquency to *any* conclusion concerning predatory criminal acts by adults (Farnworth et al., 1994).

Fourth, it should be recognized that official statistics are limited and give only a partial picture of the class distribution of crime. In particular, official data are notorious for understating the frequency of certain crimes, some of which are characteristically committed with greater frequency by members of the middle class (for example, occupationally related theft) and representatives of the powerful segments of society (such as consumer fraud). So official statistics distort the true relationship between class and crime since the crimes of higher-status persons may be less visible (Nettler, 1984) and, therefore, less likely to come to the attention of the official agents of social control. And, of course, class position may also influence the likelihood of official intervention (Tittle and Villemez, 1977), particularly for those crimes more typically committed by those higher in status.

Criminologists have not paid sufficient attention to the many meanings and measures of class. Class position has most often been equated by criminologists with occupational status or prestige, at least for purposes of measurement. Class is thereby reduced to a handful of occupational categories, such as blue-collar, white-collar, or professional/managerial. These categories lump together some quite diverse positions in the labour market on questionable grounds, while at the same time excluding those not in the labour force, such as the unemployed.

Some criminologists have questioned these conventions (Clelland and Carter, 1980), and others have proposed alternative conceptualizations. For example, Quinney (1977) argues for the adoption of a Marxist orientation, with a focus on the relative surplus population of a capitalist economy as the locus for much of the conventional personal and property crime. Those most marginal to the labour market—rather than those in less skilled occupations, with less education or fewer financial resources—are, from this perspective, most at risk for turning to conventional, predatory crime. This is precisely the population segment typically ignored in criminological research on class and crime, partly because this segment is difficult for researchers to locate and survey (Clelland and Carter, 1980), and partly on account of the fuzzy thinking that has characterized much of the empirical research on this topic. Quinney also identifies a second category of crime in capitalist society: the crimes of domination. These include offences committed by members of the so-called ruling class, such as violations of human rights not currently defined as crimes, as well as illegal acts engaged in by government authorities and law enforcement officials. These crimes of domination most often go undetected and/or unpunished, and hence rarely appear in official statistics. Quinney and others argue that the negative correlation between class and crime found in such statistics applies only to the crimes of the underclass or marginalized segment of the population. So class position may be related to crime in something of a curvilinear fashion—high crime at both the bottom and the top of the class hierarchy—depending on how one defines and measures both class position and criminal behaviour. In fact, Tittle et al. (1978) have gone so far as to suggest that it is *only* at the extremes of the class hierarchy that class is a significant factor in crime in a mass society with a mass culture such as that found in North America. It's a bit paradoxical, then, that these same authors conclude their paper by stating that criminology should shift away from class-based theories. Rather, what seem to be required "are class-based theories which explain why certain types of crime are perpetrated almost disproportionately by the powerless, while other forms of crime are almost exclusively the prerogative of the powerful" (Braithwaite, 1981, 49).

REGION

UNCJIN (United Nations Crime and Justice Information Network)
www.uncjin.org

Criminal behaviour is correlated with geographic region. That is, crime rates are higher in certain nations of the world, regions within a country, communities, and urban neighbourhoods (Brantingham and Brantingham, 1984).

It is difficult to compare the crime rates of different countries. There are major differences in criminal codes, in police practices, in the willingness of citizens to report crime, and in record keeping that make most international comparisons meaningless. The only figures that can be compared with any degree of confidence are homicide statistics, and even these are not completely reliable for many countries. Table 5.2 shows the homicide rates for selected countries in 2000. Although Canada's homicide rate is generally three to four times lower than the U.S. rate, it is still higher than rates in many European countries, such as Switzerland and Italy (Fedorowycz, 2001). The highest rates of murder are generally found in the less economically developed countries. This conclusion is consistent with the pattern of high levels of violent crime in the less developed

TABLE 5.2 Homicide Rates for Selected Countries, 2000

Country	Homicide rate per 100 000
Russia	19.68
United States	5.50
Finland	2.80
Hungary	2.14
Sweden	2.00
Australia	1.80
France	1.78
Canada	**1.76**
England and Wales	1.37*
Italy	1.32
Switzerland	0.95
Japan	0.52
* estimated number	

Source: Statistics Canada. Adapted from the Statistics Canada publication, "Homicide in Canada—2000." *Juristat*, Catalogue 85-002, Vol. 21, No. 9, October 2001. Reproduced with permission of the Minister of Industry, 2003.

nations and high levels of property crime in the economically more developed nations evident in Interpol statistics for several decades. While a number of variables are no doubt involved in the explanation of this pattern, income inequality and economic opportunity seem particularly relevant. Countries with greater inequality in the distribution of income have higher homicide rates (Krahn et al., 1986), but economic development creates many more opportunities for property crime (Brantingham and Brantingham, 1984; Hartnagel, 1982).

Crime rates show a definite regional pattern within Canada, with the highest rates of both violent and property crime in the west (see Figure 5.5). Saskatchewan and Manitoba reported the highest violent crime rates in 2001, but all three territories had violent crime rates that were more than double these high rates. Quebec and Prince Edward Island continued to report the lowest violent crime rates. British Columbia continues to show the highest property crime rate (Savoie, 2002). These patterns persist, with only occasional exceptions, over time and for both violent and property crime (Lindsay, 1986). Victim survey data generally confirm the regional patterns found in the official statistics. The victimization rates for both household property crime and violent crime are highest in British Columbia and the Prairie provinces (Mihorean et al., 2001).

These regional differences have not received much research attention to date. Provincial differences in the age and sex composition of populations and degree of urbanization may contribute to these crime rate differences. Provinces with a higher proportion of young males and urban residents could be expected to have higher crime rates, but the evidence does not suggest that these variables are of major importance (Hartnagel, 1978; Giffen, 1965; 1976). Kennedy et al. (1991) attributed regional variation in homicide rates to differences in economic inequality and social disorganization. They found a convergence of murder rates among eastern, central, and western Canada in Census

FIGURE 5.5   Violent and Property Crime, Canada, Provinces, and
Territories, 2002

Source: Statistics Canada. Adapted from the Statistics Canada publication, "Crime Statistics in
Canada, 2002." *Juristat*, Catalogue 85-002, Vol. 23, No. 5. Reproduced with permission of the
Minister of Industry, 2003.

Metropolitan Areas where there were higher levels of inequality and disorganization. Provincial differences in crime rates are at least partly a function of differences in the amount of geographic mobility experienced in different
provinces (Hartnagel, 1997). Provinces with higher amounts of migration of
population from other provinces have higher rates of both violent and property
crime, controlling for urbanization, age composition, police per capita, and
percentage of the provincial population with low income.

    Crime rates also vary by community size: rates of many crimes are higher in
larger-sized communities than in smaller towns and rural areas. In 1995, rates for
larger cities were notably higher than those of smaller cities and towns for
attempted murder, robbery, breaking and entering, motor vehicle theft, and prostitution. However, smaller cities and towns had higher rates for such offences as
sexual assault, common assault, weapons and explosives offences, and impaired
driving (Leonard, 1997). The correlation between community size and crime is
stronger for property crime than violent crime (Hartnagel and Lee, 1990). Urban
residents continue to report higher rates of both personal and, in particular,
household victimization than do rural residents. Overall in 1999, 27 percent of

the urban population and 18 percent of the rural population reported being the victim of at least one crime in the preceding 12 months (Mihorean et al., 2001).

Research examining differences in crime rates by community size has a long history. However, several potential explanations for these differences can be summarized (Hartnagel and Lee, 1990). Social disorganization theory (see Chapter 13) proposes that urbanization—the increasing size, density, and heterogeneity of a community—leads to a weakening of community cohesiveness and normative consensus, thereby undermining informal mechanisms of social control and increasing crime (Wirth, 1938; Skogan, 1977). Economic deprivation arguments locate the causes of urban crime in poverty and/or the degree of inequality in the distribution of income (Braithwaite, 1979; Blau and Blau, 1982). Routine activities theory (see Chapter 14) (Cohen and Felson, 1979) suggests that features of urban locations, such as the density of potential targets, increased potential for social interaction, greater anonymity, and ease of transportation, are particularly conducive to crime. Finally, the demographic composition of cities may affect their crime rates. Since urban populations are disproportionately young and childless, behaviours such as crime to which they are especially at risk should be more evident in urban areas (Fischer, 1976). Hartnagel and Lee (1990) tested these arguments with data from 88 Canadian cities with a population of 25 000 and over. The results provided strong support for routine activities theory, although the authors qualify this conclusion by noting some of the study's limitations. Cities with a greater dispersal of work and leisure activities away from households offer more opportunities for direct contact, predatory crimes of violence, and crimes against property. The structure of urban opportunities for crime deserves further investigation as an explanation for differences in community crime rates.

Within urban centres, crime rates vary by neighbourhood (Brantingham and Brantingham, 1984; Bursik and Grasmick, 1993). Criminal areas where many criminals reside exist in most cities and persist for long time periods (Brantingham and Brantingham, 1984). These areas tend to be located adjacent to the central business district, although this can vary depending upon local land-use patterns (Shaw and McKay, 1969). The early research of Shaw and McKay (1942) in Chicago found these areas to be characterized by physical deterioration, low income, a heterogeneous population, high density, population mobility, and the presence of many renters in multiple-family dwellings. Later studies have generally replicated these findings (Kornhauser, 1978; Stark, 1987; Byrne and Sampson, 1986). There has been virtually no Canadian research on urban neighbourhoods and crime, although Jarvis and Messinger (1974) examined delinquency rates in the census tracts of London, Ontario. Their findings were consistent with the U.S. research. The 1985 survey of crime victims in Edmonton found that reports of violent victimization were twice as high for residents of the downtown area as for residents of suburban areas (Solicitor General Canada, 1987). However, reports of property crime victimization were not greatly different in the two areas (Solicitor General Canada, 1988).

Neighbourhood variation in crime rates has most often been interpreted from a social disorganization perspective. Neighbourhoods of low economic status, ethnic heterogeneity, and residential mobility experience a disruption of local social organization and informal control since residents have few stakes in the local area and experience difficulty in forming primary relationships and groups to solve common problems (Kornhauser, 1978). Although Shaw and McKay (1942) and early replications of their work did not directly test this model of social disorganization, more recent research has examined indicators of neighbourhood structure and control with generally favourable results (Sampson and Groves, 1989; Bursik and Grasmick, 1993). However, the neighbourhood distribution of criminal opportunities may also affect the distribution of criminal acts within cities (Bursik and Grasmick, 1993). For example, Sampson and Wooldredge (1987) discovered that high levels of target attractiveness were related to neighbourhood burglary rates, and individuals were most at risk of personal theft in areas with high levels of street activity. Ouimet (2000) tested the ability of the social disorganization and criminal opportunities perspectives to explain juvenile offender rates (where delinquents live) and juvenile crime rates (where crimes are committed) at both the census tract (495) and neighbourhood (84) levels of aggregation in the city of Montreal. Social disorganization variables predicted offender rates fairly well while opportunity variables were generally unimportant. On the other hand, opportunity variables helped explain juvenile crime rates, along with the social disorganization variables. More of the variation in both offender rates and crime rates was explained at the neighbourhood rather than the census tract level. As yet, however, there has been little investigation of the dynamics involved in the convergence of offenders and suitable targets at the neighbourhood level (Bursik and Grasmick, 1993).

SUMMARY

- Correlates of crime are those phenomena that are associated with, or related to, criminal behaviour. Among the most important correlates of crime are age, sex, race, social class, and region.

- Crime is strongly associated with age. After peaking in late adolescence/early adulthood, crime decreases with age.

- Sex is also strongly associated with crime. Males are much more likely to be involved in criminal behaviour than females, particularly for violent crimes and for serious property offences. However, in the past three decades, women have increased their involvement in both violent and property crime, although their highest rates continue to be found among the less serious property crimes.

- Canadian Aboriginal people are greatly over-represented in our criminal justice system. This is most evident when looking at the population of jails and prisons. Alcohol plays a major role in the crimes of Aboriginal people and, directly or indirectly, contributes to this over-representation. Both cultural and structural explanations have been given for the disproportionate involvement of Aboriginal people in crime, as has the possibility of biased enforcement of the law.

- The evidence on the relationship between social class and crime is conflicting. Some criminologists deny that there is such a relationship, while others conclude that there is at least a moderate negative correlation between these two variables. Recent research suggests that those at the very bottom of the social class ladder have higher rates of involvement in violent crimes and in property crimes such as break and enter and theft. Also, some types of corporate and white-collar crimes are disproportionately committed by those in the highest social class. For the majority of people between these two extremes, there is likely no correlation between crime and social class.

- Finally, crime varies by region. Violent crime rates are higher in less economically developed countries, while property crime is higher in more developed nations. Crime in Canada varies by region, with the highest rates occurring in the west and the north. Crime rates are also correlated with community size. Larger communities generally have higher crime rates, particularly for property crime. Neighbourhoods within cities differ in their rates of crime, with high-rate neighbourhoods tending to be located near the city centre. A combination of theories stressing economic inequality, social disorganization, and opportunities for crime has been used to explain these regional patterns.

QUESTIONS FOR CRITICAL THINKING

1. Define correlation, distinguish it from causation, and illustrate the difference with a criminological example.
2. Describe maturational reform, and discuss its application to the age distribution of criminal behaviour.
3. Summarize the trends in the sex differences in criminal behaviour, and discuss the concept of role convergence as applied to these trends.
4. Should data on the race of criminal offenders be routinely collected by criminal justice agencies in Canada?
5. Discuss and evaluate several possible explanations of Aboriginal over-representation in the Canadian criminal justice system.
6. Describe and evaluate the evidence concerning the relationship between social class and criminal behaviour.
7. Discuss how provincial variation in crime rates could be explained.

NET WORK

Statistics Canada provides a great deal of information about crime and its correlates over the Internet. To learn more about correlates of crime, first go to the Statistics Canada home page at **www.statcan.ca/start.html**. Click on "Canadian Statistics." Scroll down the page until you reach "The State." Then click on "Justice and Crime" and scroll down to "Victims, Accused, and Criminals." Using the data on the tables in this section, answer the following questions:

1. Has the ratio of youths to adults charged for Criminal Code offences changed over the past two years? If so, what is the nature of this change?
2. Now look at the rate of adults and youths charged for violent and property crimes. Have the rates of these crimes committed by adults and by youths changed over the past two years?
3. Now look at homicide accused. What is the five-year trend for male and female involvement in homicide? Do the same analysis for homicide victims.

KEY TERMS

correlate   over-representation
correlation   role convergence
cultural explanation   structural explanation
maturational reform

SUGGESTED READING

Boritch, Helen. (1997). *Fallen Women: Female Crime and Criminal Justice in Canada.* Toronto: ITP Nelson. A text reviewing the patterns and trends in female offending and victimization, as well as the theoretical perspectives on female criminality and the response of the criminal justice system to it.

Braithwaite, John. (1981). "The Myth of Social Class and Criminality Reconsidered." *American Sociological Review* 46:36–57. A comprehensive survey of the evidence concerning the relationship between social class and criminality, which concludes that the evidence for such a relationship is persuasive.

Farrington, David P. (1986). "Age and Crime." In Michael Tonry and Norval Morris (eds.), *Crime and Justice* (pp. 189–250). Chicago: University of Chicago Press. A detailed analysis of the age–crime relationship.

Hartnagel, Timothy F., and G.W. Lee. (1990). "Urban Crime in Canada." *Canadian Journal of Criminology* 32:591–606. A research article testing several alternative explanations of the variation in urban crime rates in Canada.

LaPrairie, Carol. (1996). *Examining Aboriginal Corrections in Canada.* Ottawa: Supply and Services Canada. A discussion and evaluation of the evidence concerning the disproportionate involvement of Aboriginal peoples in the Canadian justice system, with a review of policy options and recommendations for responding to this over-representation.

BIBLIOGRAPHY

Adler, F. (1975). *Sisters in Crime.* New York: McGraw-Hill.

Austin, R.L. (1993). "Recent Trends in Official Male and Female Crime Rates." *Journal of Criminal* Justice 21:447–66.

Baron, S.W. (1994). "Street Youth and Crime: The Role of Labour Market Experiences." Unpublished Ph.D. dissertation, Department of Sociology, University of Alberta.

Bell-Rowbotham, B., and C.L. Boydell. (1972). "Crime in Canada: A Distributional Analysis." In C.L. Boydell, C.F. Grindstaff, and P.C. Whitehead (eds.), *Deviant Behavior and Societal Reaction* (pp. 93–116). Toronto: Holt, Rinehart and Winston.

Besserer, S. and C. Trainor. (2000). "Criminal Victimization in Canada, 1999." *Juristat* 20(10):1–27.

Bienvenue, R.M., and A.H. Latif. (1974). "Arrests, Disposition and Recidivism: A Comparison of Indians and Whites." *Canadian Journal of Criminology and Corrections* 16(2):105–16.

Blackburn, C. (1993). "Aboriginal Justice Inquiries, Task Forces and Commissions: An Update." In *Royal Commission on Aboriginal Peoples, Aboriginal Peoples and the Justice System* (pp. 15–41). Ottawa: Minister of Supply and Services Canada.

Blau, J.R., and P.M. Blau. (1982). "The Cost of Inequality." *American Sociological Review* 47:114–29.

Bloch, H.A., and A. Niederhoffer. (1958). *The Gang*. New York: Philosophical Library.

Boldt, E.D., L.E. Hursh, S.D. Johnson, and K.W. Taylor. (1983). "Presentence Reports and the Incarceration of Natives." *Canadian Journal of Criminology* 25:269–76.

Boritch, H. (1997). *Fallen Women*. Toronto: ITP Nelson.

Boritch, H., and J. Hagan. (1990). "A Century of Crime in Toronto." *Criminology* 28:567–99.

Box, S. (1987). *Recession, Crime and Punishment*. London: Macmillan Education.

Box, S., and C. Hale. (1984). "Liberation/Emancipation, Economic Marginalization, or Less Chivalry." *Criminology* 22(4):473–97.

Braithwaite, J. (1979). *Inequality, Crime, and Public Policy*. London: Routledge.

———. (1981). "The Myth of Social Class and Criminality Reconsidered." *American Sociological Review* 46:36–57.

———. (1989). *Crime, Shame and Reintegration*. New York: Cambridge University Press.

Brantingham, P., and P. Brantingham. (1984). *Patterns in Crime*. New York: Macmillan.

Brody, H. (1971). *Indians on Skid Row*. Ottawa: Information Canada.

Bursik, R.J., and H.G. Grasmick. (1993). *Neighborhoods and Crime*. Toronto: Maxwell Macmillan.

Bureau of Justice Statistics. (1993). *Highlights from 20 Years of Surveying Crime Victims*. Washington, D.C.: U.S. Department of Justice.

Byrne, J.M., and R.J. Sampson (eds.). (1986). *The Social Ecology of Crime*. New York: Springer-Verlag.

Campbell, G. (1990). "Women and Crime." *Juristat* 10(20):1–14.

Canadian Centre for Justice Statistics. (1991). *Crime in Aboriginal Communities, Saskatchewan, 1989*. Ottawa: Statistics Canada.

Canadian Corrections Association. (1967). *Indians and the Law*. Ottawa: Canadian Corrections Association.

Carrington, P.J. (2001). "Population Aging and Crime in Canada, 2000–2041." *Canadian Journal of Criminology* 43:331–56.

Clelland, D., and T.J. Carter. (1980). "The New Myth of Class and Crime." *Criminology* 18(3):319–36.

Cohen, L.E., and M. Felson. (1979). "Social Change and Crime Rate Trends." *American Sociological Review* 44:588–608.

Cohen, L.E., and K.C. Land. (1987). "Age Structure and Crime." *American Sociological Review* 52:170–83.

Correctional Service of Canada. (1991). Patterns of Alcohol and Drug Use Among Federal Offenders as Assessed by the Computerized Lifestyle Screening Instrument. Ottawa: Correctional Service of Canada.

Daly, M., M. Wilson, and S. Vasdev. (2001). "Income Inequality and Homicide Rates in Canada and the United States." *Canadian Journal of Criminology* 43:219–236.

Demers, D.J. (1978). "Discretion, Disparity and the Parole Process." Unpublished Ph.D. dissertation, University of Alberta.

Doob, A.N., M.G. Grossman, and R.P. Auger. (1994). "Aboriginal Homicides in Ontario." *Canadian Journal of Criminology* 36(1):29–62.

Dumont, J. (1993). "Justice and Aboriginal People." In *Royal Commission on Aboriginal Peoples, Aboriginal Peoples and the Justice System* (pp. 42–85). Ottawa: Minister of Supply and Services Canada.

Elliott, D.S., and S. Ageton. (1980). "Reconciling Differences in Estimates of Delinquency." *American Sociological Review* 45(1):95–110.

Empey, L. (1982). *American Delinquency.* Homewood, Ill.: The Dorsey Press.

Fagan, J. (1990). "Intoxication and Aggression." In M. Tonry and J.Q. Wilson (eds.), *Drugs and Crime* (pp. 241–320). Chicago: University of Chicago Press.

Farnworth, M., T.P. Thornberry, M.D. Krohn, and A.J. Lizotte. (1994). "Measurement in the Study of Class and Delinquency." *Journal of Research in Crime and Delinquency* 31:32–61.

Fedorowycz, O. (2001). "Homicide in Canada—2000." *Juristat* 21(9):1–18.

Fischer, C.S. (1976). *The Urban Experience.* New York: Harcourt Brace Jovanovich.

Fisher, J. (1986). "Canadian Trends in Selected Female Crimes." Unpublished M.A. thesis, University of Alberta.

Fox, J., and T. Hartnagel. (1979). "Changing Social Roles and Female Crime in Canada." *Canadian Review of Sociology and Anthropology* 16(1):96–104.

Fréchette, M. (1983). "Delinquency and Delinquents." In R.R. Corrado et al. (eds.), *Current Issues in Juvenile Justice* (pp. 49–60). Toronto: Butterworths.

Frideres, J.S. (1988). *Native Peoples in Canada.* Scarborough: Prentice Hall.

Giffen, P.J. (1965). "Rates of Crime and Delinquency." In W.T. McGrath (ed.), *Crime and Its Treatment in Canada.* Toronto: Macmillan.

———. (1966). "The Revolving Door." *Canadian Review of Sociology and Anthropology* 3(3):154–66.

———. (1976). "Official Rates of Crime and Delinquency." In W.T. McGrath (ed.), *Crime and Its Treatment in Canada* (pp. 66–110). Toronto: Macmillan.

Gomme, I.M. (1985). "Predictors of Status and Criminal Offences among Male and Female Adolescents in an Ontario Community." *Canadian Journal of Criminology* 27(2):147–59.

Gomme, I.M., M.E. Morton, and W.G. West. (1984). "Rates, Types, and Patterns of Male and Female Delinquency in an Ontario Community." *Canadian Journal of Criminology* 26(3):313–23.

Gordon, R.A. (1976). "Prevalence: The Rare Datum in Delinquency Measurement and Its Implications for the Theory of Delinquency." In M.W. Klein (ed.), *The Juvenile Justice System* (pp. 201–84). Beverly Hills: Sage.

Greenaway, W.K. (1980). "Crime and Class: Unequal Before the Law." In J. Harp and J.R. Hofley (eds.), *Structured Inequality in Canada* (pp. 247–65). Scarborough: Prentice Hall.

Greenberg, D. (1979). "Delinquency and the Age Structure of Society." In S.L. Messinger and E. Bittner (eds.), *Criminology Review Yearbook* (pp. 586–620). Beverly Hills: Sage.

Griffiths, C.T., D.S. Wood, E. Zellerer, and J. Simon. (1994). *Aboriginal Policing in British Columbia.* Victoria: Ministry of Attorney General.

Hagan, J. (1974). "Criminal Justice and Native People." *Canadian Review of Sociology and Anthropology* Special Issue (August):220–36.

———. (1975a). "The Social and Legal Constitution of Criminal Justice." *Social Problems* 22(5):620–37.

———. (1975b). "Parameters of Criminal Prosecution." *Journal of Criminal Law and Criminology* 65(4):536–44.

———. (1975c). "Law, Order and Sentencing." *Sociometry* 38(2):374–84.

———. (1977). "Criminal Justice in Rural and Urban Communities." *Social Forces* 55(3):597–612.

———. (1985). *Modern Criminology: Crime, Criminal Behavior, and Its Control.* New York: McGraw-Hill.

Hagan, J., A.R. Gillis, and J. Simpson. (1985). "The Class Structure of Gender and Delinquency." *American Journal of Sociology* 90(6):1151–78.

Hagan, J., and B. McCarthy. (1990). "Streetlife and Delinquency." Paper presented to American Society of Criminology.

Hagan, J., J. Simpson, and A.R. Gillis. (1979). "The Sexual Stratification of Social Control." *British Journal of Sociology* 30:25–38.

Hartnagel, T.F. (1978). "The Effect of Age and Sex Compositions of Provincial Populations on Provincial Crime Rates." *Canadian Journal of Criminology* 20(1):28–33.

———. (1982). "Modernization, Female Social Roles, and Female Crime." *Sociological Quarterly* 23:477–90.

———. (1997). "Crime Among the Provinces: The Effect of Geographic Mobility." *Canadian Journal of Criminology* 39(4):387–402.

———. (1998). "Labour Market Problems and Crime in the Transition from School to Work." *Canadian Review of Sociology and Anthropology* 35(4):435–59.

Hartnagel, T.F., and G.W. Lee. (1990). "Urban Crime in Canada." *Canadian Journal of Criminology* 32:591–606.

Havemann, P., K. Couse, L. Foster, and R. Matonovich. (1985). *Law and Order for Canada's Indigenous People.* Regina: Prairie Justice Research, School of Human Justice, University of Regina.

Hendrick, D., and L. Farmer. (2002). "Adult Correctional Services in Canada, 2000/01." *Juristat* 22(10):1–24.

Hindelang, M.J., T. Hirschi, and J.G. Weis. (1979). "Correlates of Delinquency." *American Sociological Review* 44(6):995–1014.

Hirschi, T., and M. Gottfredson. (1983). "Age and the Explanation of Crime." *American Journal of Sociology* 89(3):552–84.

Hirschi, T., and H. Selvin. (1966). "False Criteria of Causality in Delinquency Research." *Social Problems* 13(3):254–68.

Hylton, J.H. (1982). "The Native Offender in Saskatchewan." *Canadian Journal of Criminology* 24(2):121–31.

Indian and Northern Affairs Canada. (1980). *Indian Conditions.* Ottawa: Minister of Indian Affairs and Northern Development.

Irvine, M.J. (1978). *The Native Inmate in Ontario.* Toronto: Ministry of Correctional Services, Province of Ontario.

James, J.T.L. (1979). "Toward a Cultural Understanding of the Native Offender." *Canadian Journal of Criminology* 21(4):453–62.

Jarvis, G.K., and H.B. Messinger. (1974). "Social and Economic Correlates of Juvenile Delinquency Rates." *Canadian Journal of Criminology and Corrections* 16:361–72.

Jensen, G.F., J.H. Stauss, and V.W. Harris. (1977). "Crime, Delinquency, and the American Indian." *Human Organization* 36(3):252–57.

———. (1986). *Women and Crime in Canada.* Ottawa: Solicitor General Canada.

Johnson, H. (1987). "Getting the Facts Straight." In E. Adelberg and C. Currie (eds.), *Too Few to Count* (pp. 23–46). Vancouver: Press Gang Publishers.

———. (1996). *Dangerous Domains: Violence Against Women in Canada.* Scarborough: Nelson Canada.

Johnston, P. (1994). "Academic Approaches to Race–Crime Statistics Do Not Justify Their Collection." *Canadian Journal of Criminology* 36:166–73.

Kennedy, L.W., and D.G. Dutton. (1989). "The Incidence of Wife Assault in Alberta." *Canadian Journal of Behavioural Science* 21(1):40–54.

Kennedy, L.W., R.A. Silverman, and D.R. Forde. (1991). "Homicide in Urban Canada." *Canadian Journal of Sociology* 16:397–410.

Kong, R. (1998). "Canadian Crime Statistics, 1997." *Juristat* 18(11):1–22.

Kornhauser, R. (1978). *Social Sources of Delinquency.* Chicago: University of Chicago Press.

Krahn, H., T.F. Hartnagel, and J.W. Gartrell. (1986). "Income Inequality and Homicide Rates." *Criminology* 24:269–95.

LaPrairie, C.P. (1983). "Native Juveniles in Court." In T. Fleming and L.A. Visano (eds.), *Deviant Designations* (pp. 337–50). Toronto: Butterworths.

———. (1990). "The Role of Sentencing in the Overrepresentation of Aboriginal People in Correctional Institutions." *Canadian Journal of Criminology* 32:429–40.

———. (1992). "Aboriginal Crime and Justice." *Canadian Journal of Criminology* 34:281–97.

———. (1995). *Seen But Not Heard: Native People in the Inner City.* Ottawa: Minister of Public Works and Government Services Canada.

———. (1996). *Examining Aboriginal Corrections in Canada.* Ottawa: Supply and Services Canada.

LeBlanc, M. (1975). "Upper Class vs. Working Class Delinquency." In R.A. Silverman and J.J. Teevan Jr., *Crime in Canadian Society* (pp. 102–18). Toronto: Butterworths.

———. (1983). "Delinquency as an Epiphenomenon of Adolescence." In R.R. Corrado et al. (eds.), *Current Issues in Juvenile Justice* (pp. 31–48). Toronto: Butterworths.

Leonard, T. (1997). "Crime in Major Metropolitan Areas, 1991–1995." *Juristat* 17(5):1–13.

Lester, D. (1999). *Crime and the Native American.* Springfield, Ill.: Charles Thomas.

Linden, R., and C. Fillmore. (1981). "A Comparative Study of Delinquency Involvement." *Canadian Review of Sociology and Anthropology* 18(3):343–61.

Lindsay, C. (1986). "Trends in the Crime Rate in Canada, 1970–1985." *Canadian Social Trends* (Autumn):33–38.

Loeber, R., and M. LeBlanc. (1990). "Toward a Developmental Criminology." In M. Tonry and N. Morris (eds.), *Crime and Justice*, Vol. 12. Chicago: University of Chicago Press.

Lupri, E. (1989). "Male Violence in the Home." *Canadian Social Trends* 14:19–31.

Lupri, E., E. Grandin, and M.B. Brinkerhoff. (1994). "Socioeconomic Status and Male Violence in the Canadian Home." *Canadian Journal of Sociology* 19(1):47–73.

"Manitoba Public Inquiry into the Administration of Justice and Aboriginal People." (1991). *Report of the Aboriginal Justice Inquiry of Manitoba.* Winnipeg: The Inquiry.

Merton, R. (1938). "Social Structure and Anomie." *American Sociological Review* 3:672–82.

Métis and Non-Status Indian Crime and Justice Commission. (1978). *Report.* Ottawa: Minister of Supply and Services.

Mihorean, K., S. Besserer, D. Hendrick, J.A. Brzozowski, C. Trainor, and S. Ogg. (2001). *A Profile of Criminal Victimization: Results of the 1999 General Social Survey.* Ottawa: Minister of Industry.

Monture-Angus, P.A. (1996). "Lessons in Decolonization." In D.A. Long and O.P. Dickason (eds.), *Visions of the Heart* (pp. 335–54). Toronto: Harcourt Brace and Company.

Mosher, J., and D. Jernigan. (2001). "Making the Link: A Public Health Approach to Preventing Alcohol-Related Violence and Crime." *Journal of Substance Use* 6:273–89.

Native Counselling Services of Alberta. (1982). "Native People and the Criminal Justice System." *Canadian Legal Aid Bulletin* 5(1):55–63.

Nettler, G. (1982). *Explaining Criminals.* Cincinnati: Anderson Publishing.

———. (1984). *Explaining Crime.* New York: McGraw-Hill.

Nielsen, M.O. (1992). "Introduction." In R.A. Silverman and M.O. Nielsen (eds.), *Aboriginal Peoples and Canadian Criminal Justice.* Toronto: Butterworths.

O'Brien, R.M. (1999). "Measuring the Convergence/Divergence of 'Serious Crime' Arrest Rates for Males and Females: 1960–1995." *Journal of Quantitative Criminology* 15:97–114.

Osgood, D.W., P.M. O'Malley, J.G. Backman, and L.D. Johnston. (1989). "Time Trends and Age Trends in Arrests and Self-Reported Illegal Behaviour." *Criminology* 27:389–417.

Ouimet, M. (2000). "Aggregation Bias in Ecological Research." *Canadian Journal of Criminology* 42:135–56.

———. (2002). "Explaining the American and Canadian Crime 'Drop' in the 1990s." *Canadian Journal of Criminology* 44:33–50.

Parker, R.N., and K. Auerhahn. (1998). "Alcohol, Drugs, and Violence." *Annual Review of Sociology* 24:291–311.

Pollak, O. (1950). *The Criminality of Women.* Philadelphia: University of Pennsylvania Press.

Quinney, R. (1977). *Class, State and Crime.* New York: David McKay Company.

Rand, A. (1987). "Transitional Life Events and Desistance from Delinquency and Crime." In M.E. Wolfgang and T.P. Thornberry (eds.), *From Boy to Man: From Delinquency to Crime* (pp. 134–62). Chicago: University of Chicago Press.

Reed, M., and J.V. Roberts. (1998). "Adult Correctional Services in Canada, 1996–97." *Juristat* 18(3):1–12.

Roberts, J. (1994). "Crime and Race Statistics: Toward a Canadian Solution." *Canadian Journal of Criminology* 36:175–85.

Roberts, J.V., and A.N. Doob. (1997). "Race, Ethnicity, and Criminal Justice in Canada." In M. Tonry (ed.), *Ethnicity, Crime, and Immigration* Vol. 21 (pp. 469–522). Chicago: University of Chicago Press.

Robinson, D., F.J. Porporino, W.A. Millson, S. Trevethan, and B. MacKillop. (1998). "A One-Day Snapshot of Inmates in Canada's Adult Correctional Facilities." *Juristat* 18(8):1–14.

Rowe, A.R., and C.R. Tittle. (1977). "Life Cycle Changes and Criminal Propensity." *The Sociological Quarterly* 18:223–36.

Royal Commission on Aboriginal Peoples. (1996). *Report of the Royal Commission on Aboriginal Peoples* Vol. 1, *Looking Forward, Looking Back.* Ottawa: Minister of Supply and Services Canada.

Sagi, P.C., and C.F. Wellford. (1968). "Age Composition and Patterns of Change in Criminal Statistics." *Journal of Criminal Law, Criminology and Police Science* 59:29–36.

Sampson, R.J., and W.B. Groves. (1989). "Community Structure and Crime." *American Journal of Sociology* 94:774–802.

Sampson, R.J., and J.H. Laub. (1990). "Crime and Deviance over the Life Course." *American Sociological Review* 55:609–27.

———. (1992). "Crime and Deviance in the Life Course." *Annual Review of Sociology* 18:63–84.

Sampson, R.J., and J. Wooldredge. (1987). "Linking the Micro- and Macro-Level Dimensions of Lifestyle-Routine Activity and Opportunity Models of Predatory Victimization." *Journal of Quantitative Criminology* 3:371–93.

Savoie, J. (2002). "Crime Statistics in Canada, 2001." *Juristat* 22 (6):1–22.

Shaw, C.R., and H.D. McKay. (1942). *Juvenile Delinquency and Urban Areas.* Chicago: University of Chicago Press.

———. (1969). *Juvenile Delinquency and Urban Areas,* 2nd ed. Chicago: University of Chicago Press.

Short, J.F., Jr., and F.I. Nye. (1957). "Reported Behavior as a Criterion of Deviant Behavior." *Social Problems* 5:207–13.

Silverman, R., and L. Kennedy. (1993). *Deadly Deeds.* Scarborough: Nelson Canada.

Simon, R.J. (1975). *Women and Crime.* Lexington, Mass.: D.C. Heath.

Skogan, W.G. (1977). "The Changing Distribution of Big-City Crime." *Urban Affairs Quarterly* 13:33–48.

Smart, C. (1976). *Women, Crime and Criminology.* London: Routledge and Kegan Paul.

Smith, D.A., and C.A. Visher. (1980). "Sex and Involvement in Deviance/Crime." *American Sociological Review* 45 (4):691–701.

Smith, M.D. (1990). "Sociodemographic Risk Factors in Wife Abuse." *Canadian Journal of Sociology* 15(1):39–58.

Solicitor General Canada. (1987). *Patterns in Violent Crime: Canadian Urban Victimization Survey,* Bulletin No. 8. Ottawa: Ministry of Solicitor General.

———. (1988). *Correctional Issues Affecting Native Peoples.* Ottawa: Solicitor General Canada.

Stack, S. (1984). "Income Inequality and Property Crime." *Criminology* 22:229–57.

Stark, R. (1987). "Deviant Places." *Criminology* 25:893–909.

Steffensmeier, D. (1978). "Crime and the Contemporary Woman." *Social Forces* 57(2):566–83.

———. (1980). "Sex Differences in Patterns of Adult Crime, 1965–77." *Social Forces* 58(4):1080–1108.

Steffensmeier, D., and E. Allan. (1995). "Criminal Behavior: Gender and Crime." In J.F. Sheley (ed.), *Criminology: A Contemporary Handbook,* 2nd ed. (pp. 83–113). Belmont, Calif.: Wadsworth.

Steffensmeier, D.F., E.A. Allan, M.D. Harer, and C. Streifel. (1989). "Age and the Distribution of Crime." *American Journal of Sociology* 94:803–31.

Steffensmeier, D.J., and M.D. Harer. (1991). "Did Crime Rise or Fall During the Regan Presidency?" *Journal of Research in Crime and Delinquency* 28:330–59.

Steffensmeier, D., and C. Streifel. (1992). "Time-series Analysis of the Female Percentage of Arrests for Property Crimes, 1960–1985." *Justice Quarterly* 9(1):77–103.

Steffensmeier, D., R.H. Steffensmeier, and A.S. Rosenthal. (1979). "Trends in Female Violence, 1960–1977." *Sociological Focus* 12(3):217–27.

Sutherland, E., and D. Cressey. (1978). *Criminology*. New York: J.P. Lippincott.

Tanner, J., and H. Krahn. (1991). "Part-Time Work and Deviance among High-School Seniors." *Canadian Journal of Sociology* 16:281–302.

Task Force on Aboriginal Peoples in Federal Corrections. (1989). *Final Report*. Ottawa: Minister of Supply and Services.

Task Force on the Criminal Justice System and Its Impact on the Indian and Métis People of Alberta. (1991). *Report of the Task Force on the Criminal Justice System and Its Impact on the Indian and Métis*. Edmonton: The Task Force.

Thomas, D. (1993). "The Foreign Born in the Federal Prison Population." Canadian Law and Society Association Conference, Ottawa, June 8.

Thomas, M. (2002). "Adult Criminal Court Statistics, 2000/01." *Juristat* 22(2):1–15.

Tittle, C.R., and W.J. Villemez. (1977). "Social Class and Criminality." *Social Forces* 56 (2):474–502.

Tittle, C.R., and D.A. Ward. (1993). "The Interaction of Age with the Correlates and Causes of Crime." *Journal of Quantitative Criminology* 9:3–53.

Tittle, C.R., W.J. Villemez, and D.A. Smith. (1978). "The Myth of Social Class and Criminality." *American Sociological Review* 43(5):643–56.

Tonry, M. (1995). *Malign Neglect: Race, Crime and Punishment in America*. New York: Oxford University Press.

Trasler, G. (1980). "Aspects of Causality, Culture, and Crime." Paper presented at the 4th International Seminar at the International Centre of Sociological, Penal and Penitentiary Research and Studies, Messina, Sicily.

Tremblay, S. (1999). "Illicit Drugs and Crime in Canada." *Juristat* 19(1):1–14.

Trevethan, S. (1993). *Police-Reported Aboriginal Crime in Calgary, Regina and Saskatoon*. Ottawa: Canadian Centre for Justice Statistics.

Tribble, S. (1972). "Socio-Economic Status and Self-Reported Juvenile Delinquency." *Canadian Journal of Criminology and Corrections* 14:409–15.

Verdun-Jones, S.N., and G.K. Muirhead. (1979/80). "Natives in the Canadian Criminal Justice System." *Crime and Justice* 7/8(1):3–21.

Vold, G.B., and T.J. Bernard. (1986). *Theoretical Criminology*. New York: Oxford University Press.

Wallace, M. (2003). "Crime Statistics in Canada, 2002." *Juristat* 23(5). Ottawa: Statistics Canada.

Warr, M. (1993). "Age, Peers, and Delinquency." *Criminology* 31:17–40.

Wellford, C.F. (1973). "Age Composition and the Increase in Recorded Crime." *Criminology* 11:61–70.

West, W.G. (1984). *Young Offenders and the State*. Toronto: Butterworths.

Wirth, L. (1938). "Urbanism as a Way of Life." *American Journal of Sociology* 44:3–24.

Wolff, L., and B. Reingold. (1994). "Drug Use and Crime." *Juristat* 14(6):1–19.

Wood, D.S., and C.T. Griffiths. (1996). "Patterns of Aboriginal Crime." In R.A. Silverman, J.J. Teevan, and V.F. Sacco (eds.), *Crime in Canadian Society*, 5th ed. (pp. 222–33). Toronto: Harcourt Brace and Company.

Wortley, S. (1999). "A Northern Taboo: Research on Race, Crime, and Criminal Justice in Canada." *Canadian Journal of Criminology* 41:261–74.

Wynne, D.F., and T.F. Hartnagel. (1975). "Race and Plea Negotiation." *Canadian Journal of Sociology* 1(2):147–55.

6

Feminism and Criminology

ELIZABETH COMACK
University of Manitoba

Like other academic disciplines, criminology has been a male-centred enterprise. Despite the use of generic terms such as "criminals," "defendants," and "delinquents," most of criminology has really been about what *men* do. As a consequence, women have been rendered invisible in much criminological inquiry. When women are looked at as offenders, their small numbers relative to men have typically been used to justify or rationalize this neglect. In 2001, for instance, females constituted only 17 percent of adults charged with Criminal Code offences in Canada (Statistics Canada, 2002). When women were looked at as victims, violence against them was traditionally not a major area of concern. Official statistics on crime indicated that offences such as rape were relatively infrequent, and victim surveys reported young males to be the group most at risk from crime. Perhaps even more significant is that even though the subject matter of criminology has been men, criminologists have done very little work on men *as* men. In short, they have neglected to consider the "maleness" of their subjects. Over the past three decades, there has been a growing awareness of the implications that these omissions hold for the discipline. This has come about largely through the feminist engagement with criminology: the efforts of feminist criminologists to move women—and an analysis of gender—from the periphery to the centre of criminological inquiry. The purpose of this chapter is to recount this history with a view to clarifying the kinds of issues and questions that are now commanding criminologists' attention.

LEARNING OBJECTIVES

After reading this chapter, you should be able to

- Explain the various theories that have been developed to understand women's involvement in crime.

- Understand the social, cultural, and legal factors that pertain to the issue of male violence against women.

- Appreciate some of the connections between a woman's law violations and her history of abuse.

- Evaluate the claim that women are "men's equals" in violence and some of the problems raised with the use of the Conflict Tactics Scale for researching violence between intimate partners.

THE INVISIBILITY OF WOMEN

The feminist engagement with criminology began over 30 years ago, when pioneers in the discipline, such as Marie-Andrée Bertrand (1967) and Frances Heidensohn (1968), first called attention to criminology's amnesia when it came to women. Heidensohn (1968, 171), for instance, described the analysis of women and crime as "lonely uncharted seas" and suggested that what was needed was a "crash programme of research which telescopes decades of comparable studies of males." In its initial phases, however, the feminist engagement with criminology consisted of a critique of the existing approaches to explaining crime. This critique took two paths. Initially, writers like Dorie Klein (1973) and Carol Smart (1976, 1977) focused attention on the **sexism** of the small body of theories that had been developed to explain women's crime. Other writers soon broadened the focus to include the invisibility of women in the mainstream theories within the discipline.

sexism
Attributing to women socially undesirable characteristics that are assumed to be intrinsic characteristics of that sex.

Theories of Women's Crime

The Conservative Approach

Historically, a particular pathway can be followed when tracing the initial attempts to explain women's criminality. It begins with the publication of Cesare Lombroso and William Ferrero's *The Female Offender* in 1895 and is followed by W.I. Thomas's *The Unadjusted Girl* in 1923, Sheldon and Eleanor Glueck's *500 Delinquent Women* in 1934, and Otto Pollak's *The Criminality of Women* in 1950. Each of these works reflects a **conservative approach** to understanding differences between men and women. Specifically, "difference" is rooted in biology. Women are viewed as "naturally" inferior to men, and it is this inferiority that is used to explain women's criminality.

conservative approach
An approach that understands "difference" between men and women as biologically based sex differences. Women are viewed as "naturally" inferior or unequal to men.

For example, in applying the concepts of atavism and social Darwinism (see Chapter 7, "Early Theories of Criminology"), Lombroso and Ferrero suggested that women possessed limited intelligence. They were also less sensitive to pain than men, full of revenge and jealousy, and naturally passive and conservative. Women's natural passivity, for instance, was caused by the "immobility of the ovule compared to the zoosperm" (Lombroso and Ferrero, 1895, 109). Atavistically, women were seen as displaying fewer signs of degeneration than men. The reason, according to Lombroso and Ferrero, was that women (and nonwhite males) had not advanced as far along the evolutionary continuum as (white) males and so could not degenerate as far. Given that women were relatively "primitive," the criminals among them would not be highly visible. However, those women who were criminal were cast as excessively vile and cruel in their crimes. They combined the qualities of the criminal male with the worst characteristics of the female: cunning, spite, and deceitfulness. Lacking the "maternal instinct" and "ladylike qualities," criminal women were seen as genetically more male than female.

First published in 1923, W.I. Thomas's (1967) work on female delinquency was premised on a similar kind of biological determinism. Thomas suggested that human behaviour was based on four "wishes": for adventure, security, response, and recognition. These wishes corresponded to features in the nervous system, which were expressed as biological instincts of anger, fear, love, and the will to gain status and power respectively. However, Thomas asserted that men's and women's instincts differed both in quantity and quality. Since women had more varieties of love in their nervous systems, their desire for response was greater than men's. According to Thomas, it was the need to feel loved that accounted for women's criminality, and especially prostitution.

Sheldon and Eleanor Glueck (1934) continued in this same tradition with *500 Delinquent Women*. The Gluecks described the women in their study as a "sorry lot. Burdened with feeblemindedness, psychopathic personality, and marked emotional instability, a large proportion of them found it difficult to survive by legitimate means" (299). The view of criminal women as "Other" is clearly evident in the Gluecks' work: "This swarm of defective, diseased, antisocial misfits . . . comprises the human material which a reformatory and a parole system are required by society to transform into wholesome, decent, law-abiding citizens! Is it not a miracle that a proportion of them were actually rehabilitated?" (303).

Otto Pollak's (1961) work attempted to account for what he described as the "masked" nature of women's crime. Sceptical of the official data on sex differences in crime, Pollak suggested that women's crime was vastly undercounted. He put forward the view that female criminality was more likely to be hidden and undetected. Women were more often the instigators than perpetrators of crime. Like Eve in the Garden of Eden, they manipulated men into committing offences. Women were also inherently deceptive and vengeful: they engaged in prostitution, blackmailed their lovers, as domestics they stole from their employers, and as homemakers they carried out horrendous acts on their families (like poisoning the sick and abusing children). According to Pollak, woman's devious nature was rooted in her physiology. While a man must achieve erection in order to perform the sex act, and hence will not be able to conceal orgasm, a woman can fake orgasm (10). This ability to conceal orgasm gave women practice at deception. Pollak also suggested that female crime was caused by the vengefulness, irritability, and depression women encountered as a result of their generative phases. For example, menstruation drove women to acts of revenge by reminding women of their inferior status (and their ultimate failure to become men) (see Box 6.1). The concealed nature of their crimes, the vulnerability of their victims, and their chivalrous treatment by men who could not bear to prosecute or punish them, all combined to "mask" women's offences. When these factors are taken into account, according to Pollak, women's crimes are equal in severity and number to those of men.

As Heidensohn (1985, 122) notes, these early approaches to explaining women's crime lent an aura of intellectual respectability to many of the old folk tales about women and their behaviours. They reflected the widely held assumptions about "women's nature," including the good girl/bad girl duality and a

BOX 6.1

FOCUS

The "Women Problem"

In the following passage, Otto Pollak offers us an illustration of a male-centred view of what has been traditionally referred to as the "woman problem" and its relationship to female criminality.

The student of female criminality cannot afford to overlook the generally known and recognized fact that [women's] generative phases are frequently accompanied by psychological disturbances which may upset the need satisfaction balance of the individual or weaken her internal inhibitions, and thus become causative factors in female crime. Particularly because of the social meaning attached to them in our culture, the generative phases of women are bound to present many stumbling blocks for the law-abiding behaviour of women. Menstruation with its appearance of injury must confirm feelings of guilt which individuals may have about sex activities which they have learned to consider as forbidden. As a symbol of womanhood, it must also, because of its recurrent nature, aggravate any feeling of irritation and protest which women may have regarding their sex in a society in which women have had, and still have, to submit to social inequality with men. In both instances, it must lead to a disturbance of the emotional balance of the individual and this becomes potentially crime-promoting. Pregnancy in a culture which frowns upon illegitimacy and fosters in large sectors of society limitation in the number of children or even childlessness must become a source of irritation, anxiety, and emotional upheaval in many instances. The menopause in a society which makes romance and emotional gratification the supreme value in a monogamous marriage system must be experienced, at least by married women, frequently as a threat to the basis of their emotional security if not to their general marital existence. In view of these cultural implications of the generative phases and their psychological consequences, it is difficult to understand why the existing literature contains so little discussion of their possible crime-promoting influence.

Source: Otto Pollak. (1961). *The Criminality of Women.* New York: A. S. Barnes, pp. 157–58. Originally published by University of Pennsylvania Press (Philadelphia) in 1950.

double standard that viewed sexual promiscuity as a sign of "amorality" in women but "normality" in men. Relying on "common-sense," anecdotal evidence, and circular reasoning—that is, "things are as they are because they are natural, and they are natural because that is the way things are" (Smart, 1976, 36)—the early theorists failed to call into question the structural features of their society and the gendered nature of the roles of men and women. Instead, sex (a biological difference) and gender (a cultural prescription) were equated as one and the same, with the "ladylike qualities" of the middle- and upper-class white woman used as the measuring rod for what was inherently female. In the process, the theories constructed were not only sexist, but classist and racist as well.

While we can look back on these early theories of women's crime with some amusement, it bears noting that the kinds of assumptions and beliefs reflected in them have not disappeared. As Klein (1973, 7) comments, "The road from Lombroso to the present is surprisingly straight." Throughout the 1960s, researchers continued to rely on the assumptions and premises of the earlier approaches (see, for example, Cowie, Cowie, and Slater, 1968; Konopka, 1966).

Following in the footsteps of Otto Pollak, a more contemporary version of this conservative approach to understanding difference between men and women links hormonal changes associated with women's menstrual cycles to their involvement in crime.

Premenstrual syndrome or PMS has been described as a condition of "irritability, indescribable tension" and a "desire to find relief by foolish and ill-considered actions" that is thought to occur during the preceding week or two prior to the onset of menstruation (Frank cited in Osborne, 1989, 168). There have been some 150 different symptoms (behavioural, psychological, and physiological) associated with PMS, and estimates of its incidence vary from 20 to 95 percent of the female population. There are no biomedical tests for determining the existence of PMS; it is the only "disease" not dependent on a specific type of symptom for its diagnosis. Nevertheless, premenstrual syndrome has been argued to be a cause of violent behaviour in women who suffer from it. It gained popularity as a cause of women's criminality in the 1980s, when PMS was introduced in two British court cases as a mitigating factor in homicide (Luckhaus, 1985).

While research linking PMS to women's criminality has been criticized for its methodological deficiencies (Morris, 1987), feminist criminologists have questioned the validity of framing explanations for women's criminality that isolate the source of the problem in women's bodies, thereby ignoring the cultural meanings (especially with regard to menstruation) and social contexts that are at play (Kendall, 1991; 1992). So long as women are pathologized as "sick" or "diseased," the broader structural factors that impinge upon women's lives—and are thereby implicated in their offending behaviours—will be ignored.

The Liberal Approach

liberal approach

Distinguishes sex (biological) from gender (cultural) and sees differences between men and women as resulting from gender roles and socialization patterns.

In the 1970s, theories of women's crime began to shift toward a more sociological orientation. Rather than focusing on biology, attention shifted to culture. In this **liberal approach**, differences between men and women are not necessarily innate or inborn, but are learned by individuals through the process of socialization. It is the culture that marks off the differences between men and women by proscribing certain roles and behaviours as "male appropriate" and "female appropriate." "Gender" was therefore separated from "sex" and made the key focus of inquiry. This liberal approach to understanding difference took the form of role theory as an explanation for female criminality. Dale Hoffman-Bustamante (1973), for example, suggested that the lower rate of delinquency of girls can be accounted for by differential socialization and child-rearing practices. Whereas boys are encouraged to be aggressive, outgoing, and ambitious and are allowed greater freedom, girls are taught to be passive and domesticated and are more closely supervised. Since girls are taught to be non-violent, they do not acquire the skills, technical ability, or physical strength to engage in violent acts such as gang fighting. When women do engage in violent behaviour, their actions reflect their greater domesticity. For example, women who murder are more likely to use kitchen knives than guns. The finding that women are more likely to be charged with shoplifting offences was similarly explained with reference to their gender roles and socialization. Women are traditionally the consumers in society and, when they steal, girls are more likely to take small items like make-up. Role theory, then, offered an explanation in terms of the differential gender socialization for both the types and nature of offences that females commit.

Another version of role theory was put forward by John Hagan and his colleagues (Hagan et al., 1979; 1987; Hagan et al., 1985) in the form of a power-control theory of sex and delinquency. Power-control theory is designed to explain the sex differences in delinquency by drawing linkages between the variations in parental control and the delinquent behaviour of boys and girls. More specifically, Hagan and his colleagues suggest that parental control and adolescents' subsequent attitudes toward risk-taking behaviour are affected by family class relations. They distinguish two ideal types of family: the *patriarchal family* in which the husband is employed in an authority position in the workforce and the wife is not employed outside the home, and the *egalitarian family* in which both husband and wife are employed in authority positions outside the home. Hagan and his colleagues suggest that in the former, a traditional gender division exists, whereby fathers and especially mothers are expected to control their daughters more than their sons. Given the presence of a "cult of domesticity," girls are socialized to focus their futures on domestic labour and consumption activities, while boys are prepared for their participation in production activities. In the latter form, parents redistribute their control efforts so that girls are subject to controls more like those imposed on boys. "In other words, in egalitarian families, as mothers gain power relative to husbands, daughters gain freedom relative to sons" (1987, 792). As such, the authors predict that these different family forms will produce differing levels of delinquency in girls: "patriarchal families will be characterized by large gender differences in common delinquent behaviours, while egalitarian families will be characterized by smaller gender differences in delinquency" (1987, 793).

Carol Smart (1976) has commented that role theory can offer only a partial explanation of women's crime. Because of a failure to situate the discussion of gender roles in broader structural terms, little attention is devoted to *why* socialization patterns are gender differentiated and *how* they have come to be that way. In the absence of a structural analysis, it is too easy to fall back on explanations that view such differences as biological, and not social, in their origins: "role is destiny" can therefore act as a ready substitute for "biology is destiny" (Morris, 1987, 64). While Hagan and his colleagues endeavour to place role theory in a broader structural context (by attending to the labour force participation of parents), they make an important assumption: if a woman is working for wages, there will be "equality" within the household. Their formulation does not pay enough attention to the nature of women's paid work and to other variables that might be in operation (such as how power and control may be exercised between males and females within the household).

In addition to engaging in critical evaluations of the specific theories that had been developed to explain women's involvement in crime, feminist criminologists drew attention to the invisibility of women in the mainstream approaches within the discipline.

The Mainstream Theories of Crime

Since the 1970s, mainstream approaches to explaining crime have come under increasing scrutiny. Writers such as Eileen Leonard (1982), Frances Heidensohn (1985), Allison Morris (1987), and Ngaire Naffine (1987) have highlighted the general failure of mainstream theories in criminology to adequately explain or account for women's involvement in crime; "mainstream" was, in effect, "malestream."

For example, in explaining crime in relation to the strain that results from the disjunction between culture goals (like monetary success) and institutionalized means (education, jobs), Robert Merton's anomie theory (see Chapter 10, "Strain Theories") reflected a sensitivity to the class inequalities that exist in society. The same could not be said, however, with regard to an awareness of gender inequalities. If lower-class individuals were more likely to engage in crime because of a lack of access to the institutionalized means for achieving monetary success, then it follows that women—who as a group experience a similar lack of access—should also be found to commit crime as a consequence of this strain. This is not the case.

Like strain theory, Edwin Sutherland's differential association theory is presented as a general theory of crime (see Chapter 12, "Interactionist Theories"). In focusing on the processes by which individuals learn definitions of the legal codes as either favourable or unfavourable, Sutherland posited the existence of a "cultural homogeneity" in society with regard to pro- and anti-criminal associations. While this cultural heterogeneity accounted for men's involvement in crime, women were the anomaly or exception in that they displayed a "cultural homogeneity." In Sutherland's view, women were more altruistic and compliant than men. As Naffine (1987) has noted, Sutherland missed a great opportunity when he neglected to explore this apparent cultural homogeneity in females. Given his critical outlook on the individualism and competition that he felt characterized American society, an examination of women's conformity could have provided Sutherland with clues to better understand crime and its causes.

Travis Hirschi's work on social control theory is also characterized by a neglect of the female (see Chapter 13, "Social Control Theory"). While other criminologists focused their attention on explaining deviance, Hirschi set out to explain conformity. In this regard, since women appear to be more conformist than men, it would have made sense to treat women as central to his analysis. Nevertheless, despite having collected data on female subjects, Hirschi set these data aside and—like his colleagues—concentrated on males.

With the advent of the labelling and conflict theories during the 1960s and 1970s, the potential for a more inclusive approach to crime increased. Yet, while Howard Becker's labelling perspective raised the question of "Whose side are we on?" and advocated an approach to deviance that gave a voice to those who were subject to the labelling process, it was never fully realized in the case of women. Similarly, Ian Taylor, Paul Walton, and Jock Young's *The New Criminology*

(1973), which offered up a devastating critique of the traditional criminological theories, failed to give any mention to women.

In general, when sex differentials in crime are considered by the mainstream theorists, the tendency has been to rely on stereotypical constructions of masculinity and femininity: men are aggressive, independent, daring, and adventurous; women are submissive, dependent, and compliant. In the process, female offenders are classed as a rather "dull lot." Even in their deviance, they are less interesting than men. Moreover, such stereotypical depictions of women have been considered "so obvious" that they require no further discussion (see, for example, Cohen, 1955, 142)—let alone theoretical or empirical concern.

We have seen in Chapter 5 that females commit less serious offences, in smaller numbers, and with less frequency than males. Criminologists have typically responded to these findings by formulating their theories to account for only male crime and delinquency. The ramifications of this tendency have been spelled out by Lorraine Gelsthorpe and Allison Morris:

> Theories are weak if they do not apply to half of the potential criminal population; women, after all, experience the same deprivations, family structures and so on that men do. Theories of crime should be able to take account of both men's and women's behaviour and to highlight those factors which operate differently on men and women. Whether or not a particular theory helps us to understand women's crime is of *fundamental*, not marginal importance for criminology. (Gelsthorpe and Morris, 1988, 103; emphasis added)

The Generalizability Problem

One issue raised by this critique of the mainstream theories is referred to by Kathleen Daly and Meda Chesney-Lind (1988) as the **generalizability problem**: can theories generated to explain male offending be modified to apply to women? Several criminologists responded to this problem by attempting to make the mainstream theories of crime "fit" women. Eileen Leonard (1982), for example, in a reformulation of Merton's strain theory, suggested that females may be socialized to aspire to different culture goals than males, in particular, relational ones concerning marriage and having children. If this is the case, then women's low rate of criminality would be explained by the relatively easy manner in which females can realize their goals. Nevertheless, as Morris (1987) notes, such a formulation relies on an idealized and romanticized version of women's lives. Not only does it display an insensitivity to the strains and frustrations associated with women's familial role, but it also fails to acknowledge the economic concerns that women confront. Such efforts to revise mainstream theories of crime to include women have been referred to as the "add women and stir" approach. Part of the difficulty with this endeavour is that women are presented as afterthoughts, not as integral to the arguments being developed (Gelsthorpe and Morris, 1988). A more significant problem with this effort is captured by Naffine (1997, 32): "The point of these exercises has been to adapt to the female case, theories of crime which purported to be gender-neutral but

generalizability problem

Raises the issue of whether mainstream theories of crime—which have largely been developed with men in mind—can be made to "fit" women.

were in fact always highly gender specific. Not surprisingly, the results have been varied and generally inconclusive."

The Gender-Ratio Problem

gender-ratio problem

Poses the question of why are there sex differences in rates of arrest and types of criminal activity between men and women.

A second issue raised by the feminist critique of mainstream criminology is one which Daly and Chesney-Lind (1988, 119) refer to as the **gender-ratio problem**. Why are women less likely than men to be involved in crime? What explains the sex difference in rates of arrest and in the variable types of criminal activity between men and women? Attention to the gender-ratio problem sparked a plethora of studies in the 1970s and 1980s on the processing of men and women by the criminal justice system (see, for example, Scutt, 1979; Kruttschnitt, 1980–81 and 1982; Steffensmeier and Kramer, 1982; Zingraff and Thomson, 1984; Daly, 1987 and 1989). The main question that guided much of this research stemmed from Pollak's assertion of the "chivalry" on the part of criminal justice officials: Are women treated more leniently than men? Like the generalizability problem, the results have been mixed. For instance, research that supports the chivalry hypothesis indicates that when it does exist, chivalry benefits some women more than others, in particular, the few white middle- or upper-class women who come into conflict with the law. It also appears to apply only to those female suspects who behave in a stereotypical fashion, that is, "crying, pleading for release for the sake of their children, claiming men have led them astray" (Rafter and Natalazia, 1981, 92). In this regard, Rafter and Natalazia have argued that chivalrous behaviour should be seen as a means of preserving women's subordinate position in society, not as a benign effort to treat women with some special kindness. Naffine (1997, 36), however, points to a larger problem with this research. By turning on the question of whether women were treated the same as or different than men, the chivalry thesis (and its rebuttal) took men to be the norm: "Men were thus granted the status of universal subjects, the population of people with whom the rest of the world (women) were compared."

The Women's Liberation Thesis

While research on the chivalry thesis drew the attention of criminologists in the 1970s and 1980s, another thesis was attracting considerable attention. The women's liberation thesis posits that women's involvement in crime will come to more closely resemble men's as differences between men and women are diminished by women's greater participation and equality in society. As reflected in the work of Rita Simon (1975) and Freda Adler (1975), the thesis suggests that changes in women's gender roles will be reflected in their rates of criminal involvement. Simon suggested that the increased employment opportunities that accompanied the women's movement would also bring an increase in opportunities to commit crime (such as embezzlement from employers). Adler linked the apparent increase in women's crime statistics to the influence of the women's movement and suggested that a "new female criminal" was emerging: women were becoming more violent and aggressive, just like their male counterparts.

Naffine (1997, 32) refers to the thesis that "women's liberation" causes crime in women as "perhaps the most time-consuming and fruitless exercise" in criminology. The numerous empirical difficulties with the thesis have already been discussed at some length in Chapter 5. For feminist criminologists, the main difficulty with the women's liberation thesis—similar to the chivalry thesis—was that it posed a question that took males to be the norm: were women becoming more "liberated" and thus more like men, even in their offending?

Given the difficulties encountered in the efforts to respond to the generalizability and gender-ratio problems, many feminist criminologists saw the need to "bracket" these issues for the time being in order to understand better the social worlds of women and girls (Daly and Chesney-Lind, 1988, 121). Maureen Cain (1990) took this suggestion further. She noted that while feminist criminologists needed to understand women's experiences, there were no tools in existing criminological theory with which to do this. Cain therefore advocated a "transgressive" approach, one that started from outside the boundaries of criminological discourse.

Criminalized Women

For many feminist criminologists, starting from outside criminology has meant resisting the temptation to fashion theories of women's involvement in crime that take crime categories (such as crimes against the person or crimes against property) as their starting point. As writers such as Carol Smart (1989), Danielle Laberge (1991), and Karlene Faith (1993) have pointed out, "crime" is not a homogenous category. There are notable differences between women in the nature and extent of both their criminal involvement and their contacts with the criminal justice system. As well, crime categories are legal constructions, the end result of a lengthy process of detection, apprehension, accusation, judgement, and conviction. They represent one way of ordering or making sense of social life. Crime categories are also premised on a dualism between "the criminal" and "the law-abiding," which reinforces the view of criminal women as "Other" and thereby misses the similarities that exist between women. In this respect, criminal women are in very many ways no different from the rest of us. They are mothers, daughters, sisters, girlfriends, and wives, and they share many of the experiences of women collectively in society. Since crime is the outcome of interactions between individuals and the criminal justice system, writers like Laberge (1991) have proposed that we think not in terms of "criminal women" but "criminalized women."

In these terms, women may commit a variety of crimes for a variety of reasons; there is no single or special theory for their criminality. As Pat Carlen (1985, 10) has emphasized, "The essential criminal woman does not exist." In contrast to the conservative and liberal approaches that have dominated criminologists' thinking about "difference" between men and women, a **feminist approach** understands "difference" as rooted in the structure of society. More specifically, the lives of criminalized women are located within a broader social context characterized by inequalities of class, race, and gender.

feminist approach
Understands "difference" between men and women as structurally produced by inequalities of class, race, and gender that condition and constrain women's lives.

With regard to their class location, criminalized women tend to be young, poor, undereducated, and unskilled. They are most likely to be involved in property crimes. Holly Johnson and Karen Rodgers (1993, 98) suggest that "women's participation in property offences is consistent with their traditional roles as consumers and, increasingly, as low income, semi-skilled, sole support providers for their families. In keeping with the rapid increase in female-headed households and the stresses associated with poverty, greater numbers of women are being charged with shoplifting, cheque forging and welfare fraud."

In contrast to the women's liberation thesis, feminist criminologists have suggested that increases in women's involvement in crime are more directly connected with the "feminization of poverty" than with women's emancipation. Indeed, several writers have called attention to how government cutbacks to social assistance have left increasing numbers of women and children at risk. In the province of Ontario, for example, social assistance payments were cut by 21.6 percent in 1995, "workfare" programs were implemented, and a zero-tolerance policy on welfare fraud was put in place. The feminization of poverty has been accompanied by the "criminalization of poverty." Next to homicide, individuals convicted of welfare fraud now have the greatest likelihood of receiving a sentence of incarceration. A 1997 study of 50 cases of welfare fraud convictions found that 80 percent were sentenced to time in prison (Martin, 1999). One individual caught up in this process was Kimberly Rogers (see Box 6.2).

Justice with Dignity—includes articles and information on the inquest on the death of Kimberly Rogers
http://dawn.thot.net/Kimberly_Rogers/

BOX 6.2

FOCUS

We've Learned Little from Kimberly Rogers' Death

By JoAnne Frenschkowski

It was sweltering hot this time last year when Kimberly Rogers, 40 years old and eight months pregnant, died in her Sudbury apartment. She was serving a six-month sentence of house arrest after pleading guilty to defrauding the Ontario Works program (she'd collected welfare while receiving student loans to cover her studies in the social services program at Cambrian College).

What have Canadians learned since she died? The B.C. government has actually reduced welfare benefits and tightened eligibility criteria; single-parents' cheques have been trimmed along with allowances for clothing and school supplies. Ontario has continued to ban other people convicted of fraud from collecting welfare benefits, and some of those bans are for life (three cases are being challenged in court). Could Kimberly Rogers' tragedy happen again? Yes.

Under the Ontario Works Act, student loans are considered income, despite the fact that the primary goal is to cover the cost of tuition and books, and are to be repaid. Never mind that Ms. Rogers had taken the initiative to change the direction of her life, had graduated near the top of her college class and had excellent prospects for moving into the workforce.

Her sentence was strict. She was only allowed to leave her house for three hours a week. A restitution order also required her to pay back the excess amount she had received. And she was placed on probation for 18 months.

Her guilty plea also triggered a newly enacted section of the Ontario Works Act, which banned her from receiving welfare for three months. This left her with no income—at a time when she was prohibited from leaving her house to work or look for work. Along with the ban on welfare benefits, she lost her drug card and could no longer afford the medications prescribed for her

(continued)

migraines, insomnia, anxiety and depression (the Elizabeth Fry Society was able to get the card reinstated).

Pregnant and desperate, Ms. Rogers found only a few charities willing to help. Had she gone to jail, she and her unborn child would have at least had the necessities of life.

On May 31, 2001, as a part of a constitutional challenge, a judge temporarily lifted the ban, reasoning that the act of forcing a pregnant woman into destitution would harm both Ms. Rogers and the public at large. Ms. Rogers began to receive benefits again. But because she had to repay welfare, her debt was deducted off each monthly cheque, reducing $520 to $468. Her rent cost $450 a month, leaving $18 a month for food and other expenses.

A year ago she was found dead in her apartment.

What has society learned?

Ontario's welfare rates remain as low as they have been since they were cut by 21.6 per cent in 1995 (there hasn't even been a cost of living adjustment). A single person still receives a maximum of $520 per month.

Just months before Kimberly's death, Ontario introduced further amendments to its social assistance laws. Now, for anyone convicted of welfare fraud committed after April 2000, there is a lifetime ban. Those convicted can never receive welfare again. Ever. Not even if they need it to survive. The fiscal savings that result from clamping down on welfare remain a greater political priority to government than the lives of citizens who are left without shelter and food.

And the Ontario government is still crowing about the success of "workfare" in helping welfare recipients return to work. But the reality is different: Instead of integrating people into the new, knowledge-based economy, workfare is geared toward pushing people into low-paying, insecure jobs.

Still, some things have changed.

Opposition to the province's treatment of welfare recipients is growing. To date, 10 Ontario municipalities have passed resolutions to oppose the lifetime ban. Recently, the Court of Appeal determined that the province can't discriminate against welfare recipients simply because they are welfare recipients and dependent on government programs for support—in other words, a government does not have carte blanche to impose stricter conditions on welfare recipients than any other citizen. And later this year the Ontario Superior Court will consider the cases of three people who are appealing their lifetime welfare-benefit bans.

What the government did to Kimberly Rogers, it did in the name of Ontario's citizens. So her case forces all citizens to think about what kind of society we want. One that truly gives us all opportunities to participate in all aspects of society? Or one that condemns the most vulnerable to die alone? We cannot ignore these questions even if we wish to: An inquest into Kimberly Rogers's death is set to begin Oct. 7.

Source: JoAnne Frenschkowski. (August 9, 2002). "We've Learned Little from Kimberly Rogers's Death," *The Globe and Mail.* Reprinted by permission of the author.

Locating women's involvement in crime in its broader social context also involves attending to racial inequality. Aboriginal people in Canada are disproportionately represented in crime statistics, but the over-representation of Aboriginal women in Canadian prisons is even greater than that of Aboriginal men. Aboriginal women are incarcerated for more violent crimes than non-Aboriginal women. And alcohol has played a role in the offences of twice as many Aboriginal women in prison than Aboriginal men (La Prairie, 1993; Comack, 1996). The historical forces that have shaped Aboriginal communities—the processes of colonization, of economic and political marginalization, and of forced dependency on the state—have culminated in a situation where violence and drugging and drinking have reached epidemic proportions in many Aboriginal centres. As Patricia Monture Angus (1999, 27) has noted, "Aboriginal people do not belong to communities that are functional and healthy (and colonialism is significantly responsible for this fact)."

Attention to gender inequality—and its interconnections with race and class—assists in explaining prostitution or sex trade work (Brock, 1998). According to Johnson and Rodgers, women's involvement in prostitution is a reflection of their subordinate social and economic position in society: "Prostitution thrives in a society which values women more for their sexuality than for their skilled labour, and which puts women in a class of commodity to be bought and sold. Research has shown one of the major causes of prostitution to be the economic plight of women, particularly young, poorly educated women who have limited *legitimate* employment records" (Johnson and Rodgers, 1993, 101, emphasis in original).

The structured inequalities in society that contour and constrain the lives of criminalized women provide an important backdrop for understanding their involvement in crime. As Carlen (1988, 14) notes, women set about making their lives within conditions that have certainly not been of their own choosing. Indeed, in their efforts to transgress criminology, feminist criminologists have become increasingly aware that to understand women's lives we must bring into view women's experiences of violence at the hands of men. This violence needs to be understood as a manifestation of **patriarchy** or the systemic and individual power that men exercise over women (Brownmiller, 1975; Kelly, 1988).

patriarchy

A system of male domination that includes both a structure and an ideology that privileges men over women. For example, men exercise control over women both overtly by objectifying women's bodies in pornography and covertly in the form of a "monogamous heterosexuality" that legitimates male control over women and children and reinforces the ideology that women are dependent on men for both their economic and sexual needs.

cultural construction

A perspective on a subject that is shaped by cultural assumptions rather than having a natural or objective basis. For example, concepts of "masculine" and "feminine" suggest how men and women should behave, but very few of these gender differences are determined by biological sex.

VIOLENCE AGAINST WOMEN

At the same time that feminist criminologists were criticizing criminology for its neglect of women, feminists in the women's movement were raising the issue of male violence against women. This is an issue that historically has not been a matter of societal, legal, or academic concern.

The Cultural Construction of Rape

With regard to the lack of societal concern about male violence against women, feminists questioned the kinds of assumptions and beliefs that have dominated the public's understanding of sexual violence. The **cultural construction** of rape, for example, was riddled with certain myths or misconceptions about the nature of the act itself, and with stereotypical images of "true" rape victims and offenders. These myths and stereotypes—and their limitations—include the following:

■ *Women "ask for it" by their dress or their behaviour.* The absurdity of this claim is revealed when we apply the same logic to victims of robbery (see Box 6.3).

■ *Rape is a sexual act brought on by a man's uncontrollable sexual urges that cannot be halted once a woman has "turned him on."* Such a view not only

FOCUS

BOX 6.3

Was He Asking for It?

In 1975, Harper's Weekly *carried the following response to an American Bar Association finding that few rapists are punished for their crime. The article asks us to imagine a robbery victim undergoing the same sort of cross-examination that a rape victim does.*

"Mr. Smith, you were held up at gunpoint on the corner of First and Main?"

"Yes."

"Did you struggle with the robber?"

"No."

"Why not?"

"He was armed."

"Then you made a conscious decision to comply with his demands rather than resist?"

"Yes."

"Did you scream? Cry out?"

"No. I was afraid."

"I see. Have you ever been held up before?"

"No."

"Have you ever given money away?"

"Yes, of course."

"And you did so willingly?"

"What are you getting at?"

"Well, let's put it like this, Mr. Smith. You've given money away in the past. In fact, you have quite the reputation for philanthropy. How can we be sure you weren't contriving to have your money taken by force?"

"Listen, if I wanted—"

"Never mind. What time did this holdup take place?"

"About 11 p.m."

"You were out in the street at 11 p.m.? Doing what?"

"Just walking."

"Just walking? You know it's dangerous being out on the street that late at night. Weren't you aware that you could have been held up?"

"I hadn't thought about it."

"What were you wearing?"

"Let's see—a suit. Yes, a suit."

"An expensive suit?"

"Well—yes. I'm a successful lawyer, you know."

"In other words, Mr. Smith, you were walking around the streets late at night in a suit that practically advertised the fact that you might be a good target for some easy money, isn't that so? I mean, if we didn't know better, Mr. Smith, we might even think that you were asking for this to happen, mightn't we?"

Source: Harper's Weekly. (1975).

depicts male sexuality in a distorted way, it ignores the element of physical coercion and the effects of fear and threats on the victim.

- *When women say no they really mean yes.* This belief suggests that women are expected to be coy and flirtatious, and men are encouraged *not* to take no for an answer. In these terms, it legitimates the act of rape.

- *If a woman has had sexual relations in the past, she will less credible when she says she didn't consent to sex.* This myth suggests that "bad girls" or "loose women" deserve to be raped.

- *Women cannot be trusted.* For instance, they will make false accusations against innocent men. Casting all women as inherently untrustworthy acts to silence victims and exonerate rapists.

- *The act of rape really has little long-term impact on the victim.* So long as the harm of rape is denied, society can continue to ignore the issue and its effects on women's lives.

- *Men who commit "real" rape are an "abnormal" group in society.* Attributing rape to the actions of a small, disturbed minority in society effectively lets men as a group off the hook. Rape is thus cast as an isolated problem for psychologists and psychiatrists to deal with or is narrowly defined as a "women's issue"—not an issue that *all* of us need to confront.

Clearly, the more prevalent such myths and stereotypes about sexual violence are in society, the more far-reaching will be their consequences. For offenders, they can translate into less chance of detection, higher acquittal rates, and lighter sentences. Studies show, for example, that most rapists do not even believe that they have done anything wrong (Clark and Lewis, 1977; Scully and Marolla, 1985; Messerschmidt, 1986). For victims, rape myths can mean a "double victimization." Victims not only endure the humiliation and degradation inherent in the act itself, but may experience further humiliation if they choose to report the case to the authorities. Also, since cultural beliefs suggest that rape is the woman's fault, victims may feel responsible for their own victimization. For women generally, the cultural construction of rape can produce feelings of fear and vulnerability that impose restrictions on their daily activities. One study, for example, reported that 24 percent of women (compared with only 3 percent of men) stay at home at night because they are afraid to go out alone (Johnson, 1996).

The Law's Role in Condoning Male Violence Against Women

Recognition of the pervasiveness of these myths and stereotypes led to a questioning of the role that law has played in condoning male violence against women. Feminists noted, for example, that women have historically been viewed as the "property" of men. The law upheld this view by granting husbands certain legal rights, in particular, the "right to consortium" and the "right to chastise" their wives.

Consortium generally refers to the companionship, affection, and assistance that one spouse in a marriage is entitled to receive from the other. According only husbands the right to consortium meant that wives had a legal obligation with respect to the "consummation of marriage, cohabitation, maintenance of conjugal rights, sexual fidelity, and general obedience and respect for his wishes" (Dobash and Dobash, 1979, 60). The husband's right to consortium was reflected in Canadian law until 1983. Under the old rape law, a rape was defined to have occurred when "[a] male person has sexual intercourse with a female person *who is not his wife*, (a) without her consent, or (b) with her consent if the consent (i) is extorted by threats or fear of bodily harm, (ii) is obtained by impersonating her husband, or (iii) is obtained by false and fraudulent representations as to the nature and quality of the act" (s. 143, emphasis added). It made no sense, under law's logic, to prevent men from "consorting" with their own property; wives did not have the legal right to say no.

In addition to granting a husband's immunity from rape charges, the rape law also reinforced the cultural construction of rape. For instance, reflecting the belief that "women cannot be trusted" when they claim they have been raped, the legislation included a corroboration requirement, whereby the accused could not be found guilty in the absence of corroborating evidence (such as cuts and bruises) that would support the testimony of the victim. As well, under the doctrine of recent complaint, it was assumed that a victim who complained at the first reasonable opportunity was more credible or believable than one who complained some time after the rape had taken place. Because the key element in establishing the guilt of the accused in rape cases was consent, the focus of the trial rested on the credibility of the victim. Her moral character came under the scrutiny of the court in the attempt to determine whether she could be believed when she said she did not consent. Defence lawyers were permitted to ask questions about the past sexual history of the victim, reinforcing the belief that women who have had sexual relations in the past are "less credible" when they say they didn't consent to sex.

With regard to the right to chastise, law historically has given a husband the authority to use force in order to ensure that his wife fulfilled her obligations. The only restraint law placed upon a husband was that he did so in a moderate manner. As English jurist Sir William Blackstone explained in 1765, since the husband was obliged under law to answer for his wife's misbehaviour (as she was his property), "the law thought it reasonable to intrust him with his power of restraining her, by domestic chastisement, in the same moderation that a man is allowed to correct his apprentices and children, for whom the master or parent is also liable in some cases to answer" (Blackstone cited in Dobash and Dobash, 1979, 61). When husbands went too far, and their wives died as a result, the British courts were inclined to leniency. On the other hand, if a wife killed her husband, it was considered a "species of treason" akin to killing the king, as she was going against his authority (Edwards, 1985). Law, in essence, reflected and reinforced patriarchal relations between men and women. This view continued to inform legal practice into the latter part of the 20th century. Because police officers were inclined to view violence in the home between intimate partners as a "private trouble" that was not the law's business, they were reluctant to intervene or to define the situation as a criminal matter.

Criminology's Complicity

Within criminology, male violence against women was similarly not seen as a social problem. Official statistics suggested that crimes like rape were relatively infrequent in their occurrence. Victim surveys—which asked respondents whether they had been victimized by crime—indicated that the group most at risk of victimization was young males, and not women. When criminologists' attention did turn to crimes like rape, the focus was on the small group of men who had been convicted and incarcerated for the offence, and these men were typically understood as an abnormal and pathological group. Much of traditional criminology, then, tended to mirror the cultural construction of rape. In his "classic" study of rape, for example, Menachem Amir (1971) introduced the notion of "victim precipitation." The concept suggests that some women are "rape prone" or invite rape, and Amir's work essentially blamed the victim for the violence she encountered.

Canadian Association of Sexual
Assault Centres
www.casac.ca

Breaking the Silence

In combination, the absence of societal, legal, and academic concern about the issue of male violence against women had the effect of silencing women. One of the main goals of the women's movement, as it gained momentum in the 1970s, was to break this silence. As women came together to share their stories, and with increasing efforts devoted to providing support and services to women (such as rape crisis centres, crisis lines, and shelters for abused women), it soon became evident that the incidence of sexual violence far exceeded what was reported in the official crime statistics. In 1980, for example, the Canadian Advisory Council on the Status of Women (CACSW) estimated that one in every five Canadian women will be sexually assaulted at some point in her life, and one in every seventeen will be the victim of forced sexual intercourse. Yet only one in ten sexual assaults was ever reported to the police (Kinnon, 1981). A year later, the CACSW released its report, *Wife Battering in Canada: The Vicious Circle*. Linda MacLeod (1980), the author of the report, estimated that every year, one in ten Canadian women who is married or in a relationship with a live-in lover is battered. Yet when this finding was reported in the House of Commons (on May 12, 1982), it was met with laughter from Members of Parliament. Public outrage ensued and, over the next decade, wife abuse was gradually transformed from a "private trouble" into a "public issue."

The growing awareness of male violence against women led to pressures for legislative reform. Two major changes occurred in 1983. First, the old rape law was repealed and three new categories were added to the offence of assault: sexual assault (s.246.1); sexual assault with a weapon, threats to a third party, and bodily harm (s. 246.2); and aggravated sexual assault (s. 246.3). Under this new legislation, husbands could now be charged with sexually assaulting their wives, limitations were placed on the ability of the defence to ask questions about the past sexual history of the victim, the corroboration requirement was dropped, the doctrine of recent complaint was formally removed, and there was provision for a publication ban on any disclosure of the identity of the complainant. These changes were designed to redress the apparent gender inequities in the law and to reduce the trauma experienced by the victim during the trial in an attempt to encourage the reporting of cases. Second, a national directive was issued to encourage police to lay charges in wife assault cases (previously, the decision was left to the wishes of the complainant) and police training was upgraded to stress sensitive interventions in cases of wife assault. These reforms led to increases in the number of charges for domestic assaults. In Winnipeg, for instance, there were 629 domestic assault charges laid in 1983; by 1989, the number had increased to 1137 charges laid (Ursel, 1994).

The Montreal Massacre

The reality of violence against women was made most evident on December 6, 1989, when a gunman entered a classroom at the École Polytechnique in Montreal, separated the men from the women students, proclaimed, "You're all a bunch of feminists," and proceeded to gun them down. Fourteen women were killed that day and thirteen others wounded. The gunman's suicide letter explicitly identified his action as politically motivated: he blamed "feminists" for the major disappointments in his life. Police also found a "hit list" containing the names of prominent women (see Box 6.4). The Montreal Massacre served to reinforce what women's groups across the country had been arguing for decades: that violence against women is a widespread and pervasive feature of our society. It takes many forms, including sexual harassment in the workplace, date rape, violent sexual assaults, incest, and wife abuse.

While the murder of 14 women in Montreal has understandably received the attention it deserves, it is also noteworthy that the violence that women encounter at the hands of men has become "routine." In 1993, Statistics Canada released the findings of the Violence Against Women Survey (VAWS). The first national survey of its kind anywhere in the world, the VAWS included responses from 12 300 women (see Johnson, 1996). Using definitions of physical and

BOX 6.4

FOCUS

A Time for Grief and Pain

Montreal

Fourteen women are dead for one reason: they are women. Their male classmates are still alive for one reason: they are men. While gender divides us in thousands of ways every day, rarely are the consequences of misogyny so tragic.

I found out about the murders early yesterday morning. I came home from dinner with friends about 1 a.m., and listened as usual to my answering machine. It was the last message that gave me a jolt. It was a good friend telling me that there would be a vigil last night for the 14 women who had been killed at the University of Montreal.

Not believing my ears and desperate for news, I turned on the radio. I ended up listening to an open-line show. The talk was about relationships between young men and women these days.

Most of the callers were men. They blamed the murders on everything from drugs and condom distributors in high schools to women who have made men feel insecure. Many callers said they did not understand what had happened. It's all very well and fine to be misogynous, said one caller, but you can't lose your head.

I realized, as I was listening to this show, that I was trembling. So were the voices of the female callers. I felt something I had not experienced in a long time: fear of being alone in my apartment.

There were sounds at the window I would normally ignore. Now I could not. Immobilized, I was afraid to stay alone and afraid to go out.

It does not matter that the man who decided to kill 14 women—and he clearly did decide to do that—killed himself afterward; it is not of him I am afraid. I am afraid of what he represents, of all the unspoken hatred, the pent-up anger that he expressed. Hatred and anger that is shared by every husband who beats his wife, every man who rapes his date, every father who abuses his child, and by many more who would not dare.

It happened at the École Polytechnique in Montreal but it could have been anywhere.

It would be a great mistake, I think, to see this incident as some kind of freak accident, the act of a madman that has nothing to do with the society in which we live. The killer was angry at women, at feminism, at his own loss of power. He yelled: "You're all a bunch of feminists" on his way to killing 14 women.

Now there is little that is comforting to say to women. It is a time for grief for all of us; grief for those who have died, and pain at being reminded of how deep misogyny still runs in our society.

Source: Diana Bronson. "A Time for Grief and Pain." *The Globe and Mail* (8 December 1989), A7. Reprinted with permission of the author.

sexual assault consistent with the Canadian Criminal Code, the survey found that one-half (51 percent) of Canadian women have experienced at least one incident of physical or sexual violence since the age of 16. The survey also confirmed the results of other research in finding that women face the greatest risk of violence from men they know. "Almost one-half (45%) of all women experienced violence by men known to them (dates, boyfriends, marital partners, friends, family, neighbours, etc.), while 23% of women experienced violence by a stranger (17% reported violence by both strangers and known men)" (Statistics Canada, 1993, 2). The VAWS also found that 29 percent (or 3 in 10) of ever-married women had been assaulted by a spouse. Findings such as these confirm that male violence against women continues to be a serious social problem in Canadian society. They also raise concerns about the effectiveness of the criminal justice system in responding to this pressing problem.

Recent Developments in Law's Response to Violence against Women

As the 1990s unfolded, many feminists became uncertain as to whether engaging with the criminal justice system to combat male violence against women was having the desired outcome. With respect to sexual assault, it appeared that the myths and stereotypes surrounding rape were continuing to invade the practice of law. Some judges, for instance, were making statements in court that suggested their decisions were being influenced by these myths. In a British Columbia case heard in 1991, the judge made the following statement in his written decision: "The mating practice, if I may call it that, is less than a precise relationship. At times no may mean maybe, or wait awhile" (*Letendre* cited in Boyle, 1994, 141). In June of 1998, an Alberta Court of Appeal judge upheld a lower court's acquittal of a man charged with sexually assaulting a 17-year-old girl. In his decision, the judge commented on the clothing worn by the young woman (a T-shirt and shorts), noting, "It must be pointed out that the complainant did not present herself to [the accused] in a bonnet and crinolines" (Laghi, 1998). Several decisions by the Supreme Court of Canada also raised concerns over the law's treatment of sexual assault cases.

In a 1991 ruling on the cases of *Seaboyer* and *Gayme*, the Supreme Court struck down section 276 of the Criminal Code. Known as the "rape shield" provision, section 276 was included in the 1983 sexual assault law with the aim of preventing a victim's sexual conduct from being used to discredit her testimony. The Supreme Court ruled that, while laudable in its intent, the provision went too far and could deny the accused the right to a fair trial. Critics took exception to this decision, as it left the question of whether evidence of the complainant's past sexual history would be admissible in court to the discretion of the trial judge. In response, Parliament introduced Bill C-49 in 1992, which was designed to amend the 1983 sexual assault legislation.

Under this new legislation, rules of evidence now state that evidence that the complainant has engaged in sexual activity, whether with the accused or with any other person, is not admissible to support an inference that the complainant is either more likely to have consented to the sexual activity in question or is less worthy of belief. A new test for judges is also provided for determining whether a complainant's sexual history may be admitted at trial. Bill C-49 also provided a definition of "consent" as it applies to sexual assault cases—"the voluntary agreement of the complainant to engage in the sexual activity in question"[s. 243.1 (1)]—and specified the conditions under which "no consent" is obtained (for instance, where the complainant is incapable of consenting to the activity by reason of intoxication or where the complainant expresses, by words or conduct, a lack of agreement to engage in the activity). As well, restrictions were placed on the defences available to men accused of sexual assault; the onus was now on the accused to show that he took "reasonable steps" in the circumstances to ascertain that the woman was consenting [s. 273.2 (b)].

The Supreme Court's ruling in the *O'Connor* case in 1995 had even more profound implications for victims of sexual assault. Bishop O'Connor was a priest and principal at a residential school near Williams Lake, British Columbia, where four Aboriginal women attended and worked. In 1991, the women laid charges of rape and indecent assault against O'Connor for incidents that occurred at the school between 1961 and 1967. The charges were stayed by the trial judge in 1992 when the Crown failed to release to the defence counsel the women's residential school records and all therapy and medical records since the time they had left the school (none of these records were in the Crown's possession). When the case reached the Supreme Court, the Court overturned the stay and ordered a new trial for O'Connor, but gave exceptionally large scope to defence access to complainants' records held by third parties. Subsequent to the Court's decision, women's shelters and rape crisis centres were being subpoenaed to turn over all files and counselling records relating to cases before the courts, and criminal defence lawyers were being advised by their association that they would be "negligent" if they did not subpoena complainant's files (Busby, 1997).

The Supreme Court's ruling in *O'Connor* meant that confidential records as well as personal diaries, letters, and the like could now all be accessed. The ruling also had special implications for the work of therapists and rape crisis counsellors, as they could now be required to hand over any and all records or notes relating to a complainant in a sexual assault case. Critics noted that such materials are not designed to be a written record of allegations; they are maintained for therapeutic, not evidentiary, purposes. For example, one of the issues regularly dealt with in therapy sessions is the need to explore feelings of guilt or shame that a woman may experience after a rape. In the hands of the court, this could be taken as evidence of "consent" or "complicity" on the part of the woman. To this extent, the *O'Connor* decision supports the old rape myths: that women lie or make false allegations, and that they cannot be trusted. One of the main effects of the ruling was the silencing of women. Women who were sexually assaulted had to decide whether they would seek counselling or initiate criminal prosecution of their assailant (Busby, 1997; 1999).

In response to concerns raised over the *O'Connor* decision, Parliament passed Bill C-46 in May of 1997 to limit the access of defendants to confidential records of complainants in sexual assault cases. The bill established more restrictive grounds for access, required that the defence establish that the records are relevant to the case at hand, and restricted the disclosure only to those parts that are important to the case.

This recent history of the law's treatment of sexual assault highlights a number of tensions. For one, there appears to be tension between the courts—whose decisions become binding as case law—and Parliament—which, in passing statute law, has endeavoured to be sensitive to the concerns raised from women's constituencies across the country. For another, there is a tension within the law with regard to competing rights, in particular, the right of a defendant to a fair trial compared with the right of a complainant to privacy. Clearly, the extent to which the legal system will be able to resolve these tensions and thereby offer both women and men equal protection and treatment under the law is a matter of ongoing debate.

Although the national directive to police forces in 1983 resulted in increasing numbers of domestic assault charges entering the criminal justice system, several provinces took further steps to respond to the problem of wife assault. In the city of Winnipeg, for example, a specialized Family Violence Court was established in 1990. The number of spousal assault cases dealt with by this court rose from 1302 in 1990–91 to 3543 in 1993–94, a 172 percent increase (Ursel, 1998). A large part of this increase can be attributed to the implementation of a zero-tolerance policy on domestic violence by the Winnipeg Police Service in 1993. Under this policy, police are instructed to lay a charge when there are reasonable grounds to believe that a domestic assault has occurred, whether or not the victim wishes to proceed with the matter and even in circumstances where there are no visible injuries or independent witnesses. The zero-tolerance policy resulted in increasing numbers of men—and women—being charged. Nevertheless, a large proportion of charges were resulting in a dismissal or stay of proceedings. One Winnipeg study, for instance, found that 80 percent of charges against women and 51 percent of those against men were subsequently stayed by the Crown (Comack et al., 2000). While the underlying intent of this more rigorous charging protocol was to assist victims of domestic violence (who are predominantly women), zero tolerance has opened the way for "double-charging" to occur, whereby both partners are charged with an offence when police are called to the scene. Comack et al. (2000) found that double-charging occurred in 55 percent of the cases they studied involving women accused and in 10 percent of those cases involving men. Stays of proceedings were even higher in these cases (88 percent and 70 percent respectively). In sum, while the changes that have occurred within the criminal justice system have a symbolic value—they carry a strong message of society's unwillingness to tolerate wife abuse—feminists have questioned whether the traditionally punitive and adversarial nature of the system is the most effective means for combating the problem (see, for example, Snider, 1991; 1994).

BLURRED BOUNDARIES: WOMEN AS VICTIMS AND OFFENDERS

Breaking the silence around male violence against women has had an impact on how feminist criminologists understand the lives of criminalized women. Violence against women is clearly a gender-related factor; it both reflects and reinforces women's inequality in society in relation to men. As the *War Against Women* report (1991, 9) noted, "The vulnerability of women to violence is integrally linked to the social, economic and political inequalities women experience as part of their daily lives." How, then, does this gender-based violence figure in the lives of criminalized women?

Several studies carried out in the 1990s revealed the extent of abuse experienced by criminalized women. Research conducted for the Task Force on Federally Sentenced Women, for instance, found that 68 percent of women serving a federal term of imprisonment in Canada had been physically abused as children or adults, and 53 percent were sexually abused at some point in their lives. Among Aboriginal women, the figures were considerably higher: 90 percent said that they had been physically abused and 61 percent reported sexual abuse (Shaw et al., 1991, vii and 31). Another study of women in a provincial jail found that 78 percent of the women admitted over a six-year period reported histories of physical and sexual abuse (Comack, 1993).

Qualitative research conducted by feminist criminologists explored women's accounts of their law breaking and its connections to abuse. *Women in Trouble* (Comack, 1996), for instance, was built around the stories of 24 women who were incarcerated in a provincial jail (see also, Gilfus, 1992; Adelberg and Currie, 1993; Sommers, 1995; Ritchie, 1996). The women's stories revealed the connections between a woman's law violations and her history of abuse to be complex. Sometimes the connections are direct, as in the case of women who are criminalized for resisting their abusers. Janice, for instance, was serving a sentence for manslaughter. The offence occurred at a party:

> I was at a party, and this guy, older guy, came, came on to me. He tried telling me, "Why don't you go to bed with me. I'm getting some money, you know." And I said, "No." And then he started hitting me. And then he raped me. And then [pause] I lost it. Like, I just, I went, I got very angry and I snapped. And I started hitting him. I threw a coffee table on top of his head and then I stabbed him. (Janice cited in Comack, 1996, 96)

Sometimes the connections become discernable only once a woman's law violations are located in the context of her struggle to cope with the abuse and its effects. Merideth, for example, had a long history of abuse that began with her father sexually assaulting her as a young child, and extended to several violent relationships with the men in her life. She was imprisoned for writing cheques on her bank account when she didn't have the money to cover them. The cheques were used to purchase "new things to keep her mind off the abuse":

Canadian Association of Elizabeth Fry Societies
www.web.apc.org/~kpate/

I've never had any kind of conflict with the law. [long pause] When I started dealing with all these different things, then I started having problems. And then I took it out in the form of fraud. (Merideth cited in Comack, 1996, 86)

Sometimes the connections are even more entangled, as in the case of women who end up on the street, where abuse and law violation become enmeshed in their ongoing, everyday struggle to survive. Brenda had this to say about street life:

Street life is a, it's a power game, you know? Street life? You have to show you're tough. You have to beat up this broad or you have to shank this person, or, you know, you're always carrying guns, you always have blow on you, you always have drugs on you, and you're always working the streets with the pimps and the bikers, you know? That, that alone, you know, it has so much fucking abuse, it has more abuse than what you were brought up with! . . . I find living on the street I went through more abuse than I did at home. (Brenda cited in Comack, 1996, 105–6)

In seeing the connections between a woman's law violations and her history of abuse, the traditional boundaries that divide "offenders" from "victims" become blurred. Nevertheless, this dichotomy of "offender versus victim" came under a different kind of scrutiny as the 20th century drew to a close. Increasingly, media and academic attention became focused on the issue of women's violence.

GENDERED VIOLENCE

In breaking the silence around male violence against women, feminists tended to cast men as the "offenders" and women as the "victims." This typification has been challenged in recent years. One publication that received considerable media attention was Patricia Pearson's (1997) book, *When She Was Bad: Violent Women and the Myth of Innocence.* Pearson argues not only that "women are violent, too" but also that their violence can be just as "nasty" as men's. Following in the tradition of Otto Pollak, she suggests that women's violence is more masked and underhanded than men's violence: women kill their babies, arrange for their husbands' murders, beat up on their lovers, and commit serial murders in hospitals and boarding houses (Pearson, 1997, 20–21). Yet, argues Pearson (1997, 61), when their crimes are discovered, women are more likely to receive lenient treatment from a chivalrous criminal justice system.

Pearson drew support for her analysis from studies that utilize the Conflict Tactics Scale (CTS) to measure abuse in intimate relationships. Developed by U.S. researcher Murray Straus and his colleagues (Straus et al., 1980), the scale is a quantitative instrument that consists of eighteen items and measures three different ways of handling interpersonal conflict in intimate relationships: reasoning, verbal aggression, and physical violence. The scale categorizes items on a continuum from least to most severe (for example, "discussed an issue calmly" and "cried" to "threw something," "hit with a fist," and "used a knife or a gun"). Respondents in a survey are asked how frequently they perpetrated each act in the course of conflicts or disagreements with their partners within the past year, and how frequently they had been on the receiving end. These self-reports of perpetration and victimization are then used to construct estimates of the rate of violence used by male and female partners. Most researchers who have employed the CTS have found equivalent rates for women and men on both minor and severe types of violence (Straus and Gelles, 1986; Steinmetz, 1981; Brinkerhoff and Lupri, 1988; Kennedy and Dutton, 1989). Such findings have led to the conclusion that there is a sexual symmetry in intimate violence; that is, that women are just as violent as men.

Despite its popularity, the CTS has not been without its critics (see, for example, DeKeseredy and Hinch, 1991; Dobash et al., 1992; Schwartz and DeKeseredy, 1993; and Johnson, 1996). Criminologists have noted that the CTS is an incomplete measure of intimate violence because

- it measures only incidents of violence and thus ignores the social context of the violence (such as whether a woman is acting in self-defence);

- it situates items only in the context of settling quarrels or disputes and thus misses assaults that "come out of the blue" or are motivated by the desire to control another person;

- it relies on self-reports of violence and may thereby underestimate the incidence of violence by males (who, it has been found, are more likely to under-report);

- it fails to make adequate distinctions between the severity of different forms of violence (for example, "tried to hit with something" is defined as "severe" while "slapped" is defined as "minor"); and

- it does not capture the outcome of the violence (for example, the degree of injury incurred by the participants).

Pearson, however, argues that these methodological concerns amount to unwarranted attacks by battered women's supporters who are invested in a gender dichotomy of "men as evil" and "women as good." In her view, violence is gendered only to the extent that women and men differ in the methods they use and the vocabulary of motives that accompany their actions. The problem, according to Pearson (1997, 32, 243), is that under the sway of feminists, we have failed to acknowledge that women, like men, possess a "will to power"; there are "dimensions of power that have nothing to do with formal structures of patriarchy" and to ignore women's violence is to promote a "culture of victimhood" that denies women's agency and responsibility.

The claims made by writers like Pearson, in combination with the difficulties encountered with using the CTS as a measure of violence between intimate partners, have led feminist criminologists to seek alternative strategies for determining whether, in fact, women are "men's equals" in violence. Comack et al. (2002), for instance, drew a random sample of 1002 cases from police incident reports involving men and women charged with violent crime in the city of Winnipeg over a five-year period (1991 to 1995). Women represented only

15 percent of the 23 090 violent crime charges laid against adults during that period. The aim of the study, however, was to determine whether qualitative differences exist between men's and women's violence.

One of the findings of the research was that over half (53 percent) of the cases studied involved violence between intimate partners. The large number of cases involving partner violence is, in large part, a reflection of the impact of the zero-tolerance policy on domestic violence implemented by the Winnipeg Police Service in 1993. In this respect, the policy has opened a window into the violence that occurs between intimate partners. Unlike the CTS, which approaches the issue of intimate violence from the vantage point of "settling disputes" in marital relationships, police incident reports are governed by the requirement to establish evidence (physical or otherwise) that a criminal act has occurred. As such, police officers include fairly detailed accounts in their reports of "who did what to whom." Also, because criminal law distinguishes between violent offences on the basis of their "seriousness" (for example, assault, assault with a weapon, assault causing bodily harm), police incident reports are a good source of information for measuring the degree of injury incurred by participants in a violent event—a variable that has been missing in most CTS research.

Studies that utilize the CTS have concluded that a sexual symmetry exists in intimate violence: men are as likely as women to be victims of abuse, and women are as likely as men to be perpetrators of both minor and serious acts of violence. Comack et al., however, found a different picture emerged from studying police incident reports. First, the violence tactics used by men and women differed on the basis of their seriousness. Men were more likely to use their physical strength or force against their female partners, while women were more likely to resort to the use of objects or weapons during the course of a violent event. Second, female partners of men accused of violence used violence themselves in only 23 percent of the cases, while male partners of women accused used violence in 65 percent of the cases, which suggests that the violence that occurs between intimate partners is not "mutual combat." Third, almost one-half (48 percent) of the women accused—as opposed to only 7 percent of the men accused—in partner events were injured during the course of the event, which adds weight to the conclusion that violent events between men and women are not symmetrical. Finally, in incidents involving partners, it was the accused woman who called the police in 35 percent of the cases involving a female accused (compared with only 7 percent in those involving a male accused). If calls to the police are interpreted as a form of "help-seeking behaviour" on the part of someone in trouble, this finding would suggest that in more than one-third of the cases involving a woman accused, she was the one who perceived the need for police intervention. Nevertheless, she ended up being charged with a criminal offence. In combination, these four indicators suggest that partner violence is asymmetrical.

Comack et al.'s findings are supported by data from the General Social Survey (Statistics Canada, 2000), which show that the nature and consequences of spousal violence are more severe for women than for men. For instance, women were more likely to report severe forms of violence (25 percent of women compared with 10 percent of men reported having been beaten on at least one occasion during the five years prior to the survey) and some form of physical injury (40 percent of women compared with 13 percent of men). While a similar percentage of women and men who were married or living in a common-law relationship during the previous five-year period experienced some type of violence by their partner, the frequency of violence directed at women by their partners was significantly greater than the frequency of violence directed at men by their partners.

While women are certainly capable of violence, these findings suggest that they are not "men's equals." Writers like Pearson are to be credited for pointing to the "culture of victimhood" that is produced when feminists rest their understandings on dualistic constructions such as "victim versus offender." Yet, in her efforts to call attention to women's capacity for violence, Pearson goes to the other extreme. By casting women as scheming, underhanded manipulators who engage in violence "to defend their aspirations, their identity and their place on the stage" (Pearson, 1997, 20), she effectively replaces the "men as evil" image that she so roundly criticizes feminists for with a "woman as evil" imagery.

Violence is "gendered." Its manifestations are tied to social and cultural distinctions attributed to men and women in our society. In these terms, the concept of patriarchy—a system of male domination—allows us to understand some of the pervasive patterns of male violence in society. This does not mean, however, that women are without agency or bereft of power. Indeed, there is no

TABLE 6.1 Theories of Women's Crime

Theory	*Theorists*	*Key Elements*
Early theorists	Lombroso/Ferrero, Thomas, Glueck/Glueck, Pollak	Women's "inherent nature" and their natural inferiority to men account for the nature and extent of their criminality.
Sex role socialization	Hoffman-Bustamante	Differential socialization of females is reflected in the types of offences they commit and the nature of their participation in crime.
Power-control theory	Hagan/Simpson/Gillis	Gender differences in delinquency can be explained by variations in parental control. Girls in patriarchal families will be less free to deviate than those in egalitarian families.
Women's liberation thesis	Adler, Simon	Women's changing gender roles are reflected in the nature and extent of their criminal involvement. Women are becoming "more like men"—more aggressive and violent—and have greater opportunities to commit crime.
Feminist theories	Carlen, Chesney-Lind, Comack, Daly, Morris, Naffine	Structured inequalities of class, race, and gender (including experiences of male violence) condition and constrain the lives of criminalized women.

reason to believe that women are not influenced by the cultural messages that permeate our society—especially when those messages herald violence as a means of "getting your way." So long as violence is held up as a resource to be used when someone is confronted with problems and conflicts in life, we should not be surprised when women act out violently.

SUMMARY

- One of the primary aims of the feminist engagement with criminology has been to bring women into view. This has involved a re-evaluation of the accumulated knowledge about female offenders, the nature of their offending, and the claims made about their "differences" from males. In the process, mainstream criminologists have been forced to consider how their traditional subject matter—men and male criminality—has influenced their theories and research.

- Feminist criminologists have argued that understanding women's involvement in crime requires an awareness of the larger social context, specifically, the structured inequalities of class, race, and gender that condition and constrain the lives of criminalized women.

- Breaking the silence around male violence against women has meant questioning the ways in which societal and legal responses reinforce and reproduce the problem.

- Making women more visible in criminology requires not simply letting women into the mainstream of the discipline but developing alternative ways of conceptualizing and studying the social world so that the interests and concerns of *both* men and women are included. In the process, the criminological enterprise is itself transformed.

QUESTIONS FOR CRITICAL THINKING

1. How does the way in which "difference" between men and women is understood influence our understanding of women's involvement in crime?
2. To what extent is the "cultural construction of rape" evident in films, music videos, advertising, and other aspects of Canadian culture? To what extent does it influence your own thinking about sexual violence?
3. In what ways have rape myths and stereotypes been evident in law and legal practice?
4. Is the criminal justice system the most effective strategy for responding to the problem of domestic violence?
5. How would making gender a central focus of criminological inquiry affect the ways in which criminologists study male criminality?

NET WORK

Are you interested in finding more information about the issues of domestic violence and sexual assault? To find a variety of sites that deal with these issues, first visit the Womennet.ca (The Canadian Women's Virtual Information Centre) home page at **www.womennet.ca**. Here you will find various links to domestic violence sites and sites dealing with sexual assault.

Using these links or any of the links found throughout this chapter, answer the following questions:

1. Describe some of the programs that are offered in Canada to serve victims of domestic violence and sexual assault.
2. Identify some of the controversies concerning domestic violence. Can you find sites on the Internet that present different perspectives on this problem? How can you assess the validity of the information presented on different websites?

KEY TERMS

conservative approach
cultural construction
feminist approach
gender-ratio problem

generalizability problem
liberal approach
patriarchy
sexism

SUGGESTED READING

Adelberg, Ellen, and Claudia Currie (eds.). (1993). *In Conflict with the Law: Women and the Canadian Justice System.* Vancouver: Press Gang Publishers. An edited collection including papers on such issues as theories of women's crime, the over-representation of Aboriginal women, prostitution, and recent efforts to reform women's prisons.

Comack, Elizabeth. (1996). *Women in Trouble: Connecting Women's Law Violations to Their Histories of Abuse.* Halifax: Fernwood Publishing. This book examines the stories of 24 women who have been incarcerated. It links the women's histories of abuse with their law violations and raises questions about imprisonment and our efforts to respond to violence against women.

Daly, Kathleen, and Lisa Maher (eds.). (1998). *Criminology at the Crossroads: Feminist Readings in Crime and Justice.* New York: Open University Press. A compilation of 14 articles that raise some of the key issues and unresolved problems for feminist work in criminology.

McKenna, Kate, and June Larkin (eds.). (2002). *Violence Against Women: New Canadian Perspectives.* Toronto: Ianna Publications. This collection presents some of the most recent Canadian research and policy initiatives on violence against women.

Smart, Carol. (1989). *Feminism and the Power of Law.* London: Routledge. In her classic work, Smart approaches law as a discourse and a claim to power capable of disqualifying alternative worldviews such as feminism. Smart challenges us to think about law and the prospects of law reform in an entirely new way.

BIBLIOGRAPHY

Adelberg, Ellen, and Claudia Currie. (1993). "In Their Own Words: Seven Women's Stories." In E. Adelberg and C. Currie (eds.), *In Conflict with the Law: Women and the Canadian Justice System.* Vancouver: Press Gang.

Adler, Freda. (1975). *Sisters in Crime.* New York: McGraw-Hill.

Amir, Menachem. (1971). *The Patterns of Forcible Rape.* Chicago: University of Chicago Press.

Bertrand, Marie-Andrée. (1967). "The Myth of Sexual Equality Before the Law." Fifth Research Conference on Delinquency and Criminality. Montreal, Centre de Psychologies et de Pédagogie (pp. 129–61).

Boyle, Christine. (1994). "The Judicial Construction of Sexual Assault Offences." In J. Roberts and R. Mohr (eds.), *Confronting Sexual Assault: A Decade of Social and Legal Change.* Toronto: University of Toronto Press.

Brinkerhoff, Merlin, and Eugen Lupri. (1988). "Interspousal Violence." *Canadian Journal of Sociology* 13(4):407–34.

Brock, Deborah. (1998). *Making Work, Making Trouble: Prostitution as a Social Problem.* Toronto: University of Toronto Press.

Brownmiller, Susan. (1975). *Against Our Will: Men, Women and Rape.* New York: Bantam Books.

Busby, Karen. (1997). "Discriminatory Uses of Personal Records in Sexual Violence Cases." *Canadian Journal of Women and the Law* 9(1):149–77.

———. (1999). " 'Not a Victim Until a Conviction Is Entered': Sexual Violence Prosecutions and Legal Truth." In E. Comack (ed.), *Locating Law: Essays on the Race/Class/Gender Connections.* Halifax: Fernwood Publishing.

Cain, Maureen. (1990). "Towards Transgression: New Directions in Feminist Criminology." *International Journal of the Sociology of Law* 18:1–18.

Carlen, Pat (ed.). (1985). *Criminal Women.* Cambridge: Polity Press.

———. (1988). *Women, Crime and Poverty.* Milton Keynes: Open University Press.

Clark, Lorenne, and Debra Lewis. (1977). *Rape: The Price of Coercive Sexuality.* Toronto: Women's Press.

Cohen, Albert. (1955). *Delinquent Boys.* Glencoe, Ill.: The Free Press.

Comack, Elizabeth. (1993). "Women Offenders' Experiences with Physical and Sexual Abuse: A Preliminary Report." Criminology Research Centre, University of Manitoba.

———. (1996). *Women in Trouble: Connecting Women's Law Violations to Their Histories of Abuse.* Halifax: Fernwood Publishing.

Comack, Elizabeth, Vanessa Chopyk, and Linda Wood. (2000). "Mean Streets? The Social Locations, Gender Dynamics and Patterns of Violent Crime in Winnipeg." Winnipeg: Canadian Centre for Policy Alternatives (Manitoba) (*www.policyalternatives.ca*).

———. (2002). "Aren't Women Violent Too? The Gendered Nature of Violence." In B. Schissel and C. Brooks (eds.), *Marginality and Condemnation: An Introduction to Critical Criminology.* Halifax: Fernwood Publishing.

Cowie, John, Valerie Cowie, and Eliot Slater. (1968). *Delinquency in Girls.* London: Heinemann.

Daly, Kathleen. (1987). "Discrimination in the Criminal Courts: Family, Gender, and the Problem of Equal Treatment." *Social Forces* 66(1):152–75.

———. (1989). "Rethinking Judicial Paternalism: Gender, Work-Family Relations, and Sentencing." *Gender and Society* 3(1): 9–36.

Daly, Kathleen, and Meda Chesney-Lind. (1988). "Feminism and Criminology." *Justice Quarterly* 5(4):101–43.

DeKeseredy, Walter, and Ronald Hinch. (1991). *Woman Abuse: Sociological Perspectives.* Toronto: Thompson.

Dobash, R. Emerson, and Russell Dobash. (1979). *Violence Against Wives: A Case against Patriarchy.* New York: Free Press.

Dobash, Russell, R. Emerson Dobash, Margo Wilson, and Martin Daly. (1992). "The Myth of Sexual Symmetry in Marital Violence." *Social Problems* 39(1)(February):71–91.

Edwards, Susan. (1985). "Gender Justice? Defending Defendants and Mitigating Sentence." In S. Edwards (ed.), *Gender, Sex and the Law.* Kent: Croom Helm: (pp. 129–54).

Faith, Karlene. (1993). *Unruly Women: The Politics of Confinement and Resistance.* Vancouver: Press Gang Publishers.

Frenschkowski, JoAnne. (2002). "We've Learned Little from Kimberly Rogers's Death." *Globe and Mail,* (August 9:A13).

Gelsthorpe, Lorraine, and Allison Morris. (1988). "Feminism and Criminology in Britain." *British Journal of Criminology* 23:93–110.

Gilfus, Mary. (1992). "From Victims to Survivors to Offenders: Women's Routes of Entry and Immersion into Street Crime." *Women and Criminal Justice* 4(1): 63–89.

Glueck, Eleanor, and Sheldon Glueck. (1934). *Five Hundred Delinquent Women.* New York: Alfred A. Knopf.

Hagan, J., A.R. Gillis, and J. Simpson. (1985). "The Class Structure of Gender and Delinquency: Toward a Power-Control Theory of Common Delinquent Behavior." *American Journal of Sociology* 90:1151–78.

Hagan, J., J. Simpson, and A.R. Gillis. (1979). "The Sexual Stratification of Social Control: A Gender-Based Perspective on Crime and Delinquency." *British Journal of Sociology* 30:25–38.

———. (1987). "Class in the Household: A Power-Control Theory of Gender and Delinquency." *American Journal of Sociology* 92(4)(January):788–816.

Heidensohn, Frances. (1968). "The Deviance of Women: A Critique and an Enquiry." *British Journal of Sociology* 19(2):160–75.

———. (1985). *Women and Crime.* London: Macmillan.

Hoffman-Bustamante, Dale. (1973). "The Nature of Female Criminality." *Issues in Criminology* 8:117–36.

Johnson, Holly. (1996). *Dangerous Domains.* Toronto: Nelson.

Johnson, Holly, and Karen Rodgers. (1993). "A Statistical Overview of Women in Crime in Canada." In Ellen Adelberg and Claudia Currie (eds.), *In Conflict with the Law: Women and the Canadian Justice System* (pp. 95–116). Vancouver: Press Gang.

Kelly, Liz. (1988). *Surviving Sexual Violence.* Minneapolis: University of Minnesota Press.

Kendall, Kathleen. (1991). "The Politics of Premenstrual Syndrome: Implications for Feminist Justice." *Journal of Human Justice* 2(2)(Spring):77–98.

———. (1992). "Dangerous Bodies." In D. Farrington and S. Walklate (eds.), *Offenders and Victims: Theory and Policy.* British Society of Criminology: (pp. 45–61).

Kennedy, Leslie, and Donald Dutton. (1989). "The Incidence of Wife Assault in Alberta." *Canadian Journal of Behavioural Science* 21:40–54.

Kinnon, Dianne. (1981). *Report on Sexual Assault in Canada.* Ottawa: CACSW.

Klein, Dorie (1973). "The Etiology of Female Crime: A Review of the Literature." *Issues in Criminology* 8(3).

Konopka, Gisella. (1966). *The Adolescent Girl in Conflict.* Englewood Cliffs, N.J.: Prentice Hall.

Kruttschnitt, Candace. (1980/81). "Social Status and Sentences of Female Offenders." *Law and Society Review* 15(2):247–65.

———. (1982). "Women, Crime and Dependancy." *Criminology* 195:495–513.

Laberge, Danielle. (1991). "Women's Criminality, Criminal Women, Criminalized Women?: Questions in and for a Feminist Perspective." *Journal of Human Justice* 2(2):37–56.

Laghi, Brian. (1998). "Alberta Judge Stirs Outrage in Sex Case." *The Globe and Mail* (February 23): A1, A11.

LaPrairie, Carol. (1993). "Aboriginal Women and Crime in Canada: Identifying the Issues." In Ellen Adelberg and Claudia Currie (eds.), *In Conflict with the Law: Women and the Canadian Justice System* (pp. 235–46). Vancouver: Press Gang.

Leonard, Eileen. (1982). *Women, Crime and Society: A Critique of Theoretical Criminology.* New York: Longman.

Lombroso, C., and W. Ferrero. (1895). *The Female Offender.* London: Fischer Unwin.

Luckhaus, Linda. (1985). "A Plea for PMT in the Criminal Law." In S. Edwards (ed.), *Gender, Sex and the Law.* Kent: Croom Helm (pp. 159–81).

MacLeod, Linda. (1980). *Wife Battering in Canada: The Vicious Circle.* Ottawa: CACSW.

Martin, Dianne. (1999). "Punishing Female Offenders and Perpetuating Gender Stereotypes." In Julian V. Roberts and David P. Cole (eds.), *Making Sense of Sentencing.* Toronto: University of Toronto Press.

Messerschmidt, James. (1986). *Capitalism, Patriarchy and Crime: Toward a Socialist Feminist Criminology.* Totowa, N.J.: Rowman and Littlefield.

Monture Angus, Patricia. (1999). "Women and Risk: Aboriginal Women, Colonialism, and Correctional Practice." *Canadian Women's Studies* 19(1)(Spring/Summer):24–29.

Morris, Allison. (1987). *Women, Crime and Criminal Justice.* Oxford: Basil Blackwell.

Naffine, Ngaire. (1987). *Female Crime: The Construction of Women in Criminology.* Sydney: Allen and Unwin.

———. (1997). *Feminism and Criminology.* Sydney: Allen and Unwin.

Osborne, Judith. (1989). "Perspectives on Premenstrual Syndrome: Women, Law and Medicine." *Canadian Journal of Family Law* 8:165–84.

Pearson, Patricia. (1997). *When She Was Bad: Violent Women and the Myth of Innocence.* Toronto: Random House.

Pollak, Otto. (1961). *The Criminality of Women.* New York: A.S. Barnes.

Raftner, N.H., and E.M. Natalazia. (1981). "Marxist Feminism: Implications for Criminal Justice." *Crime and Delinquency* 27(January):81–98.

Ritchie, Beth. (1996). *Compelled to Crime: The Gender Entrapment of Battered Black Women.* New York: Routledge.

Schwartz, Martin, and Walter DeKeseredy. (1993). "The Return of the 'Battered Husband Syndrome' Through the Typification of Women as Violent." *Crime, Law and Social Change* 20:249–65.

Scully, D., and J. Marolla. (1985). "'Riding the Bull at Gilly's': Convicted Rapists Describe the Rewards of Rape." *Social Problems* 32:251–63.

Scutt, Jocelyn. (1979). "The Myth of the 'Chivalry Factor' in Female Crime." *Australian Journal of Social Issues* 14(1):3–20.

Shaw, Margaret, Karen Rogers, Johannes Blanchette, Tina Hattem, Lee Seto Thomas, and Lada Tamarack. (1991). *Survey of Federally Sentenced Women: Report on the Task Force on Federally Sentenced Women: The Prison Survey.* Ottawa: Ministry of the Solicitor General of Canada. User Report No. 1991-4.

Simon, Rita. (1975). *Women and Crime.* Lexington, Mass.: D.C. Heath.

Smart, Carol. (1976). *Women, Crime and Criminology: A Feminist Critique.* London: Routledge and Kegan Paul.

———. (1977). "Criminological Theory: Its Ideology and Implications Concerning Women." *British Journal of Sociology* 28(1):89–100.

———. (1989). *Feminism and the Power of Law.* London: Routledge.

Snider, Laureen. (1991). "The Potential of the Criminal Justice System to Promote Feminist Concerns." In E. Comack and S. Brickey (eds.), *The Social Bias of Law: Critical Readings in the Sociology of Law* (2nd ed.) (pp. 238–60). Halifax: Fernwood Publishing.

———. (1994). "Feminism, Punishment and the Potential of Empowerment." *Canadian Journal of Law and Society* 9(1):74–104.

Sommers, Evelyn. (1995). *Voices from Within: Women Who Have Broken the Law.* Toronto: University of Toronto Press.

Statistics Canada. (2002). CANSIM II, table 252-0002 and Catalogue no 85-205-XIE. Canadian Statistics: Youths and adults charged in criminal incidents. www.statcan.ca/english/Pgdb/legal14a.htm.

Statistics Canada. (1993). "The Violence Against Women Survey." *The Daily* (18 November).

———. (2000). "Family Violence." *The Daily.* (25 July). www.statcan.ca/Daily/English/000725/d000725b.htm

Steffensmeier, Darryl, and J. Kramer. (1982). "Sex-based Differences in the Sentencing of Adult Criminal Defendants." *Sociology and Social Research* 663:289–304.

Steinmetz, Suzanne. (1981). "A Cross-cultural Comparison of Marital Abuse." *Journal of Sociology and Social Welfare* 8:404–14.

Straus, Murray, and Richard Gelles. (1986). "Societal Changes and Change in Family Violence from 1975 to 1985 as Revealed by Two National Surveys." *Journal of Marriage and the Family* 48:465–80.

Straus, Murray, Richard Gelles, and Suzanne Steinmetz. (1980). *Behind Closed Doors: Violence in the American Family.* New York: Doubleday.

Taylor, I., P. Walton, and J. Young. (1973). *The New Criminology.* London: Routledge and Kegan Paul.

Thomas, W.I. (1967). *The Unadjusted Girl.* New York: Harper and Row.

Ursel, Jane. (1994). "The Winnipeg Family Violence Court." *Juristat,* Canadian Centre for Justice Statistics 14:12.

———. (1998). "Eliminating Violence Against Women: Reform or Co-optation in State Institutions." In L. Samuelson and W. Antony (eds.), *Power and Resistance: Critical Thinking About Canadian Social Issues* (2nd ed.). Halifax: Fernwood Publishing.

The War Against Women. (1991). Report of the Standing Committee on Health and Welfare. Social Affairs, Seniors and the Status of Women. (June) Ottawa.

Zingraff, M., and R. Thomson. (1984). "Differential Sentencing of Women and Men in the U.S.A." *International Journal of the Sociology of Law* 12:401–13.

Explanations of Crime

The field of criminology is multidisciplinary. Lawyers, sociologists, political scientists, psychologists, biologists, physicians, historians, and philosophers all may consider the study of crime as part of their discipline. Nowhere is this diversity more apparent than in the development theories of the causes of crime. Why some people commit crime while others do not has been addressed from each of these perspectives.

Part 2 covers many of the most popular explanations of crime. The debate over which of these explanations is "best" has often become heated, and no attempt is made to resolve this issue here. It would be premature to impose such a judgement on a field that has been described as consisting of "a number of fitful leads from one partially examined thesis to another."[*] Instead, each theory is presented by an author who has had experience (and some sympathy) with it, and who presents the theory's strengths and weaknesses. A number of researchers are now trying to synthesize several of the different approaches, and some of the authors discuss this integrative work.

Part 2 illustrates how theories of crime causation have developed over time. In Chapter 7, several of the earliest approaches to the explanation of crime are discussed. The most important point made in this chapter is that explanations of crime arise from particular historical milieus and reflect the social and intellectual fashions of the day. Chapters 8 and 9 present theories that focus on the traits of individuals. Both biological and psychological perspectives have been with us for many years and are still popular today. Chapters 10 to 13 are concerned with the sociological explanations of crime. They illustrate the diverse ways in which social structure and social processes may promote or restrain criminal behaviour.

[*] Paul Rock. (1980). "Has Deviance a Future?" In Hubert M. Blalock (ed.), *Sociological Theory and Research* (pp. 290–303). New York: Free Press.

Part 2

Early Theories of Criminology

TULLIO CAPUTO
Carleton University

RICK LINDEN
University of Manitoba

We begin this chapter by exploring the context within which modern criminology developed. Societal beliefs relating crime to superstition and sin were slowly replaced during the Enlightenment by naturalistic explanations based on the idea that people are free and rational beings. This development was consistent with the pressure for individual rights and freedoms that was gaining prominence during this period and the view that the social order reflected a social contract between the individual and the state. These changes reflected the growing power of the rising merchant classes and the reduced influence of the feudal aristocracy, whose power rested on the ownership of the land and the loyalty of the peasants who lived and worked on it.

Next we discuss the rise of the Classical School of criminology during this era. The principle of "let the punishment fit the crime" represents the core of the philosophy of the Classical School and its belief in people's ability to reason and to act rationally. Although this reform provided the basis for our modern Criminal Code, it was too inflexible. The argument of later Positive criminologists that mitigating circumstances had to be considered when dealing with crime and criminals led to further reforms in the manner in which we dealt with criminals. The chapter concludes with an examination of the early theories that searched for the causes of crime in the biological make-up of individual offenders.

LEARNING OBJECTIVES

After reading this chapter, you should be able to

- Discuss the context within which modern explanations of crime and criminality were developed.
- Identify the founders of the Classical School of criminology, the key principles of this approach, and the impact of this school on our legal system.
- Outline the criticisms of the Classical approach and the changes in the legal process that were influenced by the Positive criminologists.
- Describe the basic features of the Positive School of criminology, and outline their approach and key principles.

- Show how the ideas advanced by the Positive School influenced other researchers to search for the biological causes of crime.

- Discuss how biological explanations of criminality influenced the development of this field at the beginning of the 20th century.

Prior to the 18th century, theories about crime were inspired primarily by religious beliefs and superstition. As Zilborg (1969, 11) notes,

> [F]rom the most primitive beginnings of human history, man [*sic*] believed in the existence of spirits and magic, and ... from the earliest days of his existence on earth, he began to ascribe various unusual phenomena of nature to the activities of evil spirits. This naturally led him to believe that any pathology in human behavior must be due to an evil spirit.

The link between evil spirits and wrongdoing is an important one for many religions. For example, Judeo-Christian teachings provide two powerful explanations outlining the role of evil spirits in sinful behaviour: temptation and possession. The idea of temptation is based on the belief that people exercise their free will and choose to act in particular ways, even ways they know to be wrong. Indeed, the Devil is thought to be at work tempting people. Of course, righteous believers can resist the Devil's powerful allure by drawing strength from their faith. They are encouraged to do this by religious leaders who employ images of hell-fire and threats of eternal damnation to help steel the spines of the faithful who might otherwise waiver. These images and beliefs about temptation imply that people who succumb are weak and morally inferior beings. In this way, the poor, the destitute, and other unfortunate members of society have been held responsible for their situations throughout much of history. Their misfortunes are seen as the result of their own moral failures. These beliefs also provide the basis for our ideas about deterrence. Thus, most people believe that the threat of severe punishment should be enough to persuade people to avoid engaging in misdeeds.

The second, and equally powerful Judeo-Christian imagery linking sin to evil spirits is that of possession. Wrongdoers were often suspected of being possessed by the Devil or some other malevolent spirit. These unfortunate individuals were thought to have little hope of recovering and were treated quite harshly. A host of horrifying tortures were used to drive the evil spirits from their bodies, and evidence of guilt was determined through a series of trials designed to differentiate between the righteous and the sinner. These included trial by battle, trial by ordeal, trial by fire, and trial by water. In most cases, the accused had little to look forward to, whether innocent or guilty, since these trials were extremely severe and often fatal.

These practices reflect a belief in the power of supernatural forces. They reached their zenith during the Middle Ages with the introduction of the notorious Inquisition and the witch craze that it spawned. This was a period marked by tremendous social upheaval and rapid social change. Western Europe was in the midst of the transition from feudalism to capitalism. Confusion and fear followed the revolution that was underway in the material and intellectual worlds of the day. Those in power—the political and religious elites—used every means at their disposal to protect their positions and privileges. They sought to preserve the status quo and maintain the existing order. This included using both religious and civil laws. As Angell (1965, 118) notes,

> The development of a common criminal law was aided by the close connection between crime and sin.... [P]unishment meant expiation. It is only one step from the fear of gods' displeasure to the desire for reassurance concerning the integrity of the moral order.

The changes underway in medieval society were based on the inability of the existing social arrangements to meet the needs of a growing European population. Poverty, misery, wars, and sickness ravaged the masses. These problems led people to question and even to challenge longstanding practices and beliefs, including those related to civil and religious authority. For example, the Protestant Reformation shook the foundations of the Christian world by challenging the power and authority of the Catholic Church. Throughout Europe, those in power were increasingly being held to account for deteriorating material conditions and social problems. It is in this context that the Inquisition and the witch craze found fertile ground. The religious and political elites began to seek ways of diverting attention away from themselves and of silencing the rebellious members of society. Blaming the existing social problems on the influence of the Devil and other evil spirits provided a means of meeting both objectives. First, this diverted the public's attention away from the elites and helped to place blame for social problems on individuals who were identified as being possessed or otherwise in league with the Devil. Second, those in power made themselves indispensable by arguing that they alone had the knowledge and ability to deal with the threat of the Devil on earth (Harris, 1974).

Importantly, these developments helped to blur the distinctions between sin and crime, and provided ideal conditions for the confluence of civil and religious authority. In medieval England, for example, there existed

> an almost paranoid concern for order in society, and a close association between crime and sin. The Reformation and the increased power of the Puritans changed perceptions of crime and justice both in government and in the popular mind. Religion and morality became matters of state law and potential sources of rebellion; although sin and crime were usually dealt with by different courts (crime by the civil court, sin by the ecclesiastical court), they were in some ways almost indistinguishable. (Best, 1998)

By linking morality to rebellion, the authorities were effectively preventing anyone from challenging the status quo. Those who did were likely to be accused of heresy and as a result, subjected to extremely harsh punishments, including death. This is precisely what happened to those accused of witchcraft and offers a partial explanation of how more than half a million people could be put to death during the 300 years in which the witch craze flourished. Indeed, the plight of those accused of being witches illustrates how charges of heresy were used to silence critics and quash any rebellious inclinations in the population.

Witches had been active in western Europe for centuries, although they were never prosecuted. This changed as a result of the growing challenge to both religious and civil authorities during the 15th century. Witches provided a convenient scapegoat against whom the masses could vent their anger. Importantly, it was usually the less powerful members of a community who were most susceptible to accusations of witchcraft. Although this group included the elderly, the infirm, and children, the witch craze mainly victimized women. As Pfohl (1985) points out, women made up 85 percent of the people executed for witchcraft throughout history. He suggests that "it is hardly surprising that during times in which the great male mastery over nature seemed least secure, times of economic hardship and political instability, the priestly finger of men often found bewitching women to blame"(39). He goes on to note that this led to horrific ritual punishments, including "baths in boiling water, crushing by heavy weights, tearing the flesh from the breasts with searing-hot pincers, and torture of the female sex organs" (39).

Economically independent women and women who lived alone and outside the protection of men were most susceptible to charges of witchcraft. Their presence in a community disrupted and threatened the male-dominated power structures. Charges of witchcraft and public executions served to reassert the authority of male leaders and remind community members of their subordinate positions in the social hierarchy. At the same time, however, the cruelty and sheer barbarism of the courts and their punishments fuelled the cries for reform across western Europe.

Early theorizing about crime and the beginnings of our modern system of criminal justice began to emerge during this tumultuous period of European history. "It was an era of racing industrial revolution, enclosure movements, growing capitalism and growing cities" (Sylvester, 1972). These developments were hastened by a rapidly expanding population and by the growth of trade and manufacturing.

The feudal economy was based on agricultural production, with clearly established relations between the aristocracy, who owned the land, and the peasants, who worked it. A system of mutual rights and obligations bound these two classes together, and when this relationship was challenged, the entire system was threatened. Increasingly, feudalism was unable to meet the needs of the growing population. It is estimated that England's population soared from 2.8 million in 1500 to 8.9 million in 1800. Similar increases were reported for the rest of Europe (Pfohl, 1985). This surge in population fuelled a period of colonial expansion as European monarchs sought havens for their surplus population and access to the markets and raw materials that colonies could provide. Europe's merchant classes gained considerable power during this period, as their economic activities offset the mounting economic shortfall (see Chapter 2).

Changes in the economy were mirrored by changes throughout the society. Revolutionary developments had taken place in philosophy, art, music, literature, and other intellectual pursuits. Progressive thinkers of the day fought to usher Europe into a new era. They argued against fanaticism and religious superstition, advocating "naturalistic" explanations of the world based on people's ability to reason. The Enlightenment philosophers believed that people were free and rational beings. This belief led them to call for the establishment of individual rights and freedoms. In their view, society was based on a social contract under which people chose to relinquish a small portion of their individual autonomy in order to ensure their own safety and the well-being of the entire group. These ideas were clearly contrary to the collectivist orientation of feudalism and the notion of noble privilege held by its rulers. If realized, a system based on rights and freedoms could seriously undermine the bonds of fealty, which held feudalism together. At the same time, these bonds restricted the availability of labour and hampered the development of manufacturing and industry. Herein lies the essence of the conflict between the aristocracy and the merchants. What was useful for one was detrimental to the other. Each group fought to advance its own interests.

The merchant classes enjoyed little political influence despite their growing economic power. Participation in the legislatures of the day was restricted to landowners, and since the merchants owned little land, they were barred from political power. Land was not considered a commodity, that is, as something that could be bought and sold. It was held primarily for its immediate use in agricultural and other pursuits. Given their lack of access to political power, the merchants turned to the legal arena to have their interests served.

In an ironic twist, the merchant classes found an opportunity to strengthen their position in society by financing the costly wars being fought by European monarchs over new colonies. The European aristocracy was forced to turn to the merchants for funds as their own resources were depleted. In exchange for their financial assistance, the merchants were able to gain significant legal concessions. While many of these concessions were aimed specifically at enhancing mercantile activities, a number of important legal principles were established, which reflected the ideals of the Enlightenment philosophers. It was within this milieu that the **Classical School** of criminology made its most significant contributions to the establishment of our modern criminal justice system.

"Cesare Beccaria (1738–1794)"
The Internet Encyclopedia of Philosophy
www.utm.edu/research/iep/b/ beccaria.htm

Classical School

Considered to be the first formal school of criminology, Classical criminology is associated with 18th and early 19th century reforms to the administration of justice and the prison system. Associated with authors such as Cesare Beccaria (1738–1794), Jeremy Bentham (1748–1832), Samuel Romilly (1757–1818), and others, this school brought the emerging philosophy of liberalism and utilitarianism to the justice system, advocating principles of rights, fairness, and due process in place of retribution, arbitrariness, and brutality.

THE CLASSICAL SCHOOL

In 1764, Cesare Beccaria published his major work, *An Essay on Crimes and Punishments.* Although this work contained little that was novel, "it captivated the attention of Europe, much more than did the voluminous lucubrations of theologians and publicists ... for it summed up in a masterly, unanswerable manner the conceptions and aspirations of the progressive minds of the age" (Phillipson, 1970). Beccaria provided a focus for the humanitarian reform movement that was gaining momentum throughout Europe with his criticism of the cruelty and inhumanity that characterized the criminal justice system of his day.

Abuses in the administration of justice were routine. Practices established in the notorious Court of Star Chamber and the institutionalized terror of the Inquisition had become commonplace. "The existence of criminal law of eighteenth-century Europe was, in general, repressive, uncertain, and barbaric. Its administration encouraged incredibly arbitrary and abusive practices"

(Mannheim, 1972). Few safeguards existed for the accused, and judicial torture was a routine method of securing confessions and discovering the identities of accomplices (Langbein, 1976). "A great many crimes were punished by death not infrequently preceded by inhuman atrocities" (Mannheim, 1972). This was particularly evident in the fanatical attack against heresy and witchcraft that swept across Europe.

The more popular forms of torture for these crimes included the rack, the ducking stool, thumbscrews, and other mechanical devices designed to inflict severe pain. The death penalty was administered in a number of ways, including burning at the stake, hanging, decapitation, and drawing and quartering.

In 18th-century England, as many as 350 offences were punishable by death. About 70 percent of death sentences were given for robbery and burglary (Newman, 1978). Practices in the colonies were similar in the early 1800s. The first person executed in Toronto was hanged for passing a bad cheque.

Clamour for the reform of such practices had started long before Beccaria's book was published. Humanitarian appeals were heard from jurists, writers, and philosophers of the era, including Hobbes, Locke, Montesquieu, and Voltaire. The administration of the criminal law, in particular, embodied practices that were in direct contrast to many of the principles advocated by the Classical theorists. It was contrary to the ideals of the social contract, as it denied the average citizen fair and impartial treatment at the hands of the state. European society was ripe for the liberating ideas of the Classical theorists and their humanitarian reforms. Beccaria's book served as a catalyst for these sentiments. The reform of a barbaric

BOX 7.1

FOCUS

Witchcraft and Torture

It is estimated that five hundred thousand people were convicted of witchcraft and burned to death in Europe between the fifteenth and seventeenth centuries. Their crimes: a pact with the Devil; journeys through the air over vast distances mounted on broomsticks; unlawful assembly at sabbats; worship of the Devil; kissing the Devil under the tail; copulation with incubi, male devils equipped with ice-cold penises; copulation with succubi, female devils.

Other more mundane charges were often added: killing the neighbor's cow; causing hailstorms; ruining the crops; stealing and eating babies. But many a witch was executed for no crime other than flying through the air to attend a sabbat....

Torture was routinely applied until the witch confessed to having made a pact with the Devil and having flown to a sabbat. It was continued until the witch named other people who were present at the sabbat. If a witch attempted to retract a confession, torture was applied even more intensely until the original confession was reconfirmed. This left the person accused of witchcraft with the choice between dying once and for all at the stake or being returned repeatedly to the torture chambers. Most people opted for the stake. As a reward for their cooperative attitude, penitent witches could look forward to being strangled before the fire was lit.

Source: Marvin Harris. (1974). *Cows, Pigs, Wars and Witches.* New York: Vintage Books. Copyright © by Marvin Harris. Reprinted by permission of Random House, Inc.

system of justice provided an excellent vehicle through which the ideas of the Classical theorists could be focused.

The Classical Theory of Crime

The roots of Classical criminology lie in the philosophy of the Enlightenment. Social contract theory represented a new way of looking at the relationship between people and the state. To avoid living in a state of nature that was, to use Hobbes's famous description, "solitary, poor, nasty, brutish, and short" (1958, 107), people voluntarily entered into a social contract with the state. This involved giving up some of their freedom to the state. In return, the state agreed to protect the citizen's right to live in security. The social contract was made with the consent of both parties, and neither had the right to break it. The state had to provide protection but could not violate the rights of citizens. The citizen had to obey the rules or face punishment from the state. In the opening chapter of his book, Beccaria writes:

> Laws are the conditions whereby free and independent men unite to form society. Weary of living in a state of war, and of enjoying a freedom rendered useless by the uncertainty of its perpetuation, men will willingly sacrifice a part of this freedom in order to enjoy that which is left in security and tranquility. (quoted in Monachesi, 1972)

The reforms proposed by the Classical theorists were based on a very well-developed theory of the causes of crime, a theory that represented a significant break with earlier theories. The Classical theorists had a simple explanation for crime. People broke the law because they thought that doing so would advance their own interests. In other words, deviance is the natural result of our rational self-interest. If it suits us, and if we think we can get away with it, we will break the law. Crime was understood to be a rationally calculated activity and not the result of some supernatural force or demonic possession.

Having addressed the causes of crime, the Classical theorists turned to the problem of finding ways to control it. The solution was to set up a system of punishment that would deter people from breaking the law. The Classical theorists believed that humans were rational beings who carefully calculated the consequences of their behaviour. Thus a person who might be tempted to break the law would consider the positive and negative consequences of his or her actions. A well-crafted criminal code would ensure that most people would choose to be good rather than evil. One might think that the extremely brutal justice system of the time should have been an effective deterrent, but its excessive harshness was contrary to the Enlightenment view that citizens should not be treated unfairly by the state. Instead, Beccaria proposed that the punishment should fit the crime, that is, it should be proportional to the harm done to society. Beccaria argued this on two grounds: that this amount of punishment would be the most effective deterrent; and that this was the fairest way to punish those who were not deterred and who chose to break the law. Unfair punishment would be a violation of the social contract and would be perceived as unjust by the individual and by other members of society. In the following quotation, Beccaria describes how this would affect the social contract and reduce the deterrent effect of law:

In proportion as torments become more cruel, the spirits of men, which are like fluids that always rise to the level of surrounding objects, become callous, and the ever lively force of the passions brings it to pass that after a hundred years of cruel torments the wheel inspires no greater fear than imprisonment once did.... The countries and times most notorious for severity of penalties have always been those in which the bloodiest and most inhumane of deeds were committed, for the same spirit of ferocity that guided the hand of the legislators also ruled that of parricide and assassin. (1963, 43–44)

Crime would be reduced if these reforms were implemented in law because calculating criminals would see that they would not profit from their actions. The punishment would cost them more than they could gain from their criminal behaviour. Beccaria also proposed that punishment should be swift and certain. If punishment followed too long after the act, or if it was unlikely to happen at all, then the law would not be an effective deterrent to crime. Finally, the law would be most effective in preventing crime if it was clear and simple enough that people could understand it.

With regard to specific reforms, Beccaria felt that the brutality of torture and the practice of executing people for minor offences must be abolished, as they were abuses of state power. Criminal matters should be dealt with in public according to the dictates of the law. Beccaria wanted to restrict the power of judges, which had been exercised in an arbitrary manner, in private, and generally without recourse for the defendant. He sought to restrict this power by separating the lawmaking power of the legislature from the activities of the judges. In his view, the law should be determined by the legislature; it should be accessible to all; trials should be public; and the role of the judiciary should be restricted to the determination of guilt and the administration of punishment set out in law.

The reforms suggested by Beccaria represented a call for equality and for the establishment of due-process safeguards. The creation of graded punishments effectively restricted the arbitrariness and inequality that characterized the existing system. By arguing that the punishment should "fit the crime," Beccaria shifted the focus away from the actor and onto the act. In this way, both noble and peasant would be judged on the basis of what they did and not who they were. Moreover, the judiciary was stripped of its discretion in sentencing since judges were bound to give punishments that were fixed by law. This was a powerful directive for equality since the preferential treatment formerly accorded to those of wealth and power could no longer be granted. However, as you have read in Chapter 2, those with wealth and power had the most influence in shaping the law, so the reforms in the justice system did little to alter the fundamental inequalities based on ownership of property.

Assessing the Contributions of the Classical School

The Classical School and Legal Reform

The ideals of the social contract theorists were translated into progressive criminal justice policy in the reforms promoted by the Classical School. In the process, the excesses and injustices that existed were attacked, and the foundations of our modern legal system were established. The due-process safeguards, which are taken for granted today, as well as reforms such as the guarantee of individual rights, equality before the law, the separation of judicial and legislative functions, and the establishment of fixed penalties, remain as the legacy of the Classical School of criminology. Canada's Criminal Code and our modern criminal justice system still reflect the work of the Classical theorists.

Limitations of the Classical School

Despite this success, the influence of the Classical School was not all positive. A serious problem with Classical theory was Beccaria's insistence that the degree of punishment must be proportional to the degree of harm that was done to society. While at first glance this proposal seemed reasonable, it meant that the personal characteristics of the offender and the circumstances of the offence could not be considered when courts determined punishments (Roshier, 1989). Also, by removing the flexibility of judicial discretion, the reforms actually gave more power to the state, which was responsible for passing very specific sentencing laws (Newman and Marongiu, 1990).

Although punishments could be rationally determined on paper, their application in real life often resulted in gross injustices. The courts were bound to follow the letter of the law and could not use discretion to temper the justice being meted out. For example, the hardship that results from having to pay a $1000 fine varies dramatically depending on whether a person is wealthy or poor. The courts, however, could not take this into account. Further, they were unable to consider mitigating circumstances or factors such as motive or mental competence, which would alter the responsibility of the convicted person. In this way, attempts to enforce equality resulted in a system that produced a great deal of injustice.

Changing this rigid system was one of the goals of Neoclassical criminologists, including the French magistrate Gabriel Tarde. Tarde contributed a number of ideas to criminology, most notably his "laws of imitation," but his main contribution came from his criticism of the legal system established by proponents of the Classical School (Beirne, 1993). Tarde rejected the notion of free will and proposed a modification of the system of punishment to recognize that there must be some individual treatment of offenders. As a result of the work of Tarde and other Neoclassical writers, courts began to take into account factors such as age (children were held less accountable), mental competence, motive, and mitigating circumstances. For example, in France, the Penal Code of 1791, which reflected the views of the Classical School, was revised in 1810 and again in 1819. With each revision, the rigid nature of the code was modified to include more discretion for judges as well as consideration of extenuating circumstances.

deterrence

As used in criminal justice, it refers to crime prevention achieved through the fear of punishment.

Another problem with the Classical School is its emphasis on **deterrence**. The approach the Classical School advocated was based more on a theory of deterrence than on a theory of crime, and it can be assessed on these grounds. The issue of deterrence continues to be an important element of this approach as modern-day Classical theorists emphasize its message. The work of James Q.

Wilson, for example, is a current example of Classical thinking. "He argues that penalties need not be long and severe as long as they are swift and certain" (Pfohl, 1985). However, for most offences, the likelihood of punishment is so small, and the time between the criminal event and any punishment that is given is so great, that the Classical theorists' hopes of reducing crime by changing the legal codes have not been met.

An additional problem with the Classical School is its overly simplified view of human nature and the theory of human behaviour that this supports (Thomas and Hepburn, 1983). The Classical theorists wholly accepted the image of the free and rational human being. This view completely ignores the objective realities faced by different individuals as they make their choices, the inequalities they experience, the state of their knowledge at any given time, and a multitude of other factors that may influence their decisions.

Finally, the emphasis on the rational dimension of human behaviour did not stem from the collection of empirical evidence but was based mostly on philosophical speculation. Little effort was made to examine these theoretical ideas in the real world. The notion of deterrence based on a rationally calculated set of punishments was assumed to work because it was felt that most reasonable people would follow the same logic.

In spite of the problems with the ideas of the Classical School, their contribution to our modern criminal justice system cannot be denied. Legal principles such as due process and equality before the law are fundamental to our legal system. Beccaria's work had a direct influence on the drafting of the legal code of France following the French Revolution and on the U.S. Bill of Rights, and Classical principles remain as part of the legal systems of many countries. For example, in section 15 of our Charter of Rights and Freedoms, Canadians are guaranteed the right to equal treatment before and under the law. We are protected from cruel and unusual punishment by section 12. In sections 7 through 11, a whole array of procedural safeguards are outlined that guarantee Canadians the right to due process of law. Clearly, modern criminal justice owes a great debt to the Classical theorists and the reforms that they introduced. However, our legal system also incorporates the changes suggested by the Neoclassical reformers.

"Canadian Charter of Rights and Freedoms"
Department of Justice Canada
canada.justice.gc.ca/Loireg/charte/ const_en.html

THE STATISTICAL SCHOOL: SOCIAL STRUCTURE AND CRIME

The first half of the 19th century saw the emergence of an approach to criminology that differed markedly from that of the Classical School. This was evident in the work of André-Michel Guerry (1802–1866) in France, Adolphe Quetelet (1796–1874) in Belgium, and Henry Mayhew (1812–1887) in England. These researchers believed that crime, like other human behaviour, was the result of natural causes. Once discovered, these causes could be altered through the application of scientifically derived knowledge. Guerry, Quetelet, and Mayhew's reliance on objective empirical data, as opposed to philosophical conjecture or speculation, identified them as positivists.

BOX 7.2

What Happens to Old Theories? Classical Theory Today

Beccaria's book *Dei Delitti E Delle Pene* was written in 1764. You have learned that the work of Beccaria and the other Enlightenment writers had a lasting impact on our legal system, but what other elements of the theory remain? While many of the other early theories have deservedly disappeared, the work of the Classical School continues to guide two related streams of criminological theory and research. The first is deterrence theory, the second is rational choice theory.

You will recall that the heart of Classical theory was the belief that humans were rational beings who carefully calculated the consequences of their behaviour. Crime would be prevented if the potential criminal realized that the costs of committing the crime would be greater than the potential rewards. Classical theorists had great faith in the ability of a well-designed criminal code to deter criminal behaviour.

How effective is the law as a deterrent? Because our legal system operates in large part on the basis of its ability to deter, one might think there was a large body of research on this topic. In fact, because the Classical School quickly fell out of fashion among academics and was replaced by a succession of positivist theories that minimized the importance of rational choice, we know surprisingly little about deterrence, though the rebirth of classical thinking in recent years has begun to change this. Research has focused on two different types of deterrence—specific deterrence and general deterrence.

Specific deterrence refers to the impact of deterrence on the individual. For example, a judge may sentence a burglar to six months in jail to teach him not to repeat his offence. Will punishment of a person who breaks the law actually deter him or her from breaking the law again in the future? The research on specific deterrence has been ambiguous. The fact that most people in prison have long prior records and that most people released from prison continue to reoffend tells us that deterrence is far from perfect. One reason for this is that most crimes do not result in punishment, so offenders correctly assume that their chances of getting away with a particular offence are good. Also, you may be surprised to learn that some research suggests that those who are more severely punished are more likely to reoffend than those who receive milder punishment for the same offences (Gibbs, 1975). Labelling theorists (see Chapter 12) would suggest that this is because punishment may stigmatize people so that their opportunities for a life in the noncriminal world may be reduced.

General deterrence refers to the effect of punishment on the public at large. The existence of a system of punishment will deter most of us from committing crimes. Thus a judge may decide that burglaries are getting out of hand and give one burglar a severe sentence to set an example for others. We do know that at one level, general deterrence is effective. You do not deliberately park where you know your car will be towed away and you do not speed if you see a police car behind you. Further, when the police have gone on strike crime has risen dramatically. In one notable police strike in Montreal, armed robberies began to occur within minutes of the strike and on several occasions huge mobs of people ran through the shopping district, breaking windows and stealing whatever they could get their hands on. However, such strikes are rare and the more important question is not whether the law deters, but whether we can change our current system to make it more effective as a deterrent.

The research that has been done on this issue suggests that certainty of punishment is more important than the severity of punishment, a finding that would have been predicted by the Classical theorists. A simple example is that obscene and harassing telephone calls declined dramatically after the introduction of caller ID because this new technology made it much easier to identify the offending caller. Unfortunately, it is difficult to increase the certainty of punishment for most offences so policy-makers have turned their attention to severity. "Get tough" politicians regularly assure us that cracking down on crime by increasing the penalties will enable us to solve

(continued)

our crime problems. The evidence suggests otherwise, probably because the likelihood of being arrested, convicted, and punished for any offence is so low that tinkering with the level of punishment makes no difference. Also, it may be the case that the existing level of punishment is severe enough for most of us. To cite just one example, there is no evidence that capital punishment is any greater deterrent to crime than lengthy terms of imprisonment. In fact, one international study found that homicide rates actually went down after capital punishment was abolished (Archer et al., 1983).

The second area where the concerns of the Classical School are enjoying a resurgence is in the growing popularity of the rational choice theory of crime. (You can learn more about this theory in the Net Work exercise at the end of this chapter and in Chapter 14.)

Members of the **Statistical School** did not share the image of the rational individual held by the Classical theorists. Instead, they saw behaviour as the product of a whole host of factors. They systematically analyzed the statistical information available to them and tried to find a relationship between this information and crime. They analyzed such things as population density, education, and poverty (Thomas and Hepburn, 1983). A great deal of their work was based on geographical or cartographic analysis, which involved the plotting of various crime rates onto maps.

These theorists went far beyond simply describing what they learned from their maps and graphs. Many of their ideas anticipated the work of modern sociologists as they addressed issues related to criminal careers, delinquent subcultures, and social learning theory. They provided a critical and insightful perspective, as well as a thorough statistical analysis of criminal behaviour in their work.

Perhaps the most significant contribution of these theorists is their discovery of the remarkable regularity of phenomena such as crime. Countries, provinces, cities, and towns all had rates of crime that were remarkably stable from one year to the next. Even murder, a highly individualistic act, varied little over time. They attributed this stability to elements of the social structure. Quetelet, for example, argued that "rather than being the result of our individual free wills, [our behaviour] is the product of many forces that are external to us" (Thomas and Hepburn, 1983). The fact that these forces appeared in regular and recurring patterns prompted these theorists to believe that human behaviour was governed by certain laws akin to those found in the natural or physical sciences.

In a style that anticipated much of our contemporary thinking about crime, these theorists focused on inequalities and other structural features of their society. People in unfavourable social circumstances were seen to have few options open to them. In Quetelet's words, "The crimes which are annually committed seem to be a necessary result of our social organization ... the society prepares the crime and the guilty are only the instruments by which it is executed" (Bierne, 1993, 88).

The influence of the Statistical School was, unfortunately, limited. This was not the result of any shortcomings on their part; rather, it reflected the wider

Statistical School

Associated with early social scientists such as Adolphe Quetelet (1795–1874) and André-Michel Guerry (1802–1866), who began to explore the structure of emerging European societies with the assistance of statistical methods. While their early use of statistics is important, they also developed a *structural explanation* of crime and other social problems.

appeal of the biological theories of Cesare Lombroso and his colleagues. Nevertheless, these early pioneers of statistical analysis of criminology provided a uniquely sociological contribution to this emerging field of inquiry and demonstrated the value of testing theoretical formulations with empirical observations.

LOMBROSO AND THE POSITIVE SCHOOL

Positive School

The first scientific school consisting of the Italian criminologists Cesare Lombroso (1836–1909), Raffaelo Garofalo (1852–1934), and Enrico Ferri (1856–1929). They supported the assumptions of positivism and argued that criminality is determined—the effect in a cause–effect sequence—and that the mandate of criminology should be to search for these causes. It was believed that with the exception of those deemed to be born criminals, the discovery of the causes of crime would allow for effective treatment.

"Cesare Lombroso"
Centre for Interactive Multimedia, James Cook University
www.cimm.jcu.edu.au/hist/stats/lomb/index.htm

The **Positive School** of criminology is also known as the Italian School because its most influential members were the Italian criminal anthropologist Cesare Lombroso (1836–1909) and his students Enrico Ferri (1856–1929) and Raffaelo Garofolo (1852–1934). Lombroso was influenced by the evolutionary theories of Charles Darwin, by the positivist sociology of Auguste Comte, and by the work of the sociologist Herbert Spencer, who attempted to adapt Darwin's theory to the social world.

Like the members of the Statistical School, Lombroso brought the methods of controlled observation to the study of criminals, comparing them with non-criminals in order to isolate the factors that caused criminality. His own research was badly flawed, and his work is remembered because of his use of the scientific method rather than because of the specific findings he reported. Despite their flaws, Lombroso's ideas were widely accepted at the end of the 19th century. Their popularity was partly due to the growing influence of science, particularly to the awareness of Darwin's theory of evolution. It was likely also due to the comfort of the ruling classes with the view that criminals were not produced by society's flaws, as Quetelet and his colleagues had shown; rather, criminals were genetic misfits who were born to break the rules that governed the lives of civilized people (Radzinowicz, 1966).

Lombroso had worked as an army doctor and as a prison physician. He was interested in psychology and at one stage of his career was a teacher of psychiatry. These diverse interests are reflected in his theory of criminality. Lombroso's interest in physiology led him to note certain distinct physical differences between the criminals and soldiers with whom he worked. His thoughts on the subject came together during an autopsy he was performing on the notorious thief Vilella. He noted that many of the characteristics of Vilella's skull were similar to those of lower animals. In a remarkable description of the moment of discovery, Lombroso recalled:

> This was not merely an idea, but a revelation. At the sight of that skull, I seemed to see all of a sudden, lighted up as a vast plain under a flaming sky, the problem of the nature of the criminal—an atavistic being who reproduces in his person the ferocious instincts of primary humanity and the inferior animals. Thus were explained anatomically the enormous jaws, high cheek-bones, prominent superciliary arches, solitary lines in the palms, extreme size of the orbits, handle-shaped or sessile ears found in criminals, savages, and apes, insensibility to pain, extremely acute sight, tattooing, excessive idleness, love of orgies, and the irresistible craving for evil for its own sake, the desire not only to extinguish life in the victim, but to mutilate the corpse, tear its flesh, and drink its blood. (Wolfgang, 1972)

This discovery led Lombroso to believe that criminals were throwbacks to an earlier stage of evolution, or "**atavisms**." His theory has been succinctly described by Gould (1981):

> These people are innately driven to act as a normal ape or savage would but such behaviour is deemed criminal in our civilized society. Fortunately, we may identify born criminals because they bear anatomical signs of their apishness. Their atavism is both physical and mental, but the physical signs, or stigmata as Lombroso called them, are decisive. Criminal *behaviour* can also arise in normal men, but we know the "born criminal" by his anatomy. Anatomy, indeed, is destiny, and born criminals cannot escape their inherited taint.

The contrast between the primitive nature of the criminal and the more completely evolved contemporary man is shown in Lombroso's explanation of the use of professional slang, or argot, by criminals. Born criminals talk differently because they experience the world differently. "They talk like savages because they are veritable savages in the midst of this brilliant European civilization" (Parmelee, 1912).

To support his theory, Lombroso had to show that organisms lower on the evolutionary ladder were naturally criminal. Thus, primitive humans were described as "savages." Even when evidence of their savagery was absent, Lombroso was able to save his theory by speculating that among honourable primitives, the conditions for criminality simply did not yet exist. For example, "it is not possible ... to steal when property does not exist or to swindle when there is no trade" (Lombroso, 1912). Once these supposed savages take on a little civilization, their criminality is inevitable. Lombroso went even further down the evolutionary ladder, finding evidence of criminality in the behaviour of animals, insects, and even insectivorous plants.

Lombroso tested his ideas by observing many imprisoned criminals. In one study, he compared the physical characteristics of a group of criminals with those of a group of soldiers and found that the criminals had many more of the atavistic **stigmata** than did the soldiers. In another piece of research, he found that stigmata were present in 30 to 40 percent of anarchists, but in less than 12 percent of members of other extremist movements (Taylor et al., 1973). He also concluded that different types of offenders were characterized by different physiological characteristics. For example, "robbers have ... small, shifting, quick-moving eyes; bushy connecting eyebrows; twisted or snub noses, thin beards ... and foreheads almost receding," while "habitual homicides have glassy, cold, motionless eyes, sometimes bloodshot and injected. The nose is often aquiline, or rather hawklike, and always voluminous" (Lombroso, 1972). Lombroso felt that women had fewer stigmata and lower crime rates than males because women were closer to their primitive origins. Although he concluded that women were vengeful, deceitful, and jealous, he said that their crime rates were relatively low because these negative traits were neutralized by their maternal instinct, piety, and lack of passion.

Lombroso initially postulated two types of offenders—born criminals and occasional criminals. However, in response to his critics, he later added several more categories, including the following:

atavism

Cesare Lombroso (1836–1909) believed that some criminals were born criminals; they were atavistic. This suggested that they were throwbacks to an earlier stage of human evolution and that this limited evolutionary development meant that they were morally inferior. This inferiority could be identified through a series of physical *stigmata*.

stigmata

Physical signs of some special moral position. Cesare Lombroso (1836–1909) used the term to refer to physical signs of the state of *atavism* (a morally and evolutionary inferior person).

1. *Epileptics.* In addition to their disability, epileptics also had the atavistic characteristics of criminals.

2. *Criminal insane.* This is the category of those whose insanity has led to their involvement in crime.

3. *Criminals of passion.* These are criminals who contrast completely with born criminals in that they lack any of the criminal stigmata. They commit crimes because of "noble and powerful" motives such as love or politics.

4. *Criminaloids.* This is a grab-bag category, which includes anyone who commits a crime but does not fall into one of the other classifications. Lombroso felt that precipitating factors other than biological ones caused criminality among this group.

Some have interpreted this expansion of categories as a softening of Lombroso's commitment to his biological theory. This view seems to be supported by his last major work, *Crime: Its Causes and Remedies*, in which he discusses social and environmental causes of crime along with biological causes. However, examination of these modifications suggests that this change was more apparent than real. While there were differences between atavistic criminals, the insane, and the epileptics, all three categories had elements of degeneration that stemmed from epilepsy, which he called the "kernel of crime" (Lombroso, 1912). Criminaloids may lack some of the stigmata, but they differ from born criminals only in degree, not in kind. After long periods in prison, criminaloids may even come to resemble born criminals. While those who commit crimes out of passion do not show any of the stigmata, they show some points of resemblance with epileptics. The only category that has no connection with atavism or epilepsy is that of the occasional criminals. Even these pose no threat to Lombroso's theory, however, for he suggests that they should not be called criminals at all.

The Contribution of the Positive School

In its day, Lombroso's work attracted a large following among those interested in studying the causes of criminality. The stigmata were used as indicators of criminality in many trials, and Lombroso himself appeared as an expert witness on several occasions. In one case, the court had to decide which of two brothers had killed their stepmother. Lombroso's testimony that one of the men had the features of a born criminal helped secure the man's conviction.

BOX 7.3

FOCUS

A "Novel" Theory

Criminal anthropology reached the attention of novelists as well as theorists. Bram Stoker and Lombroso were contemporaries, but Stoker's *Dracula* was published almost 20 years after Lombroso's most famous work. Compare Stoker's description of Count Dracula with Lombroso's description of the born criminal:

Dracula: "His face was ... aquiline, like the beak of a bird of prey."

Lombroso: "[The criminal's] nose on the contrary is often aquiline like the beak of a bird of prey."

Dracula: "His eyebrows were very massive, almost meeting over the nose ..."

Lombroso: "The eyebrows are bushy and tend to meet across the nose."

Dracula: "... his ears were pale and at the tops extremely pointed ..."

Lombroso: "with a protuberance on the upper part of the posterior margin ... a relic of the pointed ear...."

Source: Leonard Wolf. (1981). In Stephen Jay Gould, *The Mismeasure of Man.* New York: W.W. Norton.

However, Lombroso's theory of criminal anthropology has not stood up to empirical test. Lombroso's research was poorly done by today's standards. His comparison groups were chosen unsystematically, his statistical techniques were crude, his measurements were often sloppy, and he assumed that those in prison were criminals and those out of prison were noncriminals. Many of the stigmata he mentioned in his research, such as tattooing, were social factors that could not possibly have been inherited. Yet despite these weaknesses, his work did represent an attempt at providing a scientific explanation of the causes of criminality.

Perhaps the most lasting contribution of Lombroso was his discussion of the criminal justice system. The Classical theorists felt that crime could be controlled if society could design punishments to fit the crime. Positive theorists, on the other hand, felt that the punishment should fit the *criminal*. Radzinowicz and King (1977) have nicely outlined the difference between the two perspectives: "The Classical School exhorts men to study justice, the Positivist School exhorts justice to study men."

Because Lombroso believed that people became involved in criminality for different reasons, he felt that they should be treated differently by the criminal justice system. If a respectable man committed murder because of passion, honour, or political belief, no punishment was needed as that man would never repeat the crime. For other offenders, indeterminate sentences would best ensure rehabilitation. Born criminals should not be held responsible for their actions, though they needed to be incarcerated for the protection of society. However, this was to be done in a humane way. He recommended that "sentences should show a decrease in infamy and ferocity proportionate to their increase in length and social safety" (Lombroso-Ferrero, 1972).

Some born criminals could be channelled in a socially useful direction. For example, banishment and transportation to one of the colonies might allow their tendencies to be redirected toward the difficult business of building settlements in a hostile environment. For others, more severe sanctions were required. "There exists, it is true, a group of criminals, born for evil, against whom all social cures break as against a rock—a fact which compels us to eliminate them completely, even by death" (Lombroso, 1912).

A number of features of our current criminal justice system stem from the concern of Lombroso and his followers with individualizing the treatment of offenders. Probation, parole, indeterminate sentences, and the consideration of mitigating circumstances by the court were all influenced by Lombroso's work as well as by the work of Neoclassical criminologists. The rational person of Classical theory now had a past and a future.

BIOLOGICAL THEORIES IN THE EARLY 20TH CENTURY

Crime and Physical Characteristics

During his lifetime, Lombroso's theories came under frequent attack. In 1889, he responded to his critics by challenging them to compare 100 born criminals, 100 people with criminal tendencies, and 100 normal people. He promised to retract his theories if the criminals did not turn out to be different from the other groups. His challenge was ultimately taken up by an English prison medical officer, Dr. G.B. Griffiths, and completed by his successor, Dr. Charles Goring, who succeeded Griffiths in 1903 shortly after the project began.

Goring carefully measured and compared the physical and mental characteristics of 3000 English convicts with those of diverse samples of "normals," including British university students, schoolboys, university professors, insane Scots, German Army recruits, and British Army soldiers (Goring, 1972). Based on his comparison of these groups on 37 physical and 6 mental traits, Goring concluded that there was no evidence of a distinct physical type of criminal. Lombroso's "anthropological monster has no existence in fact" (Goring, 1913). Criminals were no more or less likely to possess stigmata than were members of the control groups. Goring did find that criminals were physically inferior to normals, but attributed this fact to social selection processes.

Goring's most important finding was the high correlation between criminality and low intelligence. This led to his own explanation that crime was inherited and that the most important constitutional mechanism through which crime was genetically transmitted was mental inferiority. Unlike Lombroso, Goring did feel that hereditary predispositions could be modified by social factors such as education. However, he also supported eugenic measures, which would restrict the reproduction of the constitutional factors leading to crime.

In some respects, Goring's research represented a major advance over the work of Lombroso. His measurement was far more precise, and he had access to statistical tools that were not available to Lombroso. However, his work also contained a number of serious methodological flaws. Among them was the fact that he was comparing officially labelled criminals, who were not a representative sample of all criminals, with diverse groups of other people who did not represent the noncriminal population. While many of the other criticisms of Goring's research are quite technical, they are serious enough to cause doubt both about his own theories and about his refutation of Lombroso (Driver, 1972).

The search for individual differences as the cause of crime did not end with Goring. This theme was picked up again in the 1930s by Ernest A. Hooton, a Harvard anthropologist. He compared more than 13 000 criminals with a sample of noncriminals drawn from groups of college students, firemen, hospital out-patients, militiamen, mental hospital patients, people using the change house at a public beach, and others. On the basis of this comparison, Hooton concluded that "criminals as a group represent an aggregate of sociologically and biologically inferior individuals" (1939). Among the new stigmata he attributed to criminals were such characteristics as "low foreheads, high pinched nasal roots, nasal bridges and tips varying to both extremes of breadth and narrowness," and "very small ears" (1939).

While Hooton was not as concerned as some of his predecessors with the policy implications of his research, he did not hesitate to draw the obvious conclusion. Since "crime is the resultant of the impact of environment upon low grade human organisms ... it follows that the elimination of crime can be effected only by the expiration of the physically, mentally, and morally unfit, or by their complete segregation in a socially aseptic environment" (1939).

Hooton's work stirred up a great deal of controversy. His findings were challenged on a variety of grounds. He was accused of using poor scientific methods and circular reasoning. For example, he used conviction of a crime as a method of separating criminals from noncriminals; he then examined the convicted groups and concluded they were inferior; finally, he used this finding of inferiority to account for their criminality (Empey, 1982). Only in this way could a trait such as thin lips be turned into an indicator of criminality.

There are several other criticisms of Hooton's methods worth considering. His control group did not represent the general population. Students, firefighters, and mental patients have particular characteristics that distinguish them from the rest of the population. Furthermore, his findings show tremendous differences within the various control groups he used. In fact, the differences between his control groups drawn from Boston and Nashville were actually greater than between prisoners and controls (Pfohl, 1985). As in the case of Lombroso, Hooton's attempt to link criminal behaviour to physical types was thoroughly discredited.

This kind of research has made periodic appearances in a variety of forms since the days of Lombroso and Hooton. In the 1950s, William Sheldon attempted to re-establish the link between body type and criminality in his elaboration of a "somatotype" theory. He described three basic body types, which, he argued, were related to particular types of personalities and temperament. These consisted of endomorphs, with fat, round bodies and easygoing personalities; ectomorphs, who are tall and lean individuals with introverted personalities and nervous dispositions; and mesomorphs, who have well-built, muscular bodies with aggressive personalities and who are quick to act and insensitive to pain. Sheldon related each of these types to particular kinds of criminal behaviour. He found that the muscular mesomorphs were the type most likely to become involved in delinquent or criminal behaviour.

Sheldon fared no better than his predecessors, however, when his work was subjected to scrutiny. It was found that he had done an extremely poor job of measuring delinquency among the young people he had studied. He had used vague and inconsistent categories that have been described as scientifically meaningless.

These criticisms could not be levelled at the Gluecks, who followed up on Sheldon's ideas. They applied his somatotype theory to a study of 500 juvenile delinquents. In their study, they compared the bodies of 500 adjudicated delinquents with a matched sample of nondelinquents. The Gluecks concluded from their work that delinquents were more likely to be mesomorphs. However, this finding may have raised more questions than it answered. Putting aside a whole host of methodological criticisms levelled at the Gluecks, it may be that mesomorphs actually look more like stereotypical delinquents than either endomorphs or ectomorphs. As a result, people may respond to mesomorphs differently and they may be more likely to be labelled delinquent than those who are nonmesomorphs. Also, other social selection factors may have been involved. Youths who are athletic, muscular, and active may be better candidates for Little League baseball, hockey, or delinquency than their less athletic peers.

Crime and Intelligence

Other examples of biological approach have focused on a variety of factors that have been associated with individual differences. Goring proposed one such point of view when he suggested that instead of looking for defective body types, the focus should be on genetic weaknesses demonstrated by low intelligence.

In one famous study of family and heredity, the American psychologist Henry Goddard traced the legitimate and illegitimate offspring of an army lieutenant, Martin Kallikak. Young Martin fathered an illegitimate son with a feeble-minded barmaid before he settled down and married a "respectable" woman. The study compared the family trees of the descendants of Kallikak's feeble-minded mate to those of his "normal" wife. The offspring of the feeble-minded barmaid produced a collection of deviants and feeble-minded degenerates. By contrast, the family of his wife showed no such weakness (Goddard, 1912).

Even if the enormous methodological weaknesses of Goddard's study are ignored (Gould [1981] has shown that even the photographs showing the "depraved" Kallikaks had been retouched to make them look like defectives), little is left of scientific consequence. It is hardly surprising that children raised under difficult and impoverished circumstances should be less than model citizens. In fact, a requirement for life under these conditions may be that an individual learns a great deal of undesirable behaviour simply to survive. The absence of any consideration of the social factors involved in this comparison clearly undermines the findings of Goddard's research.

Goddard continued his work using the Binet-Simon intelligence test, which had recently been developed in France. This IQ test was based on the notion of "mental age." Goddard studied the residents of a New Jersey mental institution and, on the basis of this work, established the mental age of 12 as the cutoff point for determining feeble-mindedness. Goddard then applied this IQ test to the inmates of jails and prisons throughout the New Jersey area. He found that in approximately half of the institutions, 70 percent of the inmate population was at or below the mental age of 12. From these findings, he concluded that IQ was an important determinant of criminal behaviour. He also concluded that feeble-mindedness was directly inherited and could only be eliminated by denying those he called "morons" the right to reproduce (1914). Goddard also argued that "criminal imbeciles" should not be held criminally responsible for their actions. His expert testimony helped to acquit at least one murderer on grounds of criminal imbecility (Rafter, 1997).

The acceptance of Goddard's position was short-lived. In 1926, Murchinson published the results of a study in which he compared IQ data from World War I army recruits with that of a group of inmates (Pfohl, 1985). He found that 47 percent of the recruits, compared with only 30 percent of the prisoners, had IQ scores that fell below the mental age of 12. This startling finding implied that almost half of a very large sample of normal American men could be considered mentally feeble. The absurdity of these findings forced Goddard to lower his cutoff point for feeble-mindedness from 12 years to 9. This reduction resulted in the disappearance of any significant differences between inmates and soldiers, or anyone else for that matter (Pfohl, 1985).

Despite evidence so convincing that even Goddard disavowed his earlier work, governments responded to their fear of those with low IQs by passing legislation controlling their behaviour. These laws resulted in thousands of mentally retarded people in North America being forced into institutions and, in many cases, being involuntarily sterilized. In Canada, sterilization laws were passed in Alberta in 1929 and in British Columbia in 1933. The Alberta law was not repealed until 1972. In 1995, Leilani Muir, an Alberta woman of normal intelligence, sued the Alberta government. As a child, Muir was incorrectly labelled as mentally retarded. She was kept in an institution and was sterilized without her knowledge or consent. This case shows the problems with developing policies based on notions of individual inferiority.

The controversy over IQ tests has continued. A number of serious flaws in the assumptions behind this approach have been realized. For example, it has been suggested that high scores on these tests may have more to say about test-taking ability than they do about intelligence. Furthermore, the composition of these tests has been found to be biased in favour of the cultural groups of the designers of the tests. In a dramatic demonstration, Adrian Dove, a black sociologist, devised an IQ test based on the cultural referents and language of the black ghetto (Pfohl, 1985). Black respondents who were familiar with this culture did well on the tests, but white middle-class respondents did poorly. The validity of IQ tests remains suspect, and their use has often been linked with racist ideology and propaganda.

A number of other recent formulations have sought to re-establish a link between individual characteristics and criminal behaviour. These include a focus on such things as chromosomes, unusual EEG results, hypoglycemic disorders, and premenstrual tension. These theories, and others, will be considered in Chapter 8.

The results in many of these cases are similar. While it would be foolhardy to deny the biological or psychological dimensions of human behaviour, the evidence supporting a link between pathology and criminal behaviour is weak. Moreover, this approach ignores the essentially political nature of social control, for what one society praises and rewards, another may condemn. Given this variability in what we define as crime, an assessment of the underlying social and political context is indispensable.

The continued search for individual differences and the erroneous identification of a normal "us" and a criminal "them" carries with it distinct political overtones. The emergence of a positive science coincided with the rise of a powerful capitalist class and expanded colonial activity. Both of these developments welcomed the ideological justification contained within the Darwinian notion of survival of the fittest. Social Darwinism and a positivist criminology flourished in this environment.

This approach offered a ready-made and "humane" way of dealing with the problems of social control. This was extremely important at a time when the population was being transformed into a disciplined industrial labour force. Rather than applying the harsh and barbaric punishments of the past, a scientifically designed technology of control could be used to "treat" troublesome

TABLE 7.1   Early Theories of Crime

Theory	Theorists	Key Elements
Classical theory	Beccaria	Humans were rational thinkers. Those who contemplated breaking the law considered the positive and negative consequences of their actions. A measured system of punishments was needed to deter crime.
Neoclassical theory	Tarde	Helped to develop a more individualized system of criminal justice.
Statistical School	Guerry, Quetelet, Mayhew	Explored the social causes of crime. Related structural factors such as inequality to crime.
Positive School	Lombroso	Criminals were born, not made. They were atavisms who were less evolved than the law-abiding.
Early 20th-century biological	Goring, Hooton, Sheldon, Goddard	Related criminality to several types of theories of biological inferiority including intelligence and body shape.

individuals. This focus on the pathologies of individuals also serves to conveniently remove one's gaze from the social structure. If it is certain that problems like crime are the result of individual deficiencies, then it is not necessary to be concerned with the social structure. If, on the other hand, the structural sources of inequality, such as racism, sexism, and other social ills, are examined, the very nature of the society may be called into question.

SUMMARY

- Early theories of crime were based on superstition and religious beliefs.
- This view of crime changed when the Classical School of criminology became popular. Members of this school argued that people were free and rational actors and proposed that the key to preventing crime was the establishment of a criminal code based on the principle that the punishment should fit the crime.
- The Classical School had a major impact on legal systems in many countries. However, the resulting legal codes were rigid and inflexible. Other scholars proposed a series of Neoclassical reforms that have now been incorporated in the legal systems of many countries.
- Lombroso and other members of the Positive School brought scientific methods to the study of crime. While Lombroso's biological theory has not stood up to scientific scrutiny, the application of science to criminology represented a major shift in the discipline.

- Lombroso's work was followed by a number of other researchers who sought to blame crime on the biological inferiority of criminals. As with Lombroso's theory, research has not supported these early 20th-century biological theories. However, they did have a major impact on the legal system, as measures such as involuntary sterilization and lengthy incarceration for "defectives" were passed in many jurisdictions.

QUESTIONS FOR CRITICAL THINKING

1. How did the development of the Classical School of criminology reflect the wider changes taking place in European society at the time? Consider how the social, economic, and ideological forces influenced the founders of the Classical School.
2. What changes did the Positive School of criminology introduce? How did these alter the existing explanations of crime and criminality? What are the implications of the Positive School for the way we treat people who break the law today?
3. What were the major biological explanations of criminality that emerged early in this century? How were these explanations received by social scientists?
4. Discuss the social policy implications of the early biological theories. In other words, if the theories were correct, what should societies do to deal with crime?
5. In general, what have you learned in this chapter about the relationship between theories of criminality and social policy concerning the treatment of criminals?

NET WORK

In Box 7.2 you learned about contemporary work that is in the tradition of the Classical School. Rational choice theory (discussed in detail in Chapter 14) is based on the assumption that criminal behaviour is the result of a rational choice between good and evil. Prior to committing the offence, the potential offender calculates the probability of being caught and the likely penalty and weighs these against the potential rewards of committing the offence. Crime-prevention specialists have used this theory as the basis for a wide variety of prevention programs directed at increasing the cost of crime or at decreasing its rewards. This has been called situational crime prevention.

To learn more about this approach, visit **www.preventingcrime.org.** This site contains a major report on crime prevention—"Preventing Crime: What Works, What Doesn't, What's Promising."

On the home page, search for the keyword "situational." When the references for this material appear on your screen, click on "Chapter 8." Use this chapter to answer the following questions:

1. What does the author of this chapter tell us about the relationship between place and crime? How can we use our knowledge of this relationship to prevent crime? Can you think of any places in your own community that have high rates of crime?

2. Find three different types of situational-crime-prevention programs. For each of these programs, describe one study that measures the program's success or lack of success.

3. Read the section on crime and public transportation. Based on the research cited in the report, list three recommendations you would make to reduce crime on the public transportation system in your community.

4. Many of our politicians suggest that the best way to deal with crime is to toughen up the Young Offenders Act and increase the penalties for crime. After reading this report on situational crime prevention, do you think these politicians are correct?

KEY TERMS

atavism

Classical School

deterrence

Positive School

Statistical School

stigmata

SUGGESTED READING

Beccaria, Cesare Bonesana, Marquis. (1819). *An Essay on Crimes and Punishments*. Philadelphia: Philip H. Nicklion Publishers. This is Beccaria's major work. It is important to read the original text since it contains the ideas that inspired many of the criminal justice reforms of the period.

Lombroso-Ferrero, Gina. (1972). *Criminal Man According to the Classification of Cesare Lombroso*. Montclair, N.J.: Patterson Smith. Lombroso's daughter Gina compiled this work, which contains the major ideas developed by her father. First published in 1911, it provides a number of vivid examples of how Lombroso applied his theory to a whole range of offenders.

Maestro, Marcello T. (1942). *Voltaire and Beccaria as Reformers of Criminal Law*. New York: Columbia University Press. An excellent source for delineating the ideas of Beccaria in relation to the intellectual developments of the era. Maestro presents a clear and thorough treatment of Beccaria's work in light of both social contract and Classical theories.

Monachesi, Elio. (1972). "Cesare Beccaria." In Hermann Mannheim (ed.), *Pioneers in Criminology* (pp. 36–50). Montclair, N.J.: Patterson Smith. A useful introduction to Beccaria and his ideas. This article is informative and concise and helps the reader to appreciate the conditions that existed when Beccaria was writing.

Phillipson, Coleman. (1970). *Three Criminal Law Reformers*. Montclair, N.J.: Patterson Smith. An excellent source on the contributions of Beccaria. It presents a thorough discussion of his work and the conditions surrounding the rise of the Classical School.

Sylvester, F. Sawyer, Jr. (1972). *The Heritage of Modern Criminology*. Cambridge, Mass.: Schenkman Publishing Company. This book contains short selections from the major works of such early criminologists as Beccaria, Lombroso, Quetelet, and Mayhew.

Vold, George B. (1979). *Theoretical Criminology*. New York: Oxford University Press. In this classic text in criminology, Vold presents a colourful description of Lombroso and the development of the Positive School of criminology.

BIBLIOGRAPHY

Angell, Robert. (1965). *Free Society and Moral Crisis*. Ann Arbor: University of Michigan Press.

Archer, Dane, Rosemary Gartner, and Marc Beittel. (1983). "Homicide and the Death Penalty: A Cross-National Test of a Deterrence Hypothesis." *Journal of Criminal Law and Criminology* 74:991–1014.

Beccaria, Cesare. (1963). *On Crimes and Punishments*. Translated by H. Paolucci. Indianapolis: Bobbs-Merrill. (First published as *Dei Delitti E Delle Pene* in 1764.)

Beirne, Piers. (1993). *Inventing Criminology*. Albany: State University of New York.

Best, Michael. (1998). "What Did Elizabethans Consider a Crime?" Shakespeare's Life and Times Home Page. Internet Shakespeare Editions 2001. web.uvic.ca/shakespeare/Library/SLTnoframes/history/crime.html. Accessed July 14, 2003.

Driver, Edwin D. (1972). "Charles Buckman Goring." In Hermann Mannheim (ed.), *Pioneers in Criminology* (pp. 429–42). Montclair, N.J.: Patterson Smith.

Empey, LaMar T. (1982). *American Delinquency: Its Meaning and Construction*. Homewood, Ill.: The Dorsey Press.

Gibbs, Jack R. (1975). *Crime, Punishment, and Deterrence*. New York: Elsevier.

Goddard, H.H. (1912). *The Kallikak Family: A Study in the Heredity of Feeble-Mindedness*. New York: Macmillan.

———. (1914). *Feeble-Mindedness: Its Causes and Consequences*. New York: Macmillan.

Goring, Charles. (1913). *The English Convict*. London: His Majesty's Stationery Office.

———. (1972). *The English Convict*. Montclair, N.J.: Patterson Smith.

Gould, Stephen Jay. (1981). *The Mismeasure of Man*. New York: W.W. Norton.

Harris, Marvin. (1974). *Cows, Pigs, Wars and Witches*. New York: Vintage Books.

Hobbes, Thomas. (1958). *Leviathan, Parts I and II*. Indianapolis: Bobbs-Merrill. (First published in 1651.)

Hooton, Ernest Albert. (1939). *The American Criminal: An Anthropological Study*. Cambridge, Mass.: Harvard University Press.

Langbein, John H. (1976). *Torture and the Law of Proof*. Chicago: University of Chicago Press.

Lombroso, Cesare. (1912). *Crime: Its Causes and Remedies*. Boston: Little, Brown and Company.

———. (1972). "Criminal Man." In S.F. Sylvester (ed.), *The Heritage of Modern Criminology* (pp. 67–78). Cambridge, Mass.: Schenkman.

Lombroso-Ferrero, Gina. (1972). *Criminal Man According to the Classification of Cesare Lombroso*. Montclair, N.J.: Patterson Smith.

Mannheim, Hermann (ed.). (1972). *Pioneers in Criminology* (pp. 36–50). (2nd ed.). Montclair, N.J.: Patterson Smith.

Monachesi, Elio. (1972). "Cesare Beccaria." In Hermann Mannheim (ed.), *Pioneers in Criminology*. Montclair, N.J.: Patterson Smith.

Newman, Graeme. (1978). *The Punishment Response.* New York: J.B. Lippincott.

Newman, Graeme, and Pietro Marongiu. (1990). "Penological Reform and the Myth of Beccaria." *Criminology* (May):325–46.

Parmelee, Maurice. (1912). "Introduction to the English Version." In Cesare Lombroso, *Crime: Its Causes and Remedies* (pp. xi–xxxii). Boston: Little, Brown and Company.

Pfohl, Stephen J. (1985). *Images of Deviance and Social Control.* New York: McGraw-Hill.

Phillipson, Coleman. (1970). *Three Criminal Law Reformers.* Montclair, N.J.: Patterson Smith.

Radzinowicz, Sir Leon. (1966). *Ideology and Crime.* London: Heinemann.

Radzinowicz, Sir Leon, and Joan King. (1977). *The Growth of Crime.* London: Pelican Books.

Rafter, Nicole Hahn. 1997. *Creating Born Criminals.* Urbana: University of Illinois Press.

Roshier, Bob. (1989). *Controlling Crime: The Classical Perspective in Criminology.* Philadelphia: Open University Press.

Sylvester, F. Sawyer, Jr. (1972). *The Heritage of Modern Criminology.* Cambridge, Mass.: Schenkman.

Taylor, Ian, Paul Walton, and Jock Young. (1973). *The New Criminology: For a Social Theory of Deviance.* London: Routledge and Kegan Paul.

Thomas, Charles W., and John R. Hepburn. (1983). *Crime, Criminal Law and Criminology.* Dubuque, Iowa: Wm. C. Brown Company Publishers.

Wolfgang, Marvin E. (1972). "Cesare Lombroso." In Hermann Mannheim (ed.), *Pioneers in Criminology* (pp. 232–91). Montclair, N.J.: Patterson Smith.

Zilborg, Gregory. (1969). *The Medical Man and the Witch During the Renaissance.* New York: Cooper Square Publishers.

Biological Factors in Criminal Behaviour

SHEILAGH HODGINS

Institute of Psychiatry, King's College, University of London

A s you have read in Chapter 7, many of the early theories of criminality were based on biological characteristics. However, these theories were not supported by research, so their popularity waned in favour of psychological and sociological explanations of crime. The policy implications of some of the biological theories, culminating in the eugenics movement and policies such as involuntary sterilization, also made biological theories unpopular. However, in recent years, biological theories have once again become scientifically and politically respectable.

This chapter discusses the role of biological factors in crime causation. Some theorists have proposed that factors such as brain damage, epileptic disorders, and endocrine disorders are direct causes of criminal behaviour. Other biological factors are believed to be indirectly related to criminality. These factors are felt to interact with social influences to produce criminality. Among these factors are perinatal damage, minimal brain damage, brain neurochemistry, and endocrine factors. The chapter also discusses the biological elements involved in psychopathy and the role of major mental disorders in criminality.

After reading this chapter, you should be able to

- Understand the role of biological factors in human behaviour.
- Describe the way in which some biological factors may directly cause criminal behaviour.
- Describe how biological factors may interact with social influences to cause criminal behaviour.
- Understand the biological factors involved in psychopathy.
- Understand how major mental disorders are related to criminality.

LEARNING OBJECTIVES

THE ROLE OF BIOLOGICAL FACTORS IN BEHAVIOUR

Biological factors play a role in the development of all human behaviour, but, like all factors involved in determining behaviour, they do not act alone. Rather, each factor interacts with numerous other biological and nonbiological factors in a complex causal chain. Biological factors mediate nonbiological factors;

"Crime Times"
Research reviews and information
on biological causes of criminal,
violent, and psychopathic
behaviour.
www.crime-times.org

incoming stimuli are modulated, and responses are made based on an interaction between the individual and his or her environment. Thus, each of us perceives and reacts to the world in a unique way.

The importance of biological factors in determining behaviour varies enormously. In Down's syndrome, for example, a chromosomal abnormality is responsible for the multiple symptoms—limited intelligence, small stature, cardiovascular malformations—that characterize the disorder. Consider a second example in which an endocrine disorder is partially responsible for the behaviour of a 15-year-old who develops a robot to clean the garage. Owing to low thyroid levels, the boy reacts slowly. As a small boy, he realized that he was a poor athlete, so he spent much of his time alone, reading and playing with electrical equipment. In the first example, the biological variable is an important determinant, while in the second, it has some, but not much, importance. Even in the first example, however, other factors play a key role. Depending on the learning experiences, the individual with Down's syndrome could spend his or her life in an institution being cared for by others or living independently. In the second example, other determinants of the boy's skills include the influence of his older brother, who was studying electrical engineering, and the presence of electronics magazines and old equipment that the brother left lying around.

To sum up, biological factors play a role in determining all human behaviours. In so doing, they interact among themselves and with nonbiological factors. Their importance varies depending on the behaviour in question.

OBSTACLES TO RESEARCH

Three major obstacles hinder the study of the role of biological factors in determining criminality. The first is that the methods available to study biological factors are limited. There is often no way to observe biological factors as they interact with other factors to determine behaviour. Nor is it possible to conduct experiments to discover if a biological factor will produce a criminal. Only relations among variables can be investigated and inferences drawn about the importance of each factor in determining a behaviour.

The second obstacle is the definition of *criminal*. Crime is defined socially. Each society defines it somewhat differently. In addition, different societies have different rates of crime resolution, and some offenders are more likely to be arrested than others. For example, large numbers of men who assault their female partners and their children never come to the attention of the criminal justice system. Crime is a very heterogeneous category including very different behaviours. However, in order to discover the role played by biological factors, it is important to study precisely defined behaviours, not a socially defined generic term such as "a conviction for armed robbery," which lumps together many very different behaviours. Consequently, studies examining biological factors usually focus on individuals who are described as showing a consistent pattern of antisocial behaviour (whether or not it has led to criminal charges), or aggressive behaviour, or conduct disorder (persistent antisocial behaviour in children), rather than on convicted offenders. These categories are **operationally defined**, and the behaviours are objectively measured.

Crime is socially defined, and furthermore, arrest, prosecution, and conviction are social phenomena. Consequently, the likelihood that an illegal behaviour will lead to conviction depends on many factors, including the circumstances surrounding the crime and the characteristics of the offender. The fact that not all who engage in illegal behaviour are equally likely to be prosecuted seriously hinders research. For example, while it has been consistently shown that little boys who are antisocial grow up to be adult offenders, many antisocial little girls do not become adult offenders. Does their antisocial behaviour go away, or is their adult antisocial behaviour hidden? If their antisocial behaviour does disappear with age, it is important to identify how and why this comes about so that it can be applied to boys. If, on the other hand, the antisocial behaviour of girls does remain stable across the life span (like that of the males), then there are important social and moral reasons for uncovering it.

The third obstacle in studying the role of biological factors implicated in criminal behaviour is a conceptual one. The assumption that there is a single cause of crime is unreasonable. Given the very different behaviours that are defined as illegal, it is likely that there are many different causal pathways, each involving complex interactions of numerous factors. Even when the criminal behaviour is the same, subgroups with distinct determinants are found. For example, in a study of a cohort of adolescent murderers in Quebec, three subgroups were identified: boys who committed homicides while committing another crime, those who committed the homicide in the midst of an interpersonal conflict, and boys with mental disorders. These groups differed on measures of psychosocial adjustment before the homicide and on **recidivism** (Toupin, 1993). Consequently, as will be noted throughout the chapter, most research in this area attempts to identify homogeneous subgroups of individuals that have distinct causal pathways toward adult criminality.

To sum up, research designed to tease apart biological factors that determine criminal behaviour is limited to nonexperimental methods except in those rare instances where experimental situations exist in nature. Such investigations advance knowledge insofar as they examine specific behaviours rather than socially or legally defined categories of persons who exhibit very different kinds of behaviour. It is reasonable to propose that each of these kinds of behaviour is determined by different combinations of factors.

Generalizing Results

Before we begin to look at the data, one final comment is necessary. As you have seen in Chapter 5, rates and types of crimes vary widely from one society to another. Even different regions in the same country may have quite different rates of crime. Such differences are very important to an understanding of the determinants of criminal behaviour. Biological factors interact with nonbiological ones to determine behaviour. One society may exaggerate the importance of a biological factor, while another may limit it. For example, in countries such

operationally defined

To define some concept of study in such a way that it can be observed and measured. For example, well-being might be measured by asking people to rate their overall satisfaction with their lifestyle, or antisocial behaviour might be measured by frequency of arrest or criminal prosecution.

recidivism

Where an individual commits new criminal offences after having been sentenced for previous crimes. Although difficult to measure, the rate of recidivism is a basic tool in evaluating the effectiveness of various corrections programs.

as the United States, where firearms are relatively accessible, an individual inherited tendency to get angry easily and behave impulsively may be potentially more lethal than in a country such as Japan, where weapons are relatively rare, and where from a very young age, children are taught not to show their negative emotions and not to behave impulsively. The environments in which research, even biological research, is carried out are thus important in understanding the findings.

In this light, it is essential to note differences and similarities in research findings from different countries. For example, a number of prospective **longitudinal studies** have followed unbiased cohorts of subjects from birth, or from a very young age, through adulthood. These studies have been conducted in countries with very different cultures, attitudes to crime, and criminal justice systems—England, Sweden, Finland, Denmark, New Zealand, Norway, and the United States. Despite the differences, all these studies have identified a small group of males who are antisocial and aggressive at an early age and who become persistent adult offenders. Consider now another example, where unexpected differences between relatively similar cultures have been documented. Psychopathy, as defined by Hare's Checklist (which will be discussed later in this chapter), is diagnosed among approximately 22 percent of male penitentiary inmates in Canada, but among only 3 percent of Scottish prisoners serving sentences of comparable length (Cooke, 1997). For both of these types of offenders, biological factors are thought to be important in determining the development of adult criminality.

longitudinal study

This measures relationships between variables over a period of time. For example, one might follow a group of males from birth to age 30 to measure their involvement with the criminal justice system over time.

BIOLOGICAL FACTORS DIRECTLY RELATED TO CRIMINAL BEHAVIOUR

Destructive Brain Processes

Research with humans and with several nonhuman species (see, for example, Moyer, 1976) has shown that there are specific brain structures that elicit and terminate aggressive behaviour. Different forms of aggressive behaviour are associated with different structures. If these structures are impinged upon by tumours, inflammatory processes, or other brain diseases, aggressive verbal and physical behaviour will result. For example, several recent studies have identified some older women who show antisocial behaviour as a result of degenerative brain disease (Hodgins et al., 1986). However, such conditions are extremely rare (Shah and Roth, 1974). More frequent may be destructive brain processes that result from environmental pollutants. For example, it has been shown that children who are exposed to lead over long periods of time absorb it. The lead damages the brain and the children develop a persistent pattern of delinquent behaviour (Needleman et al., 1996).

Brain Damage

Violent behaviour is one possible result of head traumas severe enough to cause loss of consciousness (Detre et al., 1975). Following brain injury, patients are often described as aggressive, irritable, and unable to control their tempers (Lezak and O'Brien, 1988). Such patients, however, are not usually convicted of crimes as they live in institutions and not in the community. More minor brain damage resulting from injury has been found to be prevalent among adult male offenders (Templer et al., 1992). In a study of men who requested treatment for wife battering, 61 percent had suffered head traumas of sufficient severity as to cause brain injury (Rosenbaum and Hoge, 1989). Among serious delinquent offenders referred for psychiatric evaluation, an elevated rate of treatment for head trauma was documented (Lewis et al., 1979). It is unlikely, although possible, that such trauma is a direct cause of the aggressive behaviour. Head trauma at an early age, however, may very likely be the cause of the minor brain damage that characterizes children who become offenders. This research is reviewed in a subsequent section of the chapter.

In these studies of offenders, it is difficult to discern whether the brain injury preceded the illegal behaviour or whether it was simply the result of behaviour such as frequent fighting. In order to more accurately document the relationship between brain injury and violent behaviour, a group of Finnish investigators examined the criminal records of men who had been soldiers. It was found that soldiers who had sustained a brain injury were more likely than others to be convicted subsequently of a violent offence (Virkkunen et al., 1977). Taken together, the existing findings do suggest that head trauma in adulthood may well be a determinant of violent behaviour in some people. More minor forms of alterations to the developing brain in utero and in early childhood are very likely associated with stable antisocial behaviour, which is first evident in childhood.

Epileptic Disorders

There is some evidence that if the brain structures that elicit and terminate aggressive behaviour are activated by abnormal electrical activity, aggressive behaviour will result (Monroe, 1970). This condition, the dyscontrol syndrome, is very rare.

Epilepsy is a disorder in which a small number of brain cells have been damaged. As a result, they sometimes produce excessive electrical activity, which provokes a seizure. In some cases, depending on the location of the damaged cells, the seizure may take the form of aggressive behaviour. When epilepsy is accompanied by diffuse brain damage, there appears to be a relation with aggressive behaviour. However, even in those cases where brain damage is evident, it has been shown that other nonbiological factors, such as social class, learning, and family functioning, contribute to the development of aggressive behaviour (Shah and Roth, 1974). While violent and criminal behaviour related to epilepsy can occur, current findings suggest that it is very rare (Borum and Appelbaum, 1996; Mendez et al., 1993).

Endocrine Disorders

Dalton (1961) and d'Orban and Dalton (1980) have reported that a disproportionate number of women convicted of crimes committed the illegal acts in the days preceding menstruation or on the first day of menstruation. Epps (1962), studying shoplifters, found no such relation. Dalton (1961) has argued that some women suffer from premenstrual syndrome and that treatment with progesterone eliminates their antisocial behaviour. However, recent studies, using better control methods, have not found that progesterone is any more effective than placebos (Maddocks et al., 1986). In looking at all the findings in this area, it appears that only some female offenders are prone to aggressive behaviour during the premenstrual and menstrual periods. It is more likely that the endocrine changes present during these periods act as triggers to exaggerate characteristics such as aggressivity (Asso, 1984; Dougherty et al., 1997).

To sum up, biological states and factors that are directly related to criminal behaviour are very rare. Tumours, inflammation, brain disease, certain forms of epilepsy (when accompanied by diffuse brain damage), and one endocrine disorder have all been associated with various types of criminal behaviour.

BIOLOGICAL FACTORS INDIRECTLY RELATED TO CRIMINAL BEHAVIOUR

As previously noted, longitudinal studies conducted in several countries throughout the world—England (Farrington and West, 1990), Finland (Pulkkinen, 1988), Sweden (Janson, 1989; Kratzer and Hodgins, 1999; Magnusson, 1988), and the United States (McCord, 1979; Robins, 1979)—have consistently shown that a small number of boys begin offending early and continue doing so through early adulthood. While few in number, they are responsible for the majority of crimes committed. For example, in a prospective longitudinal study of an unselected birth cohort composed of 1037 children in New Zealand, 5 percent of the boys were consistently rated (by themselves, their teachers, and their parents) as antisocial at ages 3, 5, 7, 9, 11, 13, and 15 (Moffitt, 1993). Similarly, I studied a Swedish birth cohort composed of 15 117 subjects followed from pregnancy to age 30. Among the boys rated by their teachers in Grades 6 and/or 9 as having problem behaviour, 70 percent had at least one conviction as adults. Among boys who were identified for delinquent behaviour in the community but not at school, 72.2 percent had at least one conviction as an adult. Among boys identified both by their teachers for problem behaviour and by community agencies for delinquency, 92.7 percent were convicted as adults for at least one offence. Among the boys who were identified by neither their teachers nor the community agency, 27.6 percent had criminal records by age 30. Most of this latter group had only one or two convictions, whereas three-quarters of the identified groups had three or more convictions (Hodgins, 1994).

cross-sectional investigation

A study, survey, or measurement of a phenomenon or a population taken at one point in time. For example, a census survey is cross-sectional.

The results of these longitudinal studies and of numerous **cross-sectional investigations** suggest that before they begin offending, these boys are different from their peers on a number of biological and behavioural measures. Their families behave differently toward them than families of boys who do not subsequently offend behave toward their sons. This constellation of factors, individual and familial, predicts adult criminality (for reviews see Moffitt, 1993; Stattin and Magnusson, 1996). This group of boys who are antisocial from a young age is not homogeneous. Existing data suggest that it includes at least four different types of persistently antisocial boys: (1) boys with low intelligence who have a great deal of difficulty learning as quickly as other children (Crocker and Hodgins, 1997); (2) boys who have difficulty concentrating and are restless (unable to stay still) from a very young age (Farrington et al., 1989; Klinteberg et al., 1993); (3) boys whose male relatives suffer from alcoholism (Pihl and Peterson, 1991; Virkkunen et al., 1994); and (4) pure antisocial boys (Hodgins et al., 1998; Crocker and Hodgins, 1997). It is presumed that determinants of the criminality among these four groups of boys are different. However, in all cases, biological factors (hereditary, pre- and postnatal injury) are hypothesized to interact with nonbiological factors—both individual factors (personality factors, cognitive ability, problem-solving capacities) and family factors (supervision, violence, chronic stress)—to determine the behaviours that are labelled criminal. Much less is known about delinquency, which begins and ends in adolescence (Patterson and Yoerger, 1993). However, recent findings suggest that social rather than individual factors are the most important determinants of criminal behaviour limited to the adolescent period (Kratzer and Hodgins, 1999).

Hereditary Factors

Most human characteristics are partially determined by hereditary factors. This is true of personality traits and intelligence. However, any predisposition is either brought out or suppressed by events that occur subsequent to conception. For example, although an individual's height is largely determined by one's genes, the mother's eating habits during pregnancy as well as the individual's own nutritional history interact with the hereditary factor to determine the individual's height as an adult. The mother's nutritional habits in turn have been influenced by her social class origins as well as by her social class at the time of the pregnancy, her attitudes toward the pregnancy, and so on. Even in this case, where the genetic factor is powerful, many other factors interact with it to determine an individual's height.

Chromosome Studies

At conception, each human receives 23 chromosomes from each parent for a total of 46. Each chromosome carries numerous genes, or proteins, which are active at specific times during the course of the person's life. The current knowledge about the role of hereditary factors in the determination of complex adult behaviours has happily ended an era marked by the search for chromosomal abnormalities that might cause criminality. Such abnormalities, which involve many genes, lead to severe disorders, each characterized by a highly stable pattern of symptoms. The last vestige of this kind of research involved the study of men possessing an extra male, or Y, chromosome. These men, known as XYY men, were said to be highly aggressive and disproportionately represented among prison inmates and security-hospital patients. What appears to be true, however, is simply that XYY males are taller and less intelligent than the average male. The investigation, which put to rest this line of research, included all men who had been born in Copenhagen in 1944, 1945, 1946, and 1947 (Witkin et al., 1977). In 1975, the chromosomes of all the 4139 men who were over 184 cm tall were examined. Twelve were identified who had an XYY profile. While these 12 men had more criminal convictions than did XY men of their age, height, intelligence, and social class, there was no evidence of violent behaviour on their part.

Family Studies

It has been repeatedly noted that criminals have numerous close relatives who are also criminals. Several well-known studies (for example, Farrington et al., 1996) have noted that a large proportion of adult criminals have parents and siblings who were convicted offenders. Although such investigations suggest that the family is important in determining criminal behaviour, they do not help us to separate its specific determinants such as learning, social class, heredity, and so on.

Twin Studies

Studies of the similarities between twin pairs with respect to criminal behaviour have been carried out in an effort to discover if a genetic factor can be implicated as a determinant of adult criminality. Such investigations compare concordance rates (proportion of twin pairs in which both twins manifest the characteristic under study) for **monozygotic twins** (twins who have the same genes) with those of **dizygotic twins** (twins who have, on average, half the same genes). If monozygotic pairs have higher concordance rates for criminal behaviour than dizygotic pairs, it is reasonable to postulate that a genetic factor may partially determine the criminal behaviour. In all the published investigations of this kind (see review by Bock and Goode, 1996), concordance rates for monozygotic twins are greater than those for dizygotic twins, clearly suggesting that a genetic factor is involved in determining the behaviour of adults. Such studies also provide information about the importance of the genetic factor. Concordance rates for the monozygotic pairs never reach 100 percent, thereby indicating that other factors play a causal role.

Twin studies also indicate that heritable factors associated with criminality are more powerful among women than among men. In other words, among women who are antisocial, the hereditary factor has to be more powerful than that observed among antisocial males in order to overcome socialization, which strongly discourages antisocial behaviour among women. Similarly, hereditary factors associated with criminality are stronger among twins from higher social classes and from rural areas in which the social factors associated with criminality are less important. By contrast, twin studies have also demonstrated that there is no hereditary factor associated with offending that is limited to adolescence (Lyons, 1996).

These data are not, however, conclusive proof that a genetic factor is implicated in the determination of criminal behaviour. All of the twin pairs in these studies had been reared together, thereby confounding possible causal factors.

monozygotic twins

Commonly known as identical twins, they are from a single egg that has divided after fertilization to create two embryos; consequently, they share exactly the same genetic material and are of the same sex.

dizygotic twins

Commonly known as fraternal twins, they are from two fertilized eggs; consequently they share no more genetic material than any other siblings and may be of different sexes.

The monozygotic twins may have been treated more similarly than the dizygotic pairs because they look so much alike. Such an interpretation would suggest that psychosocial factors, not a genetic factor, explain the higher concordance rates for monozygotic twins. However, further analyses have shown that both genetic factors and sibling interactions are important determinants of criminal behaviours (Carey, 1992).

Adoption Studies

Cross-fostering studies provide a naturally occurring experimental design that separates genetic factors from all the others. The most recent example of such an investigation was carried out by Mednick et al. (1984). All 14 427 nonfamilial adoptions that took place in Denmark between 1927 and 1947 were examined. A small number of subjects were lost because their date and/or place of birth was unknown. Court records were obtained for 65 516 biological parents, adoptive parents, and adopted children. As can be seen in Table 8.1, the children of biological parents with criminal records were more likely to have been convicted of criminal offences themselves than those whose parents had no such records. (The female adoptees are excluded from these analyses because of their low conviction rates.) This relation between biological parent convictions and adoptee convictions remains significant within each socioeconomic level.

   As Figure 8.1 indicates, the relation between the convictions of the male adoptees and the degree of recidivism of their biological parents is **statistically significant** for property crimes but not for violent offences. Similarly, in an adoption study conducted in Sweden, a hereditary factor was found to be associated with property crime but not with violent crime (Bohman et al., 1982).

   For purposes of the analysis, chronic offenders were defined as those with three or more convictions. Although they represented 4.1 percent of the male adoptees, they were responsible for 69.4 percent of all the male adoptees' convictions. As can be seen in Figure 8.1, the proportion of chronic adoptee offenders increases as a function of recidivism in the biological parent. But this genetic influence is not sufficient to produce a criminal adoptee. Seventy-five percent of the adoptees whose biological parents had three or more convictions were never convicted of a crime. Of the other 25 percent, 16 percent had one or two convictions, while 9 percent had three or more.

   The importance of these results is increased when the following methodological issues are considered. The cohort studied was very large, and the follow-up period was lengthy. The country in which the data were collected has very accurate criminal registers and a high rate of crime resolution. The adoptees who were excluded do not appear to differ from those who were included in the cohort: both had similar conviction rates and similar rearing status. Age of transfer to the adoptive home did not interact with the genetic influence. There was not an effect due to labelling the adopted child "criminal": the fact that the adoptive parents were informed of the biological parents' criminality did not alter the likelihood that the adoptee would be convicted of a crime. Children of biological mothers with criminal records were at greater risk

"Crime Genes: The Danish Adoption Studies"
The Gene Letter
www.geneletter.com/archives/
danishcrime.html

statistically significant

When researchers study differences within or between groups, they need a technique to determine if these differences would have occurred by chance. Various statistical techniques can determine this, and if it is unlikely that the differences could have occurred by chance, it is called a statistically significant difference. Usually, a .05 level of significance is used (there are five chances of 100 trials that this difference would occur by chance), but other levels can be used.

TABLE 8.1 "Cross-Fostering" Analysis: Percentage of Adopted Sons Who Have Been Convicted of Criminal Law Offences

	Are Biological Parents Criminal?	
Are Adoptive Parents Criminal?	*Yes*	*No*
Yes	24.5 (143)	14.7 (204)
No	20.0 (1226)	13.5 (2492)

Note: The numbers in parentheses are the total *N*s for each cell.

Source: W.F. Gabrielli and S.A. Mednick. (1983). "Genetic Correlates of Criminal Behavior." *American Behavioral Scientist* 27(1):61. Copyright © 1983. Reproduced with permission of Sage Publications, Inc.

of becoming criminals themselves than were the children of biological fathers with criminal records. However, the risk of criminality in the offspring did not differ depending on whether it was the adoptive mother or father who was criminal (Baker et al., 1989).

FIGURE 8.1 Percentage of Adoptees Convicted of Violent and Property Offences as a Function of Biological Parents' Convictions

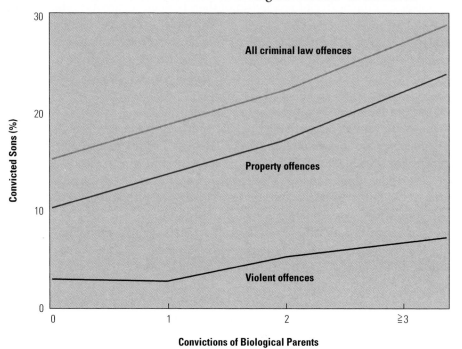

Source: S.A. Mednick, W.F. Gabrielli, and B. Hutchings. (1984). "Genetic Influences in Criminal Convictions: Evidence from an Adoption Cohort." *Science*: 893. Copyright © 1984 by the American Association for the Advancement of Science. Reprinted with permission of the American Association for the Advancement of Science. www.sciencemag.org.

Using this same cohort, the relations between social class and crime were analyzed (Van Dusen et al., 1983). The rates of conviction of the adopted sons varied inversely with the social class of their biological parents and with that of their adoptive parents. These relations held for property offences but not for violent offences, in which neither the social class of the biological parents nor that of the adopted parents was related to the adoptees' violent behaviour. The class–crime relation identified for overall conviction rates and for convictions for nonviolent offences is not specific to adoptees, but has been demonstrated for a cohort of 31 434 Danish men (Moffitt et al., 1981).

Social class of the biological parents and social class of the adoptive parents contribute independently to the criminal behaviour of the adoptees. However, the social class of the adoptive parents can exaggerate or mitigate the influence of the biological parents' social class. Similarly, it has been shown (Gabrielli and Mednick, 1984) that an urban environment can potentiate the genetic factor, and a rural environment can compensate for it. Again, in this latter investigation, no interaction was found between the genetic factor and the social one. Each contributed independently to the determination of criminal behaviour.

In a large adoption study (Sigvardsson et al., 1982) carried out in Sweden, it has been shown that the genetic factor related to adult criminality is the same for both sexes, but the nonbiological factors differ. While male criminality is more prevalent, female criminals have more relatives who are criminals than do male criminals. This finding indicates that the predisposition to criminality in a woman must be greater than that of a man in order for her to manifest criminal behaviour. It is suggested that because boys are encouraged to behave aggressively and independently while girls are taught the opposite, the adult women who do behave aggressively and independently have a greater genetic predisposition to these behaviours than their male counterparts.

While unstable pre-adoptive placement and low socio-economic status have been shown to relate to male criminality, no such relation exists for female criminality. However, prolonged early institutional care and being reared in an urban environment increase the risk of female criminality, but not that of male criminality (Sigvardsson et al., 1982; Wolkind, 1974). For males, the social class of the adoptive parents has more influence than that of the biological parents, but the reverse is true for females. These findings correspond to others in the child development literature which suggest that little boys are more fragile and reactive to family functioning (and dysfunctioning) than are girls (Maccoby and Jacklin, 1974).

These sex differences in the determination of adult criminal behaviour alert us to the probable complexity of the causal process. As noted at the beginning of the chapter, it is unlikely that all criminals have followed the same developmental path. In a study in Sweden (Bohman et al., 1982; Cloninger et al., 1982; Sigvardsson et al., 1982) of a cohort of adoptees, it was found that genetic as well as certain social antecedents of petty nonviolent criminal activity are different than those of alcohol-related criminality, which is more often violent and repetitive. Another adoption study (Crowe, 1974) carried out in the United States also distinguished these two kinds of criminality.

It may be more precise to speak about hereditary factors, rather than a single factor, associated with criminality. Research findings suggest that a number of traits that characterize those who become adult offenders are partially determined by their genes. For example, twin studies have revealed hereditary factors associated with aggressive behaviour. The boys identified in the longitudinal studies with early onset, persistent antisocial behaviour across the life span, are characterized by their frequent aggressive behaviour. However, animal studies have consistently shown that there are different hereditary factors associated with different types of aggressive behaviour (for example, aggressive behaviour to defend a territory versus aggressive behaviour in a fear-provoking situation). Similarly in humans, different hormonal patterns are associated with different types of aggressive behaviour. The other point to remember about aggressive behaviour is that it is one of the most, if not the most, stable of all human traits across the life span. In other words, in very large measure, aggressive children grow up to be aggressive adults (Olweus, 1979).

Studies are now beginning to identify particular genes associated with aggressive behaviour in humans. In a large Dutch family, it was observed that over six generations, a number of the men, but not the women, had low IQ scores and repetitive outbursts of severe aggressive behaviour. The aggressive men, but none of the other family members, have a mutated gene on the X chromosome that was failing to produce the enzyme necessary to break down the neurotransmitters (Morell, 1993). Another example of a trait that characterizes many offenders, and that is partially determined by genes, is impulsivity (Lyons et al., 1995). In addition, the early-start offenders who have been identified in the longitudinal studies meet the criteria for what is called antisocial personality disorder. This diagnosis is given to individuals who show a stable pattern of antisocial behaviour from a young age. This pattern of behaviour is at least partially heritable, both when it occurs in a pure form and when it is combined with attention-deficit hyperactivity disorder (Faraone et al., 1995).

To sum up, data from recent investigations point to the existence of hereditary factors in determining criminal behaviour. These factors, while consistently present, act in concert with a multitude of other biological and nonbiological factors. Therefore, even if a hereditary factor is present, the individual does not necessarily become a criminal. Genetic factors appear to be neither necessary nor sufficient to determine adult criminality. Just as the genetic factor differs by type of criminality, the other **etiological factors**, too, appear to vary by gender and by type of criminality. Such results clearly indicate that there is not one causal pathway to adult criminality but several different ones.

These findings have important implications for **social intervention programs**. It appears that some individuals who have a constitutional predisposition to adult criminal behaviour never manifest this predisposition. This suggests that other, nongenetic factors have protected them. If we could identify these factors, we could attempt to create experiences and/or environments that would mitigate the influence of genetic factors. Genes do not cause criminal behaviours. Genes code for proteins and enzymes, which in turn determine biological characteristics and processes. The goal is to understand how the hereditary factor or factors associated with criminality affect the individual's

etiological factor

A factor that encourages or causes a particular outcome. For example, addiction to hard drugs is a factor that can lead people into prostitution or criminal behaviour; being raised in a violent home is a factor that can lead to violent behaviour or being victimized by violence.

social intervention program

Activity by governments, social agencies, and volunteers designed to change and improve the social situation of individuals, groups, and communities; strengthen social bonds; and encourage internalization of social control.

biology, which in turn influences his or her perception of the world and response to it. Genes could, for example, render individuals vulnerable to brain damage either pre- or postnatally, which would in turn make it difficult for them to concentrate and to sit still; or genes could alter the neurochemistry of the brain, rendering the individual irritable and impulsive; or genes could alter the reactivity of the autonomic nervous system so that an individual reacts so little to events that are stressful to others that he or she cannot learn from individual experience; or genes could alter the brain's response to alcohol and thereby increase the likelihood that the individual will behave aggressively when intoxicated and in a conflict situation. Recent and ongoing research on twins and adoptees focuses on understanding how these hereditary predispositions are activated and suppressed by other nongenetic factors (see, for example, Cadoret et al., 1995).

Perinatal Factors

Evidence is now accumulating that the developing brain of a fetus is relatively fragile and sensitive to insult. This can be directly biological, for example, when the mother abuses alcohol and/or drugs, or indirectly biological, when the mother experiences a severe psychological stress and the physiological consequences are experienced by both her and the baby (Huttunen and Niskanen, 1978). Because so many violent offenders show signs of minor brain damage, it has been hypothesized that the damage resulted not only from their many fights, but was also a consequence of perinatal insult. Litt (1971) examined a birth cohort composed of 1944 individuals. He found that perinatal trauma predicted the number of impulsive criminal offences committed by age 36. In another prospective longitudinal investigation, perinatal factors have been found to be a precursor of impulsivity measured at age 18 (Baker and Mednick, 1984).

However, just as hereditary factors interact with social factors to determine behaviours, perinatal factors lead to damage, which interacts with the individual's environment. Birth complications in interaction with maternal rejection have been found to be associated with violent crime. However, this was true only for early-start offenders (Raine et al., 1994; 1997). Similarly, in another investigation, it has been shown that children who experienced perinatal trauma were more aggressive if they were being raised in nonintact families but not if their family was intact (Baker and Mednick, 1984). It has been hypothesized that children who have experienced complications during pregnancy and/or birth will grow up to be violent offenders if their parents modelled aggressive behaviour, but not in the absence of parental violence (Mednick et al., 1988). The developing brain sensitive not only to insult, but also to hormones from the mother. These may influence traits in the child such as sensation seeking and the tendency to respond with physical aggression (Resnick et al., 1993).

Minimal Brain Damage

Neuropsychological tests measure various cognitive functions and indicate brain dysfunction, which may be general or limited to one specific brain area. A recent review (Moffitt, 1990) found that in all but one of 32 studies, juvenile

National Perinatal Information Centre (U.S.A.)
www.npic.org

delinquents scored poorly on a substantial proportion of the tests administered. The more methodologically rigorous the study, the clearer the indication that boys and girls who become juvenile offenders show deficits in verbal functions (receptive and expressive language, oral and written) and in executive functions (abstraction, planning, inhibition of inappropriate responses, mental flexibility, sequencing, attention, and concentration) before offending. In a study of an unselected birth cohort composed of more than a thousand 15-year-old New Zealand children, neuropsychological testing revealed that verbal, memory, and visual-motor integration deficits characterized those boys and girls who reported offending. Self-reports of offending correlated highly with parental reports. This relation between brain function and self-reported delinquency was independent of social class, family adversity, and IQ (Moffitt, 1990). Similarly, in a prospective longitudinal investigation of boys in Montreal, those who displayed a stable pattern of aggressive behaviour throughout childhood performed poorly on measures of executive functions (tasks that challenge the frontal lobes). These aggressive boys were unable to organize several different concepts simultaneously, to uncover complex rules, to anticipate the consequences of their choices and behaviours, and to reflect abstractly in order to solve interpersonal and social problems (Séguin et al., 1995).

Intelligence (IQ) tests, if used with subjects matched to those on whom the test was developed and standardized, reflect the quality of brain functioning. Many studies (for a review, see Wilson and Herrnstein, 1985; Moffitt, 1990) have found that juvenile delinquents have lower IQs than nondelinquents. For example, in a longitudinal study of working-class boys in London (West and Farrington, 1973), Farrington found that low IQ characterized those convicted at the earliest ages (10 to 13 years) and those who offended repeatedly. This association between low IQ scores and delinquency was independent of family income and family size. Similarly, in two Swedish longitudinal studies of entire birth cohorts, it was found that three different measures of global intelligence were negatively related to being an extreme multiple offender. The relationship between intelligence and official criminality was unaffected by differences in population size, density, and homogeneity of the community in which the subject is raised (Reichel, 1989). In the Pittsburgh Youth Study, it was again found that lower IQ scores characterize delinquents and precede the delinquency, and that this relation is independent of race, socio-economic status, and observed test motivation (Lynam et al., 1993).

However, the relation between cognitive functioning and criminality is not direct or simple. Individual differences in cognitive functioning are partially determined by hereditary factors and in turn interact with the environment to determine the individual's behaviour. For example, Walsh (1992) studied male delinquents. He found that among those from very disadvantaged backgrounds, differences in performance and verbal IQ scores had no relation to violent crimes, while a lack of love and nurturing from their parents was highly related. Among those from advantaged families, the opposite was true: the difference in performance and verbal IQ scores was highly related to violent offending, and a lack of love or nurturing was not related.

The minor brain damage reflected by neuropsychological and IQ tests could be due to various kinds of insults to the brain during pregnancy or early life—for example, the mother's falling during pregnancy, the effects of instrument delivery, the young child's falling, or the child's being beaten. Some studies show that many aggressive offenders have suffered severe head injuries. As well, children who were physically abused are at increased risk for adult criminality, and particularly violence (Spatz Widom, 1989). This could be due to head injuries that they sustained.

In this regard, it is interesting to note that in all cultures, most offences are committed by boys and men. It is now known that the central nervous system of boys, from conception to puberty, is more fragile than that of girls (Jacklin, 1989). Thus, an event occurring either during or after pregnancy that damages a boy's brain does not always injure a girl's brain.

Another indication of minor brain damage in children is the presence of motor restlessness, impulsivity, and difficulty in paying attention. Boys who at age 13 were judged by their teachers to show these three characteristics and often to behave aggressively were significantly more likely than the others to be juvenile offenders. They were also more likely to become adult criminals (Magnusson, 1988).

In another longitudinal study in Finland, Pulkkinen (1983) obtained similar results using teacher ratings made when boys were only eight years old. Similarly, in a U.S. study (Loeber and Bowers, 1985), it was shown that teacher and parent ratings of motor activity, impulsivity, attention problems, and aggressive behaviour predict rates of juvenile offending. In addition, in a longitudinal study in London, England (Farrington et al., 1989), motor activity, impulsivity, and attention problems were found to be predictive of juvenile offending. Boys who show this constellation of factors—motor hyperactivity, impulsivity, attention problems, and aggressive behaviour—and who offend as juveniles also show significant impairment in neuropsychological tests (Moffitt, 1990).

Attention Deficit Disorder (sometimes called hyperactivity, hyperkinesis, or minimal brain damage) is a syndrome involving severe difficulty in paying attention and concentrating, impulsivity, fidgeting, restlessness, constant activity, aggressive behaviour, and, in adolescence, low self-esteem. This syndrome, which is from four to nine times more prevalent among boys than girls (American Psychiatric Association, 1994), is thought to result from minor damage to the central nervous system. Follow-up studies (see for example, Klinteberg et al., 1993; Hechtman et al., 1984; Hechtman and Weiss, 1983) indicate that a subgroup of these individuals become antisocial adults presenting many of the same symptoms that they did in childhood. Such children, who begin life with limited verbal and executive abilities, and who are impulsive, unable to sit still, frequently aggressive, and unable to pay attention, are difficult to deal with, both for parents and teachers. Unless the child has direct training to improve his or her self-control and concentration difficulties and to learn how to deal with conflict without resorting to physical violence, and unless the family can consistently respond to his behaviour, the problems will persist. Studies have often shown that children with these difficulties are raised in families that tolerate rather than sanction their aggressive behaviour. Such a child may become more and more frustrated at school because he or she cannot cope with the demands of the classroom. Low self-esteem, marginalization, lack of interest in school, and low academic achievement follow.

Brain Neurochemistry

The brain is composed of several circuits, each of which functions with a different chemical called a neurotransmitter. One of these circuits uses the neurotransmitter serotonin. In humans, a low level of brain serotonin has consistently been associated with impulsive violence and with traits of impulsivity and irritability. Among primates and nonprimates, it is associated with aggressive behaviour. Serotonin probably has its effect on behaviour by increasing the individual's sensitivity to aversive stimuli. Adults with low levels of brain serotonin have been shown to have a history of aggressive behaviour (Brown et al., 1979), to have more frequent police contacts than other subjects (van Praag, 1986a; 1986b), to be irritable (Brown and Goodwin, 1986), and to be hostile (Roy et al., 1988). Studies of impulsive violent offenders (Linnoila et al., 1983; Virkkunen et al., 1987) have found that these men have low levels of brain serotonin compared with offenders who *planned* similar crimes.

Brain serotonin is probably related to violent behaviours in several different ways. The results of a series of investigations by a group of Finnish investigators are presented in Table 8.2. These findings illustrate the complexity of the interactions of biological and nonbiological factors in determining aggressive behaviour, and also the necessity of identifying homogeneous subgroups of offenders with similar characteristics and determinants of violent behaviour. The research focused on offenders with a history of frequent, heavy drinking because in Finland, as in most countries in the Western world, alcohol-intoxicated individuals are involved in the majority of violent crimes and incidents of domestic violence (Pihl and Peterson, 1993). As can be noted in Table 8.2, three subgroups of alcoholic, violent offenders were distinguished: those whose violence was impulsive and who had a history of antisocial behaviour going back to at least early adolescence; those whose violence was impulsive but did not have a history of antisocial behaviour; and those whose violence was not impulsive. While the impulsive, violent offenders had low levels of serotonin and high scores on the trait of impulsivity, the nonimpulsive offenders did not. Other differences among these subgroups composed of male, alcoholic, violent offenders were also found. For example, the impulsive offenders with a history of antisocial behaviour going back to childhood had lower levels of corticotrophin. This hormone plays an active role in the process of consolidating memories. This is of great interest because, as was noted earlier, individuals with a stable pattern of antisocial behaviour from a young age do not learn from experience, particularly from negative experiences. This same group—male, alcoholic, impulsive, violent offenders with a history of stable antisocial behaviour—are also distinguished from other groups by high testosterone levels. Testosterone is not, as was previously thought, directly related to aggression. Rather, it is related to social dominance (Schaal et al., 1996). Individuals

TABLE 8.2 A Comparison of Violent, Alcoholic Male Offenders and Healthy Male Volunteers

Alcoholic Impulsive Violence Antisocial	Alcoholic Impulsive Violence Not Antisocial	Alcoholic Nonimpulsive Violence	Nonalcoholic Nonoffender Not Antisocial
↑serotonin[1]	↓serotonin[1]	↑serotonin[1]	=serotonin[1]
↓corticotropin[2]	=corticotropin	=corticotropin	=corticotropin
↑testosterone	=testosterone	=testosterone	=testosterone
↓physical activity during the day	equal amounts of physical activity during the day and the night	=physical activity during the day	=physical activity during the day
		↑physical activity at night	↓physical activity at night
↓IQ	↑IQ	=IQ	=IQ
↑impulsiveness[3]	=impulsiveness[3]	=impulsiveness[3]	=impulsiveness[3]
↓monotony avoidance[3]	=monotony avoidance[3]	=monotony avoidance[3]	=monotony avoidance[3]
↓↓ socialization[3]	↓↓ socialization[3]	↓socialization[3]	=socialization[3]
↑irritability[3]	↑irritability[3]		=irritability[3]
↑verbal aggression[3]	=verbal aggression[3]	=verbal aggression[3]	=verbal aggression[3]
↑psychic anxiety	↑psychic anxiety	=psychic anxiety[3]	=psychic anxiety[3]

1 5-HIAA (A metabolite of brain serotonin measured in the cerebrospinal fluid. Serotonin is associated with impulsive, violent behaviour.)

2 Corticotropin is produced in the pituitary gland. (In the brain, it is necessary for the consolidation of memory.)

3 Scores on subscales of the Karolinska Scales of Personality.

Source: Based on M. Virkkunen et al. (1994). "Personality Profiles and State Aggressiveness in Finnish Alcoholic, Violent Offenders, Fire Setters, and Healthy Volunteers," *Archives of General Psychiatry* 51:28–33 and "C.S.F. Biochemistries, Glucose Metabolism, and Diurnal Activity Rhythms in Alcoholic, Violent Offenders, Fire Setters, and Healthy Volunteers," *Archives of General Psychiatry* 51:20–27.

who are socially dominant consistently put themselves in frustrating situations. If, in addition to high testosterone levels, they also have low serotonin levels, they will have a tendency to behave aggressively (without thinking about the consequences) when they are frustrated (Bernhardt, 1997).

Thus, the findings in Table 8.2 provide evidence that the determinants of violent behaviour among three groups of alcoholic men differ. Males with a history of stable antisocial behaviour from a young age, who develop alcoholism and impulsively commit violent offences, have both lower-than-average IQ scores and low levels of corticotrophin, which suggest difficulties in learning; low levels of brain serotonin and stable traits of impulsiveness and irritability; and high levels of testosterone. The alcoholic men who also had committed impulsive, violent offences, but who did not have a stable pattern of antisocial behaviour from childhood, had average IQ scores and average levels of corticotrophin. These latter subjects showed low levels of brain serotonin but not the associated personality traits, and average levels of testosterone. However, they had very disturbed diurnal levels of activity. The alcoholic, violent offenders who planned their offences had higher-than-average brain serotonin levels, average levels of corticotrophin and testosterone, average diurnal activity levels, and average scores on the scales of personality traits. Children who receive diagnoses of Attention Deficit Disorder, Conduct Disorder, or Oppositional Defiant Disorder—characterized by hyperactivity, impulsivity, attention problems, and aggressive behaviour—have been shown to have low brain serotonin levels. In the first study of this kind, it was found that the children's levels of brain serotonin were negatively related to self-reports of the total number of aggressive incidents toward others (Kruesi et al., 1990). Low levels of brain serotonin were associated with repetitive and severe aggressive behaviour over the next two years, while low skin conductance and heart rate levels were associated with incarceration. These relationships remained even when other factors associated with criminality/aggression such as age, previous aggressive behaviour, previous antisocial behaviour, IQ, and family factors were controlled (Kruesi et al., 1992). These abnormal serotonin levels could result from the genes that have been associated with these childhood disorders that predate the adult offending.

The brain directs and controls peripheral body functions. If different subtypes of offenders have different abnormalities of the brain, depending on the particular abnormality, differences would be expected in physiological functions measured outside of the brain. Consequently, much research has focused on measures of the autonomic nervous system and the endocrine system.

Psychophysiological Factors

electrodermal response
Electrical activity of the sweat glands in the skin. Tests of electrodermal activity have indicated correlation between skin conductivity and tendency to delinquency, aggressiveness, and recidivism.

Several recent studies demonstrate distinctive functioning of the autonomic nervous system in some adult male criminals. (The autonomic nervous system is composed of the parts of the peripheral and central nervous systems that regulate visceral functions.) Just as we all have different faces, we all have different autonomic nervous systems. These characteristics of the autonomic nervous system are largely determined by genetic factors. Studies of the **electrodermal responses** (electrical activity of the sweat glands in the skin) show that slow recovery to baseline rates measured in young boys relates to delinquency (Loeb and Mednick, 1977) and to aggressiveness (Siddle et al., 1977; Clark, 1982), while among adult male criminals, it predicts recidivism (Hare, 1978). Further, in a longitudinal study, it was shown that those boys who became adult offenders had lower baseline skin conductance, lower heart rates, and slower brain activity than the other boys (Raine et al., 1990a; 1990b). Low pulse rate at age 11 has been related to severe delinquency at age 21 (Wadsworth, 1976). Those boys who subsequently committed violent crimes or sex offences had particularly low pulse rates at age nine. Similarly, low heart rate has been found to characterize boys who display a stable pattern of aggressive behaviour from middle childhood through adolescence (Mezzacappa et al., 1997) and to be predictive of juvenile offending (Raine and Venables, 1988). This relation appears to hold equally well for girls (Hume, 1986).

The characteristics of the autonomic nervous system interact with social factors to determine antisocial behaviour. For example, among pro-social children, those from families of lower socio-economic strata were found to have low skin conductance responses during a learning situation, while those from families of higher socio-economic strata learned easily, showing large skin conductance responses. Among the antisocial children, the pattern was reversed: those from families of lower socio-economic strata learned the skin response easily, while those from families of higher socio-economic strata had difficulty learning and showed small skin conductance responses (Raine and Venables, 1981). A similar interaction between heart rate levels, socio-economic status of the family of origin, and pro-social and antisocial behaviour has been demonstrated (Raine and Venables, 1984).

Mednick (Mednick and Finello, 1983; Mednick, 1977) has proposed a theory that illustrates the role these psychophysiological anomalies might play in the development of criminality. Based on knowledge of how learning occurs, Mednick argues that in order to learn to behave in accordance with social norms, a child requires (1) a censuring agent; (2) an adequate fear response; (3) the ability to learn the fear response in anticipation of an antisocial act; and (4) fast dissipation of fear to provide a natural positive reinforcement for the inhibitory response. Mednick's hypothesis of the absence of a censuring agent has received experimental support. Longitudinal studies have demonstrated that the families of children who become delinquent have failed to track and to censure their inappropriate behaviours from a young age (Patterson, 1986). Mednick proposes that the offender has inherited an autonomic nervous system that cannot react as in (2), (3), and (4). The results of many investigations suggest that this hypothesis explains the development of criminality among at least one subgroup of offenders.

Endocrine Factors

There is some evidence to suggest that boys who offend as juveniles and as adults have abnormally low levels of adrenaline. (This hormone is produced by the adrenal glands during states of general excitement or anxiety.) In a longitudinal study in Sweden (Magnusson, 1988), individuals who offended as juveniles and as adults showed lower levels of adrenaline at age 13 than those who never offended. The children with low adrenaline levels were rated by teachers and peers as being aggressive and restless. Olweus (1985) has shown that low adrenaline levels characterize boys who behave aggressively when not provoked. In three separate studies carried out in England (Woodman and Hinton, 1978; Woodman et al., 1977a; 1977b), it has been found that men convicted of violent offences show low levels of adrenaline and high levels of noradrenaline. (Noradrenaline, the chemical precursor of adrenaline, is also produced by the adrenal glands.) These findings are consistent with more general knowledge indicating that high adrenaline levels are associated with good social and personal adjustment (Bergman and Magnusson, 1979; Lambert et al., 1969).

Testosterone, a male sex hormone, has been related in animal studies to aggressive behaviour. While the results of the investigations presented in Table 8.2 are robust and clear, most findings on testosterone from studies of humans are notoriously contradictory (Archer, 1991; Scerbo and Kolko, 1994; Schaal et al., 1996). These contradictions most likely result because different researchers use different measures of testosterone (blood, urine, saliva), fail to control the time of day when the measure is taken, and attempt to relate the level directly to aggressive behaviour rather than to social dominance. Despite these methodological problems, the research with humans suggests that some violent offenders have elevated testosterone levels. For example, it was found that prisoners who had a history of violent crimes had higher salivary testosterone levels than prisoners with histories of nonviolent offending (Dabbs et al., 1995). In another investigation, a group of violent offenders had higher levels of testosterone than did nonviolent offenders, who in turn had higher levels than did nonoffenders (Schiavi et al., 1984). Elevated testosterone levels may be related only to certain forms of aggressive behaviour. Olweus (1983) found that plasma testosterone in adolescent boys related only to ratings of aggression "involving a response to provocation, including threat or unfair treatment." Scaramella and Brown (1978) studied hockey players and obtained similar results. Given that different forms of aggression are associated with different neural structures, it is not surprising that other biological correlates differ as well.

Ever since the appearance of a report by Hill and Sargant in 1943, a link between hypoglycemia (a low level of sugar in the blood) and aggressive behaviour has been suspected. More recently, a group of 60 habitually violent offenders and 47 percent of a sample of arsonists have been shown to react abnormally on a glucose tolerance test (Virkkunen and Huttunen, 1982; Virkkunen, 1982; 1984). It is proposed that low blood sugar levels, exacerbated by inadequate nutrition and high alcohol intake, lead to confusion, memory loss, and impulsive violent behaviour in certain vulnerable individuals. Similarly, but probably more prevalent, low cholesterol has been found to be associated with violent offending and violent suicide attempts (Golomb et al., 2000). Given the large number of persons who take medications that lower cholesterol levels, this biological factor could be a determinant of a significant amount of violent behaviour. The levels of another hormone, T3, triiodothyronine, have been found to distinguish early-start offenders (Alm et al., 1996). This finding is just another example of a peripheral biological measure that reflects the different biological functioning of males who display a stable pattern of antisocial behaviour from childhood through adulthood.

To resume, our knowledge of the biological factors that are indirectly related to criminal behaviour indicates that many different biological factors are involved. The most systematic and impressive finding in the large body of literature that has accumulated on this subject is that there are numerous developmental pathways to adult criminality, all of which include biological factors of one kind or another. Most research on the biological factors associated with criminality has focused on persistent behaviours that begin in early life. Genetic factors have been implicated in the determination of adult criminal behaviour. One of these factors is associated with repetitive property crime. Evidence to date would suggest that such a factor may operate by altering the chemistry of the brain and, as a consequence, other peripheral physiological functions, so that the individual fails to learn from his or her experience or is impulsive or lacking in self-control. Other hereditary factors are associated with aggressive behaviour. The extensive literature on aggressive behaviour among animals suggests that there are probably different genetic factors associated with different types of aggressive behaviour, and that these factors operate largely by altering the endocrine system. Another hereditary factor has been associated in males with a combination of alcoholism and persistent antisocial behaviour from a young age. It is important to remember that such hereditary factors can be present without the individual becoming a criminal. The hereditary factor is modified by the child's environment. Disturbances in fetal development may lead to changes in the baby's brain. Some of these changes appear to be associated with various types of aggressive behaviour. While both hereditary and perinatal factors can alter the biology of the individual in ways that contribute to the development of criminal behaviour, such changes in biology can also result from other factors such as physical abuse, severe psychological stress, and inappropriate parenting. Regardless of the cause, if the brain is altered, peripheral physiological systems such as the autonomic nervous system and the endocrine system will also be altered, and in turn will alter behaviour.

BIOLOGICAL FACTORS IMPLICATED IN PSYCHOPATHY

In recent years, a group of criminals fulfilling the criteria for psychopathy have been studied. Most of these investigations employed different methods for identifying psychopaths, thereby limiting the generalizations that can be made from the results. Robert Hare, at the University of British Columbia, has developed a scale to select psychopaths, which has proven to be both reliable and valid (Hare, 1991). The scale is presented in Table 8.3. As noted earlier, men who meet these diagnostic criteria for psychopathy represent about 22 percent of penitentiary inmates. There are no differences in the rates between French-speaking inmates in Quebec and English-speaking inmates in the rest of Canada. These men

"Without Conscience: The Website of the Hare Lab at UBC" **www.hare.org**

TABLE 8.3 The 20 Items of the Psychopathy Checklist

1. Glibness/superficial charm[p]	14. Impulsivity[ab]
2. Grandiose sense of self-worth[p]	15. Irresponsibility[ab]
3. Need for stimulation/proneness to boredom[ab]	16. Failure to accept responsibility for own actions[ab]
4. Pathological lying[p]	17. Many short-term marital relationships
5. Conning/manipulative[p]	18. Juvenile delinquency[ab]
6. Lack of remorse or guilt[p]	19. Revocation of conditional release[ab]
7. Shallow affect[p]	20. Criminal versatility
8. Callous/lack of empathy[p]	
9. Parasitic lifestyle[ab]	The checklist is composed of two factors: [p] identifies the items that define personality traits, and [ab] identifies items descriptive of antisocial behaviour.
10. Poor behavioural controls[ab]	
11. Promiscuous sexual behaviour	
12. Early behavioural problems[ab]	
13. Lack of realistic, long-term goals[ab]	

Source: R.D. Hare. (1991). "The Hare Psychopathy Checklist—Revised." Multi-Health Systems, Inc. Adapted from R.D. Hare. (1980). "A Research Scale for the Assessment of Psychopathy in Criminal Populations." *Personality and Individual Differences* 1:111–19. Oxford: Pergamon Press. © 1990 R.D. Hare. Reprinted with permission from Elsevier Science Ltd.

commit more crimes and more crimes of violence than penitentiary inmates who score lower on the Psychopathy Checklist (Hare and McPherson, 1984). Persons diagnosed psychopathic by Hare's Checklist would receive a diagnosis of Antisocial Personality Disorder (American Psychiatric Association, 1994; Hare, 1985). However, not all persons receiving a diagnosis of Antisocial Personality Disorder would be diagnosed psychopathic on Hare's Checklist.

There is evidence that a genetic factor contributes to the development of psychopathy (Schulsinger, 1977). Fifty-seven adult men who had been adopted away from their biological parents shortly after birth were clinically diagnosed as psychopaths. Their biological fathers—but not the biological mothers or the adopted parents—included a large number of psychopaths.

Overall, the autonomic nervous system of psychopaths does not differ from that of nonpsychopaths. However, three very specific differences have been discovered. First, psychopathic inmates show lower tonic electrodermal activity levels. Second, some studies have indicated that psychopaths react little or not at all in anticipation of positive and negative events. However, when psychopathic subjects were paid to play a game involving the avoidance of shock, their electrodermal responses were similar to those of nonpsychopaths in anticipating the aversive stimulus. Third, the psychopath's electrodermal activity returns to baseline levels of abnormality slowly after a response. In addition to these differences in the psychopaths' electrodermal responses, their heart rate responses in anticipation of a noxious stimulus appear to differ from those of nonpsychopaths (Hare, 1998). In 1978, Hare proposed that these autonomic nervous system differences indicate that psychopaths tune out or attenuate incoming stimuli and thereby inhibit fear. This hypothesis is supported by recent findings showing that psychopaths fail to show autonomic reactions (skin conductance, heart rate, muscle tension) to fearful imagery (Patrick et al., 1994).

More corroborating evidence for Hare's proposition comes from work by a group of Swedish researchers (Lidberg et al., 1978). They measured levels of adrenaline and noradrenaline in the urine of psychopathic and nonpsychopathic men waiting to appear in criminal court. The psychopaths showed no elevation of the hormone levels. Again, the researchers interpreted this finding as suggesting that psychopaths do not experience fear in anticipation of noxious events.

Despite the fact that male criminals who meet the criteria for psychopathy have average or above-average IQ scores, and that they show no deficits in brain functioning on standard neuropsychological tasks, historically there has been speculation that psychopathy is caused by inadequate functioning of the frontal lobes of the brain. In recent years, it has been shown that different parts of the frontal lobes are associated with different functions. In 1984, Hare showed that the performance of psychopathic inmates on cognitive tasks, which are indicative of dorsolateral prefrontal lobe functioning, did not differ from that of nonpsychopathic inmates or noncriminal control subjects. Recently, researchers compared the performance of male penitentiary inmates—one group diagnosed psychopaths by Hare's Checklist and the others nonpsychopaths—on a series of neuropsychological tests. It was found that the psychopaths performed worse than the nonpsychopaths on three tasks indicative of ventral frontal lobe functioning, but equally well on tests measuring functioning associated with other areas of the frontal lobes and other brain areas. For some reason, as yet undiscovered, psychopaths cannot activate the ventral part of the frontal lobes, and consequently, the capacities associated with these brain areas—impulsive control and odour detection—are reduced (LaPierre et al., 1995).

While these studies indicate that psychopaths have a specific deficit related to one small area of the frontal lobes, some evidence suggests that other parts of their brains may be functioning even better than those of nonpsychopaths. It has been shown that the parietal lobes of psychopaths attend longer to meaningful stimuli and that psychopaths achieve higher than average scores on tasks that require parietal lobe involvement (Raine and Venables, 1988).

Other differences in the functioning of the psychopath's brain have also been identified. For example, one study (Jutai and Hare, 1983, reported in Hare and McPherson, 1984) involved the recognition and categorization of words presented to either the right or left visual field. (Information presented to the right visual field is processed by the left hemisphere of the brain in which the structures related to verbal abilities are found. Information presented to the left visual field is processed by the right hemisphere.) In another of these studies (Hare and McPherson, 1984), auditory tasks were employed, and again, the information going to one or the other of the brain hemispheres was controlled. Psychopathic inmates, like nonpsychopathic inmates and noncriminal subjects, showed left-hemisphere superiority for simple verbal tasks, but unlike the nonpsychopaths, they showed right-hemisphere superiority when carrying out a more complex verbal task. The results of the auditory tasks also suggest that the brain hemispheres of the psychopathic subjects are less specialized than those of most people, at least for language functions.

Other experiments have shown that psychopaths do not distinguish neutral and emotionally charged words. Their brains actually process these two types of words similarly compared to nonpsychopaths, whose brains process these words differently. Consequently, it is hypothesized that when they lie, their words are not invested with any emotional content, and consequently, they show none of the physiological reactions usually associated with lying in other people. Further, psychopaths have been found to speak more quietly and more quickly, and biological measures of their speaking patterns indicate that they fail to distinguish between neutral and emotionally charged words (Louth et al., 1998). This hypothesis, that semantic and emotional processes are disassociated in psychopaths, is further supported by the findings reported above that their autonomic nervous systems do not react in anticipation of noxious stimuli or when imagining fearful stimuli. These findings suggest that language exerts little control over the psychopaths' behaviour. This line of thinking is intriguing not only because it has produced substantial findings, but also because it relates to numerous clinical descriptions of the psychopath as a person whose eloquent verbal discourses in no way correspond to his or her behaviour.

Men diagnosed as psychopaths commit more crimes generally and more violent crimes than nonpsychopaths. Research has implicated a genetic factor in the determination of psychopathy. Psychopaths show differences in electrodermal response when compared to nonpsychopaths. They have lower baseline levels, no reaction in anticipation of negative events (except when rewarded for doing so), and slow recovery to baseline levels after a response. Their cardiovascular response and adrenaline and noradrenaline levels in anticipation of negative events are also different from those of nonpsychopaths. Their autonomic nervous systems react little to imagined fearful situations. Recent neuropsychological studies suggest that the cognitive functioning of psychopaths differs in only very specific ways from that of equally intelligent nonpsychopaths. A deficit in ventral frontal lobe functioning that is related to impulsivity and odour discrimination has been identified. Other experiments have shown that psychopaths speak differently than nonpsychopaths, that their brains do not distinguish neutral and emotionally charged words, and that language capacities are spread across two hemispheres rather than being restricted to the left, which is the case in most humans.

Trasler (1978) has proposed a theory to account for psychopathy. He presumes initially that the prime characteristic of the psychopath is an "insusceptibility to social influences." The psychopath simply does not learn from negative experiences or punishment. Trasler suggests that law-abiding behaviour is learned principally by a procedure that is called passive avoidance learning—that is, learning not to make a response that would elicit punishment. Even though one may be tempted to make such a response (for example, to steal a handsome shirt), one inhibits the response after realizing the negative consequences (being arrested) that would ensue. The emotional reactions (fear, shame, and anxiety) accompanying the thoughts of the negative consequences are relieved when the response is inhibited so that one doesn't steal the shirt. Thus, the behaviour of not stealing is positively reinforced by the reduction of the feelings of fear, shame, and anxiety. This kind of learning is controlled by specific structures and pathways in the brain. Trasler theorizes that psychopaths are poor passive avoidance learners: they fail to learn not to commit illegal acts because they feel little or no fear. Trasler interprets the findings that the electrodermal and cardiovascular systems of psychopaths react abnormally in anticipation of a noxious stimulus as suggesting that they do not anticipate negative consequences emotionally. This theory, while intriguing, accounts for only part of what is now known about psychopaths. It does not account for the recent findings on impulsivity and language.

MAJOR MENTAL DISORDERS

Six follow-up studies of unselected birth cohorts have now shown that more people, both male and female, who develop major mental disorders (schizophrenia, bipolar disorders, major depression) commit crimes and crimes of violence compared to those who never develop these disorders. On average, the offenders with major mental disorders are convicted for more offences than, or as many as, the nondisordered offenders. They commit all types of crimes (Hodgins, 1998; Hodgins, 1995). There is evidence that those with major mental disorders are at particular risk to commit homicide (Côté and Hodgins, 1992).

It is not surprising then that recent investigations of representative samples of U.S. jail inmates, prison inmates, and Canadian penitentiary inmates (Hodgins and Côté, 1990; 1995) have shown that the prevalence of major mental disorders within these populations exceeds that in the general population. In the Canadian study, the prevalence rate of schizophrenia among inmates was seven times higher than among nonoffender males, the rate of bipolar illness was four times higher, while the rate of major depression was about three times higher.

Looking at the same phenomenon from the opposite point of view, studies that have tracked persons with major mental disorders after discharge from a psychiatric ward have consistently shown that they commit more offences than nondisordered persons living in the same community (Hodgins, 1993).

Thus, many convicted offenders suffer from severe, chronic mental disorders, which devastate individuals throughout their lives, beginning in late adolescence. The determinants of these disorders include biological factors. Powerful genetic factors have been implicated in all three disorders. Perinatal disturbance has been identified as a determinant of schizophrenia. The interactions of the biological and nonbiological factors in determining these disorders remain to be identified. The relationship of the mental disorder to the criminality is at present unknown. The process appears to be rather complicated. There appear to be two types of offenders with major mental disorders (Hodgins and Côté, 1993; Hodgins et al., 1998). The "early starters" display a stable pattern of antisocial behaviour from a young age, while the "late starters" begin offending only when the mental disorder is present. It is further hypothesized that while the symptoms of the mental disorder are determinants of the offending of the late starters, the major mental disorder is not associated with the offending of the early starters. You will read more about the relationship between mental illness and crime in Chapter 9, "Psychological Perspectives on Criminality."

ALCOHOL AND DRUG ABUSE

In the study referred to previously (Hodgins and Côté, 1990) of a representative sample of Canadian penitentiary inmates, it was found that among those who had never suffered from a major mental disorder, 67 percent had met or did meet the medical criteria for alcohol abuse and/or dependence. Almost half (49 percent) of the inmates had, at least one time in their lives, met the medical criteria for drug abuse and/or dependence. This over-representation of substance abusers among criminals has often been documented (see, for example, Janson, 1989). Substance abuse is associated both with violent criminal offending (Janson, 1989; Toch and Adams, 1989) and with violent behaviour that does not lead to criminal charges (see, for example, Hodgins and Larouche, 1980). Genetic factors leading to abnormal brain processing of alcohol are determinants of alcoholism. The antisocial men described in the left column of Table 8.2 who committed impulsive violent offences may well suffer from an inherited form of early onset alcoholism. Many of the same childhood factors that are associated with adult offending are also associated with drug abuse (Magnusson, 1988). Recently, genes associated with the trait of novelty seeking have been identified (Ebstein et al., 1996). The genes affect behaviour by altering neurotransmitters in the brain so that novel events—for example, intoxication by drugs—are especially positive.

CONCLUSION

The role of biological factors in the development of human behaviour is still poorly understood. Consequently, our limited knowledge of those biological factors implicated in the development of criminal behaviour is not surprising. Biological factors interact with one another and with other nonbiological factors in complex causal chains to determine behaviour. The more precisely the behaviour in question is defined, the more likely it is that the determinants can be identified. Many different behaviours are defined as criminal, and each has a distinct combination of determinants. Investigations of the biological factors involved in determining such behaviours often fail to take into account characteristics of the society that may alter the importance of the biological factor.

As has been discussed, biological states and factors are in some rare cases directly implicated as causes of behaviours labelled criminal. However, in most instances, biological factors act indirectly in determining such behaviours. In all cases, they interact with numerous other factors. Longitudinal studies of unselected birth cohorts from early age until late adulthood are beginning to provide invaluable documentation on these various pathways to crime. The findings from these studies are powerful: factors are measured before offending

TABLE 8.4 Biological Perspectives on Crime

Theory	Biological States	Key Elements
Direct biological disorders	Destructive brain processes Brain damage Epileptic disorders Endocrine disorders	Certain rare types of biological states are believed to directly cause criminal behaviour. Typically, these operate by triggering aggressive behaviour.
Indirect biological factors	Hereditary factors Perinatal factors Minimal brain damage Brain neuro chemistry Psychophysiological factors Endocrine factors	The contribution of most biological factors to crime is typically mediated by the social environment. Some people may be biologically predisposed to crime, but social factors such as family, peer associations, school, and neighbourhood characteristics may suppress these antisocial tendencies. Similarly, people who do not have a biological predisposition may become criminal if their environment is criminogenic.
Biological factors in psychopathy	Autonomic nervous system factors	There is evidence that a genetic factor contributes to psychopathy. Autonomic nervous system differences suggest that psychopaths may be less responsive to incoming stimuli that normally result in a fear reaction.
Major mental disorders	Schizophrenia Bipolar disorders Major depression	The prevalence of major mental disorders is higher among prison inmates than among the general population. The determinants of these disorders include biological factors.

begins, and factors both internal and external to the subject are examined simultaneously. These investigations are providing an understanding of the complex interactions of factors that determine criminal behaviours. Such information is necessary for the development of successful prevention programs.

SUMMARY

- Biological factors play a role in determining behaviour. These factors interact among themselves and with other nonbiological factors in complex causal chains. Most biological factors are related only indirectly to criminal behaviour.

- Biological factors directly related to criminal behaviour exist but are very rare. These include tumours, brain disease, and certain forms of epilepsy when accompanied by diffuse brain damage.

- Young children who have difficulty sitting still and paying attention and who are impulsive and aggressive are at risk for antisocial behaviour as adults.

These children's endocrine systems react differently from those of other children. Also, children who become juvenile delinquents have fewer verbal and executive abilities than other children. These deficits are indicative of minor brain damage.

■ Some studies have shown that the electrodermal system, the cardiovascular system, and the adrenal glands of criminals react differently in some situations from those of noncriminals. These findings have been interpreted as manifestations of a hereditary factor that has been implicated in criminal behaviour. The influence of this hereditary factor that has been implicated in criminal behaviour is mediated by the social environment, particularly family factors.

■ Investigation of male inmates fulfilling the criteria for psychopathy has uncovered several biological characteristics specific to them. These results have led some researchers to conclude that psychopaths are unable to learn to passively avoid making a response that will lead to negative consequences.

■ Several studies have found that persons who suffer from major mental disorders are at greater risk than nondisordered persons to commit crimes, particularly crimes of violence.

QUESTIONS FOR CRITICAL THINKING

1. Crime is socially defined—our informal rules and our formal laws are developed by members of society and are constantly changing. How can biological factors be related to socially defined behaviour such as crime?
2. Give examples of hereditary factors, perinatal factors, and early childhood factors that may affect the development of offending.
3. Consider three of the biological factors that are related to criminality. What are the social policy implications of each of these theories? In other words, how should society deal with people whose biological make-up is a cause of their criminality?

NET WORK

The disorders of psychopathy and Antisocial Personality Disorder are discussed both in this chapter and in Chapter 9. You can learn more about the work of Robert Hare at his website: **www.hare.org.**

For this Net Work exercise, go to the Internet Mental Health website at **www.mentalhealth.com**. Considering the material in the "Research" and "Magazine Articles" sections at this website and some of the content of Robert Hare's site, discuss how recent work on psychopathy has tried to deal with the problem you have identified in the first part of the exercise.

KEY TERMS

cross-sectional investigation
dizygotic twins
electrodermal response
etiological factor
longitudinal study

monozygotic twins
operationally defined
recidivism
social intervention program
statistically significant

SUGGESTED READING

Raine, A., P.A. Brennan, D.P. Farrington, and S.A. Mednick (eds.). (1997). *Biosocial Bases of Violence.* New York: Plenum. This book focuses on interactions between biological and nonbiological factors that contribute to the development of violent behaviour. Twenty-nine chapters, written by the leading researchers in the world in this field, critically review what is known about the etiology of violent behaviour and violent criminality. Many of the chapters are good illustrations of multidisciplinary collaboration, which furthers our understanding of the causes of violence.

Stoff, D.M., J. Breiling, and J.D. Maser (eds.). (1997). *Handbook of Antisocial Behavior.* New York: John Wiley and Sons. This book with 50 chapters is authored by the leading researchers in this field. They present up-to-date critical reviews of empirical investigations of antisocial behaviour, its etiology, and its management. The chapters vary in their accessibility to nonspecialist readers, but they are generally quite comprehensible. More information on any of the topics covered in the present chapter can be found in this very comprehensive handbook.

Volavka, J. (1995). *Neurobiology of Violence.* Washington, D.C.: American Psychiatric Press. This is a specialized volume that synthesizes an enormous body of work on neuroscience and violence. It uses many technical terms but the explanations of how and why certain brain processes are relevant to our understanding of violent behaviour are clear and concise and, with effort, can be understood by the nonspecialist.

BIBLIOGRAPHY

Alm, P.O., B. Klinteberg, K. Humble, J. Leppert, S. Sörensen, R. Tegelman, L.H. Thorell, and L. Lidberg. (1996). "Criminality and Psychopathy as Related to Thyroid Activity in Former Juvenile Delinquents." *Acta Psychiatrica Scandinavica* 92:1–6.

American Psychiatric Association. (1994). *Diagnostic and Statistical Manual of Mental Disorders* (3rd ed.), Revised (DSM-IV). Washington, D.C.

Archer, J. (1991). "Influence of Testosterone on Human Aggression." *British Journal of Psychology* 82:1–28.

Asso, D. (1984). *The Real Menstrual Cycle.* Toronto: Wiley.

Baker, L.A., W. Mack, T.E. Moffitt, and S. Mednick. (1989). "Sex Differences in Property Crime in a Danish Adoption Cohort." *Behavior Genetics* 19:355–70.

Baker, R.L., and B.R. Mednick. (1984). *Influences on Human Development: A Longitudinal Perspective.* Boston: Kluwer-Nijhoff Publishing.

Bergman, L.R., and D. Magnusson. (1979). "Overachievement and Catecholamine Excretion in an Achievement-Demanding Situation." *Psychosomatic Medicine* 41:181–88.

Bernhardt, P.C. (1997). "Influences of Serotonin and Testosterone in Aggression and Dominance: Convergence with Social Psychology." *Current Directions in Psychological Science* 6:44–48.

Bock, G.R., and J.A. Goode. (1996). *Genetics of Criminal and Antisocial Behaviour.* Chichester, U.K.: John Wiley and Sons.

Bohman, M., R. Cloninger, S. Sigvardsson, and A.-L. Von Knorring. (1982). "Predisposition to Petty Criminality in Swedish Adoptees: I. Genetic and Environmental Heterogeneity." *Archives of General Psychiatry* 39:1233–41.

Borum, R., and K.L. Appelbaum. (1996). "Epilepsy, Aggression, and Criminal Responsibility." *Psychiatric Services* 47:762–63.

Brown, G.L., J.C. Ballanger, M.D. Minichiello, and F.K. Goodwin. (1979). "Human Aggression and Its Relationship to Cerebrospinal Fluid 5-Hydroxyindoleacetic Acid, 3-Methoxy, 4-Hydroxyphenylglycol, and Homovanillic Acid." In M. Sandler (ed.), *Psychopharmacology of Aggression* (pp. 131–48). New York: Raven Press.

Brown, G.L., and F.K. Goodwin. (1986). "Cerebrospinal Fluid Correlates of Suicide Attempts and Aggression." In J.J. Mann and M. Stanley (eds.), *Psychobiology of Suicide. Annals of the New York Academy of Sciences* 487:175–88.

Cadoret, R.J., W.R. Yates, E. Troughton, G. Woodworth, and M. Stewart. (1995). "Genetic-Environmental Interaction in the Genesis of Aggressivity and Conduct Disorders." *Archives of General Psychiatry* 52:916–24.

Carey, G. (1992). "Twin Imitation for Antisocial Behaviour: Implications for Genetic and Family Environment Research." *Journal of Abnormal Psychology* 101:18–25.

Clark, F. (1982). "Relationship of Electrodermal Activity at Age 3 to Aggression at Age 9: A Study of Physiological Sellstrate of Temperament." Unpublished doctoral dissertation, University of Southern California.

Cloninger, C.R., S. Sigvardsson, M. Bohman, and A.-L. Von Knorring. (1982). "Predisposition to Petty Criminality in Swedish Adoptees: II. Cross-Fostering Analysis of Gene-Environment Interaction." *Archives of General Psychiatry* 39:1241–47.

Cooke, D. (1997). "Psychopaths: Over-sexed, Overplayed But Not Over Here?" *Criminal Behaviour and Mental Health* 7:3–111.

Côté, G., and S. Hodgins. (1992). "The Prevalence of Major Mental Disorders Among Homicide Offenders." *International Journal of Law and Psychiatry* 15:89–99.

Crocker, A.G., and S. Hodgins. (1997). "The Criminality of Noninstitutionalized Mentally Retarded Persons: Evidence from a Birth Cohort Followed to Age 30." *Criminal Justice and Behavior* 24:432–54.

Crowe, R.R. (1974). "An Adoption Study of Antisocial Personality." *Archives of General Psychiatry* 31:785–91.

Dabbs, J.M., T.S. Carr, R.L. Frady, and J.K. Riad. (1995). "Testosterone, Crime, and Misbehavior among 692 Male Prison Inmates." *Personality and Individual Differences* 18:627–33.

Dalton, K. (1961). "Menstruation and Crime." *British Medical Journal* 2:1752–53.

Detre, T., D.J. Kupfer, and J.D. Taub. (1975). "The Nosology of Violence." In W.S. Fields and W.H. Sweet (eds.), *Neural Bases of Violence and Aggression.* St. Louis, Mo.: Warren H. Green.

d'Orban, P.T., and J. Dalton. (1980). "Violent Crime and the Menstrual Cycle." *Psychological Medicine* 10:353–59.

Dougherty, D.M., J.M. Bjork, D. Huang, and F.G. Moeller. (1997). "The Relationship between Self-Reported Menstrual Symptomatology and Aggression Measured in the Laboratory." *Personality and Individual Differences* 22:381–91.

Ebstein, R.P., O. Novick, R. Umansky, B. Priel, Y. Osher, D. Blaine, E.R. Bennett, L. Nemanov, M. Katz., R.H. Belmaker. (1996). "Dopamine D4 Receptor (D4DR) Exon III Polymorphism Associated with the Human Personality Trait of Novelty Seeking." *Nature Genetics* 12:79–80.

Epps, P. (1962). "Women Shoplifters in Holloway Prison." In T.C.N. Gibbens and J. Prince (eds.), *Shoplifting* (pp. 132–45). London: Institute for the Study of the Treatment of Delinquency.

Faraone, S.V., J. Biederman, W.J. Chen, S. Milberger, R. Warburton, and M.T. Tsuang. (1995). "Genetic Heterogeneity in Attention-Deficit Hyperactivity Disorder (ADHD): Gender, Psychiatric Co-Morbidity, and Maternal ADHD." *Journal of Abnormal Psychology* 104:334–45.

Farrington, D.P., G.C. Barnes, and S. Lambert. (1996). "The Concentration of Offending in Families." *Legal and Criminological Psychology* 1:47–63.

Farrington, D.P., R. Loeber, and W.B. van Kammen. (1989). "Long-Term Criminal Outcomes of Hyperactivity-Impulsivity-Attention Deficit and Conduct Problems in Childhood." In L.N. Robins and M. Rutter (eds.), *Straight and Devious Pathways from Childhood to Adulthood* (pp. 62–81). Cambridge: Cambridge University Press.

Farrington, D.P., and D.J. West. (1990). "The Cambridge Study in Delinquent Development: A Long-Term Follow-up of 411 London Males." In H.-J. Kerner and G. Kaiser (eds.), *Criminality: Personality, Behavior, Life History* (pp. 115–38). Berlin: Springer Verlag.

Gabrielli, W.F., Jr., and S.A. Mednick. (1983). "Genetic Correlates of Criminal Behavior." *American Behavioral Scientist* 27:59–74.

———. (1984). "Urban Environment, Genetics, and Crime." *Criminology* 22:645–52.

Golomb, B.A., H. Stattin, and S. Mednick. (2000). "Low Cholesterol and Violent Crime." *Journal of Psychiatric Research* 34 (4–5):301–9.

Hare, R.D. (1978). "Electrodermal and Cardiovascular Correlates of Psychopathy." In R.D. Hare and D. Schalling (eds.), *Psychopathic Behaviour: Approaches to Research* (pp. 107–44). Toronto: Wiley.

———. (1984). "Performance of Psychopaths on Cognitive Tasks Related to Frontal Lobe Function." *Journal of Abnormal Psychology* 93:133–40.

———. (1985). "A Comparison of Procedures for the Assessment of Psychopathy." *Journal of Consulting and Clinical Psychology* 53:7–16.

———. (1991). *The Hare Psychopathy Checklist Revised.* Toronto: Multi-Health Systems, Inc.

———. (1998). "Psychopathy, Affect and Behavior." In D.J. Cook, A.E. Forth, and R.D. Hare (eds.), *Psychopathy: Theory, Research and Implications for Society* (pp. 105–38). Dordrecht, The Netherlands: Kluwer.

Hare, R.D., and L. McPherson. (1984). "Violent and Aggressive Behaviour by Criminal Psychopaths." *International Journal of Law and Psychiatry* 7:35–50.

Hechtman, L., and G. Weiss. (1983). "Long-Term Outcome of Hyperactive Children." *American Journal of Orthopsychiatry* 53:532–41.

Hechtman, L., G. Weiss, and T. Periman. (1984). "Hyperactives as Young Adults: Past and Current Substance Abuse and Antisocial Behavior." *American Journal of Orthopsychiatry* 54:415–25.

Hill, D., and W. Sargant. (1943). "Homicide in Hypoglycaemia." *Lancet* i:526–27.

Hodgins, S. (1993). "The Criminality of Mentally Disordered Persons." In S. Hodgins (ed.), *Mental Disorder and Crime.* Newbury Park, Calif.: Sage.

———. (1994). "Early Identification of Children With Conduct Problems." *Studies of Crime and Crime Prevention* 3:41–62.

———. (1995). "Major Mental Disorder and Crime: An Overview." *Psychology, Crime and Law* 2:5–17.

———. (1998). "Epidemiological Investigations of the Association between Major Mental Disorders and Crime: Methodological Limitations and Validity of the Conclusions." *Social Psychiatry and Epidemiology* 33(1):29–37.

Hodgins, S., and G. Côté. (1990). "The Prevalence of Mental Disorders Among Penitentiary Inmates." *Canada's Mental Health* 38:1–5.

———. (1993). "The Criminality of Mentally Disordered Offenders." *Criminal Justice and Behavior* 28:115–29.

———. (1995). "Major Mental Disorder Among Canadian Penitentiary Inmates." In L. Stewart, L. Stermac, and C. Webster (eds.), *Clinical Criminology: Toward Effective Correctional Treatment* (pp. 6–20). Toronto: Solicitor General and Corrections Canada.

Hodgins, S., G. Côté, and J. Toupin. (1998). "Major Mental Disorders and Crime: An Etiological Hypothesis." In D. Cooke, A. Forth, and R.D. Hare (eds.), *Psychopathy: Theory, Research and Implications for Society* (pp. 231–56). Dordrecht, The Netherlands: Kluwer Academic Publishers.

Hodgins, S., J. Hébert, and R. Baraldi. (1986). "Women Declared Incompetent to Stand Trial and/or Not Guilty by Reason of Insanity: A Follow-Up Study." *International Journal of Law and Psychiatry* 8:203–16.

Hodgins, S., and G. Larouche. (1980). *Violence conjugale: Antécédents et conséquences.* Rapport de recherche soumis au Solliciteur général du Canada.

Hume, W.I. (1986). "Heart Rate Levels in Female Subjects and Their Associations with Antisocial Behaviour and Eysenck's Three Personality Dimensions." Unpublished manuscript, University College, London, Department of Psychology.

Huttunen, M., and P. Niskanen. (1978). "Prenatal Loss of Father and Psychiatric Disorders." *Archives of General Psychiatry* 35:429–31.

Jacklin, C.N. (1989). "Female and Male: Issue of Gender." *American Psychologist* 44(2):127–33.

Janson, C.G. (1989). "Psychiatric Diagnoses and Recorded Crimes." In C.G. Janson and A.M. Janson (eds.), *Crime and Delinquency in a Metropolitan Cohort* (pp. 31–55). Stockholm: University of Stockholm.

Jutai, J.M., and R.D. Hare. (1983). "Psychopathy and Selective Attention During Performance of a Complex Perceptual-Motor Task." *Psychomyology* 20(2):146–51.

Klinteberg, B., T. Andersson, D. Magnusson, and H. Stattin. (1993). "Hyperactive Behavior in Childhood as Related to Subsequent Alcohol Problems and Violent Offending: A Longitudinal Study of Male Subjects." *Personality and Individividual Differences*, 4:381–88.

Kratzer, L., and S. Hodgins. (1999). "A Typology of Offenders: A Test of Moffitt's Theory Among Males and Females from Childhood to Age 30." *Criminal Behaviour and Mental Health* 9:57–73.

Kruesi, M.J.P., E.D. Hibbs, T.P. Zahn, C.S. Keysor, S.D. Hamburger, J.J. Bartko, and J.L. Rapoport. (1992). "A 2-Year Prospective Follow-up Study of Children and Adolescents with Disruptive Behavior Disorders." *Archives of General Psychiatry* 49:429–35.

Kruesi, M.J.P., J.L. Rapoport, S., Hamburger, E. Hibbs, W.Z. Potter, M. Lenane, and G.L. Brown. (1990). "Cerebrospinal Fluid Monoamine Metabolites, Aggression, and Impulsivity in Disruptive Behavior Disorders of Children and Adolescents." *Archives of General Psychiatry* 47:419–26.

Lambert, W.W., G. Johansson, M. Frankenhaeuser, and I. Klackenberg-Larsson. (1969). "Catecholamine Excretion in Young Children and Their Parents as Related to Behavior." *Scandinavian Journal of Psychology* 10:306–18.

LaPierre, D., C.M.J. Braun, and S. Hodgins. (1995). "Ventral Frontal Deficits in Psychopathy: Neuropsychological Test Findings." *Neuropsychologia* 33:139–51.

Lewis, D.O., S.A. Shanok, and D.A. Balla. (1979). "Perinatal Difficulties, Head and Face Trauma, and Child Abuse in the Medical Histories of Seriously Delinquent Children." *American Journal of Psychiatry* 136:419–23.

Lezak, M.D., and K.P. O'Brien. (1988). "Longitudinal Study of Emotional, Social, and Physical Changes after Traumatic Brain Injury." *Journal of Learning Disabilities* 21:456–63.

Lidberg, L., S. Levander, D. Schalling, and Y. Lidberg. (1978). "Urinary Catecholamines, Stress, and Psychopathy: A Study of Arrested Men Awaiting Trial." *Psychosomatic Medicine* 40:116–25.

Linnoila, M., M. Virkkunen, M. Scheinin, A. Nuutila, R. Rimon, and F.K. Goodwin. (1983). "Low Cerebrospinal Fluid 5-Hydroxyindoleacetic Acid Concentration Differentiates Impulsive from Nonimpulse Violent Behavior." *Life Science* 33:2609–14.

Litt, S.M. (1971). "Perinatal Complications and Criminality." Unpublished doctoral dissertation, University of Michigan.

Loeb, J., and S.A. Mednick. (1977). "A Prospective Study of Predictors of Criminality. 3. Electrodermal Response Patterns." In S.A. Mednick and K.O. Christiansen (eds.), *Biosocial Bases of Criminal Behavior* (pp. 245–54). New York: Gardner Press.

Loeber, R. (1988). "Behavioral Precursors and Accelerators of Delinquency." In W. Buikhuisen and S.A. Mednick (eds.), *Explaining Criminal Behavior* (pp. 51–67). New York: E.J. Brill.

Loeber, R., and B. Bowers. (1985). "A Five Year Follow-Up Evaluation of the Multiple Gating Procedure." Unpublished manuscript, Western Psychiatric Institute and Clinic, Pittsburgh, Pa.

Louth, S.M., S.E. Williamson, M. Alpert, E.R. Pouget, and R.D. Hare. (1998). "Acoustic Distinctions in the Speech of Psychopaths." *Journal of Research in Psycholinguistic Research* 273(3):37–84.

Lynam, D., T. Moffitt, and M. Stouthamer-Loeber. (1993). "Explaining the Relation between IQ and Delinquency: Class, Race, Test Motivation, School Failure, or Self-Control?" *Journal of Abnormal Psychology* 102:187–96.

Lyons, M.J. (1996). "A Twin Study of Self-Reported Criminal Behaviour." In G.R. Bock and J.A. Goodeman (eds.), *Genetics of Criminal and Antisocial Behaviour* (pp. 61–70). Chichester, England: John Wiley and Sons.

Lyons, M.J., W.R. True, S.A. Eisen, J. Goldberg, J.M. Meyer, S.V. Faraone, L.J. Eaves, and M.T. Tsuang. (1995). "Differential Heritability of Adult and Juvenile Antisocial Traits." *Archives of General Psychiatry* 52:906–15.

Maccoby, E., and C.N. Jacklin. (1974). *The Psychology of Sex Differences*. Stanford, Calif.: Stanford University Press.

Maddocks, S., P. Hahn, R. Moller, and R.L. Reid. (1986). "A Double-Blind Placebo-Controlled Trial of Progesterone Vaginal Suppositories in the Treatment of Premenstrual Syndrome." *American Journal of Obstetrics and Gynecology* 154(3):573–81.

Magnusson, D. (ed.). (1988). Individual Development from an Interactional Perspective. Hillsdale, N.J.: Lawrence Erlbaum Associates.

McCord, J. (1979). "Some Child-Rearing Antecedents of Criminal Behavior in Adult Men." *Journal of Personality and Social Psychology* 37:1477–86.

Mednick, S.A. (1977). "A Biosocial Theory of Learning of Law-Abiding Behavior." In S.A. Mednick and K.O. Christiansen (eds.), *Biosocial Bases of Criminal Behavior* (pp. 1–8). New York: Gardner Press.

Mednick, S.A., P. Brennan, and E. Kandel. (1988). "Predisposition to Violence." *Aggressive Behavior* 14:25–33.

Mednick, S.A., and K.M. Finello. (1983). "Biological Factors and Crime: Implications for Forensic Psychiatry." *International Journal of Law and Psychiatry* 6:1–15.

Mednick, S.A., W.F. Gabrielli, Jr., and B. Hutchings. (1984). "Genetic Influences in Criminal Convictions: Evidence from an Adoption Cohort." *Science* 224:891–94.

Mendez, M.F., R.C. Doss, and J.L. Taylor. (1993). "Interictal Violence in Epilepsy: Relationship to Behavior and Seizure Variables." *Journal of Nervous and Mental Disease* 181:566–69.

Mezzacappa, E., R.E. Tremblay, D. Kindlon, J.P. Saul, L. Arseneault, J. Séguin, R.O. Pihl, and F. Earls. (1997). "Anxiety, Antisocial Behavior, and Heart Rate Regulation in Adolescent Males." *Journal of Child Psychology and Psychiatry* 38:457–69.

Moffitt, T.E. (1990). "The Neuropsychology of Juvenile Delinquency: A Critical Review." In M. Tonry and N. Morris (eds.), *Crime and Justice—A Review of Research* (pp. 99–169). Chicago: University of Chicago Press.

———. (1993). "Adolescence-Limited and Life-Course-Persistent Antisocial Behavior: A Developmental Taxonomy." *Psychological Review* 100:674–701.

Moffitt, T.E., W.F. Gabrielli, S.A. Mednick, and F. Schulsinger. (1981). "Socioeconomic Status, IQ and Delinquency." *Journal of Abnormal Psychology* 90:152–56.

Monroe, R.R. (1970). *Episodic Behavioural Disorders: A Psychodynamic and Neurophysiologic Analysis.* Cambridge, Ma.: Harvard University Press.

Morell, V. (1993). "Evidence Found for a Possible Aggression Gene." *Science* 260:1722–23.

Moyer, K.E. (1976). *The Psychobiology of Aggression.* New York: Harper and Row.

Needleman, H.L., J.A. Riess, M.J. Tobin, G.E. Biesecker, and J.B. Greenhouse. (1996). "Bone Lead Levels and Delinquent Behavior." *Journal of the American Medical Association* 275:363–69.

Olweus, D. (1979). "Stability of Aggressive Reaction Patterns in Males: A Review." *Psychological Bulletin* 86:852–75.

———. (1983). "Testosterone in the Development of Aggressive Antisocial Behavior in Adolescents." In K.T. Van Dusen and S.A. Mednick (eds.), *Prospective Studies of Crime and Delinquency* (pp. 237–47). Boston: Kluwer-Nijhoff.

———. (1985). "Aggression and Hormones. Behavioral Relationships with Testosterone and Adrenaline." In D. Olweus, J. Block, and M. Radke-Yarrow (eds.), *The Development of Antisocial and Prosocial Behavior: Research, Theories, and Issues* (pp. 237–48). New York: Academic Press.

Patrick, C.J., B.N. Cuthbert, and P.J. Lang. (1994). "Emotion in the Criminal Psychopath: Fear Image Processing." *Journal of Abnormal Psychology* 3:523–34.

Patterson, G.R. (1986). "Performance Models for Antisocial Boys." *American Psychologist* 41(4):432–44.

Patterson, G.R., and K. Yoerger. (1993). "Development Models for Delinquent Behavior." In S. Hodgins (ed.), *Mental Disorder and Crime* (pp. 140–72). Newbury Park, Calif.: Sage Publications.

Pihl, R.O., and J.B. Peterson. (1991). "Attention-Deficit Hyperactivity Disorder, Childhood Conduct Disorder, and Alcoholism." *Alcohol, Health and Research World* 15:25–31.

———. (1993). "Alcohol/Drug Use and Aggressive Behavior." In S. Hodgins (ed.), *Mental Disorder and Crime* (pp. 263–83). Newbury Park, Calif.: Sage.

Pulkkinen, L. (1983). "Search for Alternatives to Aggression in Finland." In A.P. Goldstein and M. Segall (eds.), *Aggression in Global Perspective* (pp. 104–44). New York: Pergamon Press.

———. (1988). "Delinquent Development: Theoretical and Empirical Considerations." In M. Rutter (ed.), *Studies of Psychosocial Risk* (pp. 184–99). Cambridge: Cambridge University Press.

Raine, A., P. Brennan, and S.A. Mednick. (1994). "Birth Complications Combined with Early Maternal Rejection at Age 1 Predispose to Violent Crime at Age 18 Years." *Archives of General Psychiatry* 51:984–88.

———. (1997). "Interaction Between Birth Complications and Early Maternal Rejection in Predisposing Individuals to Adult Violence: Specificity to Serious, Early-Onset Violence." *American Journal of Psychiatry* 154:1265–71.

Raine, A., and P.H. Venables. (1981). "Classical Conditioning and Socialization—A Biosocial Interaction." *Personality and Individual Differences* 2:273–83.

———. (1984). "Tonic Heart Rate Level, Social Class, and Antisocial Behaviour in Adolescents." *Biological Psychology* 18:123–32.

———. (1988). "Enhanced P3 Evoked Potentials and Longer P3 Recovery Time in Psychopaths." *Psychophysiology* 25:30–38.

Raine, A., P.H. Venables, and M. Williams. (1990a). "Relationships Between Central and Autonomic Measures of Arousal at Age 15 Years and Criminality at Age 24 Years." *Archives of General Psychiatry* 47:1003–7.

———. (1990b). "Autonomic Orienting Responses in 15-Year-Old Male Subjects and Criminal Behavior at Age 24." *American Journal of Psychiatry* 17:933–37.

Reichel, H. (1989). "The Intelligence-Criminality Relationship: A Comparative Study." *Crime and Delinquency in a Metropolitan Cohort.* (Research Rep. no. 26). Stockholm: University of Stockholm.

Resnick, S.M., I.I. Gottesman, and M. McGue. (1993). "Sensation Seeking in Opposite-Sex Twins: An Effect of Prenatal Hormones?" *Behavior Genetics* 23:323–29.

Robins, L.N. (1979). "Study Childhood Predictors of Adult Outcomes: Replications from Longitudinal Studies." In J.E. Barrett et al. (eds.), *Stress and Mental Disorder* (pp. 219–35). New York: Raven Press.

Rosenbaum, A., and S.K. Hoge. (1989). "Head Injury and Marital Aggression." *American Journal of Psychiatry* 146(8):1048–51.

Roy, A., B. Adinoff, and M. Linnoila. (1988). "Acting Out Hostility in Normal Volunteers: Negative Correlation with Levels of 5-HIAA in Cerebrospinal Fluid." *Psychiatry Research* 24:187–94.

Scaramella, T.J., and W.A. Brown. (1978). "Serum Testosterone and Aggressiveness in Hockey Players." *Psychosomatic Medicine* 40:262–65.

Scerbo, A.S., and D.J. Kolko. (1994). "Salivary Testosterone and Cortisol in Disruptive Children: Relationship to Aggressive, Hyperactive, and Internalizing Behaviors." *Journal of the American Academy of Child and Adolescent Psychiatry* 33:1174–84.

Schaal, B., R.E. Tremblay, R. Soussignan, and E.J. Sussman. (1996). "Male Testosterone Linked to High Social Dominance but Low Physical Aggression in Early Adolescence." *Journal of the American Academy of Child and Adolescent Psychiatry* 34:1322–30.

Schiavi, R.C., A. Theilgaard, D.R. Owen, and D. White. (1984). "Sex Chromosome Anomalies, Hormones, and Aggressivity." *Archives of General Psychiatry* 41:93–99.

Schulsinger, F. (1977). "Psychopathy: Heredity and Environment." In S.A. Mednick and K.O. Christiansen (eds.), *Biosocial Bases of Criminal Behavior* (pp. 109–25). New York: Gardner Press.

Séguin, J.R., R.O. Pihl, P.W. Harden, R.E. Tremblay, and B. Boulerice. (1995). "Cognitive and Neuropsychological Characteristics of Physically Aggressive Boys." *Journal of Abnormal Psychology* 104:614.

Shah, S., and L. Roth. (1974). "Biological and Psychophysiological Factors in Criminality." In D. Glaser (ed.), *Handbook of Criminology* (pp. 101–71). Chicago: Rand McNally and Company.

Siddle, D.A.T., S.A. Mednick, A.R. Nicol, and R.H. Foggitt. (1977). "Skin Conductance Recovery in Antisocial Adolescents." In S.A. Mednick and K.O. Christiansen (eds.), *Biosocial Bases of Criminal Behavior* (pp. 213–16). New York: Gardner Press.

Sigvardsson, S., C.R. Cloninger, M. Bohman, and A.-L. Von Knorring. (1982). "Predisposition to Petty Criminality in Swedish Adoptees: III. Sex Differences and Validation of the Male Typology." *Archives of General Psychiatry* 39:1248–53.

Spatz Widom, C. (1989). "The Cycle of Violence." *Science* 244:160–66.

Stattin, H., and D. Magnusson. (1996). "Antisocial Development: A Holistic Approach." *Development and Psychopathology* 8:617–45.

Templer, D.I., J. Kasiraj, N.H. Trent, A. Trent, B. Hughey, W.J. Keller, R.A. Orling, and S. Thomas-Dobson. (1992). "Exploration of Head Injury Without Medical Attention." *Perceptual and Motor Skills* 75:195–202.

Toch, H., and K. Adams. (1989). *The Disturbed Violent Offender*. London: Yale University Press.

Toupin, J. (1993). "Adolescent Murderers: Validation of a Typology and Study of Their Recidivism." In A.V. Wilson (ed.), *Homicide: The Victim Offender Connection* (pp. 135–36). Cincinnati: Anderson.

Trasler, G. (1978). "Relations Between Psychopathy and Persistent Criminality— Methodological and Theoretical Issues." In R.D. Hare and D. Schalling (eds.), *Psychopathic Behaviour: Approaches to Research* (pp. 273–98). Toronto: Wiley.

Van Dusen, T., S.A. Mednick, W.F. Gabrielli, Jr., and B. Hutchings. (1983). "Social Class and Crime in an Adoption Cohort." *The Journal of Criminal Law and Criminology* 74:249–69.

van Praag, H. (1986a). "Affective Disorders and Aggression Disorders: Evidence for a Common Biological Mechanism." *Suicide and Life-Threatening Behavior* 16:21–50.

———. (1986b). "Aggression and CSF 5-HIAA in Depression and Schizophrenia." *Psychopharmacology Bulletin* 22:669–73.

Virkkunen, M. (1982). "Reactive Hypoglycemic Tendency among Habitually Violent Offenders." *Neuropsychobiology* 8:35–40.

———. (1984). "Reactive Hypoglycemic Tendency Among Arsonists." *Acta Psychiatrica Scandinavica* 69:445–52.

Virkkunen, M., and M.O. Huttunen. (1982). "Evidence for Abnormal Glucose Tolerance Test Among Violent Offenders." *Neuropsychobiology* 8:30–34.

Virkkunen, M., A. Nuutila, F.K. Goodwin, and M. Linnoila. (1987). "Cerebrospinal Fluid Metabolite Levels in Male Arsonists." *Archives of General Psychiatry* 44:241–47.

Virkkunen, M., A. Nuutila, and S. Huusko. (1977). "Brain Injury and Criminality. A Retrospective Study." *Diseases of the Nervous System* 38:907–8.

Virkkunen, M., E. Kallio, R. Rawlings, R. Tokola, R.E. Poland, A. Guidotti, C. Nemeroff, G. Bissette, K. Kalogeras, S.-L. Karonen, and M. Linnoila. (1994). "C.S.F. Biochemistries, Glucose Metabolism, and Diurnal Activity Rhythms in Alcoholic, Violent Offenders, Fire Setters, and Healthy Volunteers." *Archives of General Psychiatry* 51:20–27.

Wadsworth, M. (1976). "Delinquency, Pulse Rates and Early Emotional Deprivation." *British Journal of Criminology* 16:245–56.

Walsh, A. (1992). "Genetic and Environmental Explanations of Juvenile Violence in Advantaged and Disadvantaged Environments." *Aggressive Behavior* 18:187–99.

West, D.J., and D.P. Farrington. (1973). *Who Becomes Delinquent?* London: Heinemann.

Wilson, J.Q., and R.J. Herrnstein. (1985). *Crime and Human Nature.* New York: Simon and Schuster.

Witkin, H.A., S.A. Mednick, R. Schulsinger, E. Bakkestrom, K.O. Christiansen, D. Goodenough, K. Hirschhorn, C. Lundsteen, D.R. Owen, J. Phillips, D.B. Rubin, and M. Stocking. (1977). "Criminality, Aggression and Intelligence Among XYY and XXY Men." In S.A. Mednick and K.O. Christiansen (eds.), *Biosocial Bases of Criminal Behavior* (pp. 165–88). New York: Gardner Press.

Wolkind, S.N. (1974). "Sex Differences in the Aetiology of Antisocial Disorders in Children in Long-Term Residential Care." *British Journal of Psychiatry* 125:125–30.

Woodman, D., and J. Hinton. (1978). "Catecholamine Balance During Stress Anticipation: An Abnormality in Maximum Security Hospital Patients." *Journal of Psychosomatic Research* 22:447–83.

Woodman, D.D., J.W. Hinton, and M.T. O'Neill. (1977a). "Abnormality of Catecholamine Balance Relating to Social Deviance." *Perceptual and Motor Skills* 45:593–94.

———. (1977b). "Relationship Between Violence and Catecholamines." *Perceptual and Motor Skills* 45:702.

9

Psychological Perspectives on Criminality

PATRICIA A. ZAPF
John Jay College of Criminal Justice

DAVID N. COX
Simon Fraser University

RONALD ROESCH
Simon Fraser University

Many different theories have been proposed to explain why people commit criminal acts. This chapter reviews different psychological perspectives on criminality. We begin with a discussion of the characteristics of psychological theories and then review different psychological theories that have been proposed to explain criminality. Next, antisocial personality and psychopathy are described, and the differences between the two are illustrated through the use of three case studies—Charles Manson, Ted Bundy, and Canada's most notorious criminal, Clifford Olson. We conclude with a discussion of crime and mental illness, including a review of research in this area and a discussion of the prevalence of mental illness in jail and prison populations.

LEARNING OBJECTIVES

After reading this chapter, you should be able to

- Describe the different psychological theories that have been used to explain criminal behaviour, including psychoanalytic theory, moral development theory, Eysenck's theory, social learning theory, and operant conditioning theory.

- Understand what is meant by the term "antisocial personality."

- Describe the difference between Antisocial Personality Disorder and psychopathy.

- Describe the most current theories linking crime and mental illness.

PSYCHOLOGICAL THEORIES OF CRIME

There has been considerable debate over psychological explanations of criminal behaviour. Psychologists typically approach the problem of understanding, explaining, and predicting criminality by developing theories of personality or learning that account for an individual's behaviour in a specific situation. One extensive review of a decade of published research on offenders (Reppucci and Clingempeel, 1978) found that nearly all the research could be characterized as reflecting one of two value assumptions. The first is the "**assumption of offender deficit**," which asserts that theories and interventions are premised on the notion that there is something psychologically wrong with offenders. The second is the "**assumption of discriminating traits**," which holds that criminals differ from noncriminals, particularly in such traits as impulsivity and aggression. Research based on this assumption would involve studies of offender and nonoffender populations, and would utilize a number of personality tests in an attempt to find traits that differentiate the two groups.

Critics have taken issue with psychology's reliance on these two assumptions. Reppucci and Clingempeel (1978) point to two major omissions in psychological research. One is that there is typically very little emphasis placed on studies of the strengths of offenders. Most of the research and interventions focus on the deficits rather than on the positive characteristics of individuals. Another is that the psychological research tends to ignore the potential importance of situational and environmental factors that affect individual behaviour. Sarbin (1979) has also been critical of the approach taken in developing psychological theories of crime, which is essentially based on the expectation that it is possible to classify individuals as criminals and noncriminals. Sarbin argues that this cannot be done reliably. He points to studies of self-reported delinquency, white-collar crime, and corporate crime as examples of the pervasiveness of criminal behaviour.

Conversely, the work of David Farrington (1978; 1979; 2002) illustrates the importance of understanding individual differences. Farrington views criminal behaviour as the outcome of several different social and psychological factors (see also Loeber et al., 2001a; 2001b). According to him, the motivation to commit delinquent acts arises primarily out of a desire for material goods or a need for excitement. If these desires cannot be satisfied in a socially approved manner, an illegal act may be chosen. The motivation to commit delinquent acts will be influenced by psychological variables, including the individual's learning history and the beliefs he or she may have internalized regarding criminal behaviour. Eysenck and Gudjonsson (1989) support this position, suggesting that "psychological factors and individual differences related to the personality are of central importance in relation to both the causes of crime and its control." They contend that psychology, with its focus on individual differences, is the central discipline in the study of criminal behaviour and that "no system of criminology has any meaning that disregards this central feature of all criminology: the individual person whom we are trying to influence."

While the individual perspective is clearly the dominant one in psychology, there are other psychological perspectives, such as those of **community psychology** (Roesch, 1988), that are quite closely akin to sociological perspectives. Commonly, such psychologists view social problems from what Rappaport (1977) has termed a "levels of analysis" perspective. Briefly, the four levels are (1) *individual level,* in which social problems are defined in terms of individual

assumption of offender deficit

The view that offenders who break the law have some psychological deficit that distinguishes them from normal law-abiding citizens.

assumption of discriminating traits

The view that offenders are distinguished from nonoffenders by, for example, their high levels of impulsiveness and aggression.

community psychology

A perspective that analyzes social problems, including crime, as largely a product of organizational and institutional characteristics of society. It is closely related to sociology.

deficit; (2) *small-group level*, which suggests that social problems are created by problems in group functioning, essentially problems in interpersonal communication and understanding; (3) *organizational level*, in which the organizations of society have not accomplished what they have been designed to accomplish; and (4) *institutional or community level*, in which it is suggested that social problems are created by institutions rather than by persons, groups, or organizations. At this level the emphasis is on the values and policies underlying institutional functioning.

An example that cuts across these four levels would be the way in which "victimless" crimes, such as drug abuse and prostitution, are defined. If the problem is defined at the first level, individuals would be examined to determine what psychological problems they have. Once this has been determined, direct interventions could be employed in changing these individuals so that they might fit into society better and conform to the existing laws. At the small-group level, the influence of peers, such as drug-abusing friends, could be viewed as influencing the individual's behaviour. At the next level, organizations such as law enforcement agencies would be seen as having insufficient resources to prevent or deter individuals from engaging in criminal behaviour. Finally, if this problem is defined at the institutional level, it might be said that the problems that individuals face are caused by the laws their society has created. Therefore, the focus would be on changing the laws so that they do not affect people negatively. If the problem is defined at the institutional level, therapy for an individual would be inappropriate if the cause of the problem was, for example, related to socio-economic factors (Seidman and Rabkin, 1983). Community psychologists tend to define social problems at the organizational and institutional levels and have a theoretical perspective that has much in common with that of sociologists.

These concerns and alternative perspectives should be kept in mind as different psychological theories of criminal behaviour are considered. These theories focus, for the most part, on individual-level variables and explanations. The remainder of this chapter will review psychological theories that can be directly related to understanding criminal behaviour.

Psychoanalytic Theory

Sigmund Freud is the figure most associated with psychoanalytic theory, but he did not make any significant attempts to relate his theory specifically to criminal behaviour. Other psychoanalysts have, however, attempted to explain criminal behaviour with psychoanalytic concepts (Alexander and Healey, 1935; Bowlby, 1953; Friedlander, 1947; Polansky et al., 1950; Redl, 1966).

A basic premise of psychoanalytic theory is that people progress through five overlapping stages of development. These are the oral, anal, phallic, latency, and genital stages. Freud believed that personality is composed of three forces: the **id** (biological drives); the **ego** (which screens, controls, and directs the impulses of the id and acts as a reality tester); and the **superego** (conscience). Psychoanalytic theory holds that the ego and superego are developed through the successful resolution of conflicts presented at each stage of development. It

id

A psychoanalytical term that denotes the most inaccessible and primitive part of the mind. It is a reservoir of biological urges that strive continually for gratification. The ego mediates between the *id* and the *superego*.

ego

A psychoanalytical term that denotes the rational part of the personality. It mediates between the *id* and the *superego* and is responsible for dealing with reality and making decisions.

superego

A psychoanalytical term that denotes the ethical and moral dimensions of personality; an individual's conscience. The *ego* mediates between the superego and the *id*.

is believed that both biological and social factors are involved in the resolution of each stage. (See Figure 9.1.)

Psychoanalytic theory presents an elaborate, comprehensive view of the psychological functioning of individuals. It deals with all aspects of human behaviour, but the discussion here will be limited to its impact on the study of criminal behaviour. Briefly, this theory suggests that criminal behaviour occurs when "internal (ego and superego) controls are unable to restrain the primitive, aggressive, antisocial instincts of the id" (Nietzel, 1979). Criminal behaviour is the consequence of an individual's failure to progress through the early stages of development, which leaves the superego inadequately developed or deficient. The individual is left susceptible to antisocial behaviour (Martin et al., 1981).

"Freud Net"
The Abraham A. Brill Library of
The New York Psychoanalytic
Institute
www.psychoanalysis.org/lib.htm

FIGURE 9.1 Freud's Theory of Personality

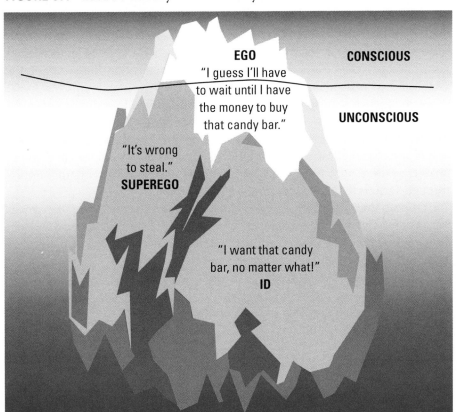

This illustration shows how Freud might picture a person's internal conflict over whether to commit an antisocial act such as stealing a candy bar. In addition to dividing personality into three components, Freud theorized that our personalities are largely unconscious—hidden away outside our normal awareness. To dramatize this point, Freud compared conscious awareness (portions of the ego and superego) to the visible tip of an iceberg. Most of our personality—including all of the id, with its raw desires and impulses—lies submerged in our subconscious.

Source: Diana Kendall, Rick Linden, and Jane Lothian Murray. (1998). *Sociology in Our Times: The Essentials* (with InfoTrac), 2nd ed., p. 81. Reprinted with permission of Wadsworth, a division of Thomson Learning. www. thomsonrights.com. Fax 800-730-2215.

Warren and Hindelang (1979) have summarized five other interpretations of criminal behaviour that can be derived from psychoanalytic theory:

(1) criminal behavior is a form of neurosis which does not differ in any fundamental way from other forms of neuroses (e.g., while some neurotics work too hard, others set fires); (2) the criminal often suffers from a compulsive need for punishment in order to alleviate guilt feelings and anxiety stemming from unconscious strivings; (3) criminal activity may be a means of obtaining substitute gratification of needs and desires not met inside the family; (4) delinquent behavior is often due to traumatic events whose memory has been repressed; and (5) delinquent behavior may be an expression of displaced hostility.

Schoenfeld (1971) offered a theory of juvenile delinquency that illustrates psychoanalytic theory. Schoenfeld proposed that delinquent behaviour reflects a weak, defective, or incomplete superego that is unable to control the oral, anal, and phallic impulses that are resurrected at puberty. Schoenfeld believes that parental deprivation and lack of affection, especially during the first few years of a child's life, is the cause of a weak superego. Boys raised in a fatherless home, he adds, will be especially prone to deviant behaviour as they attempt to establish their male identity.

socialization

The interactive process whereby individuals come to learn and internalize the culture of their society or group.

A number of studies support the view that family life is important in the process of **socialization**. Bowlby (1953) stressed that a stable attachment to a mother in the first few years of life allows the child to show affection toward others and to care for them. If this attachment does not occur, the child will be unable to show affection and, thus, may damage others without remorse through various forms of victimization.

One of the difficulties in assessing psychoanalytic theory is that many aspects of it are untestable because they rely on unobservable underlying constructs. As Cohen (1966) points out, "Aggressive or acquisitive acts are often explained by underlying aggressive or acquisitive impulses."

This explanation is a tautology in that aggressive acts are explained by aggressive impulses, but the only evidence of the aggressive impulses is the occurrence of aggressive acts. Further, studies have failed to demonstrate that criminals desire to be punished or suffer from guilt or anxiety, as one psychoanalyst (Abrahamsen, 1944) suggested. In fact, as Nietzel (1979) asserts, "criminals are very successful in their efforts to prevent detection or if detected, elude official prosecution and conviction. Most offenders do not appear unduly frustrated or further guilt-ridden by the fact that their 'crime pays' at least some of the time." Despite these problems, psychoanalytic theory is regarded by some as a useful conceptual framework for understanding the importance of early development on later behaviour of all types, including criminal behaviour.

Theories of Moral Development

According to moral development theorists, if we wish to understand criminal and delinquent behaviour, we need to ask how it is that individuals develop, or fail to develop, a sense of morality and responsibility. One of the first contemporary moral development theorists was the French psychologist Jean Piaget (1932), whose research focused on the moral lives of children. In order to determine how children developed their ideas about right and wrong, Piaget studied how children developed the rules to the games they played. He concluded that moral reasoning developed in stages. The thinking of young children was characterized by egocentrism. That is, they projected their own thoughts and wishes onto others because they were unable to take the perspective of those others. Through their interaction with others, by the ages of 11 or 12, children will normally have progressed to the stage of cooperation with others. Based on this research, Piaget concluded that the schools should teach moral reasoning by allowing students to work out the rules through problem solving in the classroom.

Kohlberg, expanding on Piaget's theory, has hypothesized that there are six stages of moral development (see Table 9.1). The stages are age related, and progression through the stages occurs as "the developing child becomes better able to understand and integrate diverse points of view on a moral-conflict situation and to take more of the relevant situational factors into account" (Jennings et al., 1983). Kohlberg believes that all individuals go through the same sequence of stages, although the pace may vary and some individuals may never progress beyond the first few stages.

Kohlberg categorizes the six stages into three levels of moral judgement development, each with two stages of moral reasoning.

The first is the *preconventional* level, characteristic of children under age 11 and of many adolescent and adult offenders. At this level, the morals and values of society are understood as "do's" and "don'ts" and are associated with punishment. The preconventional person is one for whom roles and social expectations are something external to the self.

The *conventional* level reflects the average adolescent and adult in our society and others. He or she understands, accepts, and attempts to uphold the values and rules of society. For a conventional person, the self is identified with or has internalized the rules and expectations of others, especially those of authorities.

"Moral Development: Reasoning, Judgment, and Action"
Yvonne L. Lamar
Cornell University
http://rochim.human.cornell.edu/gallery/lamar/lamar1.htm

TABLE 9.1 Kohlberg's Theory of Moral Development

Level	Stage	Description	
I.	Preconventional	1. Punishment 2. Instrumental Hedonism	Egocentric (What happens to me?)
II.	Conventional	3. Approval of others 4. Authority maintaining morality	Social Expectations (What do others expect of me?)
III.	Postconventional	5. Democratically accepted law 6. Principles of Conscience	Universality (What is best for all?)

Source: D.A. Andrews and James Bonta. (1994). *The Psychology of Criminal Conduct.* Cincinnati: Anderson Publishing.

The *postconventional* level is the one at which customs are critically examined with regard to universal rights, duties, and moral principles. It is characteristic of a minority of adults after the age of 20. The postconventional person has differentiated his or her self from the rules and expectations of others and defined his or her value by means of self-chosen principles (Jennings et al., 1983).

Carol Gilligan (1982) has criticized Kohlberg's theory of moral development, stating that it is biased in favour of males. Gilligan argues that there is variation in moral standards by gender, with females taking a more care-oriented approach to morality, while males typically use a more justice-oriented approach. She believes that Kohlberg's theory does not take into consideration the more care-oriented approach of females, and that as a result females rarely obtain the higher stages of moral development in Kohlberg's theory. To support her argument, she points out that females were not taken into consideration when Kohlberg was developing his theory, as the development of moral judgement was based on an empirical study of 84 males whom Kohlberg followed for a 20-year period. Gilligan states that females typically reach only the second level (third stage) in Kohlberg's theory, which is characterized by goodness being equated with helping and pleasing others and is consistent with the care-oriented approach of females to morality. She argues that Kohlberg and Kramer (1969) have looked at this concept of goodness and concluded that this level of moral reasoning would be adequate for women whose lives will take place in the home. They indicate that only when women enter the "traditional arena of male activity" do they realize that this level of moral reasoning is not sufficient, and therefore go on to progress toward the higher stages as men do. Gilligan points out that "herein lies a paradox, for the very traits that traditionally have defined the 'goodness' of women, their care for and sensitivity to the needs of others, are those that mark them as deficient in moral development" (1982, 18).

Considerable research has been done on the relationship between moral development and delinquency. Kohlberg believes that people with high moral development are more likely to make individual choices and be less influenced by friends or by consequences of actions. Thus, there should be an inverse relationship between moral development and delinquency. Jennings et al. (1983) reviewed a large number of studies on this relationship and concluded that "the overwhelming weight of the empirical data reviewed here supports the notion that juvenile delinquents' moral judgement is at a less advanced level than that of non-delinquent controls matched on a variety of variables." But they are careful to point out that a cause–effect relationship has not been established. Individuals at the same level of moral development may or may not become delinquent. They add that

> these studies lend support to the more modest claims that moral reasoning of increased maturity has an insulating effect against delinquency. Advanced stages of moral judgment cause one's moral orientation to be more integrated, stable and consistent. Higher reasoning makes one a more reliable moral agent and thus better able to withstand some incentives to illegal conduct postulated by a variety of sociological and psychological theories of the etiology of delinquency.

This last statement suggests that **moral development theory** has considerable relevance for a sociological explanation of criminal behaviour. Indeed, Morash (1983) has discussed at length the possible integration of moral development and sociological theories, suggesting that it may be more fruitful to study the interaction of personal and situational variables. She concludes:

> Most serious delinquency would result from social conditions, primarily those that are enduring, that impinge on youths who possess the personality factors and the pre-conventional reasoning conducive to serious delinquent behavior. An advantage of this explanation is that it allows for the many pre-conventional individuals who do not break the law regularly or not at all, and it accounts for different patterns in delinquency—that is, the repeated serious delinquency and sporadic and/or less serious delinquency.

In conclusion, there is evidence to suggest that level of moral reasoning is related to behaviour (see also Hogan, 1973). However, the correlations reported in many studies are often quite low. Moral development may affect how an individual behaves in a given context, but it is clear that other characteristics of the individual, as well as the situation, will also be important determinants of behaviour.

Eysenck's Theory of Crime and Personality

Hans Eysenck, a noted British psychologist, has developed an elaborate theory of how personality characteristics are related to criminal behaviour (Eysenck, 1977). This theory has generated considerable research, in large part because it lends itself quite readily to the identification of groups of offenders and to predictions about their behaviour.

Eysenck believes that illegal, selfish, or immoral behaviour is simple to explain. These behaviours are inherently reinforcing and, hence, it is more fruitful to try to explain why people do *not* commit crimes. Eysenck claims that children will naturally engage in such acts and only refrain from doing so if they are punished. Eysenck's theory is based on **classical conditioning**. Each time a child is punished, he or she may experience pain and fear. This pain and fear may be associated with the act itself. Thus, whenever the child contemplates the act, he or she will experience fear, which will tend to inhibit the response. Eysenck equates this conditioned fear with conscience. Delinquents and criminals do not readily develop this conditioned response, either because of lack of exposure to effective conditioning practices by parents and others, or because they are less susceptible to conditioning. Eysenck (1990) states:

> Depending on the frequency of pairings between the conditioned and unconditioned stimulus in the field of social behavior, and on the precise content of the conditioning program, children will grow up to develop appropriate types of behavior. Conditionability is a crucial factor on the social or environmental side. In a permissive society where parents, teachers, and magistrates do not take seriously the task of imposing a "conscience" which would lead them to behave in a

moral development theory

Refers generally to theories of individual psychology that investigate how moral reasoning emerges in the individual and develops as the individual matures.

"Hans Eysenck and Other Temperament Theorists"
C. George Boeree, Shippensburg University of Pennsylvania
www.ship.edu/~cgboeree/ eysenck.html

classical conditioning

A basic form of learning whereby a neutral stimulus is paired with another stimulus that naturally elicits a certain response; the neutral stimulus comes to elicit the same response as the stimulus that automatically elicits the response.

socialized manner, a large number of individuals with poor or average conditionability will acquire a "conscience" too weak to prevent them from indulging in criminal activities, although had they been subjected to a stricter regime of conditioning, they might have grown up to be perfectly respectable and law-abiding citizens.

As Eysenck points out, the concept of "strictness" is not a function of excessive strength of the conditioning process, but a result of the certainty and frequency of pairings of the conditioned and unconditioned stimulus.

There are three dimensions of personality, according to Eysenck. **Extraversion** is a personality characteristic with highly sociable, impulsive, and aggressive people at one extreme of the continuum. Highly introverted, introspective, and inhibited people are the other extreme. *Neuroticism* is linked to the psychiatric concept of neurosis. People who are high on this dimension are characterized by such symptoms as anxiety, restlessness, and other emotional responses. The opposite extreme of neuroticism is referred to as stability. The third dimension, *psychoticism*, is a recent addition. According to Eysenck and Eysenck (1976), a person who is high on this dimension is "cold, impersonal, hostile, lacking in sympathy, unfriendly, untrustful, odd, unemotional, unhelpful, antisocial, lacking in human feelings, inhumane, generally bloodyminded, lacking in insight, strange, with paranoid ideas that people are against him."

A number of hypotheses have been generated about the relationship of these dimensions to criminal behaviour. Extraverts, because of their high need for excitement, their impulsivity, and relatively weak conscience, are believed to be more prone to criminal behaviour. In addition, persons high on both neuroticism and extraversion would be predicted to be delinquents or criminals. Persons high on psychoticism would tend to be more serious offenders, with a propensity for violence. Hare (1982) investigated the relationship between these three dimensions and psychopathy. While neuroticism and extraversion did not correlate with measures of psychopathy, psychoticism did. It is concluded that this may be because each taps a common element of psychopathy (criminal and antisocial tendencies) rather than those psychological features that are assumed in the diagnosis of psychopathy (for example, lack of remorse, lack of empathy).

Eysenck and others have developed psychological measures of each of these dimensions. Research in testing predictions about offenders has produced mixed results. In their extensive and excellent review of Eysenck's theory, Farrington et al. (1982) summarized data from 16 studies, most of which were conducted in Great Britain, and found that while some studies support the predictions of Eysenck's theory, other studies do not. Bartol (1980) comes to a similar conclusion. Nevertheless, Eysenck's theory is important because it shows how psychological and social variables can be interrelated. Individuals who may have a psychological propensity to commit crime may be effectively socialized if they grow up in an environment that provides effective conditioning. Similarly, individuals with a low propensity for criminality may become criminal if their environment is too permissive. Although Eysenck argues strongly for the importance of individual differences, he recognizes the importance of societal influences: "Crime ... is essentially a function of the ethos of the society in which we live; it reflects the practices of positive and negative reinforcement, of reward and pun-

extraversion

A personality characteristic associated with sociability, impulsiveness, and aggression.

ishment, of teaching and conditioning, which are prevalent, and these in turn are mirrored and reflected by the types of films we see, television programs we watch, books and newspapers we read, and teaching and examples we receive at school." In the next section, it will be seen that social learning theory reflects this perspective more explicitly.

Social Learning Theory

Another theory that lends itself to an integration of sociology and psychology is social learning theory. Although this theory focuses on individual behaviour, it takes into account the influence of the environment and of social conditions on the individual. Cognitive functioning, the ability to think and make choices, is central to social learning theory.

An important element of social learning theory is the role of **modelling**. Individuals can learn new behaviours through direct experience or by observing the behaviour of others. The latter, also referred to as vicarious learning, can be a most effective and efficient way to acquire new behaviours. Albert Bandura, a Stanford University professor of psychology, is a leading social learning theorist. He suggests that "virtually all learning phenomena resulting from direct experiences can occur on a vicarious basis through observation of other persons' behavior and its consequences for them" (Bandura, 1979).

Social learning theory has been used to explain how aggression is learned. Since this is of great concern to criminology theory, aggression will be used as an example of an application of social learning theory.

Bandura (1979) suggests that aggressive behaviour can be learned from three sources. The *family* is one source, with a number of studies showing that children of parents who respond aggressively to problems will tend to use similar tactics. Bandura also points to research on child abuse, which shows that many children who have been abused will later become abusers themselves. Another source of aggressive behaviour can be referred to as *subcultural influences*, or the influence of social models and peers. Bandura suggests that "the highest incidence of aggression is found in communities in which aggressive models abound and fighting prowess is regarded as a valued attribute." The third source of learned aggressive behaviour is through *symbolic modelling*. An example of this is violence on television, which provides models of aggressive behaviour (Skoler et al., 1994).

Bandura's research on the role of film models reinforced existing concerns about the effects of television on aggressive behaviour. Geen (1983) reviewed the research on the relationship between viewing television violence and aggression. He first looked at the vast number of correlational studies, the majority of which support the conclusion that there is a positive relationship between viewing violence and aggressive behaviour. A typical study is the one by Teevan and Hartnagel (1976), which showed that high school students who described their favourite television shows as violent also reported committing more aggressive acts than students whose favourite shows were nonviolent.

The problem with correlational research, as Geen points out, is that the direction of causation is unknown. It is possible that people who are more likely to behave aggressively simply prefer more violent television shows. Thus, it

modelling
A form of learning that occurs as a result of watching and imitating others.

"Albert Bandura (1925–present)" C. George Boeree, Shippensburg University of Pennsylvania **www.ship.edu/~cgboeree/ bandura.html**

"Television Violence: A Review of the Effects on Children of Different Ages" Child and Family Canada **www.cfc-efc.ca/docs/mnet/ 00001068.htm**

cannot be concluded through correlational studies alone that viewing violence is the cause of aggressive behaviour. Cook et al. (1983) re-analyzed data from several large-scale studies of the effects of television violence. They concluded that an association between television viewing and aggression by children can be found regularly, but the level of association is typically quite small and often not statistically significant. Nevertheless, they conclude that the association is most probably a causal one, that watching violence on television does have an effect on children's aggressive behaviour. The same can be said for violence in music videos (Smith and Boyson, 2002).

In addition to its direct effect on aggressive behaviour, it is also possible that exposure to television violence increases one's tolerance toward violence and decreases one's sensitivity to acts of violence. Thomas et al. (1979) found that both adult and child subjects showed less **autonomic reactivity** to a scene of real-life interpersonal aggression if they had first watched a violent scene from a television show. Malamuth and Check (1981) reported similar results in their study of the effects of film violence on attitudes toward violence. Male and female university students were randomly assigned to view either a violent-sexual or a control feature-length film. The films were shown as part of the regular campus film program, and subjects believed they were viewing the films as a film-rating task. Several days later, they were asked to respond to a number of attitude measures, but were unaware of any relationship between the film and the questionnaire. Malamuth and Check found that exposure to the film portraying violent sexuality was associated with a greater acceptance of interpersonal violence against women. This finding was true only for male subjects. Female subjects had a nonsignificant tendency in the opposite direction, as women exposed to violence tended to be less accepting of interpersonal violence than control females. It is important to realize, however, that this study does not provide any data on whether males exposed to violence would actually behave differently toward women. But the study does demonstrate that such exposure may have a significant effect on attitudes.

In his analysis of antisocial behaviour, Bandura (1986) suggests that the best deterrent to such activity is the provision of more attractive pro-social alternatives. However, he acknowledges that "when inducements to criminal acts are strong, when personal sanctions against such conduct are weak, and when people lack socially acceptable means of getting what they want, fear of punishment serves as a major deterrent to transgressive conduct." Deterrence may take two forms—direct or vicarious. In the former, punishment is used to discourage current transgressors of such activity in the future. In the latter, punishment serves as a general deterrent to others. Bandura identifies three major sources of deterrence against criminal activity: legal sanction, social sanction, and self-sanction. Legal sanctions derive from the belief that there are legal consequences to transgressions despite the reality that most crime goes unpunished. Bandura cites research by Clastner (1967) in stating that "people who are not in the habit of breaking the law share a distorted perception of legal threats, in which they greatly overestimate the risks of getting caught and punished for unlawful acts. In contrast, offenders judge personal risks to be lower and more in line with the actual probabilities." Social sanctions reflect the neg-

autonomic reactivity

A measurement of the extent to which an individual's physical organism reacts to external stimuli.

ative social consequences that criminal stigmatization can have for an individual and the powerful deterrent effect this risk has. Self-sanctions are self-imposed moral standards; they are seen as the most effective deterrent as they are operative even when there is no risk of detection involved. Bandura (1986) states, "In the absence of self-sanctions rooted in societal standards, whenever personal desires conflict with societal codes, external threats in the form of legal and social sanctions, and extensive social surveillance are needed to insure that the rights and welfare of others are not completely disregarded."

Operant Conditioning

Another learning theory is based on the principle of **operant conditioning**. This involves the use of rewards and punishments to increase the probability or frequency of a given response. B.F. Skinner is the psychologist most identified with this theory, and his research forms the basis for both the theoretical and the applied applications of operant conditioning.

One way a response can be learned is through a process referred to as shaping. This involves rewarding approximations of a target behaviour until the behaviour gradually progresses to the desired response. Behaviour can also be learned through punishment, which can be either a withdrawal of a positive reinforcer or the introduction of a negative stimulus such as an electric shock. There have been a number of attempts to use operant conditioning theory to account for the acquisition of criminal behaviour. Notable among this work is that of Jeffery (1965) and that of Burgess and Akers (1966).

Burgess and Akers (1966) and Akers (1990) conceptualize criminal behaviour in terms of operant conditioning and imitation. The main component in Akers's (1990) social learning theory is differential reinforcement. This refers to the balance of rewards and punishments that govern behaviour. In this theory, operant conditioning is the basic process by which an individual's behaviour is shaped, and this can occur through both reinforcement and punishment. Reinforcement refers to any process that strengthens a behaviour, while punishment is any process that weakens a behaviour. As applied to deviance and crime, Akers (1990) states that

> social learning is a behavioral approach to socialization which includes individuals' responses to rewards and punishments in the current situation, the learned patterns of responses they bring to that situation, and the anticipated consequences of actions taken now and in the future in the initiation, continuation, and cessation of those actions. It is a "soft behaviorism" that allows for choice and cognitive processes. It views the individual's behavior as responding to and being conditioned by environmental feedback and consequences. It does not view the individual as unreasoning and only passively conditioned.

Considerable research has been conducted on the application of learning theory to the treatment of delinquents. The "teaching-family" group-home model begun in the late 1960s has been at the centre of group-home development. The approach

operant conditioning
The basic process by which an individual's behaviour is shaped by reinforcement or by punishment.

"Operant (Instrumental) Conditioning"
Bill Huitt, Valdosta State University
http://chiron.vladosta.edu/whuitt/col/behsys/operant.html

rests on the view that an adolescent's behavior patterns, behavior discriminations, and skills are functions of past behavior-environment interactions (learning history), currently ongoing behavior-environment interactions, and genetic organismic variables (Braukman et al., 1980). In this conceptualization, inherited characteristics and environmental features in childhood, particularly parenting practices (relationship development, teaching, supervision, and discipline) affect later development. In adolescence, earlier developed antisocial patterns tend to persevere (indeed, are self-perpetuating) and can be maintained further by ongoing behavior-environment interactions associated with inappropriate parenting, deviant peers, and school failure. (Braukman and Wolf, 1987)

The group home provides the reinforcing environment designed to change existing behavioural interactions in the direction of functional and pro-social skills. The emphasis is on learning social and family life skills. The best known of these programs is Achievement Place, a cottage-style treatment facility for delinquents (Phillips, 1968). Youth in this program live in residence with trained "houseparents." The heart of the program is a **token economy** system in which points can be earned (or lost). For example, residents can earn points for being at class on time, cleaning their bedroom, and engaging in other positive behaviours. Disruptive behaviour in the classroom, making aggressive statements or fighting, and being late for class can result in a loss of points. The points can be used to purchase privileges and material goods. Research on Achievement Place has demonstrated that "contingent token consequences could both establish behaviors basic to participation in lawful, productive intra- and extra-treatment activities, and eliminate behaviors likely to get the participants in further trouble" (Braukman and Wolf, 1987). A comprehensive outcome study on the teaching-family program (Braukman et al., 1985) indicates that this approach has considerable short-term positive effects. However, the long-term implications are less positive since it is very difficult to control reinforcement following release from the institution. Because of this, increased emphasis has been placed on systematic aftercare to help maintain treatment effects.

token economy

A behaviour therapy procedure based on operant learning principles. Individuals are rewarded (reinforced) for positive or appropriate behaviour and are disciplined (punished) for negative or inappropriate behaviour.

ANTISOCIAL PERSONALITY

The study of antisocial personality provides a good example of how psychological theory can be applied to criminal populations. Some confusion has resulted from the variety of terms used to describe basically the same set of behaviours: sociopathy, psychopathy, moral insanity, antisocial personality, and **Antisocial Personality Disorder**. There has also been a tendency for some to use the term very loosely as a "wastebasket" category for antisocial individuals generally. There is, however, strong empirical evidence that the traits underlying this disorder form a valid and clinically meaningful cluster (Hare and Cox, 1978; Skilling et al., 2002). For many, this term is associated with images of violent and sadistic murderers as portrayed countless times on television or, all too often, demonstrated in real life. The brutal murders committed by Ted Bundy (see Box 9.1), Clifford Olson (see Box 9.3), and Charles Manson and his followers in California are frequently cited

Antisocial Personality Disorder

A personality disorder that involves disregard for the rights of others, as well as impulsive, irresponsible, and aggressive behaviour.

BOX 9.1

FOCUS

Ted Bundy—Why?

Born in 1946, Theodore Robert Bundy seemed destined for a charmed life; he was intelligent, attractive, and articulate (Holmes and DeBurger, 1988). A Boy Scout as a youth and then an honor student and a psychology major at the University of Washington, he was at one time a work-study student at the Seattle Crisis Clinic. Later he became assistant to the chairman of the Washington State Republican Party. It is likely that about this time he claimed his first victim; a college-age woman was viciously attacked while sleeping, left alive but brain-damaged. During the years from 1974 through 1978, Bundy stalked, attacked, killed, and then sexually assaulted as many as 36 victims in Washington, Oregon, Utah, Colorado, and Florida. Apparently some of the women were distracted when the good-looking casual Bundy approached, seeming helpless because of being on crutches or with an apparent broken arm. He usually choked them to death and then sexually abused and mutilated them before disposing of their bodies in remote areas (Nordheimer, 1989).

It is characteristic of the psychopathic personality or sociopath to maintain a facade of charm, so that acquaintances will describe him (as they did Bundy) as "fascinating," "charismatic," and "compassionate." At his trial for the murder of two Chi Omega sorority sisters in their bedrooms at Florida State University, he served as his own attorney (Bundy had attended two law schools). But he was convicted; he was also found guilty of the kidnapping, murder, and mutilation of a Lake City, Florida, girl who was 12 years old.

Bundy was sentenced to death. Shortly before he was executed on January 24, 1989, Bundy gave a television interview to California evangelist James Dobson in which he attributed the cause of his problems to pornography. He said: "Those of us who are ... so much influenced by violence in the media, in particular pornographic violence, are not some kind of inherent monsters. We are your husbands, and we grew up in regular families" (quoted by Lamar, 1989, p. 34). Bundy claimed that he spent his formative ages with a grandfather who had an insatiable craving for pornography.

He told Dr. Dobson, "People will accuse me of being self-serving but I am just telling you how I feel. Through God's help, I have been able to come to the point where I much too late, but better late than never, feel the hurt and the pain that I am responsible for" (quoted by Kleinberg, 1989, p. 5A).

The tape of Bundy's last interview, produced by Dobson and titled "Fatal Addiction," has been widely disseminated, especially by those who seek to eliminate all pornography. (Dr. Dobson served on a federal pornography commission during the Reagan administration.) But Bundy's claim that pornography was the "fuel for his fantasies" has been received skeptically by others, who saw it as one last manipulative ploy to gain further time. Even his mother stated that no evidence existed in her son's first 28 years (before he became a murder suspect for the first time) that hinted at any aberrant behavior (Nordheimer, 1989). In none of his previous interviews, including extensive conversations in 1986 with Dorothy Lewis, a psychiatrist he had come to trust, did he ever cite "a pornographic preamble to his grotesqueries" (Nobile, 1989, p. 41). Bundy had decided at that time that he needed psychiatric testimony in order to escape the electric chair—that is, by being diagnosed as not competent to stand trial because he was supposedly too confused and irrational to assist in his own murder defense. Despite Dr. Lewis's testimony in 1986, the judge would not declare Bundy incompetent. Thus, perhaps at that time he decided to portray himself as a normal youth who had been corrupted by pornography (Nobile, 1989).

According to psychiatrist Park Dietz, most serial sexual killers have two distinct qualities: sexual sadism and psychopathy, or the lack of normal inhibitions about acting on that desire (quoted by Nobile, 1989). This classification seems a succinct summary of Ted Bundy.

Source: Adapted from L.S. Wrightsman, M.T. Nietzel, and W.H. Fortune. (1991). *Psychology and the Legal System*, 2nd ed. Copyright © 1991. Reprinted with permission of Wadsworth Publishing, a division of Thomson Learning: www.thomsonrights.com. Fax 800-730-2215.

examples of psychopathy. Indeed, while there is some debate over the most appropriate diagnosis for Manson, many would argue that his behaviour best fits the clinical picture of psychopathy. As Nathan and Harris (1975) point out:

> Charles Manson acted upon society in an unbelievable variety of antisocial ways. At one time or another he robbed, deceived, assaulted, exploited, seduced—and murdered. But despite the extraordinary range of antisocial acts for which he had been responsible, perhaps his most surprising characteristic was that at no time did he show guilt or remorse about anything he had done. During his trial for the Tate murders, he said, "I've considered innocence and guilt and I know the difference between them and I have no guilt" (quoted from the *New York Times*, Dec. 25, 1969). A man who could be charming and captivating, brutal and ruthless, Manson could not be guilty, at least in his own eyes. What kind of human being feels no remorse over murder? Why would a person keep committing crimes despite repeated punishment? How can a man charm so many people and yet never relate with genuine feeling to anyone?

These questions are difficult to answer because the crimes Manson, Olson, and Bundy committed seem so senseless to society. However disturbing they may be, it is possible for most people to understand murders motivated by greed or passion; but the murder of Sharon Tate and others by Manson cannot be explained by either of these motivations.

Similarly, it is difficult to understand the motivations of "Canada's Ken and Barbie Killers"—Paul Bernardo and Karla Homolka—who were responsible for the grotesque rape and murder of three young women, including Karla Homolka's own sister. Although the prevalence of female psychopaths is lower than that of males, we are especially intrigued by these women. In recent parole board reports, Karla Homolka has been deemed a psychopath (see Box 9.2), though the motivation for her actions remains unclear.

This section began with a discussion of Charles Manson because it is this image that best fits the common conception of persons with an antisocial personality. It is a misleading picture, however, because many individuals with diagnoses of antisocial personality do not have a history of violence and, even among those who do, very few would exhibit the extreme forms that Manson did. The term *sociopath* was later used instead of the term *psychopath* to convey this less violent picture. More recently, the use of the term *Antisocial Personality Disorder* has become common (see Chapter 8).

The current edition of the American Psychiatric Association's *Diagnostic and Statistical Manual of Mental Disorder* (DSM-IV) defines Antisocial Personality Disorder in the following manner:

> The essential feature of Antisocial Personality Disorder is a pervasive pattern of disregard for, and violation of, the rights of others that begins in childhood or early adolescence and continues into adulthood.

Lying, stealing, fighting, truancy, and resisting authority are typical early childhood signs. In adolescence, unusually early or aggressive sexual behaviour, excessive drinking, and use of illicit drugs are frequent. In adulthood, those

BOX 9.2

FOCUS

Psychologists Suggest Bernardo and Homolka Are Psychopaths

TORONTO—Prosecutors painted a picture of a battered woman and a controlling, abusive husband who forced her to take part in unspeakable crimes. But some experts suspect that both Karla Homolka and Paul Bernardo are psychopaths—people who aren't mentally ill but lack any conscience and single-mindedly pursue their own pleasure.

In Bernardo, they suggest, psychopathic qualities combined with sexual sadism to form an explosive mix. Some psychologists who have followed the Bernardo trial say the crimes Homolka and Bernardo admitted to committing, and their almost total lack of emotion in the witness box, suggest psychopathic tendencies.

"What bothers me about him, and her, too, is the casual way these horrific things are described on the witness stand," said psychologist Robert Hare of the University of British Columbia, one of the world's leading experts on psychopaths.

"When a psychopath commits a violent act, they're not doing it because they're malicious or malevolent or evil. They're doing it because they don't give a damn."

Bernardo was "such a good psychopath" that he found a woman who had a penchant for submissive sex that complemented his urge to dominate, said psychologist Marnie Rice of Ontario's Penetanguishene Mental Health Centre. Homolka may not have got into trouble with another man. But hooked up with Bernardo, it's possible she agreed to take part in three-way sex with kidnapped teenage girls as part of a willingly subservient role, said Rice, whose hospital houses some of the province's most dangerous offenders.

"It appears the two found each other."

Homolka testified Bernardo beat her into submission and blackmailed her over her role in the death of her sister, who was drugged and raped by the couple. Two psychologists called by the Crown suggested Homolka suffered from battered women's syndrome. Rendered helpless and hopeless by repeated beatings, someone in her shoes could feel obliged to take part in the most heinous crimes, they said. Hare is skeptical.

"We look for very simple explanations for complex behavior," he said. "To me, battered women's syndrome does not explain what she did."

Even a psychiatrist retained by the prosecution—but not called as a witness at Bernardo's trial—said Homolka's role in the horrific crimes can't be fully explained by the abuse she suffered.

"Karla Homolka remains something of a diagnostic mystery," Dr. Angus McDonald wrote in his report, which the Bernardo jury never saw.

"Despite her ability to present herself very well, there is a moral vacuity in her which is difficult, if not impossible, to explain."

In Bernardo's case, it appears there were no ethical restraints to hold him back from sex that inflicted pain, terror and humiliation on his partner, psychologists say. Among evidence ruled inadmissible at his trial was a statement the Crown says Bernardo made to two witnesses.

"I have no conscience," prosecutors quoted him as saying. "I could kill anybody."

Experts also say his videotaping of the sexual assaults is typical of many rapists and sex killers, who keep souvenirs of their victims such as jewelry, clothing or hair. Serial killer Harvey Murray Glatman used photographs of the women he murdered in Los Angeles during the 1950s to relive his sexual fantasies.

"They're like stamp collectors," said psychologist Vern Quinsey of Queen's University in Kingston. "They look at them and think about them and try to do better next time."

Psychopaths tend to be egocentric, lack remorse or guilt and constantly seek excitement, said Hare. They're also unable to empathize with others and tend to be deceitful and emotionally shallow. Only a small percentage are physically violent, he said.

"They are predators—emotional and physical and sexual predators."

(continued)

Bernardo's cool, confidant and sometimes condescending demeanor in the witness box was typical, Hare said.

"A psychopath who has committed a crime and is caught is now on stage. He doesn't see himself as any sort of pariah, he sees himself as a victim of the system.... He's on stage, he's enjoying it, he's loving it.

"What these people do is confuse fame and infamy."

Source: Tom Blackwell. (n.d.) "Psychologists Suggest Bernardo and Homolka are Psychopaths." Printed with permission of The Canadian Press.

kinds of behaviour continue, with the addition of inability to sustain consistent work performance or to function as a responsible parent and failure to accept social norms with respect to lawful behaviour. After age 30, the more flagrant aspects may diminish, particularly sexual promiscuity, fighting, criminality, and vagrancy. It is estimated that between 15 and 30 percent of the inmate population in Canadian prisons could be considered psychopathic (Ogloff et al., 1990).

In his book *The Mask of Sanity*, Cleckley (1976) provided a clinical description of the antisocial personality and described the psychopath using the following criteria: unreliability; insincerity; pathological lying and deception; egocentricity; poor judgement; impulsivity; a lack of remorse, guilt, or shame; an inability to experience empathy or concern for others and to maintain warm, affectionate attachments; an impersonal and poorly integrated sex life; and an unstable life plan with no long-term commitments.

Since the 1960s, Hare and his colleagues have devoted considerable attention to the development of a reliable and valid procedure for the assessment of psychopathy. This program has culminated in the Revised Psychopathy Checklist (PCL-R) (Hare, 1991), a 20-item checklist of traits and behaviours associated with psychopathy (see Table 8.3). Research has continued to support the use of this scale in prison populations. An excellent review of the use, and misuse, of the PCL-R has been provided by Hare. In discussing the PCL-R and its screening version, the PCL-SV (Hart et al., 1995), he concludes that these checklists "provide reliable and valid assessments of the traditional construct of psychopathy. They are used widely for research purposes and for making decisions in the mental health and criminal justice systems. They are strong predictors of violence and recidivism in offenders and psychiatric patients, form a key part of current risk assessment procedures, and play an important role in many judicial decisions" (Hare, 1998c, 99).

DSM-IV estimates that the prevalence of Antisocial Personality Disorder is 3 percent for men and less than 1 percent for women. However, estimates of this diagnostic classification in prison populations are, not surprisingly, considerably higher. Indeed, depending on how one interprets the diagnostic criteria, virtually all inmates could be so classified. The differences in interpretation may partly account for the large disparity in prison studies of this disorder, reflecting, in part, changes in diagnostic procedures and criteria. In a Canadian study of the prevalence of Antisocial Personality Disorder, Hare (1983) had two clinicians examine a provincial and a federal prison inmate sample. The clinicians found that approximately one-third of the provincial sample and 42 percent of the federal sample met the criteria for Antisocial Personality Disorder. Overall, 39 percent of the total prison sample received this diagnosis. However, in a previous study described in the same paper, Hare, using the initial criteria proposed in a draft of DSM-III-R, found that 76 percent of a sample of 145 white male criminals met the criteria for Antisocial Personality Disorder. The reason for the difference is that the published version of DSM-III-R required that more stringent criteria be met before a diagnosis of Antisocial Personality Disorder could be made. Hare's work was influential in the decision to change the criteria. The two studies provide a clear illustration of how changes in diagnostic criteria and procedures can influence the perceived prevalence of antisocial personality.

A leading theory about antisocial personality is that these individuals do not learn from negative experiences because they do not become anxious in circumstances that should elicit anxiety. Also, they do not have sufficient fear of the consequences of their behaviour (Brodsky, 1977; Hare, 1970). Applying Eysenck's model, reviewed earlier in this chapter, the psychopath can be viewed as an extravert who does not easily acquire conditioned responses or, if he or she acquires them, extinguishes them very rapidly. Given these characteristics, particularly the inability to learn from punishment or to experience fear or anxiety, it is understandable that Brodsky (1977) concludes that imprisonment is unlikely to have much effect on the postrelease behaviour of such individuals. Newman (1998) reviews a position suggesting that psychopaths exhibit deficits in information processing that limit their ability to use contextual cues appropriately in the implementation of goal-directed behaviour and interfere with effective self-regulation. Hare (1998b) suggests that while a great deal remains to be done, there is a convergence emerging with regard to etiologic bases of psychopathy, which forms "a reasonably coherent conceptual/empirical package that helps us understand how and why psychopaths differ from others in the processing and use of semantic and affective information, and in their capacity for callous, predatory behaviour" (1998b, 131).

Heilbrun (1979) conducted an interesting study of the influence of intelligence on the relationships between psychopathy, violence, and impulsiveness. His sample of 76 white male prisoners was divided into psychopathic and nonpsychopathic groups (N=38). Two personality measures were used (one of which, incidentally, was validated in a study by Craddick [1962] using a Canadian prison sample). He further divided the groups into high-intelligence and low-intelligence subgroups. Heilbrun found that intelligence level does indeed have an influence on violence and impulsiveness among psychopaths. The more intelligent psychopaths were neither violent nor impulsive, and were more likely to have attained educational goals. This study points to the importance of viewing persons with the label of psychopath, or antisocial personality, in multidimensional ways. Not all such individuals should be expected to be violent or impulsive.

The Heilbrun study should also serve as a reminder that studies of prison populations may present a misleading picture of antisocial personality. Most of the research on antisocial personality has used samples obtained from institutional populations. This may give a distorted view because the impressions one has about people with antisocial personalities are, thus, based on people who committed criminal acts but were not able to avoid apprehension. Furthermore, it is certainly true that not all persons with this label are criminals (Cleckley, 1976). An exception to the focus on institutionalized populations is the work of Cathy Spatz Widom (Widom, 1977; Widom and Newman, 1985). In one study, Widom placed an advertisement in a local newspaper asking for "charming, aggressive, carefree people who are impulsively irresponsible but are good at handling people and at looking after number one." Twenty-nine applicants were interviewed. The demographic and personality test data applied to these people revealed some interesting information about this noninstitutionalized population. Only two subjects had not finished high school, and most had some college. Nearly two-thirds had at least one arrest, but the conviction rate was quite low (18 percent), even though many of the charges were felonies. While 50 percent had been incarcerated, most had been in jail less than two weeks. The subjects scored high on the extraversion and neuroticism scale of Eysenck Personality Inventory, consistent with Eysenck's (1977) notions of psychopathy. Scores on the Minnesota Multiphasic Personality Inventory (MMPI), an objective personality test, fit the classic profile of psychopathy (high scores on the psychopathic deviate and manic scales). Subjects had low scores on the measure of socialization, and most also had low scores on the empathy scale.

While many of the results of Widom's study were similar to those found in institutional populations, Widom's study presents a picture of somewhat more successful antisocial persons. That is, they are better educated and more successful at avoiding conviction and lengthy incarceration. These results support the conclusion of Widom and Newman (1985) that research on the antisocial personality must avoid a primary focus on the incarcerated criminal. Her methodology seems to have been successful in drawing a sample of noninstitutionalized persons who meet the antisocial personality criteria. This is important as it is vital for us to become more aware of the prevalence of psychopathy within the general population and to begin to understand better the noncriminal manifestations of this personality. However, at this time, the fascination with such individuals continues to be mostly a consequence of the overwhelmingly antisocial nature of their acts. In *Without Conscience*, Hare (1998a) captures the essence of this in his description of Clifford Olson (see Box 9.3).

A final note on treatment seems appropriate. Losel (1998) reviews a position taken by Suedfeld and Landon (1978) that no effective treatments exist for this disorder. While acknowledging that our understanding of issues related to concerns such as assessment, etiology, prediction, and the biological, cognitive, emotional, and behavioural correlates has advanced greatly in the past 20 years, he indicates that treatment of such individuals remains an area of uncertainty.

"MMPI-2 Workshops and Symposia"
Department of Psychology, University of Minnesota
Click on "Current Newsletter" and "Past Editions."
www1.umn.edu/mmpi/

CRIME AND MENTAL ILLNESS

We begin this discussion of crime and mental illness with a most extreme statement: all crime is symptomatic of mental illness. While this may seem a preposterous statement to some, many mental health professionals have held this belief. Hakeem (1958) has summarized these views:

BOX 9.3

FOCUS

Clifford Olson—The Prototypical Psychopath

Canada's most notorious and reviled criminal is Clifford Olson, a serial murderer sentenced in January 1982 to life imprisonment for the torture and killing of eleven boys and girls. These crimes were the latest and most despicable in a string of antisocial and criminal acts extending back to his early childhood. Although some psychopaths are not violent and few are as brutal as he, Olson is the prototypical psychopath.

Consider the following quotation from a newspaper article written around the time of his trial: "He was a braggart and a bully, a liar and thief. He was a violent man with a hairtrigger temper. But he could also be charming and smooth-tongued when trying to impress people.... Olson was a compulsive talker.... He's a real smooth talker, he has the gift of gab.... He was always telling whoppers.... The man was just an out-and-out liar.... He always wanted to test you to the limits. He wanted to see how far he could go before you had to step on him.... He was a manipulator.... Olson was a blabbermouth.... We learned after a while not to believe anything he said because he told so many lies" (Farrow, 1982). A reporter who talked with Olson said, "He talked fast, staccato.... He jumped from topic to topic. He sounded glib, slick, like a con trying to prove he's tough and important" (Ouston, 1982).

These reports by people who knew him are important, for they give us a clue to why he was able to get his young, trusting victims alone with him. They may also help to explain the Crown's decision to pay him $100 000 to tell them where he hid the bodies of seven of the eleven young people he had killed. Not surprisingly, public outrage greeted disclosure of the payment. Some typical headlines were: KILLER WAS PAID TO LOCATE BODIES; MONEY-FOR-GRAVES PAYMENT TO CHILD KILLER GREETED WITH DISGUST.

In the years since his imprisonment Olson has continued to bring grief to the families of his victims by sending them letters with comments about the murders of their children. He has never shown any guilt or remorse for his depredations; on the contrary, he continually complains about his treatment by the press, the prison system, and society. During his trial he preened and postured whenever a camera was present, apparently considering himself an important celebrity rather than a man who had committed a series of atrocities. On January 15, 1983, the *Vancouver Sun* reported, "Mass killer Clifford Olson has written to the *Sun* newsroom to say he does not approve of the picture of him we have been using ... and will shortly be sending us newer, more attractive pictures of himself." (Quotes are from articles by R. Ouston, *Vancouver Sun*, January 15, 1982; and M. Farrow, *Vancouver Sun*, January 14, 1982.)

At this writing Olson has written to several criminology departments in Canada offering to help them establish a course devoted to studying him.

Source: Robert D. Hare. (1998). *Without Conscience: The Disturbing World of the Psychopaths Among Us.* New York: Guilford Press, pp. 132–34. Reprinted with permission of the author.

So powerful is the conviction of some psychiatrists that crime stems from mental disease, that they have held that the commission of crime in itself constitutes evidence of the presence of mental disease. Again, this aspect of the ideology usually draws on the medical analogy. The thesis runs as follows: just as fever is a symptom of physical disease, so crime is a symptom of mental disease.

Today, most would disagree with this position. Indeed, the current view is that while some criminals exhibit symptoms of mental illness, the majority do not (Corrado et al., 2000; Freeman and Roesch, 1989). In the remainder of this

"Mental Disorders and Crime: The Connection Is Real"
Crime Times
www.autismtv.com/crimetimes/ 96c/w96cp1.htm

section, some of the current theories of crime and mental illness will be reviewed. In particular, the extent to which persons charged with crimes are in need of mental health intervention will be examined.

Studies of the prevalence of mental illness in jail or prison populations are difficult to assess because of the diversity of findings. Teplin (1991) reported the prevalence rates of mental disorder among jail detainees range from about 5 to 12 percent for severe mental disorders and from 16 to 67 percent for any mental illness. Silber (1974) argues that the rate of severe mental illness is quite low, as do Brodsky (1972) and Guze (1976). Monahan and Steadman (1983) reviewed a number of studies addressing the issue of prevalence and concluded that the rates of mental illness in jails or prisons are no higher than the rates in the general population, controlling for social class.

The above studies are based on U.S. prison samples. There have been only a few studies in Canada on the extent of mental health problems in jail populations. Allodi et al. (1977) reported that increases in referrals of jail inmates to a jail psychiatric unit were associated with decreases in mental hospital populations in the Toronto area. Statistics Canada data on the number of admissions to psychiatric units within correctional facilities also support the view that the referral rate has increased (see Borzecki and Wormith, 1985, for a review of this issue). A study by Hodgins and Côté (1990) of 650 inmates in Quebec prisons revealed a high rate of mental disorder. Indeed, these researchers report that "the prevalence of schizophrenic disorders ... is about seven times that observed in samples of non-incarcerated adult males." Hodgins and Côté also comment on the fact that most of the inmates diagnosed with a major mental disorder did not receive any mental health treatment during their confinement in prison (see Steadman et al., 1988, for similar conclusions based on a national survey of American jails). In a study using a pretrial population, Roesch (1995) found that the prevalence of major mental disorders was 15.6 percent. As well, the prevalence of substance use disorders was exceptionally high, with over 77 percent considered to have alcohol use or dependence disorders, and over 63 percent with drug use disorders. Many of these individuals had co-occurring disorders (e.g., schizophrenia and substance abuse), further compounding the mental health and social problems these individuals experience. This finding is consistent with the results of a study by Abram and Teplin (1991), which found considerable overlap between mental disorders and drug or alcohol abuse in jail populations. This has been referred to as co-occurring disorders. The high rate of individuals with co-occurring disorders suggests the need for treatment programs both within the jail and after release. Abram and Teplin suggested that these individuals might be particularly appropriate for alternatives to prosecution, such as pretrial diversion programs.

There is little question that individuals with mental health problems are increasingly involved with the legal system. The first contact is usually by police officers. These officers have considerable discretion in responding to the mentally ill, although changes in the civil commitment laws have placed some limits on them. Jacobsen et al. (1973) found that police rarely arrested persons they

"The Prison Careers of Offenders with Mental Disorders"
Correctional Service of Canada
www.csc-scc.gc.ca/text/rsrch/ reports/r33/r33e_e.shtml

suspected of being mentally ill, indicating that they believed that hospitalization was more helpful than jail. The police officers frequently looked for alternatives to jail, such as contacting a responsible person, family counselling, or not taking any action at all.

There is some evidence, however, that the discretionary powers of the police in dealing with the mentally ill have been affected by the deinstitutionalization movement. This movement resulted in the release of large numbers of patients from mental hospitals. At the same time, the civil commitment laws were changed so that commitment had to be based on findings of mental illness and dangerousness. As a consequence, police could no longer use the mental hospital as an alternative disposition to jail and were often forced to arrest a mentally ill person.

If this is true, does it suggest that there is a significant relationship between crime and mental disorder? In his study of the rates of mental disorder in prisons, Gunn (1977) answers this question with a note of caution, suggesting that, as other alternatives for the placement of mentally ill persons were blocked off, it would be expected that a greater number of persons previously detained in mental hospitals would now end up in prisons. As Roesch and Golding (1985) point out, the increased rate of mental disorder in prisons is the result of "institutional and public policy practices that have nothing to do with individual deviance *per se*. In fact, the individual behavior may not have changed at all. What has changed, however, is the manner in which institutions of our society react to that individual behavior."

With these cautions in mind, it will be instructive to review some studies on the extent to which persons considered to be mentally ill are arrested for criminal offences. Most of the research on arrest rates of the mentally ill has relied on police or court records. Such research is limited by the availability of information in the files, which are often incomplete and inaccurate. One of the few researchers to actually observe how the police dealt with the mentally ill was Linda Teplin (1984). She was interested in examining the probability of arrest for mentally ill persons as compared to persons who were not mentally ill.

Teplin's sample was 1382 police–citizen encounters involving 2555 citizens. Overall, the probability of arrest was low, occurring in only 12 percent of 884 encounters (traffic-offence and public-service incidents were deleted from the total). In individual terms, 506 of the 1798 citizens involved were considered suspect, but only 29 percent were arrested.

Does the presence of symptoms of mental illness affect the probability of arrest? Teplin's data suggest that it does. Of 506 suspects, 30 were considered by observers to be mentally ill. Nearly one-half (14) were arrested, compared to an arrest percentage of 27.9 percent for those not mentally ill. Furthermore, this difference was not accounted for by differences in type of charge. In other words, mentally ill suspects were not arrested more often because they were suspected of committing more serious crimes. The difference held up across types of crime.

Lamb (1982) also examined police arrests of mentally ill persons. The sample was 102 inmates who had been referred to a forensic unit within a county jail. Ninety percent had a history of prior hospitalization, and 92 percent had prior arrests. Lamb was interested in why the police chose to arrest rather than hospitalize these individuals. About one-half were arrested for felonies, so police had little choice since persons who have allegedly committed serious crimes are almost uniformly arrested, regardless of mental condition. Lamb argues that police have become reluctant to take persons charged with less serious crimes to mental health treatment centres, as they have learned through experience that the centres frequently release such people because of bed shortages, or because they do not meet the criteria for civil commitment. Lamb concluded that "the police may well book the person into jail—which is less time-consuming and ensures the person's removal from the community pending further evaluation—rather than take him to the hospital."

Once arrested, do mentally disordered offenders recidivate at a high level? In a recent meta-analysis of a large number of empirical studies, Bonta et al. (1998) found that mentally disordered offenders on average showed lower recidivism rates than other offenders. A diagnosis of Antisocial Personality Disorder was found to be a more potent predictor than any other clinical diagnosis. However, with respect to violence after release from custody, Borum (1996) notes that mental disorder is now considered a robust and significant risk factor for predicting violent recidivism, as mentally disordered offenders have a greater probability of committing violent offences after release. But Borum adds that most persons with mental disorders are not violent, so it is a relative rather than an absolute risk factor. It is important to keep in mind that most mentally disordered offenders are not violent and may have a decreased risk of general recidivism.

In conclusion, it is likely that theories of criminal behaviour that rely on models of mental illness will not account for the behaviour of most criminals. It is certainly true that some people who commit crimes can be considered mentally ill, but these individuals make up only a small percentage of the total criminal population. In a legal sense, most criminals are responsible for their actions in that they are aware of their behaviour and can distinguish between right and wrong.

Each of the psychological theories reviewed in this chapter makes a contribution to the understanding of criminal behaviour. However, there is a need for greater integration of sociological and psychological perspectives so that both situational determinants and individual differences can be taken into account in attempts to explain criminal behaviour (Monahan and Splane, 1980). A study by Conger (1976) provides an excellent example of an attempt to integrate the two approaches. Conger examined the relationship between two models of delinquent behaviour: the social control model (which is discussed in Chapter 13) and a social learning model. Based on data collected from a sample of Grade 7 boys, Conger demonstrated how social learning theory, particularly the effects of differential reinforcement and punishment, can be used to explain how an individual's bonds to society can be strengthened or weakened. Conger argued that the combination of the two theories can provide a more comprehensive theory of delinquent behaviour than can either theory by

TABLE 9.2 Psychological Theories

Theory	Theorists	Key Elements
Psychoanalytic theory	Freud	Crime results when the ego and superego cannot control the antisocial instincts of the id. This occurs because the individual has not been adequately socialized in early childhood.
Moral development theory	Piaget Kohlberg	Each individual must go through a sequence of moral development. Those with a high level of moral development will be more likely to make responsible choices when faced with the opportunity to get involved in criminal behaviour.
Personality theory	Eysenck	Law-abiding people must develop a conditioned fear of deviance. Those who become delinquents and criminals do not develop this fear because of poor conditioning by parents or because they are less susceptible to conditioning.
Social learning theory	Bandura	Deviant behaviour such as aggression can be learned through direct experience or through modelling the behaviour of others.
Operant conditioning theory	Skinner	Individual behaviour is shaped through both reinforcement and punishment. Behaviour that is rewarded will tend to be continued; behaviour that is punished will cease.
Psychopathy	Cleckley Hare	Psychopaths seem to lack empathy for their victims and do not feel guilty about their crimes. They do not learn from their experience or fear the consequences of their behaviour.

itself. It is likely that the same arguments can be made for any of the theories reviewed in this chapter.

SUMMARY

- Psychological theory is primarily concerned with explanations of behaviour at the level of the individual. Some psychological theories have been criticized for relying too much on trying to explain crime at the level of the individual and for not placing enough emphasis on environmental and situational factors.

- Certain psychological perspectives, such as community psychology, view social problems from a "level of analysis" perspective. Such levels include individual, small-group, organizational, and institutional or community levels.

- The premise for psychoanalytic theory is a series of five stages of development (oral, anal, phallic, latency, and genital) and three components of personality (id, ego, and superego). Psychoanalytic interpretations of criminality suggest that criminal behaviour occurs when the ego and superego are unable to restrain the id.

- Kohlberg has proposed a six-stage theory of moral development, with two stages occurring at each of three levels (preconventional, conventional, and postconventional). This theory has been criticized from a feminist perspective for not adequately considering the different approaches of males (more justice-oriented) and females (more care-oriented) to morality.

- Eysenck's theory of crime and personality is based on the premise of classical conditioning. He has proposed three dimensions of personality (extraversion, neuroticism, and psychoticism), has developed measures of each of the three dimensions, and has generated a number of hypotheses about the relationship of these dimensions of personality to criminal behaviour. Eysenck's work offers a comprehensive model or theory of criminal behaviour that remains to be validated.

- Social learning theory integrates sociology and psychology in explaining criminal behaviour. Modelling is an important aspect of social learning theory. Family, subcultural influences, and symbolic modelling are all important sources from which an individual can learn aggressive behaviour. Deterrence, on the other hand, can occur through legal sanction, social sanction, and self-sanction.

- Operant conditioning is a subset of learning theory that has been proposed to explain criminal behaviour. Reinforcement and punishment are theorized to play a large part in strengthening or weakening criminal behaviours. A token economy is one method that has been used to change existing behavioural interactions of individuals.

- Antisocial Personality Disorder is a diagnostic label that refers to a cluster of traits that underlie a pervasive pattern of disregard for the rights of others. Such traits include lying, stealing, fighting, and truancy. Behaviours that may be characteristic of this disorder include excessive drinking or the use of illicit substances, aggressive sexual behaviour, inconsistent work performance, and a failure to accept social norms with respect to lawful behaviour.

- Psychopathy is a term that is often confused with antisocial personality. Psychopathy refers to a pattern of behavioural features that are similar to those associated with Antisocial Personality Disorder. However, in addition to these behavioural features, psychopathic individuals also display certain attitudinal features such as grandiosity, glib and superficial charm, lack of empathy, and a lack of remorse, guilt, or shame.

■ The majority of criminals do not display any symptoms of mental illness. The prevalence of mental illness in jails and prisons is difficult to assess. However, some studies have estimated it to be between 5 and 12 percent for severe disorders and between 16 and 67 percent for any mental disorder.

QUESTIONS FOR CRITICAL THINKING

1. Describe how each of the major psychological theories would explain criminal behaviour (i.e., psychoanalytic theory, theories of moral development, Eysenck's theory of crime and personality, social learning theory, and operant conditioning). What are the social policy implications of each of these theories?
2. Describe what is meant by Antisocial Personality Disorder and psychopathy, and discuss how these two disorders differ from each other.
3. Discuss the relationship between crime and mental illness, and describe the prevalence of mental illness in criminal populations. Is prison the most appropriate place to deal with people with mental illness?

NET WORK

In this chapter, you have learned about theories of moral development. You can read more about these theories at **http://tigger.uic.edu/~lnucci/MoralEd/ overview.html.**

Go to the "Overview" section of this website to read more about the work of Piaget, Kohlberg, and Gilligan. Then do the following:

1. Go to the "Classroom Practices" section of the website. Describe one of the programs that has been used to teach moral development in the schools. How does this differ from the teaching program that you experienced when you were in school?
2. In the same section, you will see a link to a site called "Leading Moral Discussions." Can you think of a moral dilemma from fiction or from real life that would be suitable if you were doing a moral development session with first-year university students?
3. Go the "Articles of the Month" section of the website. Using the articles for this month as well as the "Archives," can you find two different contexts to which proponents feel moral development should be applied? Do you think moral development training would be useful in these contexts?

KEY TERMS

Antisocial Personality Disorder
assumption of discriminating traits
assumption of offender deficit
autonomic reactivity
classical conditioning
community psychology
ego
extraversion

id
modelling
moral development theory
operant conditioning
socialization
superego
token economy

SUGGESTED READING

Andrews, D.A. (2002). *The Psychology of Criminal Conduct.* Cincinnati: Anderson Publishing. A text by two Canadian psychologists that presents an interdisciplinary general psychology of criminal conduct.

Bartol, C.R. (2003). *Criminal Behavior: A Psychological Approach.* Englewood Cliffs, N.J.: Prentice Hall. An overview of the contributions of psychology to the field of criminology. The emphasis is on the interactionist approach in which criminal behaviour is viewed as the interaction of dispositional and learning factors with social and environmental factors.

Cooke, D.J., A.E. Forth, and R.D. Hare. (1998). *Psychopathy: Theory, Research and Implications for Society.* Dordrecht, The Netherlands: Kluwer Academic Publishers. Each chapter in this text is devoted to a particular issue that has relevance to the study of psychopathy.

Feldman, M.P. (1977). *Criminal Behaviour: A Psychological Analysis.* London: Wiley. This book provides a good analysis of the application of learning theories in explaining criminal behaviour. Both psychological and sociological approaches are reviewed, and there is a chapter on treatment approaches.

Hilton, N.Z., M.A. Jackson, and C.D. Webster (eds.). (1990). *Clinical Criminology: Theory, Research and Practice.* Toronto: Canadian Scholar's Press. This is an edited text that brings together papers and articles representing a decade (the 1980s) of work by influential theorists in the field of forensic psychiatry and psychology. The exception is a 1953 paper by the late B.F. Skinner that outlines the basic principles of operant conditioning.

Hollin, C.R. (1989). *Psychology and Crime.* London and New York: Routledge. Topics include reviews of psychological approaches to criminal behaviour, mental disorder and crime, psychology in the courtroom, psychology and the police, and crime prevention.

Jacks, I., and S.G. Cox (eds.). (1984). *Psychological Approaches to Crime and Its Correction: Theory, Research, Practice.* Chicago: Nelson-Hall. This is an edited volume with contributions by well-known theorists (Eysenck, Rosenthal, Eron, Quay, and Rosenhan, among others) on aggression, heredity, and television and violence, as well as sections on treatment approaches.

Laufer, W.S., and J.M. Day. (1983). *Personality Theory, Moral Development, and Criminal Behavior.* Lexington, Mass.: Lexington Books. This is an edited volume with a chapter on interpersonal maturity theory, one by Eysenck on antisocial personality, and several chapters on moral development theory.

Roesch, R., J.R.P. Ogloff, P.A. Zapf, S.D. Hart, and R. Otto. (1998). "Mental Health Issues for Jail and Prison Inmates: A Review of Prevalence, Assessment, and Treatment." In N.N. Singh (ed.), *Comprehensive Clinical Psychology: Applications in Diverse Populations.*

Oxford: Elsevier. The authors provide a comprehensive review of the literature and the research on mental health issues with respect to offender populations, including a section on female offenders.

BIBLIOGRAPHY

Abrahamsen, D. (1944). *Crime and the Human Mind.* New York: Columbia University Press.

Abram, K.M., and L.A. Teplin. (1991). "Co-Occurring Disorders Among Mentally Ill Jail Detainees: Implications for Public Policy." *American Psychologist* 46:1036–45.

Akers, R. (1990). "Rational Choice, Deterrence, and Social Learning Theories in Criminology: The Path Not Taken." *Journal of Criminal Law and Criminology* 81:653–76.

Alexander, F., and M. Healey. (1935). *Roots of Crime.* New York: Knopf.

Allodi, F., H. Kedward, and M. Robertson. (1977). "Insane But Guilty: Psychiatric Patients in Jail." *Canada's Mental Health* 25:3–7.

American Psychiatric Association. (1994). *Diagnostic and Statistical Manual of Mental Disorders* (4th ed.). Washington, D.C.: American Psychiatric Association.

Bandura, A. (1979). "The Social Learning Perspective: Mechanisms of Aggression." In H. Toch (ed.), *Psychology of Crime and Criminal Justice* (pp. 198–236). New York: Holt, Rinehart and Winston.

———. (1986). *Social Foundations of Thought and Action: A Social Cognitive Theory.* Englewood Cliffs, N.J.: Prentice Hall.

Bartol, C.R. (1980). *Criminal Behavior: A Psychosocial Approach.* Englewood Cliffs, N.J.: Prentice Hall.

Bonta, J., M. Law, and K. Hanson. (1998). "The Prediction of Criminal and Violent Recidivism Among Mentally Disorders Offenders: A Meta-Analysis." *Psychological Bulletin* 123:123–42.

Borum, R. (1996). "Improving the Clinical Practice of Violence Risk Assessment: Technology Guidelines, and Training." *American Psychologist* 51:945–46.

Borzecki, M., and J.S. Wormith. (1985). "The Criminalization of Psychiatrically Ill People: A Review with a Canadian Perspective." *Psychiatric Journal of the University of Ottawa* 10:241–47.

Bowlby, J. (1953). *Child Care and the Growth of Love.* Baltimore: Penguin Books.

Braukman, C.J., K.A. Kirigin, and M.M. Wolf. (1980). "Group Homes Treatment Research: Social Learning and Social Control Perspectives." In T. Hirschi and M. Gottfredson (eds.), *Understanding Crime: Current Theory and Research.* Beverly Hills, Calif.: Sage.

Braukman, C.J., and M.M. Wolf. (1987). "Behaviorally Based Group Homes for Juvenile Offenders." In C.J. Braukman and M.M. Wolf (eds.), *Behavioral Approaches to Crime and Delinquency.* New York: Plenum Press.

Braukman, C.J., M.M. Wolf, and K.K. Ramp. (1985). "Follow-Up of Group Home Youths into Young Adulthood." (Progress Report, Grant MA 20030). Achievement Place Research Project. Lawrence, Kan.: The University of Kansas.

Brodsky, S.L. (1972). *Psychologists in the Criminal Justice system.* Urbana, Ill.: University of Illinois Press.

———. (1977). "Crime and Dangerous Behavior." In D.C. Rimm and J.W. Somervill (eds.), *Abnormal Psychology.* New York: Academic Press.

Burgess, R.L., and R.L. Akers. (1966). "A Differential Association Reinforcement Theory of Criminal Behavior." *Social Problems* 14:128–47.

Clastner, D.S. (1967). "Comparison of Risk Perception Between Delinquents and Nondelinquents." *The Journal of Criminal Law, Criminology and Police Science* 58:80–86.

Cleckley, H. (1976). *The Mask of Sanity.* St. Louis: Mosby.

Cohen, A.K. (1966). *Deviance and Control.* Englewood Cliffs, N.J.: Prentice Hall.

Conger, R.D. (1976). "Social Control and Social Learning Models of Delinquent Behavior: A Synthesis." *Criminology* 14:17–40.

Cook, T.D., D.A. Kendzierski, and S.V. Thomas. (1983). "The Implicit Assumptions of Television Research: An Analysis of the 1982 NIMH Report on Television and Behavior." *Public Opinion Quarterly* 47:161–201.

Corrado, R.R., I. Cohen, S.D. Hart, and R. Roesch. (2000). "Comparative Examination of the Prevalence of Mental Disorders among Jailed Inmates in Canada and the United States." *International Journal of Law and Psychiatry* 23:633–47.

Craddick, R. (1962). "Selection of Psychopathic from Non-Psychopathic Prisoners Within a Canadian Prison." *Psychological Reports* 10:495–99.

Eysenck, H.J. (1977). *Crime and Personality.* London: Routledge and Kegan Paul.

———. (1990). "Crime and Personality." In N.Z. Hilton, M.A. Jackson, and C.D. Webster (eds.), *Clinical Criminology: Theory Research and Practice* (pp. 85–99). Toronto: Canadian Scholars' Press.

Eysenck, H.J., and S.B. Eysenck. (1976). *Psychoticism as a Dimension of Personality.* London: Hodder and Stoughton.

Eysenck, H.J., and G.H. Gudjonsson. (1989). *The Causes and Cures of Criminality.* New York and London: Plenum Press.

Farrington, D.P. (1978). "The Family Background of Aggressive Youths." In L.A. Hersov, M. Berger, and D. Shaffer (eds.), *Aggression and Antisocial Behavior in Childhood and Adolescence.* Oxford: Pergamon.

———. (1979). "Environmental Stress, Delinquent Behavior, and Conviction." In I.G. Sarason and C.D. Spielberger, (eds.), *Stress and Anxiety,* vol. 6. Washington, D.C.: Hemisphere.

———. (2000). "Multiple Risk Factors for Multiple Problem Violent Boys." In R.R. Corrado, R. Roesch, S.D. Hart, and J.K. Gierowski (eds.), *Multi-problem Violent Youth: A Foundation for Comparative Research on Needs, Interventions and Outcomes* (pp. 23–34). Amsterdam, Netherlands Antilles: IOS Press.

Farrington, D.P., L. Biron, and M. LeBlanc. (1982). "Personality and Delinquency in London and Montreal." In J. Gunn and D.P. Farrington (eds.), *Abnormal Offenders, Delinquency, and the Criminal Justice System.* Chichester, U.K.: Wiley.

Freeman, R.J., and R. Roesch. (1989). "Mental Disorder and the Criminal Justice System: A Review." *International Journal of Law and Psychiatry* 12:105–15.

Friedlander, K. (1947). *The Psychoanalytic Approach to Juvenile Delinquency.* New York: International Universities Press.

Geen, R.G. (1983). "Aggression and Television Violence." In R.G. Geen and E.I. Donnerstein (eds.), *Aggression: Theoretical and Empirical Reviews.* New York: Academic Press.

Gilligan, C. (1982). *In a Different Voice: Psychological Theory and Women's Development.* Cambridge, Ma.: Harvard University Press.

Gunn, J. (1977). "Criminal Behaviour and Mental Disorder." *British Journal of Psychiatry* 130:317–29.

Guze, S. (1976). *Criminality and Psychiatric Disorders.* New York: Oxford University Press.

Hakeem, M. (1958). "A Critique of the Psychiatric Approach to Crime and Correction." *Law and Contemporary Problems* 23:650–82.

Hare, R.D. (1970). *Psychopathy: Theory and Research.* New York: Wiley.

———. (1982). "Psychopathy and the Personality Dimensions of Psychoticism, Extraversion and Neuroticism." *Personality and Individual Differences* 3:35–42.

———. (1983). "Diagnosis of Antisocial Personality Disorder in Two Prison Populations." *American Journal of Psychiatry* 140:887–90.

———. (1991). *The Hare Psychopathy Checklist—Revised.* Toronto: Multi-Health Systems.

———. (1998a). *Without Conscience: The Disturbing World of the Psychopaths Among Us.* New York: Guilford Press.

———. (1998b). "Psychopathy, Affect and Behavior." In D.J. Cooke, A.E. Forth, and R. Hare (eds.), *Psychopathy: Theory, Research and Implications for Society* (pp. 105–37). Dordrecht, The Netherlands: Kluwer Academic Publishers.

———. (1998c). "The Hare PCL-R: Some Issues Concerning Its Use and Misuse." *Legal and Criminological Psychology* 3:101–19.

Hare, R.D., and D.N. Cox. (1978). "Clinical and Empirical Conceptions of Psychopathy, and the Selection of Subjects for Research." In R.D. Hare and D. Schalling (eds.), *Psychopathic Behavior: Approaches to Research.* Chichester, England: Wiley.

Hart, S.D., D.N. Cox, and R.D. Hare. (1995). *The Hare Psychopathy Checklist: Screening Version.* Toronto: Multi-Health Systems.

Heilbrun, A.B., Jr. (1979). "Psychopathy and Violent Crime." *Journal of Consulting and Clinical Psychology* 47:509–16.

Hodgins, S., and G. Côté. (1990). "Prevalence of Mental Disorders among Penitentiary Inmates in Quebec." *Canada's Mental Health* (March):1–4.

Hogan, R. (1973). "Moral Conduct and Moral Character: A Psychological Perspective." *Psychological Bulletin* 79:217–32.

Jacobsen, D., W. Craven, and S. Kushner. (1973). "A Study of Police Referral of Allegedly Mentally Ill Persons to a Psychiatric Unit." In J.R. Snibbe and H.M. Snibbe (eds.), *The Urban Policeman in Transition: A Psychological and Sociological Review.* Springfield, Ill.: C.C. Thomas.

Jeffery, C.R. (1965). "Criminal Behavior and Learning Theory." *Journal of Criminal Law and Criminology* 56:294–300.

Jennings, W.S., R. Kilkenny, and L. Kohlberg. (1983). "Moral-Development Theory and Practice for Youthful and Adult Offenders." In W.S. Laufer and S.M. Day (eds.), *Personality Theory, Moral Development, and Criminal Behavior.* Lexington, Mass.: Lexington Books.

Kohlberg, L., and R. Kramer. (1969). "Continuities and Discontinuities in Child and Adult Moral Development." *Human Development* 12:93–120.

Lamb, H.R. (1982). *Treating the Long-Term Mentally Ill.* San Francisco: Jossey-Bass.

Loeber, R., D.P. Farrington, and M. Stouthamer-Loeber. (2001a). "Male Mental Health Problems, Psychopathy, and Personality Traits: Key Findings from the First 14 years of the Pittsburgh Youth Study." *Clinical Child and Family Psychology Review* 4:273–97.

———. (2001b). "The Development of Male Offending: Key Findings from the First Decade of the Pittsburgh Youth Study." In R. Bull (ed.), *Children and the Law: The Essential Readings* (pp. 336–78). Malden, Mass.: Blackwell Publishers.

Losel, F. (1998). "Treatment and Management of Psychopaths." In D.J. Cooke, A.E. Forth, and R. Hare (eds.), *Psychopathy: Theory, Research and Implications for Society* (pp. 303–54). Dordrecht, The Netherlands: Kluwer Academic Publishers.

Malamuth, N.M., and J.V.P. Check. (1981). "The Effects of Mass Media Exposure on Acceptance of Violence Against Women: A Field Experiment." *Journal of Research in Personality* 15:436–46.

Martin, S.E., L.E. Sechrest, and R. Redner (eds.). (1981). *New Directions in the Rehabilitation of Criminal Offenders.* Washington, D.C.: National Press Academy.

Monahan, J., and S. Splane. (1980). "Psychological Approaches to Criminal Behavior." In E. Bittner and S. Messinger (eds.), *Criminology Review Yearbook.* Beverly Hills, Calif.: Sage.

Monahan, J., and H.J. Steadman. (1983). "Crime and Mental Disorder: An Epidemiological Approach." In M. Tonry and N. Morris (eds.), *Crime and Justice: An Annual Review of Research.* Chicago: University of Chicago Press.

Morash, M. (1983). "An Explanation of Juvenile Delinquency: The Integration of Moral-Reasoning, Theory and Social Knowledge." In W.S. Laufer and J.M. Day (eds.), *Personality Theory, Moral Development, and Criminal Behavior.* Lexington, Mass.: Lexington Books.

Nathan, P.E., and S.L. Harris. (1975). *Psychopathology and Society.* New York: McGraw-Hill.

Newman, J.P. (1998). "Psychopathic Behavior: An Information Processing Perspective." In D.J. Cooke, A.E. Forth, and R. Hare (eds.). *Psychopathy: Theory, Research and Implications for Society* (pp. 81–104). Dordrecht, The Netherlands: Kluwer Academic Publishers.

Nietzel, M.T. (1979). *Crime and Its Modification: A Social Learning Perspective.* New York: Pergamon.

Ogloff, J.R.P., S. Wong, and A. Greenwood. (1990). "Treating Criminal Psychopaths in a Therapeutic Community Program." *Behavioral Sciences and the Law* 8:181–90.

Phillips, E.L. (1968). "Achievement Place: Token Reinforcement Procedures in a Home Style Rehabilitation Setting for 'Pre-Delinquent' Boys." *Journal of Applied Behavior Analysis* 1:213.

Piaget, J. (1932). *The Moral Judgment of the Child.* New York: Free Press.

Polansky, N., R. Lippitt, and F. Redl. (1950). "An Investigation of Behavioral Contagion in Groups." *Human Relations* 3:319–48.

Rappaport, J. (1977). *Community Psychology: Values, Research, and Action.* New York: Holt, Rinehart and Winston.

Redl, F. (ed.). (1966). *When We Deal With Children: Selected Writings.* New York: Free Press.

Reppucci, N.D., and W.G. Clingempeel. (1978). "Methodological Issues in Research with Correctional Populations." *Journal of Consulting and Clinical Psychology* 46:727–46.

Roesch, R. (1988). "Community Psychology and the Law." *American Journal of Community Psychology* 16:451–63.

———. (1995). "Mental Health Interventions in Pretrial Jails." In G.M. Davies, S. Lloyd-Bostock, M. McMurran, and C. Wilson (eds.). *Psychology and Law: Advances in Research* (pp. 520–31). Berlin: De Greuter.

Roesch, R., and S.L. Golding. (1985). "The Impact of Deinstitutionalization." In D.P. Farrington and J. Gunn (eds.), *Aggression and Dangerousness.* New York: Wiley.

Sarbin, T.R. (ed.). (1979). "The Myth of the Criminal Type." In *Challenges to the Criminal Justice System: The Perspectives of Community Psychology* (pp. 1–27). New York: Human Sciences Press.

Schoenfeld, C.G. (1971). "A Psychoanalytic Theory of Juvenile Delinquency." *Crime and Delinquency* 19:469–80.

Seidman, E., and B. Rabkin. (1983). "Economics and Psychosocial Dysfunction: Toward a Conceptual Framework and Prevention Strategies." In R.D. Felner et al. (eds.), *Preventive Psychology* (pp. 175–98). Elmsford, N.Y.: Pergamon.

Silber, D.E. (1974). "Controversy Concerning the Criminal Justice System and Its Implications for the Role of Mental Health Workers." *American Psychologist* 29:239–44.

Skilling, T.A., G.T. Harris, M.E. Rice, and V.L. Quinsey. (2002). "Identifying Persistently Antisocial Offenders Using the Hare Psychopathy Checklist and DSM Antisocial Personality Disorder Criteria." *Psychological Assessment* 14:27–38.

Skoler, G.D., A. Bandura, and D. Ross. (1994). "Aggression." In W.A. Lesko (ed.), *Readings in Social Psychology: General, Classic, and Contemporary Selections* (2nd ed., pp. 296–326). Boston, Mass.: Allyn & Bacon.

Smith, S.L., and A.R. Boyson. (2002). "Violence in Music Videos: Examining the Prevalence and Context of Physical Aggression." *Journal of Communication* 52:61–83.

Steadman, H.J., D.W. McCarty, and J.P. Morrissey. (1988). *The Mentally Ill in Jail: Planning for Essential Services.* New York: Guilford.

Suedfeld, P., and P.B. Landon. (1978). "Approaches to Treatment." In R.D. Hare and D. Schalling (eds.), *Psychopathic Behaviour: Approaches to Research* (pp. 347–76). Chichester, England: Wiley.

Teevan, J.J., and T.F. Hartnagel. (1976). "The Effects of Television Violence on the Perceptions of Crime by Adolescents." *Sociology and Social Research* 60:337–48.

Teplin, L.A. (1983). "The Criminalization of the Mentally Ill: Speculation in Search of Data." *Psychological Bulletin* 94:54–67.

———. (1984). "Criminalizing Mental Disorder: The Comparative Arrest Rate of the Mentally Ill." *American Psychologist* 7:794–803.

———. (1991). "The Criminalization Hypothesis: Myth, Misnomer, or Management Strategy." In S.A. Shah and B.D. Sales (eds.), *Law and Mental Health: Major Developments and Research Needs* (pp. 149–83). Rockville, Md.: U.S. Department of Health and Human Services.

Thomas, M.H., R.W. Horton, E.C. Lippincott, and R.S. Drabman. (1979). "Desensitization to Portrayals of Real-Life Aggression as a Function of Exposure to Television Violence." *Journal of Personality and Social Psychology* 35:450–58.

Warren, M.Q., and M.J. Hindelang. (1979). "Current Explanations of Offender Behavior." In H. Toch (ed.), *Psychology of Crime and Criminal Justice* (pp. 166–82). New York: Holt, Rinehart and Winston.

Widom, C. (1977). "A Methodology for Studying Non-Institutionalized Psychopaths." *Clinical Psychology* 45:674–83.

Widom, C., and J.P. Newman. (1985). "Characteristics of Non-Institutionalized Psychopaths." In D.P. Farrington and J. Gunn (eds.), *Aggression and Dangerousness* (pp. 57–80). New York: Wiley.

10

Strain Theories

JAMES C. HACKLER
University of Victoria

consensus perspective

Also known as functionalism, the foundation of this perspective is the assumption that societies have an inherent tendency to maintain themselves in a state of relative equilibrium through the mutually adjustive and supportive interaction of their principal institutions. The approach also assumes that effective maintenance of a particular form of society is in the common interest of all its members.

conflict perspective

Sociological perspectives that focus on the inherent divisions of societies based on social inequality and the way these social divisions give rise to different and competing interests. The central assumption is that social structures and cultural ideas tend to reflect the interests of only some members of society rather than society as a whole. This contrasts with consensus or functionalist perspectives that assume a foundation of common interest among all members of society. Marxism and feminism are examples of conflict perspectives.

strain theory

The proposition that people feel strain when they are exposed to cultural goals that they are unable to obtain because they do not have access to culturally approved means of achieving those goals.

Most of the theories you have read about in the preceding chapters have tried to explain the criminality of individuals. With the growth of sociology, scholars began to look at the wider relationship between crime and social structure. Two broad theoretical perspectives have guided this work. The older tradition can be called the **consensus perspective**. This approach maintains that the vast majority of the population shares similar values regarding right and wrong. Morality is universal, and important values are shared by all members of society. Customs persist, and the law represents a codification of societal values.

The **conflict perspective** questions such assumptions and argues that the criminal law does not necessarily represent the moral values of the majority but rather reflects the interests of the groups that are in a position to create and enforce those laws. The character of laws, the kinds of conduct they prohibit, and the types of sanctions depend on the nature of the powerful groups that influence legislation. The social values that receive the protection of the criminal law are ultimately those that are treasured by the dominant interest groups. It is not the *majority*, but rather the most *powerful*, whose values and concerns will be represented in the justice system. Ronald Hinch discusses these ideas in the next chapter. This chapter reviews some historical traditions that reflect the consensus perspective. While authors differ in their use of terms, recent discussions of **strain theory** fit this general orientation.

Consensus theorists assume a reasonable degree of agreement on things that matter in society. They also assume that social institutions such as the family, education, government, religion, and the economy normally all contribute to the smooth running of society. Crime occurs when something unusual happens that affects some or all of these institutions. This results in strains, stresses, or frustrations that affect people's behaviour.

While it is convenient to separate the consensus and conflict perspectives, you should be aware that this arbitrary classification oversimplifies reality. It may be more appropriate to think of particular crimes as being of the conflict or consensus type. In most societies, there is a high level of agreement that robbing someone and doing them bodily harm is a crime. Other crimes, such as smoking marijuana and gambling, will lead to less agreement regarding the need for criminalization. Laws regarding homosexuality illustrate not only varying attitudes but changes in attitudes and laws over time. Thus, elements of consensus and conflict are always present in modern societies.

After reading this chapter, you should be able to

- Understand the differences between conflict and consensus perspectives of crime.
- Describe Durkheim's pioneering work dealing with the relationship between crime and social structure. Of particular importance is his conception of anomie or normlessness.
- Discuss how Robert Merton modified Durkheim so that anomie theory became a theory of relative deprivation rather than a theory of a lack of social regulation.
- Note that strains can arise from features in the society or from situations surrounding individuals.
- Outline the role played by community opportunities in the theories of Kobrin and Cloward.
- Explain the role played by the school and by peers in Cohen's theory of lower-class delinquency.
- Understand the strengths and weaknesses of strain theories.
- Describe the social policy implications of strain theories.

DURKHEIM: THE FUNCTIONS OF CRIME AND ANOMIE

In his book *Division of Labor in Society*, first published in France in 1893, Émile Durkheim argued that social solidarity—social groups working together toward agreed-upon goals—was an essential characteristic of human societies (1933). These agreed-upon goals led to a set of shared norms. Without norms to guide them, societies function poorly. Such "normlessness," or anomie, occurs during periods of rapid change when social solidarity or social cohesion is reduced. The lack of a sense of community and a collective conscience leads to a breakdown in society and increases in suicide and crime.

Although some crime is normal, even necessary, to define the boundaries of acceptable behaviour, there must be a balance between the functional and dysfunctional aspects of deviance. Excessive crime and deviance would destroy a society, but if there were none at all, society would almost be compelled to create some. Even in a society of saints, someone would have to be defined as pushing the limits of proper behaviour. Although behaviour is restrained, there will be someone who violates that code. For Durkheim, every society needs its quota of deviants.

Maintaining Boundaries by Creating "Crime Waves"

In a study of the early Puritan colonies in the United States, Kai Erikson (1966) described three "crime waves" during the first 60 years of settlement in Massachusetts. Each of these occurred at a time when unity in the colonies was waning. Erikson argued that the crime rates actually remained fairly stable during that period but that crime in the colonies served certain boundary definition and maintenance functions. By creating or exaggerating a crime, such as accusing someone of being a witch, and by reacting to it in a vigorous way, the new and fragile society was able to identify the boundaries of acceptable behaviour and offer a sense of stability.

One must be careful about this functionalist approach to crime. Excessive punitive reactions to deviants can lead to repressive societal conditions that stifle the creativity that deviance often represents (Mead, 1918). By repressing deviant behaviour, a society may be less able to examine itself and make changes to face new situations. For modern heterogeneous societies, crime may be the price one pays for diversity.

Anomie and Normlessness

anomie

A concept developed by Émile Durkheim (1858–1917) to describe an absence of clear societal norms and values. Individuals lack a sense of social regulation: people feel unguided in the choices they have to make. American sociologist Robert Merton (1910–) used the term more narrowly to refer to a situation in which people's goals—what they wanted to achieve—were beyond their means. Their commitment to the goal was so strong that they would adopt deviant means to achieve it.

Durkheim popularized the concept of **anomie** to explain crime in more advanced and differentiated urban societies. Heterogeneity and increased division of labour weakened traditional societal norms. The resultant changes loosened the social controls on people, allowing a greater materialism and individualism. When social cohesion breaks down in society and social isolation is great, society loses its traditional social control mechanisms and eventually suffers from a high rate of crime.

MERTON: THE GAP BETWEEN ASPIRATIONS AND MEANS

social structure

The patterned and relatively stable arrangement of roles and statuses found within societies and social institutions. The idea of social structure points out the way in which societies, and institutions within them, exhibit predictable patterns of organization, activity, and social interaction.

culturally prescribed aspiration

A rejection of the notion that aspirations are entirely self-created; rather, they are defined by culture and transmitted by other members of the society.

In the 1950s and 1960s, the most-cited article in criminology was a paper in which Robert K. Merton (1938) discussed **social structure** and anomie. For Merton, crime is a symptom of the gap between **culturally prescribed aspirations** and the socially structured means for realizing those aspirations. The culturally prescribed aspirations are the goals that are held up for all members of society. Merton argues that in America, the accumulation of money, and the status that results from material wealth, is a universal goal. Socially structured avenues such as schooling are the accepted institutionalized means of reaching such goals. The socially structured avenues to achieve these goals may not be a problem for certain members of the society. If one comes from a family in which the father is a medical doctor, it may be realistic for the son or daughter to aspire to the same occupation and social status. The family may live in a nice neighbourhood, the children may attend schools that condition students toward thinking about a university or college education, and there may be a home environment that encourages reading and getting good grades. Although certain individual characteristics, such as a certain level of intelligence, may be required, the means to achieve culturally prescribed aspirations may be available to many middle-class youths.

By contrast, the child of a poor family, especially a racial minority family, could find things a bit more difficult. If the father has abandoned the family, if an older sibling has already been in trouble with the law, and if the mother has been on welfare, the means to achieve success may not be readily available. A youth coming from such an environment may not respect the school system and may have poor grades and minimal likelihood of entering university or college. However, he or she might aspire to become a doctor and to have both the material and social rewards that accrue to that occupation.

The gap between goals and means is small for certain portions of the society but large for others. The strain resulting from the gap between goals and means to achieve those goals could result in some sort of innovation, usually deviant in nature. In simpler terms, when society encourages people to want things but makes it difficult for certain groups to get them, members of these groups are more likely to steal or go into prostitution.

Merton's argument seems to fit many forms of lower-class crime, particularly among marginally employed people. Robert Crutchfield (1995) points out that the lack of work influences crime. In addition, if these marginally employed people reside in concentrations of similarly underemployed people, the propensity to engage in crime is greater. This description fits certain ethnic groups in the United States and Canada.

The argument may also fit certain upper-class crimes in which people in business, and others, aspire to great wealth. The legitimate avenues to success may not be sufficient because of severe competition; other businesspeople may be "cutting corners" in a variety of ways. Thus, if there is a gap between the desired goals and the means, innovation or illegitimate tactics are more likely.

> **FOCUS**
>
> **BOX 10.1**
>
> ## Durkheim's General Model of Deviance
>
> In his classic work on suicide, Durkheim argues that individualism, in contrast to community-oriented or collective thinking, leads to a lack of social cohesion. Suicide, crime, and general deviance are inhibited in cohesive communities. His research showed that Protestant communities, which are more individualistic, had higher suicide rates than Catholic communities, which are more oriented toward collective thinking. One can generalize the argument from the specific act of suicide to deviance and crime in general, as illustrated in the sequence below:
>
> **An Oversimplified Model of Durkheim's Explanation of Suicide as a General Explanation of Crime**
>
> Greater Individualism → Lack of Social Cohesion → Suicide and Crime

Strain as a Feature of Society (Rather Than of Individuals)

Debates have arisen over what Merton meant. Were his ideas intended to explain the behaviour of individuals or, as Thomas Bernard (1987) argued, the behaviour of aggregates or groups? Bernard argued that it was not correct to interpret strain or anomie in psychological or social psychological terms; rather, these were properties of social structures. According to Bernard, Merton's theory would predict that societies whose cultures overemphasized the goal of monetary success and underemphasized adherence to legitimate means would have high rates of instrumental crime. If legitimate opportunities to achieve those monetary goals were unevenly distributed, instrumental crime would be unevenly distributed.

One must note the distinction between *cultural* factors and *structural* factors in society. In societies in which structural features create an uneven distribution of legitimate opportunities—that is, where there are many blocked opportunities—there will be pockets of instrumental crime, regardless of cultural values. In a culture that emphasizes the ruthless pursuit of wealth, even if everyone has an equal opportunity, crime will be widespread, and such a society will have a high rate of crime.

Steven Messner and Richard Rosenfeld (1997a; 1997b) extend this argument with their institutional-anomie theory. American culture emphasizes monetary success, but in addition, there is a weak emphasis on the importance of legitimate means for the pursuit of that success. This combination of strong pressures to succeed monetarily and *weak restraints on the means* is intrinsic to the "American Dream." It contributes to crime directly by encouraging people to use illegal means to achieve culturally approved goals, especially monetary goals. It also exerts an indirect effect on crime through its links with, and impact on, the institutional structure, or "the institutional balance of power." One institution—the economy—dominates all others (Rosenfeld and Messner, 1997), and such an emphasis has created a greater potential for crime.

The modern corporation may increase this tendency toward crime even more by splitting the production aspects from the financing. In the past, many companies were created by individuals who were primarily concerned with producing a product or service. Of course, they hoped to make a profit. Today, one can make money trading shares while disregarding the productive activities of a company. Shareholders play no part in daily operations. Nor are they committed to the long-term success of the company. They are simply entitled to a share of the profits. In fact, investors who "buy low and sell high" are admired. Northern Telecom, which became Nortel, illustrated this mentality when it was dominating business news in 2000 and 2001. A person selling Nortel stock at $125 in 2000 would have been congratulated. However, if one bought Nortel at its peak only to watch it drop to $1 in 2002, such an investor might be seen as stupid and greedy. Concern for the many people who lost their jobs, as well as genuine interest in the production of fibre optics, was secondary to the interest in the financial bubble that expanded and then burst.

Stock markets also create a new potential criminal—the inside trader. Those with intimate knowledge of a company are not supposed to profit from that insider knowledge. Terry Hungle, chief financial officer of Nortel, traded shares of the company just before the corporation announced some bad news, including the layoff of 15 000 employees (*Globe and Mail*, February 12, 2002). Similarly, Bill Bennett, former premier of British Columbia, had close relations with the forestry company Doman Industries. He unloaded his shares in Doman, thus reaping a $6-million windfall, minutes before those shares plummeted in value when a previously announced sale of the company was called off by the buyer. Bennett testified that the owner of Doman Industries never called him (even though phone records show that someone called him from Doman's office) just before he sold the stock.

Robber barons of the past might ruthlessly exploit others to build a railway, oil company, or steel mill; modern entrepreneurs with deviant tendencies might find fraudulent stock deals a faster way of achieving monetary goals. At age 32, Mark Valentine had achieved wealth and social standing. He came from a privileged family. Valentine could draw enough friends and sports celebrities, such as Eric Lindros, to a Valentine Golf Invitational to raise $800 000 in one year for the Children's Wish Foundation. His father, a former ambassador, was director of the World Trade Centre in Toronto. In August 2002 he was accused of conspiring to sell $29.4 million (U.S.) of stock at inflated prices to an FBI agent posing as a corrupt mutual fund manager (*Globe and Mail*, August 24, 2002).

Garth Drabinsky surrendered to police to face 19 counts of fraud, totalling half a billion dollars, for allegedly cooking the books at Livent Inc., his defunct live-theatre company (*Maclean's*, November 4, 2002). Drabinsky illustrates the weak restraints on the means to achieve wealth described by Rosenfeld and Messer. But things have perhaps been exacerbated by new opportunities to manipulate finances. Bernie Ebbers, a former Edmonton milkman, was able to steal from his company, WorldCom, much faster than Leland Stanford and his railway could pillage California in the 19th century.

Similarly, cultural factors, such as the nature of our mass media, may minimize the impact of public opinion. Fraud at Enron was very much in the news for a short time. The coverage dwindled rapidly as the conflict with Iraq dominated the media. One must be wary of conflict theories that suggest the "war on Iraq" was designed to distract the public from corporate wrongdoing, but Vice-President Dick Cheney has been accused of being aware of accounting irregularities while he was CEO of Halliburton. George W. Bush was a director of Harken Energy and sold stock worth $850 000 just before the company released bad news. The company was also accused of hiding $10 million in debt to make the balance sheet look good. Is it also a coincidence that the accounting firm of Arthur Anderson, which has been charged with encouraging unethical practices, was advising Enron, WorldCom, Halliburton, Harken Energy, and many other well-known companies (*Maclean's*, July 22, 2002)? If world leaders and law makers are part of a culture that condones or at least tolerates these activities, is it likely that corrective action will be taken in Canada or the United States? Is it any wonder that George W. Bush's claims that he wants to clean up corporate wrongdoing have been met with scepticism?

Compared with other societies, economic institutions dominate North America. Other important institutions—the family, education, and the political system—are relegated to secondary roles. Although these other institutions traditionally curbed criminal tendencies and imposed controls over the conduct of individuals, economic factors overwhelm those institutions which socialize people into pro-social behaviour. In other nations, such as Japan and India, the family appears to rank higher on the hierarchy of institutions and to be more influential relative to economics. Thus, North America produces higher levels of serious crime than those countries in which the institutional balance of power leans toward non-economic institutions.

Strain as a Feature of Individuals

Perhaps Bernard is correct in arguing that Merton was applying his ideas to structures, but many of us find it useful to apply his ideas to individuals. As one applies strain theory to individuals, one can see a convergence with differential association (Chapter 12) and control theory (Chapter 13). An attempt in this direction, using strain theory as a base, is offered by Robert Agnew (1992). Strain triggers negative emotions, which in turn require that the individual cope with those emotions. Usually we are able to deal with our stresses. For example, strain could result from failing an exam. A legitimate coping strategy might be to accept the fact that one should have studied more. Another illustration: a boy develops a crush on a girl. She ignores him, so he works extra hard to become a top athlete. But if legitimate coping strategies are ineffective or unavailable, one may adopt illegitimate coping strategies.

Adolescents located in unpleasant environments, such as school, from which they cannot escape are more likely to be delinquent. Parental rejection, unfair or inconsistent discipline, parental conflict, and unsatisfactory relations with peers can be sources of strain. Often adolescents have few means to cope. If the coercive treatment is perceived as unjust or arbitrary, the resulting anger can lead to the defiance of authority.

Agnew and others (Brezina, 1998; Mazerolle and Piquero, 1997; 1998) call attention to the intervening role of anger in the relationship between strain and delinquency. If the strain doesn't make you mad, you may simply endure it rather than search for illegitimate alternatives. If the strain does lead to anger that cannot be handled legitimately, because opportunities are not available or are ineffective, crime becomes more likely.

Strain has usually been defined in the past in terms of blocked opportunities in education and jobs, but Agnew reminds us that other negative experiences also lead to stress and hence a search for illegitimate alternatives. In addition, different types of strain are more relevant to different subgroups (1991; 1992). There is also empirical support for the interaction of strain variables and social psychological ones, such as having delinquent friends (Agnew and White, 1992). Bonds with both delinquent and nondelinquent friends can lead to other stresses.

As more sophisticated measures of strain/anomie are developed, these ideas are being applied to different populations (Agnew et al., 1996). Recent empirical studies suggest that strain, or anomie, theory is more complex than the simplified versions presented here. We are learning more about the sources of individual strain and the macro-level determinants of such strain (Agnew, 1997; Jensen, 1995). The nature of the relationships among these variables is probably more complex than even the elaboration of strain theory offered by Agnew. This chapter, however, will simplify these arguments.

Coercion and Strain

Colvin et. al (2002) point out that coercive forces, such as economic pressures, can produce strains that in turn produce desperation and anger. Hagan and McCarthy (1997b) noted such forces among homeless youth in Canada. These coercive forces can be consistent or erratic as well as varying in strength (Colvin, 2000). Erratic coercion teaches individuals that they cannot control consequences because the strain is not predictable. Thus, there is no pattern and no incentive to learn self-control. Erratic coercion is particularly conducive to chronic predatory crime.

One might argue that consistent coercion produces conformity. Dictatorships may be able to produce temporary conformity. Or the successful indoctrination of a social philosophy, such as communism, may result in a low crime rate. East Germany seemed to have a low crime rate, but with reunification the former East Germany has experienced a growing crime rate. The reunified eastern Germany may provide more erratic coercion, fewer legitimate opportunities, and less social support for legitimate activities.

Women in Afghanistan under the Taliban may have conformed under consistent coercion, but in a democracy, it is difficult to constantly monitor people to detect noncompliance. Thus consistent but mild coercion that is seen as fair, coupled with legitimate coping opportunities, combined with social support that reduces strain and anger, would lead to less crime.

Let us oversimplify by suggesting that some consistent coercion produces anger that is directed toward the self (Colvin, 2000). This could produce depression. Outward expressions of anger are likely to be met with a painful reprisal. Erratic coercion, which heightens the sense of injustice, produces anger directed against others. Since stresses are influenced by different settings, let us turn to the nature of opportunity structures.

THE SHIFT FROM CONTROL TO OPPORTUNITY STRUCTURES

Durkheim argued that human aspirations had to be regulated and channelled. Since human aspirations were boundless, and people could not always have what they want, they had to be persuaded to accept what they received. When people were not persuaded, the society became anomic. The moral guidelines were unclear. Social control broke down, and some people violated the norms established by those in power.

While Durkheim emphasized the restraints that control crime, Merton focused on **opportunity structures**. He suggested that American society had an overriding dominant goal—material success—but the guidelines for achieving that success were not always clear. If this type of anomie was so widespread, however, why wasn't crime distributed evenly through society? Merton accepted the argument that crime was distributed unevenly—that it was higher in the urban slums, for instance. To explain this social-class-specific crime by anomie, he redefined anomie as the disjuncture between the cultural goal of success and the opportunity structures by which this goal might be achieved. Anomie was shifted from normlessness to **relative deprivation**, whereby it was not the entire community that was anomic but rather specific individuals who were committed to the goal of wealth while being barred from the means that would realize that goal. However, different opportunity structures may facilitate breaking the law. Some communities, or some situations, may not provide opportunities for crime even though individuals are discontented. In one of the seminal articles in criminology, Sol Kobrin (1951) argues that opportunities differ in various types of communities.

opportunity structure
Opportunity is shaped by the way the society or an institution is organized or structured.

relative deprivation
Relative deprivation and absolute deprivation are often contrasted. Absolute deprivation refers to the inability to sustain oneself physically and materially. However, in relative terms, deprivation is not judged against some absolute standard of sustainability but against deprivation in relation to others around you. You may have sufficient money to meet your needs and even meet them adequately, but you may feel relatively deprived because others around you have more.

Kobrin: Opportunities in the Community

Kobrin points out that we live in communities that sometimes offer a variety of opportunities, both legitimate and illegitimate. No community entirely lacks legitimate opportunities for its inhabitants to attain their aspirations or entirely lacks illegitimate opportunities. All communities offer a mixture of possibilities. Table 10.1 oversimplifies those possibilities to make its point. If communities have legitimate opportunities and/or illegitimate opportunities, four types of communities are possible. Although communities exist that approximate these four types, this typology oversimplifies reality, in which there will always be a gradation in opportunities. Nonetheless, it is useful to think in terms of ideal types.

In Type I communities, there are illegitimate opportunities as well as legitimate ones. One might call this type of community a "stable slum," where prostitution, gambling, and a variety of other illegal activities are well organized. The organized criminal element may concentrate on certain activities and avoid, or even discourage, violence and other types of crime that would upset the community and the forces of control. In such stable lower-class neighbourhoods, one would expect to find a number of legitimate opportunities that reflect the normal ongoing activities of a city. These would include restaurants, stores, repair shops, and all the other normal economic functions that arise to meet the needs of any urban society.

The Type II community might be called a "transitory slum," as typified by a decaying housing project. In such a disorganized community, there is extensive unemployment. No business dares to establish a store in the neighbourhood because of the fear of robbery. Paper carriers do not deliver in the area because customers would probably lose their papers, the deliverers might be attacked, and the newspaper would find it unprofitable. Restaurants are not established; thus, there are few opportunities for servers, dishwashers, or cooks. In other words, it is an area with very few legitimate opportunities for earning money. Even the illegitimate opportunities are minimal because the neighbourhood is poorly organized. Prostitutes find it dangerous to work there, those who wish to gamble go to the more stable slum areas, and although the residents may occasionally attack one another, the pickings are rather slim. In these disorganized areas, there is little sense of community life, and families

TABLE 10.1 Typology of Community Opportunity Structures Implicit in Kobrin (1951)

	I	II	III	IV
Type of Community	*"Stable Slum"*	*"Transitory Slum"*	*"Suburbia"*	*Unlikely*
Legitimate opportunities	Yes	No	Yes	No
Illegitimate opportunities	Yes	No	No	Yes

Source: Adapted from Sol Kobrin. (1951). "The Conflict of Values in Delinquency Areas." *American Sociological Review* 16:653–61.

tend to be poorly integrated. Minimal opportunities exist for either legitimate or illegitimate enterprise.

The Type III community has legitimate opportunities but practically no illegitimate ones. Perhaps "suburbia" fits this description. A teenager can find work mowing lawns, especially if the neighbours know that the teenager comes from a good, solid family. Paper routes are available, and through their contacts in the community, juveniles may learn of opportunities for summer work and other part-time jobs. Adults and adolescents are involved in economic activities that create opportunities for work and the anticipation of future work. Illegitimate opportunities are rare. A would-be suburban prostitute might find difficulty in approaching customers out peacefully walking their dogs. A university or college student may not find much success trying to sell an armful of stolen hubcaps door-to-door in his or her suburban neighbourhood. Such a community can be expected to be lacking in illegitimate opportunities.

What about the Type IV community? Although such a combination is theoretically possible, it is probably unlikely that any neighbourhood could develop a wide range of illegitimate opportunities without also spawning some legitimate ones. If the illegitimate opportunities were well organized, we would expect restaurants, stores, laundries, and other facilities to develop to provide those stable lower-class communities with normal services. If either organized crime or the citizenry had things fairly well under control, the community could become viable. While the control mechanisms may differ in such neighbourhoods, the suggestion is that it would be very unlikely to find a community with well-organized illegitimate opportunities alone.

Kobrin (1951) emphasizes the *dual* characteristics of lower-class communities. Both legitimate and illegitimate opportunities exist together in greater or lesser degree. Questions regarding how these two structures interact and what draws people to one rather than another have generated considerable debate among sociologically oriented criminologists. Policy-makers must take community characteristics into account and be aware that a uniform strategy is unlikely to work because all communities are different.

Richard Cloward: Illegitimate Opportunity Structures

Just as there are differences between legitimate and illegitimate opportunities, there are different types of illegitimate opportunities. Cullen (1984) points out the importance of "structuring variables." Cloward asserts that simply being subjected to socially generated strain does not enable a person to deviate in any way he or she chooses. People can participate in a given adaptation only if they have access to the means to do so (Cullen, 1984, 40). Even though members of the lower class may be under a great deal of strain, they are unlikely to engage in violations of financial trust, political corruption, and other white-collar crimes in order to achieve their goals. In an article (1959) and then in a book with Lloyd Ohlin entitled *Delinquency and Opportunity* (1960), Cloward extended the ideas of Merton by combining them with themes found in Sutherland's "differential association" (see Chapter 12). Sutherland argued that criminal behaviour is learned through associations with others who define criminal activity favourably. While Merton emphasized legitimate means, Sutherland concentrated on illegitimate means (Cullen, 1988). People under strain cannot become any kind of criminal they choose; they are limited by the opportunities available to them. Dealing in drugs is not automatically available to a "square" college or university professor as a means of supplementing her income; she probably lacks the skills and contacts to obtain a source of illegal drugs. In other words, illegitimate means are not readily available to people simply because they lack legitimate means. While Durkheim and Merton developed plausible theories of structurally induced pressures, it remained to Cloward to try to explain the resulting adaptive behaviour.

Merton appreciated Cloward's insights and extension of his ideas, as was apparent in the commentary Merton wrote in the *American Sociological Review*, which appeared immediately after Cloward's article. Merton noted that some earlier research showed that there were five times as many fraud convictions in Texas as in Massachusetts. Perhaps, he went on, it was more difficult to sell someone a dry oil well in Massachusetts than in Texas. Illegal opportunities for certain types of fraud are more available in some areas than others.

Opportunity theory fits many different types of deviance, but Cloward and Ohlin are best known for the application of these ideas to juvenile delinquency. Although undergoing strain, juveniles face different barriers to resolving that strain than adults do. The way they respond to social barriers for achieving goals could lead to three different types of gangs or **subcultures**: *criminal, conflict*, and *retreatist* gangs. Herbert Costner, in lectures at the University of Washington, used the diagram shown in Figure 10.1 to explain how these gangs are formed.

subculture

A group of people who share a distinctive set of cultural beliefs and behaviours that differs in some significant way from that of the larger society.

There are pressures toward conventional goals and there are pressures toward achieving middle-class values, such as respectability and conventional success. When juveniles overcome those barriers, as most middle-class juveniles do, they commit little crime. However, lower-class males may actually have different goals. Instead of respectability, they may be more interested in money, a car, and showing off for their girlfriends. Under certain economic conditions, this might be achieved by working in areas in which their skills are scarce, working in a hazardous occupation, or possibly being fortunate as an athlete. In other words, it is possible to be successful in a working-class style of life. These ideas differ somewhat from Merton's in that aspirations are not universal, as Merton has argued. Striving for success can mean different things to different people.

However, Cloward emphasizes the barriers to lower-class as well as middle-class goals. Not only is there an opportunity structure for the goals of the lower class, but crime also has an opportunity structure of its own. If legitimate opportunities are blocked, the next step may be to search for illegal success, but even here there are barriers. Without certain contacts, it may be difficult to get into illegal gambling or learn the skills of a successful safecracker. Many juveniles will have difficulty learning the skills necessary to succeed in these areas. However, if there are barriers to profitable property crime, juveniles can still turn to conflict as a means of attaining status, at least among their peers.

Juveniles who are unskilled as thieves can show their bravery by fighting for their "turf." This will show others that they have "heart"; their courageous

FIGURE 10.1   Barriers to Legal and Illegal Opportunities Implicit in the Work of Cloward and Ohlin (1960)

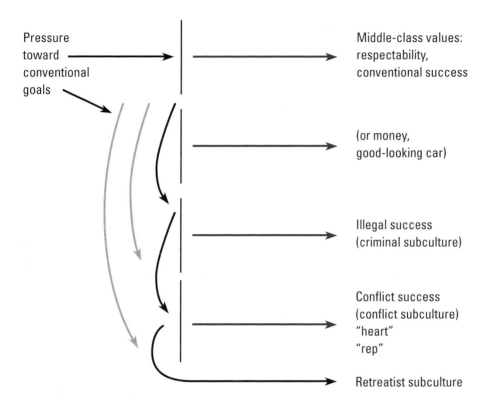

behaviour will give them a "rep." But even conflict success has barriers. Not every juvenile is keen on wielding a bicycle chain in a gang war. Some may lack strength or courage or both. These juveniles may employ a third delinquent alternative: the use of drugs. In the drug or retreatist subculture there are practically no barriers.

Individual characteristics, such as race, will be related to some of these barriers. Thus, Asian youth in Vancouver may have opportunities to work with Asian gangs who extort money from restaurant owners. Blacks who have lived in Nova Scotia since the American Revolution, Jamaican youth in Toronto, and Haitian immigrants in Montreal probably have a realistic view of the barriers to legitimate and illegitimate success. Violence and drugs may be the only things left. In Canada, the abuse of alcohol by First Nations people may also be influenced by barriers to both legitimate and illegitimate opportunities.

Marginal Opportunity Structures

Francis Cullen (1988) believes that many scholars have not fully appreciated the contributions made by Cloward because they are focused primarily on the gap between aspirations and perceived opportunities. In fact, other deviant styles of adaptation to illegitimate opportunities become apparent when one looks beyond traditional types of crime and at different settings. Fred Desroches describes the way some men adapt to pressures related to homosexual activity in public restrooms in Ontario (1995). The "tearoom," a public washroom where homosexual activity takes place, provides an opportunity structure for those under certain types of strain. Alternatives do not seem to fill the need; thus, this marginal opportunity structure is used with the risk that police action will create additional problems in their lives.

Street life offers another type of marginal or illegitimate opportunity structure (Hagan and McCarthy, 1997a; 1997b). Youth in families that are functioning well do better in school as well as in finding work. Negative family experiences increase the likelihood of "hanging out" on the street. The interactions among parental employment, weakened marital ties, neglect, and abuse increase the likelihood of crime directly, but they also expose such youth to additional new stresses when they leave one negative environment for another. Seeking food and shelter on the street, these vulnerable youth meet seasoned offenders, who coach the newcomers in criminal activities. The police will also view them as criminally inclined.

Street life increases exposure to networks of seasoned offenders who offer tutelage in offending and a means of acquiring "criminal capital"—that is, information (e.g., where to sell stolen goods) and skills (e.g., how to use burglary tools). Physical and sexual abuse, the erratic coercion suggested by Colvin (2000), has conditioned them to respond to police confrontations with defiance and rage. Hagan and McCarthy show how employment, a source of social and **human capital**, in contrast to criminal capital, can reduce involvement in crime and street life. (See Chapter 13.)

human capital

The talents and capabilities that individuals contribute to the process of production. Companies, governments, and individuals can invest in this capital, just as they can invest in technology and buildings or in finances.

Cloward's work may also offer an explanation of certain marginal activities, such as being an oil company spy. In Alberta, where many oil companies drill wells in the wilderness and try to keep their findings secret, spies from rival companies sometimes pose as hunters or wilderness trekkers to observe drilling operations without being detected. This often-hazardous activity highlights the presence of particular opportunities and barriers to potentially profitable tasks. Kobrin and Cloward have applied these ideas to conventional crime, but there may be a much wider range of marginal behaviours that would fit these models.

In Figure 10.1, one can see that there are a number of barriers or "structuring variables" that influence the choice of activities. If all opportunities are blocked, skid row may be the alternative. P.J. Giffen (1966) describes the "revolving door" in Toronto where skid row alcoholics go in and out of jail on a regular basis. If the retreatist subculture is the end of the line for certain types of delinquents, we might argue that skid row represents a similar situation for those who find other barriers insurmountable.

The question of opportunity structures, including illegitimate ones, poses an interesting policy question for society. Which is more desirable: having skid row alcoholics with no opportunities, or having prostitutes and gamblers engaging in activities that are seen as deviant by society? While legitimate opportunities are clearly preferable to illegitimate ones, is it possible that the integration of some borderline, or even obvious, deviance would be better than the total breakdown represented by some of society's rejects? In a society that must sometimes choose between levels of evils, would policy-makers be wise to consider the nature of different opportunity structures and assess the impact of selected illegitimate opportunities on society?

ALBERT K. COHEN: THE MIDDLE-CLASS MEASURING ROD

Strain theories focus on a given situation without paying much attention to the way the situation develops. A more dynamic approach to barriers to success is presented in the very influential book by Albert K. Cohen entitled *Delinquent Boys: The Culture of the Gang* (1955). Cohen differs from Cloward in that he feels that lower-class boys aspire to middle-class goals when they enter the education system. Cloward's work tends to neglect the opportunity structure of schools and the ways in which schools block opportunity. According to Cohen, schools are dominated by the "**middle-class measuring rod**," which sets up a certain set of standards: sophistication, good appearance, selling oneself, controlling aggression, respect for authority, deferred gratification, and those general characteristics that make young boys and girls a success in the middle-class world. If a student follows these standards, he or she is likely to have success in school. The clear implication is that this will lead to success in the larger society. This process begins early. The lower-class child begins school with desires and goals that are similar to those of other young children. The difference is that the lower-class child may have difficulty meeting the standards set by the middle-class measuring rod. While middle-class children are taught to respect books and be polite, the lower-class child may have been taught to stand up for her rights and not let people push her around. The middle-class child has been taught to "save for a rainy day," but the lower-class child has learned that men who win money gambling spend it quickly and treat their friends.

Other strain theorists have attempted to identify sources of stress but have spent less time explaining the dynamics of how an individual adapts to that stress. A lower-class student could make an effort to change his or her behaviour to please the teacher, but there may be little support from home and from peers. A second alternative is to withdraw from the contest and lead an isolated existence. Cohen argues that male juveniles who fail in the educational system when they cannot meet middle-class standards can gain status by reversing those standards. In this third alternative, juveniles try to modify the goals and begin looking for others who are in the same predicament. If the goals have been turned upside down, "good" boys become "squares" and teachers' pets. Instead of respecting authority, one challenges it. "Tough" guys gain prestige. Fighting becomes important; "rep" and "heart" are important to show that a boy is capable of participating in a gang rumble. The juvenile strives for higher prestige among the gang. Instead of saving money and developing economical habits, one shares with fellow gang members. Destroying property shows contempt for those whose goals one has rejected. Instead of being courteous, the gang member emphasizes discourtesy and dresses in a manner to provoke middle-class teachers.

middle-class measuring rod

A phrase suggesting that children and young people from the lower class often find themselves in situations in which they are measured against middle-class standards.

reaction formation

In Freudian terms, it is an adaptation in which the *ego* unconsciously develops attitudes and interests the direct opposite of those in the *id* striving for expression. In Albert Cohen's theory, lower-class children who cannot succeed when measured by middle-class criteria collectively reverse these values and obtain status by doing the opposite.

mutual conversion

A phrase suggesting that conversion to deviance (and perhaps to other lifestyles) is not a solitary activity but is achieved through a process of interaction with others.

Reaction formation is a psychological mechanism for redefining goals when the individual cannot meet the standards expected of him or her. However, reversing middle-class standards cannot be done by one individual alone. This is a collective process brought about through **mutual conversion**. In relations with others, people generally explore the nature of the response from others before they commit themselves too far. The juvenile who is doing poorly in school notices that there are others who are not succeeding in school. While walking home together, two boys might explore their feelings about school. "What do you think about the teacher?" The other responds cautiously, "I dunno, do you like him?" Response: "Not much, how about you?" "I don't like him at all."

The mutual conversion continues. Each boy commits himself a bit more until they have mutually agreed that the teacher is unfair, the teacher's pet is a

TABLE 10.2 Strain Theories

Theory	Theorists	Key Elements
Anomie: weak social regulation	Durkheim	When social cohesion breaks down, society loses its traditional mechanisms of social control and eventually suffers from a high rate of crime.
Anomie: the gap between aspirations and means	Merton	Crime occurs when there is a gap between culturally prescribed aspirations and socially structured means for realizing those aspirations.
Institutional-Anomie	Messner, Rosenfeld	Strong pressures to succeed monetarily and weak restraints on the means to succeed in a society emphasizing economics leads to crime.
General strain	Agnew	Adolescents in unavoidable unpleasant environments face strain leading to anger and delinquency.
Coercion and strain	Colvin	Erratic coercion heightens a sense of injustice, produces anger against others and destroys social bonds.
Opportunity structures	Kobrin, Cloward	In addition to strains that create a pressure toward criminal behaviour, there are also different opportunity structures that may facilitate breaking the law. These structures are both legitimate and illegitimate.
The middle-class measuring rod	Cohen	Lower-class youth are unable to meet the middle-class standards of the school. As a result, they collectively build a new set of values and standards that are the opposite of those of the middle class.

creep, and so is the boy who gets good grades. As the process continues, they can rebuild a new set of values and different standards, which they can meet more easily than middle-class standards.

It is important to note that as these boys achieve new status among gang members, such status is limited to the inner group. Outside of the gang, their status is low and becomes even lower. As a result, they turn more to the gang for gratification and become even more separated from the middle-class orientation of the school.

ASSESSING STRAIN THEORIES

When Durkheim introduced his ideas, scholars were still explaining crime primarily by genetics and inner psychological forces. Durkheim focused attention on social forces, a radical idea at the time, but now the dominant methodology for explaining crime. His attempts to explain the link between crime and modernization may or may not be accurate, but it seems that the basic patterns of crime that have evolved in western Europe have also occurred in eastern European countries and in the emerging nations of Asia, Africa, and Latin America as they move toward modernization (Shelley, 1981).

Durkheim was less accurate in his description of premodern nations as stable, crime-free societies. In fact, many had high levels of violence. Furthermore, Western countries seem to have experienced a long-term decline in crime over the past few centuries (Gurr, 1981). Despite the continual complaints we hear today, during the 17th century, the average citizen in most cities in western Europe would rarely leave the security of a locked home after dark.

Gwynne Nettler feels that the concept of "opportunity" is vague. Is there a difference between perceived opportunities and real ones? "Opportunities are by their nature much easier to see after they have passed than before they are grasped" (1984, 209). If people do not end up equally happy and rich, is this due to differences in opportunities? We must avoid the circular argument of explaining the cause by using the outcome.

Merton's strain theory does not help us explain the lower crime rates of women. Merton takes into account differences in opportunity that arise out of social class, but he does not apply the same reasoning to blocked opportunities based on gender (Comack, 1992). Women, like disadvantaged lower-class males, might be expected to be more criminal as a means to achieve universal goals. While many conventional theorists have assumed that women experience less strain than men in the struggle to achieve through institutionalized means, many feminist scholars reject these statements as assumptions and biases rather than fact (Morris, 1987; Naffine, 1987). While the strains women are subject to may differ from those experienced by men, they may be just as severe. Unless one assumes women have more modest goals, strain theory does not explain why women are less criminal.

Strain theories that link coercion with social support may be more compatible with less female crime (Colvin et al., 2002). Females may get more social support from families and from one another, which may help them cope and may lead to less anger. In one sense, women have had considerable experience coping with injustice.

The Static State of Strain Theories

With the exception of Cohen, Agnew, Colvin, and some recent authors, the traditional strain theorists offer rather static explanations without taking into account the dynamic nature of social interaction. Cohen moves the thinking in that direction, but most strain theories tend to ignore group dynamics, making them inadequate for explaining certain types of crime. Imagine, for example, that a group of boys have gained entry to a feed-mill warehouse to play tag among the stacks of feedbags.

> Soon the motorized fork-lift trucks were discovered, and the boys began having fun driving them. They didn't *deliberately* drive them into the feed bags, but they were unskilled pilots of the fork-lift trucks. The first time the grain sacks were damaged, the boys may have hesitated, perhaps a bit anxious about what they had done; but they may have also wondered how deeply you could drive the forks on the trucks into a bag of grain if you really took a run at it. The challenge, the dare, the competition, and the perverse pleasure in the destruction stimulated others to go further than they had earlier planned. This is *mutual excitation.* (Hackler, 2003, 83–84)

In earlier studies of collective behaviour, Blumer (1951) suggested the term *circular reaction.* This is the type of interstimulation in which the actions of one individual stimulate another, which in turn is reflected back to the first person, providing reinforcement. Soon there is *group contagion.* Andrew Wade (1967) provides an explanatory argument for vandalism that is quite compatible with these ideas.

Traditional strain theory is clearly lacking in its power to incorporate the dynamic elements of social interaction. While some of the static variables may have been relevant at the beginning, the interstimulation, the dynamics of the events seem to play a much more powerful role. These factors may also provide tools for preventing crime. What are the conditions that lead to a potential participant refusing to take part right from the beginning and possibly changing the entire direction of the process? While Albert Cohen takes some of these interactive factors into account with *reaction formation* and *mutual conversion,* these dynamic elements are lacking in most structural–functional explanations of crime, which may be their greatest weakness. Explanations that do consider these elements are presented in Chapter 12, which discusses interactionist theories.

The Convergence of Strain Theory and Other Perspectives

Despite the criticisms of strain theory, these ideas have been of considerable interest to criminologists. More recent elaborations of strain theory (Agnew,

1992; Colvin et al., 2002), have led to some convergence with other theories, including control theory and differential association theory. There is considerable agreement that the contributions emerging from Merton, Kobrin, and Cloward are still useful (Bernard, 1987; Agnew, 1997; Agnew et al., 1996; Menard, 1997; Messner and Rosenfeld, 1997a; Vaughan, 1997; Cullen, 1988; Farnworth and Leiber, 1989). Nor do traditional theoretical perspectives have to be seen as distinct and competing explanations. There has been a convergence of ideas that permits strain theory, differential association, and control theory to complement one another. In addition, the policy implications of the different theories can be similar. For example, enabling the disenfranchised to participate more fully in what society has to offer is probably related to greater social bonding with others and a stronger belief in the rules that guide the larger society. However, if social bonds are primarily with people who condone or rationalize criminal behaviour, and with those who face similar blocked opportunities, criminal behaviour is likely. In such situations, control theory, differential association, and strain theory complement one another.

Nikos Passas (1997) suggests such a blend when he links together anomie, reference group, and relative deprivation theory. For structural strains to translate into individual deviant behaviour, people must *experience* the gap between means and ends. The culture of the American Dream and high rates of social mobility foster *nonmembership*, that is, unrealistic, reference groups. For example, it would be unrealistic for me to aspire to the lifestyle of the chief executive officer of the Royal Bank of Canada. Wealthy business executives are a nonmembership reference group for me. Symbolic interactionists have noted that people falsely identify with groups even when they obviously do not belong. This leads to unfavourable comparisons, *feelings* of relative deprivation, and deviant responses. Such experiences, interactions, and responses may crystallize into deviant subcultures and thereby produce *deviance without strain*. Thus, business executives engaged in white-collar crime, which they feel is necessary in order to compete, may be able to rationalize their behaviour without feeling guilty. Using *reaction formation* and *mutual conversion*, as suggested by Albert Cohen, they translate a structural strain into a personal response.

There is similar logic in the work of Robert Agnew (1992; 1997). He argues that adolescents located in unpleasant environments, such as school, from which they cannot escape are more likely to be delinquent. Although strain has usually been defined in the past in terms of blocked opportunities in education and jobs, Agnew reminds us that there are other negative experiences that lead to stress. This can lead to the search for illegitimate alternatives. In addition, different types of strain are more relevant to different subgroups. Furthermore, there is empirical support for the interaction of strain variables and social psychological ones, such as having delinquent friends (Agnew and White, 1992). Differential association emphasizes ties with delinquents (Chapter 12). Social control theory (Chapter 13) focuses on the lack of social bonds juveniles have with nondeviant members of society. Agnew and White note that some of these bonds could lead to strain. Furthermore, some criminologists have measured reciprocal effects (Thornberry, 1987). One variable affects another, which in turn has a further impact on the previous variable.

A vast oversimplification of these ideas might be as follows: (1) learning theories (Chapter 12), such as differential association, explain delinquency by *positive* relations with deviant others; (2) social control theories (Chapter 13) argue that delinquency occurs when juveniles have *little or no* attachment or social bonds to others; (3) Agnew's elaboration of strain theory emphasizes that *negative* relations and experiences in situations beyond their control lead juveniles to delinquency; (4) all three conditions can reinforce one another and can have a reciprocal impact increasing the likelihood of criminal behaviour.

USES OF STRAIN THEORY

Modern society creates many illegitimate opportunities for those wishing to take advantage of them. Credit cards, computers, and the flow of information across borders make new forms of theft possible. The terrorist attacks of September 11, 2001, on the World Trade Center created opportunities for fraud. There have been more than 200 arrests for defrauding agencies that were trying to help victims and relatives. A lawyer stole $78 000 from several agencies. A morgue manager was accused of stealing coffins and reselling them. However, most normal people do not avail themselves of the vast opportunities for theft in complex societies. Strain theories may be less adequate in explaining non-deviance.

Messner and Rosenfeld (1997a) argue that the emphasis on material wealth in North America encourages crime, but other countries may have a different value structure. In one informal study done by *Reader's Digest*, 1100 wallets were "lost" in about a dozen countries. Each wallet contained $50 in local currency and the name and phone number of the owner. About 44 percent of the wallets disappeared. However, in Norway and Denmark, every single wallet was returned. Do some societies create a climate that produces more good Samaritans and where illegitimate opportunities are ignored?

John Braithwaite: Greater Class Mix and the Reduction of Crime

Braithwaite (1979) argues that one must look at the interaction between the social class of individuals and the social class of the neighbourhood in order to answer the question of whether an increase in class heterogeneity in neighbourhoods would reduce crime. He offers two propositions. The first is that crime is most likely when both exposure to illegitimate opportunities is high and exposure to legitimate opportunities is low. The second states that crime is unlikely either when legitimate opportunities are high or when illegitimate opportunities are low. In other words, in three out of the four possible combinations, there are factors that would inhibit crime. Only when both illegitimate opportunities and a lack of legitimate opportunities exist would there be a marked increase in crime.

Braithwaite also argues that belonging to the lower class has more effect on delinquency for youth in lower-class areas than for youth in middle-class areas.

Consequently, cities with relatively large numbers of lower-class people living in predominantly middle-class areas and relatively large numbers of middle-class people living in predominantly lower-class areas have relatively low crime rates. That is, greater class mix results in less crime.

This implies that if the middle classes could keep together, they would be better off; on the other hand, if the lower classes stay together, they will be even worse off. Hence, it may be to the advantage of those with power and influence to keep themselves segregated. The quality of life for the society as a whole, however, would be improved if residential heterogeneity characterized the society.

Braithwaite's ideas seem more applicable to property crime, but another study shows that if there is a culture of violence, its roots are to be found in racial and economic inequalities (Blau and Blau, 1982). Spatial mixing in neighbourhoods would be more easily achieved with a reduction of racial and economic inequalities. Some observers have suggested that Canada has a lower crime rate than the United States in part because our housing policies have been less likely to "ghettoize" the poor in areas that could develop very high crime rates.

Reducing Upper-Class Crime

Braithwaite also offers an interesting idea about crime among the upper classes. He argues that "too little power and wealth creates problems of living, and this produces crime of one type; too much power corrupts, and this produces crime of another type" (1979, 200). This does not mean that upper-class people are more criminal than lower-class people. If lower-class people were exposed to the same vast opportunities as white-collar criminals, they, too, would engage in large-scale "power" crimes. Powerful people abuse their occupational power. Lawyers, business owners, pharmacists, and medical doctors all have unique opportunities to commit crimes with very little risk. It makes little sense to ask which social class commits more crime. Rather, opportunities differ by social class. However, the class-mix logic described above applies to the upper class as well. If we reduced the power of these people, that is, reduced their opportunities for crime, white-collar crime would also be reduced. If lower-class people commit crimes because of a lack of power and wealth, increasing their influence and well-being might help. Braithwaite (who admits a socialistic bias) argues that greater economic equality and a greater distribution of influence among people would modify to some extent those factors that lead to crime.

Lower-class crime may be caused by the failure to achieve success goals. By contrast, upper-class crimes arise from an unprincipled overcommitment to success goals. One study of college students found that those most dedicated to monetary success were those most likely to argue that they "can't afford to be squeamish about the means." Similarly, certain occupational structures can increase commitment to illegitimate success. Richard Quinney (1963) found that retail pharmacists tended to fall into two divergent categories with different role expectations: professional and business. Those who were oriented toward the professional role were bound by guidelines for compounding and dispensing prescriptions. Those oriented toward the business role subscribed to the popular belief that self-employment carries with it independence and freedom from control. For them, professional norms exercised less control. Prescription violations occurred more frequently among the business-oriented pharmacists. As both Quinney and Braithwaite would argue, the mutual support of like-minded individuals insulated from the broader society, and from their professional colleagues, increased the likelihood of crime.

POLICY IMPLICATIONS

Four decades ago, crime-prevention projects utilized strain theories to change opportunity structures. In hindsight, the narrow focus of these projects made it difficult to obtain significant impacts, but they illustrate attempts to apply some of the ideas reviewed in this chapter.

In the 1960s, the Mobilization for Youth Project was launched in New York City following the principles outlined by Cloward and Ohlin. This project attempted to improve education, create work opportunities, organize lower-class communities, and provide a variety of social services. There is little evidence to suggest that the project was successful in an overall sense (Short, 1975; Helfgot, 1981). It is extremely difficult to alter the social-structural arrangements that create barriers to opportunity. Moreover, the programs were later taken over by traditional social service bureaucracies that normally act to protect and enhance their own interests. Under their jurisdiction, actual implementation involved attempts to change individuals instead of making basic changes in the structure of society. In his book *The Betrayal of the Poor*, Rose (1972) argues that the War on Poverty in the United States failed because it was transformed to serve the interests of poverty-serving agencies.

Opportunities for Youth (OFY) in Seattle was another attempt to use work opportunities to reduce delinquency that met with little success (Hackler, 1966). One might argue that temporary job programs do not have a meaningful impact on the larger community. However, this same project had an impact on the attitudes of the adults living in the four communities in which the project was conducted (Hackler and Linden, 1970). Furthermore, parents of black children seemed particularly responsive to the idea of job opportunities for their children. Like so many programs launched during the 1960s, OFY attempted to utilize strain theories. Lower-class populations did respond and became involved. Although evidence of crime reduction in the short term is lacking, the opportunity structure was altered for some lower-class families. We should not be overly cynical or sceptical. Early childhood education programs implemented in the 1960s have demonstrated that they can have a significant effect on later school achievement and, eventually, success in the adult world (Schweinhart et al., 1993).

Unfortunately, opportunities for the lower classes may have decreased in North America in the past decade. While there has been a dramatic increase in the wealth of the upper classes, the frequent display of a luxurious lifestyle, especially on television, creates all the more strain for those who aspire to a share of that material wealth.

It may be difficult to alter the structure of society, but governments could support those institutions that ease some of the strains that arise from blocked opportunities. Public policies could provide visiting nurses, training and support for disadvantaged mothers, paid family leave, and universal health care. The work done by Richard Tremblay and his colleagues at the Université de Montréal on early childhood development is consistent with preschool "head start" programs that help reduce the strains caused by the challenges of education (Tremblay and Craig, 1995). Young people could be involved in national service programs, such as the Peace Corps, which lead to government funding for higher education or training in skilled occupations. Workplaces could offer continuing training and upgrading. In other words, some of the strains experienced in the family, school, and workplace do not have to lead to anger and attacks on society if institutions provide alternatives.

Other strains are created by the criminal justice system itself, which is based largely on coercion (Colvin et al., 2002). Disintegrative shaming pervades our current coercive criminal justice operations (Braithwaite, 1989). Social support is the key ingredient in "reintegrative shaming." Andrews and Bonta (1998) show that individuals can control their behaviour with rehabilitation programs that use cognitive and behavioural therapies. Given the right setting, this can lead to positive outcomes and legitimate ways of coping. In fact, most current crime control measures produce an erratic coercive cycle, which increases strain and anger. Unfortunately, moving toward a noncoercive, socially supportive criminal justice system does not seem likely at the present time.

Scholars do not have to be in complete agreement regarding strain theory before applying many of its principles to public policy in the important pursuit of reducing the gap between rich and poor. Nor should we ignore the warning Merton voiced in his 1938 article: *The ruthless pursuit of profit creates a criminogenic society.* Increasing opportunities for the less privileged members of society makes a great deal more sense than rewarding the wealthy to encourage them to invest (for a profit, of course) so that some of the wealth will trickle down to the poor. The self-serving policies advocated by many powerful people in North America in recent years should, according to any version of strain theory, lead to more crime.

SUMMARY

- Two broad theoretical perspectives have guided sociological theories of crime. The consensus perspective maintains that the vast majority of the population share similar values regarding right and wrong. The law represents a codification of societal values. The conflict perspective questions such assumptions and argues that the criminal law does not necessarily represent the moral values of the majority but rather reflects the interests of the groups that are in a position to create and enforce those laws.

- Strain theory is part of the consensus tradition. Strain theorists assume that social institutions such as the family, education, government, religion, and the economy normally all contribute to the smooth running of society. Crime occurs when something unusual happens that affects some or all of these institutions. This results in strains, stresses, or frustrations that affect people's behaviour.

- Durkheim saw crime and other deviance as a consequence of modernity. Changes associated with modernity led to a weakening of social controls, and consequently rates of deviance increased.

- Merton began with Durkheim's concept of anomie but modified Durkheim's theory to account for what he felt were the realities of American society. In Merton's anomie theory, crime resulted from the gap between culturally prescribed aspirations and the socially structured means for realizing those aspirations.

- Messner and Rosenfeld argued that American culture emphasizes monetary success. When combined with weak restraints on illegitimate means this encourages economic crimes.

- Agnew suggests that adolescents located in unpleasant and stressful environments, such as school, from which they cannot escape become frustrated and angry. If legitimate coping alternatives are not available, violent outbursts and delinquency are likely.

- Kobrin extended Merton's theory by introducing the idea of community opportunity structures. Some communities provide more legitimate opportunities than do others. Cloward pointed out that illegitimate opportunities were also not equally accessible to all. As a result, he hypothesized that there would be three different types of delinquent subcultures: criminal, conflict, and retreatist.

- Albert Cohen took a more dynamic approach to the problems created by strain. Lower-class youth are unable to meet the middle-class standards of the school. As a result, they collectively build a new set of values and standards that are the opposite of those of the middle class. This inversion of middle-class standards often results in delinquency.

- While most strain theorists have looked exclusively at crime committed by members of the lower class, the theory can also be used to explain white-collar and corporate crime. Upper-class crimes can arise from an unprincipled overcommitment to success goals. Even successful people may feel pressure to make more money and may choose to break the law in order to achieve these financial goals.

QUESTIONS FOR CRITICAL THINKING

1. In this chapter, you have read about the consensus and conflict perspectives to crime. Think of three different laws that prohibit behaviour that most

people would agree is wrong. Can you think of any circumstances under which these acts might be permissible? Now think of three different laws that prohibit behaviour that a significant number of Canadians think should be tolerated. Why do these behaviours remain against the law?

2. How would Merton's anomie theory explain the higher rates of deviance and crime among Canada's Aboriginal people? Does the theory help you to think of any possible solutions to this problem?

3. Researchers who have studied delinquent gangs have failed to find the three distinct criminal, conflict, and retreatist subcultures predicted by Cloward and Ohlin. Why do you think these distinct types of gangs do not exist?

4. Discuss some of the strengths and weaknesses of strain theory.

5. Merton, and those who followed him, developed strain theory to explain lower-class crime and delinquency. However, some might argue that strain theory actually provides a better explanation of white-collar and corporate crime. Describe how strain theory can be used to explain the crimes of the rich and powerful.

NET WORK

Go to the website of the National Crime Prevention Strategy at **www.prevention. gc.ca/en/.** Look at the section of the website headed "Crime Prevention Practices." This section outlines a variety of programs designed to prevent crime and delinquency. Which of these programs address issues raised by strain theorists? How likely do you think it is that these programs will have an impact on crime? Why?

KEY TERMS

anomie

conflict perspective

consensus perspective

culturally prescribed aspiration

human capital

mechanical solidarity

middle-class measuring rod

mutual conversion

opportunity structure

organic solidarity

reaction formation

relative deprivation

social structure

strain theory

subculture

SUGGESTED READING

Agnew, Robert. 1997. "The Nature and Determinants of Strain." In Nikos Passas and Robert Agnew (eds.), *The Future of Anomie Theory*. Boston: Northeastern University Press. This essay broadens the traditional discussion of anomie.

Bernard, Thomas. (1987). "Testing Structural Strain Theories." *Journal of Research in Crime and Delinquency* 24:262–80. This article debates the application of strain theory to individuals or groups.

Cohen, Albert K. (1955). *Delinquent Boys: The Culture of the Gang.* Glencoe, Ill.: Free Press. One of the classic studies of delinquency that linked ideas of opportunity structure to the subculture of gang delinquency. Extensively influenced later studies of delinquency.

Cohen, Deborah. (1995). "Ethics and Crime in Business Firms: Organizational Culture and the Impact of Anomie." In Freda Adler and William S. Laufer (eds.), *Advances in Criminological Theory. Vol. 6: The Legacy of Anomie.* New Brunswick, N.J.: Transaction. Strain theory applied to the business world.

Hagan, John, and Bill McCarthy. (1997). *Mean Streets: Youth Homelessness and Crime.* New York: Cambridge University Press. Being on the street leads to a variety of illegitimate and dangerous opportunities.

Merton, Robert. (1968). *Social Theory and Social Structure.* (2nd ed.). New York: Free Press. The third revision of Merton's classic anomie theory of crime.

Messner, Steven F., and Richard Rosenfeld. (1997). *Crime and the American Dream.* (2nd ed.). Belmont, Calif.: Wadsworth. Economic factors are pervasive in North America, and there are only weak restraints on ethical behaviour.

BIBLIOGRAPHY

Agnew, Robert. (1991). "A Longitudinal Test of Social Control Theory and Delinquency." *Journal of Research in Crime and Delinquency* 28:126–56.

———. (1992). "Foundation for a General Strain Theory of Crime and Delinquency." *Criminology* 30:47–87.

———. (1997). "The Nature and Determinants of Strain." In Nikos Passas and Robert Agnew (eds.), *The Future of Anomie Theory.* Boston: Northeastern University Press.

Agnew, Robert, and Helene Raskin White. (1992). "An Empirical Test of General Strain Theory." *Criminology* 30:475–99.

Agnew, Robert, Francis T. Cullen, Velmer S. Burton Jr., T. David Evans, and R. Gregory Dunaway. (1996). "A New Test of Class Strain Theory." *Justice Quarterly* 13:681–704.

Andrews, Donald A., and James Bonta. (1998). *The Psychology of Criminal Conduct* (2nd ed.). Cincinatti, Oh: Anderson.

Bernard, Thomas. (1987). "Testing Structural Strain Theories." *Journal of Research in Crime and Delinquency* 24:262–80.

Blau, Judith, and Peter Blau. (1982). "Metropolitan Structure and Violent Crime." *American Sociological Review* 47 (February):114–29.

Blumer, Herbert. (1951). "Collective Behaviour." In A.M. Lee (ed.), *Principles of Sociology.* New York: Barnes and Noble.

Braithwaite, John. (1979). *Inequality, Crime and Public Policy.* London: Routledge and Kegan Paul.

Brezina, Timothy. (1998). "Adolescent Maltreatment and Delinquency: The Question of Intervening Processes." *Journal of Research in Crime and Delinquency* 35:71–99.

Cloward, Richard. (1959). "Illegitimate Means, Anomie, and Deviant Behavior." *American Sociological Review* 24 (April):164–76.

Cloward, Richard, and Lloyd Ohlin. (1960). *Delinquency and Opportunity.* Glencoe, Ill.: Free Press.

Cohen, Albert K. (1955). *Delinquent Boys: The Culture of the Gang*. Glencoe, Ill.: Free Press.

Colvin, Mark. (2000). *Crime and Coercion: An Integrated Theory of Chronic Criminality*. New York: St. Martin's Press.

Colvin, Mark, Francis T. Cullen, and Thomas Vander Ven. (2002). "Coercion, Social Support and Crime: An Emerging Theoretical Consensus." *Criminology* 40:19–42.

Comack, Elizabeth. (1992). "Women and Crime." In Rick Linden (ed.), *Criminology: A Canadian Perspective* (2nd ed.). Toronto: Harcourt Brace.

Crutchfield, Robert D. (1995). "Ethnicity, Labor Markets and Crime." In Darnell F. Hawkins (ed.), *Ethnicity, Race and Crime: Perspectives Across Time and Place*. Albany: State University of New York Press.

Cullen, Francis. (1984). *Rethinking Crime and Deviance Theory: The Emergence of a Structuring Tradition*. Totowa, N.J.: Rowman and Allanheld.

———. (1988). "Were Cloward and Ohlin Strain Theorists? Delinquency and Opportunity Revisited." *Journal of Research in Crime and Delinquency* 25:214–41.

Desroches, Fred. (1995). "Tearoom Trade: A Law Enforcement Problem." *Canadian Journal of Criminology* 33(1):1–21.

Durkheim, Émile. (1933). *The Division of Labor in Society*. New York: Free Press.

Erikson, Kai. (1966). *Wayward Puritans*. New York: Wiley.

Farnworth, Margaret, and Michael Leiber. (1989). "Strain Theory Revisited." *American Sociological Review* 54:263–74.

Giffen, P.J. (1966). "The Revolving Door: A Functional Interpretation." *Canadian Review of Sociology and Anthropology* 3 (August):154–66.

Gurr, Ted. (1981). "Historical Forces in Violent Crime." In Michael Tonry and Norval Morris (eds.), *Crime and Justice*, Vol. 3 (pp. 295–353). Chicago: University of Chicago Press.

Hackler, James C. (1966). "Boys, Blisters, and Behavior." *Journal of Research in Crime and Delinquency* 3 (July):155–64.

———. (2003). *Canadian Criminology: Strategies and Perspectives* (3rd ed.). Toronto: Prentice Hall Canada.

Hackler, James C., and Eric Linden. (1970). "The Response of Adults to Delinquency Prevention Programs: The Race Factor." *Journal of Research in Crime and Delinquency* 7 (January):31–45.

Hagan, John, and Bill McCarthy. (1997a). *Mean Streets: Youth Homelessness and Crime*. New York: Cambridge University Press.

———. (1997b). "Anomie, Social Capital, and Street Criminology." In Nikos Passas and Robert Agnew (eds.), *The Future of Anomie Theory*. Boston: Northeastern University Press.

Helfgot, Joseph. (1981). *Professional Reforming: Mobilization for Youth and the Failure of Social Science*. Lexington, Mass.: Heath.

Jensen, Gary F. (1995). "Salvaging Structure Through Strain: A Theoretical and Empirical Critique." In Freda Adler and William S. Laufer (eds.), *Advances in Criminological Theory, Vol. 6: The Legacy of Anomie*. New Brunswick, N.J.: Transaction.

Kobrin, Sol. (1951). "The Conflict of Values in Delinquency Areas." *American Sociological Review* 16 (October):653–61.

Mazerolle, Paul, and Alex Piquero. (1997). "Violent Responses to Strain: An Examination of Conditioning Influences." *Violence and Victims* 12:323–43.

———. (1998). "Linking Exposure to Strain with Anger: Investigation of Deviant Adaptations." *Journal of Criminal Justice* 26:195–211.

Mead, George Herbert. (1918). "The Psychology of Punitive Justice." *American Journal of Sociology* 23 (March):577–602.

Menard, Scott. (1997). "A Developmental Test of Cloward's Differential Opportunity Theory." In Nikos Passas and Robert Agnew (eds.), *The Future of Anomie Theory*. Boston: Northeastern University Press.

Merton, Robert K. (1938). "Social Structure and Anomie." *American Sociological Review* 3 (October):672–82.

Messner, Steven F., and Richard Rosenfeld. (1997a). *Crime and the American Dream* (2nd ed.). Belmont, Calif.: Wadsworth.

———. (1997b). "Political Restraint of the Market and Levels of Criminal Homicide: A Cross-National Application of Institutional-Anomie Theory." *Social Forces* 75:1393–416.

Morris, Alison. (1987). *Women, Crime, and Criminal Justice*. Oxford: Basil Blackwell.

Naffine, Ngaire. (1987). *Female Crime: The Construction of Women in Criminology*. Sydney: Allen and Unwin.

Nettler, Gwynne. (1984). *Explaining Crime*. New York: McGraw-Hill.

Passas, Nikos. (1997). "Anomie, Reference Groups, and Relative Deprivation." In Nikos Passas and Robert Agnew (eds.), *The Future of Anomie Theory*. Boston: Northeastern University Press.

Quinney, Richard. (1963). "Occupational Structure and Criminal Behavior: Prescription Violation by Retail Pharmacists." *Social Problems* 11 (Fall):179–95.

Rose, Stephen. (1972). *The Betrayal of the Poor: The Transformation of Community Action*. Cambridge, Mass.: Shenkman.

Rosenfeld, Richard, and Steven F. Messner. (1997). "Markets, Morality, and an Institutional-Anomie Theory of Crime." In Nikos Passas and Robert Agnew (eds.), *The Future of Anomie Theory*. Boston: Northeastern University Press.

Schweinhart, L.L., H.V. Barnes, and D.P. Weikart. (1993). *Significant Benefits: The High/Scope Perry Preschool Study through Age 27*. Ypsilanti, Mich.: High/Scope Press.

Shelley, Louise. (1981). *Crime and Modernization*. Carbondale, Ill.: Southern Illinois Press.

Short, James, Jr. (1975). "The Natural History of an Applied Theory: Differential Opportunity and Mobilization for Youth." In N.J. Demerath (ed.), *Social Policy and Sociology*. New York: Academic Press.

Sutherland, Edwin. (1949). *White Collar Crime*. New York: Dryden.

Thornberry, Terence P. (1987). "Toward an Interactional Theory of Delinquency." *Criminology* 25:863–91.

Tremblay, Richard E., and Wendy M. Craig. (1995). "Developmental Crime Prevention." In M. Tonry and D.P. Farrington (eds.), *Building a Safer Society: Strategic Approaches to Crime Prevention*. Vol. 19. Chicago: University of Chicago Press.

Vaughan, Diane. (1997). "Anomie Theory and Organizations: Culture and the Normalization of Deviance." In Nikos Passas and Robert Agnew (eds.), *The Future of Anomie Theory*. Boston: Northeastern University Press.

Wade, Andrew L. (1967). "Social Processes in the Act of Juvenile Vandalism." In Marshall B. Clinard and Richard Quinney, *Criminal Behavior Systems: A Typology*. New York: Holt, Rinehart, and Winston.

Conflict and Marxist Theories

11

RONALD HINCH

University of Ontario Institute of Technology

Conflict and Marxist theories challenge dominant assumptions about how the social order is maintained. Whereas consensus theory (see Chapter 10) assumes a societal-wide consensus concerning the protection and preservation of values, the theories presented in this chapter argue that no such consensus exists. They argue that contemporary societies are characterized by conflict and dissension. The extent to which the theories discussed in this chapter challenge the notion of consensus vary according to their assumptions regarding the source and nature of conflict. As a result, some of them offer a greater challenge to assumptions about social order than do others. To highlight their differences and similarities, they have been grouped under the following headings: Cultural Conflict Theories, Group Conflict Theory, Feminist Theories, and Marxist Theories.

After reading this chapter, you should be able to

LEARNING OBJECTIVES

- Understand how cultural conflict theorists proposed that bringing diverse cultures into contact within the same society results in conflict. Members of the dominant culture have the power to resolve conflict by using the law to control other cultures.

- Describe how group conflict theory emerged as a response to the failure of cultural conflict theorists to offer a full account of societal conflict and the role that conflict plays in the creation and enforcement of social rules.

- Know the differences between radical feminism and socialist feminism and the strengths and weaknesses of these two examples of feminist theories of crime.

- Explain the Marxist approach to crime.

- Show your familiarity with the strengths and weaknesses of Marxist theories of criminology, including instrumentalist Marxism, structuralist Marxism, and left realism.

CULTURAL CONFLICT THEORIES

Cultural conflict theory developed from the **Chicago School**, one of the most influential forces shaping both sociology and criminology prior to 1940. It incorporated several approaches to the study of society. One approach, symbolic

Chicago School
Refers to the main themes in research and theoretical ideas that emerged from the University of Chicago in the first half of the 20th century. In criminology, the Chicago School focused on the socio-cultural causes of urban crime and on crime prevention.

symbolic communications

All communication with others is symbolic and involves the use of language, sound, bodily gesture, and expression.

conduct norms

Specifications of proper and appropriate behaviour generally supported and shared by members of a group. Societies contain different groups whose norms of conduct are to some extent divergent.

career criminality

Where commission of criminal acts becomes a central aspect of a person's social behaviour. Career criminality is associated with an individual's exposure to deviant subcultures.

social disorganization theory

The theory that crime and other deviant behaviour is most likely to occur where social institutions are not able to direct and control groups of individuals.

individual pathology

A term used to refer to biological or psychological explanations of criminal or deviant behaviour by individuals. The assumption is that the deviant behaviour of individuals can be at least partly explained by some physical or psychological trait that makes them different from normal law-abiding citizens.

criminal definition

Refers to the fact that crime is socially defined and that this definition will vary from society to society.

interactionism (see Chapter 12), focused on the analysis of the way people learn to be members of their societies by interpreting and using **symbolic communications**. Another approach, social disorganization theory (see Chapter 13), focused on the lack of organization within and between segments of society. Each of these approaches may be found in Sellin's (1938) theory of **conduct norms**, as well as Sutherland's (1939) theory of **career criminality**.

According to Sellin (1938), all cultures establish their own behaviour codes, or conduct norms. Bringing divergent cultures into direct contact within the same society results in conflict. This conflict is heightened whenever one culture is able to have its beliefs and practices protected by inclusion in the Criminal Code. Where this happens, other cultures, whose beliefs and practices differ, must either alter their culture and behaviour or risk conflict with the dominant culture. Sellin was concerned that the conduct norms among immigrant cultures would place them in conflict with the conduct norms of their new society. For example, in some societies female circumcision is an accepted practice, but in North American society it is called genital mutilation and is a criminal act.

In addition to Sellin's theory of conduct norms, Sutherland's (1939) theory of career criminality incorporated elements of **social disorganization theory** and symbolic interactionist theory. The key elements of this theory were that behaviour is learned in association with others (a notion he borrowed from symbolic interactionism), that the various cultural groups in society establish their own conduct norms (borrowed from Sellin), and that the proliferation of cultural groups leaves both society and some of these cultural groups disorganized (see Chapter 13). Career criminality, he said, is more common in some subcultures because members of these groups are exposed to social and cultural forces that encourage behaviour patterns that place them in conflict with better organized, more powerful cultures. In this context, each culture attempts to use the law to control other cultures.

Sellin and Sutherland sought an alternative to theories of crime that said that criminality was a product of **individual pathology** and argued that culture was more important. A second objective for both Sellin and Sutherland was to expand criminological investigation beyond explanations of violations of the Criminal Code. Sellin argued that because **criminal definitions** varied from country to country, and over time, it was unreasonable to study only violations of criminal codes. To restrict criminological theory to explanations of criminal law would mean that a different theory would be needed to explain each type of rule breaking. Violations of civil law and other norms would each require a different theory. Sellin argued that rule-breaking behaviour of all types could be explained by a single theory—his theory of *conduct norms*.

Critique of Cultural Conflict Theory

Culture conflict theory has been criticized for failing to appreciate how non-cultural factors, such as economic disparity and inequalities of power, affect the power to define and enforce social norms of all kinds. While cultural conflict theorists recognize group differences on these dimensions, these differences are said to be less important than cultural differences.

Sellin has been criticized for assuming that universal laws of behaviour govern rule-violating behaviour. Tappan (1947) has argued that Sellin could not establish what these universal laws of behaviour—the conduct norms—were. In Tappan's assessment, Sellin's advocacy of conduct norms resulted in a circular argument. Sellin had argued that legal norms are too varied and variable to provide a universal standard by which to assess and judge behaviour, but then suggested that the category *conduct norms* be used as the universal standard. Implicit in Sellin's argument is the notion that most street crimes are crimes only because they violate the conduct norms of the most powerful segments of society. Crimes such as murder, robbery, and assault, however, are meant to apply to everyone, and everyone can expect these laws to protect them from wrongdoers.

Sutherland's theory was not well received. Critics were dissatisfied with the theory because of its poor linkage of symbolic interactionism, cultural conflict theory (Sellin, 1938), and social disorganization theory. Even Sutherland (1947) later rejected the concept of social disorganization because when combined with the concept of culture conflict, it implies that some cultural groups are disorganized. Rather than saying that, his later version of the theory (see Chapter 12) proposed that these groups are merely organized in different ways for different purposes.

Despite these shortcomings, cultural conflict theory played a significant role in the development of conflict theory. It paved the way for later writers to offer more comprehensive theories. For example, both Quinney (1970) and Turk (1969), two of the best-known conflict theorists, were strongly influenced by the work of the culture conflict theorists.

GROUP CONFLICT THEORY

Group conflict theory emerged primarily as a response to the failure of cultural conflict theorists to offer a full account of societal conflict and the role that conflict plays in the creation and enforcement of social rules. The most prominent group conflict theorist was George Vold (1958), who, like the cultural conflict theorists, sought to direct criminological theory away from theories of individual pathology toward explanations based on the analysis of conflicts between social groups. He argued that the number and diversity of social groups produced conflict. In order to secure its own place in society, each group forms alliances with other groups. It may even be necessary to alter alliances whenever an existing alliance is no longer useful.

Vold applied this analysis of group interaction to the specific problem of understanding how criminal laws were made and enforced. According to Vold, the ability to influence the creation and enforcement of criminal law represents the triumph of an alliance of one set of groups over others. Without the ability to influence law creation through forming alliances, the probability that any group can maintain or enhance its place in society is reduced. Those who managed to have a law passed would be the ones most likely to conform to the new law and to put pressure on law enforcement agents to enforce it. Those who opposed the law, or whose actions were the target of the new law, would be the ones least likely to obey the law and would attempt to put pressure on law enforcers to ensure that the law would not be enforced. This implies that conflict is most likely whenever groups that are organized for the purpose of promoting opposed values come into direct contact.

Criminalization is most likely when those groups Vold refers to as "minority groups" (his examples included juvenile gangs and conscientious objectors during World War II) come in contact with law enforcement agents who enforce the law according to the wishes of those who sought its passage. Conversely, so long as groups do not come into contact with groups with opposing viewpoints or behaviour patterns, they are not likely to find themselves in conflict and are not likely to become criminalized.

Vold described four patterns of conflict that result from efforts to define and control criminal behaviour. In the first, definitions of behaviour as criminal may result from expressions of political dissent or protest. This may include violent revolutionary action, burglary, bribery, perjury, and fraud undertaken to win an election. While some or all of these actions may be condemned publicly, they may still form an important part of day-to-day activity in many democratic societies and are to be considered as part of the struggle between groups. For example, members of the Quebec-based terrorist group, the FLQ, believed themselves to be engaging in political protest when they kidnapped a Quebec cabinet minister and a foreign government representative in October 1970. The reaction of the governments of Canada and Quebec to these incidents—invoking the War Measures Act and the subsequent criminal convictions of the kidnappers—clearly resulted in these protests by the FLQ being labelled as criminal actions. The FLQ's acts of protest were stripped of any claim to legitimacy in the eyes of many Canadians, particularly after they murdered the cabinet minister, Pierre LaPorte.

A second pattern of conflict emerges out of the efforts of managers to manage their organizations and the efforts of employees to obtain better wages and working conditions. It is not uncommon for both sides in labour disputes to violate the law and to offer as a defence the explanation that they were protecting their rights. Both sides may see the law that condemns their lawbreaking as less important than their conformity with the norms of their group.

A third conflict pattern emanates from the effort to unionize. When opposing labour unions attempt to organize the same group of workers, one union or the other or both may resort to violence to gain support. Those who use violence to gain group ends are generally given the support of the group. They are seen as engaging in behaviour that is consistent with group values and objectives.

A fourth conflict pattern arises from race relations. In various parts of the world, different racial groups attempt to maintain their positions of dominance by creating and enforcing laws restricting the behaviour of other races. This was evident in the old Jim Crow segregation laws in many states of the United States, and in South African apartheid laws that denied black Africans their rights. It is also evident in struggles to outlaw racial discrimination. In such disputes, both sides may attempt to use the law to promote their own viewpoint and behaviour patterns.

Critique of Group Conflict Theory

Group conflict theory has been criticized for being unable to explain irrational or impulsive criminal behaviour. For example, it cannot account for "non-utilitarian, malicious and negativistic" acts, such as vandalism, fighting, bullying, and shoplifting then throwing away the stolen item, which Cohen (1955) says lower-class gang delinquents engage in "for the hell of it." However, it should be noted that Vold had not intended his theory to explain such behaviour.

Group conflict theory has also been criticized for having a simplistic conception of power relations between and within groups. The theory does not recognize the possibility that relatively small, elite groups might control the lawmaking process, and that some members of a group might engage in behaviour condemned by the majority or might otherwise refuse to do as the group expects.

On the other hand, group conflict theory, like cultural conflict theory, contributed to later developments in criminological theory. Vold's (1958) book has been revised several times (see Vold et al., 1998) and was an important precursor of other conflict theories of crime.

FEMINIST THEORIES

Feminist theorizing about crime and criminality emerged initially as a series of critiques of mainstream criminology (see Chapter 6). Although there are several variations of feminist criminology, this chapter focuses on only two: radical feminism and socialist feminism.

Radical Feminism

The basic assumption of **radical feminism** is that **patriarchy**—a social system in which men occupy positions of power and privilege and use those positions to maintain dominance over women—is universal. Most argue that patriarchy originates in the biological differences between men and women and that this gives rise to the division of labour by sex. According to radical feminists, the sex-based division of labour was the first class structure in human societies. Men attempt to dominate women within this structure in order to assure themselves control over both women's reproductive capacity and their labour power.

Within criminology, radical feminism attempts to account for the violence perpetrated on women by men, including dating violence, wife assault, incest, and rape. It has also been used to explain why and how the laws governing male violence give greater protection to men's interests.

For example, Susan Brownmiller says that rape is an essential control mechanism by which "all men keep all women in a state of fear" (1975, 14). She argues that current marriage practices and rape laws emerged out of a bargain struck in early human societies in which women surrendered sexual access and the right to say no to one man in exchange for his protection from all other men. Thus, women became the sexual property of men, and marriage and rape laws emerged to protect male property rights. For example, Canadian law prior to 1983 did not allow a married man to be charged with raping his wife. The

radical feminism
A perspective that sees women's social situation as chiefly shaped by male dominance (i.e., patriarchy) rather than by the capitalist class structure of society. Within criminology, radical feminists focus on documenting and analyzing ways in which the content of law and practices of law enforcement have served to entrench and strengthen male dominance in society.

patriarchy
A system of male domination that includes both a structure and an ideology that privileges men over women. For example, men exercise control over women both overtly by objectifying women's bodies in pornography and covertly in the form of a "monogamous heterosexuality" that legitimates male control over women and children and reinforces the ideology that women are dependent on men for both their economic and sexual needs.

law specifically said that rape occurred only when a man perpetrated an act of sexual intercourse upon a woman who was *not* his wife without her consent.

To further emphasize how and why rape laws serve to protect male interests, radical feminists have examined the implications of specific law reform measures. For example, they have argued that the 1983 amendments to the Criminal Code championed by some as a step forward for women because they substituted gender-neutral terms (sexual assault) for the old gender-specific terms (rape, indecent assault on a female, and indecent assault on a male) actually perpetuate male domination (Boyle, 1984). Cohen and Backhouse (1980a; 1980b), as well as Lowenberger and Landau (1982), argue that gender-neutral terms trivialize rape (1) by hiding its gender-specific nature; (2) by making it appear to be no more harmful than other types of assault; and (3) by making it appear to be no more serious than minor forms of sexual assault, such as touching the breasts.

Similar kinds of analysis have been applied to the study of wife battering and incest. These crimes against women have persisted within the context of the

---

BOX 11.1

FOCUS

Sexual Assault Law and the Female Perspective

It is submitted that our law at any particular time can be analysed in terms of the interplay of the law-makers' various self-perceptions or, more accurately, their perceptions of their potential. It is to state the obvious that the people who have created our sexual assault law (until this latest reform)[1] have almost exclusively been male, and it is important to explore the significance of this fact. It would seem reasonable to suppose that, in carrying out any rule-making function, a rule-maker would try to imagine himself as one of those affected by a possible rule in order to reach some opinion of the fairness and efficacy of the rule. But since the ability to put ourselves in someone else's shoes is limited by our imagination, education, sex, class, age and many other factors, all of our law is deeply influenced by this limitation....

In the context of sexual assault, it is submitted that the law reveals that the law-maker has seen himself in various guises and not always as a potential victim. He has seen himself very vividly in the shoes of the accused, and hence the victim of a false complaint, and also in the shoes of a man who is close to the woman assaulted, as husband, father, brother, and hence as victim of the assault.

It seems to have been extraordinarily difficult, however, for him to cross the sexual barrier and put himself in the position of an assaulted woman. Hence our law, in the balancing exercise between competing values, has attached little if any weight to the simple goal of protecting women from assault. This should not be overstated. It may well have happened that some women have been protected indirectly, in the process of protecting the male as husband, father, and brother. Certainly individual men may have been able to make the imaginative leap and see the world from a female perspective but, overall, our law does not reveal that much importance has been attached to the protection of women in their own right, as human beings with a right to sexual autonomy.[2]

---

1 Boyle is referring to the amendments to the Criminal Code introduced in 1983.

2 Footnotes included in the original source have been omitted for this reprint.

Source: Christine Boyle. (1984). Sexual Assault. Toronto: Carswell Company Limited, pp. 4, 5–6. Reprinted by permission of Carswell—a division of Thomson Canada Limited.

family because men were able to use their dominance within the family to make these offences appear to be simply the private troubles of the individuals involved and to mask the extent of the problem. Radical feminists have been particularly concerned that police and court enforcement of the criminal law of assault allowed men to assault their wives. Law enforcement allowed this by effectively turning a blind eye to these assaults. Usually, only severe physical assaults would be treated as crimes. Many women have been forced to endure beatings over a prolonged period because the police and the courts refused to take the problem seriously. The exact number of women subjected to assaults at the hands of their husbands (or other partner) is difficult to determine. However, it has been estimated that at least one in ten married women, including those living with, but not married to, their partners, is beaten each year. By treating it as a private trouble, the law enforcement apparatus effectively hid the problem. Individual women subjected to the violence were made to feel that it was something that was happening only to them, or that it was something they had to endure because that was the way things were.

Radical feminists, therefore, have attempted to document and analyze the ways in which the law and law enforcement practices have been used to strengthen male dominance. They have argued that even though some laws have been created with the apparent intent of providing equality for women, the reality is that people who are politically, socially, and economically unequal cannot be made equal by the passage of laws that do nothing to remove these forms of inequality. Formal legal equality, as well as male-dominated law enforcement practices, mask the real nature of women's inequality.

Critique of Radical Feminism

One of the most frequent criticisms of radical feminism concerns its assumption that female subjugation is universal and originates in the biological differences between men and women. Hartmann (1977) and Schwendinger and Schwendinger (1983), for example, have argued that the division of labour by sex was not always hierarchical. It became hierarchical as men's production began to be associated with the public realm, thereby becoming social and kin centred, while women's production and reproduction became nuclear-family centred, or privatized within the family. Similarly, Lacombe (1988) argues that women's reproductive capacity is not in itself oppressive. It becomes so only when it is "associated with characteristics which are socially defined as unequal" (29).

Radical feminists have also been criticized for having the overly cynical view that rape is a threat used by all men to control all women. This view is based on the assumption that rape exists apart from other forms of violence in society. Hale (1990) argues that this view overstates the influence of patriarchy. This results in the abnormal becoming the normal. She agrees that there is widespread evidence of violence against women, but the evidence also says that most marriages are characterized by "mutually supportive relations" (352). Schwendinger and Schwendinger (1983) also add that rape and other forms of sexual violence against women cannot be understood apart from all other forms of violence in society. They argue that violence in society is more strongly related to the ways in which societies organize their economic affairs than it is

socialist feminism
A perspective that views women's social situation as being shaped by both patriarchal gender relations and the class structure of capitalism.

to the ways they organize relations between men and women. Hale (1990) also argues that radical feminists overstate the extent of violence against women.

Radical feminism has played a significant role in forcing other theoretical models to incorporate elements of the feminist critique. For example, radical feminism has played a significant role in forcing researchers to look at how and why rape laws were created. This helped reveal the implicit and explicit anti-woman biases in criminological thinking.

Socialist Feminism

Socialist feminism represents an attempt to merge radical feminism with Marxism. Once again, the merger has taken several forms. In its early stages, socialist feminism followed what has been called a *dual systems* approach. According to this, patriarchy and capitalism are separate but equal systems. Both must be assessed in order to fully comprehend women's place in society.

For example, Hartmann (1977; 1981) says that while it is improbable that patriarchy has been present in all human societies, patriarchal structures predate the emergence of capitalism. Once capitalism emerged, men could attempt to maintain their positions solely through patriarchy, switch their power base to the new capitalist system, or take advantage of both systems. They chose the latter. Patriarchy allowed men to continue dominating women through gender relations, while capitalism allowed men to extend control into the marketplace. Thus, in capitalist societies women may be oppressed by virtue of either their class position or their gender, or by both.

Another variant of socialist feminism argues against the dual systems approach. These feminists argue that it is impossible to conceptualize any mode of production that excludes the organization of gender relations. This conceptualization of the relation between patriarchy and capitalism gives primacy to neither. Smith writes:

> Looked at in this way, the problem of patriarchy versus class takes on a different cast. The interpersonal relations of direct dominance, between women and men, are implicated in a larger organisation of the society. Even if we see the patriarchal principle at work in each new setting, in government, business, professions, labour unions, yet that personal relation of dominance and inequality is articulated to the larger social, political and economic organisation of the society. It cannot be separated from it. (1985, 3–4)

The two are inseparably linked. As a theoretical model used to explain criminal behaviour, socialist feminism has been used to explain why men and women from different social classes commit different types of crime and to analyze how the law functions to preserve both capitalist and patriarchal relations.

Messerschmidt (1986; Beirne and Messerschmidt, 1991) says that men in all classes commit more crime than women because men have more power and more opportunity resulting from both the combined effects of their social class and their patriarchal standing. The types of crime men commit vary with their social class. Men in the upper and managerial classes are less likely to engage in conventional crimes. They are, however, more likely to participate in corporate crime because the demand for corporate profit making is the key to success. If the profits cannot be obtained legally, then illegal methods of profit making become more attractive. In many situations, this means that the corporation—that is, corporate executives—may decide that it is better to set aside ethical standards, or risk lives, than to risk reductions in corporate profits.

Men from lower socio-economic positions have little or no opportunity to commit this type of crime and confine themselves to more conventional crime. They encounter conditions that men from upper classes do not. Periods of unemployment, lower incomes, and inferior occupations all contribute to lower-class male crime. Unemployment, low incomes, and poor jobs put pressure on men, especially young men, to commit crimes such as burglary and theft. Illegal activity is sometimes easier and more profitable than finding or continuing to work at low-paying or short-term jobs.

The effects of class and patriarchy also pressure men to commit violent crime. Sexual violence, such as rape and incest, and crimes of abuse, such as dating violence and wife assault, are perpetrated against women as a means of reinforcing both patriarchal and class relations (see Luxton, 1980, 65–69). For example, as a statement of patriarchal power, rape represents male dominance and women's subordination. Women from different class positions have different risks of being raped. Both official crime data and victim survey studies show that teenage women from lower socio-economic groups are most at risk.

As for female criminality, Messerschmidt (1986; see also Beirne and Messerschmidt, 1991) says that the effects of gender mediate the impact of unemployment, low incomes, and poor jobs on women. Rather than argue that women's entry into the labour market has produced more female crime, Messerschmidt identifies poverty as a major contributing factor leading to increased female crime. Faced with such conditions as single parenthood with poor economic prospects, women engage in property crimes, such as theft, in order to satisfy their concerns about their family role. Family need and the desire to maintain a marriage are frequently given by women as their reasons for committing theft or embezzlement.

Critique of Socialist Feminism

A major criticism of socialist feminism concerns its attempted union of Marxism and radical feminism. It has been argued that this submerges feminism within Marxism (Miles, 1985). Socialist feminists are accused of reducing patriarchy to just another mechanism by which capitalism maintains control over women. Radical feminists, like Eisenstein (1979), argue that capitalist exploitation of workers and patriarchal domination of women by men are not equivalent and should not be treated as such.

Socialist feminism, however, provides a strong alternative to both radical feminism and Marxism. In so doing, it illustrates that social systems and social structures are extremely complex, and that solutions to problems are rarely as simple as they might seem. Like other forms of feminist argument, it has also forced recognition of the ways in which other theories have negated or overlooked the complexity of modern life, especially the complexity in understanding women's role and status in society.

MARXIST THEORIES

It has been argued that all conflict and Marxist theories should be grouped together under the general heading of conflict theory. However, some analysts argue that there are fundamental differences between the two perspectives, which should not be ignored (see Wood, 1983; Hinch, 1989a; 1989b). To ignore the differences is to assume that superficial similarities are more important than core propositions.

It should be noted that Marx never offered a systematic analysis of crime. When Marx did venture to comment on crime or criminals, his comments were frequently made with tongue in cheek or stated as pure sarcasm. For example, he once said that crime served the useful purpose of providing jobs for policemen and other criminal justice workers (Marx, 1979, 191). This sarcastic remark was really intended as a critique of the notion that crime does indeed serve a useful purpose. In some of his other comments, he made it very clear that criminals were essentially parasites whose behaviour left them open to becoming the "bribed tool of reactionary intrigue" (Marx and Engels, 1971, 43). Because Marx did not offer a systematic analysis of crime, some Marxists have said that crime is an inappropriate object of study for Marxists (Bankowski et al., 1977; Hirst, 1975). Other Marxists disagree (Hinch, 1983; Taylor and Walton, 1975). They argue that just because Marx did not offer a systematic analysis of crime and criminality is no reason for modern Marxists not to do so.

The place of Marxist criminology within contemporary criminology as a whole is also controversial: it poses the most direct challenge to the major assumptions and practices of the other theoretical perspectives and of Western, capitalist society itself. Marxist theories of crime are also the least understood theories. There is a strong tendency among non-Marxist scholars to assume that there is only one Marxist theory of crime and criminality, whereas in reality, there are several. Furthermore, it is assumed that this one Marxist theory is an extreme example of a style of argument known as **economic determinism** when, in fact, that is a highly contentious issue within Marxism. If there is one element common to the four examples of Marxist analysis to be presented in this chapter, it is that they all begin from the assumption that class relations are the most significant factor affecting the definition of crime and the process of criminalization.

economic determinism

The theory that all the main features of a society, including its cultural ideas and social organization, are chiefly shaped by its form of economic organization.

instrumentalist Marxism

A perspective that stresses the intimate connection between the state, its organization, and personnel and the capitalist class as the key influence on the state's role in society.

Instrumentalism

Simply stated, **instrumentalist Marxism** holds that the criminal laws are created and enforced for the protection of the capitalist class. The list of instrumentalist Marxists includes Richard Quinney (1974), Mark Kennedy (1974), David Gordon (1971; 1975), John Hepburn (1977), John Casey (1985), and many others. Instrumentalists argue that class is the most important factor affecting the definition and enforcement of criminal law. Capitalist society is divided into two great classes: the capitalists, defined as the owners of the means of production, and the proletariat, defined as those who sell their labour power for a wage to capitalists. The greater economic power of the capitalist class allows it to control the lawmaking, interpreting, and enforcement apparatus of the state. Those members of the state charged with the day-to-day tasks of making, interpreting, and enforcing the law favour the capitalists in order to enhance or protect their own privileged positions as servants of capitalism.

For example, Goff and Reasons (1978) argue that Canada's anticombines legislation was shaped to minimize government interference in corporate affairs, and furthermore, that it has been enforced in a political fashion. Even the director of investigations under the Combines Act, they say, has used his office to allow corporations to evade prosecution. According to Goff and Reasons, only 0.003 percent of corporate mergers from 1960 to 1972 resulted in charges being laid, and only 0.0005 percent were successfully prosecuted. Thus, the misdeeds of the ruling class are made to seem less significant than those of other groups.

Even the act of defining crimes such as murder, rape, assault, and theft of personal property, and the act of protecting human rights, serve the interests of capital. They do so by making it appear that the state has a general interest in defining these acts and in defending the rights of those who are victimized by violations of the protective statutes governing these acts. In fact, the state creates a smoke screen around the activities of the ruling class that renders those activities invisible and that serves to focus attention on the misdeeds of other classes. Deaths caused by deliberate violation by employers of workplace health and safety laws are treated much less seriously than deaths caused by other deliberate means. According to Laureen Snider (1988), occupational deaths are the third leading cause of death in Canada. She attributes at least half of these deaths to unsafe and illegal working conditions. The mining industry has been particularly dangerous. Decades ago, large numbers of Canadian miners died because of the failure of their employers to protect them from mine hazards. Coal miners died of black lung caused by inhaling coal dust, and fluorspar miners died as a result of inhaling silica dust in unventilated mine shafts. Not only did the mine owners fail to provide safe working conditions, but company doctors were told not to advise the miners of the seriousness of their illness. The loss of 26 miners in a preventable mine explosion at Nova Scotia's Westray mine in 1992 suggests that some mine owners have yet to put their employees' lives above profits.

The Marxist view that capitalists are protected by the state is illustrated by the case of Silco, an Edmonton-based construction company. In 1994, a Silco employee working in Manitoba fell to his death from a homemade man basket attached to an unstable crane boom. The company had received three different orders to improve safety practices earlier in the year but had ignored all of them, including a stop-work order the month of the accident. Despite Silco's obvious negligence, the company received only a $6000 fine for its part in the employee's death (Ward, 1996).

Structuralist Marxism

structuralist Marxism

The view that the state in a capitalist society is set in a context in which its actions will be determined by the necessities of the reproduction and accumulation of capital. The state serves the social order, or structure, within which it is located.

The **structuralist Marxist** approach differs from instrumentalist Marxism. In essence, structuralists reject the instrumentalist notion that the capitalist class acts as if it had one mind and body. They also reject the notion that the state directly serves the interests of the capitalist class. According to the structuralists, the role of the state is to serve the interests of maintaining capitalist relations, not necessarily the interests of specific capitalists. Sometimes laws must be created or enforced in ways that are contrary to the short-term interests of particular capitalists, but are necessary to protect the long-term interests of maintaining capitalist relations.

For example, with respect to law creation, Smandych (1985) argues that the creation of the Canadian anticombines legislation was a symbolic gesture intended to avert a clash between capital and labour. During the late 1800s and early 1900s, labour felt itself increasingly vulnerable to what it considered the excesses of monopoly capitalism. These included poor working conditions, low wages, and failure to recognize the legitimacy of trade unions and collective bargaining. As labour's efforts to resist these excesses became increasingly better organized, the government of the day took a keen interest in the voting power of the emerging labour movement. In order to maintain an image of itself as an honest broker between the two antagonists, and also to maintain capitalist interests in capital accumulation, the state created a weak law. This law gave labour the impression that its voice was being heard, but offered no significant impediment to the accumulation of capital and the continuation of the capitalist system in Canada.

Further, with respect to law enforcement, Balbus (1973) argues that state agents must satisfy the demands of formal legal rationality. State agents cannot violate the law as they see fit because of the checks and balances established in law to prevent such transgressions. The state must follow prescribed legal procedures and apply, without prejudice, universally applicable legal standards. In this way, the law acts as a significant restraint upon the actions of the state and its agents. Balbus is not saying that legal authorities always conform to legal demands. What he is saying is that even when some state agents, especially the police and prosecutors, abandon normal procedure, the people they process are given their day in court. Their appearance in court is subject to formal legal rules, which are difficult, if not impossible, to abandon in such a public forum. State agents can be, and often are, held accountable for their criminal actions and their failure to observe the legal rights of other people. When state agents behave in an unacceptable way, the people whose rights they abuse may be seen as the victims of state power. Thus, the phrase "equality before the law" has a double meaning. On the one hand, the law must treat all who come before it without obvious prejudice with respect to judgements of social or economic background, thereby protecting the disadvantaged from arbitrary decision making. On the other hand, by refusing to consider inequalities in living conditions as legitimate reasons for committing crime, the law protects the state, and thereby reinforces the capitalist system.

In essence, structuralists contend that not only does the structure of the society with its various competing parts, or classes and class fractions, prevent a group from gaining total control of the society, but the structure of the law and law enforcement apparatus itself prevents similar single-interest domination. Nonetheless, the complex structure of the society and the apparent autonomy of the law mask the underlying conflict between capital and labour. This makes the conflict appear to be either nonexistent or irrelevant as a factor contributing to the definition and enforcement of criminal law.

A Theory of Contradictions

A somewhat different approach to Marxist analysis has been adopted by William Chambliss (1986) and others. According to Chambliss, societies are composed of a number of competing interests, and "every society, nation, economic system, and historical period contain within them certain contradictory elements which are the moving force behind social changes—including the creation of law" (Chambliss and Seidman, 1982). From this viewpoint, all societies are characterized by a pattern of conflict resolution and creation, in which resolutions of existing contradictions produce new contradictions in need of solution. Chambliss and Seidman take special care to indicate that people, not systems (as in structuralist approaches), create law, and that it is people who are faced with the task of finding solutions to ever-emerging contradictions.

For example, Hinch (1988a; 1988b; 1991) argues that passage of Canada's sexual assault legislation in 1983 resulted from an attempt to resolve conflicts between men and women over the definition and enforcement of the rape law as it existed prior to 1983. Critics of the old rape law claimed it was openly sexist. Married men could not be charged with raping their wives, and the sexual history of rape victims was subject to scrutiny during a trial, while the sexual history of the offender was not. Law enforcement practices also ensured that women were often treated by the criminal justice system as if they, not the rapists, were the wrongdoers. In order to address these and other problems with the law, reformers sought to amend the law (see Hinch, 1985). Those benefiting from patriarchal and capitalist relations sought either greater protection from false accusations of rape or increased police powers. Other reformers, primarily feminists opposed to patriarchy, claimed that men's concerns over false accusations of rape were unfounded. Feminists sought law reforms, such as lower penalties for sexual assault offences and the removal of the marital privilege, which would make it easier for police to make arrests and for the courts to convict.

The reforms introduced in 1983 did little to alter the basic contradictions in the social and economic positions of men and women (Hinch, 1991). While some sources of conflict between men and women were removed, others remained. The state removed the marital privilege and gave victims of sexual assault greater protection from character assassination in court. However, women's sexual histories can still be examined in court as a means of challenging the victim's credibility, and the social pressures on women that prevent them from reporting victimization at the hands of their husbands have not been affected by the reforms. Hinch argues that these social pressures are frequently a more significant influence than the law on women's decisions to report the abuse they receive from their husbands. In the end, the contradictions of patriarchy and capitalism remain, while men and women remain enmeshed in conflicts; and although these conflicts may lead to further legal reform, it still will not deal with the contradictions that cause the conflicts. It is impossible, then, to change the contradictions by changing the law. A much more profound change in the social order is required for this.

A similar situation exists with regard to labour relations. Concern that the workplace can be dangerous for the worker has been expressed for at least two centuries. Chambliss and Seidman (1982) cite research that indicates that work-related injuries and illnesses cause five times as many Americans to be killed on the job as are murdered in the "conventional" sense. Comparable Canadian data (Reasons et al., 1981) indicate that Canadians are 18 times more likely to die from work-related illness or injury than they are to be murdered. A significant amount of the death and injury is the direct result of employers' failure to comply with existing health and safety laws and of putting profits ahead of safety. Yet the problem does not receive as much attention as conventionally defined murder, and the penalties are far less severe.

Nonetheless, in the face of organized opposition from labour, governments have taken some steps toward reclassifying work-related health hazards as illegal and occasionally criminal. Reasons et al. note that Canadian workers, through their unions and through both legal and illegal strikes, have a long history of fighting dangerous working conditions and have had some success in having legislative changes made to promote greater job safety. Despite opposition by capital, lawmakers have created legislation reducing the amount of freedom employers have in setting conditions of work.

It is also clear that this legislation created new conflicts. The new problems centre on the enforcement process and on deciding whether violations of health and safety legislation are to be labelled as simply illegal or as criminal. Further, while Chambliss and Seidman (1982), Reasons et al. (1981), and DeKeseredy and Hinch (1991) recognize that in certain circumstances, workers have been able to obtain better enforcement of health and safety legislation, they also observe that enforcement practices require further improvement. Indeed, Chambliss and Seidman claim that in some cases, law reforms have actually resulted in more, not less, job-related illness and injury. In such cases, legal bureaucracies with intimate connections to capital fail to take the problem as seriously as they do other forms of crime. Further, the law does not always provide sufficient penalties to force compliance. In some cases, this means that endangering worker safety or health may be termed illegal but not criminal. It may also mean that potential penalties, such as fines, may be interpreted as simply "another cost of doing business."

The more general point is that criminal law should not be regarded as simply the product of the interests of specific capitalists or of the system as a whole. Nor can it be seen as simply the product of struggles between capital and labour or between feminism and patriarchy. Criminal law is a product of the ongoing struggles within capital and patriarchy to control the state for the purpose of creating legislation that resolves conflicts but does not resolve basic contradictions. Given that capitalist and patriarchal forces are stronger and generally better organized than either labour or antipatriarchal forces, it is to be expected that they will have a greater (even if not absolute) influence on law creation and enforcement.

Left Realism

Left realism is the most recent development in Marxist criminology. It emerged during the early 1970s in Britain (see Lea, 1987; Lea and Young, 1984; Matthews, 1987; Young, 1979; 1987), but has also found advocates in Canada (see MacLean, 1989; Currie et al., 1990), the United States (Gross, 1982; Michalowski, 1983), and elsewhere (see Hogg and Brown, 1988). Left realism emerged as a response to a perceived inability of other forms of criminology, including the Marxist variety, to respond to the crime-control concerns of disadvantaged and repressed groups within society. Specifically, they were concerned that law and order issues were being defined by the state in ways that disadvantaged the working class, racial minorities, and women (MacLean, 1991). This was reflected in the fact that conventional criminology devoted much attention to the problem of street crime but ignored the perspectives of those who were the victims of that crime. Left realists set about to redirect the study of crime toward understanding that crime control can be accomplished without the need to adopt repressive measures.

According to Matthews, realist criminology has four central elements:

1. a commitment to detailed empirical investigation;
2. a recognition of the independence and objectivity of criminal activity;
3. an emphasis on the disorganizing effect of crime; and
4. a statement of the possibility and desirability of developing measures to reduce crime. (1987, 371)

Left realists argue that the notoriously problematic nature of crime statistics generated by the police and other sources is no reason to cease doing empirical work. Careful, critical analysis of official crime statistics is needed in order to illustrate the biased functioning of the criminal justice system and to understand the crime process itself. The empirical reality of crime, as revealed through official crime statistics, is that crime is an intraclass, not interclass, activity; that there is universal opposition to street crime; and that lower-class criminals are the most likely to be criminalized by the state (see MacLean, 1986; Young, 1979). Greater effort needs to be devoted to the empirical investigation of the crimes of the powerful, which cost far more than crimes committed by members of the lower class (see Chapter 16).

Realists' concerns over the independence and objectivity of criminal activity are focused on demonstrating that even though the concept of crime itself is problematic, it is independent of the will of particular interests and has a definite impact on social behaviour. Crimes are "conflicts or disputes which cannot be resolved within 'normal' social relations" (Matthews, 1987). Legal crimes are part of the larger process of social control and are an indication that informal control mechanisms are ineffective in controlling some types of conflicts. The objective of criminology is to understand which conflicts require informal rather than formal control strategies.

It is no secret that crime has a negative impact on the quality of human life and on the cohesiveness of society. Crime and disorder go together. In some cases, for example, where people avoid urban areas believed to be frequented by muggers, thieves, and rapists, crime also restricts people's freedom of movement and their activities to areas and situations that reduce the risk of victimization. In urban centres, high-crime areas suggest that no one cares, and so their existence incites still more crime.

Realists argue that the potential to reduce crime through implementation of effective policies is enormous. The task of the left realist is to ensure that crime reduction is achieved through the creation and implementation of policies formulated by the left and not by the right. This means finding ways to allow those most affected by crime to become involved in the crime control process. Working-class involvement in the crime control apparatus of the state risks making that apparatus a more efficient agent of repression of the working class. At the same time, however, it also creates an opportunity for the working class

---

BOX 11.2

FOCUS

Marxist and Crime Research

Traditionally, Marxists preferred historical and qualitative research and have avoided statistical research. However, the left realists have tried to adapt statistical methods to their Marxist social analysis.

One task for the left realist researcher is to determine the nature and extent of corporate crime. However, this is far from being their only concern. Some argue that it is more important to understand the everyday reality of conventional crime. They feel that leaving official agencies, such as the police or Statistics Canada, to measure the "official crime rate" amounts to leaving those with a vested interest in creating a particular image of crime free to create that image. For example, MacLean (1996) says that police data are more closely related to the needs of the agents of control, the police, and their political masters than they are to the community. To overcome the problem, MacLean outlines six principles for conducting local crime surveys: the survey must be local, based on preparatory research, longitudinal, independent, funded in partnership, and sensitive to the experiences of the disenfranchised.

Although some left realists (DeKeseredy, 1996) have conducted national crime surveys, MacLean argues that it is important for the local community to have an indication of the nature of its local crime problem. Crime rates vary from one community to another, and consequently, the policing needs of one community are not necessarily the same as all others. Similarly, the kind of concerns that one community has about its crime problems are not necessarily the same as those of other communities. As MacLean says:

> In order for the crime survey to assist in the documentation of local policing practices, the monitoring of community–police relations, the measurement of the specific patterns of victimization relevant to the community, and the monitoring of the success of various crime control and prevention strategies, in-depth surveys at the local level are required. (1996, 92)

He goes on to caution that conducting a number of local surveys in order to generate national statistics would defeat the purpose of conducting a local survey. The local survey must be able to reflect the local concerns about crime, victimization, policing, and general crime control policies.

(continued)

To meet this objective, MacLean says that local crime surveys must be preceded by a detailed qualitative study. This prestudy should be directed at documenting the concerns of the people in the community. While there may be commonalities in the crime concerns from one community to another, it is also true that specific communities may have crime concerns that are unique to them. For example, people in Vancouver may be concerned about street prostitution, while people in Montreal may have concerns about biker gangs. The concerns may change over time, but it is important to document the local crime problem so that a local crime control strategy can be developed that is best suited to control the type of crime found in that community. Once the prestudy is complete, it is possible to determine the frequency and distribution of the type of crime(s).

It is also important that the local survey be longitudinal. Patterns of crime, and concerns about crime, change over time. Today's crime rate may not be the same as it was in the past. To be able to ascertain patterns or trends in the crime rate, it is necessary to repeat the crime survey over and over again. By repeating the crime survey, it will be possible to change policing patterns and to alter crime control strategies to reflect any changes.

An important pitfall to be avoided, says MacLean, is the tendency to conduct surveys that are dedicated to the needs of the crime control apparatus. He notes that several surveys in Canada have been flawed because they lacked the proper kinds of controls. For example, he observes that the Canadian Urban Victimization Survey (Solicitor General, 1983) was flawed because it was designed to meet the vested interests of the Ministry of the Solicitor General. To overcome this problem, it is important that the survey be conducted by independent academic researchers. This is the only way to ensure that the survey meets a general community interest and not the interests of the police or other official crime control agencies such as the Ministry of the Solicitor General.

The interests of the disenfranchised are a key component in any left realist local crime survey. Disenfranchised groups, such as gays and lesbians, racial minorities, women, and working-class people, are often ignored in the creation of crime control policies and when conducting crime surveys. MacLean argues that it is possible to include the concerns and interests of these people only when the research is conducted by academic researchers who have performed sufficient preparatory research. These are the only people who can distance themselves from the crime control agencies.

to take part in the creation of crime control policies that genuinely reflect its needs. By becoming involved in the creation of crime control strategies and the crime control apparatus, the working class has the opportunity to create crime control measures that, instead of increasing the penalties for crime or increasing the coercive character of the state, *minimize* the "intervention necessary to protect the population against predatory criminal forces—and unallayed market forces" (Young, 1987, 353). Crime control, then, becomes part of the struggle to expand the ability of the working class to control its own living conditions. If it does not become involved, it abdicates this potential and must therefore live under crime control policies that reflect the concerns of the upper class.

For example, Aboriginal peoples have argued that creation of a separate criminal justice system designed by and for them would reduce the harmful effect of having an alien system forced upon them. Several provincial task forces on criminal justice have also made this recommendation. Another initiative

restorative justice

A system of justice that tries to reconcile victims and offenders and to reintegrate offenders into their communities.

compatible with left realism is **restorative justice**, a system that is intended to restore social relationships rather than simply to punish (Church Council on Justice and Corrections, 1996). Advocates of restorative justice seek to return the focus of the justice system to repairing the harm that has been done to the victim and to the community. A key element of restorative justice is the involvement of the victim and other members of the community as active participants in the process. The focus of the restorative justice approach is to reconcile offenders with those they have harmed and to help communities to reintegrate victims and offenders. Restorative justice has its roots in traditional societies where the restoration of order was crucial to society's survival. In North America, Aboriginal communities used a variety of different methods, including circle sentencing, to resolve disputes. In recent years, these traditional practices have been revived and have been modified in innovative ways. Two of the most widespread contemporary restorative justice methods are victim–offender reconciliation and family group conferencing.

Victim–offender reconciliation was devised in Elmira, Ontario, in 1974 as an initiative by two individuals to persuade a judge to deal in a positive fashion with two youths who had vandalized property belonging to 22 different victims. Rather than a normal court disposition that may well have involved incarceration, the offence was handled in the community. Mediators worked with the victims and the offenders to reach a resolution that was acceptable to all parties. As a result, the boys had to deal personally with each of their victims and to make restitution for the damage they had caused. The restorative process gave victims a chance to have a say in what happened and gave offenders the chance to make amends.

Family group conferencing is a restorative justice technique that had its origins in New Zealand and is a type of circle sentencing. The RCMP has selected family group conferencing as one of the ways its detachments will work with communities to try to reduce crime, so use of this method of conflict resolution should become common in Canada. Family group conferencing typically applies to young offenders and normally involves the victim, offender, and as many of their family and friends as possible. Professional or community workers may also participate. A typical family group conference involves about a dozen people. When adult offenders are involved, the process is called community group conferencing and is more likely to involve community members rather than families. The goal of the conference is to allow those affected by the crime the opportunity to resolve the case in an environment that is supportive of both victim and offender. A coordinator allows all parties to speak about the case and then leads the conference into a discussion of what might be done to repair the harm done to the victim. Victims and their family and friends outline their expectations, and offenders and their family and friends respond. Negotiation continues until a plan is agreed on and written down. The coordinator then establishes mechanisms for enforcing the plan. The family and friends of both the victim and offender are encouraged to offer continuing help to ensure the resolution arrived at during the conference is actually carried out in the community.

BOX 11.3

An Alternative Mi'kmaq Worldview

In the Mi'kmaq worldview, individual behaviour faithfully accommodates collective culture; there is a firm consensus of proper respect of inherent dignities. The mechanism by which individual passions are prevented from wreaking havoc on society is deference to shared values, reinforced by family opinion and rewarded with honour and respect. Order in society presupposes and evokes order in the soul. Order is a matter of kinship, education, and equal right to be heard and heeded by others. Coercive institutions are generally absent, if not vigorously opposed. Aggressiveness is considered wrongful and contrary to human dignity.

Like other Indigenous worldviews, the Mi'kmaq only recognizes binding obligations which arise from consent. The most striking trait of the consensual order is the almost exclusive commitment to custom or interactional law. Written laws, codes, and regulations are still unknown, and imposed authoritative systems are kept within strictest limits. To codify customary forms of behaviour or law is to destroy the living flexibility that is their greatest virtue.

Mi'kmaq could violate the spiritual order. But their violations are not seen as derived from a concept of wrongness. The idea of change creates an understanding of mistakes and conflicts. Violating the harmony of the natural order unleashes dangerous forces in both the spiritual and the social realm, which articulate a conflict. Being Mi'kmaq means the ability to withdraw from conflict and to think good thoughts.

Traditionally, the very fact of seeking a "political" solution to a situation was cause for concern. Most problems were resolved with the extended family, not by the Mawi'omi or district chiefs. Solutions were likewise spontaneous and contextual, not based on logical reasoning, rules, or trying to control events. Instead, like the ecosystem, resolutions were the shortest paths back to equilibrium, which depended entirely on the circumstances in each case. Usually, the families were satisfied with whatever solution presented itself—happy that the conflict was over and harmony restored. Harmony, not justice, is the ideal.

There is no concept of an "innocent" or "guilty" individual. The priority is not determining culpability, but resolving the conflict quickly to maintain harmony. If the offender repents and wishes to make peace, an exchange of presents and other suitable atonements takes away bad feeling and restores good thoughts.

Source: Klikeptin Alex Denny. (1992). "Beyond the Marshall Inquiry: An Alternative Mi'kmaq Worldview and Justice System." In Joy Mannette (ed.), *Elusive Justice: Beyond the Marshall Inquiry*. Halifax: Fernwood Publishing, pp. 103–4. Reprinted with permission.

The success of the restorative justice movement shows that ideas developed by critical criminologists can lead to a better understanding of ways of reducing crime and building healthier communities by involving citizens, including those belonging to marginalized groups, a meaningful voice in the justice system.

Critiques of Marxist Criminology

One of the most frequent criticisms of Marxist criminology, especially instrumentalism, is that it oversimplifies the complexity of capitalist societies. Toby (1980), for example, has argued that it actually glorifies predatory crime when it claims that criminals are engaged in rebellious behaviour fighting against the evils of capitalist repression. However, even some Marxists would agree that the instrumentalist conception is overly romantic (Hinch, 1983; Matthews, 1987). Hinch (1983) is also critical of the instrumentalist notion that socialist societies can be both free of crime and free of conflict. In this context, Sykes's (1974) critique of conflict theory would appear to be equally relevant as a critique of both instrumentalist and structuralist Marxism. Conflict theory and instrumentalist and structuralist Marxism have an overly simplistic conceptualization of the relation between power and social interests. Turk (1977) adds that Marxists are often guilty of relying more on assertion than on the verifiability of their claims (see also Downes and Rock, 1982).

Structuralist Marxism is also said to lack a full understanding of how real people create and sustain social systems. By placing so much emphasis on the system, structuralist argument loses contact with the real people engaged in the struggle.

The theory that criminal definitions emerge out of a continual process of finding solutions to conflicts embedded in the contradictions of patriarchy and capitalism fails to specify how the cycle of "contradiction, resolution, contradiction" can be brought to a conclusion. A central part of this thesis is that the resolution of contradictions always leaves the forces of capital in secure control, even if they must encounter new difficulties in maintaining that control. Thus, this orientation does not resolve the problems of the structuralist argument and specifically, its assumption of a relatively independent "system." Hinch's negative interpretation of the effectiveness of the 1983 reform of the Canadian sexual assault law may also be countered by the fact that the law seems to have accomplished one of its major objectives: to encourage more women to report these events to the police. Further, as Gunn and Linden (1993) indicate, the reforms did result in some transformation in the attitudes shown toward victims of sexual assault. This is most clearly seen in the improved treatment by criminal justice workers and in the finding that female victims are more likely to say that they have been treated fairly.

Left realists have been severely criticized by other Marxists who argue that any effort to utilize the state to achieve socialist aims is doomed. The state, they argue, serves the interests of those forces that created it, the interests of capital. Thus, cooperation with the state as recommended by left realists will only help the state control the working class. It will force the working class to play the game according to rules established by the state in the interests of capital.

Notwithstanding these various critiques, it can be said that Marxist criminology has done much to challenge other approaches to criminology to take issues of class and class domination seriously. For example, even though instrumentalist Marxism has been criticized for being overly simplistic and deterministic, it has forced other theorists to respond to the critique that society is dominated by a ruling elite. Similarly, structuralist Marxism has forced greater recognition of the ways in which social structures infringe upon and limit social action, especially with regard to the state and legal structures. Left realism has gone even further. It has challenged other Marxists to examine ways in which Marxian analysis can and should be used to improve social conditions for racial minorities, women, and the working class as a whole.

TABLE 11.1 Conflict and Marxist Theories

Theory	Theorists	Key Elements
Cultural conflict	Sellin, Sutherland	Crime occurs because the norms of some groups differ from those of the dominant culture.
Group conflict	Vold	Social groups try to influence the creation and enforcement of the criminal law. Those with opposing viewpoints may be criminalized.
Radical feminism	Brownmiller	The content of the law and the practices of law enforcement have strengthened and entrenched male dominance.
Socialist feminism	Messerschmidt	Men in all classes commit more crimes than women because they have more power and more opportunity.
Instrumental Marxism	Quinney	Criminal laws are created and enforced for the benefit and the protection of the capitalist class.
Structuralist Marxism	Balbus	Sometimes laws must be created and enforced in ways that are contradictory to the short-term interests of particular capitalists in order to protect the long-term interests of the capitalist system.
Contradictions theory	Chambliss, Hinch	All societies are characterized by a pattern of conflict resolution and creation in which resolutions of existing contradictions produce new contradictions in need of solution.
Left realism	Matthews, MacLean	Advocate the scientific study of crime and a system of crime control that does not involve repressive measures.

CONCLUSION

The theoretical models summarized in this chapter offer profoundly differing conceptions of contemporary social life. In each case, the theorists present data that they believe demonstrate the validity of their own theory or undermine the credibility of opposed theories. But the extent to which any one theory is accepted as an accurate statement describing the nature and origins of criminal behaviour is dependent on factors other than the accuracy of its propositions and observations. As Thomas Kuhn (1962) explains, theories may gain acceptance or be rejected for reasons other than their scientific validity. Their reception may also be based on their ability to conform to prevailing social attitudes and beliefs. Theories that conform most to prevailing beliefs or ideologies are likely to gain more acceptance than those which resist or criticize dominant ideologies.

Nonetheless, the popularity of a theory is not an accurate test of its validity. Criminologists judge the credibility of a theory by assessing the methods by which its practitioners gather data and assess and interpret the data. The disagreements that persist even after these assessments are made reflect the commitment of the assessors to their theoretical orientation, as well as the ongoing debates within criminology over appropriate research methods. For example, significant differences exist among criminologists regarding the use of official crime data as an indicator of the crime rate and of who commits crimes (see Chapters 4 and 5). So long as these kinds of differences exist, there will continue to be differences of opinion regarding theories and their acceptability.

SUMMARY

- Conflict theorists argue that contemporary societies are characterized by conflict and dissension.

- According to cultural conflict theorists, all cultures establish their own codes of behaviour. Bringing divergent cultures into contact within the same society results in conflict. This conflict may result in one culture using the law to control the behaviour of others.

- Group conflict theorists such as Vold proposed that the ability to influence the creation and enforcement of criminal law represents the triumph of an alliance of one set of groups over other groups.

- Influenced by the work of Weber, conflict theorists such as Dahrendorf and Turk argued that Marxists had transformed criminology into a partisan enterprise by overemphasizing the role of class in conflict among social groups. Their nonideological approach allows them to be critical of the processes of law creation and enforcement without necessarily calling for the destruction of societal institutions.

- Radical feminism and socialist feminism are two of the feminist approaches to crime. Radical feminists argue that patriarchy is universal and results in men using violence to maintain their dominance over women. Socialist feminists attempt to merge the radical feminist notion of patriarchy with the Marxist emphasis on social class. Women are oppressed by virtue of both gender and class.

- Instrumentalist Marxists maintain that the criminal laws are created and enforced for the protection of the capitalist class. Structuralist Marxists reject the notion that the state serves the interests of the capitalist class directly. They say that society is so divided that no single class can dominate the state. Nonetheless, the law does protect the state and preserve the capitalist system.

Left realism represents an attempt to re-orient Marxist theory to respond to the crime control concerns of disadvantaged groups.

QUESTIONS FOR CRITICAL THINKING

1. Cultural conflict theorists claim that bringing diverse cultures into contact within the same society can result in conflict. Members of the dominant culture may try to use the law to control the behaviour of the groups with less power. Can you think of an example from Canadian society where this has occurred?
2. Discuss similarities and differences between feminist theories and other conflict explanations of crime.
3. Look through your local newspaper to find cases in which white-collar criminals have been convicted and sentenced. Do you think the sentences given to these offenders are proportionate to the harm they caused? Do you think that high-status offenders are generally treated more or less harshly than low-status offenders?
4. Left realists have proposed that local crime surveys provide the best way of understanding the reality of conventional crime. How will these surveys help communities deal with their own crime problems? Why do left realists suggest that these surveys are an improvement over traditional crime statistics?
5. Many Aboriginal groups and several government commissions have proposed that the only way that Aboriginal people can obtain justice is to have a separate criminal justice system that accommodates traditional customs and practices. What do you think would be some of the advantages and disadvantages of separate systems?

NET WORK

Conflict theories focus on the lack of consensus among members of society about whether certain acts should be criminal. Use the Internet to see how two competing groups present their sides of a debate over controversial legal issues. One example is the harmfulness of marijuana:

■ Pro-marijuana:

   http://norml.org

   www.cheeo.com/pro_marijuana.htm

■ Anti-marijuana:

   ehrweb.aaas.org/~sbf/5g.htm

Another is the issue of abortion:

■ Pro-choice:

   www.caral.ca

- Pro-life:

   www.lifesite.net/clc/index.html

   Do you think the Internet is an effective way for these groups to get out their message, or do you think that these websites will attract only those who already support these points of view?

KEY TERMS

career criminality
Chicago School
conduct norms
criminal definition
economic determinism
individual pathology
instrumentalist Marxism

patriarchy
radical feminism
restorative justice
social disorganization theory
socialist feminism
structuralist Marxism
symbolic communications

SUGGESTED READING

Boyle, Christine. (1984). *Sexual Assault.* Toronto: Carswell. An excellent radical feminist review of the changes to the sexual assault laws introduced in 1983. It is must reading for anyone interested in understanding this reform measure.

MacLean, Brian D. (1996). "A Program of Local Crime Survey Research for Canada." In Brian MacLean (ed.), *Crime and Society: Readings in Critical Criminology* (pp. 73–105). Toronto: Copp Clark. A good discussion of left realism applied to the Canadian context.

McMullan, John L. (1992). *Beyond the Limits of the Law: Corporate Crime and Law and Order.* Halifax: Fernwood Publishing. An articulate assessment of the state of corporate crime research, including suggestions for methods of controlling corporate crime.

Turk, Austin. (1982). *Political Criminality.* Beverly Hills: Sage. An assessment of the context and extent of political crime by the leading advocate of nonpartisan conflict theory.

Vold, George B., Thomas J. Bernard, and Jeffrey B. Snipes. (1998). *Theoretical Criminology* (4th ed.). New York: Oxford University Press. This revision by Bernard of the classic text by Vold contains an updated version of Vold's theory, augmented by reference to contemporary conflict theorists.

BIBLIOGRAPHY

Balbus, Isaac. (1973). *The Dialectics of Legal Repression: Black Rebels before the American Criminal Courts.* New York: Russell Sage Foundation.

Bankowski, Zenon, Geoff Mungham, and Peter Young. (1977). "Radical Criminology or Radical Criminologist." *Contemporary Crises* 1(21) (January):37–54.

Beirne, P., and J. Messerschmidt. (1991). *Criminology.* San Diego: Harcourt Brace Jovanovich.

Boyle, Christine. (1984). *Sexual Assault.* Toronto: Carswell.

Brownmiller, Susan. (1975). *Against Our Will: Men, Women and Rape*. New York: Simon & Schuster.

Casey, John. (1985). "Corporate Crime and the State: Canada in the 1980s." In Thomas Fleming (ed.), *The New Criminologies in Canada: State, Crime, and Control* (pp. 100–11). Toronto: Oxford University Press.

Chambliss, William J. (1986). "On Lawmaking." In Steven Brickey and Elizabeth Comack (eds.), *The Social Basis of Law*. Toronto: Garamond Press.

Chambliss, William J., and Robert Seidman. (1982). *Law, Order and Power* (2nd ed.). Reading, Mass.: Addison-Wesley.

Church Council on Justice and Corrections. (1996). *Satisfying Justice*. Ottawa: Church Council on Justice and Corrections.

Cohen, Albert K. (1955). *Delinquent Boys: The Culture of the Gang*. New York: The Free Press of Glencoe.

Cohen, L., and C. Backhouse. (1980a). "Desexualizing Rape: A Dissenting View on the Proposed Rape Amendments." *Canadian Woman Studies* 2(4).

———. (1980b). "Putting Rape in Its Place." *Maclean's* (June 30):6.

Currie, Dawn, Walter S. DeKeseredy, and Brian D. MacLean. (1990). "Reconstructing Social Order and Social Control: Police Accountability in Canada." *The Journal of Human Justice* 2(1):29–53.

DeKeseredy, Walter. (1996). "Left Realism and Woman Abuse in Dating." In Brian MacLean (ed.), *Crime and Society: Readings in Critical Criminology* (pp. 183–206). Toronto: Copp Clark.

DeKeseredy, Walter, and Ronald Hinch. (1991). *Woman Abuse: Sociological Perspectives*. Toronto: Thomson Educational Publishers.

Downes, David, and Paul Rock. (1982). *Understanding Deviance: A Guide to the Sociology of Crime and Rule Breaking*. Oxford: Clarendon Press/Oxford University Press.

Eisenstein, Zillah. (1979). "Some Notes on the Relations of Capitalist Patriarchy." In Zillah Eisenstein (ed.), *Capitalist Patriarchy and the Case for Socialist Feminism* (pp. 5–14). New York: Monthly Review Press.

Goff, Colin, and Charles E. Reasons. (1978). *Corporate Crime in Canada*. Toronto: Prentice Hall Canada.

Gordon, David M. (1971). "Class and the Economics of Crime." *The Review of Radical Economics* 3(3):51–72.

———. (1975). "Class and the Economics of Crime." In William J. Chambliss (ed.), *Criminal Law in Action*. Santa Barbara, Calif.: John Wiley and Sons.

Gross, Bertram. (1982). "Some Anti-Crime Strategies for Progressives." *Crime and Social Justice* 19:51–54.

Gunn, R., and R. Linden. (1993). "Evaluating the Impact of Legal Reform: Canada's New Sexual Assault Laws." In J. Hudson and J. Roberts (eds.), *Evaluating Justice: Canadian Policies and Programs* (pp. 135–54). Toronto: Thompson Educational Publishing.

Hagan, John. (1974). "Criminal Justice and Native People." *Canadian Review of Sociology and Anthropology*, Special Issue (August):220–36.

Hale, Sylvia. (1990). *Controversies in Sociology: A Canadian Introduction*. Toronto: Copp Clark Pitman Ltd.

Hartmann, H. (1977). "Capitalism, Patriarchy, and Job Segregation by Sex." In N. Glazer and H.Y. Waehrer (eds.), *Woman in a Man Made World* (pp. 137–69). Chicago: Rand McNally.

———. (1981). "The Unhappy Marriage of Marxism and Feminism: Toward a More Progressive Union." In R. Dale et al. (eds.), *Politics, Patriarchy and Practice*, Vol. 2 (pp. 191–219). Milton Keynes: Open University.

Hepburn, John R. (1977). "Social Control and the Legal Order: Legitimate Repression in a Capitalist State." *Contemporary Crises* 1(1):77–90.

Hinch, Ronald. (1983). "Marxist Criminology in the 1970s: Clarifying the Clutter." *Crime and Social Justice* (Summer):65–74.

———. (1985). "Canada's New Sexual Assault Laws: A Step Forward for Women?" *Contemporary Crises* 9(1):33–44.

———. (1988a). "Enforcing Canada's Sexual Assault Laws: An Exploratory Study." *Atlantis* 14(1):109–15.

———. (1988b). "Inconsistencies and Contradictions in Canada's Sexual Assault Law." *Canadian Public Policy* xiv(3):282–94.

———. (1989a). "It's Marxism, Not Conflict Theory." *Canadian Critical Criminology* 2/3/4:2–8.

———. (1989b). "Teaching Critical Criminology and Critical Justice Studies in Canada." *Journal of Human Justice* 1(1):63–76.

———. (1991). "Contradictions, Conflicts and Dilemmas in Canada's Sexual Assault Law." In Gregg Barak (ed.), *Crimes by the State: The Politics of Governmental Control* (pp. 233–51). Albany: State University of New York Press.

Hirst, Paul Q. (1975). "Marx and Engels on Law, Crime and Morality." In Ian Taylor, Paul Walton, and Jock Young (eds.), *Critical Criminology* (pp. 203–32). London: Routledge and Kegan Paul.

Hogg, Russell, and David Brown. (1988). "Law and Order Politics, Left Realism and Criminology: An Overview." Paper presented at the Annual Conference of the American Society of Criminology, Chicago, November 9–12.

Kennedy, Mark. (1974). "Beyond Incrimination." *Catalyst* 1(1):1–37.

Kuhn, Thomas. (1962). *The Structure of Scientific Revolutions.* Chicago: University of Chicago Press.

Lacombe, D. (1988). *Ideology and Public Policy: The Case against Pornography.* Toronto: Garamond Press.

Lea, John. (1987). "Left Realism: A Defence." *Contemporary Crises* 11(4):357–70.

Lea, John, and Jock Young. (1984). *What Is to Be Done about Law and Order?* London: Penguin Books.

Lowenberger, L., and R. Landau. (1982). "A Rape by Any Other Name." *Broadside* 3(9):3.

Luxton, M. (1980). *More Than a Labour of Love.* Toronto: The Women's Press.

MacLean, Brian D. (1986). "Introduction: Critical Criminology and Some Limitations of Traditional Inquiry." In Brian D. MacLean (ed.), *The Political Economy of Crime: Readings for a Critical Criminology.* Scarborough: Prentice Hall Canada.

———. (1989). "Left Realism and Police Accountability in Canada." Paper presented at the Annual Conference of the Canadian Sociology and Anthropology Association, Quebec, June 4.

———. (1991). "The Origins of Left Realism." In Brian D. MacLean and Dragan Milovanovic (eds.), *New Directions in Critical Criminology* (pp. 9–13). Vancouver: Collective Press.

———. (1996). "A Program of Local Crime Survey Research for Canada." In Brian MacLean (ed.), *Crime and Society: Readings in Critical Criminology* (pp. 73–105). Toronto: Copp Clark.

Marx, Karl. (1979). "Apologist Conception of the Productivity of All Professions." In Maureen Cain and Alan Hunt (eds.), *Marx and Engels on Law* (pp. 191–92). London: Academic Press.

Marx, Karl, and Friedrich Engels. (1971). *Manifesto of the Communist Party*. Moscow: Progress Publishers.

Matthews, Roger. (1987). "Taking Realist Criminology Seriously." *Contemporary Crises* 11(4):371–98.

Messerschmidt, J. (1986). *Capitalism, Patriarchy, and Crime: Toward a Socialist Feminist Criminology*. Totowa, N.J.: Roman and Littlefield.

Michalowski, Ray. (1983). "Crime Control in the 1980s: A Progressive Agenda." *Crime and Social Justice* 19:13–22.

Miles, Angela. (1985). "Feminism, Equality and Liberation." *Canadian Journal of Women and the Law* 1(1):42–68.

Quinney, Richard. (1970). *The Social Reality of Crime*. Boston: Little, Brown and Company.

———. (1974). *Critique of Legal Order*. Boston: Little, Brown and Company.

Reasons, Charles E., Lois L. Ross, and Craig Paterson. (1981). *Assault on the Worker: Occupational Health and Safety in Canada*. Toronto: Butterworths.

Schwendinger, J.R., and H. Schwendinger. (1983). *Rape and Inequality*. Beverly Hills: Sage.

Sellin, Thorsten. (1938). *Culture Conflict and Crime*. New York: Social Science Research Council.

Smandych, Russell. (1985). "Marxism and the Creation of Law: Re-Examining the Origins of Canadian Anti-Combines Legislation." In Thomas Fleming (ed.), *The New Criminologies in Canada: State, Crime, and Control* (pp. 87–99). Toronto: Oxford University Press.

Smith, D.E. (1985). "Women, Class and Family." In Varda Burstyn and D.E. Smith, *Women, Class, Family and the State* (pp. 1–44). Toronto: Garamond Press.

Snider, Laureen. (1988). "Commercial Crime." In Vincent F. Sacco (ed.), *Deviance, Conformity and Control in Canadian Society* (pp. 231–83). Scarborough: Prentice Hall Canada.

Solicitor General Canada. (1983). "Victims of Crime." *Canadian Urban Victimization Survey*. Ottawa: Solicitor General Canada.

Sutherland, Edwin. H. (1939). *The Principles of Criminology* (3rd ed.). Philadelphia: Lippincott.

———. (1947). *The Principles of Criminology* (4th ed.). Philadelphia: Lippincott.

Sykes, Gresham M. (1974). "The Rise of Critical Criminology." *Journal of Criminal Law and Criminology* 65:206–14.

Tappan, Paul. (1947). "Who Is the Criminal?" *American Sociological Review* 12:96–102.

Taylor, Ian, and Paul Walton. (1975). "Radical Deviancy Theory and Marxism: A Reply to Paul Q. Hirst's 'Marx and Engels on Law, Crime and Morality.'" In Ian Taylor, Paul Walton, and Jock Young (eds.), *Critical Criminology* (pp. 95–122). London: Routledge and Kegan Paul.

Toby, Jackson. (1980). "The New Criminology Is the Old Baloney." In James Inciardi (ed.), *Radical Criminology: The Coming Crises* (pp. 124–32). Beverly Hills: Sage.

Turk, Austin. (1969). *Criminality and Legal Order*. Chicago: Rand McNally.

———. (1977). "Class, Conflict and Criminalization." *Sociological Focus* 10:209–20.

Vold, George. (1958). *Theoretical Criminology*. New York: Oxford University Press.

Vold, George B., Thomas J. Bernard, and Jeffrey B. Snipes. (1998). *Theoretical Criminology* (4th ed.). New York: Oxford University Press.

Ward, Mike. (1996). "Firm Fined $6,000 After Man Killed in Unsafe Workplace." *Winnipeg Free Press* (March 7).

Wood, Robert E. (1983). "Conflict Theory as Pedagogy: A Critique from the Left." *Teaching Sociology* 10(4):463–85.

Young, Jock. (1979). "Left Idealism, Reformism, and Beyond: From New Criminology to Marxism." In Bob Fine, Richard Kinsey, John Lea, Sol Picciotto, and Jock Young (eds.), *Capitalism and the Rule of Law: From Deviancy Theory to Marxism* (pp. 13–28). London: Hutchinson and Company.

———. (1987). "The Tasks Facing a Realist Criminology." *Contemporary Crises* 11(4):337–56.

Interactionist Theories

12

ROBERT A. STEBBINS
University of Calgary

S train and conflict theories deal with causes of crime at the level of social structure. Strain theorists related crime to variables such as cultural goals and the access to opportunities that was provided by society. For conflict theorists, the cleavages between different groups in society and the power relationships among these groups were critical in explaining criminality. Interactionist theories turn our attention to the smaller details of social life. They consider the ways in which crime is a consequence of our relationships with other people and of the social meaning of those relationships.

One of the most important concepts for interactionist theories of crime is the deviant career. This is the passage of an individual through the stages of one or more related deviant identities. This notion is at the heart of labelling theory, which explains how the social response to initial, tentative acts of deviance can move a person toward a deviant identity and a deviant career. The other important interactionist theory discussed in this chapter—differential association—outlines the ways in which people learn to be criminals through their interaction with other criminals and how they come to acquire a criminal identity.

After reading this chapter, you should be able to

- Describe primary and secondary deviation and explain how primary deviation can be transformed into secondary deviation.
- Understand the process of drift among juvenile delinquents.
- Explain the role of moral entrepreneurs in creating and enforcing the law.
- Discuss the various contingencies that criminals encounter in their deviant careers.
- Understand how people can be socialized into a life of crime.
- Outline the strengths and limitations of interactionist theories of deviance.

Interactionist theory in criminology centres on the interchanges people have with one another and on the meanings of these interchanges in the past, present, and future. Herbert Blumer (1986) notes that **symbolic interactionism**, the broader theory from which the interactionist theories of crime are derived, rests on three premises. First, people act toward the human and nonhuman objects in their lives according to the meanings that those objects have for them. Second, the meaning of those objects for each individual emerges from interactions between him or her and other people. Third, the meanings of objects

LEARNING OBJECTIVES

symbolic interactionism

A sociological perspective that focuses on the dynamics of how people interpret social situations and negotiate their meaning with others. It differs from more structurally focused perspectives in seeing individuals as actively creating the social world rather than just acting within the constraints of culture and *social structure*.

learned in this manner are applied and occasionally modified as individuals interpret how the objects and their meanings fit particular social situations with reference to them and their reasons for being there.

Much of this chapter is about criminal interactions, meanings, interpretations, and situations. Before turning to these processes, however, let us set the stage for discussion with a brief illustration of the three premises operating in the sphere of crime. The following interview with Allen, about 20 years old, shows how the meaning of a situation changed through social interaction with other people on the scene in an all-night drugstore:

> From what I understand from them, they didn't go in there with the intent to rob or beat anybody up or anything. I think they only really wanted to buy some gum and cigarettes, but by being drunk, they was talking pretty tough, and so the lady behind the counter automatically got scared.... The druggist ... got a little pushy or ordered them out of the store, and by them being all fired up, naturally the next thing they did was jump on him.
>
> So now what do you have? You've got a drugstore. You've got a scared lady in the corner somewhere with her hands over her face. You've got a beat-up druggist laying on the floor. You've got three dudes that came in for chewing gum and cigarettes, but now they got two cash registers. So what do they do? They take the cash. Wasn't nothing to stop them, and it was there. Why would they leave it? They're thieves anyway and supposed to be hustlers.... There wasn't nothing to stop them, so they just took the money. (Katz, 1990)

THE DEVIANT CAREER

labelling

According to labelling theory, deviance is not a quality of the act but of the label that others attach to the act. This raises the question of who applies the label and who is labelled. The application of a label and the response of others to the label may result in a person becoming committed to a deviant identity.

career

In common use, this refers to the sequence of stages through which people in a particular occupational sector move during the course of their employment. It has also been applied to analyzing the various stages of an individual's involvement with criminal activity.

Interactionism centres chiefly on what happens to criminals once their deviant activities commence. Interactionists have observed, for example, that some groups or individuals have enough power to force the label of deviant on other less powerful groups or individuals. The **labelling** process, however, is by no means accurate. It is not even always fair. Some people who have deviated escape public detection of their behaviour. Some who have not deviated are nonetheless labelled as having done so, despite their protests to the contrary. The application of the deviant label is sometimes subject to considerable negotiation between possibly deviant people and those in a position to apply the label of deviant to them.

Thus, interactionist theory in criminology helps explain the establishment of moral rules, their application through labelling, and the long-term consequences of these two processes for deviants and for society. In interactionist theory, labelling and its consequences are viewed as unfolding within the deviant career.

A **career**, whether in deviance or a legitimate occupation, is the passage of an individual through recognized stages in one or more related identities. Careers are further composed of the adjustment to, and interpretations of, the contingencies and turning points encountered at each stage. For example, Short

(1990) notes that careers in youth crime are likely to be prolonged after certain turning points are reached. One turning point is the early onset of delinquent activities; another is the development of an interest in drugs. The inability to find legitimate employment, a career contingency, also contributes to continued criminality. The type of offence, however, has been found to be unrelated to the length of careers in youth crime and even to the rate at which it is perpetrated. During the careers of young offenders and other deviants, there is a sense of continuity. This sense is fostered by the perception of increasing opportunities, sophistication, and perhaps recognition among one's associates for skill in, or at least commitment to, the special endeavour.

Primary Deviation

Edwin Lemert (1972) has contributed two important concepts to the study of deviant careers: **primary deviation** and **secondary deviation**. Primary deviation occurs with little change in the individual's everyday routine or lifestyle. In general, this will be the case when the individual engages in the deviance infrequently, has few compunctions about it, and encounters few practical problems when doing it. A person who occasionally smokes marijuana supplied by someone else exemplifies primary deviation.

Primary deviation occurs in the early stages of the deviant career, between the first deviant act and some indefinite point at which deviance becomes a way of life and secondary deviation (discussed later) sets in. According to Matza (1969), one precondition of deviance is the willingness to engage in it. That is, the individual must have an affinity, innate or acquired, for the intended act (for example, theft, homicide, drug use). The affinity helps him or her choose among existing options. By way of illustration, imagine an individual who believes that the rich cheat others to get their money. This individual has an affinity for stealing from the rich. That affinity could lead the individual into crimes against the rich when faced with such unpleasant alternatives as poverty, unemployment, or tedious manual labour.

Behind the willingness to engage in deviance is a weak commitment to conventional norms and identities. At the same time, few young people have a strong value commitment to deviant norms and identities. Instead, they **drift** between the world of respectability and the world of deviance. They are "neither compelled to deeds nor freely choosing them; neither different in any simple or fundamental sense from the law abiding, nor the same; conforming to certain traditions in … life while partially unreceptive to other more conventional traditions" (Matza, 1990).

Matza was writing about American males who were young offenders. He found these youths firmly attached to certain marginal, masculine, *subterranean traditions* or ways of life. They found satisfaction in drinking, smoking, renouncing work, being tough, and pursuing the hedonistic pleasures of "real" men. Matza's subjects looked upon themselves as grown and mature, but their behaviour was hardly a true picture of adult life in general in the United States.

Lemert explains how this peculiar orientation can set one adrift toward deviance:

primary deviation
Where the individual commits deviant acts but does not adopt a primary self-identity as a deviant.

secondary deviation
Occurs when an individual accepts the label of deviant. This results in the adoption of a deviant self-identity that confirms and stabilizes the deviant lifestyle.

drift
A psychological state of weak normative attachment to either deviant or conventional ways.

While some fortunate individuals by insightful endowment or by virtue of the stabilizing nature of their situation can foresee more distant social consequences of their actions and behave accordingly, not so for most people. Much human behaviour is situationally oriented and geared to meeting the many and shifting claims which others make upon them. The loose structuring and swiftly changing facade and content of modern social situations frequently make it difficult to decide which means will insure the ends sought. Often choice is a compromise between what is sought and what can be sought.... All this makes me believe that most people drift into deviance by specific actions rather than by informed choices of social roles and statuses. (Lemert, 1972)

Social control has failed for the groups of young offenders and young adults. This failure occurs because it is important for each deviant individual to be in good standing with his or her friends in the group. He or she attains good standing by honouring and practising the marginal, or subterranean, traditions that Matza describes. The quest for honour among peers helps explain how entire groups of youth can drift toward deviance (Hirschi, 1969).

It appears that much, if not all, of this is applicable to Canada. For instance, a comparative study conducted in California and Alberta indicates that ties to peers are important considerations among the sample of delinquent youth, while being in touch with home and school are valued much less (Linden and Fillmore, 1981).

The young offender subculture (see Chapter 10) is composed of many elements, some of the most important being the **moral rhetorics** (Schwendinger and Schwendinger, 1985) that are used to justify deviant behaviour. Each rhetoric consists of a set of guiding principles that is largely taken for granted, sometimes logically inconsistent, and always selectively applied according to the social situations in which youth find themselves. The rhetoric of *egoism* is most often used by those who still feel guilty about their deviant acts. These are typically early offenders, who have learned various ways to neutralize the **stigma** that comes with their behaviour, such as the claim that they steal in response to the greed and immorality of shopkeepers whose prices are unfair. Later young offenders are more likely to use the *instrumental* rhetoric to justify their acts. Here they stress the cunning and power that they can bring to bear against people who are otherwise more powerful and uncontrollable. Fraud, deceit, and violence are used in the pursuit of deviant aims whenever they appear to pay off, whenever they can take advantage of a weak moment in the lives of such people. The main point of this is that young offenders, like people in many other walks of life, can justify what they do. Though the law-abiding world sees it otherwise, the offenders have their own ways of defending their deviant acts as morally right.

During the primary deviation stages of the deviant career, young offenders and young adults drift, in part, because they lack a value commitment to either conventional or deviant values. Value commitment is an attitude toward an identity, an attitude that develops when a person gains exceptional rewards from taking on that identity (Stebbins, 1970). Young men and women drifting

moral rhetoric

In the study of crime, this is the set of claims and assertions that deviants make to justify their deviant behaviour. The moral rhetoric of a group is an important component of socialization into a deviant identity.

stigma

As used by Erving Goffman (1922–1982), a characteristic of an individual that is given a negative evaluation by others and thus distorts and discredits the public identity of the person. For example, a prison record may become a stigmatized attribute. The stigma may lead to the adoption of a self-identity that incorporates the negative social evaluation.

between criminal and respectable pursuits have found few, if any, enduring benefits in either type of activity. Nonetheless, this pattern begins to change as they begin to have more contact with the agents of social control.

Agents of Social Control

The members of society who help check deviant behaviour are known as agents of social control. They include the police, judges, lawmakers, prison personnel, probation and parole officers, and ordinary citizens who take an active interest in maintaining law and order as they define it. Groups of ordinary citizens and lawmakers sometimes join hands in the capacity of **moral entrepreneurs**:

> Rules are the products of someone's initiative, and we can think of the people who exhibit such enterprise as *moral entrepreneurs*. Two related species—rule creators and rule enforcers—will occupy our attention. (Becker, 1963)

The prototype of the rule creator, Becker observes, is the crusading reformer, whose dissatisfaction with existing rules is acute and who, therefore, campaigns for legal change (adding new laws or procedures and rescinding old ones) and, sometimes, for a change in attitude designed to produce what he or she considers proper behaviour. Canadian society is replete with crusades, both past and present. Different groups have sought to eliminate drug abuse, discourage the abuse of alcohol, reduce the availability of pornography, and stop the exploitation of women in the workplace. Organizations have been formed to stress the need for such things as protection against break and entry. Moral enterprise is currently at work in an attempt to curb electronic crime (for a further example, see Box 12.1).

To conduct an effective crusade, moral entrepreneurs must construct an argument that is capable of convincing the community that it has a deep and genuine threat in its midst. This process of collective definition (Spector and Kitsuse, 1987; Hewitt and Hall, 1973) centres largely on the "claims-making activities" of the entrepreneurs themselves. They

1. assert the existence of a particular condition, situation, or state of affairs in which human action is implicated as a cause;
2. define the asserted conditions as offensive, harmful, undesirable, or otherwise problematic to the society but nonetheless amenable to correction by human beings; and
3. stimulate the public scrutiny of the condition from the point of view advanced by the claims makers.

The claims are explained by quasi-theories that, unlike scientific theories, are selectively constructed to square with the point of view of the claims makers, are seldom responsive to **empirical evidence**, and contain simple explanations of complex and ill-defined problems.

Moral entrepreneurs also enforce rules. The rules make it possible to apply norms to those who misbehave or step out of line. The entrepreneurs' legislated rules provide the enforcers (police, security personnel) with jobs and justifications

moral entrepreneur
Someone who is engaged in the process of defining new rules and laws or who advocates stricter enforcement of existing laws. Often such entrepreneurs will have some financial or organizational interest in particular definitions or applications of law.

empirical evidence
Evidence that can be observed through the senses. That is, it can be seen, touched, heard, smelled, tasted, and, to some extent, measured. This is the only form of evidence acceptable to science.

BOX 12.1

FOCUS

Cracking Down on Crime: Could This Moral Entrepreneurship Happen in Canada?

Moral entrepreneurs often seek to increase the penalties for particular offences. For example, Mothers Against Drunk Driving (MADD) has lobbied very effectively to force the justice system to treat drinking and driving more seriously. While most people would probably support the efforts of MADD, other initiatives to make laws tougher have been more controversial. The most dramatic effort to increase penalties came in California with the passage of a very tough "three strikes you're out" law in 1994 and is far harsher than the legislation in any other state or Canada's dangerous offender legislation. The reason for the severity of the law was the power of the moral entrepreneurs responsible for its passage.

The law was passed during a period when fear of crime was high, even though crime rates had been declining for several years. The United States was becoming more politically conservative, and tougher laws were seen as the best way of dealing with the crime problem. The process that resulted in the California three strikes law began with the 1992 murder of Kimber Reynolds by a career criminal who was attempting to rob her (Vitiello, 1997). Her father, Mike Reynolds, worked with a judge to develop a draft of the Three Strikes legislation and lobbied to get the legislature to adopt it. While the Justice Committee initially defeated the bill, the kidnapping and murder of 12-year-old Polly Klaas by a repeat offender in 1993 galvanized public support for the bill. After thousands of Californians signed an initiative supporting his proposal, Mr. Reynolds returned to the legislature and was successful in getting the original bill passed with no modification. While the flaws of the legislation were well-known, in an election year few politicians were prepared to support any amendments to the bill for fear of being labelled "soft on crime" by their opponents. The legislation provides for a mandatory sentence of 25 years to life for a third felony conviction and a doubled sentence for those with a second felony conviction.

The consequences of the Three Strikes legislation can now be seen. By 2001, more than 50 000 offenders were serving time under this law. Nearly 7000 were convicted for "three strikes" and another 44 000 under a "second strike" provision that doubled the normal sentence. It costs billions of dollars to keep these people in prison, and these costs will escalate as the first three strikes offenders will not be released until 2019. By 2026, it is estimated that 30 000 three strikes offenders—a number that is close to the size of Canada's entire prison population—will be serving sentences of 25 years to life in California (King and Mauer, 2001). Most of these prisoners will be far past the age at which they represent any further threat to society but their incarceration will continue to take funds that might otherwise be used for education and health care.

As the following *Globe and Mail* editorial shows, many three strikes offenders have been sentenced for very minor offences:

Some convicted felons have the book thrown at them. Leandro Andrade had an entire library thrown at him. He was sentenced to life in prison with no hope of parole for 50 years for the crime of trying to steal several videotapes worth a total of $153.54 (U.S.) from two different stores in California.

This week, the U.S. Supreme Court upheld the sentence in a 5–4 decision. It reversed the ruling of the U.S. Court of Appeals for the Ninth Circuit, which had found the sentence unconstitutional because it amounted to "cruel and unusual punishment" under the Eighth Amendment of the U.S. Constitution.

You might suspect there is more to the story than that, and you would be right. The

(continued)

majority on the Supreme Court, including Chief Justice William Rehnquist, Justice Sandra Day O'Connor and Justice Clarence Thomas, found ways, inch by tenuous inch, to justify a sentence that is on the face of it absurd, because the judges deferred to California's right to adopt and enforce its "Three Strikes and You're Out" law.

The law says that someone convicted of a felony, who has previously committed two serious felonies, must automatically receive a sentence of 25 years to life.... To an extent, the law is similar to the Canadian law that permits serial criminals to be declared dangerous offenders, and held indefinitely in prison, if they pose a foreseeably high risk to society. The idea of Canada's rule is to protect the public by locking up predictably dangerous recidivists, and if that were the sole effect of the California law, few would object to it.

In practice, the law can run amok. In 1995, Mr. Andrade was detained while leaving a Kmart store with five videotapes. A few days later, he tried to steal four tapes from another Kmart. He had previously been in and out of prison for theft and burglary. He said he took the videos to pay for his heroin habit. His state probation officer wrote: "He says when he gets out of jail or prison he always does something stupid."

So, not an ideal citizen. But not an obvious candidate for 50 years in prison without hope of parole.

Enter the three-strikes law. The prosecutor decided to treat the tape thefts as felonies rather than misdemeanours. The jury found that his conviction on three counts of first-degree burglary in 1982 qualified as "serious felonies" under the law. He received 25 years to life for each of the two tape thefts.

On Wednesday, the Supreme Court ordered him to serve the time. After all, it said, it's not as though he has no chance of parole; he will be eligible after 50 years.

"The gross disproportionality principle reserves a constitutional violation for only the extraordinary case."

Forgive our slack-jawed incredulity. If this doesn't count as an "extraordinary case," what on Earth could? (The Supreme Court had one answer. It previously wrote that it might have trouble with a sentence of life imprisonment for "overtime parking.")

Justice David Souter, writing for his colleagues in the minority, had no problem with higher penalties for recidivists. However, he said, Mr. Andrade was a clear victim under the Eighth Amendment.

For a start, he received twice the sentence of a man who stole three golf clubs, though Mr. Andrade's offence was less serious and his criminal record less grave. "Andrade did not somehow become twice as dangerous to society when he stole the second handful of videotapes." And the judge wasn't impressed by the majority's note that Mr. Andrade will, after all, qualify for parole after 50 years—when he will be 87, if he lives that long.

"If Andrade's sentence is not grossly disproportionate," Judge Souter wrote, "the principle has no meaning."

The majority on the court may have prevailed with its states'-rights, tough-on-crime decision, but the absurdity of this case may help those in California—including a group called Families to Amend California's Three Strikes—to trim the ludicrous edges from the law.

Source: Editorial. "Where Shoplifting Means Life in Prison." *Globe and Mail* (Friday, March 7, 2003), p. A14. Other sources: Michael Vitiello. (1997). "Three Strikes: Can We Return to Rationality?" *Journal of Criminal Law and Criminology* 87 (Winter):395–482. Ryan S. King and Marc Mauer. (2001). *Aging Behind Bars: "Three Strikes" Seven Years Later*. Washington: The Sentencing Project.

for them. Since the enforcers want to keep these jobs, they are eager to demonstrate that enforcement is being carried out properly. Yet they also realize that there are more infractions than they can possibly prevent and guard against. Therefore, they must establish priorities. Thus,

> whether a person who commits a deviant act is in fact labelled a deviant depends on many things extraneous to his actual behaviour: whether the enforcement official feels that at this time he must make some show of doing his job in order to justify his position, whether the misbehaver shows proper deference to the enforcer, whether the "fix" has been put in, and where the kind of act he has committed stands on the enforcer's list of priorities. (Becker, 1963)

It is no accident, then, that the least influential members of society (for example, the poor or certain **ethnic groups**) are often caught in the web of social control and labelled deviant out of proportion to their numbers. In other words, deviance is, in part, created by people in society. Moral entrepreneurs make certain laws, and the infraction of these laws constitutes deviance. Moral entrepreneurs also apply these laws to particular people, thereby labelling them as deviants of some sort. As Becker (1963) points out: "Deviance is not a quality of the act.... The deviant is one to whom that label has successfully been applied; deviant behaviour is behaviour that people so label."

But the rules are applied to some people and not to others; the application process is sometimes biased. Hence, some people remain at large as secret, or potentially identifiable, deviants. Others go through life falsely accused of anti-social acts. To discover why only certain groups of people are labelled deviant by dint of their actions, labelling theorists also study those who make the laws that deviants violate and the ways those laws are applied.

Those publicly labelled as deviant generally meet with some sort of community or societal reaction to their misdeeds (Lemert, 1951). Depending on the nature of the deviance, one or more of the following may be the deviant's fate: imprisonment, ostracism, fines, torture, surveillance, and ridicule. All labelled deviants soon discover that they must cope with a stigma.

A *stigma* is the black mark, or disgrace, associated with a deviant identity. It is part of the societal reaction inasmuch as it is a collective construction by the agents of social control and ordinary members of the community of the supposed nature of the unlawful act and the people who perpetrate it. As Goffman (1963) and Link and Phelan (2001) note, the collective image of stigma is constructed from social, physical, or psychological attributes that the deviant is believed to possess. In this connection, imputed possession of the attributes is far more important than actual possession.

Mark Watson (1984; and Wolf, 1991) found, after years of participation observation with outlaw motorcycle gangs, that their members had a mentality and background noticeably different from that imputed to them by the general public. They were not especially hostile to most social institutions, including government, education, and the family. Most members had finished high school and had held jobs from time to time. Some had gone to college, some

ethnic group

A group of individuals having a distinct subculture in common. An ethnic group differs from a race because it implies that values, norms, behaviour, and language, not necessarily physical appearance, are the important distinguishing characteristics.

were military veterans. Nearly every member had been married at least once. They were, to be sure, not particularly successful in these areas of life—which helped account for their tendency to live for the moment, to be impulsive. And although they were basically not violent men, it was important to them to be seen as "manly" in the most traditional sense of the term.

Secondary Deviation

The existence of moral rules and the societal reaction and stigma that occur when these rules are believed to have been violated set the stage for secondary deviation. Deviation becomes secondary when deviants see that their behaviour substantially modifies their ways of living. A strong desire to deviate, or a feeling of extreme guilt, can foster this redefinition of one's deviant activities. But being accused of deviance is typically the most influential factor behind the redefinition. Being labelled by the authorities as a murderer, rapist, prostitute, or cheque forger and being sanctioned for such behaviour forces the deviant to change his or her lifestyle drastically. As Lemert (1972) puts it, "This secondary deviant ... is a person whose life and identity are organized around the facts of deviance."

What does a lifestyle of secondary deviation actually consist of? Stebbins (1997) defines lifestyle as

> a distinctive set of shared patterns of tangible behaviour that is organized around a set of coherent interests or social conditions or both, that is explained and justified by a set of related values, attitudes, and orientations and that, under certain conditions, becomes the basis for a separate, common social identity for its participants.

For example, drug addicts regularly buy or produce the drugs they use, habitually follow certain practices designed to prevent discovery by the authorities, and routinely consume the illicit substance thus acquired. Some addicts, prostitutes among them, justify this lifestyle as an escape from intolerable working conditions. The identity for an addict is pejorative, however, as the label "junky" clearly indicates.

Among the factors leading to secondary deviation is the tendency of society to treat someone's criminality as a **master status** (Becker, 1963). This status overrides all other statuses in perceived importance. Whatever laudable achievements the deviant might have, such as a good job or a successful marriage, he or she is primarily judged in the community by the fact of deviance. The statuses of work and family are treated as subordinate to the master status of deviance (see Box 12.2).

Lack of success, or a perceived low probability of success, in attaining respectability among nondeviants may lead to interaction with other deviants. Here we shall consider a special aspect of this sort of interaction that takes place between the labelled deviant and the organized deviant group. There are several characteristics of this type of group life that stimulate or maintain such behaviour. These characteristics are effective partly because the wider community has rejected the deviant.

master status

A status that overrides all others in perceived importance. Whatever other personal or social qualities individuals possess, they are judged primarily by this one attribute. Criminal is an example of a master status that determines the community's identification of an individual.

BOX 12.2

FOCUS

The Master Status of Sex-Trade Workers

We think the real question is, "What effect does society's perception of women have on prostitution and pornography?" We think this is the *real* issue because the perception is there before the imagery of the trade comes into being.

Despite the efforts of women struggling for years to equalize our position in society, we are not anywhere near our goal. We do not have economic equality, our share of political power, safe and effective birth control, guaranteed access to safe abortion, adequate health care, or physical safety. In fact, in the last few years we have seen a downslide of women's power, both socially and economically. They allow a few of us to get on top, but it's on the rest of our backs that they do.

At the conference marking the end of the UN Decade of Women, held in Nairobi, the academics were talking about female sexual slavery and how to abolish it. They demanded that the governments of various countries do something about the immigration of women for the sex trade, female sexual slavery, how to get women out of it, how to reform these women, how to educate them about self-esteem. Meanwhile the women at the grassroots level, who were mostly Women of Colour, were talking about racism, feeding our children, and the economic power of women or lack thereof.

Let me say here that there is an incredible amount of racism in the sex trade at the street level. Women of Colour are in a majority on the street. It is a very clear example of the racism in this society that they even have to be in the industry. Women of Colour are the last hired, the first fired of all women. They cannot get jobs. Many are immigrants and, of course, have to be running the most. They cannot get into the escort services because of the racism in this society and because, of course, the services have to explain to the trick over the phone that this is a Woman of Colour. So it's next to impossible to get into the escort services because none of the men want the women unless it's for kinky sex. There is one escort service in Vancouver that hired Women of Colour, but it has them all advertised and labelled: Black women: "earthy"; Latinos: "hot"; Orientals: "submissive." It reflects how this society functions.

In Vancouver 50 percent of the women on the street are Women of Colour. In Calgary a large percentage are Black and Native women. In Winnipeg it's 80 percent. The police and the Fraser Committee told us it's 98 percent in Regina, mostly Native women. There are many Black women out on the street in Toronto, approximately 60 percent in Montreal. It is not a majority of women in the sex trade who are Third World women. It is just the majority of those that are on the street and in the prisons. The same is true in the United States from what we hear. Women on the street are viewed as bad girls, and so Women of Colour end up taking the rap.

We are kept apart by the good girl/bad girl thing, as Margo St. James has said. Historically, good girls have been pitted against bad girls: But men get to decide which label we receive. If we step outside the boundaries, we are already labelled. And the tables can be turned on any of the good girls very fast. One minute you're a good girl, and if you don't do it right, you're a bad girl the next. And what is good in one decade is not necessarily good in the next. Historically, women have built cities through prostitution, but men have created the situation by which women have had to turn to prostitution in order to build these cities. The next time you go through Athens, think about how prostitutes built that city.

Source: Marie Arrington. (1987). "Under the Gun." In Laurie Bell (ed.), *Good Girls/Bad Girls: Sex Trade Workers and Feminists Face to Face* (pp. 173–75). Toronto: Women's Press. Reprinted by permission of Canadian Scholars' Press Inc. and/or Women's Press.

As Becker (1963) pointed out, the individual who gains entrance to a deviant group often learns from the group how to cope with the various problems associated with deviance. This makes being a deviant easier. Furthermore, the deviant acquires rationalizations for his or her values, attitudes, and behaviour, which come to full bloom in the organized group. While these rationalizations are highly varied, it is important to note that the very existence of rationalizations seems to point to the fact that some deviants feel a need to deal with certain conventional attitudes and values that they have also internalized.

Prus and Sharper (1991) quote one of their respondents, who was explaining how he developed the callous attitude prized by professional card hustlers:

> When I first got involved in hustling, my attitudes were less calloused [*sic*]. I might be at a stag of some sort and say some fellow is losing a little money. Through the course of the evening, talking back and forth, you find out that maybe he just got married, or that he has some kids and here he's writing cheques and I would slow down. If you pull something like this with a crew [of hustlers], the other guys will want to know what the hell you are doing! They're waiting for you to take him, and you're saying, "Well gee, the guy doesn't have much money." You would get the worst tongue lashing! The position they take is that "You can't have feelings on the road." And it's true, if you start saying to yourself, "Well, maybe I better not beat this guy or that guy," you would soon be out of business or at least you would really cut down on your profits.
>
> When a crew is on the road, they have no feelings for the other players. They say, "Well, if the sucker doesn't blow it to you, he's going to blow it to somebody else, so you might as well take him for his money. He's going to lose it one way or the other."

Because group forces operate to maintain and even promote deviance, it should not be assumed, as Goffman (1963) apparently does, that full-fledged deviants are always members of groups. There are some who reject the label of deviant during certain phases of their career, although they may be forced into that status. Some of these individuals spend part of their career trying to re-enter conventional life, often without success. Yet the fact that they refuse to identify themselves as deviant leads them to avoid others who are so labelled (for example, shoplifters and embezzlers). There are, moreover, some forms of deviant behaviour that, whatever the reason, are enacted alone. Rape is an example of this behaviour, as is some cheque forging. It is probably true, nevertheless, that deviance has collective support in most instances.

The amount and kinds of interaction that take place between the individual who is suspected of deviant behaviour and the agents of social control are extremely important for the future course of that person's deviant career. In fact, the interaction that takes place here makes up a major set of deviant career contingencies. A **career contingency** is an unintended event, process, or situation that occurs by chance; that is, it lies beyond the control of the individual pursuing the career. Career contingencies emanate from changes in the deviant's environment, his or her personal circumstances, or both. Movement through the career is affected by the contingencies the deviant meets along the way.

Cohen (1965) has presented this process most clearly: alter (the agents of social control) responds to the action of ego (the deviant); ego in turn responds to

career contingency
An unintended event, process, or situation that occurs by chance.

alter's reaction; alter then responds to his perception of ego's reaction to him; and so forth. The final result is that ego's opportunity structure is in some way modified, permitting either more or fewer legitimate or illegitimate opportunities.

Where the opportunities for a deviant career are expanding, the steady growing apart of the deviant and the control agents leads to open conflict. Some proportion of these encounters lead in the opposite direction, however, resulting in some form of accommodation and a decrease in the opportunities for a deviant career (West, 1980).

This process of agent–deviant interaction is illustrated in the circumstances encountered by one of the respondents in Stebbins's study of nonprofessional criminals.

> The respondent arrived in Toronto shortly after being released from prison in New Brunswick, only to be stopped while walking on a main street by two policemen in a prowl car. He was apparently immediately recognized and advised to return to his home province without further delay. But since he had just come from there, the respondent politely informed the police that he had important business in Toronto that would take a few days to accomplish, and after that he would consider leaving the city. This was not the sort of reaction the police were after, so they pressed their request again in a firmer manner. The respondent's reply was likewise more adamant, and the police left without success. That evening he was called from his rented room by his landlady only to be confronted by two different but "enormous" policemen who had just arrived in an ominous-looking police van. They again questioned him about his intentions to stay in Toronto, but the respondent, who could now see that he would probably remain in that city only in jail, replied that he had decided to return to New Brunswick after all. (Stebbins, 1976)

continuance commitment

Adherence to a criminal or other identity arising from the unattractiveness or unavailability of alternative lifestyles.

Another prominent contingency in secondary deviation is **continuance commitment**. Continuance commitment is "the awareness of the impossibility of choosing a different social identity ... because of the imminence of penalties involved in making the switch" (Stebbins, 1976). Like the value commitment mentioned earlier in this chapter, continuance commitment helps explain a person's involvement in a deviant identity. Unlike value commitment, which explains this involvement by stressing the rewards of the identity, continuance commitment explains the involvement by describing the penalties that accrue from renouncing the deviant identity and trying to adopt a conventional identity.

As Ulmer (1994) notes, such penalties may be structural—they flow from the social structure of the community—or personal—they flow from the person's attitudes and sense of self. Stebbins's (1976) study of male, nonprofessional property offenders in Newfoundland reveals a number of commitment-related penalties of both types. As ex-offenders with prison records, the men in the study had difficulty finding jobs within their range of personally acceptable alternatives. The work they found was onerous, low in pay, and low in prestige. Many of the men had accrued sizable debts before they went to prison, which tended to discourage their return to a conventional livelihood upon release. Also penalizing were the questions from casual acquaintances about the nature of criminal life and the insulting remarks these people occasionally made about those who have been in jail. Even where their records were unknown, these nonprofessional offenders often heard people express unflattering opinions about men like them.

For these reasons and others, the man with a criminal record was often inclined to seek the company of those who understood him best—namely, other criminals—and to seek the way of life that afforded him at least some money and excitement—namely, crime. The police knew all this, and they would question local ex-offenders to determine whether they were possibly guilty of certain crimes. The ex-offenders, who were trying to "go straight," saw this as an additional penalty.

What is experienced as a string of penalties to the ex-offender is, from another perspective, a set of expressions of the societal reaction. In the everyday lives of ex-offenders, these expressions, when defined by the ex-offenders as penalizing, affect their deviant careers. The expressions force many of them into the company of other deviants. Here they find greater understanding for their circumstances. Here, also, is at least the possibility of a better living than they believe they can get in the conventional world.

What import does the process of continuance of commitment have for that of drift? Those teenagers and young adults who fail to drift out of crime into a more or less conventional way of life drift into a more or less solid commitment to crime. With a prison record and several years of secondary deviation, continuance commitment develops. Most deviants in this stage of their moral careers appear to be trapped in a self-degrading form of continuance commitment. The image they have of themselves is unflattering. It is one they wish they could abandon if only they could find a palatable way of leaving the world of crime (see also Schwendinger and Schwendinger, 1985).

But some criminals, including professional offenders, are quite attached to their deviant activities. Since the professionals find leaving crime for a conventional way of life no easier than it is for the nonprofessional offender, they are also committed to deviance. Nonetheless, theirs is a self-enhancing commitment. For the professionals, continuance commitment is of minor consequence, for they enjoy what they do and are disinclined to give it up.

Reactions to Commitment

Generally speaking, **self-enhancing commitment** presents no problem for deviants in spite of the fact that they are more or less forced to retain their social role. There is little motivation to leave this role for reasons of self-conception. Self-degrading commitment, however, presents a dramatically different situation. A number of alternatives are open to an individual committed to an identity in this manner.

First of all, a person motivated by **self-degrading commitment** has the objective alternative of redefining the values and penalties associated with the committed identity in such a way that he or she becomes attached to them. Basically, this alters the individual's perception of the balance of penalties. Such

self-enhancing commitment
Commitment leading to a better opinion of oneself.

self-degrading commitment
Commitment leading to a poorer opinion of oneself.

a psychological leap from self-degrading to self-enhancing commitment in the same deviant identity is exemplified by some in Shover's (1983) sample of repeat offenders. These offenders wrestled with the frustrating gap between their legitimate aspirations and what they could actually achieve in life. Since conventional work offered them little, they turned to living from day to day, with crime being one of their more enjoyable activities.

Without really switching to a form of self-enhancing commitment, it is occasionally possible for the deviant to adjust psychologically to self-degrading commitment. This depends, of course, on how strong a motivating force the current state of self-degrading commitment actually is for the deviant. Some types of mildly rejected deviants seem to manage this form of adaptation. Lemert (1972) refers to them as "adjusted pathological deviants." The subsequent development of character disorders is another possibility under these circumstances (Griffiths and Verdun-Jones, 1994). Successful adjustment apparently depends, in part, on the availability of a role for them to play in the community.

Lemert also considers "self-defeating and self-perpetuating deviance." He cites alcoholism, drug addiction, and systematic cheque forgery as examples of this sort of vicious circle of cause and effect, characterized by an almost complete absence of durable pleasure for those involved. Finally, if the desire to escape self-degrading commitment is exceptionally high, and none of the alternatives mentioned so far appeals to the committed individual, suicide becomes a prominent alternative. Perhaps this was the motive behind some or all of the 45 prison suicides reported by the Canadian Centre for Justice Statistics (Statistics Canada, 2001) for the period 1999 to 2000.

Undoubtedly, there are many other alternatives to self-degrading commitment besides the ones discussed here. Much, it seems, depends on the nature of the identity to which the deviant is committed. There are different ways in which commitment can manifest itself. Extensive research is still needed to isolate the kinds and circumstances of commitment and the various reactions to it.

For many deviants, however, commitment is not a lasting contingency in their careers once they become aware of their entrapment in that identity. In fact, this is one of the reasons for stating the case for commitment in subjective terms. The deviant feels this way, but this does not always correspond to the objective state of affairs. Criminological theory and research support this notion. For instance, Matza (1990) contends that delinquents generally end their deviant career at maturation, with very few continuing on to adult crime (for supporting evidence, see Shannon, 1988). West (1980) and Wolfgang et al. (1987) found that many adult criminals also mature out of their antisocial ways. This occurs when they take up a serious romantic relationship, find a legitimate job they like better than crime, or simply decide "to settle down" (see Chapter 13). Thus, even deviants attached to their way of life often undergo disillusionment and shifts of interest (Sommers, 2001), which is what "maturation" means in everyday terms in the world of crime (Jankowski, 1991). There is always the possibility of therapy for alcoholics, gamblers, and drug addicts. And, of course, some deviance requires youthful vigour, a quality lost with increasing years (Inciardi, 1974).

Undoubtedly, the same can be said for many other committed identities. The worker committed to his or her job by a pension plan and seniority arrangements is often relieved of this condition if in no other way than by retirement. Divorce and remarriage are always possibilities for those in an unhappy union.

It is possible that self-enhancing commitment lasts longer than the self-degrading variety. Underlying this suggestion is the assumption that self-degrading commitment, while preferable to certain alternatives in the conventional world, is still undesirable in itself. A mortifying self-conception acts as a special penalty. It furnishes a significant part of the pressure to deal with an unpleasant state of affairs. Commitment to an identity or expectation that creates a negative self-image is viewed as a lesser-evil choice when initially compared with certain alternatives, and as a greater-evil choice when subsequently compared with certain others. The strength of the individual's desire to abandon an unpleasant status is an important consideration in determining whether the transition will be made.

Figure 12.1 summarizes the ideas presented thus far in this chapter.

SOCIALIZATION INTO CRIME

The theories of criminality discussed elsewhere in this book help explain why people start a life of crime. By contrast, interactionism has been interested chiefly in what happens to criminals once their deviant activities commence. Still, two areas of interactionist theory, though not causal, can be properly seen as contributions to the study of socialization into crime. They are the processes of differential association and acquisition of a **criminal identity**.

Differential Association

Edwin H. Sutherland first set out his theory of differential association in the 1939 edition of *Principles of Criminology*. The statement he made in that edition differs little from the most recent version written by Sutherland and Cressey (1978). The theory consists of nine propositions that describe the complicated pattern of interaction Sutherland called **differential association**: (1) people learn how to engage in crime; (2) this learning comes about through interaction with others who have already learned criminal ways; (3) the learning occurs in small, face-to-face groups; (4) what is learned is criminal technique (for example, how to open a safe), motives, attitudes, and rationalizations; (5) among criminals, one important learned attitude is a disregard for the community's legal code; (6) one acquires this attitude by differentially associating with those who hold it and failing to associate with those who do not; (7) differential associations with criminals and noncriminals vary in frequency, duration, priority, and intensity; (8) learning criminal behaviour through differential association rests on the same principles as learning any other kind of behaviour; and (9) criminal behaviour is a response to the same cultural needs and values as noncriminal behaviour. For instance, one individual steals to

criminal identity

This social category is imposed by the community and correctly or incorrectly defines an individual as a particular type of criminal. The identity will pervasively shape his or her social interactions with others. It is similar in concept to *master status*.

differential association

Developed by Edwin Sutherland in the 1930s, this theory argues that crime, like any social behaviour, is learned in association with others. If individuals regularly associate with criminals and are relatively isolated from law-abiding citizens, they are more likely to engage in crime themselves. They learn the specific skills needed to commit crime and the ideas that justify and normalize crime.

FIGURE 12.1   Commitment

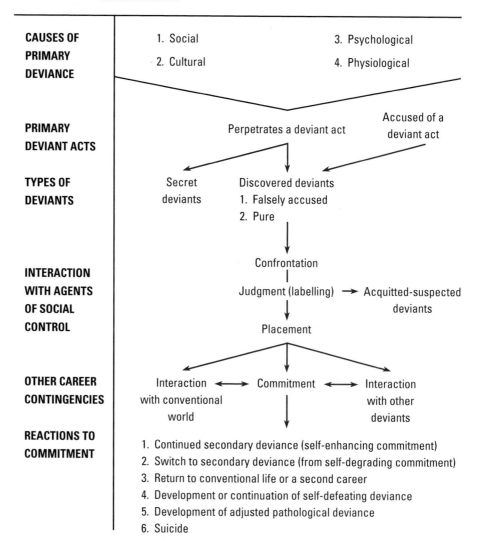

Source: Robert A. Stebbins. (1976).*Commitment to Deviance. The Nonprofessional Criminal in the Community*. Westport, Conn.: Greenwood Press, p. 66.

acquire money for a new suit of clothes, while another works as a carpenter to reach the same goal. Consequently, tying societal needs and values to crime fails to explain it.

Based on what is known about the antecedents of crime, Sutherland's theory offers a valuable, albeit partial, explanation of theft, burglary, prostitution, and marijuana use. Also, differential association is often a major antecedent in the use of addictive drugs and dependence on alcohol. It may even play an explanatory role in some mental disorders.

However, many other factors, which dilute the importance of differential associations, must be considered when explaining these kinds of behaviour. For example, two processes discussed earlier in this chapter—drift and primary and secondary deviation—indicate that deviant motives and meanings are often gradually learned and tentatively applied and modified over time in interaction with both deviants and nondeviants. The motives and meanings are not mere causal antecedents of criminal acts and memberships in criminal groups (Davis, 1980). Another set of factors was recently reviewed by Birkbeck and LaFree (1993). Symbolic interactionism, they note, further contributes to our understanding of crime by directing attention to the motives and meanings operating in the situations in which crimes are committed. In this connection, Katz (1990) found that the expressive reasons behind many criminal acts such as thrill and enjoyment are as important as the instrumental reasons such as money and status. Additionally, precisely how a crime is committed and even which crimes are committed depend, in part, on decisions made on the spot by the criminal. These decisions may be made with reference to the possibility of being apprehended, serving a longer or shorter sentence, or enduring a hostile reaction from the community to the deviant act or acts.

Although various tests of the theory of differential association have been carried out, convincing support for it has always been blocked by the difficulty of operationalizing for empirical study some of Sutherland's key concepts (for example, frequency, intensity, and duration of criminal and noncriminal associations). Nonetheless, in Matsueda's (2001) words,

> differential association theory represents one of the most important theoretical traditions in criminology. Historically, the theory brought a sociological perspective to the forefront of criminology and, with his path-breaking work on white-collar crime, established Edwin Sutherland as perhaps the most important criminologist of his generation.... Over 50 years later, differential association theory continues to stimulate revisions, extensions, and original research into the causes of crime.

The major contribution of differential association is its emphasis on the role of ties to deviant peers in the persistence of a criminal career. Daniel Wolf, an anthropologist who rode with the Rebels, an Edmonton biker gang, described how the willingness of peers to stand up for one another can be critical in maintaining power in the face of violent opposition from competitors:

> For an outlaw biker, the greatest fear is not of the police; rather, it is of a slight variation of his own mirror image: the patch holder of another club. Under slightly different circumstances those men would call each other "brother." But when turf is at stake, inter-club rivalry and warfare completely override any considerations of the common bonds of being a biker—and brother kills brother. None of the outlaws that I rode with enjoyed the prospect of having to break the bones of another biker. Nor did they look forward to having to live with the hate–fear syndrome that dominates a conflict in which there are no rules. I came to realize that the willingness of an outlaw to lay down his life in these conflicts

goes beyond a belligerent masculinity that brooks no challenge. When a patch holder defends his colours, he defends his personal identity, his community, his lifestyle. When a war is on, loyalty to the club and one another arises out of the midst of danger, out of apprehension of possible injury, mutilation, or worse. Whether one considers this process as desperate, heroic, or just outlandishly foolish and banal does not really matter. What matters is that, for patch holders, the brotherhood emerges as a necessary feature of their continued existence as individuals and as a group. (1991, 11)

There is a great deal of research evidence showing that having young offenders as friends is one of the strongest correlates of deviant behaviour. Several recent studies have also found that among at-risk youth, gang membership contributes to delinquency above and beyond the influence of associating with deviant peers. Sutherland's work helps us to understand why this is the case. Differential association theory also points to the need to learn the skills of committing certain crimes. These range from very simple techniques such as hitting a man over the head and stealing his watch to taking an unlocked bicycle to sophisticated computer crimes. According to Sutherland, people learn the necessary techniques and the motives, drives, rationalizations, and attitudes of deviant behaviour from others with whom they associate. Peter Letkemann (1973), for example, described how a former Canadian penitentiary resident learned the now-obsolete art of safecracking:

> Prior to doing his first "can" [safe] [he] bugged an older safecracker in prison "until he finally divulged how to do it." This instruction, he added was "not like a teacher-student, it was just a matter of discussion during work."
>
> When he left the prison he went back to his regular partner and described to him what he had learned about safes. His partner said this was ridiculous but [he] persuaded him to come along: "I followed the instructions to the letter. It opened—we were both overcome with it all—the ease of it all!"
>
> This first job had been a punch job [breaking into a safe without explosives]—technically the simplest. Following this [he] and his partner "opened many doors by trial and error" … This went on for four years; they had not yet used explosives, nor had they ever been caught punching safes. They became increasingly eager to try explosives since they found so many safes that couldn't be opened any other way.
>
> During this time, [he] was associating with other safecrackers…. He eventually asked another safecracker whether he could borrow some grease [nitroglycerine]. "I wouldn't admit that I knew nothing about it." He obtained the grease and chose a small safe, but was unsuccessful. The next day, he discussed his problem with some more experienced safecrackers. He found he had used too long a fuse and was advised to use electric knockers [detonators]. This he did with success. (Letkemann, 1973, 136)

Criminal Identities

A *criminal identity* is a social category into which deviants are placed by others in the community and into which, eventually, they may place themselves. That is, the process of identification of an individual as deviant is a two-sided coin. Based on a variety of criteria (for example, appearance, actions, associates, and location), members of the community come to view someone as a particular kind of criminal. The woman wearing garish, suggestive clothing, who frequents a street corner in the red-light district, is identified as a prostitute. The man with long, unkempt hair, dirty jeans, and a black leather jacket who rides a Harley-Davidson motorcycle is identified, as we saw earlier, as a member of a gang bent on rape, violence, and drunkenness.

Moreover—and this is the other side of the coin—community identification of people tends to be very persuasive, even for the deviant. That is, with officials, neighbours, relatives, and others asserting that an individual is some sort of social outlaw, it becomes increasingly difficult for him or her to deny the charge. At the very least, the alleged prostitute must accommodate her everyday life to such opinion, whether or not she is selling sex. The biker has the same problem (Watson, 1984; Wolf, 1991).

Acquiring a community reputation, or identity, for unsavoury behaviour often helps to further individual criminality. This is especially likely to happen when the reputed criminal is forced into association with others of similar reputation and away from those who are "respectable." Once deviant ties are forged and nondeviant ties sufficiently weakened, the socializing potential of differential association begins to take effect. Interactionists see social interaction and definitions of situation as underlying the processes of identification and differential association.

LIMITATIONS

Like all theories of crime and deviance, interactionist theory has its limitations. That is to say, it is not in itself a complete explanation of crime. It falls well short of explaining all crime under all the conditions in which it is committed. Throughout this chapter, we have discussed the strengths of the theory (for a summary see Table 12.1). Drawing on Barry Glassner's (1982) review of the various critiques of this theory, we will now examine its limitations. These are discussed with reference to three categories: neo-Marxist, empiricist, and ethnomethodological. Each critique is also the nucleus of still another approach to the study of crime.

The Neo-Marxist Critique

The principal neo-Marxist objection to interactionist theory is that it fails to relate crime and other forms of deviance to the larger society. It fails to account for historical and contemporary political and economic interests. After all, deviant acts and careers do take place within such a context.

TABLE 12.1 Interactionist Theories

Theory	Theorists	Key Elements
Labelling	Lemert Becker	Primary deviance is infrequent deviance that involves little change in routine or lifestyle. Secondary deviance occurs when deviance becomes a way of life and a part of the deviant's self-image.
Differential association	Sutherland	Crime and delinquency are primarily learned in interaction association with others in small, face-to-face groups. This involves learning the techniques of deviance and the justifications for deviant behaviour.

It is further charged that labelling theorists overlook the division between the powerful and the powerless in explaining deviance. Powerful members of society also violate laws and other norms even while establishing some of them in their role as moral entrepreneurs. Consider the case of Henri Marchessault, former head of the Montreal Police Drug Squad. In November 1983, he was convicted of stealing and selling hashish and cocaine, which were available to him from a police vault. He was a detective captain at the time (*Calgary Herald*, November 26, 1983).

The concept of moral entrepreneur and the categories of secret and falsely accused deviants suggest, however, that interactionists have some understanding of the power differences in society. Perhaps the fairest criticism is that they have failed to go as far as they might in linking power to such ideas as labelling, deviant career, and agent of social control. Still, the observation that labelling theory overlooks the larger social context of deviance is apt. This exposes the predominantly social-psychological character of the perspective.

The Empiricist Critique

The empiricists find several research weaknesses in labelling theory and its empirical support. Glassner (1982) discusses three of these. First, interactionists are said by the empiricists to examine only, or chiefly, labelled deviants—those who have been *officially* identified as having deviated (charged and convicted, or examined and hospitalized). It is true that labelling theorists have frequently followed this narrow conception of the labelling process. Some deviants—for example, religious fanatics or occultists—are deviant and labelled by the community as such, even though they rarely if ever gain official recognition. This exposes interactionists to the criticism that community labelling makes no practical difference to the individual.

Second, the empiricists argue that labelling as a cause of deviance is inadequately conceptualized. This is a misunderstanding. As this chapter points out, labels are seen by interactionists as interpretations, not causes. The label of deviant is a career contingency, an event, a process, or a situation interpreted by the deviant as having a significant impact on his or her moral career.

Third, the empiricists claim that labelling theory lacks testable propositions. Consequently, data in this area can be explained in many different ways. Glassner notes that the empiricists hold that tests by quantitative, statistical means are the only definitive way of confirming propositions. Interactionists defend their approach by pointing out that qualitative methods, particularly participant observation, are more appropriate for the study of interaction, labelling, career, and self-conception. These phenomena rest on definitions of the situation, images of self and others, negotiations of reality, and similar processes that are difficult to measure and, therefore, largely unquantifiable. Nevertheless, qualitative research often proceeds from the intense examination of individual groups and cases. Such studies are difficult and time-consuming. As a result, there are relatively few of them. There is only suggestive, and still unconfirmed, evidence for many interactionist propositions.

The Ethnomethodological Critique

The ethnomethodologists and conversational analysts are the modern-day inheritors of the phenomenology of Alfred Schutz. (In fact, Glassner refers to them as "phenomenologists" in his review of interactionist theory.) The chief concern of the ethnomethodologists with labelling theory is its tendency to neglect this question: How do people make sense of their social world?

Kenneth Leiter (1980) defines **ethnomethodology** as the study of common-sense knowledge. Three phenomena are encompassed by this definition: ethnomethodologists study the stock of knowledge that people have of the social and physical world around them; with this stock of knowledge, people engage in common-sense reasoning about the events, processes, things, and characteristics experienced in everyday life; when people reason together on a common-sense basis, their thoughts often combine to form a suprahuman reality—a social reality. This social reality transcends the thoughts of those in the situation who are doing the reasoning.

Ethnomethodologists do not seek to confirm the validity of common sense. Rather, they note that whether common sense is scientifically right or wrong, it is the way in which "we experience the social world as a factual object" (Leiter, 1980). By studying these three phenomena, we find answers to the question of how people make sense of their social world.

However, the people of interest to the ethnomethodologist are not always deviant. Rather, ethnomethodologists are interested in how agents of social control and ordinary citizens make sense of deviants and deviant acts. Interactionists are accused of ignoring the ways in which the conventional world identifies and classifies morally offensive individuals and their behaviour. The important data for ethnomethodologists are the clues people use to identify kinds of deviants and deviant acts. People use this knowledge to reach such conclusions as "guilty" or "innocent." Studying these two processes demonstrates how we will construct special social realities—the realities of who did what to whom, at what time, and at what place.

ethnomethodology

A sociological theory developed by Harold Garfinkel. Roughly translated, the term means the study of people's practices or methods. The perspective does not see the social world as an objective reality but as something that people must build and rebuild constantly in their thoughts and actions. Ethnomethodologists try to uncover the methods and practices that are used by people as they create the taken-for-granted world.

To some extent, interactionists are guilty as charged. Although there are occasional hints of ethnomethodological thinking in the interactionist literature on deviance, there has been until recently a tendency to rely heavily on official definitions, or labels, of what and who is deviant. But even official definitions and their applications are informed by common sense. They, too, warrant ethnomethodological analysis.

IMPLICATIONS

The most profound implication of interactionist theory is practical only in a general sense. The theory offers a unique perspective on deviance, which enhances understanding of this phenomenon. For instance, observations on moral enterprise underscore the arbitrariness of criminal law and call attention to patterns of local and national power (though rarely to the extent neo-Marxists would like). Practically speaking, there is little that can be done to counteract most moral enterprise. But interactionist research, at least, exposes its existence.

On a more practical level, interactionist theory stresses the pernicious effects of the deviant label. These effects are of at least two types. One, the label (to the extent that the wider community is aware of it) makes re-entry into that community problematic after sanctioning. Nondeviants are inclined to avoid known deviants. They do so because their own reputations could be damaged from being seen with deviants and, possibly, because they are revolted by the deviant's lifestyle and moral behaviour. Deviants are more than rule violators. They are also outcasts.

Two, labels colour the judgements many people make of those who are labelled. Labels are names for stereotyped images. Both the images and the labels help nondeviants, including practitioners, define situations involving deviants. These two effects of the deviant label have led Empey et al. (1999), among others, to argue that the juvenile courts should be used as a last resort for only the most serious cases. Juvenile diversion and decriminalization programs are a practical response to this implication of interactionist theory.

Interactionist theory calls attention to the deviant career as a set of factors that helps explain deviance beyond its initial causes. One practical implication stemming from this part of the theory is that, over time, people often become committed to certain lifestyles. To the extent that they have made substantial "side bets" (Becker, 1963) in one or more conventional identities, they are unlikely to deviate. Their possible deviance, if discovered and labelled, could ruin their reputations in the conventional world (for example, the politician exposed in the press for patronizing a prostitute). One antidote to initial or continued deviance, then, is to give people every possible opportunity to build a strong side bet in a "respectable" pursuit. By this reasoning, the juvenile should be encouraged to drift toward conventional interests. The adult ex-offender should also be encouraged to find noncriminal employment in new surroundings, away from his or her former deviant associates.

SUMMARY

- Interactionist theory centres on the deviant interchanges people have with one another and the meanings of these interchanges in the present, past, and future.

- A deviant career is the passage of an individual through recognized stages in one or more related deviant identities.

- Primary deviation occurs in the early stages of the deviant career. Here, deviance is enacted with little change in the person's everyday routine or lifestyle.

- The deviant drifts between two moral worlds. In youth offender subcultures, deviance is facilitated by certain moral rhetorics and by other aspects of the subterranean tradition.

- Agents of social control help check deviant behaviour. Moral entrepreneurs create and enforce rules, the violation of which constitutes deviance. Thus, some people are labelled deviant, whereas others are not.

- When the deviant sees his or her life as substantially modified by deviance, he or she has moved into secondary deviation. The rules are applied to some people and not to others. Those who are publicly labelled as deviant generally meet with some sort of community or societal reaction to their misdeeds. Labelled deviants may find they must cope with a stigma.

- Continuance commitment, or forcing a person to remain in an identity, is sometimes the outcome of these encounters. When self-degrading continuance sets in, it motivates those so affected to redefine commitment penalties or adjust in some other way to this unsettling frame of mind.

- Although the theory of criminal socialization has not been a central concern of the interactionist perspective, interactionists have contributed to the theory in two major ways. People learn crime through differential association with others who are already criminal. They are further socialized into it by acquiring a criminal identity by being placed in such a category by other people and by coming to accept (often grudgingly) this placement.

- Limitations to the interactionist theories have been noted by the neo-Marxists, empiricists, and ethnomethodologists. At the moment, however, none of these approaches has progressed beyond the concern with finding weaknesses in the interactionist perspective such that it could become a distinct orientation itself.

- Interactionist theory also has certain theoretical and practical implications. One of these is that, wherever possible, continuance commitment to deviance should be avoided for juveniles by avoiding the official label of criminal.

QUESTIONS FOR CRITICAL THINKING

1. Identify and describe a recent change in existing criminal law or a recent passing of a new criminal law that is founded in the efforts of a group of moral entrepreneurs.
2. Select a vulnerable category (e.g., lower-class male youth, Aboriginal peoples, Asian youth from immigrant families, motorcycle gangs) and develop an explanation of how they could be falsely accused of certain crimes. How does such an explanation relate to deviant identity?
3. What are some of the factors contributing to secondary deviation among heroin users?
4. Identify some of the legitimate "side bets" (Becker, 1963) people make that help them avoid committing criminal acts and that criminals might make to help them avoid further criminality.
5. Because of the influence of labelling theory, our society has become more sensitive to the costs of a deviant label. Can you think of measures that have been taken in our youth and adult courts to reduce the number of people who are officially labelled by those institutions?

NET WORK

Moral entrepreneurs are individuals or groups who try to have their personal values reflected in law and the legal process. Gun control is one issue that has seen groups of people with different viewpoints trying to influence lawmakers. Bill C-68, the Firearms Act, has been particularly controversial, and both sides have worked very hard to have their views accepted. On one side of the issue is the National Firearms Association, which strongly objects to the restrictions on the ownership and use of firearms that are part of Bill C-68. The website of this association is at **www.nfa.ca**.

On the other side of the debate is the Coalition for Gun Control. Some of the arguments in favour of gun control can be found at their website at **www.guncontrol.ca** and at the government's Canadian Firearms Centre website at **www.cfc-ccaf.gc.ca**. On the government site, look particularly at the section "Information for the General Public."

1. What are the claims made by the two sets of moral entrepreneurs in this debate?
2. What do you think are some of the reasons for the conflicting views of the two sides in this debate?
3. What are some of the strategies that have been adopted by the National Firearms Association to fight the implementation of Bill C-68? Find some of the arguments used by the Coalition for Gun Control in their successful fight to convince the government to pass Bill C-68.

KEY TERMS

career

career contingency

continuance commitment

criminal identity

differential association

drift

empirical evidence

ethnic group

ethnomethodology

labelling

master status

moral entrepreneur

moral rhetoric

primary deviation

secondary deviation

self-degrading commitment

self-enhancing commitment

stigma

symbolic interactionism

SUGGESTED READING

Becker, Howard S. (1963). *Outsiders*. New York: Free Press. A collection of key articles written by Becker, several of which contain original statements on labelling, the deviant career, moral entrepreneurs, and types of deviants.

Foster, Janet. (1990). *Villains: Crime and Community in the Inner City*. London: Routledge. A field study of local and family traditions of petty crime among middle-aged and teenage males and females in southeast London.

Goffman, Erving. (1963). *Stigma*. Englewood Cliffs, N.J.: Prentice Hall. An essay on the nature and consequences of stigma for deviants, the handicapped, and those with physical blemishes.

Matza, David. (1990). *Delinquency and Drift*. New Brunswick, N.J.: Transaction. This book contains Matza's fullest development of the concepts of drift and subterranean tradition, as well as an introduction that links it with the 1964 edition.

Rubington, Earl, and Martin G. Weinberg (eds.). (2001). *Deviance: The Interactionist Perspective* (8th ed.). Boston: Allyn and Bacon. An anthology of theoretical and empirical articles written from the interactionist perspective.

BIBLIOGRAPHY

Becker, Howard S. (1963). *Outsiders: Studies in the Sociology of Deviance*. New York: Free Press.

Birkbeck, Christopher, and Gary LaFree. (1993). "The Situational Analysis of Crime and Deviance." In Judith Blake and John Hagan (eds.), *Annual Review of Sociology* 19. Palo Alto, Calif.: Annual Reviews, Inc.

Blumer, Herbert. (1986). *Symbolic Interactionism*. Berkeley: University of California Press.

Cohen, Albert K. (1965). "The Sociology of the Deviant Act." *American Sociological Review* 30:5–14.

Davis, Nanette J. (1980). *Sociological Constructions of Deviance* (2nd ed.). Dubuque, Iowa: Wm. C. Brown.

Empey, Lamar T., Mark C. Stafford, and Carter H. Hay. (1999). *American Delinquency: Its Meaning and Construction* (4th ed.). Belmont, Calif.: Wadsworth.

Glassner, Barry. (1982). "Labelling Theory." In M. Michael Rosenberg, Robert A. Stebbins, and Allan Turowetz (eds.), *The Sociology of Deviance.* New York: St. Martin's Press.

Goffman, Erving. (1963). *Stigma: Notes on the Management of Spoiled Identity.* Englewood Cliffs, N.J.: Prentice Hall.

Griffiths, Curt T., and Simon N. Verdun-Jones. (1994). *Canadian Criminal Justice* (2nd ed.). Toronto: Harcourt Brace Canada.

Hewitt, John P., and Peter M. Hall. (1973). "Social Problems, Problematic Situations, and Quasi-Theories." *American Sociological Review* 38:367–74.

Hirschi, Travis. (1969). *Causes of Delinquency.* Berkeley: University of California Press.

Inciardi, James A. (1974). "Vocational Crime." In Daniel Glaser (ed.), *Handbook of Criminology.* Chicago: Rand McNally.

Jankowski, Martin S. (1991). *Islands in the Street: Gangs and American Urban Society.* Berkeley, Calif.: University of California Press.

Katz, Jack. (1990). *Seductions of Crime: Moral and Sensual Attractions in Doing Evil.* New York: Basic Books.

Leiter, Kenneth. (1980). *A Primer on Ethnomethodology.* New York: Oxford University Press.

Lemert, Edwin. (1951). *Social Pathology.* New York: McGraw-Hill.

———. (1972). *Human Deviance, Social Problems, and Social Control* (2nd ed.). Englewood Cliffs, N.J.: Prentice Hall.

Letkemann, Peter. (1973). *Crime as Work.* Englewood Cliffs, N.J.: Prentice Hall.

Linden, Rick, and Cathy Fillmore. (1981). "A Comparative Study of Delinquency Involvement." *Canadian Review of Sociology and Anthropology* 18:343–61.

Link, Bruce G., and Jo C. Phelan. (2001). "Conceptualizing Stigma." In Karen S. Cook and John Hagan (eds.), *Annual Review of Sociology*, Vol. 27. Palo Alto, Calif.: Annual Reviews.

Matsueda, Ross L. (2001). "Differential Association Theory." In Patricia A. Adler, Peter Adler, and Jay Corzine (eds.), *Encyclopedia of Criminology and Deviant Behavior*, Vol. 1. Philadelphia: Brunner-Routledge.

Matza, David. (1969). *Becoming Deviant.* Englewood Cliffs, N.J.: Prentice Hall.

———. (1990). *Delinquency and Drift.* New Brunswick, N.J.: Transaction.

Prus, Robert C., and C.R.D. Sharper. (1991). *Road Hustler: Grifting, Magic, and the Thief Subculture* (expanded edition). New York: Kaufman and Greenberg.

Schwendinger, Herman, and Julia S. Schwendinger. (1985). *Adolescent Subcultures and Delinquency.* New York: Praeger.

Shannon, Lyle W. (1988). *Criminal Career Continuity.* New York: Human Sciences Press.

Short, James F. (1990). *Delinquency and Society.* Englewood Cliffs, N.J.: Prentice Hall.

Shover, Neal. (1983). "The Later Stages of Ordinary Property Offender Careers." *Social Problems* 31:208–18.

Sommers, Ira B. (2001). "Criminal Careers." In David Luckenbill and Dennis Peck (eds.), *Encyclopedia of Criminology and Deviant Behavior*, Vol. 2. Philadelphia: Brunner-Routledge.

Spector, Malcom, and John I. Kitsuse. (1987). *Constructing Social Problems.* Hawthorne, N.Y.: Aldine de Gruyter.

Statistics Canada. (2001). *Juristat.* Cat. No. 85-002-XIE, Vol. 21, No. 5.

Stebbins, Robert A. (1970). "On Misunderstanding the Concept of Commitment: A Theoretical Clarification." *Social Forces* 48:526–29.

———. (1976). *Commitment to Deviance: The Nonprofessional Criminal in the Community*. Westport, Conn.: Greenwood.

———. (1997). "Lifestyle as a Generic Concept in Ethnographic Research." *Quality and Quantity* 31:347–60.

Sutherland, Edwin H., and David R. Cressey. (1978). *Principles of Criminology* (10th ed.). Philadelphia: Lippincott.

Ulmer, Jeffery T. (1994). "Revisiting Stebbins: Labeling and Commitment to Deviance." *The Sociological Quarterly* 35:135–57.

Watson, J. Mark. (1984). "Outlaw Motorcyclists: An Outgrowth of Lower Class Cultural Concerns." In Delos H. Kelly (ed.), *Deviant Behavior* (2nd ed.). New York: St. Martin's Press.

West, W. Gordon. (1980). "The Short Term Careers of Serious Thieves." In Robert A. Silverman and James J. Teevan, Jr. (eds.), *Crime in Canadian Society* (2nd ed.). Toronto: Butterworths.

Wolf, Daniel R. (1991). *The Rebels: A Brotherhood of Outlaw Bikers*. Toronto: University of Toronto Press.

Wolfgang, Marvin E., Terence P. Thornberry, and Robert M. Figlio. (1987). *From Boy to Man, from Delinquency to Crime*. Chicago: University of Chicago Press.

13

Social Control Theory

RICK LINDEN
University of Manitoba

In this chapter, we begin by examining some of the early social disorganization theories exploring the relationship between social structure and deviance. Those who developed these theories felt that disorganized communities did not provide meaningful employment to residents and did not have strong families, schools, and churches. This lack of effective social controls led to high rates of crime and other types of deviance. While the early theorists looked at the relationship between community characteristics and crime, later theorists focused more on the social bonds of individuals. The discussion of these later theories will focus on the ways in which social bonds to conventional institutions such as the family and the school help to constrain crime and delinquency. Final sections of this chapter deal with some of the criticisms that have been made of control theory and with the policy implications of the theory.

After reading this chapter, you should be able to

- Understand the early social disorganization theories that sought to explain why crime rates were highest in neighbourhoods characterized by poverty, physical deterioration, and ethnic conflict.

- Know the importance of the social bonds of attachment, involvement, commitment, and belief in the causation of delinquency and crime.

- Explain the role of the family, the school, and the church in the causation of delinquency and crime.

- Describe the criticisms that have been made of social control theory and understand the validity of these criticisms.

- Understand the social policy implications of social control theory.

social control theory

The theory that people do not become criminal because they do not want to jeopardize their bonds to conventional society.

Social control theory assumes that human beings are neither good nor evil. Rather, we are born with the capacity to do wrong. Unlike most theories of criminality, control theory requires no special motivation to impel people to deviate. Since our natural propensity is to gratify ourselves with no concern for right and wrong, and since the "wrong" way may be the quickest and most efficient way of achieving our goals, it is conformity rather than deviance that must be explained. Other theorists ask, "Why do they do it?"; the control theorist is concerned with the question "Why don't we *all* do it?" The answer given by control theory is "We all would, if only we dared, but many of us dare not because we have loved ones we fear to hurt and physical possessions and social reputations we fear to lose" (Box, 1971, 140). All societies have developed ways of making people conform, and the control theorist is concerned with these processes that bind people to the social order.

THEORIES OF SOCIAL DISORGANIZATION—DURKHEIM, THRASHER, AND SHAW AND MCKAY

Durkheim and Social Integration

The earliest social control theories explained how some types of social structure led to high rates of crime and deviance. Communities characterized by poverty, physical deterioration, and racial or ethnic conflict were too disorganized to exert effective control over the behaviour of residents. Social disorganization theorists included Durkheim, Thrasher, and Shaw and McKay.

In his monograph *Suicide* (1951), Durkheim pointed out the importance of **social bonds** in the understanding of deviant behaviour. Egoistic suicide results from a situation in which a person's social ties are weakened to the extent that the person is freed from social constraints and acts only on the basis of private interests. Anomic suicide occurs when a lack of social integration, caused by factors such as rapid economic change, leaves a society without a clear system of moral beliefs and sentiments. In each case, social organization is weak, and the individual lacks moral guidance. If the rules are strong and if there is consensus about their validity, there will be little deviance. If the rules are weak and if there is minimal agreement about their applicability, society will be unable to regulate morality effectively, and deviance will be common. Without socially regulated goals, deviance is more likely, as people either pursue their aspirations without check or succumb to the mindlessness of pursuing unattainable goals.

We saw in Chapter 10 that in Merton's reformulation of anomie theory, he shifted from Durkheim's emphasis on a society's failure to define appropriate goals to an emphasis on the failure to define the appropriate means of reaching common culture goals, and on the unequal distribution of legitimate means of reaching these goals. More faithful to Durkheim's view of the effects of the social bond on deviance were the social disorganization theorists—among them Thrasher, and Shaw and McKay.

Thrasher and *The Gang*

Thrasher and Shaw and McKay focused their attention on ecological studies of the city. Thrasher's classic study *The Gang* is still the most extensive study of juvenile gangs ever done. Thrasher located gangs both geographically and socially where there are breaks in the structure of social organization. They occur "in city slums characterized by physical deterioration, rapid succession of inhabitants, mobility, and disorganization; along economic and ecological boundaries; along political frontiers; ... and during adolescence, an interstitial period between childhood and maturity" (Kornhauser, 1978, 51). Gangs arise spontaneously in areas where social controls are weak. Gangs are not necessarily delinquent, though delinquency will often be the natural result of the

social bond

The degree to which an individual has ties to his or her society. In Hirschi's theory, social bonds include *attachment, commitment, involvement,* and *belief.*

National Youth Gang Center (U.S.A.)
www.iir.com/nygc/

activities of groups of adolescents in communities where social institutions are not able to direct and control their behaviour (Thrasher, 1963). In the slum setting, delinquency was often the most exciting and interesting thing for these youths to do.

Shaw and McKay—Ecological Analysis

In one of the earliest sociological explanations of crime and delinquency, Shaw and McKay saw the origins of deviance not in the pathology of individuals, but in social disorganization. They concluded that the social structure of a community would affect its rates of crime and delinquency.

In their ecological analyses of the city of Chicago, Shaw and McKay found that some areas had disproportionately high rates of officially recorded crime and delinquency. Rates were highest in slum areas near the city centre and generally declined as one moved outward. Areas with high crime and delinquency rates were characterized by "physical deterioration, decreasing population, high rates of dependency, [and a] high percentage of foreign-born and Negro population" (Thrasher, 1963, 361). In many of these neighbourhoods, crime rates remained high over a long period of time, even though the racial and ethnic characteristics of the residents changed as new waves of immigrants moved into the city. Shaw and McKay attributed these high rates of crime to the failure of neighbourhood institutions and organizations such as families, schools, and churches to provide adequate social controls.

While control theory was not fully developed in the work of Thrasher and Shaw and McKay from the 1930s to the 1960s, subcultural and strain theories so dominated the field that there were very few additions to the social disorganization model (Kornhauser, 1978). Several reasons explain why control theory all but disappeared from the scene following this rather promising beginning. The most important of these was that the early research was methodologically flawed. The relationships among **independent variables** such as social class, mobility, and community diversity were consistent with social control theory, but they also were consistent with other perspectives such as strain theory, and Shaw and McKay never directly measured the degree of social control that existed in a particular community. They inferred, but did not demonstrate, that higher-income communities were better organized than were lower-class slums. The type of research done by Shaw and McKay was also subject to the problem of the **ecological fallacy**. For example, consider the finding that official crime rates are higher in lower-class than in middle-class areas. The conclusion usually drawn from this finding is that being a member of the lower class makes one more likely to become involved with crime. However, this inference is not necessarily true. Perhaps most crimes in lower-class areas are committed by middle-class residents of those census tracts. Perhaps the resident population is not responsible for crime at all. In his study of the impact of licensed hotels, bars, and shopping centres on Edmonton crime rates, Engstad (1975) showed that certain facilities, which may be attractive to people from other parts of the city, provide opportunities for crime. Chambliss (1973) found that middle-class adolescents migrated to other parts of the city to commit their delinquencies.

"Shaw and McKay: Social Disorganization Theory" **www.crimetheory.com/Soc1/ Chic2.htm**

independent variable

A presumed cause of a dependent variable. If unemployment is thought to cause crime rates to increase, unemployment is the independent variable, and crime rates the dependent variable.

ecological fallacy

A research error made when data or information is gathered at a group level (the unemployment rate of various communities or neighbourhoods) and then conclusions are drawn about individuals (the unemployed person). Areas with high unemployment may have high crime rates, but this does not tell us that those crimes are necessarily committed by unemployed persons.

Shaw and McKay studied only officially recorded crime and delinquency. The development of self-reporting measures and the discovery that crime was also commonly committed by the middle and upper classes made their claim that crime was primarily a lower-class slum phenomenon questionable. At least part of the over-representation of these areas in official statistics may be due to the behaviour of law enforcement agencies. For example, Hagan et al. (1978) have shown that an official police response was made to a higher proportion of complaints in areas Shaw and McKay might have called disorganized than in other areas. Finally, the vague and often value-laden term "social disorganization" fell into disrepute among sociologists.

Despite these problems, Thrasher and Shaw and McKay did lay the foundations for a control theory of crime and delinquency. They found that delinquents come from communities that are poorly organized and whose institutions are not well integrated. Families are unable to adequately socialize their children, and their schools are poor. These elements all reappear in the work of later theorists.

EARLY SOCIAL CONTROL THEORIES—REISS AND NYE

Albert Reiss

While the social disorganization theorists had been concerned with controls at the community and family level, Reiss (1951) was the first to distinguish between *social* controls, which include ties to primary groups such as the family and to the community and its institutions, and *personal* controls, which have been internalized by an individual. If these controls are absent, if they break down, if they are in conflict, or if they cannot be enforced, delinquency will result. Using information collected in the court files of a group of male juvenile probationers, Reiss found that success or failure on probation was associated with the absence of both social and personal controls.

Ivan Nye

Theoretically, the work of Nye (1958) simply expanded on that of Reiss. However, methodologically, it represented a great advance. While Reiss had relied on court records of youth who were officially defined as delinquent, Nye developed a technique for measuring self-reported delinquency and gathered his data from a random sample of high school students in three small American cities. His book represented one of the first attempts at unravelling the causes of delinquency using this approach.

While Reiss did not elaborate on the theory underlying personal and social controls, Nye was quite explicit in stating his theoretical perspective. To Nye, "control theory assumes delinquency is not caused in a positive sense (motivated by the gains to be derived from it) but prevented (determined by the relative costs of alternative benefits).... Weak controls free the person to commit delinquent acts by lowering their cost relative to available alternatives" (Kornhauser, 1978, 140–41). Individuals are motivated to achieve certain goals as quickly as possible but are prevented from doing so by the laws and customs that societies establish to protect their members.

In expanding on Reiss's distinction between personal and social controls, Nye outlined four types of controls:

1. Direct control from outside, such as that imposed by the police and parents.
2. Internalized control, which is self-enforcing and is exercised through one's conscience. Violations of internalized values will cause a child to feel guilt.
3. Indirect control, which is a function of the degree to which a child has affective ties with parents and other conforming individuals. Fear of embarrassing or hurting the person to whom the child has ties encourages conformity.
4. Availability of alternative ways of reaching one's goals.

Nye considered the family to be the most significant group in the development of social controls. The extent to which the family enforced external controls and the degree to which family members got along with one another determined the extent to which a child would develop internal controls. Some of Nye's specific findings will be discussed later in this chapter, but it should be mentioned here that the results of his research did support his hypotheses concerning the relationship between the family and delinquency. Children who came from families that were close and in which there was agreement on basic values were unlikely to be delinquent.

The work of Reiss and Nye provided a promising beginning for contemporary control theory. The work of other researchers such as the Gluecks (1950), the McCords (1959), and Gold (1963) provided evidence that was, for the most part, consistent with the theory. In fact, control theory received much more empirical support than did the theories of Merton, Cohen, Cloward and Ohlin, Miller, and Sutherland, which dominated the field. However, it took a number of years before control theory became widely accepted by criminologists as one of the major paradigms in explaining crime and delinquency.

HIRSCHI AND THE SOCIAL BOND

It was not until the publication of Travis Hirschi's *Causes of Delinquency* in 1969 that control theory began to receive wider attention. Hirschi developed a clear and concise version of control theory and presented an empirical examination of his theory, demonstrating that it explained delinquency better than did competing theories. Like earlier control theorists, Hirschi postulates that individuals are more likely to turn to illegitimate means if their bond to society is weak or broken. For Hirschi, four interrelated aspects of the social bond constrain our behaviour: attachment, commitment, involvement, and belief.

attachment

The degree to which an individual has affective ties to other persons. One of the social bonds in Hirschi's theory.

Attachment

Attachment refers to the degree to which the individual has affective ties to other persons, particularly those who belong to their primary groups. If an individual is sensitive to the feelings of others and close to those others, this attachment will constrain his or her behaviour because that individual will not want to hurt or embarrass the people he or she likes. Those lacking such ties will not have to consider the feelings of others and will be free to deviate. Thus, the person who dislikes his or her spouse will be more likely to have an affair than the person whose marriage is close. Youths who do not get along with their parents will be more free to commit acts of delinquency than those who are close to their families.

Commitment

The essence of **commitment** lies in the pursuit of conventional goals. "The idea, then, is that the person invests time, energy, himself, in a certain line of activity—say, getting an education, building up a business, acquiring a reputation for virtue" (Hirschi, 1969, 20). If a person decides to engage in deviance, that person will be putting his or her investment at risk. Thus, the student who has worked hard in school and who aspires to become a professional may avoid the temptations of delinquency for fear of jeopardizing this future career. However, the youth who is failing in school and who has no career aspirations may not feel as constrained. For the second youth, the immediate rewards of delinquency might outweigh the potential costs. Both commitments and attachments can change over time. For example, the phenomenon of maturational reform—as we get older, we behave better—can be explained by the fact that adults typically have a greater investment in conventional lines of activity than do adolescents so their deviance may have higher costs.

commitment
The degree to which an individual pursues conventional goals. One of the social bonds in Hirschi's theory.

Involvement

Hirschi felt that people's level of **involvement** has an impact on delinquency. According to control theory, if people are busy with conventional activities, they will not have time to engage in deviant behaviour. For example, if a student is busy at school and is involved in extracurricular activities, that student will not have as much opportunity to commit delinquencies as will peers who are not as involved.

involvement
The degree to which an individual is active in conventional activities. One of the social bonds in Hirschi's theory.

Belief

Our **belief** in conventional values, morality, and the legitimacy of the law will constrain our behaviour. Unlike cultural deviance theorists, who believe that deviants are tied to value systems different from those of the rest of the population, Hirschi claims that society does have a common value system. However, individuals vary in the degree to which they believe they should obey the rules. While cultural deviance theorists tell us that acts that are deviant from the perspective of those who have the power to make and enforce the rules are *required* by the beliefs of members of certain subcultures, the control theorist says that deviant acts are made possible by the *absence* of beliefs forbidding them.

For the most part, research has supported Hirschi's theory, particularly for the variables of attachment and commitment. Belief in the law has also been

belief
The degree to which an individual believes in conventional values, morality, and the legitimacy of law. One of the social bonds in Hirschi's theory.

found to be related to delinquency (Gomme, 1985). The evidence concerning involvement is mixed in that involvement in school activities is related to lower involvement in delinquency, while participation in sports, hobbies, and part-time jobs is not (Hirschi, 1969).

Self-Control—The General Theory of Crime

Hirschi's early work focused on external sources of social control such as family, friends, and school. In 1990 Gottfredson and Hirschi published *A General Theory of Crime,* in which they proposed that individuals with low self-control have a greater propensity to commit crimes when they have the opportunity to do so. They will also be more likely to engage in other risky behaviour such as smoking, drinking, and dangerous driving. Gottfredson and Hirschi believe this theory applies to all types of crime.

Individuals who lack self-control are impulsive people who focus on the moment rather than planning for the future, who have unstable personal relationships, and who are less likely to feel shame or remorse when their actions hurt others. As Gottfredson and Hirschi have stated, when "desires conflict with long-term interests, those lacking self-control opt for the desires of the moment, whereas those with greater self-control are governed by the restraints imposed by the consequences of acts displeasing to family, friends, and the law" (1990, xvi).

Why do some people lack self-control? For Gottfredson and Hirschi, the answer lies in early childhood socialization. Children will have low self-control if they have poor relationships with their parents or if their parents do not have good parenting skills. Those who fail to develop self-control in childhood will be more likely to be involved in crime throughout their entire lives, so the impact of poor early socialization may persist for many years. Their behaviour will be constrained only by the lack of opportunities to commit crimes and other deviant acts.

Several Canadian researchers have studied the relationship between self-control and criminal behaviour. Using data collected during a nighttime roadside survey of Ontario drivers, Keane et al. (1993) found that men and women who were lower in self-control had higher levels of blood alcohol than other drivers. Sorenson and Brownfield (1995) also found a correlation between self-control and drug use. However, they found that ties to delinquent friends were correlated more strongly with drug use than any of their self-control variables. Marc LeBlanc (1997) has suggested that low self-control is just one of several psychological traits that should be a part of a comprehensive social control theory of offending. In his own research in Quebec, LeBlanc found that youth with "egocentric personalities"—a construct similar in some respects to Gottfredson and Hirschi's notion of low self-control—have weaker social bonds and higher levels of delinquency than their peers (LeBlanc et al., 1988). In their study of young people in Edmonton, LaGrange and Silverman (1999) found that self-control explained part of the difference in delinquency involvement between males and females.

While some research does support this theory, other evidence suggests that it will not replace more traditional versions of control theory. In the general

"Risk or Threats to Children"
National Crime Prevention
Strategy
www.prevention.gc.ca/en/library/
publications/children/risk/

theory of crime, Gottfredson and Hirschi turned away from Hirschi's earlier view that ongoing social bonds will make involvement in crime and delinquency less likely. Instead, they proposed that early childhood experiences can produce low levels of self-control that will result in higher levels of deviance throughout the entire life course. However, Sampson and Laub (1993) have cast doubt on this hypothesis. Their study followed boys from ages 17 to 25 and found that those who developed adult social bonds, including stable jobs and cohesive marriages, were less likely to be involved in criminality than their peers who did not develop these ties. Thus, rather than remaining stable over the life course, the propensity to deviate appears to be variable and to depend on changes in one's social bonds. Childhood patterns of deviance are not necessarily carried into adulthood. Several other studies, including the work by LaGrange and Silverman (1999) and a thorough review of 21 studies by Pratt and Cullen (2000), suggest that self-control provides at best only a partial explanation of crime and delinquency and does not explain "all crime, at all times," as Gottfredson and Hirschi claim (117).

In the remainder of this chapter, we will look in detail at some of the research evidence bearing on control theory, discuss the weaknesses of the theory, suggest ways in which the theory might be revised, and consider its social policy implications.

FAMILY RELATIONSHIPS

Social control theory places a major emphasis on family relationships since these provide children with the attachments necessary to restrain their involvement in delinquency. A number of aspects of family relationships are related to delinquency. Among these are strength of family ties, parental supervision and discipline, and the role model provided by parents.

Strength of Family Ties

Strong ties within the family are important in the development of the social bond. If parents are close to their children and provide a congenial atmosphere in the home, family relationships should act as a deterrent to delinquency. Children in such families should be concerned about what their parents think of them and should be less likely to become involved in delinquency.

A number of studies confirm this view. Warm, affectionate family relationships are associated with low rates of delinquency, while mutual rejection and hostility are typical of the families of delinquents (Glueck and Glueck, 1950; Nye, 1958; Gold, 1963; McCord, 1979; Gove and Crutchfield, 1982). Several of these researchers have also found that conflict between the parents also characterizes the families of delinquents. A study of Edmonton youth discovered that boys who found their families attractive and who were concerned with pleasing their parents were less likely to be delinquent than boys who did not have such close ties to their parents (Kupfer, 1966).

"A Summary of Family Life, Delinquency, and Crime: A Policymaker's Guide"
Office of Prevention, Texas Youth Commission
www.tyc.state.tx.us/prevention/ famlife.htm

Parental Supervision and Discipline

Children who are adequately supervised by their parents and whose parents discipline them in an appropriate fashion will have lower delinquency rates than will their peers who do not share these advantages. A large number of studies have demonstrated the importance of parents' knowing what their children are doing and ensuring that they play with friends whom the parents consider suitable (Glueck and Glueck, 1950; Nye, 1958; Hirschi, 1969; West and Farrington, 1973; Wilson, 1980). Studies of delinquency in Montreal and Edmonton have found that supervision was more strongly related to delinquency than any other family variable (Caplan, 1977; Biron and LeBlanc, n.d.; Kupfer, 1966).

Closely related to supervision is parental discipline. While critics of control theory have complained that the theory advocates the harsh treatment of children, control theorists do not view physical punishment as the major means of controlling behaviour. Rather, they see that "disapproval by people one cares about is the most powerful of sanctions. Effective punishment by the parent or major caretaker therefore usually entails nothing more than explicit disapproval of unwanted behaviour" (Gottfredson and Hirschi, 1990, 99–100). Studies have consistently found the disciplinary practices of delinquent families to be different from those of non-delinquent families. Those families in which discipline was inconsistent or lax were much more likely to have delinquent children (Glueck and Glueck, 1950; Nye, 1958; West and Farrington, 1973). Children do not appear to learn from discipline unless it is administered in a clear, consistent manner.

There is also some evidence of association between higher rates of delinquency and very strict discipline, particularly if it is associated with harsh physical punishment (Fischer, 1980) and if parental warmth and supportiveness is lacking (Simons et al., 2000). Very strict discipline is likely seen as unfair and may lead to feelings of frustration and resentment on the part of the child. Harsh punishment may be effective in gaining immediate compliance, but more moderate discipline is more effective in encouraging children to internalize a set of values that will ensure long-term compliance (Aronson, 1984).

In his study of youth in a poor inner-city community, Elijah Anderson describes how what he calls "street-oriented" parents—those who do not try to emulate the "decent-family model"—discipline their children:

> In these circumstances, a woman—or a man, although men are less consistently present in children's lives—can be quite aggressive with children, yelling at them and striking at them for the least little infraction of the rules she has set down. Often little, if any, serious explanation follows the verbal and physical punishment. This response teaches children a particular lesson. They learn that to solve any kind of interpersonal problem, one must quickly resort to hitting or other violent behaviour. (Anderson, 1994, 83)

The importance of parenting style is clearly shown in a major study that is being conducted by Statistics Canada (1998). The National Longitudinal

Survey of Children and Youth (NLSCY) is following the development of more than 23 000 children. The researchers asked parents of these children about several dimensions of their parenting styles, including punitiveness, hostility, consistency, and the amount of positive interaction. Parenting style had a strong correlation with relationship and behavioural problems in children. For example, children who were exposed to hostile or ineffective parenting in both the 1994 and the 1996 survey periods were *nine* times more likely to have behavioural problems than were children who were not exposed to these parenting styles. Parenting style, particularly hostile parenting, was more strongly related to behavioural problems than other factors, including income and family structure.

"National Longitudinal Survey of Children and Youth"
Statistics Canada
www.statcan.ca/Daily/English/981028/d981028.htm#ART1

Parental Role Model

In his initial formulation of control theory, Hirschi argued that ties to parents will act as a deterrent to delinquency involvement regardless of the criminality of the parents. However, there does appear to be a relationship between the criminality of the parent and that of the child. For example, West and Farrington (1973) found that boys with at least one parent convicted of a criminal offence were more than twice as likely to become delinquent as those whose parents had no convictions. "Youthful crime often seems to be part of a family tradition" (West, 1982, 44). West does not attribute these findings to the parents' deliberately transmitting criminal values to their offspring since few of the children were involved in their parents' criminality, and the parents expressed disapproval of their children's involvement in delinquency. The relationship is at least partially explained by the fact that parents with criminal records were lax in applying rules and did not supervise their children effectively. In light of West's findings that criminal fathers were likely to be on social assistance and unemployment benefits and that this dependency was repeated among their sons, it would appear that families with criminal parents may have a variety of problems that are manifested in both parental criminality and poor family relationships. West and Farrington (1977) also suggest that part of the relationship between parental criminality and delinquency may be due to labelling because an act of delinquency leading to arrest was more likely to result in a conviction if a boy came from a criminal family.

While there is little to suggest that direct modelling of parental behaviour is a major cause of delinquency, it may be a factor in some types of offences. Rutter and Giller suggest that "criminal parents may provide a model of aggression and antisocial attitudes, if not of criminal activities as such" (1984, 183). The fact that a high proportion of abusive parents were themselves abused as children provides support for the view that family violence is learned in childhood in the home (Steinmetz and Straus, 1980). Abusive parents contribute to delinquency in another way. In a study of homeless youth in Toronto, Hagan and McCarthy (1997) found that some of their respondents were living on the streets in order to escape abuse at home. Once they were on the street, their need for food, shelter, and money led to delinquent behaviour.

career criminal

An individual with a long criminal history who organizes many aspects of his or her life around criminality. These individuals tend to commit a large portion of the total amount of crime in a community.

Family Relationships and Adult Criminality

While most juvenile delinquents do not become adult **career criminals**, most of those who do become career criminals begin as juveniles. Further, the earlier the age at which serious delinquency begins, the more likely it is to continue in adult life (Petersilia, 1980). Longitudinal studies confirm the relationship between childhood family relationships and adult criminality. McCord (1979) followed up a group of men who had been part of the Cambridge–Somerville study 30 years earlier. She found that variables describing family atmosphere (parental aggression, paternal deviance, maternal self-confidence, supervision, mother's affection, and parental conflict) were related to criminal behaviour. Interestingly, family relationships may be important factors in the rehabilitation of adult criminals. Wright and Wright (1992), having found that rates of reoffending are lower among adult offenders who have established and maintained healthy family relationships, recommend that probation and parole officers work with families to try to strengthen these ties.

SCHOOLING

Like the family, the school plays a primary role in socializing young people and is an important determinant of delinquency. The school is a pervasive influence in a young person's life. For most of the year, children spend all day in classes and return to school after hours for other activities such as sports and dances. More important, the school is an arena in which an adolescent's performance is constantly being judged. Those who are successful enjoy the prestige conferred by teachers, parents, and other adults as well as by many of their classmates. Those who fail may feel that they have been rejected by the adult world as well as by their peers (Hargreaves, 1967; Polk and Richmond, 1972). For those who are successful in school and who enjoy their educational experience, the school provides a stake in conformity. However, those who fail do not have this stake and hence are more likely to become involved in delinquency. The correlation between school failure and delinquency is relatively strong and has been replicated in Canada (Kupfer, 1966; Gomme, 1985), Britain (Hargreaves, 1967), and the United States (Hirschi, 1969; Polk and Schafer, 1972).

The school has an impact on delinquency in two distinct but interrelated ways. The first is that the school is "one of the fundamental determinants of an individual's economic and social position" (Polk and Schafer, 1972, 10). The school has taken over many of the occupational socialization functions that in earlier times were performed by the family. Over the past hundred years, formal educational qualifications have become the basis for entry into most occupations. Thus, a child's experiences in school will have a profound impact on that child's future life chances. The second way the school is related to delinquency is through its effects on the daily life of the child. For some, the experience is interesting, pleasant, and enriching. For others, it is irrelevant, degrading, and humiliating.

Both types of impact have an effect on a student's stake in conformity. Those whose school experiences will clearly not qualify them for meaningful occupations may not have the same degree of commitment as their peers whose expectations are higher. The daily consequences of failure and the resulting lack of attachment to the school also affect the child. In fact, research suggests that the daily problems of coping with school failure may be more strongly related to delinquency than is concern about the future. Linden (1974) found that measures reflecting present school status (whether the child liked school, finished homework, skipped school, thought good grades were important, and got along with teachers) were more highly correlated with delinquency than were measures of educational aspirations and expectations. A recent study by Arum and Beattie (1999) showed that students who experienced a school environment with small class sizes and course work that was relevant to their lives had lower rates of adult incarceration than those with less positive school experiences, even when their education did not provide any labour market benefit.

Some criminologists see a broader relationship between the school system and delinquency. From a structural perspective, the school "cuts adolescents off from participating in the social and economic life of the community: it reduces their commitments and attachments" (West, 1984, 169). Even within the school, the educational process involves the student in only a passive way. Polk and Schafer (1972) illustrate the irrelevance of the student role by asking what happens when a student dies. The student disappears without leaving a social ripple aside from family bereavement. The student's role is not one that has to be filled by someone else. This marginality may contribute to delinquency by leaving the adolescent relatively free of the commitments that constrain deviance.

RELIGION

Conventional wisdom has long held that people with strong religious commitment are not likely to become criminals. In the early penitentiaries that were the predecessors of our current prison system, Bible study was a major rehabilitative tool (Rothman, 1971). The first educational programs in prisons were implemented in order to provide inmates with the basic literacy skills needed to read the Bible and other religious literature, which was expected to motivate the offender to mend his ways.

Support for this common-sense view was provided by several early studies that showed a modest negative relationship between religious involvement and criminal behaviour. However, in 1969, Hirschi and Stark reported the results of a study that found that religious commitment was not related to delinquency. Neither church attendance, nor the belief in supernatural sanctions for those who broke the rules, nor the religiosity of parents was associated with delinquency. Because the work of Hirschi and Stark was methodologically superior to that of earlier researchers (and perhaps because of a secular bias among criminologists), the results of this study were commonly accepted as definitive. Most contemporary theories of the causes of crime do not consider religion to be an important explanatory factor.

However, subsequent studies found strong negative correlations between church attendance and delinquency (Higgins and Albrecht, 1977; Albrecht et

"Religion and Crime Examined" International Center for the Integration of Health & Spirituality
www.nihr.org/programs/ researchreports/ religionandcrime.cfm

al., 1977). How are we to reconcile these conflicting findings? One plausible answer has been given by Stark et al. (1982), who concluded that the key to resolving the contradiction was to look at differences in the communities in which the research was carried out. The studies that found no relationship between religiosity and delinquency were done in areas where religious participation was low, while those communities in which a relationship was found had high religious participation.

Using data collected by other researchers, Stark et al. provided additional evidence to support this view. They compared samples of boys from Provo, Utah, where the church membership rate is very high, with boys from Seattle, where church membership rates are among the lowest in the United States. In Provo, the correlation (gamma) between church attendance and delinquency was −.45, while in Seattle, it was only −.13. This means that the relationship was much stronger in Provo than in Seattle. The relationship also holds for adult crime. In another paper (Stark et al., 1980), they found a relationship between church membership and crime rates for 193 U.S. cities. Stark et al. conclude that religiosity is related to crime and delinquency in communities where religion is important, but not in highly secularized communities.

Their explanation of why this should be the case is worth considering as it has broader implications for social control theory. Stark et al. believe that an **individualistic**, psychological view of the manner in which religion constrains behaviour has led researchers astray. Rather than looking at religion as affecting deviance through an individual's fear of religious sanctions, they suggest that "religion only serves to bind people to the moral order if religious influences permeate the culture and the social interactions of the individuals in question" (Stark et al., 1982). Religion will have its greatest impact where it serves to bind its adherents into a moral community. In such a community, religious teachings will be salient and are likely to be consistently reinforced. Under these circumstances, an individual is less likely to consider deviant behaviour. The costs to someone who does decide to violate community norms may be high, and the likelihood of finding reference groups that support such a violation will be relatively low. Religion will have a greater impact if it is part of the community's institutional order than if it is a private matter.

It seems clear that religion does constrain involvement in delinquent and criminal behaviour. However, this relationship is complex—it is greatest where there is a strong religious community; to some extent, it is mediated by one's relationships with family and friends (Elifson et al., 1983); and it has the most impact on behaviour (such as marijuana use) that may not be universally condemned by other segments of society (Linden and Currie, 1977).

individualistic

A theory that focuses on explaining the behaviour of individuals and using factors or features of the individual in explaining this behaviour.

FEMALE CRIMINALITY

Since control theory views conformity rather than deviance as its central question, the fact that women have higher levels of conformity than men should have played an important part in the development of the theory. However, this has not been the case. While some control theorists have looked at female crime and delinquency, most have not looked explicitly at sex differences in the degree of adherence to social bonds. In fact, Hirschi excluded females from his analysis even though he had collected data from them.

A number of studies comparing male and female delinquency have been done using a control framework. Typical of the results was Linden's (1974) finding, using Hirschi's California data, that social bond variables were correlated with the delinquency of both boys and girls, though the magnitude of the correlations was generally lower for girls. Part of the sex difference in delinquency involvement was related to higher levels of parental supervision and a lower level of attachment to delinquent peers reported by the girls, as compared with the boys. However, there were still differences between the sexes that could not be accounted for by control variables.

This type of research has been extended by Hagan et al. (1985). Since their work has been discussed at length in Chapters 5 and 6, it will be sufficient here to recall that the theory dealt with socially structured differences in sex roles and that parents were more likely to place controls on the activities of daughters than of sons.

Naffine (1987) has suggested an interesting new line of inquiry that may shed more light on the causes of female criminality. She is critical of the view of control theorists that "it is the stereotypically female qualities (passivity, compliance, dependence) which bond women to the conventional order" (131). She contends that the new idea for feminism is that law-abiding women are not vapid, biddable creatures, clinging helplessly to conventional society. Instead, they are, to use Hirschi's description of conforming men, responsible, hardworking, engrossed in conventional activities and people, and perfectly rational in their calculation not to place all of this at risk by engaging in crime. She observes that women are heavily involved in conventional activities, including both work and child rearing, and hypothesizes that their intense involvement in nurturing children provides them with more powerful attachments to the conventional order. While Naffine's thesis is only speculative, it should generate research that will have an important impact on future versions of social control theory as well as on our understanding of female criminality.

CRITICISMS OF SOCIAL CONTROL THEORY

The evidence we have reviewed in this chapter is generally supportive of control theory—in fact, many observers believe that empirical research provides more support for control theory than for any of its competitors. However, a number of questions have been raised about the theory that will be addressed in this section. While we can fairly take issue with specific versions of control theory—for example, many researchers have raised questions about some aspects of Hirschi's theory—we will limit discussion to more general criticisms of the control perspective. Among these criticisms are that the theory does not explain upper-world crime; it does not adequately account for the motivation to deviate; it ignores the deterrent effects of law; its emphasis is too individualistic; and it is too conservative.

Control Theory Does Not Explain Upper-World Crime

The focus of control theory has been on street crime and juvenile delinquency, not on occupational crime committed by high-status adults. In fact, upper-world crime would appear to contradict control theory's emphasis on the role of commitment in preventing crime because high-status people have a great stake in conformity. However, control theory can be used to understand such crime.

In his analysis of the Watergate cover-up in the United States, John Hagan (1985, 171–73) has provided us with a control theory of upper-world crime. The Watergate affair took place over a two-year period from 1972 to 1974. It involved the attempt by highly placed U.S. government officials to conceal their involvement in an unsuccessful plot to break into the offices of the Democratic National Committee. Ultimately, these events led to the resignation of President Richard Nixon and to the imprisonment of a number of his senior advisors.

From a control perspective, such illegal events could have been prevented by the belief that such acts were wrong. However, North American society has not clearly defined upper-world morality. Politicians and business leaders rarely receive more than token punishments for illegal activities and are more likely to see their behaviour as only technically wrong than to consider themselves criminals. Transcripts of tapes made by Nixon reveal no concern with morality or ethics. In the absence of moral constraints, "the occurrence of such behaviors will depend largely on the risk and rewards ... associated with violating public and financial trust" (173). As you will see in Chapter 16, the rewards of upper-world crime are often very great. What, then, about the risks?

> The situational controls operative at the time of the initial Watergate offenses were inadequate. White House aides were able to manipulate funds and personnel for criminal political reasons with little expectation of detection. One reason why there was so little expectation of detection, of course, was that the criminals in this case were people who controlled the institutions of legal control (who could have been better positioned to deviate than those who controlled the FBI, the Justice Department, etc.?). Furthermore, once "caught," punishment became problematic in an atmosphere confused by promiscuous discussions of pardons. The uncertainties surrounding these events emphasize, then, the porous nature of the controls operative in one upperworld setting. (173)

In the discussion of the policy implications of social control theory in the next section of this chapter, you will learn that the theory has a message for those who wish to control deviant behaviour: monitor behaviour, recognize deviance, and punish deviant behaviour. While these principles are intended as advice for parents raising children, they seem applicable in the control of upper-world crime as well. As Hagan tells us: "If there is a message to the policy-minded in the Watergate experience ... it is that checks and balances on power are crucial. Upperworld vocations, particularly politics and business, often carry with them a freedom to deviate unparalleled in the underworld. As control theory reminds us, unchecked freedom is a criminogenic condition" (173).

Control Theory Does Not Account for the Motivation to Deviate

While there has been strong research support for control theory, critics have noted that a theory should also account for the motivation to deviate. To the control theorist, we would *all* be criminal or delinquent but for the restraints provided by various types of social controls. However, it does appear that this is only a partial explanation. Several factors can be postulated to increase the likelihood of deviance among those who lack ties to the conventional order (Box, 1981). We shall consider just one of these here—ties to deviant peers, which have been found to be one of the strongest correlates of delinquency. For example, Sorenson and Brownfield (1995) found that ties to delinquent peers were a better predictor of drug use among Seattle youth than several measures of social control. Thornberry et al. (1993) studied a group of youths in Rochester, New York, and found that these youths were more likely to have committed acts of delinquency while they were active members of juvenile gangs than they were either before or after their gang membership.

One way to deal with this is to integrate differential association (see Chapter 12) and control theories. These two theories present conflicting notions about the causation of crime and delinquency. For the differential association theorist, the crucial concept is ties to others who provide a source of definitions favourable to violation of the law; the pure control theorist claims that it is those individuals with no ties to others—not even deviant others—who are most likely to become deviant.

Control theory conceives of an individual's social bond as having only a single dimension, weak to strong. When we incorporate differential association's emphasis on the importance of ties to deviant peers into the control theory analysis, however, we should see the social bond as multidimensional: conventional—weak to strong; unconventional—weak to strong. In bringing the two perspectives together, it is proposed that the first step in delinquency involvement is a weakness in the controls that bind an individual to the conventional system. An individual without these ties does not have to consider the consequences his or her actions will have on institutional and personal relationships. With the person "adrift" in this way (Matza, 1964), delinquency is a possible alternative. We are then faced with the problem of accounting for the motivation to commit acts of crime and delinquency (if we wish to go beyond the control theorists' reliance on natural motivation) and with explaining how one learns the techniques and rationalizations that facilitate deviance.

At least part of the answer to these questions can be found in differential association theory. We can postulate that the adolescent's lack of ties to the conventional order will increase the likelihood of association with deviant peers since the adolescent no longer has anything to lose by such affiliation. These ties will, in turn, increase the probability that the adolescent will be involved in deviance. The relationship between the variables is shown in Figure 13.1.

This extension of control theory has been found to explain more of the variation in delinquency than can either of its parent theories alone (Linden and Hackler, 1973; Linden and Fillmore, 1981). However, both of these studies

FIGURE 13.1   Control-Differential Association Theory

Source: Rick Linden and Cathy Fillmore. (1981). "A Comparative Study of Delinquency Involvement." *Canadian Review of Sociology and Anthropology* 18:343–61.

utilized cross-sectional data rather than the longitudinal data that are more appropriate to the sequential theory we have proposed.

The sequential model proposed here is more consistent with control theory than with Sutherland's differential association. The control–differential association model does not necessarily entail the strong element of normative approval required by Sutherland's cultural deviance perspective. Even if this normative approval is not a factor, delinquency may be fun and profitable and is not disapproved of by the delinquent's peer group. The internal dynamics of the group are such that it would be difficult for a reluctant member not to go along. Several researchers, including Short and Strodtbeck (1965) and Velarde (1978), have found that delinquent boys may try to look "bad" or "tough" in front of the group, even though they may express different views privately, because each believes the others are committed to such values. "An individual delinquent may wonder if or even think that his/her friends are not committed to delinquencies, but he/she can never confront the others to be sure of the degree of commitment they have" (Velarde, 1978).

Other sociologists have also attempted to integrate control theory with competing perspectives. Glaser (1978) has also tried to link control and differential association theories, and Akers (1977) and Conger (1980) have linked control theory with social learning theory. The most comprehensive extension of control theory has been carried out by Marc LeBlanc and several colleagues at the University of Montreal (LeBlanc, 1997; LeBlanc and Tremblay, 1985; Caplan and LeBlanc, 1985; Fréchette and LeBlanc, 1985). In addition to control and differential association variables, these researchers have also included the variables of external social control, personality traits, and the structural conditions of sex and social status. Most recently, Hardwick (2002) has shown that personality variables such as childhood temperament and self-control interact with social bonding variables and other social variables to produce delinquent and criminal behaviour. Because none of the theories you have studied in this text provides a complete explanation of crime and delinquency, it is likely that this integrative work will continue.

Control Theory Ignores the Deterrent Effects of Law

With their emphasis on the informal sanctioning system that is part of the process of socialization, most social control theorists pay little attention to formal legal sanctions. In fact, some have gone so far as to almost deny their effectiveness altogether: "For the great mass of infractions of the law ... the fear of consequences or the fear of punishment probably enters very little into causation" (Reckless, 1967). A more realistic view can be found in the work of Werner Stark, who has written extensively on the nature of the social bond:

> The assertion that a well-functioning and perfected legal system is the best safeguard of sociality and culture may at the first blush appear extravagant, but a short consideration will unavoidably prove it to be correct. The law, it is true, depends on social life, but social life in its turn depends for its continued existence on the law which it has created. If, in a thought experiment, we think away the law, and especially the executive organs of the law, we come face to face with the fact that in this case, chaos would replace order, and universal insecurity, security. (Stark, 1980, 225–26)

To provide a more concrete example, consider the consequences of a police strike. In Canada there have been several, the most notable occurring in 1969 in Montreal, during which thousands of apparently "law-abiding" citizens went on a rampage of theft and destruction (Clark, 1971). While it is true that most of the time, most of the people obey the law without consciously thinking of the formal consequences, such sanctions are necessary to reinforce the social controls that are operative most of the time.

Some control theorists have dealt with notions of deterrence. They have asked whether there is a relationship between an individual's perception of the likelihood of being caught and punished, and deviant behaviour. Jensen (1969) found that boys whose attachments and commitments were low were less likely to be delinquent if they perceived that offenders faced a strong likelihood of being caught. While the work of Jensen and others has shown that perception of the likelihood of formal sanctions must be considered, it is a variable that has been largely ignored by control theorists.

Control Theory Is Too Individualistic

Recent work in control theory has focused on the social processes that tie individuals to the social order and has emphasized relationships with family, school, peer group, and church. Some have been critical of the theory for not examining larger structural factors that affect crime and delinquency (Box, 1981).

While this is a fair criticism of recent work, it is certainly not one that necessarily applies to a theory that has its roots in the work of Durkheim and the social disorganization theorists, who were quite concerned with the relationship between social structure and crime. What has been lacking since the 1930s is research on the linkage between structural factors and the individual. This would enable the question of why different groups vary in their rates of deviance to be addressed. Some work has been done in this area. For example, Linden et al. (1985) have studied the structural characteristics of Mennonite society that contribute to its low rate of problem drinking. The work by Hagan et al. (1979) discussed in Chapter 5 suggests that the informal social controls provided by the family are greater for females than for males and at least partly account for their lower rates of involvement in delinquency. This conclusion has also been supported by Gomme (1985).

More work of this type must be done if control theory is to provide the beginnings of a comparative sociology of crime. For example, we might ask whether control theory can account for differences in crime rates between different countries. Are the differences in crime rates between Japan and the United States due to differences in family structure or to the relevance of the school experience? Does the greater homogeneity of Japanese society make it easier to control deviance? Is there a stronger belief among Japanese in the morality of law, and does the type of loyalty shown by the Japanese corporation to its employees create stronger bonds to society?

Control Theory Is Too Conservative

The preceding chapters have shown that there is no simple explanation of crime. Research on the causes of crime is far from conclusive, and there are many different perspectives that can teach us something about these causes. In the absence of any consensus, some criminologists have taken an ideological approach in which theories are accepted or rejected on the basis of whether they are sufficiently conservative or radical. Robert Bohm has observed that "political and value preferences, ideology, empiricism, and positivism ... stand in the way of any unity between traditional and radical criminologists" (1987, 327). For example, some radical criminologists have been very critical of theories of crime, such as control theory, which do not focus on the political and economic structures that produce crime.

To some degree, this critique is a fair one and is related to the criticism that control theory is too individualistic. Control theorists have emphasized people's immediate environment, and since the time of Shaw and McKay, they have not considered the political and economic structures of their communities. However, the mistake these critics make is to reject the theory rather than recognize the fact that there is ample scope for incorporating control variables within a structural perspective. For example, Shaw and McKay pointed out the importance of community variables in the development of social bonds. The ways in which control theory explains individual differences in criminal involvement are compatible with any number of structural theories, including radical theories, and provide the link between society and individual that these structural theories lack.

While the focus of control theory is on an individual's relationships with social institutions, it is obvious that there are structural factors that condition these relationships. Thus, although crime involves the behaviour of individuals, it has its origins in the social structure in which these individuals live. Lynch and Groves point out that "persons are more likely to conform when they stand to gain by doing so. But to make conformity attractive, society must do something for the individual; it must provide minimal satisfaction for both human and culturally defined needs. Social structures that provide for these needs are more likely to encourage conformity" (1989, 78).

In a society with low rates of deviance, social institutions will work together to encourage and to support conforming behaviour. If these institutions do not work together and if individuals and groups are alienated from their society's institutions, rates of deviance will be high. Consider, for example, the problems faced by Canada's Aboriginal people. They have far less power and fewer resources than other Canadians. They must cope with systems of education and religion imposed from outside that are not compatible with Aboriginal customs and traditions. Forced attendance at residential schools and forced adoption outside of the community have destroyed family ties, and crippling rates of unemployment mean no job ties. School curricula that are irrelevant to Aboriginal students mean that children do not become attached to their schools. Many Aboriginal Canadians must face daily encounters with racism. They must submit to government policies that have not allowed Aboriginal communities to achieve effective institutional integration. Under these conditions, strong social bonds are very difficult to develop, and the high rates of crime described in Chapter 5 can be expected. As Manitoba's Aboriginal Justice Inquiry has concluded: "From our review of the information available to us, including the nature of the crimes committed by aboriginal people, and after hearing the hundreds of submissions presented to us in the course of our hearings, we believe that the relatively high rates of crime among aboriginal people are a result of the despair, dependency, anger, frustration, and sense of injustice prevalent in aboriginal communities, stemming from the cultural and community breakdown that has occurred over the past century" (Hamilton and Sinclair, 1991, 91). The impact of structural conditions on social bonds and on rates of crime and other deviant behaviour is illustrated in the discussion of life on the Grassy Narrows reserve presented in Box 13.1. By incorporating control elements within a structural perspective, it demonstrates the complementarity of the control and radical approaches.

"Manitoba Aboriginal Justice Inquiry 1991 Summary"
www.ajic.mb.ca/volume.html

POLICY IMPLICATIONS OF CONTROL THEORY

One additional criticism that has been made of social control theory is that it has few implications for social policy. Critics question the usefulness of a theory

BOX 13.1

FOCUS

The Grassy Narrows Reserve

On July 25, 1991, Ontario Provincial Police Sergeant Tom Cooper was shot to death on the Grassy Narrows reserve near Kenora in northern Ontario. The murder was committed by a resident of the reserve whom other residents had said was addicted to gas sniffing. Behind this shooting lies a tragic story that illustrates the problems that have faced Aboriginal people in Canada. The two excerpts that follow are from a book by Anastasia Shkilnyk, *A Poison Stronger Than Love: The Destruction of an Ojibway Community*. First, Shkilnyk describes some of the symptoms of the problems in Grassy Narrows:

> People who have never lived under such conditions may find it difficult to comprehend that there could be a human settlement in which odds of dying a natural death from sickness, old age, or misadventure hover around 25 percent. Yet, at Grassy Narrows, if the trend continues, three out of every four persons will die from an act of violence. This extraordinary probability of violent death spares no one, regardless of age. For people under nineteen, the odds of dying violently are even greater, and their deaths still more disturbing because they will probably die by their own hand.
>
> There are other indications that Grassy Narrows is a deeply disturbed community. Cases of acute child neglect, for example, are in general extremely rare among Indian peoples, who are known for their indulgent devotion to their young. At Grassy Narrows, however, in just one year, the Children's Aid Society had to take away over a third of all children between the ages of five and fourteen because they had been physically abused, severely neglected, or simply abandoned. When this evidence of a discontinuity in the ability of people to care for and protect their offspring is viewed alongside the data on the extent of

alcoholism and alcohol-related illness among adults, the inescapable conclusion emerges that aberrant and self-destructive behaviour has become the collective norm for this community. Social pathology, usually confined to a minority of the population becomes represented by the majority. The data speak for themselves. The social conditions at Grassy Narrows are very serious, far worse than those found among other Indian bands in the region, and comparable to those documented for indigenous populations that have been through a major upheaval or disaster. (Shkilnyk, 1985, 10)

What caused the decline of Grassy Narrows? In his introduction to Shkilnyk's book, sociologist Kai Erikson reviews the history of the Grassy Narrows people. Erikson had spent many years studying the impact of natural disasters on people's lives and had been invited to Grassy Narrows to examine the impact of the dumping of thousands of pounds of highly toxic methyl mercury into the lakes and rivers surrounding the reserve. Not only had this mercury poisoned people, but it had destroyed the fishery that many reserve residents depended on for their livelihood. As Erikson comments: "The closing of the waters meant the end of meaningful employment at the reserve, and by the time I visited Grassy Narrows, that proud band of hunters and trappers and fishermen had begun a slide into dependency and humiliation that is the main subject of this book" (in Shkilnyk, 1985, xiii). Tragic as it was, the impact of the poisoning of the waterways was magnified by several other events that had weakened the fibre of the community:

> In the 60 or so years that had preceded the relocation, the people of Grassy Narrows had experienced several shocks that served to weaken the fibre of Ojibway society. Each of these shocks can be traced directly

(continued)

or indirectly to white contact, and each of them can be justly described as a disaster from the point of view of the people exposed to it. There was an awful influenza epidemic in 1919, for example, that not only killed off more than half the population, but placed an enormous strain on the Ojibwa belief system because traditional ways of controlling the rages of nature proved powerless. At the same time, Indian children were being taken to residential schools many miles from the reserve and, as a matter of deliberate policy, were being stripped of their language, their native skills, and their very identity as Indians. And, meanwhile, a combined force of missionaries and Royal Canadian Mounted Police—not such good guys as the movies of my youth taught me—did everything it could to discourage the practice of Ojibwa religion, raiding sacred ceremonies and harassing other religious activities until the old faith had been driven underground. In the end, then, Native religion became a private preoccupation of the aging rather than an integrative force for the young, and the people of Grassy Narrows, like their Indian neighbours elsewhere, lost much of the spiritual insulation that had been their ancestors' major

protection against the effects of disaster and disruption. (Shkilnyk, 1985, xiv)

Finally, a relocation of the reserve in 1963 mixed up traditional clan alignments. According to Erikson, "The new reserve is laid out in such a way as to disturb the ancient relationship between the Ojibwa and the rest of nature, for people now feel separated from the land and the water and the creatures of the forest with which they have always felt a special kinship. They are, in a very real sense, removed from their natural habitat" (Shkilnyk, 1985, xv).

In looking at the tragic story of Grassy Narrows, we can see the complementarity of the control and radical approaches. At one level, members of groups with high crime rates typically lack the social bonds that tie the rest of us to the social order. However, if we ask why the strength of social bonds is less among those who, like aboriginal people, are forced to live on the margins of society, we must turn to the work of radical theorists and their analyses of the political and economic forces that have created the poverty, powerlessness, and inequality that shape their lives.

of the causes of delinquency if that theory implies no recommendations concerning what can be done about it (West, 1984). While not necessarily agreeing that this is a fair criticism (many sociologists argue that knowledge is of value in its own right and that even apparently useless knowledge may be of practical value in the future), control theory is not as bereft of policy implications as its critics believe. In fact, early control theorists were strongly aware of the policy implications of their work. For example, Shaw established and worked for many years with the Chicago Area Project, which was set up to strengthen community ties in a slum community. To illustrate some of the possible uses to which the findings of research done from a social control perspective might be put, we can consider the role of the family and the school in delinquency prevention.

Policy Implications—The Family

Research has shown the importance of family relationships in the causation of delinquency. However, we are a long way from knowing what to do about this

Oregon Social Learning Center
www.air-dc.org/cecp/teams/
stratpart/oslc.htm

problem. How can we strengthen the family and make sure that parents love and care for their children? If anything, we are living in an era in which the family is becoming less stable as an institution.

While many of the problems in the family relationships of delinquents may require structural solutions, some small beginnings have been made in the task of trying to re-establish a bond between parent and child. One of the best examples of this is the work of Gerald Patterson and his colleagues at the Oregon Social Learning Center.

Based on his experiences treating several hundred families of antisocial children and on very detailed observation of interaction patterns within these families, Patterson concluded that since "antisocial acts that are not punished tend to persist" (1980, 89), the key to changing the behaviour of these trouble-some children was to punish their misdeeds. Hirschi observed that "this con-clusion may come as no surprise to those millions of parents who have spent years talking firmly to their children, yelling and screaming at them, spanking them, grounding them, cutting off their allowances, and in general doing what-ever they could think of to get the little bastards to behave; but it is exceedingly rare among social scientists, especially those who deal with crime and delin-quency" (1983, 53).

While this approach might seem disturbingly authoritarian to some, Patterson is, in fact, merely advocating techniques used by families that are suc-cessful in avoiding delinquency. You will recall that parental supervision and dis-ciplinary practices were strongly related to delinquent behaviour. Patterson has determined that the key aspects of this process involve several steps that have been summarized as "(1) monitor the child's behavior; (2) recognize deviant behavior when it occurs; and (3) punish such behavior" (in Hirschi, 1983, 55). In a properly functioning family, the parents understand this process, and the system is activated by the bonds of affection and caring that exist between parent and child. The key is not just punishment—many parents of problem children were found to punish them more often and more harshly than did the parents of normal children. However, the parents of problem children did not know *how* to punish their children, and punishment actually made things worse. Discipline was used, but it was erratic and unpredictable and not directed specifically at the child's misbehaviour. "The failure of parents to use reasonable reinforcements contingent on steadily monitored behaviour places the child in a situation in which he comes to understand that he cannot control by his own actions what happens to him" (Wilson, 1983, 53). As a result, the children in effect train their parents (and others, such as teachers) to accept their misbehaviour.

Working with the families of pre-adolescent problem children, Patterson has developed a program in which parents are taught how to shape their chil-dren's behaviour by using non-physical punishments (such as time-outs), by rewarding good conduct, and by interacting more positively as a family. This training process is often long and difficult. Many of the parents did not like their children, did not identify with the role of parent, and refused to recognize that their children were deviant (Patterson, 1980). Many were trying to cope with difficult economic and family situations as well as with the problems cre-ated by their antisocial children, and they resisted help.

The results suggest that this program has potential. One evaluation showed that stealing was reduced from an average of 0.83 incidents per week to 0.07 incidents per week after the parent training program. The treatment effects persisted for six months, but within one year, stealing rates had gone back to pretreatment levels (Moore et al., 1979). This suggests that parental retraining may be necessary. Longer-term results were obtained with children diagnosed as aggressive, with whom program effects lasted longer than 12 months. The program also had a positive impact on siblings, indicating that the parenting skills of the parents had improved.

Richard Tremblay and his colleagues (1991) have evaluated a program similar to Patterson's in which preventive treatment was provided for disruptive kindergarten boys in a low-income community in Montreal. The treatment combined teaching social skills to the boys with training their parents to be consistent and constructive toward their children. Two years after the treatment, the treated boys reported less fighting and less theft than comparison groups of boys who did not receive the treatment. The classroom behaviour of the treated boys also showed improvement.

Programs like these may be too expensive to be implemented on a broad scale. However, given the high concentration of criminality in a relatively small

BOX 13.2

FOCUS

Parenting Delinquent Youth

"When I met him, he was six and a half years of age. There was nothing about his appearance that identified him as the boy who had set the record." The words are those of Gerald R. Patterson, a family therapist at the Oregon Social Learning Center in Eugene. The "record" to which he referred was the frequency—measured with painstaking care by the Learning Center's staff—with which Don, a small boy, displayed rotten behavior. Nearly four times a *minute* while in his home, Don would whine, yell, disobey, hit, or shove. When he was not at home, telephone calls from teachers and merchants would mark his progress through the neighborhood: "He left school two hours early, stole candy from a store, and appropriated a toy from a neighborhood child."

Don had "a sleazy look about him," Patterson wrote, "like a postcard carried too long in a hip pocket." His violent outbursts were frightening; any simple request or minor provocation would trigger obscene shouts, attacks on other children, or assaults on the furniture. His mother was tired, depressed, and nearly desperate as a result of coping unaided with this monster—no babysitter would take on the job of minding Don, whatever the pay. She nevertheless persevered, changing his wet sheets, bathing and dressing him, even feeding him, all the while talking to him in tones that vacillated between cajolery and scolding, murmurs and shouts. When her seemingly bottomless patience was at last at an end, she would threaten or hit him with a stick. That produced only temporary compliance. When the father was home, things were not much different. The shouting and fighting between Don and his younger brother continued, occasionally punctuated by the father slapping both children.

Children like Don are the youthful precursors not only of difficult teenagers, but sometimes of delinquents and adult criminals. The progression from violent, dishonest youngster to violent, dishonest teenager is not automatic, but it is common.

Source: James Q. Wilson. (1983). "Raising Kids." *The Atlantic* (October), p. 45.

proportion of families (as shown by West and others), they do have some potential for reducing overall crime rates. The demonstration that improved parenting can have an impact on misbehaviour should encourage those advocating structural changes (e.g., less unemployment) that are aimed at least in part at providing more family stability and programs (e.g., day care) that provide substitute parents for children who might otherwise be left on their own. The results also suggest that research should be done on other methods of increasing parenting skills, such as providing training in high schools and for the parents of newborn children.

THE SCHOOLS AND SOCIAL POLICY

In their assessment of the role of the school in delinquency, Schafer and Polk suggest that the school fails in two ways: "The school not only fails to offset initial handicaps of lower-income and minority group children, but actively contributes to education failure and deterioration. If this is true, the school itself becomes an important active force in the generation of delinquency insofar as it is linked to failure" (1967, 236).

Research suggests that some schools and some teachers are better than others in helping children to function both educationally and behaviourally. Rutter and Giller (1984) have suggested a number of factors differentiating good and bad schools. These include the standards and values set and maintained by the school; the degree to which the students are allowed to participate in decision making; school and class size; staff turnover; and the degree of concentration of intellectually and socially disadvantaged pupils. Each of these factors has rather obvious policy implications.

A number of studies have looked at the impact of the teacher–student relationship on students' behaviour. British researchers (Hargreaves et al., 1975) have found that some teachers provoked deviance, while others were able to get students to cooperate more easily. Failure to get along with teachers may weaken an adolescent's commitment to school. It may also affect grades by leading teachers to make negative judgements about a youth's abilities and character. Thus, the classroom process may help to weaken an adolescent's attachment and commitment to the school.

Others have proposed changes in the type of curriculum and in the manner in which this curriculum is taught. Weis and Hawkins (1979) have recommended that schools make greater use of programs such as performance-based education, which involves establishing learning goals for each student and developing individually paced programs with rewards for improvement. They also suggest the use of cross-age tutoring and other ways of involving students in the operation of the school to enhance their level of commitment.

Other research (Elliott, 1966; LeBlanc, 1983) suggests the importance of mechanisms for ensuring a transition from school to work, especially among those students who are not going on to university.

Schools must also ensure that their curriculum is relevant to the lives of their students. An example of irrelevancy can be found in the system of residential schools that serve Aboriginal youth in the Canadian North. A child who grows up in a small settlement on the Arctic coast will be flown south to Yellowknife or another southern point for high school. Besides being cut off from family and community, the student is educated into a way of life that is very different from that which exists in the home village. As a result, students may no longer fit into their home communities, but, at the same time, they are not completely acculturated into southern ways (Brody, 1975). Increasing rates of crime and other deviance among people who lack strong community ties are consequences of this system.

We should not conclude that it will be easy to make changes in the schools to reduce the likelihood that students will get involved in delinquency and subsequent adult criminality. It is difficult to make significant changes in large institutions that reflect an uneasy balance between a number of different interest groups. Even if we could make changes quickly, we could not be certain that they would have the desired effect. For example, programs that separate misbehaving students may have unintended consequences. Schafer and Polk (1967) discuss a program in which students with academic and behaviour problems were placed in special classes and provided with individual instruction by specially selected teachers. The outcome of the program was negative—placement in a class with other poorly motivated students compounded their problems and further alienated them from the mainstream of school life. The students may also have suffered from being labelled as troublemakers.

Despite these potential problems, there is merit in trying to work within the school system. The research that has been done represents a promising

TABLE 13.1 Social Control Theories

Theory	Theorists	Key Elements
Social disorganization theories	Durkheim Thrasher, Shaw and McKay	Deviance will be highest in disorganized communities that lack social controls.
Early social control theories	Reiss, Nye	Stresses the importance of personal controls, particularly those provided by the family.
Social bond theory	Hirschi	The four elements of the social bond: attachment, commitment, involvement, and belief.
General theory of crime	Gottfredson Hirschi	Individuals with low self-control have a greater propensity to commit crimes when they have the opportunity to do so.
Control-differential association theory	Linden	Lack of ties to the conventional order will increase the likelihood of association with deviant peers. These ties will, in turn, increase the probability of delinquency involvement.

beginning, but what is needed is a program in which the lessons learned are systematically applied to the schools on an experimental basis. The types of reforms that would be most likely to succeed would be beneficial to all students and possibly reduce delinquency as well.

SUMMARY

- Rather than asking "Why do some people break the law?", social control theorists ask "Why don't we all do it?" The answer to this question lies in the processes that bind people to conventional society.

- Early theorists, including Thrasher and Shaw and McKay, looked at community-level controls. Disorganized communities that did not provide meaningful employment to residents and did not have strong families, schools, and churches could not provide adequate social controls and would have high rates of crime and other types of deviance.

- Later social control theories focused on the social bonds of individuals. Travis Hirschi described four interrelated aspects of the social bond that constrain our behaviour: attachment, commitment, involvement, and belief.

- Research on social control theory has pointed to the importance of the family and the school in restraining involvement in delinquency. While less research has been done with adults, it suggests that stable employment and a cohesive marriage are important factors.

- Among the criticisms of social control theory are these: it does not adequately explain white-collar crime; it does not account for the motivation to deviate; it is too individualistic; and it is too conservative.

- Recent theoretical work has returned to the social disorganization tradition and has once again linked societal and community factors to individual-level bonds.

QUESTIONS FOR CRITICAL THINKING

1. How could you apply the principles of social control theory to reduce the amount of white-collar and corporate crime in Canada?
2. Discuss three of the criticisms that have been made of social control theory. How would you defend the theory against these criticisms?
3. Several of the theorists discussed in this chapter have looked at the relationship between the community and crime. Starting with the example of the tragic situation in Grassy Narrows, discuss some of the government policies that have led to high rates of crime and other types of deviance among Canada's Aboriginal people.
4. Based on your knowledge of social control theory, what changes would you make to the public school system to help reduce delinquency?

NET WORK

In 1998, the Canadian government established a $100 million fund to support the Aboriginal Head Start program. The program is intended to help reserve communities meet the educational, emotional, social, health, and nutritional needs of children under the age of six. Some early childhood education programs have proven very successful in reducing rates of crime and delinquency. You can find out more about Head Start at **www.acf.dhhs.gov/programs/hsb/**.

Using some of the evaluations you will find on this link, do the following exercises:

1. What has been the impact of Head Start programs on delinquency and crime? Are they a cost-effective way of reducing crime?
2. The most effective early childhood education program is the Perry Preschool program. Go to **www.highscope.org/Research/PerryProject/perrymain.htm.** What lessons can those running Head Start programs learn from the Perry Preschool program?
3. How important do you think it is to involve parents in Head Start programs? Does the research show that programs involving parents are more effective than those based only in the schools?

KEY TERMS

attachment	independent variable
belief	individualistic
career criminal	involvement
commitment	social bond
ecological fallacy	social control theory

SUGGESTED READING

Gottfredson, Michael R., and Travis Hirschi. (1990). *A General Theory of Crime*. Stanford, Conn.: Stanford University Press. An extension of Hirschi's earlier work on social control theory, which includes an extensive discussion of the relationship between self-control and crime.

Hagan, John. (1994). *Crime and Disrepute*. Thousand Oaks, Calif.: Pine Forge Press. This book sets out Hagan's new sociology of crime and disrepute showing the relationship between crime and the growing disparities of income and wealth. The book also describes the globalization of white-collar crime and provides a critique of the contemporary American justice system.

Hirschi, Travis. (1969). *Causes of Delinquency*. Berkeley: University of California Press. The classic statement of contemporary social control theory. Hirschi explains the theory and tests it against its major competitors.

Shkilnyk, Anastasia M. (1985). *A Poison Stronger Than Love: The Destruction of an Ojibwa Community*. New Haven, Conn.: Yale University Press. The book is a portrait of a community in trouble. It provides a graphic account of the social problems that affect a community after its social institutions have been destroyed.

Thrasher, Frederic M. (1963). *The Gang.* Chicago: University of Chicago Press. First published in 1927, this book remains the classic study of urban gang delinquency.

BIBLIOGRAPHY

Akers, Ronald L. (1977). *Deviant Behavior: A Social Learning Approach.* Belmont, Calif.: Wadsworth.

Albrecht, Stan I., Bruce A. Chadwick, and David S. Alcorn. (1977). "Religiosity and Deviance: Application of an Attitude–Behavior Contingent Consistency Model." *Journal for the Scientific Study of Religion* 16:263–74.

Anderson, Elijah. (1994). "The Code of the Streets." *The Atlantic Monthly* (May):81–94.

Aronson, Elliot. (1984). *The Social Animal.* New York: W.H. Freeman.

Arum, Richard, and Irenee R. Beattie. (1999). "High School Experience and the Risk of Adult Incarceration." *Criminology* 37(3):515–36.

Biron, Louise, and Marc LeBlanc. "Family and Delinquency." Unpublished paper, Université de Montréal.

Bohm, Robert. (1987). "Comment on 'Traditional Contributions to Radical Criminology' by Groves and Sampson." *Journal of Research in Crime and Delinquency* 24 (November):324–31.

Box, Steven. (1971). *Deviance, Reality and Society.* London: Holt, Rinehart and Winston.

———. (1981). *Deviance, Reality and Society* (2nd ed.). London: Holt, Rinehart and Winston.

Brody, Hugh. (1975). *The People's Land.* Markham, Ont.: Penguin Books.

Caplan, Aaron. (1977). "Attachment to Parents and Delinquency." Paper presented at the annual meeting of the Canadian Sociology and Anthropology Association, Fredericton, N.B.

Caplan, Aaron, and Marc LeBlanc. (1985). "A Cross-Cultural Verification of a Social Control Theory." *International Journal of Comparative and Applied Criminal Justice* 9(2):123–38.

Chambliss, William. (1973). "The Saints and the Roughnecks." *Society* 11:24–31.

Clark, Gerald. (1971). "What Happens When the Police Strike." In Donald R. Cressey (ed.), *Crime and Criminal Justice* (pp. 58–76). Chicago: Quadrangle Books.

Conger, Rand. (1980). "Juvenile Delinquency: Behavior Restraint or Behavior Facilitation." In Travis Hirschi and Michael Gottfredson (eds.), *Understanding Crime: Current Theory and Research* (pp. 131–42). Beverly Hills, Calif.: Sage.

Durkheim, Émile. (1951). *Suicide.* Translated by John A. Spaulding and George Simpson. New York: Free Press.

Elifson, Kirk W., David M. Petersen, and C. Kirk Hadaway. (1983). "Religiosity and Delinquency: A Contextual Analysis." *Criminology* 21:505–27.

Elliott, Delbert S. (1966). "Delinquency, School Attendance and Dropout." *Social Problems* 13 (Winter):307–14.

Empey, LaMar T. (1982). *American Delinquency: Its Meaning and Construction.* Homewood, Ill.: Dorsey Press.

Engstad, Peter A. (1975). "Environmental Opportunities and the Ecology of Crime." In Robert A. Silverman and James J. Teevan (eds.), *Crime in Canadian Society* (pp. 193–211). Toronto: Butterworths.

Erikson, Kai. (1985). "Foreword." In Anastasia M. Shkilnyk, *A Poison Stronger Than Love* (pp. xiii–xvii). New Haven, Conn.: Yale University Press.

Fischer, Donald G. (1980). *Family Relationship Variables and Programs Influencing Juvenile Delinquency*. Ottawa: Ministry of the Solicitor General.

Fréchette, M., and Marc LeBlanc. (1985). *Des délinquantes: émergence et développement.* Chicoutimi: Gaëtan Morin.

Glaser, Daniel. (1978). *Crime in Our Changing Society.* New York: Holt, Rinehart and Winston.

Glueck, Sheldon, and Eleanor Glueck. (1950). *Unraveling Juvenile Delinquency.* Cambridge, Mass.: Harvard University Press.

Gold, Martin. (1963). *Status Forces in Delinquent Boys.* Ann Arbor: University of Michigan Press.

Gomme, Ian. (1985). "Predictors of Status and Criminal Offences Among Male and Female Delinquency in an Ontario Community." *Canadian Journal of Criminology* 26:313–23.

Gottfredson, Michael R., and Travis Hirschi. (1990). *A General Theory of Crime.* Stanford, Conn.: Stanford University Press.

Gove, Walter R., and Robert D. Crutchfield. (1982). "The Family and Juvenile Delinquency." *The Sociological Quarterly* 23:301–19.

Hagan, John. (1985). *Modern Criminology: Crime, Criminal Behavior and Its Control.* New York: McGraw-Hill.

Hagan, John, A.R. Gillis, and Janet Chan. (1978). "Explaining Official Delinquency: A Spatial Study of Class, Conflict and Control." *The Sociological Quarterly* 19:386–98.

Hagan, John, A.R. Gillis, and John Simpson. (1985). "The Class Structure of Gender and Delinquency: Toward a Power-Control Theory of Common Delinquent Behavior." *American Journal of Sociology* 90:1151–78.

Hagan, John, and Bill McCarthy. (1997). *Mean Streets: Youth Crime and Homelessness.* Cambridge: Cambridge University Press.

Hagan, John, John Simpson, and A.R. Gillis. (1979). "The Sexual Stratification of Social Control." *British Journal of Sociology* 30:25–38.

Hamilton, A.C., and C.M. Sinclair. (1991). *Report of the Aboriginal Justice Inquiry of Manitoba.* Vol. 1. Winnipeg: Queen's Printer.

Hardwick, Kelly. (2002). *Unravelling 'Crime in the Making': Re-examining the Role of Informal Social Control in the Genesis and Stability of Delinquency and Crime.* Unpublished Ph.D. Thesis. University of Calgary.

Hargreaves, David H. (1967). *Social Relations in a Secondary School.* London: Routledge and Kegan Paul.

Hargreaves, David H., Stephen K. Hester, and Frank J. Mellor. (1975). *Deviance in Classrooms.* London: Routledge and Kegan Paul.

Higgins, Paul C., and Gary L. Albrecht. (1977). "Hellfire and Delinquency Revisited." *Social Forces* 55:952–58.

Hirschi, Travis. (1969). *Causes of Delinquency.* Berkeley: University of California Press.

———. (1983). "Crime and the Family." In James Q. Wilson (ed.), *Crime and Public Policy* (pp. 53–68). San Francisco: ICS Press.

Jensen, Gary F. (1969). "Crime Doesn't Pay: Correlates of a Shared Misunderstanding." *Social Problems* 17:189–201.

Keane, Carl, Paul S. Maxim, and James J. Teevan. (1993). "Drinking and Driving, Self-control and Gender: Testing a General Theory of Crime." *Journal of Research in Crime and Delinquency* 30:30–46.

Kornhauser, Ruth Rosner. (1978). *Social Sources of Delinquency.* Chicago: University of Chicago Press.

Kupfer, George. (1966). "Middle Class Delinquency in a Canadian City." Unpublished Ph.D. dissertation, Department of Sociology, University of Washington.

LaGrange, Theresa, and Robert Silverman. (1999). "Low Self-Control and Opportunity: Testing the General Theory of Crime as an Explanation for Gender Differences in Delinquency." *Criminology* 37(1):41–72.

LeBlanc, Marc. (1983). "Delinquency as an Epiphenomenon of Adolescence." In Raymond R. Corrado, Marc LeBlanc, and Jean Trepanier (eds.), *Current Issues in Juvenile Justice* (pp. 31–48). Toronto: Butterworths.

———. (1997). "A Generic Control Theory of the Criminal Phenomenon." In Terence P. Thornberry (ed.), *Developmental Theories of Crime and Delinquency* (pp. 215–85). New Brunswick, N.J.: Transaction Publishers.

LeBlanc, Marc, Marc Ouimet, and Richard Tremblay. (1988). "An Integrative Control Theory of Delinquent Behavior: A Validation 1976–1985." *Psychiatry* 51:164–76.

LeBlanc, Marc, and Richard Tremblay. (1985). "An Integrative Control Theory of Delinquent Behavior: A Validation 1976–1985." Paper presented at the annual meeting of the American Society of Criminology, San Diego.

Linden, Eric. (1974). "Interpersonal Ties and Delinquent Behavior." Unpublished Ph.D. dissertation, University of Washington.

Linden, Rick, and Raymond Currie. (1977). "Religiosity and Drug Use: A Test of Social Control Theory." *Canadian Journal of Criminology and Corrections* 19:346–55.

Linden, Rick, Raymond F. Currie, and Leo Driedger. (1985). "Interpersonal Ties and Alcohol Use Among Mennonites." *The Canadian Review of Sociology and Anthropology* 22: 559–73.

Linden, Rick, and Cathy Fillmore. (1981). "A Comparative Study of Delinquency Involvement." *Canadian Review of Sociology and Anthropology* 18:343–61.

Linden, Rick, and James C. Hackler. (1973). "Affective Ties and Delinquency." *Pacific Sociological Review* 16:27–46.

Lynch, Michael, and W. Byron Groves. (1989). *A Primer in Radical Criminology* (2nd ed.). Albany, N.Y.: Harrow and Heston.

McCord, Joan. (1979). "Some Child-Rearing Antecedents of Criminal Behavior in Adult Men." *Journal of Personality and Social Psychology*:1477–86.

McCord, William, and Joan McCord. (1959). *Origins of Crime: A New Evaluation of the Cambridge–Somerville Youth Study.* New York: Columbia University Press.

Matza, David. (1964). *Delinquency and Drift.* New York: Wiley.

Moore, D.R., B.P. Chamberlain, and L. Mukai. (1979). "Children at Risk for Delinquency: A Follow-up Comparison of Aggressive Children and Children Who Steal." *Journal of Abnormal Child Psychology* 7:345–55.

Naffine, Ngaire. (1987). *Female Crime: The Construction of Women in Criminology.* Sydney: Allen and Unwin.

Nye, F. Ivan. (1958). *Family Relationships and Delinquent Behavior.* New York: Wiley.

Patterson, G.R. (1980). "Children Who Steal." In Travis Hirschi and Michael Gottfredson (eds.), *Understanding Crime: Current Theory and Research*. Beverly Hills, Calif.: Sage.

Petersilia, Joan. (1980). "Career Criminal Research: A Review of Recent Evidence." In Norval Morris and Michael Tonry (eds.), *Crime and Justice: An Annual Review of Research* (pp. 321–79). Chicago: University of Chicago Press.

Polk, Kenneth, and F. Lynn Richmond. (1972). "Those Who Fail." In Kenneth Polk and Walter E. Schafer (eds.), *Schools and Delinquency* (pp. 55–69). Englewood Cliffs, N.J.: Prentice Hall.

Polk, Kenneth, and Walter E. Schafer. (1972). *Schools and Delinquency*. Englewood Cliffs, N.J.: Prentice Hall.

Pratt, Travis, and Francis T. Cullen. (2000). "The Empirical Status of Gottfredson and Hirschi's General Theory of Crime: A Meta-Analysis." *Criminology* 38(3):501–34.

Reckless, Walter C. (1967). *The Crime Problem* (4th ed.). New York: Appleton-Century-Crofts.

Reiss, Albert J., Jr. (1951). "Delinquency as the Failure of Personal and Social Controls." *American Sociological Review* 16:196–207.

Rothman, David J. (1971). *The Discovery of the Asylum*. Boston: Little, Brown and Company.

Rutter, Michael, and Henri Giller. (1984). *Juvenile Delinquency: Trends and Perspectives*. New York: The Guilford Press.

Sampson, Robert J., and John H. Laub. (1993). *Crime in the Making: Pathways and Turning Points Through Life*. Cambridge, Mass.: Harvard University Press.

Schafer, Walter E., and Kenneth Polk. (1967). "Delinquency and the Schools." In *The President's Commission on Law Enforcement and Administration of Justice, Task Force Report: Juvenile Delinquency and Crime* (pp. 222–77). Washington, D.C.: U.S. Government Printing Office.

Simons, Ronald, L.Chyi-In Wu, Kuei-Hsui Lin, Leslie Gordon, and Rand D. Conger. (2000). "A Cross-Cultural Examination of the Link Between Corporal Punishment and Adolescent Antisocial Behavior." *Criminology* 38:47–80.

Shkilnyk, Anastasia M. (1985). *A Poison Stronger Than Love: The Destruction of an Ojibwa Community*. New Haven, Conn.: Yale University Press.

Short, James, Jr., and Fred Strodtbeck. (1965). *Group Process and Gang Delinquency*. Chicago: University of Chicago Press.

Sorenson, Ann Marie, and David Brownfield. (1995). "Adolescent Drug Use and a General Theory of Crime: An Analysis of a Theoretical Integration." *Canadian Journal of Criminology* 37:19–37.

Stark, Rodney, Daniel P. Doyle, and Lori Kent. (1980). "Rediscovering Moral Communities: Church Membership and Crime." In Travis Hirschi and Michael Gottfredson (eds.), *Understanding Crime: Current Theory and Research* (pp. 43–52). Beverly Hills, Calif.: Sage.

———. (1982). "Religion and Delinquency: The Ecology of a 'Lost' Relationship." *Journal of Research in Crime and Delinquency* 19:4–24.

Stark, Werner. (1980). *An Investigation into the Bases of Law-Abidingness*, Vol. III. New York: Fordham University Press.

Statistics Canada. (1998). "National Longitudinal Study of Children and Youth." *The Daily* (October 28).

Steinmetz, Suzanne K., and Murray A. Straus. (1980). "The Family as a Cradle of Violence." In Delos H. Kelly (ed.), *Criminal Behavior* (pp. 130–42). New York: St. Martin's Press.

Thornberry, Terence P., Marvin D. Krohn, Alan J. Lizotte, and Deborah Chard-Wierschem. (1993). "The Role of Juvenile Gangs in Facilitating Delinquent Behavior." *Journal of Research in Crime and Delinquency* 30:55–87.

Thrasher, Frederic M. (1963). *The Gang.* Chicago: University of Chicago Press.

Tremblay, Richard E., Joan McCord, Helene Boileau, Pierre Charlebois, Claude Gagnon, Marc LeBlanc, and Serge Larivee. (1991). "Can Disruptive Boys Be Helped to Become Competent?" *Psychiatry* 54:148–61.

Velarde, Albert J. (1978). "Do Delinquents Really Drift?" *British Journal of Criminology* 18.

Weis, Joseph G., and J. David Hawkins. (1979). *Preventing Delinquency: The Social Development Approach.* Seattle: Center for Law and Justice, University of Washington.

West, D.J. (1982). *Delinquency: Its Roots, Careers, and Prospects.* London: Heinemann.

West, D.J., and D.P. Farrington. (1973). *Who Becomes Delinquent?* London: Heinemann.

———. (1977). *The Delinquent Way of Life.* London: Heinemann.

West, W. Gordon. (1984). *Young Offenders and the State: A Canadian Perspective on Delinquency.* Toronto: Butterworths.

Wilson, Harriet. (1980). "Parental Supervision: A Neglected Aspect of Delinquency." *British Journal of Criminology* 20:30–39.

Wilson, James Q. (1983). "Raising Kids." *The Atlantic Monthly:*45–56.

Wright, Kevin N., and Karen E. Wright. (1992). "Does Getting Married Reduce the Likelihood of Criminality—A Review of the Literature." *Federal Probation* 56(3):50–56.

Patterns of Criminal Behaviour

Many different types of behaviour are illegal but they vary widely in seriousness. Murder, for instance, is in a different category than not putting enough change in a parking meter. In Part 3, we look at some of the kinds of misconduct that frequently occur in Canada.

When the average citizen thinks of crime, the images that most commonly come to mind are the so-called street crimes—robbery, assault, break and enter, and so on. These are also the kinds of offences that occupy most of the time and attention of the criminal justice system. In Chapter 14, many of these crimes are discussed. The routine activities approach, an attempt to account for patterns of criminal victimization, is also discussed using data collected on these conventional crimes.

Chapter 15 looks at the "organized" criminals who are in the business of providing access to illegal goods and services. Chapter 16, the final chapter in the text, looks at crimes committed by "respectable" people: many of our leading citizens are white-collar criminals, and many of our largest businesses are corporate offenders. This chapter makes the important point that the power we give to those in positions of authority and ownership in modern corporations may encourage them to become involved in illegal activities that cause a great deal of social harm.

In Part 2, it was noted that the classification of theories into different categories is somewhat artificial. However, some classification system is useful in organizing the work of different theorists. In Part 3, different patterns of crime are described and they too are classified into types, though here as well there is overlap between the different categories.

14

Conventional or "Street" Crime

DANIEL J. KOENIG
Formerly of University of Victoria

RICK LINDEN
University of Manitoba

conventional crime

Those traditional, illegal behaviours that most people think of as crime. Nonconventional crime may be organized crime, white-collar crime, political crime, etc.

When most people think of crime, they have in mind offences such as murder, robbery, break and enter, assault, sexual assault, theft, and motor vehicle theft. These offences are sometimes called "street crimes" or "**conventional crimes**" to distinguish them from other categories of crime such as organized crime and white-collar and corporate crime.

Each of these conventional crimes involves an immediate and clearly identifiable victim and often results in a complaint to the police. In fact, much of the caseload of the police is made up of these offences. Most of the media reports about crime also focus on conventional crimes. In this chapter, police statistics and victimization survey data will be used to describe patterns of conventional crimes. Because these offences affect the lives of so many of us, it is important to learn as much about them as we can.

This chapter will also introduce you to a new perspective on crime that has its roots in the rational choice theory discussed in Chapter 7. In Part 2 of this text, you read about a variety of theories that try to explain why people break the law. These theories focused on the motivations of offenders. The theory introduced in this chapter, the routine activities approach to crime, looks instead at specific criminal events and so focuses more on the crimes than on the criminals. This theory does not compete with the others, as without motivated offenders no crimes would occur, but it looks at criminal events from a different perspective. As you will learn later in this chapter, the routine activities approach has been particularly useful in helping develop ways of preventing crime. This approach to crime tells us that crime will not occur unless there is a motivated offender, a suitable target, and ineffective guardianship of that target. It will be used to help understand patterns of conventional crime in Canada. The routine activities approach will also be used to suggest ways of reducing crime. This discussion may help you reduce the likelihood that you will be victimized by crime.

After reading this chapter, you should be able to

- Discuss the routine activities approach to crime and understand the role of the motivated offender, suitable target, and ineffective guardianship in any criminal event.

- Know who is most likely to be victimized by different types of conventional crime.

- Describe where the most important types of conventional crime are most likely to occur.

- Understand the legal definitions of each of the different types of conventional crime.

- Discuss how you can use your knowledge of causes and patterns of crime to develop prevention programs.

THE ROUTINE ACTIVITIES APPROACH

After reading Part 2 of this book, you know that there are many competing and sometimes contradictory explanations of why offenders commit crimes. In recent decades, many criminologists have asked why one person is more likely than another to be victimized by crime. This has led to a search for patterns of crime, such as when and where it occurs, the immediate circumstances of crime, and the relationship between victims and offenders.

Hindelang et al. (1978) used this approach to develop the **lifestyle/exposure theory** to account for personal victimization. This theory states that the lifestyle and routine activities of people place them in social settings with higher or lower risks of being victimized. For example, people who spend a lot of time in public places at night have a higher risk of being robbed than do people who spend most of their evenings at home. Similarly, people whose lifestyles put them in frequent contact with people who commit crimes are more likely to be victimized than those whose time is spent with law-abiding companions. For example, as you will see in Chapter 15, members of Quebec biker gangs likely have higher rates of homicide victimization than any other Canadians. They have chosen a lifestyle in which violence is used as a means of settling disputes and in which factors like the competition for the exclusive right to sell drugs in particular areas ensures that there will be many disputes to settle. While much of the gang violence in Quebec has been between competing gangs, it is also used as a means of settling accounts within gangs.

Cohen and Felson (1979) refined the lifestyle exposure theory into the **"routine activities approach."** This approach begins with the observation that three factors must be present simultaneously for a crime to occur:

- A *motivated offender*. Unless someone wants to commit a crime, it will not take place. Most of the theories of criminal behaviour that you have read

lifestyle/exposure theory

A theory of victimization that acknowledges that not everyone has the same lifestyle and that some lifestyles expose people to more risks than others do. If you go to bed early, you are less at risk of robbery or assault than if you like to visit the bars several nights a week. Similar to *routine activities approach.*

routine activities approach

Similar to the *lifestyle/exposure theory,* this approach assumes that crimes are the expected outcomes of routine activities and changing social patterns. For example, those with more property can expect to be the victims of property crime more often than those with less property. Young people who like to hang out in the evenings are more likely to be victims than are those who go to organized activities or remain at home to study.

about in earlier chapters try to explain why some people are motivated to commit crimes.

- A *suitable target.* A theft will not take place unless there is property to steal and an assault cannot happen unless there is someone to attack.

- A *lack of guardianship* of that target. If a target is well-guarded, it will be much less likely to be victimized. **Effective guardianship** refers to actions such as removing ignition keys from a car and locking the door (by motorists), drawing a steel mesh curtain overnight across glass display windows of jewellery (by shopkeepers), and taking evening walks on busy, well-lit streets rather than walking alone in an isolated park or down a dark alley (by pedestrians).

effective guardianship

An aspect of the *routine activities approach* to understanding crime victimization that argues that three key factors are required for crime to happen: a motivated offender, a suitable target, and ineffective guardianship of that target. Effective guardianship would include having locks on bikes, security lights in the backyard, or putting goods in the trunk of the car. Measures like this should reduce the risk of being victimized.

Changes in any of these factors can lead to increases or decreases in crime. Thus even without additional motivated offenders, an increase in the number, the value, or the accessibility of suitable targets can result in increases in crime. For example, 30 years ago, electronic equipment was bulky, heavy, and difficult to carry. Today, potential criminals have the opportunity to steal laptop computers, portable CD and MP3 players, DVD players, automobile CD players, and other valuable electronics that weigh very little and that are easy to conceal. Cohen and Felson predicted that unless small, attractive items are carefully protected, theft rates will increase as these items become more common; their data support this view. Less suitable targets are less frequently stolen. For example, Cohen and Felson observed that not many people steal refrigerators and washing machines because these are worth far less per pound than electronic equipment. Another example of the importance of suitable targets was the discovery by young people in Winnipeg and Regina that some models of Chrysler vehicles built in the 1990s were very easy to steal. As you will read later in this chapter, this discovery helped to fuel a boom in joyriding that saw rates of motor vehicle theft soar in both cities (Anderson and Linden, 2002). On the other hand, vehicles that are protected by electronic ignition immobilizers that make them virtually impossible to start without a key are very rarely stolen unless the owners leave their keys in the car.

To illustrate how changes in guardianship affect crime rates, Cohen and Felson showed that as daytime occupancy of homes decreased because of factors such as the increased employment of women outside the home and increases in the length of vacations, there was a substantial increase in daytime residential burglaries at the same time as the proportion of commercial burglaries declined. Thus besides explaining patterns of victimization, routine activities theory also offers a way of understanding changes in crime patterns over time. Crime trends are seen as expected outcomes of routine activities and changing social patterns. Cohen and Felson take offender motivation as a given. Their objective is to demonstrate the relationship between crime trends and changes in **target suitability** and effective guardianship.

target suitability

Because of their vulnerability, some potential crime targets are more attractive than others. A home that is unlit, has shrubs blocking a view of the front door, and has no alarm system will be seen as a more suitable target than a well-protected home.

The research findings to be reported in this chapter are consistent with a routine activities approach. Before looking at specific types of crimes in detail, we will provide a brief overview of some of these findings.

Who

For most crimes of violence, including assault, robbery, and homicide, rates of both victimization and offending are highest among younger people, males, and those who spend a large number of evenings in activities away from the home. Statistics Canada's 1999 General Social Survey (GSS) revealed that the rate of violent victimization among those 15 to 24 was over twice that of those 25 to 34 and 20 times that of those over 55 (Mihorean et al., 2001).

Income was also related to victimization. For example, theft of household property was much higher among respondents living in households with incomes in excess of $60 000 than in households with incomes under $15 000 per year. However, violent victimizations were 70 percent higher in the lowest household income category than in the next highest category. Marital status was another influential variable. Rates of personal victimization for single or separated/divorced respondents were much higher than rates for those who were married or living common law. Aboriginal people had much higher rates of victimization than other Canadians, while the rates for visible minorities were slightly lower than average (Mihorean et al., 2001).

GSS results from 1993 also indicate that alcohol consumption and illicit drug use increase one's likelihood of being a victim of crime. Those who consumed 14 or more alcoholic drinks per week experienced twice as many incidents of personal victimization during the preceding 12 months as did nondrinkers (Wright, 1995). In addition, 26 percent of illicit drug users experienced a personal victimization, in contrast to only 10 percent of those who did not use any illicit substances during the preceding 12 months. For each type of violent victimization, a majority of victims thought that the crime was due to their own or someone else's alcohol or drug use.

If people with certain lifestyles are going to be more exposed to criminal victimization as they go about their routine activities, the probability of becoming a victim of crime will not be randomly distributed. People who have been victimized once, therefore, should have a higher probability of being victimized a second time than people who have not been victimized at all. These probabilities will change, of course, if the typical lifestyle and exposure of the already victimized person changes to reduce the risk of subsequent victimization.

Repeated victimization of the same victim (or victim's household), by both the same type of crime and different crimes, has been observed frequently in surveys both in the United States (U.S. Dept. of Justice, 1974a, 1974b; Hindelang et al., 1978; Sparks, 1981) and in Canada (Koenig, 1977; Sacco and Johnson, 1990). The 1993 GSS was no exception. Of those who stated that they had been victimized by a crime during the preceding 12 months, the majority reported that they had been victimized more than once (exclusive of repeated victimization of the same nature, referred to as "series crimes" by Statistics Canada). This pattern of repeat victimization held for both male and female victims. Such patterns provide support for the lifestyle/exposure theory, as does the finding that the risk of violent victimization was significantly higher for those who participated in evening activities outside the home 10 or more times per month.

Where

Rates of victimization for both personal and household victimization were highest in British Columbia and lowest in the Atlantic provinces (Mihorean et al., 2001). Approximately 40 percent of violent incidents reported in the 1993 GSS took place in or around a private residence; one-third took place in bars, restaurants, malls, schools, hospitals, arenas, public transit, and so forth; and one-quarter took place in other public places such as on the street, in parks, or in parking garages (Kong, 1994). Crimes involving personal contact were more likely to occur in less guarded surroundings than they were in the home, in the neighbourhood, or at work.

When

According to the 1993 GSS, personal victimizations were most likely to occur during the summer months (Wright, 1995). With longer days and warmer weather, people are more likely to place themselves at risk as suitable targets by being outdoors, or to have windows and doors open if they are at home. Another peak for some crimes occurs in December, when people are likely to increase their interpersonal contacts during the Christmas season by shopping, visiting, or going to parties.

The **incidence** per hour of most crimes is highest in the evening, particularly from 6 p.m. to midnight. These are the hours when effective guardianship is minimized: as darkness reduces visibility, and fewer people go about their routine activities in public places so there are fewer people to observe what is happening.

incidence

Incidence tells us the frequency of new occurrences of some event during a particular time period. For example, there were 554 criminal homicides in Canada in 2001.

"Patterns of Crime"
Malaspina University-College
web.mala.bc.ca/crim/stats/

PATTERNS OF SPECIFIC CRIMES

To what extent is the routine activities approach to understanding crime consistent with known facts about patterns of specific types of crime? To answer that question, we will examine several types of conventional crimes that are commonplace or a source of public concern.

MURDER AND OTHER CRIMINAL HOMICIDES

Legal Meanings of Types of Homicide

Homicide is a legal term having somewhat different meanings in different countries and in different eras. In Canada, it is a general category that refers to an act in which the life of one person is lost at the hands of another. In Canada, criminal homicide refers to first- and second-degree murder, manslaughter, and infanticide.

Criminal homicide is classified as murder when the person who causes death means to cause death or means to cause bodily harm likely to result in death. Murder is first degree when the killing is planned and deliberate; when the victim is employed in certain occupations concerned with the preservation

Handwritten notes:

Homicide

Who: mostly male adults
What: an act in which the life of one person is lost at the hands of another
When: has declined over the years
Where: highest in the Western provinces and territories and in the household
Why: Gangs, being out at night, domestic abuse, alcohol and drugs

NEL

and maintenance of public order (for example, public police officer or correctional worker) and acting in that capacity; or when the killing occurs in connection with certain specific offences such as sexual assault, kidnapping, or hijacking. Other murders are second-degree murders. Manslaughter is a type of criminal homicide in which one person kills another in the heat of passion caused by a sudden provocation or when a person is too intoxicated to form intent. Infanticide is an archaic category of criminal homicide applying to deaths of newborn children caused by women who are in a disturbed state of mind as a consequence of giving birth.

Police statistics probably underestimate the true number of criminal homicides. Some missing persons, particularly young women and children, likely have been murdered. However, if neither a body nor other evidence of a murder is discovered, it is difficult to conclude that a specific missing person has been murdered. This has been tragically illustrated in the case of women who have gone missing from Vancouver's Downtown East Side. This community has high rates of poverty along with serious problems of addiction, HIV/AIDS, and prostitution. Over a period of 25 years, a large number of women, most of whom were drug addicts working as prostitutes, disappeared and only recently has it been established that many of these women were murdered. For many years, the Vancouver police refused to treat the disappearances as possible homicide cases. The cases were difficult ones because many of the women were transients and some were not officially reported as being missing until years after they had last been seen on the street. However, in 2001 the police finally responded to pressure from relatives and friends of the missing women. They put together a list of 54 women and began to conduct an intensive investigation of their disappearances. This work finally resulted in the arrest of Robert Pickton, who has so far been charged with 15 murders and may be charged with more. At this writing, nearly 100 workers are sifting through the soil covering Pickton's 10-acre farm near Vancouver looking for the remains of other victims. While a few of the women on the original list have been discovered alive, as of the spring of 2003 the original list has been expanded to 63 women in addition to those whose remains have already been discovered on Pickton's farm.

Homicides also may be disguised as accidental deaths or suicides, although the police are skilful at detecting the differences. Despite these problems, and despite the limitations inherent in all official police crime statistics, such statistics are the primary source of data about criminal homicides.

Incidence

What do police statistics tell us about homicide? There were 582 criminal homicides in Canada during 2002 (Wallace, 2003b). Criminal homicide should not be trivialized, but the risk should be kept in perspective. For example, there are six times more suicide deaths and five times more deaths from motor vehicle accidents than from homicides (Statistics Canada, 2003). During 2002, homicides accounted for less than 1 percent of all violent crimes.

The Canadian criminal homicide rate for 2002 of 1.9 homicides per 100 000 population was down significantly from the peak of 3.0 recorded in 1975. Canada's homicide rate is comparable to the rates in France and England

(1.8 and 1.7 respectively) but far below that in the United States. While the U.S. rate has fallen by about 30 percent since 1992, the 2001 rate of 5.6 was over three times the Canadian rate.

In Canada, homicide rates are highest in the western provinces and in the territories and lowest in the Atlantic provinces. The highest homicide rates during 2002 were recorded in the Northwest Territories (9.7) and Nunavut (7.0). Among the provinces, Manitoba (3.1) had the highest rate followed by Saskatchewan (2.7) and B.C. (3.0). Newfoundland and Labrador had only two homicides in 2002, which gave the province a rate of 0.4, and there were no homicides in the Yukon (Wallace, 2003b).

Pattern

Nationally, shootings and stabbings (both 13 percent) were the most frequent methods used to commit homicide in 2001. The next most common methods were beatings (22 percent) and strangulation (9 percent). The proportion of homicides committed by firearms is lower in Canada than in the United States but higher than in the United Kingdom. The FBI (2002) reported that 63 percent of murders in the United States during 2001 were committed by a firearm, usually a handgun.

During 2001, almost 60 percent of Canadian homicides for which the location was known took place in a private residence, most commonly in the victim's residence (Dauvergne, 2002). The location of Canadian homicides is consistent with the fact that homicide victims and their assailants usually know each other and that homicide is frequently the culmination of an argument engaged in by people as they go about their routine daily activities.

Contrary to impressions sometimes conveyed by news media and entertainment programs that focus on mass murder, 94 percent of the 515 homicide incidents reported to the police during 2001 involved a lone victim. Of the others, twenty-six involved two victims, three involved three victims, one involved four victims, and one involved five victims. The majority of multiple-victim homicides were family related (Dauvergne, 2002).

Gang-related homicides declined slightly from 72 in 2000 to 62 in 2001, but were still much higher than in the early 1990s (Dauvergne, 2002). Between 1991 and 1997, gang-related homicides averaged 22 a year—a figure that nearly tripled to 58 by 2000–01. The vast majority of gang-related homicides are in Quebec, where there has been active competition for territory between Hells Angels and the Rock Machine (now the Bandidos). However, in 2001 there were nearly as many gang-related homicides in Ontario as in Quebec.

Victims

Most Canadian victims knew their assailants. For homicides solved in 2001, 43 percent of victims were killed by an immediate family member or relative, and 45 percent were killed by some other acquaintance. Only 13 percent were killed by a stranger.

Males are more than twice as likely to be murdered as females (Dauvergne, 2002). In 2001, 71 percent of homicide victims were male and 29 percent were female. Victims were relatively young, with a median age of 33 for males and 37 for females. The most common single age of victims was 22. Males 20 to 24 were considerably more likely to be murdered than any other group (with males 25 to 29 second most likely); the age of female victims was much more equally distributed (see Figure 14.1).

The differences in the age distribution between male and female homicide victims reflects differences in the nature of their victimization. Female victims are much more likely than male victims to be killed by an intimate partner. In 2001, 52 percent of female victims and 8 percent of male victims were killed by a person with whom they had an intimate relationship at one time. By contrast, male victims were much more likely to be killed by strangers (17 percent compared with 4 percent for females) or by casual acquaintances. Thirty-nine children were murdered in 2001; three-quarters of them were killed by a parent. Contrary to what you might assume from the extensive media coverage of child victims, only three children were killed by strangers.

Over half the victims had consumed alcohol and/or drugs prior to the offence (Dauvergne, 2002). Male victims were more likely than females to have used an intoxicant, a fact that is again consistent with the different patterns of victimization.

Suspects

Police solved 77 percent of Canadian homicides in 2001. Almost all of these were cleared by laying a charge against an accused (89 percent); 10 percent of the suspected perpetrators had committed suicide.

Males made up 87 percent of those charged. Ninety-four percent of those charged were adults, and only 6 percent were young offenders. The median age of those charged was 29 for males and 28 for females. The percentage of killers drops off sharply past 40 years of age. Alcohol and drugs play a significant role in homicide; three-quarters of the accused were known to have consumed alcohol, drugs, or both at the time of the offence. The role played by alcohol is tragically illustrated by a recent case in which a 38-year-old Winnipeg man kicked a drinking companion to death because he got "bored" at a Valentine's Day drinking party (McIntyre, 2003). After his wife, daughter, and a family friend passed out, the man began kicking the friend in the head to try to wake her up. He continued to alternate between beating the woman and drinking throughout the rest of the evening until she finally died. The accused, who had a lengthy record of violence, pleaded guilty to manslaughter for the offence and received a sentence of five years in prison.

The overall pattern of Canadian homicide is consistent with a lifestyle/exposure, routine activities orientation. Homicide is often the final word in an argument arising between people who know each other and who are engaged in their normal activities. Even the location of homicide (most often the victim's own home) is where most people spend the greatest proportion of their time. Finally, both homicide suspects and victims are disproportionately young, male, and unmarried—characteristics that are associated with less structured lifestyles and higher levels of physical aggression.

The different patterns of male and female victimization are also consistent with this approach. Those who have the highest risk of victimization are young males who are users of alcohol and/or drugs and who are living lifestyles that include involvement with gangs or other criminal activities; all of these things expose them to a higher risk of homicide. Females are most likely to be killed by an intimate partner (or former partner); this is consistent with the more even age distribution of female victims (see Figure 14.1).

The Dynamics of Homicide

The routine activities perspective helps us understand the patterns of homicide and other crimes, but it does not tell us much about how and why these crimes actually occur. Why do some encounters between people result in homicide? What are the dynamics of situations that result in the death of one or more of the persons involved? Following the interactionist approach (see Chapter 12), researchers have interviewed violent offenders and analyzed the accounts of homicides contained in police files to achieve a better understanding of the dynamics of the criminal event. David Luckenbill (1977) has examined the typical roles played by offenders, victims, and bystanders in situations that resulted in homicide. He looked at the social context in which homicides occurred and concluded that many of them were confrontations that escalated into "character contests;" that is, violence became a means of saving face for the individuals.

FIGURE 14.1   Victim Homicide Rates by Age Group and Sex, 2001

Source: Statistics Canada. (September, 2002). "Victim Homicide Rates by Age Groups and Sex, 2001," adapted from the Statistics Canada publication "Homicide in Canada, 2001," Catalogue no. 85-002, Vol. 22, No. 7, September 2002, p. 13. Reprinted with permission from the Minister of Industry.

These events tended to occur during leisure time while individuals were engaged in unstructured activities such as spending time at home with others, drinking in a tavern, or just hanging out on the street. In most cases, the individuals involved were with family, friends, or acquaintances. Often the victim and the offender had previous histories of disputes that led them to anticipate or even to seek out confrontation with the others involved. In some cases, one of the parties insulted the other either intentionally or inadvertently; in others, there was a refusal to carry out some requested action. This was interpreted as being offensive; rather than ignoring the insult or leaving the scene, the offended individual responded aggressively in order to save face. In some cases, other people at the scene either encouraged a violent response or did nothing to try to defuse the situation. These points are illustrated in one of Luckenbill's examples:

> The offender, victim, and three friends were driving in the country drinking beer and wine. At one point the victim started laughing at the offender's car which he, the victim, scratched a week earlier. The offender asked the victim why he was laughing. The victim responded that the offender's car looked like junk. The offender stopped the car and all got out. The offender asked the victim to repeat his statement. When the victim reiterated his characterization of the car, the offender struck the victim, knocking him to the ground. (1977:181)

What is striking about this incident is just how trivial it was. A joking remark made among friends ultimately led to the death of one young man and a long prison sentence for another. This case is not like most of those you see on television or in movies or read about in the headlines, but it is more representative of the "typical" Canadian homicide than are the cases of Paul Bernardo or Clifford Olson or the biker killings that get so much of the media's attention. For a similar example of the circumstances surrounding a homicide, Box 14.1 describes the events leading to a recent murder in Toronto.

These cases illustrate the complexity of explaining criminal behaviour. At one level, the routine activities approach tells us that young males who engage in alcohol or drug use and other high-risk behaviours and who regularly associate with people with criminal records are more likely to be victimized by violent crime than other people. At another level, the interactionist perspective represented by Luckenbill allows us to understand the dynamics of the criminal event from the perspective of those involved. However, we still need to know more to adequately explain homicide and other serious crimes. We need to understand why some people respond violently, while others avoid such situations, walk away from them when they develop, or defuse the hostility with a friendly or conciliatory remark. We also need to understand the social circumstances in which people learn to define violence as a way of resolving problems and why homicide is more prevalent among some segments of society than others. Can you think of some reasons why "respect" was so important to the young men involved in the homicide case discussed in this section? The theories you studied in Chapters 8 to 13 all shed some light on the complex issues involved in explaining homicide and other violent offences.

BOX 14.1

Doesn't Take a Lot to Get You Killed

TORONTO—When prosecutor Laura Bird began speaking yesterday, it sounded for all the world as though she had borrowed her story line from a violent video game or, in another age, a Bugs Bunny and Road Runner cartoon.

Hers was a tale of characters with childish nicknames who seethed with preening masculinity, nourished ridiculous grievances over months and whose ludicrous code of behaviour is redolent with more ritual gestures than a formal audience with royalty.

It would have been comic, but Ms. Bird was a describing the real lives of real people and the terrible and senseless death of one of them.

Wayne Anthony Reid, a young black man, died in a hail of bullets on June 15 last year and, Ms. Bird said, he died because the friend he was with that night had, almost a full year earlier, either not nodded in respect, or not nodded vigorously enough, or not been seen to nod, in deference to a friend of the man now alleged to have killed him.

The prosecutor was delivering her opening address, designed to give jurors an overview of her case, in the second-degree murder trial of Leon Patrick Boswell....

The victim, the alleged killer and their two friends either lived or grew up in the notorious housing complexes of the Jamestown area of northwest Toronto, a neighbourhood where territory is so clearly marked that, Ms. Bird said, "When you walked through the turf of someone else you were expected to acknowledge the other person in order to show your respect for them. Failure to nod, or otherwise hail them up, could be considered to be extremely disrespectful."

And, she said, "Disrespect was taken seriously and could be expected to result in violent retaliation" such that a code of silence envelops the whole community, "preventing citizens from coming forward to report crimes for fear that they may be next in line at the morgue."

Ms. Bird's story began in the late summer of the year 2000 when, she said, Mr. Reid's friend, one Shaun Sharp (known as Cookie), who was

friends with various groups of young men in the area, was walking through Jamestown with a pal from another group.

This was the turf of Mr. Boswell's friend, Jermaine Grant (known as J-Bug), and Cookie apparently claims to have nodded at J-Bug, but J-Bug did not see him do it, and "confronted Cookie and accused him of disrespecting him." Cookie tried to explain that he had nodded, but J-Bug didn't believe him, and this marked the beginning of their bad relationship, and, allegedly, also of Mr. Reid's end.

The next time the two men saw one another, Ms. Bird said, "J-Bug demanded Cookie go around the corner with him, allegedly to talk," but Cookie "believed that J-Bug was carrying a gun, and that he would be killed" if he went. So he refused, which J-Bug purportedly took as a further disrespect.

By this time, Cookie was terrified of J-Bug, and the next time he spotted him, from inside a pool hall, he actually looked for a place to hide in case J-Bug "started shooting" through the windows.

"After this," Ms. Bird said, " the word on the street was that J-Bug was looking for Cookie. Cookie believed absolutely that J-Bug wanted him dead."

On June 15, Cookie was hanging around with Mr. Reid, who was now living in Mississauga but visiting his old neighbourhood of Jamestown that day.

The two men passed what was for them—neither were "model citizens," Ms. Bird said, and both were "low-level drug dealers"—a normal day. They had an impromptu party at Cookie's house, stood around talking in the sun, playing dominoes and drinking beer until it ran out, whereupon they headed out to buy more. En route, they spotted a girl, flirted with her and thought they had made arrangements to meet up with her later—and incurred the wrath of Mr. Reid's girlfriend, who spotted them with the girl and then chased them through the complex for a while.

Then they went back to Cookie's house, where Mr. Reid's girlfriend blasted him, partied some

(continued)

more until, later that evening, they headed out to try to meet up with the girl they had met. After a false start at finding her place, they decided to try Jamestown, what Ms. Bird called "the worst decision of their lives."

Cookie had barely parked the car when they were confronted by J-Bug and his friend, Mr. Boswell (known as Bluenose).

Now, at 26, Mr. Reid was older than the others, and had even known J-Bug as a child, and promptly stepped in, telling J-Bug and Mr. Roswell they were not going to bother Cookie so long as he was around. Cookie and Mr. Reid walked away, and as they did, Cookie told Mr. Reid that J-Bug wanted to kill him.

J-Bug and Mr. Boswell, now, were furious at being left, so they followed the two men, again confronting them. Again, Mr. Reid told them not to trouble Cookie, and again they walked away, highly disrespectful, Ms. Bird said, "particularly since all of this was happening on the turf of J-Bug" and Mr. Boswell.

Mr. Reid and Cookie continued on, through the narrow paths that wind through the complex of townhouses, and arrived at the home of the girl they had met hours earlier. They talked to her a while on the doorstep, she went in to answer the phone, and they were standing there when J-Bug and Mr. Boswell again showed up.

"They now proceeded to stare down" Cookie and Mr. Reid, Ms. Bird said. Mr. Reid was frustrated by now, and again told them to leave Cookie alone, but where J-Bug appeared to respect Mr. Reid, Mr. Boswell did not. Mr. Reid approached them, and again said he had been in Jamestown longer than either one of them.

At this point, J-Bug tried to lead Mr. Boswell away, Ms. Bird said, but Mr. Boswell "pulled out his revolver and fired five shots into the right side of Mr. Reid's body."

In the panic that followed, Cookie ran into the girl's house, Mr. Reid, bleeding, managing to follow him there. Cookie dragged him inside, shouted for someone to call 911 and then did so himself, but Mr. Reid died of his injuries in hospital some short time later. As Ms. Bird put it, "The bullets that ripped through his body had simply caused too much damage."

Source: Adapted from Christie Blatchford. (November 27, 2002). "Doesn't Take a Lot to Get You Killed," in *National Post*. Reprinted with permission of *National Post*.

ASSAULTIVE BEHAVIOURS

Assault

Amendments to the Criminal Code of Canada in 1983 created three levels of assault: aggravated assault (level 3), assault with a deadly weapon or causing bodily harm (level 2), and common assault (level 1). The least serious assaults are the most common. Thus, in 1997 just over 1 percent were level 3 aggravated assaults and an additional 18 percent were level 2 assaults (with a weapon or causing bodily harm). The least serious—level 1 common assaults—accounted for 81 percent of all assaults and 63 percent of all police-reported violent incidents reported during 1997.

Incidence

There were 749 police-reported assaults per 100 000 Canadian population during 2002 (Wallace, 2003b). This compares with the 5100 assaults per 100 000 Canadians at least 15 years of age that were reported in the 1999 General Social Survey (Mihorean et al., 2001). The GSS defined assault as

[Handwritten margin notes:]

Assault

who: mostly male offenders
50/50 male, female
victims

what: weapon, attack, or
threatened attack

when: slight increase with
a slight decrease in
2002

where: Canada

why: alcohol related,
personal matter, gangs,
workplace

involving the presence of a weapon, an actual attack, or a threatened attack. An attack, in turn, could involve anything from being hit, slapped, pushed, or grabbed to being shot or beaten. However, the GSS report excluded spousal violence, which makes up a high proportion of police-reported assaults, so the actual GSS figure would be much higher than 5100 per 100 000.

Assaults increased rather dramatically through the 1980s and early 1990s and continued to rise slowly in 2000 and 2001 before declining slightly in 2002. However, some of this increase in police-reported assault is attributable to an increased probability of reporting assaults to the police. Many behaviours that are now reported to the police and treated as crimes were in the past considered to be private or noncriminal matters. Domestic assaults, child abuse, schoolyard fights, sibling violence, and elder abuse are examples (as are date rape, child molesting, and unwanted touching, in the case of sexual assaults). Zero-tolerance policies, which require the police to lay charges in domestic violence cases, are responsible for much of the increase in recorded assaults (Linden, 1994). These policies mean that incidents that would not previously have been recorded by the police are recorded now and become part of UCR assault statistics.

Victims

Victims of assault seem to be about evenly split by gender. Police-reported crime statistics for 1997 indicated that a slight majority (52 percent) of victims were males, while the 1993 GSS indicated that women were slightly more likely than men to report having been victimized. Both police statistics and the GSS reported that the victims tended to be young. The GSS found that the average victim was just under 20. This is considerably younger than the median age of 26 for male and 29 for female victims of assaults registered by police during 1997.

The 1993 GSS indicated that a slight majority of those who were assaulted one or more times were women, single, had a personal income of less than $15 000 per year, and were working at a job (an additional 20 percent were students during the week the assault occurred). Eighty percent lived in urban areas, 74 percent were childless, and 60 percent lived in households of three or fewer members. Approximately half the victims participated in 30 or more evening activities outside of the home per month, and another three out of ten took part in 15 to 29 such activities. Three of eight victims said they felt unsafe walking alone in their area after dark, and more than one-quarter reported routinely carrying something for self-defence or to alert people.

Offenders

Police statistics for assaults during 2002 indicated that 81 percent of those charged were males and that 85 percent were adults (Wallace, 2003b). In 1997 the median age of those charged was 30 for males and 27 for females. Two of five victims reported that their assailants were strangers. However, almost as many victims reported that their assailant was someone well known to them. Another 15 percent of assailants were casual acquaintances, and 8 percent were somebody known by sight. More than four out of five assault victims in the

1993 GSS reported that they were assaulted by a lone offender. The majority of the other victims reported that there were two offenders; almost 10 percent reported that there were three or more offenders.

Pattern

Victims in 1993 GSS assault incidents overwhelmingly reported that they were the sole victim of the assault, which most commonly occurred between 6 p.m. and midnight. A majority of victims thought that their victimization was influenced by somebody's drug or alcohol use. A substantial minority of victim-reported assaults occurred in the victim's home, but most occurred in some kind of public setting. This included 10 percent in a bar or restaurant, 24 percent in another type of commercial location, and 27 percent in a public place such as a park, parking garage, or on the street (Gartner and Doob, 1994). Of those assaulted in a residence, almost half the perpetrators lived with their victims. Most of the remaining assailants were let into the residence by someone.

Almost two-thirds of the victims reported being attacked, and almost all of the rest were threatened, usually face to face. Most of those who were threatened believed that the threat would be carried out. More than one in seven victims reported that a weapon was present, most commonly a knife or a gun. Close to half the victims were hit, kicked, slapped, or knocked down; almost as many reported that they were grabbed, held, tripped, or jumped. Nearly 30 percent of the victims were physically injured. Of all assault victims (including those sexually assaulted), 11 percent received medical attention at a hospital, and 16 percent had to stay in bed all or most of a day. One out of four victims found it difficult to carry out their main activity for all or most of a day, about half of these for three or more days.

Fewer than 30 percent of the GSS assault victims reported that the police were notified. Almost half the victims said that police were not notified because no police involvement was wanted. The main reasons listed by victims for not reporting assaults to the police were that the matter was dealt with otherwise (37 percent), the matter was not important enough (21 percent), or it was a personal matter (14 percent).

Domestic Assault

Domestic assaults, particularly "series assaults" (those carried out on a repeated basis), have long been of concern to women's groups and others. Spousal violence has been discussed in Chapter 6, but several other types of domestic assaults will be discussed here.

In recent years, several types of family violence have been recognized as problems requiring intervention. These include parental assaults on adolescents and violence by children directed against one another and against parents. As with spousal assaults, many assaults are not perceived as crimes when committed against other family members.

Historically, little attention has been paid to these assaults, and we know little about them. Even when they have been studied, they have typically been studied more from a child welfare than a criminological perspective. Consequently, past

[Handwritten margin notes:]
Domestic Assault
who: parents and their children
what: physical abuse against children
when: currently
where: in the home
why: for discipline

studies have tended to lump together both criminal and noncriminal types of behaviour under the rubric of "child abuse and neglect." In recent years, the issue of parental discipline has been raised by those who feel that physical punishment should not be allowed. While the courts have thus far supported the rights of parents to discipline their children, they have been setting limits on the nature of physical punishment. Box 14.2 discusses the judge's ruling in a case in which parents and their minister insisted that physical punishment of children was required by their religion. In this ruling the judge upheld the rights of the Children's Aid Society to remove the children from their home. In a later ruling the judge prohibited the parents from using physical punishment.

Elder Abuse

The abuse of elderly people can take place in both domestic and institutional living situations. Moreover, like child abuse, there are many types of abuse that are not necessarily violations of any criminal law. Some types of neglect—psychological abuse or even material abuse—are examples of antisocial behaviours that may not be criminal matters. But most authorities agree that physical violence toward elders constitutes a criminal assault.

The 1999 General Social Survey interviewed more than 4000 seniors who were living in private households and asked if they had experienced emotional abuse, financial abuse, and physical and sexual abuse in the previous five years (Dauvergne, 2003). Seven percent of seniors reported having experienced one of these forms of abuse from an adult child, caregiver, or spouse. Emotional abuse was the most common form reported, followed by financial abuse and physical and sexual abuse. Additional data were obtained from police records for 2000 (Dauvergne, 2003). According to these data, about 25 percent of reported offences were committed by family members. Common assault was the most frequently reported offence committed against elderly victims by family members, followed by uttering threats and more serious levels of assault. Robbery was the most commonly reported crime committed by a non-family member. While rates of victimization for seniors are lower than for the rest of the population, the consequences can be much more severe. For example, seniors may be dependent on their caregivers and unable to readily escape a dangerous or threatening situation. Also, the consequences of victimization may be more serious. A young person who is knocked down by a stranger may get up unharmed, while an older person may be seriously hurt in a similar incident. Similarly, an elderly person who loses money to theft or fraud will not be able to replace the money as easily as a younger person who is still in the labour market. In response to the problem of elder abuse, most Canadian provinces and territories have passed legislation to protect seniors from victimization.

Lifestyle Factors in Assaults

Lifestyle factors, obviously, are involved in assault. Victimization is particularly high among the young, males, those who are not married (other than widowed), students, and people who are most likely to be engaging in evening activities outside of the home. Effective guardianship also plays a role in the

BOX 14.2

Judge Rules for CAS in Aylmer Spanking Case

A judge says that while the seizure of seven children from their home two years ago for fear they were being spanked was "very traumatic," a child welfare worker did not violate anyone's constitutional rights.

The worker had "reasonable and probable grounds to believe the children were in need of protection," Ontario Court Justice Eleanor Schnall said in written reasons supporting her ruling last October to admit certain evidence in the so-called "spanking case" in Aylmer, Ont.

Michael Menear and Valerie Wise, lawyer for the parents, had argued that evidence gathered by child welfare worker Shelley West was inadmissible because it was gathered in violation of the constitutional rights of their clients.

West "is not to be faulted for taking the action she did," Schnall wrote in reasons dated last Thursday.

"The rights of the parents cannot be elevated to be paramount to the rights of the children," Schnall said.

The parents had also argued that West should not have interviewed the children without their consent.

But Schnall called that "sheer nonsense."

"No community, or society, could reasonably agree with the concept that a parent who sexually abuses or physically mistreats a child should be entitled to give his/her consent to the interviewing, or examination of the child by a member of a Children's Aid Society." ...

Family and Children's Services of St. Thomas and Elgin County officials said Schnall's ruling "affirms that the right of children to be protected from abuse and neglect takes precedence over any other procedural rights for parents."

"We are pleased that Ontario's child protection legislation, regulations and accepted practice has not been compromised by the procedural arguments put forward by the parents' lawyers," Steve Bailey, executive director of the agency, said Monday in a release.

The children, devotees of a religious group called the Church of God, were taken kicking and screaming from their home in early July 2001 when child welfare workers, with the assistance of police, seized the children after the mother refused to promise she would stop using objects to discipline them.

The parents insisted they were acting in accordance with Biblical principle when they hit the children with objects, including a broken metal fly swatter described as the "spanking stick."

The children were returned home about three weeks later after their parents agreed, on an interim basis, to refrain from physical discipline and to seek medical care when necessary.

Section 43 of the Criminal Code has allowed spanking in Canada since 1892, but only for the purpose of "correction" and only within the bounds of what it calls "reasonable force."

The courts over the years have interpreted the law—which withstood a constitutional challenge earlier this year—as forbidding the use of inanimate objects such as paddles, sticks or wooden spoons.

Ultimately, Schnall will decide if the children need protection, and if so, what form it should take.

Source: Adapted from Peter Cameron. (March 3, 2002). "Judge Rules for CAS in Aylmer Spanking Case." Reprinted with permission of The Canadian Press.

probability of experiencing an assault. Not only are most assaults perpetrated on a lone victim, but the risk of assault increases—especially on the basis of risk per hour of exposure—as one moves away from the watchful eyes of family, neighbours, and work associates.

Apparent exceptions to this generalization are spousal assaults, child abuse, and assaults on the elderly. The home does not appear to be a place of effective guardianship for these victims. This is because so many of these assaults are of a domestic nature, perpetrated by a current or former spouse or parent, or a current or former dependent child who may have easy access both to the home and to the victim. Such assaults also tend to be inordinately brutal, possibly because of the nonrational, emotional affect that motivates them. However, it is likely that for most Canadians, the home remains a place of relative safety if one considers the rate of assault in various locations *per hour of risk (or exposure)*.

Sexual Assault

[handwritten margin notes:
Sexual Assault
Who! victims tend to be females, under 20 and offenders tend to be males, 12–17
What: sexual assault, sexual assault with a weapon, aggravated sexual assault
When: night time 6–12
Where: out somewhere
Why: alcohol, being alone]

The law concerning assaults involving sex was changed in 1983 by amendments to the Criminal Code of Canada (see Chapter 6). Under the new law, a variety of sex-related offences were reclassified as sexual assault, of which there are three types: sexual assault (not involving a weapon or serious injury), sexual assault with a weapon (including threats to a third person or causing bodily harm), and aggravated sexual assault (which entails wounding, maiming, disfiguring, or endangering the life of the victim).

Incidence

The rate of police-reported sexual assaults in 2002 was 78 known incidents per 100 000 population (Wallace, 2003b). Almost 98 percent of these were common sexual assaults, which include threatened, attempted, or actual sexual assaults. The remaining 2 percent were sexual assaults with a weapon and aggravated sexual assaults involving serious bodily harm. Cumulatively, sexual assaults made up about 8 percent of all violent criminal incidents known to the police during 2002. The rate of sexual assaults has declined over the past decade and is now 35 percent lower than the rate in 1993. The decline has been greatest for the two most serious categories of sexual assault.

Many feminists, criminologists, and others have long contended that police statistics grossly under-report the true incidence of sexual assault and the sexual abuse of children. They argue that many victims never report their victimization to the police. In support of their position, they cite statistics, such as that from the 1999 GSS, that 78 percent of what were classified as sexual assaults were not reported to the police. Most victimization surveys have shown that a high proportion of serious sexual assaults are never reported to the police.

Victims

Extrapolations from those who reported one or more victimizations by sexual assault in the 1993 GSS indicated that nine out of ten victims were women. Eight of ten victims were under 30, most commonly under 20, when they were victimized. Three-quarters of the victims were childless, and the majority of victims were single. Half had no personal income or an income under $10 000 per year. The main activity of two out of five was working at a job, although more than one out of three was going to school. About three of four victims were from urban areas.

Police statistics provide a somewhat different picture of sexual assault because they are not limited to experiences reported by the population at least

15 years of age (the age cutoff for respondents to the GSS Victimization Survey); also, they involve more rigorous screening to meet the legal criteria of sexual assault. For 1997, police statistics indicated that 84 percent of the victims known to the police were female (Kong, 1998b). Only 41 percent were adults; 32 percent were youths (ages 12 through 17) and 27 percent were children (under 12 years of age). The median age was 11 for male victims and 17 for female victims.

Offenders

Almost all (98 percent) of those charged by Canadian police with some type of sexual assault during 2001 were male, and about 18 percent were young offenders. Victims reported that lone offenders committed 90 percent of assaults. Three-quarters of victims knew their assailants, and almost half the assailants were either a friend or somebody else well known to the victim.

Pattern

Almost half of the GSS sexual assault incidents took place between 6 p.m. and midnight. The overwhelming majority of incidents occurred somewhere other than the victim's place of residence, and less than one in twenty involved a weapon. Wright (1995) reported that the majority of victims thought that the assault was related to somebody else's drug or alcohol use. About half of the victims reported engaging in 30 or more evening activities per month outside the home, while almost as many more engaged in 15 to 29 such evening activities.

This pattern is broadly consistent with the routine activities approach. A pool of **motivated offenders** (emotionally immature potential assailants) can be assumed to exist. Females or children (in the case of various types of child molestation) are seen as suitable targets by such motivated offenders. When the routine activities of potential victims bring them into contact with motivated offenders under situations of ineffective guardianship (being young, being out alone at night, being intoxicated, hitchhiking, going to the home of strangers, inviting potential offenders—nonstrangers as well as strangers—into their own home, and so on), the essential components for the commission of the crime are all present (Gibson et al., 1980). As with homicide, lifestyle is related to victimization.

motivated offender
A person who is ready to engage in some type of crime.

Victims of sexual assault often are indirectly victimized a second time because fear influences them to change their lifestyles and to make various types of purchases to reduce the probability of being revictimized. The victims in two-thirds of sexual assault incidents in the 1993 GSS reported that they had taken action to protect themselves against crime during the preceding year, most commonly by installing new locks. Worse, half the sexual assault victims in these incidents reported that they felt somewhat or very unsafe walking alone at night, and almost one-third reported that they routinely stayed home at night because they were afraid of being victimized by crime. It is not known whether such changes were made in response to the reported behaviour classified as sexual assault or to one or more other types of victimization.

While there may be a gender-related physiological basis for aggression, it also seems that the power (domination) component of coercive sexual assault is linked to learned gender roles. In the case of forcible rape, for example, it is almost invariably the male (or role-playing male) who is the assailant and the female (or role-playing female) who is the victim. This is as true of heterosexual rapes as it is of homosexual rapes in prisons, the vast majority of which go unreported.

ROBBERY

Robbery

who: offender is usually a young adult male

what: threatened or actual use of force or of a weapon in conjunction with taking, or attempting to take, something from another person.

when: at night

where: most common is small business like a gas station or convenience store

why: spur of moment, financial need, alcohol related

Like assault, robbery is considered a violent crime. It occurs when there is threatened or actual use of force or of a weapon in conjunction with taking, or attempting to take, something from another person. But robbery is a much rarer crime than assault. Police statistics for 2002 showed 9 percent of all violent crimes were robberies—just a bit higher than the percentage of sexual assaults.

Incidence

The police-reported rate of robberies in 2002 was 85 per 100 000 Canadians (Wallace, 2003b). About half of robberies involve no weapon; weapons other than firearms are more likely to be used in the remainder. The incidence of robbery has been declining and dropped by over 20 percent between 1991 and 2002.

Victims

In the 1993 GSS, males were twice as likely as females to report being victimized by robbery (including attempted robbery) (Wright, 1995). Single males had a rate of robbery victimization more than triple the average. Victimization rates among urban residents and those 15 to 24 were also much higher than the average. The experience of being robbed can be a very difficult one. While most robberies do not result in injury, some victims are very seriously injured and most victims suffer some emotional damage. Injuries are more likely if the victim resists the robbery. Over 60 percent of the victims interviewed by Gabor et al. (1987) reported physical symptoms because of the robbery, including chronic nervousness, insomnia, nightmares, headaches, and eating problems as well as psychological symptoms such as fear, distrust, and aggressiveness. In most cases these symptoms lasted seven months or more.

Offenders

Robbery is the only violent crime typically committed by strangers. Janhevich (1998) reported that during 1996, five out of six victims were robbed by strangers. Almost nine out of ten persons charged with robbery in 1997 were males, and three out of eight were young offenders. The median age of female offenders (16) was considerably below that of male offenders (21) (Kong, 1998b).

The robberies depicted in movies such as *Ocean's Eleven* show highly skilled crews of specialists stealing millions of dollars after months of intensive planning and practice. However, real robberies typically involve young, unsophisticated substance abusers who rarely spend more than a few minutes planning their offences and whose take is at best a few hundred dollars (Desroches, 1995). The typical targets are not banks or casinos, but vulnerable small businesses such as gas bars and convenience stores. Frequently, the victim is just a person who happens to be walking down the street when the robber decides he needs more money. Robberies can be dangerous for both victim and offender, and the chances of being caught and punished are considerably higher than for most other crimes of financial gain. In their study of robberies in Montreal and Quebec City, Gabor et al. (1987) found that in about three-quarters of the cases, the robbers did not try to disguise themselves. Although there were a few large robberies, two-thirds involved $500 or less. The vast majority of cases involved one (41 percent) or two (46 percent) offenders; the average age of offenders was 22 years.

Gabor and his colleagues asked a number of armed robbers about their motivations for committing the offence. Not surprisingly, the principal motives were financial:

> It's the fastest and most direct way to get money. There's no thrill in getting it. It's for the cash, the money that I do it. (Gabor et al., 1987, 63)

However, some robbers also enjoyed the thrill of committing a robbery and the power that the robber had over the victim:

> When I have a gun in my hands, nothing can stop me. It makes me feel important and strong. With a revolver you're somebody.

> It's funny to see the expression of people when they have a .38 in their face. Sometimes when I went home at night I thought of it and laughed. I know that it's bad to say that. Maybe I was just fascinated.(Gabor et al., 1987, 63)

No special training or skills are required to commit a robbery, and most robbers appear to underestimate the risks of being caught. Thus, robbers may see the crime as an easy way to accomplish their goals.

Gabor and his colleagues also examined the reasons why some of the robbers they interviewed decided to stop committing robberies. Occasional offenders felt that the modest rewards were not worth the long sentences involved or the risk to themselves and to others. Chronic offenders were older and decided to quit because they decided they did not want to spend increasingly longer sentences in jail and because the criminal lifestyle was no longer as attractive as it had been when they were younger. Some of those who gave up robbery completely ended their involvement in crime; others switched to different offences such as fraud and drug trafficking, which they felt were more lucrative and less risky.

Pattern

A large majority of robberies occur between 6 p.m. and 6 a.m., usually before midnight. Two of three victims in the 1993 GSS thought that their robbery was related in some way to somebody's alcohol or drug use. Thus, it is not surprising that three-quarters of the victims reported that they engaged in at least 15, and usually more than 30, evening activities outside the home in a typical month. While we must avoid blaming victims, it is apparent that these people's routine activities place them at greater risk of robbery than were people who rarely went out in the evening. Box 14.3 discusses how changes in guardianship are affecting bank robberies.

Break & Enter

Who: males, 12-17
What: private property
When: Summer months
Where: Northern Territories
Why: surveillance, and for
*   financial gain*

BREAK AND ENTER

People sometimes confuse robbery with break and enter (or burglary, as it is also called). The difference between the two is simple. Robbery involves face-to-face contact with the threat of force. Break and enter involves stealth. The typical burglar seeks to avoid all contact with anybody in the residence or building that is being illegally entered.

BOX 14.3

FOCUS

The End of Bank Robberies?

Routine activities theory would predict that if targets become less attractive or if guardianship becomes more effective there should be less crime. This is exactly what has happened to bank robberies, which used to be a major problem in Canada. In fact, two decades ago, Montreal was the bank robbery capital of North America. Well-organized and well-armed gangs were responsible for as many as 900 bank robberies a year in that city and often took their skills on the road to rob banks and jewellery stores in Toronto and other cities. Often gangs of four men would carry out precisely coordinated bank robberies. One of the men would remain in the getaway car, another would stand guard at the door with a sawed-off shotgun and count out the time remaining to the other two men who were gathering up the money. The gang assumed that the alarm had been sent to the police as soon as they entered the door, so it was critical to finish the job and leave as quickly as possible. However, the number of bank robberies in Montreal has declined to about 100 per year and has also been declining in the rest of the

country (Ha, 2002). The Montreal police department is now abolishing its specialized holdup squad, which had attracted some of the city's best police officers.

What has caused this dramatic decline in bank robberies? According to Tu Thanh Ha (2002), a number of factors were involved. First, banks have less cash on hand because of changes in banking patterns. Most people now have their paycheques deposited directly into their bank accounts so banks no longer have long lineups of people cashing their cheques at the end of the week. Also, many Canadians do their banking by using instant teller machines, debit cards, or the Internet and do not depend on getting cash at the tellers' counter. Second, banks have developed more effective security methods, including time-release locks and closed-circuit camera systems. Finally, the police make arrests in 80 to 90 percent of bank robberies (McLean, 2000), and the courts have become tougher on firearms offences, so many of the robbers have decided crimes such as drug selling are easier ways of making money.

Incidence and Patterns

The rate of break and enters has declined dramatically in Canada. From its peak of 1550 break and enters for every 100 000 Canadians in 1991, the rate has declined by 44 percent to 875 per 100 000 in 2002 (Wallace, 2003b; Kowalski, 2000). In 2002, almost six of ten break and enters targeted private residences; most of the remainder targeted commercial businesses (Wallace, 2003b). In a detailed study of break and enters that took place in 1999, Kowalski (2000) found that the highest rates were in the northern territories, followed by Saskatchewan, British Columbia, and Manitoba. Regina (2361 per 100 000) and Saskatoon (1799) had the highest city rates, followed by Vancouver (1601) and Montreal (1312). Toronto was the lowest of all cities with a rate of 612 per 100 000.

The 1999 GSS reported that 21 percent of property stolen from residences consisted of audiovisual equipment. This was followed by household tools, appliances, or furniture (18 percent), and bicycles (14 percent) (Mihorean et al., 2001).

It is unusual for stolen property to be recovered. Experienced burglars generally steal for income rather than for excitement. Consequently, they steal expensive, portable, and compact items that can easily be disposed of or sold. If such items are not available in a burgled location, often nothing will be taken. Indeed, in 1999 nothing was reported stolen in almost 20 percent of break-ins (Kowalski, 2000). The Insurance Information Centre of Canada reported that the average claim by tenants and home-owners for losses (including damages) from break and enters amounted to $2600 in 2000, and for commercial businesses, $6978. Overall, the Insurance Bureau of Canada reported that residential and commercial claims from break and enters cost the industry $290 million that year (Savoie, 2002), down from a loss of $434 million in 1992 (Kong, 1998a).

Most break and enters are not cleared by arrest. In 1999, only 16 percent of break and enters resulted in an arrest. Ninety-two percent of those charged with break and enter in 1999 were male, and about 40 percent were youths 12 to 17 (Kowalski, 2000).

Victims of break and enter found the experience very upsetting. Over half were angry, and substantial numbers were upset, shocked, or confused (35 percent); fearful (23 percent); and more cautious (16 percent) after their home had been burglarized (Mihorean et al., 2001).

A Crime of Opportunity

Research findings suggest that break and enter is largely a crime of opportunity. It is motivated less by the prospect of a large gain than by the perception of a low risk of being caught. This is consistent with the finding from the 1993 GSS that 30 percent of residential break and enters occurred in the summer months of June, July, and August, when school is out and people are most likely to be taking holidays (Wright, 1995). The perceived risk of being caught is heavily influenced by the lifestyle factors of the household occupants, by whether entrance accesses are secured, by whether a dwelling is occupied or seems to be occupied, and by a variety of environmental factors such as "surveillability."

Additional evidence of the opportunistic nature of break and enter is the fact that frequently nothing is stolen. Such a pattern suggests ease of entry rather than pursuit of any particular valuable object as the more important factor in the selection of the target. Moreover, the high frequency of attempted rather than completed break and enters would again suggest that potential targets are selected haphazardly rather than through careful planning. Clearly, many attempted break-ins are unsuccessful, presumably because of inopportune circumstances. Mayhew (1984) has suggested that such unsuccessful burglaries tell us about the value of security and target hardening. While target hardening such as enhanced hardware and security systems may not deter burglary attempts, these measures may prevent such attempts from being successful.

Bennett and Wright (1984a; 1984b) asked older, experienced burglars which factors influenced their choices of targets. They found that the prospect of a large gain was less often a consideration than the certainty that there was something present worth taking. Ease of entry was not reported to be a major consideration (though it will be recalled that many attempts at break-in apparently are foiled once begun). The majority of these older, experienced burglars also stated that they would be deterred, either conditionally or unconditionally, by the presence of dogs. The authors concluded that the major consideration in target selection was factors affecting risk: burglars would be deterred if they believed that someone was home and by the apparent "surveillability" or visibility of entrance accesses from nearby overlooking buildings or by passers-by and neighbours. For example, when Wright and Decker asked their respondents to describe unsuitable targets, most said they would avoid targets in areas where it looked like neighbours would look out for each other. Older people were considered to be especially likely to report suspicious behaviour to the police:

> The thing is if you got a lot of elderly people on one block, that'll get you killed mostly ... I wanted to do [a burglary] over here by the bakery shop, but that's a retired area. Almost everybody that live on that block is retired and they constantly lookin' out windows and watchin' [out] for each other. Ain't nothin' you can do about that. (Wright and Decker, 1992, 87)

In other words, a major factor in the risk of break and enter is the degree to which one's lifestyle decreases the exposure of the household through effective guardianship.

MOTOR VEHICLE THEFT

Motor vehicle theft is one of the few crimes that increased during the late 1990s and early 2000s. While other property crimes declined by 38 percent between 1991 and 2001, vehicle theft increased by 10 percent. There were 161 506 vehicles stolen in 2002, a decrease of 5 percent from the previous year. As with most other offences, rates of vehicle theft are highest in the territories and the western provinces and lowest in Atlantic Canada. Only about 13 percent of motor vehicle thefts result in an arrest. Those arrested are most frequently young males. Forty percent are between 12 and 17 and almost 90 percent are male (Wallace, 2003b).

We usually think of vehicle theft as a property crime, and it does cost Canadians about $1 billion per year (Wallace, 2003a). However, this offence also causes a significant number of injuries and deaths as a high proportion of stolen cars become involved in accidents. Many of those killed and injured were young people. Research conducted by the National Committee to Reduce Auto Theft (Miceli, 2002) found that between 1999 and 2001, 81 people were killed and 127 people suffered serious injuries because of collisions involving stolen vehicles. In April 2003, a particularly bad crash occurred that differed from the typical stolen vehicle accident only in the number of victims. The car was driven by a 13-year-old.

> Scars at the base of a cherry tree in full white blossom along Chilliwack River Road and a small wooden cross are the only signs left of a nightmare car crash in which six young people were trapped, screaming, inside a burning car.... Six youths died after the car they were riding in flew off the road and crashed head-on into the tree. It happened at about 10 p.m. Sunday near Cultus Lake when an unregistered, unlicenced car carrying six youths missed a sharp turn and lost control, said Chilliwack RCMP Constable David Aucoin. As soon as the car hit the tree, a fire ignited in the engine and quickly spread into the passenger area, where the six youths—aged 12 to 16—were trapped, Aucoin said ... Chilliwack RCMP would not release the age of the driver, but said the crash initially killed three boys, ages 12, 13, and 15, and two girls, aged 14 and 16. As well, a 12-year-old boy who had been on life support at B.C. Children's Hospital in Vancouver died Monday evening. (Read and O'Brian, 2003, A1)

Challinger (1987) has suggested there are three different types of motivations for motor vehicle theft: profit, transportation, and recreation. Those who steal for *profit* are often professional criminals who sell the vehicles, many of which are exported to foreign countries, or "chop" the vehicles to sell the parts. *Transportation* refers to offenders who steal cars in order get from one place to another or who use the stolen vehicle to commit another crime. *Recreational* theft is often called joyriding. This form of theft involves stealing cars for the fun of it and driving them around. This is often done in the company of friends.

The national increase in vehicle theft has largely been due to increases in thefts for joyriding and transportation. We know this because a high percentage of the cars are recovered and because many are older vehicles that have little commercial value. The increase in vehicle theft has been concentrated in a few communities and has actually declined in many other areas. Between 1991 and 2001, rates of theft quadrupled in Winnipeg, tripled in Regina, and doubled in Hamilton and London (Wallace, 2003a). In fact in 2001, Winnipeg and Regina had the highest rates of auto theft in North America. What explains this dramatic rise? A research study conducted in Winnipeg tells us a great deal about the dynamics of auto theft in some parts of Canada.

[Handwritten margin notes:]
Motor vehicle theft
Who: Young males, 12-17
What: older models for transportation and newer models for profit
When: when there is ineffective guardianship
Where: underground garages, Winnipeg
Why: profit, transportation, recreation

The most common vehicles stolen in Winnipeg in 2001 were Dodge Caravans and Plymouth Voyagers built prior to 1995, and 1995 and 1997 Dodge Neons. About 95 percent of all cars stolen in the city are recovered, most within 24 hours. The pattern of these thefts indicates that most are stolen by young people and are used for joyriding or for transportation from one part of the city to another. Anderson and Linden (2002) studied a group of young offenders who were incarcerated for vehicle theft and found that many did it just for the thrill. One of the respondents said he stole cars "for a joyride ... for the rush!" and another reported that "[stealing cars] is addicting. When you find something you're good at, you want to keep doing it." Peer influences played an important role in vehicle theft. Often cars were stolen by groups of friends, and over half the respondents reported that they had taken part in contests to see who could steal the most cars over a given period of time. Many of the young people said they sometimes took cars for basic transportation. The young offenders were also asked why they selected particular targets. As suggested by the pattern of thefts, the majority of offenders felt that Chrysler products were the easiest to steal. Although recent models are much more difficult to take, older model Chrysler vehicles can be entered and started in a few seconds using only an ordinary screwdriver.

The reason thefts increased so rapidly in Winnipeg was that vehicle theft had become a fad among many of the city's young people. After a few young people learned how easy it was to steal some models of cars and realized that the probability of arrest was very low, they told their friends and schoolmates and the number of people willing to steal cars grew quickly. Children in some neighbourhoods learned to steal cars at a very early age (a number of children under 12 have stolen dozens of vehicles), and a peer culture developed that focused on car theft. This culture was reinforced by the mass media as well as by peer groups. Most of the interviewed youth played video games such as "Grand Theft Auto" that glamorized stealing cars and using them to create mayhem on the streets. Several also said that movies such as *Gone in 60 Seconds* had helped teach them some of the techniques of stealing cars.

The dramatic increase in vehicle thefts in Winnipeg can be explained by the routine activities approach. The focus on vehicle theft among some segments of the city's youth culture led to an increase in the number of young people who were motivated to steal cars and trucks. The lack of anti-theft protection on older vehicles means that a huge number of easy targets are available, and in many parts of the city it is very difficult to guard these targets effectively, as most vehicles are stolen from parking lots and from the street, where there is little scrutiny.

The fact that almost all cars in Winnipeg, Regina, and several other cities are quickly recovered suggests that they fit this model of auto theft. However, patterns vary across the country. For example, in Montreal only 42 percent of cars were recovered in 2001. This suggests that theft in Montreal is more likely to involve professional thieves who are selling the cars or taking them apart in order to sell the parts. Tremblay et al. (1994) have explained that the greater incidence of professional vehicle theft in Quebec is likely due to circumstances that have led to an orderly market for stolen cars and car parts in that province.

From the routine activities perspective, the existence of such a market would increase the attractiveness of auto theft for those interested in making money, hence increasing the number of motivated offenders.

PREVENTING CRIME

You will recall that Cohen and Felson stated that three components—target suitability, ineffective guardianship, and a motivated offender—must converge in space and time for a crime to occur. This approach can be used to help develop ways of preventing crime (Koenig et al., 1983; Koenig and DeBeck, 1983).

   We are unlikely to see major changes in target suitability although technological advances such as ignition immobilizers in motor vehicles will help to reduce some types of crime. We live in a society that values individual freedom and mobility as well as consumer goods. We also prefer our goods, electronic and otherwise, to be compact, lightweight, and as portable as possible. The focus, therefore, must be on increasing effective guardianship and reducing the number of motivated offenders.

Effective Guardianship

Effective guardianship, or what has come to be called **situational crime prevention**, attempts to prevent an offence rather than to counter it once initiated. It is premised on the belief that much crime is opportunistic and contextual rather than on the belief that offenders are driven to commit a crime no matter what. Clarke (1995) has summarized steps people can take to reduce the opportunities for crime by requiring more effort on the part of potential offenders, increasing their risks of apprehension, or reducing the likely payoff of committing an offence (see Table 14.1). While most of Clarke's examples involve increasing guardianship, some also entail making the target less attractive. For example, the first category in the table includes ways of hardening the target, which means making it more difficult to steal. Steering locks are the devices that lock automobile steering wheels in one position until the key is placed in the lock, and slug rejector devices are mechanisms in parking meters and vending machines that reject artificial coins (which are called slugs). Both of these innovations have been shown to reduce crime. Several of the items in Table 14.1, including ID badges, baggage screening, security guards, closed-circuit TV systems, and changes in rules and regulations are among the measures that have been implemented or augmented to increase guardianship at airports and other vulnerable locations since the September 11, 2001, attack on the World Trade Center. Can you think of other changes that have been made to reduce the likelihood of this type of crime in the future? The 1999 GSS showed that fear of crime has fallen in Canada in tandem with the declines in the crime rates that you learned about in Chapter 4 (Mihorean et al., 2001). Ninety-one percent of Canadians said they were satisfied or very satisfied with their personal safety compared to 86 percent in 1993. This may explain why relatively few Canadians have taken measures to

National Crime Prevention Strategy
www.prevention.gc.ca/english/ index.asp
"International Center for the Prevention of Crime"
www.crime-prevention-intl.org/ english/icpc/index.html

situational crime prevention

Premised on the belief that most crime is opportunistic rather than being the outcome of those driven to commit a crime no matter what the circumstances. This form of prevention attempts to reduce the opportunities for crime rather than just relying on the police after the crime has occurred. An example is the exact fare system used on buses, which removes the opportunity to rob the driver.

TABLE 14.1 The Twelve Techniques of Situational Prevention

Increasing the Effort	*Increasing the Risks*	*Reducing the Reward*
1. **Target hardening** Steering locks Slug rejector device	5. **Entry/exit screening** Baggage screening Automatic ticket gates Merchandise tags	9. **Target removal** Removable car radio Exact change fares Phonecard
2. **Access control** Fenced yards Entry phones ID badges	6. **Formal surveillance** Security guards Burglar alarms Speed cameras	10. **Identifying property** Property marking Vehicle licensing Personal identification numbers for car radios
3. **Deflecting offenders** Tavern location Street closures Graffiti board	7. **Surveillance by employees** Park attendants Pay phone location Closed-circuit TV systems	11. **Removing inducements** Graffiti cleaning Rapid repair "Bum-proof" bench
4. **Controlling facilitators** Gun controls Credit card photo Caller-ID	8. **Natural surveillance** Street lighting Defensible space Neighbourhood watch	12. **Rule setting** Customs declaration Income tax returns Hotel registration

Source: Adapted from Ron Clarke. (1995). "Situational Crime Prevention." In Michael Tonry and David Farrington (eds.), *Building a Safer Society: Strategic Approaches to Crime Prevention.* Chicago: University of Chicago Press, pp. 91–150.

enhance their safety. About one-third of respondents said they had changed their routines and/or avoided certain places or had installed new locks. Less than 15 percent had taken measures such as taking a self-defence course or obtaining a dog. Only 10 percent said they stayed at home at night because they were afraid to go out.

Although defensive measures can be expected to produce an overall reduction in crime because some crime is opportunistic, some crime will simply be displaced from one victim or location to another. While some offenders are opportunistic—that is, they do not seek out potential targets but will take advantage of a target that presents itself—others are highly motivated. Offender motivation or motivated offenders must also be a focus of crime-prevention activities.

Reducing Motivated Offenders

Many criminologists argue that resources need to be targeted at social interventions that will deflect individuals at risk from becoming motivated offenders. This approach is labelled **developmental crime prevention** (Tonry and Farrington, 1995; Tremblay and Craig, 1995). Social development programs are intended to reduce the pool of motivated offenders by altering the conditions that breed crime. These programs try to focus on factors that place

developmental crime prevention

An approach to crime prevention that focuses on reducing the number of *motivated offenders* by changing the social environment. Examples include preschool education programs and effective parenting training; also called crime prevention through social development.

children at risk of criminal activity. Many of these have been mentioned in Part 2 of this book and include personality factors, family problems, peer issues, and school and community factors (Wasserman et al., 2003).

The social development approach to crime tries to deal with the root causes of crime through programs and activities that are "intended to increase positive ... motivations, attitudes or behaviour in individuals by influencing their experiences in areas such as family life, education, employment, housing or recreation" (Waller and Weiler, 1984, 4). Social development strategies are often targeted at young people, who appear to be the most amenable to intervention and who make up the next generation of offenders.

There are a wide variety of different social development programs. Some have tried to improve the parenting skills of high-risk parents, while others have provided job training and employment for young people living in poor communities. One of the most promising areas is the provision of preschool programs for children from deprived backgrounds. One of the few social development programs that has undergone a long-term evaluation is a Michigan program called the Perry Preschool Project. The students were 123 black children from poor families. Children aged three and four attended a preschool with an active learning curriculum five mornings a week, and teachers visited the children's homes once a week. The program lasted 30 weeks each year. A control group did not receive these services. Like the earlier Head Start program, this project sought to remedy the impact of the children's impoverished backgrounds on their later school success.

The most recent follow-up of the project (Schweinhart et al., 1993) looked at the participants at age 27. Only one-fifth as many program group members as controls were arrested five or more times (7 percent compared with 35 percent), and only one-third as many were ever arrested for drug dealing (7 percent compared with 25 percent). The program group had higher incomes, were more likely to own their own homes, and were less likely to have been on welfare. They had greater educational achievement and lower rates of illiteracy. Program group members were more likely to have had stable marriages, and females had lower rates of out-of-wedlock births. The costs of the program were easily recovered because of gains in reduced welfare costs and increased earnings of the graduates. Schweinhart et al. (1993) estimate that the saving was over $7 for every dollar invested in the program. Those responsible for this program strongly suggest that the intervention must be made while the children are young, and must be thorough enough to overcome the range of disadvantages faced by the participants. The Canadian government has recently responded to this research by establishing early childhood education programs in a number of communities and by providing funding for a national Aboriginal Head Start program.

Selective Incapacitation

Selective incapacitation is a very different approach that sees criminals as people for whom the usual internal and external controls against becoming a criminal have been neutralized. From this perspective it follows that until those

Perry Preschool Program
www.highscope.org/Research/ PerryProject/perrymain.htm

selective incapacitation
A philosophy of incarceration that argues that some offenders might have to be incarcerated not for what they have done, but to prevent future harm to the community. This depends on the community's ability to identify those who might re-offend. Some also argue that it is unfair to punish people for what they might do rather than for what they have done. Selective incapacitation is provided for under dangerous offender legislation.

controls have redeveloped, the most chronic motivated offenders must be incapacitated in order to prevent them from committing further offences.

During the 1980s, a Rand Corporation study claimed that the U.S. crime rate could be significantly reduced if the small proportion of highly active criminals were **incapacitated** through incarceration. Chaiken and Chaiken (1984) studied 2000 male prison and jail inmates in the United States. They found a high volume of crime committed by 15 percent of their sample who reported committing a combination of robberies, assaults, and drug deals. These prisoners, whom they labelled "**violent predators,**" were extremely young. Their average age at first incarceration was less than 23, but they had been committing serious crimes, especially violent crimes, for at least six years. They had considerably more total arrests than other offenders, including those much older than themselves. Moreover, they had spent considerable time in juvenile facilities and were more likely than other offenders to have been granted parole and to have had it revoked. Finally, they were also more socially unstable than other offenders and were unlikely to be regularly employed, married, or to have other family obligations. Drug use, particularly multiple drug use involving heroin or barbiturates, is often characteristic of violent predators. The 20 percent of highest-risk offenders in the Chaikens' sample had, on the average, robbery rates 65 times as high as those predicted to be in the lowest 20 percent of offenders; burglary rates 66 times as high; auto theft rates 346 times as high; and drug dealing rates 5 times as high.

The profile of violent predators very closely resembles the profile of psychopathic male criminals (see Chapters 8 and 9) in terms of both psychological characteristics and criminal patterns, such as more offences, more violence, earlier age at first contact, and so on. Almost certainly, there is considerable overlap among the populations of **psychopaths** and violent predators.

Most countries have laws, such as Canada's dangerous offender legislation, that enable the state to incarcerate serious habitual offenders for lengthy periods. Canada's legislation provides for indefinite sentences for dangerous offenders. This sentence is reviewed after seven years and every two years thereafter. In order to be considered a dangerous offender, a person must have committed a serious personal injury offence such as sexual assault, aggravated assault, or manslaughter and must be judged to constitute a risk to others based on the brutality of the crime, the offender's previous pattern of aggressive violent behaviour, or a failure to control sexual impulses. In most jurisdictions, very few offenders are sentenced under these provisions. (For example, in 2000 there were 276 dangerous offenders in Canadian prisons.) An exception is California's "three strikes and you're out" law, which mandates a life sentence for a third felony conviction. This has resulted in bizarre sentences, including two cases where men will spend the rest of their lives in prison, one for stealing a slice of pizza and the other for shoplifting a small package of meat. The incapacitation strategy is also very expensive. California's taxpayers will eventually be spending $6 billion each year to keep a large number of aging offenders in prison (Skolnick, 1994). Although this punishment may seem to be far too harsh, in 2003 the U.S. Supreme Court ruled that it did not violate Constitutional protection against cruel and unusual punishment in two cases involving one defendant who received a sentence of 25 years without parole for stealing three golf clubs and

incapacitation
The policy of locking offenders in jail to prevent them from repeating their crimes.

violent predator
An offender who has a very high rate of offending for serious and violent crimes.

psychopath
Psychopathy is typically classified under personality disorder. Psychopaths tend to be lacking in conscience, are unable to form emotional attachments (even to friends or family), are quite impulsive, and are only self-interested.

BOX 14.4

FOCUS

A Public Health Model or Harm Reduction Approach to Substances

Some argue that the easiest and most effective crime-prevention action would be to adopt a public health rather than a criminal approach for controlling substance use and abuse (Moore, 1995). For example, many people have concluded that the war on drugs has been an expensive failure and have recommended that treatment would be a better way to deal with the drug problem (British Columbia, 1995).

The B.C. Attorney General's Co-ordinated Law Enforcement Unit (CLEU) (1992a) estimated that the cost of illicit drug use within British Columbia for 1989 was at least $349 million (or roughly $100 per every resident in the province). Most of these costs were justice-related, including drug law enforcement services ($67.9 million) and the policing of nondrug crimes, such as break and enter or crimes of violence, that were related to illicit drug use ($151 million). Indeed, CLEU (1992b) estimated that 60 percent of nondrug crime in B.C. is drug-related. As a concrete example, CLEU (1992b, 55) cited one police officer who recounted "the case of a woman in Vancouver who supports her $1,400 per day habit with prostitution, stealing from tricks, shoplifting, forging cheques, theft and drug dealing." In contrast to these huge enforcement costs, CLEU (1992a) reckoned that in 1989, British Columbia taxpayers spent only $13.8 million on provincial programs directed at the prevention of substance abuse, of which a minuscule $1.8 million was directly targeted at the prevention of illicit drug use.

Moreover, the criminalization of drugs has fostered an environment in which contaminated needles are exchanged among users and reused. One result of this is what British Columbia's Provincial Health Officer described as "the epidemic of deaths and infections related to injection drug use" (Millar, 1998, 2). By 1996, drug overdoses had become the leading cause of death among adults between the ages of 30 and 49 within British Columbia.

The criminalization of part of the drug trade has opened an extremely lucrative market for groups of criminals to organize crime (see Chapter 15), as did Prohibition on both sides of the border earlier in the century. This, in turn, breeds numerous related crimes, ranging from thefts to murders, as well as corruption of public officials, sometimes including police.

A harm reduction approach to this problem would be to minimize criminal victimization and criminal justice system costs, as well as to reduce drug-related fatalities, disease, and health-care costs by providing heroin to addicts under controlled conditions. Following a three-year experiment with this practice that saw falling death rates and criminal involvement, as well as improved health, housing, and employment on the part of 1100 addicts, in 1997, the Swiss moved to make the change permanent. The Dutch have followed suit, though they had already been tolerating hard drug centres under controlled conditions in some cities such as Arnhem. Meanwhile, in Canada, the Chief Provincial Medical Officer for British Columbia (Millar, 1998) has also recommended legal provision of heroin to addicts as part of a larger series of recommendations. However, this approach has been rejected by lawmakers who argue that it will simply encourage the use of addictive drugs.

The election of Larry Campbell as mayor of Vancouver in 2003 has helped to ensure that a harm reduction strategy will be adopted in that city. Campbell is a former RCMP chief superintendent who became the Chief Coroner of B.C. and who was the model for the television series *Da Vinci's Inquest*. In the mid-1990s, Campbell was one of the first public figures to advocate a harm reduction approach to addiction. The Four Pillars approach to drug problems (enforcement, treatment, prevention, and harm reduction) was a key part of his election platform. Canada's first safe injection site opened in Vancouver in 2003.

a second defendant who was given two consecutive 25-year sentences (50 years in all) for stealing nine videotapes in two separate incidents (See Box 12.1).

Ethical Concerns

Some criminologists strenuously object to such proposals for selective incapacitation. They argue that it is unjust to sentence a person to a long term in prison not for something that person has done, but for what that person might do if he or she were not imprisoned. This is particularly true considering the fact that there tends to be a high rate of "**false positives**" (50 to 60 percent of the total) in most predictive studies, including the original Rand Corporation study on which the Chaikens' study was modelled. As von Hirsch (1984, 177) expressed it: "The 'false positive'—that is, the person erroneously designated to be a future recidivist—loses his liberty on account of an injury that he will not in fact commit."

Others respond that the "false positive" has lost his or her freedom for what he or she has done. The issue is for how long the offender's freedom will be lost. They contend that it is appropriate for society to protect itself by assigning longer terms to offenders whose profiles suggest a disproportionate likelihood of reoffending. Unfortunately for proponents of selective incapacitation, recent research by Auerhahn (1999) has shown that the measures used to predict which offenders should be incarcerated for long periods do not work. She concludes that sentencing is a very poor method of trying to reduce crime rates.

false positive

When trying to identify dangerous offenders (or other things as well), researchers often make mistakes. One of these mistakes is known as a false positive. The error is identifying offenders as dangerous (and possibly keeping them incarcerated or denying them parole) when they are not dangerous.

SUMMARY

- Conventional or street crime includes the offences of homicide, assault, sexual assault, robbery, break and enter, motor vehicle theft, personal theft, and household theft.

- Patterns of conventional crime can be understood with the help of lifestyle/exposure and routine activities theories. Lifestyle/exposure theory points out that the lifestyle and activities of some people place them at higher risk for crime victimization. Routine activities theory is based on the observation that crime results from the simultaneous presence of a motivated offender, a suitable target, and ineffective guardianship of that target.

- Property crimes tend to be committed disproportionately against those whose lifestyles leave their possessions least effectively guarded.

- Violent crimes are committed disproportionately against people who are exposed to individuals who have a high level of physical aggression.

- Alcohol and drug use increase the likelihood of victimization. There are two fairly distinct patterns of risk. One high-risk group are people whose family members cannot control their anger. The second group are people whose lifestyle places them in social settings with young males who use alcohol and/or drugs.

■ The routine activities approach leads to a number of crime reduction strategies. These include situational measures, crime prevention through social development, and incapacitation of high-rate offenders.

QUESTIONS FOR CRITICAL THINKING

1. Understanding patterns of crime means that you can reduce your chances of becoming a victim of crime if you change certain aspects of your lifestyle. Some people argue that they should not have to change the way they dress, work, or play to avoid being victimized. What do you think?

2. As a student at a university or college, how do you assess your risk of victimization? What changes could you or others make that might reduce your chances of being a crime victim?

3. Canada has been restricting the distribution of some drugs for almost a century, but illegal drugs are readily available across the country. Do you think that a public health model or a criminal model would be more effective for reducing harm from drug use? What are some of the weaknesses of the public health approach?

4. Is the media's portrayal of violence causally related to crime on the part of some offenders? Why or why not?

5. How do you think that social, economic, cultural, or technological changes in society will affect crime in five years' time? Why?

NET WORK

In this chapter, you have learned about the routine activities approach to crime. This approach has had an impact on the nature of crime prevention programs in North America and Europe by drawing attention to the role of the attractiveness of the target and the importance of effective guardianship. To see how these insights are used in crime prevention, go to the website of a major U.S. report on the effectiveness of crime prevention programs at **www.preventingcrime. org/report/index.htm.**

Go to Chapter 7 "Preventing Crime at Places." Find three projects that are intended to reduce the attractiveness of the target and three projects that increase effective guardianship. Have these projects been successful in reducing crime?

KEY TERMS

conventional crime
developmental crime prevention
effective guardianship
false positive

incapacitation
incidence
lifestyle/exposure theory
motivated offender

psychopath   situational crime prevention
routine activities approach   target suitability
selective incapacitation   violent predator

SUGGESTED READING

American Psychological Association Commission on Violence and Youth. (1993). *Violence & Youth: Psychology's Response. Volume 1: Summary Report of the American Psychological Association Commission on Violence and Youth.* Washington, D.C.: American Psychological Association Public Interest Directorate. This is a wide-ranging investigation of the ways in which violence affects youth, anc includes recommendations for pro-social transformations of media content.

Canadian Criminal Justice Association. (1989). "Safer Communities: A Social Strategy for Crime Prevention in Canada." *Canadian Journal of Criminology* (October). A review of factors suspected to predispose individuals to crime and recommendations for Canadian initiatives to bring about change through social development.

Erickson, Patricia G., Diane M. Riley, Yuet W. Cheung, and Patricia A. O'Hare (eds.). (1997). *Harm Reduction: A New Direction for Drug Policies and Programs.* Toronto: University of Toronto Press. A variety of contributions concerned with the emerging approach of "harm reduction." As implied by its name, the focus is on whatever is most effective at reducing harm, whether it be legal, public health, or other approaches.

Statistics Canada. *Juristat.* A serial, containing approximately 14 issues per year, which reports the latest available information about various facets of the Canadian criminal justice system.

Tonry, Michael, and David Farrington (eds.). (1995). *Crime and Justice: A Review of Research, Volume 19. Building a Safer Society: Strategic Approaches to Crime Prevention.* Chicago: University of Chicago Press. State-of-the-art reviews about various approaches to crime prevention, including community-based approaches, situational crime prevention, developmental crime prevention, and public health approaches.

BIBLIOGRAPHY

Anderson, Jeff, and Rick Linden. (2002). "Pilot Study of Juvenile Auto Theft Offenders in Winnipeg." Unpublished manuscript, University of Manitoba.

Auerhahn, Kathleen. (1999). "Selective Incapacitation and the Problem of Prediction." *Criminology* 37(4):703–34.

Bennett, Trevor, and Richard Wright. (1984a). *Burglars on Burglary.* Brookfield, Vt.: Gower Publishing.

———. (1984b). "Constraints to Burglary: The Offender's Perspective." In Ronald Clarke and Tim Hope (eds.), *Coping with Burglary* (pp. 181–200). Boston: Kluwer-Nijhoff Publishing.

British Columbia, Province of, Ministry of Attorney General, Co-ordinated Law Enforcement Unit (CLEU). (1992a). *The Costs Associated with Illicit Drug Use in British Columbia in 1989.* Victoria: The Queen's Printer.

———. (1992b). *Updates on Drug-Related Projects* (April, 1992). Victoria: The Queen's Printer.

————. (1995). *Report of the Task Force into Illicit Narcotic Overdose Drug Deaths in British Columbia.* Victoria: The Queen's Printer.

Chaiken, Marcia R., and Jan M. Chaiken. (1984). "Offender Types and Public Policy." *Crime and Delinquency* 30(2):195–226.

Challinger, D. (1987). "Car Security Hardware—How Good Is It?" *Car Theft: Putting on the Brakes, Proceedings of Seminar on Car Theft.* Sydney: National Roads and Motorists' Association and the Australian Institute of Criminology.

Clarke, Ron. (1995). "Situational Crime Prevention." In Michael Tonry and David Farrington (eds.), *Building a Safer Society: Strategic Approaches to Crime Prevention* (pp. 91–150). Chicago: University of Chicago Press.

CLEU. See British Columbia, Province of, Ministry of Attorney General, Co-ordinated Law Enforcement Unit.

Cohen, Lawrence E., and Marcus Felson. (1979). "Social Change and Crime Rate Trends." *American Sociological Review* 44:588–607.

Dauvergne, Mia. (2002). "Homicide in Canada, 2001." *Juristat* 22(7). Ottawa: Statistics Canada.

————. (2003). "Family Violence Against Seniors." *Canadian Social Trends* (Spring):10–14. Ottawa: Statistics Canada.

Desroches, Frederic J. (1995). *Force and Fear: Robbery in Canada.* Toronto: Nelson.

FBI. See U.S. Department of Justice, FBI.

Gabor, Thomas, Micheline Baril, Maurice Cusson, Daniel Elie, Marc LeBlanc, and Andre Normandeau. (1987). *Armed Robbery: Cops, Robbers, and Victims.* Springfield: Charles C. Thomas.

Gartner, Rosemary, and Anthony N. Doob. (1994). "Trends in Criminal Victimization: 1988–1993." *Juristat* 14(13). Ottawa: Canadian Centre for Justice Statistics.

Gibson, Lorne, Rick Linden, and Stuart Johnson. (1980). "A Situational Theory of Rape." *Canadian Journal of Corrections* 22(1):51–65.

Ha, Tu Thanh. (2002). "The Demise of the Bank Heist." *The Globe and Mail*, November 11:A1, A7.

Hindelang, Michael J., Michael R. Gottfredson, and James Garofalo. (1978). *Victims of Personal Crime: An Empirical Foundation for a Theory of Personal Victimization.* Cambridge, Mass.: Ballinger Publishing.

Janhevich, Derek E. (1998). "Violence Committed by Strangers," *Juristat* 18(9). Ottawa: Canadian Centre for Justice Statistics.

Koenig, Daniel J. (1977). "Correlates of Self-Reported Victimization and Perceptions of Neighbourhood Safety." In Lynn Hewitt and David Brusegard (eds.), *Selected Papers from the Social Indicators Conference, 1975* (pp. 77–90). Edmonton: Alberta Bureau of Statistics.

Koenig, Daniel J., and E. Paula DeBeck. (1983). "Proactive Police Intervention and Imminent Social Change." *Canadian Police College Journal* 7(4):310–28.

Koenig, Daniel J., E. Paula DeBeck, and Janet Laxton. (1983). "Routine Activities, Impending Social Change, and Policing." *Canadian Police College Journal* 7(2):96–136.

Kong, Rebecca. (1994). "Urban/Rural Criminal Victimization in Canada." *Juristat* 14(17). Ottawa: Canadian Centre for Justice Statistics.

————. (1998a). "Breaking and Entering in Canada, 1996." *Juristat* 18(5). Ottawa: Canadian Centre for Justice Statistics.

————. (1998b). "Canadian Crime Statistics, 1997." *Juristat* 18(11). Ottawa: Canadian Centre for Justice Statistics.

Kowalski, Melanie. (2000). "Break and Enter, 1999." *Juristat* 20(13). Ottawa: Statistics Canada.

Linden, Rick. (1994). "Deviance and Crime." In Lorne Tepperman, James E. Curtis, and R.J. Richardson (eds.), *The Social World* (3rd ed.). Whitby: McGraw-Hill Ryerson.

Luckenbill, David. (1977). "Criminal Homicide as a Situated Transaction." *Social Problems* 25(2):176–86.

Mayhew, Pat. (1984). "Target-Hardening: How Much of an Answer?" In Ronald Clark and Tim Hope (eds.), *Coping with Burglary* (pp. 29–44). Boston: Kluwer-Nijhoff Publishing.

McIntyre, Mike. (2003). "Girl, 12, Saw Father Deliver Fatal Beating." *Winnipeg Free Press*, (March12):A3.

McLean, Gene. (2000). "The New Age of Bank Security." *Canadian Banker* 107(4).

Micelli, Matthew J. (2002). *A Report on Fatalities and Injuries as a Result of Stolen Motor Vehicles (1999–2001)*. Project 6116: National Committee to Reduce Auto Theft.

Mihorean, Karen, Sandra Besserer, Dianne Hendrick, Jodi-Anne Brzozowski, Catherine Trainor, and Stacie Ogg. (2001). *A Profile of Criminal Victimization: Results of the 1999 General Social Survey*. Ottawa: Minister of Industry.

Millar, John S. Dr., British Columbia, Province of, Ministry of Health, Office of the Provincial Health Officer. (1998). *HIV, Hepatitis, and Injection Drug Use in British Columbia: Pay Now or Pay Later*. Victoria: Office of the Provincial Health Officer.

Moore, Mark H. (1995). "Public Health and Criminal Justice Approaches to Prevention." In Michael Tonry and David Farrington (eds.), *Building a Safer Society: Strategic Approaches to Crime Prevention* (pp. 237–62). Chicago: University of Chicago Press.

Read, Nicholas, and Amy O'Brian. (2003). "Six Youths Killed in Horrific Car Crash." *The Vancouver Sun*, April29:A1.

Sacco, Vincent F., and Holly Johnson. (1990). *Patterns of Criminal Victimization in Canada*. Ottawa: Statistics Canada (Housing, Family and Social Statistics Division), Minister of Supply and Services Canada.

Savoie, Josee. (2002). "Crime Statistics in Canada, 2001." *Juristat* 22(6). Ottawa: Statistics Canada.

Schweinhart, L.J., H.V. Barnes, D.P. Weikart, W.S. Barnett, and A.S. Epstein. (1993). *Significant Benefits: The High/Scope Perry Preschool Study Through Age 27*. Ypsilanti: The High/Scope Press.

Skolnick, Jerome N. (1994). "Wild Pitch: 'Three Strikes You're Out' and Other Bad Calls on Crime." *The American Prospect* 17 (Spring):30–37.

Sparks, Richard F. (1981). "Multiple Victimization: Evidence, Theory and Future Research." In National Institute of Justice, *Victims of Crime: A Review of Research Issues and Methods*. Washington, D.C.: U.S. Dept. of Justice.

Statistics Canada. (1994). *The 1993 General Social Survey—Cycle 8: Public Use Microdata File Documentation and User's Guide*. Ottawa: Minister of Industry, Science and Technology.

———. (1997). *Causes of Death, 1995* (Cat. 84-208XPB). Ottawa: Minister of Industry.

———. (2003). "Canadian Statistics—Age Standardized Mortality Rates." Ottawa: Statistics Canada, Health Statistics Division. www.statcan.ca/english/Pgdb/health30c.htm. Accessed April 25, 2003.

Tonry, Michael, and David Farrington. (1995). "Strategic Approaches to Crime Prevention." In Michael Tonry and David Farrington (eds.), *Building a Safer Society: Strategic Approaches to Crime Prevention* (pp. 237–62). Chicago: University of Chicago Press.

Tremblay, Richard E., and Wendy M. Craig. (1995). "Developmental Crime Prevention." In Michael Tonry and David Farrington (eds.), *Building a Safer Society: Strategic Approaches to Crime Prevention* (pp. 151–236). Chicago: University of Chicago Press.

Tremblay, Pierre, Yvan Clermont, and Maurice Cusson. (1994). "Jockeys and Joyriders: Changing Patterns in Car Theft Opportunity Structures." *British Journal of Criminology* 34(3):307–21.

U.S. Bureau of Justice Statistics. (1988). *BJS Data Report, 1987.* Washington, D.C.: U.S. Dept. of Justice.

———. (1990). (December). *Criminal Victimization in the United States, 1988.* Washington, D.C.: U.S. Dept. of Justice.

U.S. Department of Justice, FBI. (1997). *Uniform Crime Reports for the United States, 1996.* Washington, DC: U.S. Government Printing Office.

———. (2002). *Uniform Crime Reports, 2001.* Washington: Federal Bureau of Investigation. www.fbi.gov/ucr/01cius.htm. Accessed April 25, 2003.

U.S. Department of Justice. (1974a). *Crime in Eight American Cities.* Advance Report. Washington, D.C.: U.S. Dept. of Justice.

———. (1974b). *Crimes and Victims: A Report on the Dayton-San Jose Pilot Study of Victimization.* Washington, D.C.: U.S. Dept. of Justice.

von Hirsch, Andrew. (1984). "The Ethics of Selective Incapacitation: Observations on the Contemporary Debate." *Crime and Delinquency* 30(2):175–94.

Wallace, Marnie. (2003a). "Motor Vehicle Theft in Canada—2001." *Juristat* 23(1). Ottawa: Statistics Canada.

———. (2003b). "Crime Statistics in Canada, 2002." *Juristat* 23(5). Ottawa: Statistics Canada.

Waller, Irvin, and Dick Weiler. (1984). *Crime Prevention Through Social Development: An Overview with Sources.* Ottawa: Canadian Council on Social Development.

Wasserman, Gail, Kate Keenan, Richard Tremblay, John Coie, Todd Herrenkohl, Rolf Loeber, and David Petechuk. (2003). *Risk and Protective Factors of Child Delinquency.* Washington: Office of Juvenile Justice and Delinquency Prevention.

Wright, Christine. (1995). "Risk of Personal and Household Victimization: Canada, 1993." *Juristat* 15(2). Ottawa: Canadian Centre for Justice Statistics.

Wright, Richard T., and Scott H. Decker. (1992). *Burglars on the Job: Streetlife and Residential Break-Ins.* Evanston: Northeastern Books.

15

Organized Crime

RODNEY T. STAMLER
Assistant Commissioner RCMP (Rtd)

Over the past century, governments in North America and their enforcement agencies have become increasingly concerned about organized crime. In recent years organized crime has become more powerful because of the massive profits they have acquired from supplying illicit goods and services to a willing public. The illegal monopolistic business enterprises run by organized criminals are able to survive and grow as public demand for the illicit goods and services continues to increase. Legitimate competitors are excluded because these markets are illegal, while illegitimate competitors are controlled by force.

In this chapter, you will learn about the nature and extent of organized crime in Canada. Organized criminals are involved in a wide range of activities, including selling illegal drugs, extortion, immigration fraud, pornography, international stock and bank fraud, money laundering, and environmental crimes such as transporting and dumping hazardous waste. For a variety of reasons, the most successful organized crime groups are ethnically based. The major exceptions to this are outlaw motorcycle gangs, whose participation in organized crime has increased significantly over the past 20 years. The chapter concludes with a discussion of some of the strategies that might help to reduce the growth of organized crime.

LEARNING OBJECTIVES

After reading this chapter, you should be able to

- Describe the characteristics of organized crime and the difficulties of arriving at a precise definition of organized crime.
- Understand the roots of organized crime and the reasons why organized crime is such a profitable activity.
- Understand why many successful criminal organizations are ethnically based and why outlaw motorcycle gangs are a major exception to this trend.
- Describe the history and structure of the major organized crime groups operating in Canada.
- Explain why money laundering is such an important part of organized crime.
- Discuss the most effective ways of reducing organized crime in Canada.

WHAT IS ORGANIZED CRIME?

It is difficult to provide a precise definition of organized crime. In the past several years legislative authorities both in Canada and around the world have enacted various definitions of organized crime in order to comply with the United Nations Convention on Transnational Organized Crime. For the most part legal definitions have tended to be very narrow and limited in an attempt to define those involved in major organized crime activity.

Authors, criminologists, and legislative drafters have tried to develop all-encompassing definitions of organized crime that would include every type of crime group. Such definitions are of necessity very broad and general. Some definitions have tried to distinguish organized crime groups from petty thieves, armed robbers, and others who are involved in criminal activity. Other definitions have used the partnership or business-entity approach, which stresses organizational effort, planning, leadership, division of work, and cooperation. Still other definitions have focused on the social elements involved in organized crime and have emphasized the family-type organization in which members pledge their lifelong loyalty, trust, and obedience (Pennsylvania Crime Commission, 1980).

Some definitions of organized crime clearly delineate one organized crime network, while others confine themselves to one particular element of organized crime. Several authors, after studying or examining street gang activity, have described these groups as if they operate autonomously from any other group or level of authority. These authors tend to reach the mistaken conclusion that organized crime is not organized at all, but is a collection of uncontrolled bandits, outlaws, and crooks who work together at times in order to co-exist in the unfriendly street environment. This conclusion can be reached only if one fails to examine carefully all crime groups that operate in a given territory, from the top of the hierarchy to the street-level gang. Street groups tend to be the most visible part of an organized crime network, but, like an iceberg, the highly organized elements remain hidden from public view. Only a careful examination of the cash flow from street crimes will identify the entire criminal organization.

Jean-Pierre Charbonneau states that the underworld is not an organization but an environment. This environment consists of crooks, bandits, dealers, and outlaws of every description. Within this milieu, a multitude of gangs, clans, or organizations exist or co-exist. Some are powerful, well organized, and stable; others are loose and haphazard and may include temporary coalitions of odd-job criminals and journeyman crooks.

Margaret Beare concludes that "organized crime is a process or method of committing crimes, not a distinct type of crime in itself" (1996, 14). She goes on to say, "Organized crime is *ongoing* activity, involving a *continuing criminal conspiracy*, with a *structure greater than any single member*, with the potential for *corruption and/or violence* to facilitate the criminal process" (15).

On April 21, 1997, the Parliament of Canada passed Bill C-95 and amended the Criminal Code to create the offence of participation in a criminal organization through the commission or furtherance of certain indictable offences for the benefit of the organization. While it is still not an offence to belong to a criminal organization, Parliament did define a *criminal organization* as well as a *criminal organization offence*. In amending the Criminal Code of Canada, Parliament defined criminal organization as

"Organized Crime in Canada"
Canada Centre for Justice
Statistics
**www.statcan.ca/english/freepub/
85-556-XIE/85-556-XIE02001.pdf**

"Bill C-95—National Anti-Gang
Measures"
Department of Justice Canada
**canadajustice.gc.ca/News/factshts/
c95fs_e.html**

any group, association or other body consisting of five or more persons, whether formally or informally organized, having as one of its primary activities the commission of an indictable offence ... and any or all of the members of which engage in or have within the preceding five years engaged in the commission of a series of such offences.

In 1998 the Solicitor General of Canada used the following definition of organized crime:

Economically motivated illicit activity undertaken by any group, association or other body consisting of two or more individuals, whether formally or informally organized where the negative impact of said activity could be considered significant from an economic, social, violence generation, health and safety and/or environmental perspective. (Porteous, 1998, 2)

The INTERPOL (International Police Organization) definition adopted by the General Assembly of the member countries in 1998 defined organized crime as follows:

Any enterprise or group of persons engaged in a continuing illegal activity which has as its primary purpose the generation of profits irrespective of national boundaries.

In 1999 the United Nations adopted a new convention entitled International Transnational Organized Crime; at the present time over 120 countries have ratified this convention. The convention requires countries to enact national law that will coordinate the international control of organized crime. With more international coordination on the subject of organized crime, it has become increasingly important to distinguish organized crime from other similar criminal activities such as terrorism and other hate-related group activities. The United Nations convention defined organized crime as follows:

Organized Crime consists of groups which are bound together by language, culture and includes groups that come together for political objectives and become involved in criminal activity that produces revenue.

It becomes clear that an all-encompassing definition of organized crime must be very general if it is to include all crime groups from the street-level operators to the top-level financiers. These definitions do not adequately describe or express the complexities of major regional, national, or international crime organizations such as the Mafia, the Triads, and the North American outlaw motorcycle gangs. These organizations, with their binding ethnic ties or their binding common interests, have developed rituals and codes of conduct and secrecy that provide them with the protection and security to continue as distinctive criminal societies.

Whether for legal or academic purposes, one could do no better than to use the description developed by the U.S. Bureau of Alcohol, Tobacco and Firearms (Pennsylvania Crime Commission, 1980):

Interpol—Organized Crime
www.interpol.int

UN Convention on Transnational Organized Crime
www.unodc.org/palermo/ convmain.html

"Organized Crime" refers to those self-perpetuating, structured, and disciplined association of individuals, or groups, combined together for the purpose of obtaining monetary or commercial gains or profits, wholly or in part of illegal means, while protecting their activities through a pattern of graft and corruption.

Organized crime groups possess certain characteristics that include but are not limited to the following:

1. Their illegal activities are conspiratorial;
2. In at least part of their activities, they commit or threaten to commit acts of violence or other acts that are likely to intimidate;
3. They conduct their activities in a methodical, systematic, or highly disciplined and secret fashion;
4. They insulate their leadership from direct involvement in illegal activities by their intricate organizational structure;
5. They attempt to gain influence in government, politics, and commerce through corruption, graft, and illegitimate means;
6. They have economic gain as their primary goal, not only from patently illegal enterprises such as drugs, gambling, and loan sharking, but also from such activities as laundering illegal money through and investment in legitimate business.

When we analyze the various definitions of organized crime that have been developed for academic or legal purposes, we can clearly state that organized crime is an ongoing illegal business activity. This activity may involve what appears to be, or is in fact, a partnership, a corporation, or a sole proprietorship that is supplied by wholesalers or distributors. These may be wholesalers who purchase goods or services from other entities, who may be importers or manufacturers. If the entire business line or a portion of it is illegal, that business is an organized criminal activity and the individuals who are involved in it constitute an organized crime group. It does not matter whether the business entity sells contraband alcohol, smuggled cigarettes, or illicit drugs. The law will not enforce their contracts and their profits must be laundered to be used legitimately. In some cases, the enforcement of contracts or laundering of money actually becomes a related organized crime activity. A number of related criminal enterprises can flow from the unlawful business—for example, bribery, extortion, murder, or money laundering. While these activities are related, they can be illegal business enterprises in themselves. Thus the activities of a "Murder Incorporated" may be a stand-alone organized crime activity or it may be a way that one criminal group enforces its own directives. A money-laundering service could be a stand-alone business entity operating like a bank to service a number of criminal groups or could be directly connected to one criminal group to launder the illegal profits of that group only.

A group of thugs who break legs or cause bodily harm for various reasons, but with no intention of obtaining financial gain or benefit, is not organized crime. The infamous Ku Klux Klan would likely not be classified as part of organized crime, but could be classified as a terrorist group. A terrorist group that is involved only in a political struggle is not organized crime, unless it is also involved in illegal activities to raise funds to support its terrorist activities. An otherwise legitimate manufacturing corporation, on the other hand, which knowingly becomes involved in supplying organized crime with goods or services will certainly become part of organized crime activity, even though its main business may be supplying legal goods or services to a legitimate market. For example, the German government has begun to prosecute a German domestic tobacco manufacturing company for selling cigarettes to organized criminals for their contraband markets. Allegedly the German subsidiary of Britain's Imperial Tobacco was involved in smuggling cigarettes to several countries, including Iraq (Mansell and Boyes, 2003).

What Distinguishes an Organized Crime Group from a Terrorist Group?

Bill C-36
www.parl.gc.ca/37/1/parlbus/
chambus/house/bills/government/
C-36/C-36_3/C-36_cover-E.html

UN Convention on Terrorism
http://untreaty.un.org/English/
Terrorism.asp

Since September 11, 2001, many countries of the world, including Canada, have enacted new legislation to deal with acts of terrorism. In 2002 the Parliament of Canada enacted Bill C-36, which strengthened a number of criminal laws with respect to terrorism. This enactment created the Terrorist Financing Act and a new government agency called Fintrac. The bill also amended the Criminal Code, the Official Secrets Act, the Canada Evidence Act, the Proceeds of Crime (Money Laundering) Act, and a number of other acts, and enacted the Charities Registration (Security Information) Act. These laws have provided new definitions for terrorism and terrorist groups. In the process of restricting the financing of terrorist groups, the legislation has provided new methods for identifying and curbing money laundering, which will also apply to organized crime groups. Most of these criminal laws now conform to the various UN conventions. Because a terrorist in one country may be deemed a freedom fighter in the next country, it becomes increasingly important to distinguish terrorist groups from organized crime groups, particularly when enforcing organized activity at the international level. There are, of course, many instances when a crime group involved in organized criminal activity, such as the manufacture and distribution of illicit drugs, also becomes involved in political struggles that involve acts of terror. The profits from this organized crime activity will be directly used to finance the political acts of terror. In other instances, terrorist groups will join forces with organized crime groups to further their respective objectives.

When a terrorist group has all the elements that protect it from identification, it may easily become connected with organized crime activity. On the other hand, if funding for a terrorist group comes directly from a government or if it obtains support through demands on the public, it will not be classified as organized crime. If a terrorist group becomes involved in the commission of crimes that produce revenue or profits, that group will be included in the definition of an organized crime group.

How Organized Is Organized Crime?

Organized crime can encompass a wide range of crime groups. However, there has been a long debate about the extent to which criminal organizations fit these criteria. On one side of the debate are those who view organized crime in North America as a monolithic alliance of crime families whose members are of Italian descent. The activities of each of these families are firmly controlled by its bosses and by a commission made up of the men who control its most powerful families (Cressey, 1969). On the other side are researchers who feel that there is no centralized direction or leadership. Organized crime consists of local crime gangs, whose activities sometimes lead them to work with other groups. For example, Reuter (1983) studied bookmaking, numbers gambling, and loan sharking in New York City. He found that the Mafia did not dominate these enterprises. None of the three illegal markets was centrally controlled, and bookmaking was particularly competitive and decentralized.

The most sensible approach to the question is to recognize that the level of organization can vary widely depending on the time, place, and type of offence. Organized crime is a very broad term and can apply to a wide range of groups, from those that are structured and organized to those with fluid membership that sporadically work together to carry out specific criminal activities. Haller (1990) has found that many illegal enterprises are run as partnerships rather than as complex bureaucracies. He suggests that even the famous Capone gang was actually a complex set of partnerships directed by Al Capone, his brother Ralph, and two colleagues. These senior partners worked with many other different men to establish a variety of bootlegging, gambling, and vice activities in the Chicago area during the 1920s.

Haller concludes that the degree of organization involved in selling illegal goods and services is influenced by two factors. The first is the internal economics of the type of crime. For crimes such as the manufacture, importation, and

"Al Capone"
Marilyn Bardsley, The Crime Library
www.crimelibrary.com/capone/caponemain.htm

BOX 15.1

FOCUS

The "Virtual Corporation"

In comments at a conference on global organized crime, James Woolsey, the former director of the U.S. Central Intelligence Agency, described how drug cartels may be the model for 21st century organizations.

One could look at how drug traffickers are developing and sustaining the European market for cocaine as a model of a successful multinational business. Latin American groups know that Italian and other European groups control the drug distribution networks in Europe, networks built up over 40 years to accommodate the flow of heroin. Italian groups know that cocaine is increasing in popularity in Europe. And both groups know that cocaine sells in Europe for two to three times the U.S. price, meaning there are enormous profits to be made.

As a result, Latin American groups provide the drugs, using groups in Venezuela, Brazil, and Argentina to transship cocaine to newer markets in Europe, while distribution remains in the hands of European—primarily Italian—organized crime.

Thus the "virtual corporation" touted by management theorists as the leading contender to the dominant entrepreneurial structure of the next century takes shape: drug traffickers develop a loose network of independent companies; they share information, skills, costs, and market access and position themselves (Woolsey, 1994, 138–39).

Source: Adapted from Rick Linden. (1994). "Crime and Deviance." In L. Tepperman, J. Curtis, and J. Richardson (eds.), *The Social World* (3rd ed.). Toronto: McGraw-Hill Ryerson, pp. 188–229. Reprinted with permission of McGraw-Hill Ryerson.

distribution of illegal drugs, cooperation and coordination are required to get the product to the consumer. Other crimes such as gambling require cooperation to share the risk as street-level gamblers might not have sufficient capital to absorb a short period of heavy losses, even though the odds are strongly in their favour in the long run. The second is the involvement of law enforcement officials and politicians in supporting criminal activities. Where officials and criminals work together, competition is controlled, and there is a stable climate for illegal activity. This makes it more likely that crime groups will be well organized.

The Roots of Organized Crime

Many of the activities of organized crime result from the demand by the "law-abiding" citizenry for illegal goods and services such as illicit drugs, contraband cigarettes and alcohol, and prostitution. The opportunity of serving these illicit markets has determined the structure and scope of organized criminal activities. Consider drug trafficking, which is now the most lucrative of organized criminal activities. The basis of this activity is public demand for a product, in this case a drug such as cocaine, marijuana, or heroin. Governments of most countries have made the production, sale, and possession of these drugs illegal. Those using the drug (many of whom are addicts) have a very strong desire for it, which cannot be met by any other product, so there is a high demand for the drug. Those who are prepared to run the risk of breaking the law can charge a premium for it because competition has been restricted by laws forbidding the legal distribution of the drug.

The nature of the illicit marketplace also determines the structure of organized crime. If one intends to break into homes and to steal and sell computers and video recorders, the largest criminal network required is the thief and a "fence" who will pay for and distribute the stolen articles. However, much more is required to move a drug from the fields of Peru or Thailand to the streets of Vancouver and Toronto. Elaborate organizations must be established for this type of activity, including financiers, buyers, sellers, and people to transport the drug across international borders.

Many types of criminal activity flow out of the illicit market structure. In order to maintain or increase their share of the market, organized criminals may use violence to discourage competition. Recent gang-related shootings in any number of American cities are the result of competition for markets by rival groups. In 1991, 18 persons were shot in the Chinatown area of Toronto in battles between Chinese and Vietnamese gangs. Nine of the victims died of their wounds. Most of those shot were of Vietnamese origin (Canada, 1992). In Quebec, territorial wars among biker gangs resulted in more than 60 deaths between 1995 and 1999. Gangland shootings and bombings were regular occurrences. Violence is also used to ensure that debts are paid and other obligations are met. Normal legal channels for enforcing contracts cannot be used by organized criminals because the object of the contract is usually illegal and therefore would not be enforced in a court of law. Therefore, force is used. In addition, there is a need to conceal illegal activities. The enormous profits that can be earned from the illicit market lead to activities such as laundering money to conceal the source, loan sharking, and investment in legitimate businesses, which then come under the control of criminal syndicates. Finally, in order to prevent the legal system from interfering with these illegal activities, officials may be bribed to ignore them.

While such corruption is widespread in many countries, it is not common in Canada. Even though our politicians have not always been completely honest, there have been relatively few instances of systematic corruption involving organized criminals, police, court officials, and politicians, as has occurred in the United States. Sacco (1986) has given a number of reasons for this: political power in the United States is highly decentralized, which makes it easier to corrupt people holding certain key offices; in the United States, there are a large number of elected political, law enforcement, and court officials, many of whom are associated with political "machines" financed by organized crime; Canadians have been less inclined to try to control moral behaviour through laws than Americans, so there are fewer opportunities to establish illicit markets. To these we might also add the fact that our law enforcement agencies and court officials have worked very hard to maintain their reputations for honesty and have seldom been involved in organized corruption.

World Health Organization—
Tobacco Draft Convention
**www.who.int/gb/fctc/PDF/inb6/
einb65.pdf**

WHO IS INVOLVED IN ORGANIZED CRIME?

With the exception of outlaw motorcycle gangs, most organized crime groups are ethnically based. In North America, just about every major ethnic group has participated in organized crime over the years—Irish, English, Italians, Jews, French Canadians, blacks, Chinese, Gypsies, Chicanos, and many others (Dubro, 1985).

The Italian-based Mafia groups are perhaps the most widely known and publicized crime organizations in the Western world. The term *Mafia*, which was originally used to identify a specific Sicilian crime group, is now commonly used to identify any ethnic or regionally based crime organization. The Colombian Mafia, the Turkish Mafia, and the Asian Mafia are all major international crime groups, but they have no direct connection with the Italian-based Mafia.

There are several reasons for the ethnic connection in organized crime. You will recall from the discussion of strain theory (Chapter 10) that when people are denied legitimate access to common culture goals such as financial success, they may turn to criminal ways of achieving these goals. Frequently, minority groups have been denied access to legitimate success because of the barriers of discrimination and poverty. While visible ethnic minorities actually have lower crime rates than other Canadians (Thomas, 1992), some members of these groups choose organized crime as a way of achieving financial success.

Once this choice has been made, several structural factors increase the likelihood of ethnically based groups succeeding in the highly competitive world of organized crime. First, today's major internationally connected crime organizations started at the family or local level. It was the strong family or cultural connection that permitted these organizations to enforce their code of conduct and secrecy to counter any intrusive action from law enforcement. As the crime groups grew in size, their members moved to other regions. This migration

"Organized Crime at a Glance"
RCMP Headquarters Site
**www.rcmp.ca/organizedcrime/
overview_e.htm**

BOX 15.2

FOCUS

The Origins of an Illicit Market Structure

Over the past decade, taxes on cigarettes and alcohol have driven the prices of these products so high that many Canadians have turned to lower-priced products that are smuggled from other countries. This demand for smuggled cigarettes and alcohol has produced revenue opportunities for Canadian organized crime groups.

When governments impose high taxes on a consumer product, they create a demand for a cheaper product. Organized criminals step forward to meet that demand and black markets are created. This pattern was at the heart of the contraband tobacco crisis that gripped Canada in the early 1990s. In 1985, there was virtually no contraband tobacco for sale in Canada. However, tobacco taxes rose steeply, and by 1993 a legally sold carton of cigarettes cost about $50 compared with the $22 for an untaxed carton sold on the black market. Thus the Canadian government helped to create a booming market for smuggled cigarettes. The government did not criminalize tobacco, but attempted to reduce its consumption by imposing high taxes on it. Smuggled cigarettes saved consumers money and were lucrative for the smugglers. The federal and provincial governments were the big losers. By 1993, 30 percent of the cigarettes sold in Canada were illegally supplied. The tax revenue lost to the federal government was more than $1 billion. Smuggling was particularly out of control in Quebec, where law enforcement officials estimated that up to one-third of the cigarettes smoked were purchased illegally.

The role of government in this matter went beyond simply imposing taxes. When it did so, the federal government was aware that smuggling would increase. Most of the cigarettes smuggled into Canada are manufactured here and exported to the United States, where smugglers purchase them and bring them back illegally. The government sought to control the export of Canadian cigarettes by imposing a tax on all cigarettes exported from Canada.

Cigarette smuggling has now become a worldwide phenomenon. Organized crime has established international markets for smuggled cigarettes where products of every brand and blend can be purchased. If brands are not available from legitimate manufacturers, they are counterfeited and introduced to the marketplace through extensive illegal wholesale operations situated in various duty-free ports around the world. Mediterranean and Caribbean locations have become extremely popular for this type of shipping operation. Cigarettes are shipped to these locations and then redirected to the prime market areas of the world. The entire operations are managed and controlled by various organized crime groups. Shipments from these areas are made from countries in North America—including Canada and the United States—Europe, and Asia. Contraband cigarettes have become a source of revenue for crime groups in Afghanistan, Pakistan, the Balkans, and other countries of eastern Europe. Profits from this trade are fuelling terrorist activities.

The World Health Organization is in the process of developing an international convention to control the manufacture and international distribution of cigarettes in an attempt to control the worldwide cigarette contraband problem. The convention is currently in its development stage and is expected to be adopted in the near future. The convention is expected to be similar to the 1961 Single Convention on Narcotic Drugs. The export and import of tobacco products will likely be controlled by permits issued by government agencies to ensure that all tobacco products are under government control when shipped from a manufacturer in one country to a wholesaler in another country.

Many law enforcement officials believe that this type of control will not be successful in stopping cigarette smuggling and will actually assist organized crime in developing its own manufacturing and distribution systems similar to those that were developed to produce and distribute illicit drugs in spite of the United Nations narcotic control conventions.

served to broaden the base of the crime groups by adding new territories, which in turn resulted in the expansion of their illegal operations. Ethnic-based crime groups, which are now situated in different regions of the world, use their ties in these expanded territories to develop their international connections and penetrate the illicit markets of the world. In this way, crime groups have the advantage of developing efficient international illegal distribution systems for illicit goods and services. At the same time, they are able to set up international money laundering schemes that are used to hide and distribute their illegal profits.

Besides facilitating international networks, ethnic ties may benefit organized crime groups in other ways. For example, members of some ethnic groups have interpersonal ties, which make it difficult for strangers to infiltrate their organizations. Racial and language differences also make law enforcement much more difficult.

Biker gangs do not base their affiliation on ethnic ties, but have other bonds that exclude others and ensure the cooperation of members. Daniel Wolf, an anthropologist who succeeded in joining an Edmonton biker gang, has observed that "after repeated attempts, the police have long since discovered that infiltrating an outlaw club is a long, arduous, and risky process when it is being done for 'professional' reasons." Infiltration of the gangs is difficult. "'They have an internal discipline that makes it dangerous,' said a police officer. 'It's an area we have trouble infiltrating. The conditions of initiation make it almost impossible....'" (1991, 14).

Despite the apparent dominance of particular groups in activities such as gambling or drug sales, we should not think that doing away with any group will reduce organized crime in a community any more than closing Chrysler would seriously reduce car sales. Organized crime exists because of market demand. Groups like the Italian Mafia or the Chinese Triads may meet some of this demand at a particular time and place because their organization gives them a competitive advantage. However, if they were put out of business, other groups would quickly replace them (Sacco and Kennedy, 1994).

MAJOR ORGANIZED CRIME GROUPS IN CANADA

Major international organized crime groups have found it profitable, over the years, to establish a base of operations in Canada. In addition, crime groups that originated in Canada have grown and established ties with related groups in other parts of the world. At present, there are at least seven major types of crime groups operating in Canada. The history and development of these groups can be largely attributed to the fact that Canada has a long and open border with the United States. This allows easy access for criminals and illicit goods to move from one country to the other. Also, Canada, like the United States, enjoys a multicultural society, which extends ethnic ties to all regions of the world.

The most prominent internationally connected crime organizations with established crime bases in Canada include the Italian Mafia; Triads and other Asian organized crime groups; the South American, Colombian, and Mexican cartels; outlaw motorcycle gangs; and the Russian Mafia and other eastern European crime groups.

The Italian-Based Mafia

Mafia
A term originally used to identify a specific Sicilian crime group. It is now commonly used to identify any ethnic or regionally based crime organization.

The **Mafia** organizations of Italy are major criminal societies that are permanent, secret, and powerful. The first Mafia-style organization in Italy was the Camorra. This group was established in Sicily in the 19th century and was a direct offshoot of the 15th-century hill bandits who formed a guerrilla force known as the Garduna. The Camorra based itself on a hierarchical system of control, with the godfather at the top of the hierarchy and soldiers at the bottom. Income was derived from protection rackets, robbery, murder for hire, blackmail, kidnapping, and loan sharking. Its members were recruited from prisons. New members to the Camorra were required to serve probationary periods before entering the ranks of the society. Eventually, the Camorra gave way to the Sicilian Mafia, which had a family-based recruitment system. This organization became a powerful crime syndicate (Maclean, 1974).

In the late 19th century, members of the Sicilian Mafia found their way to the United States, Canada, and Australia. As they became established in their new homelands, they began to carry out their traditional patterns of criminal activity. Mafia members sent letters threatening serious injury or death to the recipients. The letters were signed with the outline of a black hand. This was the earliest report of organized crime activity in North America, and the "black hand" became synonymous with the Mafia (Glaser, 1978).

The first city in the United States in which a Mafia group became established as a criminal society was New Orleans. New York City became the second area, and from there, Mafia groups were quickly formed in other parts of the eastern United States (Glaser, 1978). The Mafia groups controlled gambling, narcotics, and other rackets. They became deeply involved in political patronage in Harlem and Brooklyn. By 1917, they dominated the illegal activities that took place throughout New York.

Mafia groups surfaced in Ontario as early as 1906. In this era, Toronto, Hamilton, and the Niagara Peninsula became the centres of Canadian Mafia activity. In 1909, the arrest of five so-called Black-Handers in Hamilton was a major event (Dubro, 1985). By 1920, the Mafia gangs in southwestern Ontario had increased in number and size. By 1921, murders, bombings, and extortion were common occurrences.

Prohibition in the United States caught the Mafia by surprise. They could not quickly adjust their illegal operations to supply illicit alcohol to the public. This resulted in other organized crime groups forming in the United States. In Chicago, New York, and other major cities, the groups involved in the manufacture, importation, and sale of illicit alcohol began to reap huge profits. These new organized crime groups quickly took over power and control at the expense of the Mafia.

Street wars between gangs trying to acquire or maintain control of valuable territorial rights continued for a decade. Organized crime groups with a variety of ethnic backgrounds emerged. There were Irish gangs in bootlegging, Jewish groups in money laundering, and the original Mafia families trying to regain control. In the 1930s, Lucky Luciano brought together a federation of North American Mafia families, which covered every major city in the United States and Canada. He made alliances with other major ethnic groups, which resulted in a unified crime syndicate. In the United States, this syndicate has been termed La Cosa Nostra (LCN). It invested its illegal profits in legitimate businesses, which included legal gambling casinos in Nevada and Cuba. Meyer Lansky became the chief money launderer and banker for the syndicates. He perfected money laundering systems through secret-numbered bank accounts in tax havens (Maclean, 1974).

By the 1930s, LCN was firmly based in Montreal, Toronto, and Vancouver. The Italian Mafia, as one of its main ethnic components, operates very much like a corporate entity. The godfather, capo, or family boss takes the position of the chief executive officer. The underbosses, or lieutenants, act as vice-presidents and head the various branches of the organization. These branches may be engaged in different types of criminal activity. Soldiers are given licences to operate in specific territories and are authorized to carry out specified types of criminal activity. They are required, in return, to pay a percentage of their profits to the management level of the organization. The upper levels of this criminal organization invest their laundered proceeds in legitimate businesses. They prefer to appear as legitimate business executives within their communities.

According to Carrigan (1991), pressure resulting from a U.S. Congressional committee in 1951 caused the Mafia to move its gambling headquarters to Montreal. Those involved were well connected with both the American and Italian Mafias, as well as with Quebec politicians and police. The international affiliations later facilitated drug smuggling from Montreal to the United States. The Quebec Crime Probe report of 1977 concluded that the Italian Mafia still existed in Montreal and that this organization was a significant factor in organized crime. The report went on to state:

> This secret society was reserved for criminals of Sicilian and Italian ancestry ... and is a direct descendant of similar secret societies which did and do exist in southern Italy. This statement is supported by many meetings between Mafiosi leaders from all over America and elsewhere, particularly Italy.

The report described the background and scope of the Cotroni–Violi Mafia family of Montreal and described how members of this group were recruited and selected. The report pointed out that a number of employees or independent partners of this crime family provided the infrastructure for an association of criminals from different ethnic backgrounds. Some of these associates were French Canadians, Jews, Anglo-Saxons, Slavics, and blacks; all were under the authority and control of this one Mafia family (Quebec, 1977).

In recent years, the territory controlled by Paolo Violi, who was shot to death in 1978, has been split between Montreal's Rizzuto family and Toronto's Cuntrera–Caruana family. The latter group control one of the world's largest drug-trafficking networks.

Although the Italian Mafia remains a powerful organization, its influence has been reduced over the past decade. In the United States, many of the old bosses have died or been imprisoned, and young new leaders must deal with aggressive competition from other criminal groups. For example, the majority of heroin sold in North America is imported through Asian drug-trafficking networks rather than through the Mafia-controlled French Connection route from Turkey to France and then to Montreal and New York (Dubro, 1992). In Italy, magistrates and police have conducted a concerted campaign against the Mafia, which has resulted in the conviction of hundreds of criminals and has implicated scores of politicians, government officials, and businesspeople. Public outrage over the ambush murders of prosecutors Giovanni Falcone and Paolo Borsellino in 1992 has forced the government to continue the investigations despite its natural reluctance to implicate itself and its friends (Stille, 1995).

In their 2002 annual report, the Criminal Intelligence Service Canada (CISC) stated that three main Italian-based organized crime groups participate in significant criminal activities: the Sicilian Mafia, the 'Ndrangheta, and the U.S. branch of La Cosa Nostra. Their presence in Canada is particularly prominent in Ontario and Quebec, with varying levels of activity in other provinces. These Italian-based crime groups maintain close ties with Asian and eastern European–based organized crime and with Colombian and other South American groups as well as with various domestic criminal organizations. In particular, outlaw motorcycle gangs in Quebec, Ontario, and British Columbia have had a historical relationship with the Italian crime families. These crime families are involved in a number of different organized crime activities, including drug trafficking, smuggling, contraband distribution, money laundering, illegal gaming (including Internet gaming), extortion, loan sharking, prostitution, and stock market manipulation. Unlike outlaw motorcycle gangs, the Italian-based Mafia maintains a very low profile in Canada. They mostly engage in legitimate commercial business activities to conceal their criminal activities. They participate in regular social and cultural activities in their community for the express purpose of maintaining the appearance of being respectable and legitimate to their neighbours and their community (CISC, 2002).

Outlaw Motorcycle Gangs

Motorcycle gangs began to form in North America during the late 1940s. These motorcycle enthusiasts were, for the most part, ordinary individuals who enjoyed cycling for part-time recreation. They formed the American Motorcycle Association (AMA), which in turn sponsored tours, races, and rallies. On July 4, 1947, the AMA sponsored one such event. It was a tour through California called the Gypsy Tour. On the same day, the town of Hollister, California, 60 miles south of Oakland, held its annual motorcycle "dirt hill climb races." In previous years, small groups of motorcycle enthusiasts from the surrounding area had attended these annual races. On this occasion, however, more than 3000 AMA riders invaded the small town. The AMA participants included a number of different motorcycle clubs, including a group known as Booze Fighters and another called Hells Angels. Some violent clashes broke out, causing the police to arrest many of the bikers involved. A number of police officers and bikers were seriously injured. Broken beer bottles and damaged property left the main street of the small town in a shambles.

In the days following this event, the AMA publicly drew a distinction between the legitimate members of the AMA and the now newly classified renegades. The association characterized 99 percent of its members as clean-living folks enjoying a pure sport. It condemned the other 1 percent as antisocial barbarians. The renegade groups exploited this event by publishing this condemnation with bold defiance. They developed a motorcycle patch called the "one-percenter." This patch is still worn in addition to regular "colours" and identifies the member as an "outlaw biker." This single incident clearly served to unify and develop a unique type of major organized crime society in North America. Hollywood, with the film version of the Hollister riots entitled *The Wild One* and such movies as *Easy Rider* and *Hells Angels on Wheels*, gave the motorcycle gang a distinctive image by romanticizing the outlaw biker. New chapters of outlaw groups subsequently formed in almost every part of the United States and Canada (Canada, 1980).

All groups function in the same general manner. They are tightly organized, and their hierarchical system maintains a highly exclusive control over a particular territory, either alone or through alliances with other clubs. Smaller gangs often find it more expedient to support a larger, better-organized gang.

A gang member can never fully retire from the group. New members are recruited with care to ensure that agents or informants of law enforcement or rival gangs do not penetrate the group easily. A "striker," in biker parlance, is someone aspiring to join the group. Strikers are recruited from "hangers-on," who generally ride with the gang on their tours or runs but at the back of the pack. Strikers may occasionally enter the club headquarters, but only to carry out minimal tasks. This period of "apprenticeship" may last as long as six months. Several criminal acts will likely have to be committed by the striker to the satisfaction of the peers. In addition, he may be required to attack or embarrass a rival gang member.

Crimes of violence are committed by gang members to establish territory, expand their membership through mergers, intimidate the public, or for "entertainment purposes." Most groups are involved in major traditional organized-enterprise crime activities such as extortion, prostitution, and drug trafficking. These activities can be very lucrative. Carrigan (1991) discusses one member of the Grim Reapers in Calgary who had 23 prostitutes working for him. He owned property worth over $600 000 and was once arrested with more than $200 000 in cash in his possession. Bikers are mainly responsible for the manufacture and sale of illicit chemical drugs such as ecstasy, methamphetamine (speed), and PCP (angel dust). They traffic in all types of illicit drugs, including marijuana, hashish, cocaine, and chemical drugs. In Canada the street value from the sale of these illicit drugs amounts to millions of dollars (Canada, 1985).

For many years, biker gangs in Quebec have been among the most violent in North America. The most notorious incident occurred in March 1985 when six members of the Laval chapter of the Hells Angels were murdered by some of their colleagues who suspected them of dealing drugs outside the gang. Another biker, Yves (Apache) Trudeau, became a Crown informer when he learned he was also a target. Trudeau later pleaded guilty to 43 counts of manslaughter and may have been involved in as many as 40 other deaths.

The Canadian groups connect with their American and European counterparts to facilitate their drug-trafficking operations. Unlike members of other crime organizations, outlaw bikers are usually visibly identifiable as belonging to a particular group. Yet evidence of their illegal activities is difficult for law enforcement to obtain. The very structure of outlaw motorcycle groups, their internal discipline, their intimidating behaviour, and other violent actions are the tools they use to protect themselves from prosecution. Potential witnesses and informants become the special targets of the gangs. Their intimidating approach and their barbaric behaviour make the public cautious about confronting the groups, even when they are committing crimes.

The Canadian Intelligence Service Canada (CISC) reported in 2002 that outlaw motorcycle gangs across Canada, particularly the Hells Angels, are engaged in money laundering, intimidation, assaults, murder, fraud, theft, counterfeiting, extortion, prostitution, escort agencies and strip clubs, after-hours clubs (selling alcohol illegally), telemarketing, and the possessing and trafficking of illegal weapons, stolen goods, and contraband. Hells Angels remain the largest and most criminally active organized motorcycle gang in the country with 35 full chapters. Members of this biker gang continue to be extensively involved in the importation and trafficking of cocaine; the cultivation and exportation of high-grade marijuana, and, to a lesser extent, the production and trafficking of methamphetamine; and the trafficking of ecstasy and other illicit synthetic drugs. Organized motorcycle gangs in Canada continue to be involved in violence, ranging from intimidation and assault to attempted murder and murder. Incidents of violence between the Hells Angels and another motorcycle gang, the Bandidos, continue (see Box 15.3). Several high-profile cases of intimidation against victims of crime, witnesses, and law enforcement across the country demonstrate the extent to which the gang will attempt to protect its members from law enforcement. In western Canada, the Hells Angels have dominated over the other outlaw motorcycle gangs and are in control of most gang-related organized crime activity. They continue to be extensively involved in the importation and trafficking of cocaine and the cultivation and trafficking of marijuana. They have a strong connection with the Italian-based Mafia in eastern Canada and have similar connections with Asian organized crime groups. The Winnipeg Hells Angels chapter has become increasingly active in the importation and distribution of drugs in Manitoba, particularly cocaine, marijuana, and ecstasy. In central Canada the Hells Angels have fourteen chapters; the Outlaws have ten and the Bandidos two. All three gangs, and the Hells Angels in particular, are increasingly joining alliances with various ordinary street gangs. These street gangs often perform lower-level criminal activities and security duties for the outlaw motorcycle gangs. There have been a number of violent turf wars between the Outlaws, the Hells Angels, and the Bandidos. These turf wars have extended to include their subordinate street gang affiliates. Quebec continues to be the centre of outlaw motorcycle gang activity in Canada. The groups there include the Outlaws, Hells Angels, the Bandidos, and the Nomads. All the groups continue their dominance over the illicit drug trade. The Bandidos, the Halifax chapter of the Hells Angels, and the Hells Angels Quebec City chapter, with control over other outlaw clubs in New Brunswick and Prince Edward Island, dominate biker organized crime

BOX 15.3

FOCUS

Bikers Fighting for Place Behind Bars

Police in Montreal have, to say the least, a unique problem. Members of rival motorcycle gangs, the Rock Machine [now the Bandidos] and Hell's Angels, when they are not blowing one another to smithereens, are tripping over themselves to get into jail.

In this, the Year of the Pig, the bikers' turf war has reached new heights of ferocity. For almost two months, gang members have been killed in car bombings at a rate of one a week, supplemented by the occasional machine-gun slaying and stabbing.

It's one of those paradoxes of a wintry city such as Montreal: it's too cold and snowy even for bikers, so they tend to drive trucks and minivans.

Earlier this month, when Claude (Le Pic) Rivard of the Hells Angels stopped his 4X4 at a red light, a family van pulled alongside and he died in a hail of machine-gun fire. (Those sliding doors and tinted windows are popular not only with parents but also with contract killers.) A couple of weeks earlier, the Plymouth Voyageur of Bruno (Boom Boom) Bandiera of the Rock Machine went up in a fireball. Between the two incidents, fellow Rock Machinist Daniel Senésac was blown to bits as he planted a bomb in a rival's van.

Aside from the regular bombing and shooting work, members of the leather-clad set are committing petty crimes in a bid to be sent to Bordeaux prison in east-end Montreal, the newest battleground in the nasty spat between the rival gangs.

The way the guards' union tells it, the Rock Machine, the more sophisticated and ruthless of the two, controls Bordeaux, and the Hell's Angels, a more old-fashioned bikers' group, controls Parthenais prison, also in the east end. Despite their differences in philosophy—something like the difference between the Liberals and Conservatives—neither group takes losing lightly, so the leaders have sent reinforcements to settle a few scores behind bars.

Now, why would a group such as Rock Machine, which already controls a goodly part of the drug trade in the city, including business in Montreal's glitziest bars, care about a filthy, run-down prison such as Bordeaux?

Well, consider that the jail, built in 1913 with a capacity of 800, is now home to 1014 prisoners, one of the most captive drug-consuming clienteles in the world. Prisoners will smoke, swallow and inject just about any illegal substance they can get their hands on, and they will pay dearly for the distraction.

Demand is so high, prison officials report, that pushers have taken to lobbing drug-filled tennis balls over the fence at Bordeaux, not to mention the prisoners and visitors who smuggle the booty in more traditional manners. Again, the guards' union estimates that the drug trade at Bordeaux exceeds $7-million, annually.

As it turns out, members of Rock Machine and Hells Angels, despite being purveyors of libertarian notions such as drug decriminalization, are not fond of free-market competition. Those who have the misfortune to be selling drugs in a prison that is not controlled by their gang suffer swift and harsh retribution. So, in recent weeks, the infirmary at Bordeaux has been a high-traffic area.

In an attempt to defuse the tension, members of Rock Machine and Hells Angels have been segregated in separate wings of the prison, and their leaders have been shipped to jails elsewhere in the province. Prison officials also conducted a full-scale sweep of the establishment.

They found a "pen gun" (a small pipe rigged to fire a .22-calibre bullet), a number of knives, a steel bar and numerous bits of lethally sharpened wood and glass. How someone manages to smuggle a pickaxe through a strip search boggles the mind, but there was one of those in a cell too.

Serge Ménard, the Public Security Minister, called his visit to Bordeaux on Friday "one of the most traumatizing experiences I've ever lived through." And he stayed for less than an hour.

Source: André Picard. "Bikers Fighting for Place behind Bars." *The Globe and Mail* (February 21, 1995), A8. Reprinted with permission from *The Globe and Mail*.

activity in the Atlantic provinces. Their main source of illegal activity is illegal drugs and the sex trade (CISC, 2002; **www.cisc.gc.ca**).

A number of outlaw motorcycle gangs that have become involved in highly successful crime enterprises have found it even more profitable to take on the public appearance of successful businessmen rather than the image of outlaw bikers. From their disguised position, they find it useful and more effective to use corruption than brute force to expand their enterprises' crime interests. Perhaps what is evolving is a second-level crime group in the fashion of the Triad society or the Italian-based Mafia.

Triads and Other Asian Organized Crime Groups

Just as the Mafia was founded as a guerrilla movement in Sicily, so the earliest Triad societies came into existence in Fukien Province in China in the latter part of the 17th century. They began as resistance fighters against the Manchu invaders. Although the societies' original purpose was self-protection and opposition to various Chinese dynasties, they eventually developed into crime groups (Bresler, 1980).

As the membership of the Triad societies grew, they dispersed throughout Southeast Asia. Their members were bound together by an intricate system of rituals, oaths, passwords, and a ceremonial intermingling of their blood. During the politically turbulent years of China's history, with the rise and fall of various governments, the **Triads** entrenched themselves in criminal activity for profit. This move provided them with the power to ensure their continued existence as a society. Like the Mafia, the Triads engaged in criminal activities such as gambling, narcotics trafficking, prostitution, loan sharking, and extortion.

With Chinese migration to North America, it was not long before the Triads began to develop within North American communities. In Canada and the United States, the gangs followed the basic Triad principles they had followed in China. They formed cellular groups, which were controlled by certain members operating within each group. They retained a secretive system by not disclosing details of criminal activity to other cells.

The various cells often join together for specific purposes such as opposing other groups in their attempts to acquire or maintain control over territory. Behind each cell, which is directly involved in crime activity, is a second group or cell, which provides support but is not directly involved in the criminal activity. The members of these types of cells are, however, former members of the crime cells. They are the advisors to the crime group and their approval must be solicited before any major criminal enterprise is carried out by the crime cells. The Triad groups remain almost exclusively within the Chinese communities, and very little of their criminal activity, except their illicit drug distribution activities, directly affects members of the wider public.

The Southeast Asian region involving the tri-border area of Burma, Laos, and Thailand, commonly known as the Golden Triangle, is currently a major supplier of heroin to the Western world (Buruma and McBeth, 1984–85). The Triad organizations acquired control of this illegal operation and developed major illicit drug distribution systems throughout the world. They made direct

"Understanding Asian Organized Crime"
RCMP: Learning and Development
www.rcmp-learning.org/docs/ecdd0054.htm

Triads
These Chinese groups came into existence in the 17th century as resistance fighters against the Manchu invaders. They eventually developed into crime groups.

connections with Triad groups in Canada, the United States, and Europe. Major drug shipments are made regularly between Bangkok, Hong Kong, and Vancouver or from Hong Kong via Amsterdam to Montreal and Toronto.

Hong Kong has been the centre for Triad groups throughout the world. Drug-trafficking activities have made them wealthy and powerful, and many have invested their funds in legitimate enterprises. The colony of Hong Kong came under the control of the Chinese mainland government in 1997, and this likely led to further migration by many who were not anxious to reside under the rule of the People's Republic of China. Organized crime groups, or those who have profited from this activity, are likely continuing to seek refuge in other parts of the world. This will, in all likelihood, further broaden the base of these organized crime syndicates.

Organized crime groups originating in Vietnam and Japan pattern themselves along the lines of Chinese Triads. The Japanese Yakuza (gangsters) are professional racketeers in Japan specializing in blackmail, extortion, and the sale of illicit drugs and guns. The Vietnamese crime groups originated during the Vietnam War, during which they specialized in the sale of black-market goods and illicit drugs. When the war ended, many gang members immigrated to North America. Both crime groups, attracted by the lucrative profits derived from extortion and from drug trafficking and other **consensual crime**, are beginning to emerge in Canada and the United States. Several Asian gangs, notably the Big Circle boys, have developed a business smuggling illegal immigrants into Canada and the United States. Dubro (1992) claims that this business is almost as lucrative as heroin smuggling, and the potential penalties are much less severe.

consensual crime
Any crime in which the "victim" is a willing participant (drug use, prostitution, etc.)

The Criminal Intelligence Service Canada (2002) states that members of Asian organized crime travel frequently nationally and internationally. This travel demonstrates the wide scope of their criminal activities and is also an attempt to avoid law enforcement scrutiny. Like the outlaw motorcycle gangs, the Asian crime groups recruit street and youth gangs, which they use as a labour pool for their criminal activities, for security, and as a source of recruits. There are a number of active Asian-based street gangs in British Columbia, Ontario, and Quebec. Some members of street gangs graduate to performing criminal activities for organized crime groups, typically through street-level crimes, violence, and drug trafficking. They are involved in the international illicit trade in drugs, firearms, and illegal human migrants. The Asian groups across the country remain extensively involved in the large-scale importation and trafficking of drugs, particularly heroin, cocaine, and ecstasy. Approximately 95 percent of the heroin smuggled into Canada originates in Southeast Asia, so Fukienese-based criminal groups are coming to dominate the heroin trade in Canada. All major heroin seizures in Canada in 2001 involved Asian-based crime syndicates. Southeast Asian heroin typically enters Canada through Vancouver, Toronto, or Montreal international airports or through major marine ports in British Columbia. A portion of this heroin is then smuggled to American criminal groups composed of individuals of Chinese descent, who operate on both sides of the border and who control distribution. The smuggling of heroin into the United States is expected to continue, particularly if heroin demand keeps rising. Asian groups, along with the Hells Angels in Saskatchewan, particularly in Saskatoon, are engaged in importing cocaine, ecstasy, and marijuana. In Winnipeg, Asian groups are operating cocaine trafficking rings. Most of these illicit drugs are shipped from British Columbia. The groups are also the predominant importers into Canada of opium, which originates either in Southwest Asia in the Afghanistan/Pakistan region or in Southeast Asia in the Myanmar/Thailand/Laos region.

Vietnamese-based groups continue to be extensively involved in the large-scale cultivation and exportation of marijuana through residential growing operations across Canada, particularly in British Columbia. In 2002 and 2003, Vietnamese-based marijuana operations were rapidly expanding eastward across the country to Ontario. Through marijuana brokers, the Hells Angels and Vietnamese-based crime groups control approximately 85 percent of the marijuana production and distribution in British Columbia. It is conservatively estimated that there are 15 000 to 20 000 grow operations in the B.C.'s Lower Mainland. The value of marijuana production in the Lower Mainland is estimated at $4.2 billion, with the provincial wholesale value at approximately $6 billion. Profits from the marijuana industry are frequently funnelled into other criminal activities. According to intelligence gathered from one operation, high-level gang members of Chinese descent bought marijuana from Vietnamese-based drug-trafficking gangs to transport to the United States. The Asian groups are heavily involved in manufacturing designer drugs such as ecstasy. They continue to be involved in extortions, home invasions, kidnappings, illegal migrant smuggling operations, theft, shoplifting, prostitution, assaults, illegal gambling, loan-sharking, and the production of counterfeit currency, software, manufactured goods, and credit cards. The groups are also involved in the laundering of criminal proceeds and the investment of laundered money into legitimate businesses (CISC, 2002).

Annual Report on Organized Crime in Canada, 2002 CISC (Criminal Intelligence Service Canada) **www.cisc.gc.ca/AnnualReport2002/ Cisc2002/coverpage2002.html**

The Russian Mafia and Eastern European Crime Groups

There are fears that organized crime is threatening the future of Russia. Organized criminals have been among the main beneficiaries of the transition from a communist to a capitalist economy. After the end of the Communist regime in 1991, conditions were ideal for criminals. Russia is in the midst of wrenching social change and is suffering from a troubled economy and political uncertainty. The social institutions developed under the Communist Party have disappeared or have been drastically weakened, and most people now find themselves worse off financially than they were under the old regime. The criminal justice system is corrupt and ineffective. In a country where every move was once controlled by the state police, law enforcement officials are now poorly paid, ill-equipped, and virtually powerless to have any impact on the rapidly rising crime rate.

In his analysis of the rise of the Russian mafia, Handelman concluded that Russian officials "tried to develop a free market before constructing a civil society in which such a market could safely operate.... Many activities that are considered unlawful according to Western norms, such as organized crime, are not specifically prohibited" (1994, 89). Criminal gangs were quick to fill the vacuum left by the fall of the old order. They eagerly embraced the new agenda and began to sell goods and services that were unavailable through other sources.

Statistics about organized crime cannot be very precise. Criminals try to hide their actions, and the agencies that keep such statistics may have reasons to exaggerate or to minimize criminal activities. Recognizing these inaccuracies, a study by the U.S. Department of Energy's Office of Threat Assessment provides an indication of the scope of the problem in Russia (Hersh, 1994). The study found 4000 different organized crime groups or gangs inside Russia. Organized crime groups owned half of Russia's commercial banks and similarly high proportions of other businesses. One-quarter of these groups had ties to other groups inside or outside the country, and many worked closely with corrupt police and government officials.

The close relationship between criminals and government officials is particularly troubling. The criminal establishment had existed in Russia during the Communist regime, and government officials had benefited from its operations. However, the nature of the relationship has changed. The extent of the influence of the Mafia following the 1991 coup is suggested by the comment of Peter Grinenko that "pre-coup, the government kind of ran the criminals. After-coup, the criminals are kind of running the government" (Raine and Cilluffo, 1994, 121). In April 2003 a Russian legislator was murdered in what police called a contract hit. He was the second politician to be murdered within a year, and the eighth since 1991.

In addition to its economic impact, organized crime has had a profound effect on public safety. Contract killings have added to Russia's skyrocketing murder rate, and there are fears that organized criminals may be trying to export nuclear weapons material and technology to other countries. The inability of government to control the problem has reduced the confidence of people in the democratic system of government. Box 15.4 shows how Russian organized crime has an impact even on Canada.

The Criminal Intelligence 2002 report outlines that in Canada, organized crime includes groups originating in the former Soviet Union, Poland, Hungary, Romania, Bulgaria, and the former Yugoslavia. Among these groups, power tends to be concentrated among those whose origins can be traced to the territory of the former Soviet Union. These include groups originating not only in Russia proper but also in Belarus, Ukraine, Transcaucasia (such as Georgia and Chechnya), and the former Soviet Central Asia. The centre of this activity in Canada is southern Ontario. These groups are also reported to be active in the larger urban centres of Quebec and British Columbia and are known for their entrepreneurial and opportunistic tendencies. They will engage in any type of criminal activity or attempt to penetrate any market sector they view as being vulnerable for exploitation. These crime groups are involved in a wide spectrum of criminal activities, ranging from various street-level crimes to more sophisticated economic crimes requiring specific technological expertise. To give the appearance of legitimacy, they have utilized bona fide businesses as fronts for their illegal activities. The groups have maintained a close relationship with the Italian-based Mafia, the Asian-based crime groups, and the

BOX 15.4

FOCUS

OSC Weighs YBM Directors' Duty

Mob tie would have sent reasonable person "headed for the hills"

TORONTO—A reasonable director would have "headed for the hills" when confronted with information back in 1997 that YBM Magnex International Inc.'s founding shareholders included Russian organized crime boss Semion Mogilevitch, a disciplinary panel member told a hearing yesterday.

"I'm not using hindsight. I'm saying at the time when those allegations were made, if it were me, I'd be out the door," said Ontario Securities Commission commissioner Derek Brown.

Howard Wetston, OSC vice-chairman and head of the three-man panel, asked whether YBM's board of directors had a duty to disclose the company's alleged links to organized crime.

The panel members made their remarks to James Douglas, lawyer for Owen Mitchell, a former YBM director and former investment banker at National Bank Financial Corp., who said during his closing arguments that his client took several steps to determine whether YBM was a legitimate business and to "put a box around the company" to ensure that the founding shareholders had nothing to do with it.

Certain information YBM's board learned about the company was factual but not material, Mr. Douglas said, meaning it did not have to be publicly disclosed. There was also no evidence management was involved in illegal activities, he added. You can't go to a police agency and get a sticker that says "this is an organized crime member," Mr. Douglas said.

The information that Mr. Mogilevitch and his associates owned more than one-third of the equity in YBM was contained in a report prepared in 1997 by Decision Strategies/Fairfax International LLC, a New York investigation firm hired by a special committee of the company's board.

Mr. Mitchell did not have major problems with the Fairfax report, so why would he go out of his way to try to disprove its findings, Mr. Wetston asked.

"The real issue is, faced with this information, what did [the board] do with it," he said.

"He's not motivated from the outset to bury information," Mr. Douglas responded. "We don't have a bunch of crooks on this board."

Mr. Douglas said his client and the rest of the board did not give much weight to the information about the alleged mob links because such rumours had "always evaporated in the past" and the company had a legitimate business as an industrial magnet maker. Unless you were there on YBM's board and had "watched the dream unfold," I don't think you can make the decision to just walk away, Mr. Douglas said.

"I may put my money into a questionable venture," Mr. Brown responded. "Being a director is a different thing."

The failure of the YBM board to disclose the company's reputed links to the Russian mob is at the heart of the OSC's case. OSC staff allege that the board and its underwriters failed to disclose in a prospectus for an equity financing in November, 1997, that the company was the subject of an investigation involving organized crime.

OSC staff have asked the panel to ban Mr. Mitchell for life from working in the investment industry. Mr. Douglas said Mr. Mitchell acted "honestly and in good faith." Staff "never came within a country mile" of proving that Mr. Mitchell came to the conclusion certain facts were material and then chose to ignore them, he said.

"What staff is saying is Mitchell had to achieve perfection or near perfection or suffer an economic death penalty."

OSC staff lawyer Jay Naster said during his closing arguments that YBM's board and its underwriters failed to disclose both the findings of Fairfax and its mandate, which was to try to get to the bottom of rumours about the company's links to organized crime.

The board made a decision to raise money from the public, Mr. Naster said. That "triggered" the duty to make disclosure in the prospectus, he said.

(continued)

It is up to the board to decide what information is material and should be disclosed, he added.

Mr. Wetston responded that the law has never required outside directors to be experts. They're expected to rely on experts, he said.

Mr. Naster said a board of directors cannot abdicate its responsibility by saying it got a legal opinion. "You have carved out what is a responsibility of the board."

Source: Karen Howlett, "OSC Weights YBM Directors' Duty." *The Globe and Mail* (21 November 2002), p. B4. Reprinted with permission from *The Globe and Mail.*

outlaw motorcycle gangs. This association allows them to reach criminal markets that would otherwise be inaccessible to them. Unlike other organized crime groups that have been observed to participate in either vehicle or commodities smuggling, these groups are extensively involved in both activities. These crime groups play a significant role in the organized theft and export of automobiles in Canada. In addition, they are extensively involved in the smuggling of stolen consumer goods from Canada and the United States to the former Soviet Union and other European countries, via both legitimate business and criminal operations (CISC, 2002).

South American, Colombian, and Mexican Cartels

The Colombian organized crime syndicates are situated in most cities in Colombia but are centred in Bogota, Medellin, and Cali. Although all Colombian crime families are involved in traditional organized crime activities in Colombia, their Canadian operations are centred on illicit drug trafficking. Their cocaine and marijuana crime families are organized along the same pattern as the Italian Mafia—a corporate organizational style. Each of these syndicates has related groups that act as investors, bankers, and lawyers. In addition, most have logistics experts, exporters, chemists, and specialists in wholesaling, retailing, and market development. They have separate groups that provide support services in the areas of manufacturing, transportation, distribution, finance, and security. Few of the group members are aware of the others who are involved. The loss of one member or even a whole group does not threaten the stability or security of the remaining parts. The managers or top end of each crime organization are completely removed from physical trafficking activities. They have related groups operating in the Caribbean and in major cities in the United States as well as in Canada. In addition, they have established a strong presence in Spain to facilitate cocaine distribution throughout Europe. Recent linkages with organized crime groups in Russia have increased this European foothold.

Mexican crime groups have emerged as major distributors of illicit drugs to the United States and Canada. These groups connect directly with Colombian crime families, who at one time directly supplied at least 75 percent of the cocaine that is consumed in Canada and the United States and who now channel much of that illicit market through Mexico. This market amounts to a multibillion-dollar business.

"Drugs"
RCMP Headquarters Site
www.rcmp-grc.gc.ca/drugenf/ drugs_e.htm

Members of both the Mexican and Colombian crime families are assigned to foreign illicit distribution networks on a rotational basis. Members will move into a Canadian city for a period of six months and then return to Mexico or South America and be replaced by other members. This system of constantly changing membership makes it more difficult for law enforcement to identify the size and specific drug-trafficking activities of the group.

These crime families effectively control illicit cocaine distribution in South America, the Caribbean, Europe, the United States, and Canada. They are continually expanding to develop distribution networks in other parts of the world. Their propensity to be highly organized and to commit violent crimes such as serious assaults and homicide in an effort to acquire new territory has made them potentially the most dangerous crime groups in the world. Over the past few years, the Colombian and Mexican governments, with assistance from the United States, have moved more aggressively against the cartel groups. Some leaders, including the notorious Pablo Escobar, have been killed and others imprisoned. However, Colombia remains a major cocaine supplier. With new alliances with Mexican cartels, the South American crime groups will continue to dominate crime activity in the Americas and Europe for some time to come.

Other Canadian Ethnic-Based Crime Groups

In Canada, as in the United States, many citizens or residents, because of their individual cultural backgrounds, have strong family or ethnic ties to other regions of the world. When certain organized crime enterprises emerge in those other regions, it becomes profitable for those crime groups to establish bases in Canada, and Canadian citizens or residents become members of the illegal enterprise.

Major illicit drug distribution systems controlled by strong organized crime groups currently exist in the Southwest Asian area of Pakistan, Iran, and Afghanistan; in Lebanon; and in India. These networks have now established connections with groups in Canada, the United States, South America, and Europe. Illicit drugs are supplied to Canadian-based groups, which then sell the illicit product to other organized crime groups, which then distribute the drugs in their own established territories.

Some drug-trafficking groups in drug-source countries are involved in national political violence. In such cases, there is the merging of organized crime and terrorism through the common interest of trafficking illicit drugs. The drug–terrorism link not only increases revenues for political purposes but also intensifies the political effect of the terrorist group through connections (usually ethnic) with another group that has traditionally been involved only in enterprise crime activities.

Most organized crime groups in Canada are becoming increasingly involved in criminal activities that manipulate technology and utilize the Internet to facilitate financial frauds. Credit card "skimming," e-commerce site hacking, and fraudulent credit card purchases are examples of how they exploit technology, including the Internet (CISC, 2002).

THE NATURE OF CONSENSUAL CRIME ACTIVITY

When governments use the law to curtail the distribution and supply of goods or services that are reasonably high in public demand, a so-called black market results. In this market, the traders or businesspeople become the criminals, and their business entities become the crime organizations. They will operate without regard to territorial boundaries, taxation systems, or regulations that control legitimate trade and commerce. The cost of corruption for bribes and payoffs, and of contracts for intimidation and extortion, will be the only price crime organizations will pay directly to maintain their base of control. In this environment, the consumer will pay the highest price for the lowest-quality product that the market will bear, and the crime organization will achieve its prime objective—to accumulate profit and power.

Although organized crime groups derive profits from a wide range of criminal activities including kidnapping, robbery, theft, and fraud, in North America their most sought-after criminal ventures involve consensual-type crimes. Crimes related to drug trafficking, gambling, prostitution, and pornography produce massive profits yet leave no victim behind to complain to law enforcement authorities that a financial loss has been incurred. When the criminal act has been committed, the crime group members are relatively free to use the proceeds for their own benefit. Without a victim to bring a complaint to the attention of the police and without a legitimate legal owner to bring an action of recovery for loss of property, the consensual crime will occur without creating an incident or a visible social problem in the community. Consensual crime produces more income for crime organizations than any other type of criminal activity. Drug trafficking alone accounts for most of the proceeds obtained from consensual-type crime such as prostitution, gambling, pornography, smuggling, and loan sharking.

The profitability of drug trafficking can be demonstrated by examining the increase in value of illicit drugs as they progress from the producer or manufacturer to the consumer. An illicit opium producer may receive from $1350 to $1500 for 10 kilograms of opium. This, in turn, produces one kilogram of pure heroin that sells in the production areas for up to $10 000. When that one kilogram is delivered to Canada, it will sell for as much as $200 000. The final product that emerges after being cut and diluted is a capsule dosage unit containing 5 to 6 percent pure heroin, which sells for over $35. This means that the one kilogram of pure heroin can generate retail sales that could total more than $10 million.

While the farmer who produces illicit opium may make several thousands of dollars from the annual harvest, the organized criminals who sell heroin in the illegal markets of the world will make billions of tax-free dollars annually. Judge Jean L. Dutil stated that the trade in narcotics pours tens of millions of dollars into the coffers of traffickers in Canada, financing their operations in other fields and permitting them to spread their criminal activity over a much larger area (Charbonneau, 1976; Dubro, 1985).

The United Nations estimates that revenue from the illicit drug trade worldwide is $400 billion (U.S.) per year. Illicit drugs represent approximately

8 percent of total international trade. This figure was greater than the global trade in iron, steel, and motor vehicles combined, and about the same as that of the world trade in textiles (United Nations, 1997).

Like the illicit drug trade, contraband smuggling has become a major source of revenue for organized crime. Most of the criminal groups in Canada are involved, both separately and cooperatively, in smuggling operations. While tobacco and alcohol remain the most popular commodities, the range of products is constantly increasing. The only consideration is the potential of the commodity to command a maximum profit. Among the most recent goods being smuggled are jewellery and precious stones, stolen vehicles, weapons, cigars, and illegal immigrants. A substantial market for each of these products or services exists, either within or outside Canada. One organization, whose alleged leader was arrested in the United States and is the subject of a Canada-wide arrest warrant, was responsible for smuggling tobacco and alcohol from the United States to Canada. It is estimated that this group made as much as up to $100 million in profits in five years (Criminal Intelligence Service Canada, 1997).

MONEY-LAUNDERING SCHEMES

Proceeds of crime members
members.tripod.com/~orgcrime/
genmlproc.htm

One of the few ways that a street gang's illegal activities can be connected to a national or international organized crime group is by tracing the money flow from the street-level crimes. In most organized crime groups, the transfer of the profits or proceeds is the only tangible link between the unlawful acts and the top-level organizers and planners of the group. Thus, movements of funds are carefully concealed through the use of specially devised transfer systems. These systems are usually called "money laundering schemes."

Although there are a wide variety of money laundering schemes, the most difficult to penetrate and, therefore, the most popular are those that utilize secret banking and corporate facilities in tax-haven countries.

It is now recognized by international law enforcement organizations that the only successful way to identify and prosecute organized crime figures is to trace the proceeds of crime from the source to the ultimate beneficiaries. James Dubro found that

> when the Commissos got involved in land deals they concentrated on hidden titles, a money laundering operation to hide the sources of profits made from drugs and contract murders. In one documented case, Remo and Cosimo were in secret partnership with Alberto Bentivogli in owning a Toronto restaurant, as well as 23 acres in Richmond Hill and land in Burlington. (Dubro, 1985)

In another case, law enforcement officers from the United States, Canada, Hong Kong, Singapore, and Thailand attempted to identify and seize money being transferred from North America to Thailand via the Netherlands, Hong Kong, and Singapore. They followed the transfer of $2 million, derived from heroin sales in the western United States and Canada, and transported in cash lots, first to the Netherlands and then to Hong Kong, where it was deposited in

BOX 15.5

FOCUS

Unloading Dirty Money—A Complex Process

Money laundering is a complex process. This is illustrated by a case described by Margaret Beare in her book Criminal Conspiracies: Organized Crime in Canada. *The case involved a large North American cannabis distribution network headed by Timothy Neeb and Robert Brook. Neeb and Brook were assisted in their laundering efforts by several professionals, including Toronto lawyer Donovan Blakeman. After several years of investigation, Brook was arrested and persuaded to testify against others involved in his network. For his own protection, he is now in a witness relocation program. This case demonstrates the difficulty faced by police departments in their investigations of money laundering.*

Brook estimated that between 1982 and 1987, the Neeb/Brook criminal organization exchanged $100 million through Friedberg Exchange in Toronto. (In the latter period, they were exchanging $1 million per week.). This exchange house played a critical role. The profits from drug sales were converted into U.S. dollars and bearer cheques from Friedberg Currency Exchange. Bearer cheques were used in offshore bank deposits to avoid the suspicions that large cash deposits would arise. (Although less conspicuous than large amounts of cash, these bearer cheques *should* have alerted authorities and bank officials; bearer cheques are very uncommon in legitimate transactions because they can be stolen and cashed by anyone who has them in their possession.) Some of the U.S. dollars and bearer bonds were then flown by Blakeman to Brown Shipley Inc. in Jersey Island and England, to First Trust Corporations in St. Kitts, and to Switzerland for deposit into corporate accounts. From these corporate accounts, they were transferred to corporations in the United States, Canada, Switzerland, the Caribbean, and England.

Flight records revealed that on occasion Neeb, Blakeman, and their accountant acted as couriers for these funds, flying them personally to the second stage of what was usually a long route

back home. If the Caribbean was to be the destination, the three men would rent a Learjet from Toronto's Pearson International Airport. The remaining U.S. dollars went to the United States, Mexico, and South America for the purchase of more cannabis shipments. Blakeman recognized the benefits of using international tax havens and numerous overseas corporations as vehicles for routing cash back into the criminals' hands that they could not otherwise use (RCMP case files).

The Role of Lawyers

In both the Outrage and IOU projects, investigations undertaken by the police, lawyers and ex-lawyers played a critical role. Donovan Jackson Blakeman was the main money launderer for the Neeb/Brook organization. Blakeman became involved in the organization in 1979 and retired his law practice in 1981. His role was to "manage" the illicit profits by incorporating domestic and international corporations: maintaining numerous foreign and domestic bank accounts; and concealing, laundering, and investing (in real estate in Ontario, Florida, and elsewhere) millions of dollars of criminal proceeds.

The corporations alone were registered in Liberia, the Cayman Islands, the Isle of Man, the British Virgin Islands, Ontario, Florida, and North Carolina. A chart, titled by the criminals "What We Got!—Spaghetti Jungle," was seized from Blakeman's residence. The police identified 62 Canadian corporations directly or indirectly related to accused persons in this organized criminal group. Blakeman explained to Neeb his procedure of taking the illicit funds overseas and making deposits in various banks to the credit of numerous corporations. These funds would then be repatriated to North America through offshore accounts and investments in other offshore corporations. As only an indication of their property holdings, Neeb and Brook through Blakeman owned 148 lots in West Palm Beach, Florida. Bank accounts were located in Jersey, the Channel Islands, Switzerland, St. Kitts, Bahamas,

(continued)

the Cayman Islands, Ontario, and the United States.

Major funds were put into the Brown Shipley Inc. accounts in various company names. The companies were set up with little capital and got advances through use of the "spaghetti jungle" maze of corporate entities for financing. The investigation indicated that 62 Canadian corporations, 30 U.S. corporations, and 18 foreign corporations were used (directly or indirectly) to facilitate the movement of drug money. In total, $13,408,845.00 was deposited to Brown Shipley.

Source: Margaret Beare. (1996). *Criminal Conspiracies: Crime in Canada.* Toronto: ITP Nelson, pp. 208–10. © 1995 Margaret Beare. Reprinted with permission of Nelson, a division of Thomson Learning. www.thomsonrights.com. Fax 800-730-2215.

a bank. From this bank, it was transferred to a Chinese Hong Kong import–export company that operated primarily as an underground money laundering service for the Southeast Asian Chinese community.

When the funds were received by the import–export company in Hong Kong, a corresponding credit appeared with another related import–export company in Singapore. Instructions from the company in Singapore caused a further paper transfer to occur in Thailand, where the last transaction in the chain occurred. Cash was then paid to an unidentified individual, and it was believed that the funds were moved to northern Thailand to the benefit of a major drug trafficking organized crime group. No assets were seized as a result of this investigation, but it was established that over $52 million had been moved through this one laundering system. Similar laundering systems also exist for other ethnically based organized crime groups (Stamler, 1984).

Although Europeans have been using protected banking facilities in Switzerland since the early 19th century, in North America, tax havens have grown in popularity in recent times as one of the few means of placing funds beyond the reach of government authorities or tax collectors. This guarantee of financial privacy became attractive to a wide variety of persons, including those whose primary interest was not necessarily to avoid taxes. It was not long before crime organizations found the sanctuary of tax havens too inviting to ignore. With the development of multinational banking systems and international business and commerce, it became easy to develop sophisticated laundering schemes designed to move money obtained directly from criminal activity into the foreign banks protected from intrusion by law enforcement officials. For the organized criminal, this financial privacy is an indispensable aid in concealing the proceeds of crime. Many countries and territories, at times unwittingly, provide this type of protection.

These countries and territories allow easy access to banking institutions with secret-numbered accounts; they also have extended corporate and secrecy laws to allow the establishment of an unlimited number of beneficially owned corporations. These so-called offshore corporations or international business corporations are operated by local agents or lawyers but manipulated by the beneficial owners. When these corporate entities are combined with several numbered bank accounts, a maze of financial transactions can be structured in a way that makes the tracing of assets a very complex task. If questionable funds are then moved from one tax-haven jurisdiction to another, using the combination of beneficially owned corporations with secret-numbered bank accounts, the complexities are significantly increased.

Current favourite money laundering spots include the Cayman Islands, the British Virgin Islands, the Channel Islands, and the Turks and Caicos Islands. These countries and territories have extremely permissive financial regulations that enable them to attract money laundering businesses. For example, the tiny Cayman Islands has more than 500 banks that handle massive amounts of money. Total assets held by Cayman banks in 1994 were about $430 billion (United Nations, 1998). An investigator working with a BBC TV crew visited one of the Cayman banks:

> I sat with the chairman of the bank and he described for me how to set up offshore in a way which the U.S. government could not follow what I did. He went on to explain how I could move money out of the United States by writing checks to corporations he and his bank had set up ... in the United States to receive money from people who wanted to hide it. He described how I could then, through a Caymanian corporation whose ownership was completely concealed, open up brokerage accounts and trade on stock markets anywhere I wanted to. Then finally, he described to me how I could bring money back into the United States without its being traced. (Blum, 1994)

Laundering schemes used to move illegally obtained funds vary as widely and are as complex as legitimate business and commercial transactions. Through a variety of transactions, cash can be secretly transferred anywhere in the world. This includes the use of corporations, business entities, or phony business transactions, all done under the guise of a legitimate commercial enterprise (United States Government, 1983).

CONTROLLING ORGANIZED CRIME

Legalization of Illicit Goods and Services

Legalizing the products and services supplied to meet a public demand is one of the most effective means of curbing the profits and income of crime groups. This factor has, in turn, a direct effect on the development, growth, and continuation of organized crime within a society.

There is no doubt that when the United States Congress passed the countrywide **Volstead Act** on October 28, 1919, prohibiting the manufacture and sale of alcohol, organized crime moved into the business and became the major supplier of what became then an illegal product. From 1920 to 1933, organized crime groups in the United States grew and flourished from the profits derived from the sale of illicit alcohol, only because it was a product prohibited by the government.

Volstead Act
Passed by the United States Congress on October 28, 1919, this legislation prohibited the manufacture and sale of alcohol in the United States. Since a ready market existed for this prohibited good, organized crime in America gained a ready foothold.

The United States stayed dry (at least legally) until 1933. In the 13 years that the sale of alcohol was prohibited in the United States, profits from the sale of illicit alcohol topped all other income from unlawful activities. When Prohibition ended, crime groups turned to gambling, illicit drugs, and prostitution as the high-income enterprises.

In more recent times, gambling laws in North America have been liberalized. In most Canadian provinces, gambling provides a significant portion of government revenues. In fact, some say that governments are now as addicted to gambling as are compulsive gamblers. An interesting example of how government has moved into this formerly criminal enterprise is the Pick 3 lottery. To win, you must pick a three-digit number matching the one drawn by the government lottery agency. Several years ago, this game was called the numbers racket and was the most common form of gambling in many low-income neighbourhoods. The main differences between the two are that criminals paid out a higher share of the take than the government does and that the profits now go back to the population and not into the pockets of organized criminals. With the decline in gambling revenues, organized crime is now focusing on other activities such as illicit drugs, pornography, extortion, immigration fraud, money laundering, smuggling, and international stock and bank frauds.

Although the liberalization of liquor and gambling laws in both Canada and the United States reduced the income for organized crime from those illegal activities, the dramatic increase in the demand for illicit drugs since the 1960s has more than filled the gap. Beginning in the early 1980s, drug trafficking clearly became one of the most profitable enterprises for organized crime (Canada, 1983; 1984; 1985).

Legalizing illicit drugs may, however, prove more difficult than legalizing alcohol or gambling. Canada, along with 130 countries of the world, has ratified several UN conventions agreeing to prohibit the manufacture, distribution, and sale of narcotic drugs except for medical, scientific, or research purposes. At this time, the trend at the United Nations is toward maintaining control over the manufacture and distribution of illicit drugs. In this international environment, it would be extremely difficult for one country to legalize the use of any illicit drugs other than for the purposes authorized by the UN conventions. The Netherlands has set up zones in which illicit drugs may be distributed for personal use without police intervention, but they have not legalized the distribution and sale of these drugs throughout the country. Such special zones, however, are not entrenched in law but only in police tolerance and discretion. They do not curb the activities of organized crime since the illicit drugs that are sold in these areas are produced and delivered by organized crime.

Enforcement

An effective police investigation must be proactive, especially when it is directed against an organized crime group involved in consensual crime. It must include a number of lawful covert law enforcement techniques. These covert techniques include the use of paid informants, trained undercover police officers, electronic surveillance equipment to surreptitiously record the private conversations of organized crime members, and covert physical surveillance techniques. The police and enforcement authorities must have an adequate witness protection program available so that potential witnesses will be protected from any acts of intimidation or violence by the organized crime groups. The use of financial investigations to trace, freeze, seize, and forfeit the proceeds of crime will serve to remove the profits of the criminal enterprise. This type of investigation will also assist in gathering evidence to implicate top levels of organized crime with the criminal activity carried out by the group.

Unfortunately, organized crime investigations are very expensive. Because infiltration of groups is usually impossible, the police must rely on wiretaps and constant surveillance. An investigation that resulted in the arrests in Toronto, Montreal, Italy, and Mexico of the leaders of one of the most powerful Sicilian crime families, the Cuntrera–Caruana gang, was nearly terminated for financial reasons. The difficulties of such investigations were outlined as follows by Staff Sergeant Larry Tronstad, the RCMP officer who headed the day-to-day investigation: "These guys change phones every week; it was a huge problem. At one point we had over 100 pay phones wired hoping to get these guys. They are extremely surveillance-conscious" (Appleby and Cheney, 1998, A1, A2).

Another problem was tracing the money used to purchase millions of dollars' worth of cocaine: "The money was originating in Italy, then moving to Switzerland, then to Miami, then to Caracas, then to Mexico and then on to here [Toronto]. And in each of these countries they had a network set up, opening and shutting bank accounts before we're even there" (Appleby and Cheney, 1998, A1, A2).

Limitations on police resources mean that many of the activities of organized crime groups are never investigated.

National Criminal Laws and Procedures

The enactment of new criminal laws over the past several years has provided new tools for law enforcement to combat both organized crime and terrorism in Canada. The Proceeds of Crime (Money Laundering) and Terrorist Financing Act, together with new regulations, established the Financial Transaction and Report Analysis Center of Canada (Fintrac). This agency, under the Ministry of Finance, now receives and collects reports on suspicious transactions, as well as other information relevant to money laundering. Under the provisions of this act, financial institutions and other identified private business entities are required to report all suspicious financial transactions and all money movements that are specifically outlined in the regulations. The information that is then collected and analyzed is supplied to Canadian law enforcement and intelligence agencies.

In 1997, the legislature of Quebec introduced legislation to prevent real estate from being used as a fortified or barricaded residence, which is often associated with outlaw motorcycle gangs. A similar law has since been passed by the Ontario legislature. Manitoba, on the other hand, plans to use civil law to prevent biker gangs and other organized crime groups from setting up legitimate businesses. Under the proposed legislation, police will be able to apply for court orders to cancel or withhold liquor licences and dissolve businesses that are intended to be used to advance the objectives of crime organizations.

National criminal laws and procedures along with provincial legislation are being improved to help ensure that organized crime is not able to profit from the proceeds generated by criminal activity, no matter where a crime has occurred. Canada has enacted criminal laws that make it an offence to possess the proceeds of crime. This means that it is an offence to possess anything that was obtained or derived directly or indirectly from the commission of an indictable offence or from any act committed anywhere, which, if committed in Canada, would be classified as an indictable offence. This law, combined with the laws of conspiracy, makes it possible to prosecute in Canada anyone who conspires to possess proceeds of crime within Canada, even if all the conspirators are outside Canada.

Besides empowering an attorney general to obtain an order to seize or restrain the proceeds of crime and request forfeiture, the Criminal Code makes it an offence for anyone to launder the proceeds of crime. This includes employees of banks and financial institutions. The current laws and regulations provide law enforcement with considerable authority to investigate organized crime and seize and forfeit the proceeds of crime.

International Cooperation

In 2000, the United Nations developed a convention against transnational organized crime. This convention has now been adopted by more than 120 countries.

New national laws will be required in each country to conform to the convention. These new laws and programs will make it easier for law enforcement in each country to identify and prosecute organized criminals who are operating at the international level from a base in one or two countries.

The convention also requires that national laws include in the definition of organized crime groups all persons and entities that supply and assist organized crime. This means that otherwise legitimate organizations that supply goods or services to organized crime that are subsequently distributed unlawfully will be caught up in the definition of organized crime activity. For example, the tobacco manufacturing company that sold cigarettes that it knew were being distributed in an unlawful manner in another country is being prosecuted for money laundering, because the proceeds of the smuggling operation obtained by the organized crime groups were used to purchase the next supply of cigarettes. If a conviction for money laundering is achieved, the entire amount of funds that the manufacturer received will be subject to seizure and forfeiture. In addition the manufacturer will likely be prosecuted for receiving the proceeds of crime. This situation will likely apply to any other goods or services that follow a similar pattern.

Unfortunately, as law enforcement develops more capabilities, so do the wealthy and powerful organized crime groups of the world. In the meantime, governments will likely continue to outlaw goods and services that the public demands. Organized crime will continue to build sophisticated international supply chains to bring those goods and services to a waiting public willing to part with their funds.

SUMMARY

- The demand for illegal goods and services influences the presence, size, and structure of organized crime.

- The phenomenon of organized crime is best described as the operation of illegal business entities, members of which are bound together because of their group interest and because of their desire to profit from illegal activity.

- There are a number of major organized crime groups in Canada. These groups have connections with groups in many other countries and use these connections to distribute their illicit goods and services.

- Crime organizations establish territorial distribution areas and utilize extortion and corruption to develop regions under their control and enforce their rules.

- Organized crime groups launder their illegal profits through countries whose laws are designed to protect bank and investment records. Often laundered profits are invested in legitimate businesses.

- Government control over organized crime is exercised through police enforcement and prosecution through the courts. However, because of its global nature, organized crime cannot be fought without international action and cooperation.

- The only certain way to reduce the influence of organized crime is to reduce the demand for the illicit goods and services that organized crime groups supply.

QUESTIONS FOR CRITICAL THINKING

1. Discuss the role played by governments in the creation of organized crime. Using cigarette smuggling as an example, describe several actions the government could take to reduce the profits of organized crime.
2. Why do most successful organized crime groups tend to be ethnically based?
3. Think about the theories of crime causation you studied in earlier chapters of this book. Which of these theories provides the best explanation of organized crime?
4. Find some reference material in the library or on the Internet on Russian organized crime groups. Why did these groups become so powerful in such a short time after the end of the Communist regime? How does their existence threaten the future of democracy in Russia?

5. If you were an advisor to the government of Canada, what actions would you recommend to reduce the impact of organized crime?

NET WORK

There is a good deal of material about organized crime on the Internet. A good place to start is the website of York University's Nathanson Centre for the Study of Organized Crime and Corruption at **www.yorku.ca/nathanson/default.htm.** This site has an extensive bibliography that can be searched by keyword. It also has many links to other sites.

Using the links on this site, answer the following questions:

1. Organized crime groups based in Russia are becoming more powerful. Discuss the latest information about the spread of these groups into Canada and other countries. What are the major illegal activities of Russian/Eastern European organized crime groups?
2. What new opportunities does globalization offer to organized crime? Why are organized crime groups in a good position to take advantage of these opportunities?
3. What is narcoterrorism? How does it differ from traditional organized crime?

KEY TERMS

consensual crime   Triads
Mafia   Volstead Act

SUGGESTED READING

Beare, Margaret E. (1996). *Criminal Conspiracies: Organized Crime in Canada.* Toronto: ITP Nelson. The first systematic and comprehensive examination of organized crime in Canada written by the director of York University's Nathanson Centre for the Study of Organized Crime and Corruption. The book describes the characteristics of those who get involved in organized crime and the changing nature of international organized crime, and addresses the issues of how law enforcement agencies can best deal with the problem.

Block, A.A. (1990). *Perspectives on Organized Crime.* Dordrecht, The Netherlands: Kluwer Academic Publishers. This book presents some interesting essays on some of the more recent activities of organized crime. These include toxic waste disposal and financial crimes such as tax evasion.

Carrigan, O.D. (1991). *Crime and Punishment in Canada: A History.* Toronto: McClelland & Stewart. Chapter 4 of this book is a very entertaining and informative chapter on the history of organized crime in Canada.

Cressey, D.R. (1969). *Theft of the Nation.* New York: Harper and Row. This book is drawn from Cressey's research for the influential President's Commission on Law Enforcement and the Administration of Justice. He presents his view that there was a national cartel that controlled organized crime in the United States.

Criminal Intelligence Service Canada. (2002). *Annual Report on Organized Crime in Canada.* Ottawa: Department of Supply and Services. An annual review of organized crime in Canada. Updates are available on the Internet at **www.cisc.gc.ca.**

Dubro, J. (1992). *Dragons of Crime.* Markham: Butterworths. A very readable and objective discussion of the history and activities of Asian gangs in Canada. Dubro is one of Canada's more experienced observers of organized crime.

Lavigne, Yves. (1987). *Hells Angels: Taking Care of Business.* Toronto: Deneau and Wayne. A fascinating book about the history of the Hells Angels and their Canadian operations.

Reuter, P. (1983). *Disorganized Crime.* Cambridge: MIT Press. One of the relatively few detailed research studies on organized crime. Reuter, an economist, examines the illegal markets of bookmaking, numbers gambling, and loan sharking. His results question the widely held view that the Italian Mafia has maintained firm control over these activities.

Wolf, D.R. (1991). *The Rebels: A Brotherhood of Outlaw Bikers.* Toronto: University of Toronto Press. A rare ethnographic study of a biker gang written by a Canadian anthropologist. Wolf claims that the Rebels, a group based in Alberta and Saskatchewan, commit minor criminal offences but are not involved in organized crime.

BIBLIOGRAPHY

Albini, Joseph. (1971). *The American Mafia: Genesis of a Legend.* New York: Appleton-Century.

Appleby, Timothy, and Peter Cheney. (1998). "Police Hit Crime Family." *The Globe and Mail* (July 16):A1, A2.

Beare, Margaret E. (1996). *Criminal Conspiracies: Organized Crime in Canada.* Toronto: ITP Nelson.

Blum, J. (1994). "Global Financial Systems Under Assault: Countering the $500 Billion Conspiracy." In L.P. Raine and F.J. Cilluffo (eds.), *Global Organized Crime: The New Empire of Evil* (pp. 22–25). Washington, D.C.: The Center for Strategic and International Studies.

Bresler, Fenton. (1980). *The Trial of the TRIADS: An Investigation into International Crime.* London: Weidenfeld and Nicolson.

Buruma, Ian, and John McBeth. (1984/85). "An East-Side Story." *Far Eastern Economic Review* (Dec. 27–Jan. 3).

Canada. (1980). "No Biker Problems in Canada?" *Royal Canadian Mounted Police—Gazette.* Ottawa: RCMP 42:10.

———. (1983). *RCMP National Drug Intelligence Estimate 1982.* Ottawa: Queen's Printer.

———. (1984). *RCMP National Drug Intelligence Estimate 1983.* Ottawa: Queen's Printer.

———. (1985). *RCMP National Drug Intelligence Estimate 1984/5.* Ottawa: Queen's Printer.

———. (1992). *Organized Crime Committee Report.* Ottawa: Criminal Intelligence Service Canada.

Carrigan, O.D. (1991). *Crime and Punishment in Canada: A History.* Toronto: McClelland & Stewart.

Charbonneau, Jean-Pierre. (1976). *The Canadian Connection.* Ottawa: Optimum Publishing.

Cressey, D.R. (1969). *Theft of the Nation.* New York: Harper and Row.

Criminal Intelligence Service Canada. (1997, 1998, 1999, 2000, 2001, 2002, 2003). *Annual Report on Organized Crime in Canada.* Ottawa: Department of Supply and Services Canada.

Dubro, James. (1985). *Mob Rule: Inside the Canadian Mafia.* Toronto: Macmillan.

———. (1992). *Dragons of Crime.* Markham: Butterworths.

Dutil, Jean L. (1977). Quebec Police Commission, Report of the Commission of Inquiry on Organized Crime in Quebec, "The Fight Against Organized Crime in Quebec."

Gambetta, Diego. (1993). *The Sicilian Mafia—The Business of Private Protection.* Cambridge, Mass.: Harvard University Press.

Glaser, Daniel. (1978). *Crime in Our Changing Society.* New York: Holt, Rinehart and Winston.

Haller, M.H. (1990). "Illegal Enterprise: A Theoretical and Historical Interpretation." *Criminology* 28:207–35.

Handelman, S. (1994). "The Russian 'Mafiya.'" *Foreign Affairs* 73:83–96.

Hersh, S.M. (1994). "The Wild East." *The Atlantic Monthly* (June):61–86.

Maclean, Don. (1974). *Pictorial History of the Mafia.* New York: Pyramid Books.

Mansell, Ingrid, and Roger Boyes. (2003). "Hamburg Police Raid Reemtsma Offices." *The Times of London* (January 15).

Nicaso, Antonio, and Lee Lamothe. (1995). *Global Mafia.* Toronto: Macmillan Canada.

Pennsylvania Crime Commission. (1980). *A Decade of Organized Crime.* Pennsylvania State Printer.

Porteous, Samual. (1998). *Organized Crime Impact Study: Highlights,* prepared for the Ministry of the Solicitor General, Canada.

Quebec. (1977). *The Fight Against Organized Crime in Quebec.* Quebec: Éditeur Officiel.

———. (1980). Commission de Police du Québec, Enquête sur le Crime Organisé. *Les Bandes de Motards au Québec.* Québec: Éditeur Officiel.

Raine, L.P., and F.J. Cilluffo (eds.). (1994). *Global Organized Crime: The New Empire of Evil.* Washington: The Center for Strategic and International Studies.

Reuter, P. (1983). *Disorganized Crime.* Cambridge: MIT Press.

Sacco, Vincent F. (1986). "An Approach to the Study of Organized Crime." In Robert A. Silverman and James J. Teevan (eds.), *Crime in Canadian Society* (3rd ed.) (pp. 214–26). Toronto: Butterworths.

Sacco, V.F., and L.W. Kennedy. (1994). *The Criminal Event.* Scarborough: Nelson Canada.

Stamler, Rodney T. (1984). *Background Document—Proceeds of Drug Trafficking.* Vienna: United Nations Division of Narcotic Drugs Report. DND/Wp 1984/9.

Stille, A. (1995). *Excellent Cadavers: The Mafia and the Death of the First Italian Republic.* New York: Pantheon.

Thomas, D. (1992). *Criminality Among the Foreign Born: Analysis of Federal Prison Population.* Ottawa: Immigration and Employment Canada.

United Nations. (1997). "Revenue from Illicit Drugs: $400 Billion—'8% of Total Global Trade,' says United Nations Report." United Nations Press Release, June 24, SOC/NAR/764. Vienna: United Nations.

———. (1998). "UN Laundering Report: A Global View." *The Report on Crime and Profiteering* 2(3):20–22.

United States Government. (1983) (February). Permanent Subcommittee on Investigations. *Crime and Secrecy: The Use of Offshore Banks and Companies.* Washington, D.C.: U.S. Government Printing Office.

Wolf, D.R. (1991). *The Rebels: A Brotherhood of Outlaw Bikers.* Toronto: University of Toronto Press.

Woolsey, R.J. (1994). "Global Organized Crime: Threats to U.S. and International Security." In Linnea P. Raine and Frank J. Cilluffo (eds.), *Global Organized Crime: The New Empire of Evil* (pp. 134–44). Washington: The Center for Strategic and International Studies.

16

Corporate and White-Collar Crime

JOHN HAGAN
University of Toronto

Most of us know far more about street crime and organized crime than we do about corporate and white-collar crime. While recent cases such as the multibillion-dollar Enron bankruptcy in the United States have raised the profile of these types of crime, few Canadians are aware of the harm that is done by corporate and white-collar criminals. In fact, these crimes are much more costly in dollar terms than street crime is. The $6 billion lost to investors in the Bre-X fraud discussed later in this chapter is far greater than the money lost in all the robberies in Canadian history. Few bank robbers get away with more than a few thousand dollars, but Julius Melnitzer, an Ontario lawyer, defrauded banks and friends of $90 million to support his lavish lifestyle. Corporate and white-collar crimes also cause a large number of deaths and injuries. Laureen Snider (1988) reported that occupational deaths were the third leading cause of death in Canada and attributed at least half these deaths to unsafe and illegal working conditions.

The topic of white-collar crime raises some important issues in the field of criminology. The term itself, introduced by Edwin Sutherland (1940) more than a half century ago, is probably one of the most popularly used criminological concepts in everyday life. However, despite its popularity, there is uncertainty about the precise meaning of the term. This is less important than the fact that the concept of white-collar crime has forced a reconsideration of some very basic criminological assumptions.

No longer is it possible to take for granted the way in which crime itself is defined. No longer can the official data collected on crime by agencies of crime control be accepted uncritically. No longer can it be assumed that the poor are more criminal than the rich. The criminological enterprise has taken on new form and substance now that the topic of white-collar crime has become a central part of our thinking. This chapter will consider separately issues of class, crime, and the corporations; the social organization of work; and legal sanctions. Each is part of the topic of white-collar crime.

After reading this chapter, you should be able to

- Describe the concept of white-collar crime and explain the impact the notion of white-collar crime had on the discipline of criminology.

- Understand the occupational and organizational components of white-collar crime.

- Explain the physical and social harm caused by white-collar crime in Canada.

- Analyze how the structure of the modern corporation facilitates criminal activity.

- Understand the nature and extent of occupational crime.

- Understand the causes and consequences of our weak laws concerning corporate and white-collar crime.

THE EXTENT AND NATURE OF CORPORATE AND WHITE-COLLAR CRIME

The Extent of Corporate and White-Collar Crime

The business section in your daily paper normally deals with stories involving new business developments, company profits, mergers, and other related matters. However, in recent years criminal matters have become a routine part of business reporting. To give you some idea of the extent of corporate and white-collar crime, consider the following stories from the May 9, 2003, edition of the business section of the *Globe and Mail*:

- Two Ontario men were charged with theft and fraud because of activities in the mid-1990s that resulted in over $40 million in losses. Mark Eizenga and James Sylvester were accused of selling shares to support investments in Cuba and the Caribbean. Investors were allegedly misled by the pair, and most of the money has disappeared.

- Stock traders working for a unit of the Royal Bank were accused of placing stock orders late in the day in order to artificially inflate the closing price of a stock at the end of a reporting period. This would help to make the performance of a stock portfolio look more positive than it actually was.

- The Ontario Securities Commission has accused a Peterborough man of collecting at least $25 million by falsely guaranteeing individuals a high rate of return on investments.

- There is a flaw in Microsoft's Internet Passport service that could make it possible for computer hackers to gain access to the accounts of customers visiting Internet shopping sites. The system also controls access to Microsoft's Hotmail system. The security flaw placed Microsoft in possible violation of a U.S. Federal Trade Commission order to ensure that personal consumer information was protected by the Passport system. The order resulted from previous problems with the system.

- Rupert Murdoch, owner of a global media empire that includes Fox TV, appeared before a U.S. Congressional committee seeking approval of a takeover of DirecTV, which is the largest provider of satellite television in the

United States. Critics fear that the deal would violate competition laws by allowing Murdoch's company to use its huge size to force smaller competitors out of business.

■ The U.S. government is pursuing fraud charges against HealthSouth Corporation, the largest owner of physical therapy clinics and rehabilitation clinics in the United States. Many of the company's executives have pleaded guilty to making fraudulent reports that made the company appear to be more profitable than it actually was. This inflated the stock price. Many investors who bought the stock because of its apparent profitability lost most of their money when the fraud was revealed.

■ A New York stockbroker was accused of using his clients' money to pay off former employees who had threatened to reveal his illegal stock trading. He had been previously charged with "churning" investors' accounts. "Churning" is the practice of making unnecessary trades to generate higher commissions.

■ The Dutch company Ahold NV, one of the world's largest supermarket companies, lowered its earnings estimates by $880 million after these earnings had been artificially inflated by some of its American executives in order to make the company's performance look better than it really was.

■ The U.S. Securities and Exchange Commission is looking into potential accounting fraud charges against Qwest Communications, a large phone company. The company overstated its revenues by $2.2 billion over a three-year period ending in 2001.

■ Halliburton Company, once run by U.S. Vice-President Dick Cheney, admitted paying $2.4 million in bribes to an official of the Nigerian government in order to get tax breaks for its operations in that country.

In addition to these stories involving violations and possible violations of criminal laws and securities regulations, there were also several articles dealing with ethical and regulatory issues. Among these were stories dealing with the need for better regulation of the stock market; the debate over the need to better regulate complex financial instruments known as derivatives; ethical questions about whether it was proper for Gerry Schwartz, the chief executive of the large Canadian company Onex, to appoint his wife to the board of directors of his company; the problems that were created for the Calgary-based oil company Talisman when it was accused of producing revenues that helped the Sudanese government to repress its own people in a civil war; a discussion of the reluctance of major pharmaceutical manufacturers to provide low-cost AIDS drugs for developing countries that cannot afford to pay for these treatments; and the ethics of Molson's sex-laden campaign for Bavaria beer.

The sheer volume of these stories from just one daily newspaper clearly shows that corporate and white-collar crime is a major problem. While most of these stories will remain on the business pages, many others that you will read about in this chapter have become front-page news. The public is finally starting to become aware of the harm being done by corporate and white-collar criminals.

The Nature of Corporate and White-Collar Crime

Corporate and white-collar offenders have found many ways to make money. Figure 16.1 shows the range of offences committed by corporations and by individuals in the course of practising legitimate occupations. We will not discuss all of these different crimes, but in the rest of this chapter you will first learn about corporate crimes and then about crimes committed by individual practitioners.

CLASS, CRIME, AND THE CORPORATIONS

Occupation, Organization, and Crime

White-collar crimes are often committed through, and on behalf of, corporations. The involvement of corporations in crime has been recognized at least since the early part of this century, when E.A. Ross (1907) wrote of a new type of criminal "who picks pockets with a 'rake-off' instead of a jimmy, cheats with a company prospectus instead of a deck of cards, or scuttles his town instead of his ship." Particular actions of corporations have been criminal

white-collar crime
An important concept in criminology but one with changing definitions. As used by Edwin Sutherland in 1940, the concept referred to corporate behaviour that caused social harm and for which there was a legal sanction. This sanction need not be criminal; it could be regulatory. Since that time, criminologists have also included the illegal actions of executives or employees who commit crimes against their employer or use organizational resources to gain personal benefit.

Scams and Frauds
RCMP Site
**www.rcmp-grc.gc.ca/scams/
scams_e.htm**

FIGURE 16.1   Types of Corporate and White-collar Crime

Crimes Against the Public
Corporate and Business Crime
    Price-fixing (conspiring on contract bids or on prices for selling to the public)
    Manipulation of stocks and securities
    Commercial and political bribery and rebates
    Patent and trademark infringements
    Misrepresentation and false advertising
    Fraudulent grading, packaging, and labelling
    Tax fraud
    Adulteration of food and drugs
    Illegal pollution of the environment
Crimes by Individual and Professional Practitioners
    Obtaining fees, payments, or charges through fraud and deception
    Deceiving or defrauding patients, clients, customers
    Immoral practices in relations with clients
    Unprofessional conduct and malpractice
    Falsification of statements on vital documents

Crimes within the Organization
Offences Against the Organization
    Theft of funds by employees
    Theft of inventory by employees
Offences Against Employees
    Violation of workplace health and safety laws
    Violation of labour laws
    Discriminatory employment practices
    Harassment

Source: Adapted from Ronald Akers. (1973). *Deviant Behavior: A Social Learning Approach.* Belmont: Wadsworth: 180—81. Reprinted with permission of the author.

offences in Canada since 1889 (Casey, 1985). However, it was not until after the Great Depression that Edwin Sutherland (1940) finally attached a lasting label to these offenders in his influential paper "White-Collar Crime." Sutherland proposed in this paper that white-collar crime be defined "as a crime committed by a person of respectability and high social status in the course of his occupation."

Since Sutherland came up with this term, there has been confusion about the role of *occupation* and *organization* in the study of white-collar crime. For example, Wheeler and Rothman (1982) note that two influential works—Clinard's (1952) and Hartung's (1950) studies of black-market activities during World War II—defined white-collar crime in two rather different ways. Clinard defined white-collar crime occupationally, as "illegal activities among business and professional men," while Hartung included an organizational component, defining such crimes as "a violation of law regulating business, which is committed for a firm by the firm or its agents in the conduct of its business." A distinction is still often drawn today (see, for example, Coleman, 1985, 8) between "**occupational crime**—that is, white collar crime committed by an individual or group of individuals exclusively for personal gain," and "**organizational crime**—white collar crimes committed with the support and encouragement of a formal organization and intended at least in part to advance the goals of that organization." Organizational crime is also known as **corporate crime.**

The problem is that the occupational and organizational components of many white-collar crimes cannot be easily separated. Clinard and Yeager (1980) make this point with the example of a Firestone tire official who aided his corporation in securing and administering illegal political contributions benefiting the corporation, but then embezzled much of the funds for himself. The illegal activities of lawyers (Reasons and Chappell, 1985) are another common form of white-collar crime in which it is often difficult to separate the individual component from what is done for and through the law firm. Nonetheless, it is important to note that locating white-collar offenders in their ownership and authority positions in occupational and organizational structures is a key part of the class analysis of white-collar crime (Geis, 1984; Hagan and Parker, 1985; Weisburd et al., 1990). Sutherland's emphasis on "respect" and "status" in defining white-collar crime only begins to open up the issue of class position and the role it plays in any understanding of white-collar crime. A key element of social class is the power to commit major white-collar crimes that only ownership and authority positions in occupational and organizational structures can make possible.

However, as Sutherland recognized, the problem is not only one of our conception of white-collar offenders and their class positions, but also one of our conception of white-collar crime itself (cf. Shapiro, 1990). Sometimes our confused conceptions can seem mundane, so mundane that they pass unnoticed. For example, the *New York Times* published two stories in the same edition—one that warned and possibly discouraged its readers from "pirating" computer software (Lewis, 1989), and another that informed and likely encouraged its readers to acquire newly designed devices to copy audio tapes (Fantel, 1989). The contradiction probably was unnoticed, but the latter story nonetheless began with the mildly apologetic and perhaps not entirely facetious suggestion that

occupational crime

Refers to individuals who violate the law in the course of practising a legitimate occupation.

organizational or corporate crime

White-collar crime committed with the support and encouragement of a formal organization and intended at least in part to advance the goals of that organization.

"Get Tough on Corporate Crime"
Aaron Freeman and Craig Forcese
Democracy Watch On-line
www.web.net/dwatch/camp/ corpcr94.html

among the higher animals and human beings, larceny seems to be an innate trait held in check by social conditioning. But inhibitions fail, and the primal impulse asserts itself when it comes to tape recording. Even decent folk, who refrain from pocketing silver spoons, think nothing of taping copyrighted music. (Fantel, 1989, 27)

This confusion is even more prevalent today, when a company like Sony advertises equipment that enables people to download music videos while its entertainment division fights to stop this illegal behaviour.

Sutherland (1945) insisted that insofar as there exists a "legal description of acts as socially injurious and legal provision of a penalty for the act," such acts are, for the purposes of our research and understanding, crime (cf., Tappan, 1947). This is the case even though many such acts go undetected and unprosecuted. For example, many stock and securities frauds can be prosecuted under provincial securities legislation or under the Criminal Code of Canada. The former are considered "quasi-criminal" statutes. Yet the behaviours prosecuted under either body of law may be identical. It is an act of prosecutorial discretion that determines whether these behaviours are defined clearly and officially as crimes. Sutherland insisted that such acts of official discretion were not relevant to the categorization of these behaviours for the purposes of research. In either case, the behaviours were to be regarded as criminal. Such a position can make a major difference in the relationship observed between class and crime.

Consider the issue of deaths and accidents that result from events in the workplace. Occupational deaths far outnumber deaths resulting from murder. In Canada (Reasons et al., 1981), occupational deaths accounted for more than ten times as many deaths as murder. While it cannot be assumed that all or most of such deaths result from the intentions of employers to see employees die, there nonetheless is good reason to believe that the majority of such deaths are not simply the result of employee carelessness.

One estimate (Reasons et al., 1981) holds that more than one-third of all on-the-job injuries are due to illegal working conditions, and that about another quarter are due to legal but unsafe conditions. At most, one-third of all such accidents are attributed to unsafe acts on the part of employees. There are numerous well-documented examples of employers intentionally, knowingly, or negligently creating hazards. These include failing to follow administrative orders to alter dangerous situations and covering up the creation and existence of such hazards. The penalties for these offences are very light. For example, Reasons et al. discuss the case of Quasar Petroleum of Calgary, which was fined $15 000 for violating safety regulations when three men died while cleaning out a tank containing toxic fumes. The men were not provided with protective equipment nor were they trained to recognize the need for such equipment.

The case of asbestos poisoning involving administrative decisions within the Johns-Manville Corporation is but one of the best-known examples. Swartz (1978) notes that asbestos has been recognized as a serious health hazard since the turn of the century. Nonetheless, people working with it were not informed, and the government bureaucracy and the medical community ignored the hazard. At the Johns-Manville plant in Toronto, company doctors regularly diagnosed lung diseases among the asbestos workers, but they never told the workers that their lung problems were related to asbestos. Many of the workers subsequently died of asbestos-related illnesses. The construction industry also has high rates of death and injury because of failure to implement workplace health and safety regulations. For example, in two recent Manitoba cases one company was fined $75 000 because of the death of a bridge painter who was working on a platform with no guard rails, and another was fined $27 500 for its role in the death of a young worker who was electrocuted when he was allowed to work on a high-voltage light fixture while the wires were live (McIntyre, 2001). Swartz (1978) concludes that these deaths should be recognized as a form of murder, or what is sometimes called "corporate homicide." However, as with the Westray mine disaster (Box 16.1), corporate executives are almost never held personally responsible for their negligence.

This chapter does not attempt to debate the fine points in the definition of corporate homicide or to establish with any precision how many such homicides occur. It is enough to note that such deaths occur in considerable numbers and that while the consequences of these deaths have only been (briefly) considered for employees, corporate homicides also involve many additional numbers of consumers and the general public. Corporate homicides seem likely to rival in number or even exceed those deaths resulting from homicide conceived in more traditional terms. Of immediate interest here is the meaning of corporate homicide, and crimes like it, for the relationship between class and crime.

Social Class and Crime

To pursue this interest, a fundamental point must first be made about more conventional forms of crime and delinquency. There is increasing evidence that a relatively small number of offenders account for a rather large proportion of serious street crimes (Greenwood, 1982; Wolfgang, 1972). The difficulty of including such persons in conventional research designs has probably obscured the relationship that exists between class position and this type of criminality.

A parallel point may be true of many kinds of white-collar crime. For example, crimes such as corporate homicide may occur with high incidence but low prevalence among highly selected subpopulations—that is, among particular employers in particular kinds of industries. The mining and asbestos industries are examples that have already been noted. Again, it may be difficult to pinpoint such employers in conventional research designs, and this may obscure the relationship between class position and this type of criminality.

Implicit in the preceding references to street crimes and corporate homicide is the high likelihood that crime is not a unidimensional concept. That is, these are different kinds of crime that likely have different connections to the concept of class. Among adults, class probably is negatively related to making the direct physical attacks involved in street crimes of violence, and class probably is positively related to causing harms less directly through criminal acts involving the use of corporate resources. Similarly, among juveniles, it may be that some common acts of delinquency (for example, forms of theft that include the illegal copying of computer software and music and the unauthorized use of credit and bank cards) are related positively to class (Cullen et al.,

BOX 16.1

Westray—A Disaster of Criminal Proportions

"In the early morning of 9 May 1992 a violent explosion rocked the tiny community of Plymouth, just east of Stellarton, in Pictou County, Nova Scotia. The explosion occurred in the depths of the Westray coal mine, instantly killing the 26 miners working there at the time" (Richard, 1997, vii). These words begin the report of a judicial inquiry into the Westray mine explosion that tells a shocking story of corporate and government misconduct that resulted in one of the largest occupational disasters in Canadian history.

Glasbeek and Tucker (1994) point out that the Westray explosion was not an accident, but like other occupational health and safety damage was the result of conscious decisions by those responsible for the safety of the miners. This conclusion was reinforced by the title of Justice Richard's inquiry: *The Westray Story: A Predictable Path to Disaster.*

While the explosion was not an accident, nobody intended to kill the miners. Rather, their deaths were the result of "a complex mosaic of actions, omissions, mistakes, incompetence, apathy, cynicism, stupidity, and neglect" (Richard, 1997, viii). The inquiry concluded that Westray managers "displayed a certain disdain for safety and appeared to regard safety-conscious workers as the wimps in the organization" (Richard, 1997, ix).

The mine was built in an area that was known to be treacherous because of geological faults and high levels of methane gas. However, only minimal safety precautions were taken. The mine owners and governments were more concerned about the economics of mining than about protecting the workers. While there were safety standards that should have been maintained, the government relied on the company to meet these standards and provided very limited compliance inspections. The company, Curragh Corporation, was having financial difficulties and put pressure on Westray to increase production levels in order to increase company revenues. Safety violations were common and some miners quit; others stayed because of the lack of alternative employment in the province. The state of safety of the mine was eloquently summed up by Justice Richard:

> I find that the source of ignition was sparks struck by the cutting bits of the continuous miner working in the Southwest 2 section of the mine. But it became apparent as the Inquiry proceeded that conditions at Westray were of greater significance to what happened than was the source of the ignition. Had there been adequate ventilation, had there been adequate treatment of coal dust, and had there been adequate training and an appreciation by management for a safety ethic, those sparks would have faded harmlessly. (1997, 3)

Despite clear evidence of these violations, the government did not exercise its responsibility under the Mineral Resources Act and shut down the mine until it was safe.

Five employees of the Nova Scotia Natural Resources Department and the Department of Labour were fired for their role in the explosion, but nobody from the mining company will ever be held legally responsible for the Westray tragedy. Clifford Frame, president of Curragh Corporation, refused to testify at the inquiry and was never charged with any offence. Mine managers Gerald Philips and Roger Parry were charged with manslaughter and criminal negligence, but these charges were stayed by the Nova Scotia government on the grounds that a conviction was unlikely. This is but one of many cases that illustrate the inability of our laws to control corporate crime. The weakness of the current law was addressed by Justice Richard in recommendation 73 of his report:

> The government of Canada ... should institute a study of the accountability of corporate executives and directors for the wrongful or negligent acts of the corporation and should introduce in the

(continued)

Parliament of Canada such amendments to legislation as are necessary to ensure that corporate executives and directors are held properly accountable for workplace safety. (1997, 57)

To date, the government has shown no willingness to redress this long-standing weakness in our criminal law.

2002 Fraud and Misconduct Survey
KPMG
www.kpmg.ca/english/news/docs/ webfraudsurvey.pdf

1985; Hagan et al., 1985; Hagan and Kay, 1990), while less frequent and more serious forms of delinquency are negatively related to class (see Chapter 5). It has sometimes appeared that measures of status are not related to crime and delinquency at all (Tittle et al., 1978). However, the study of white-collar crime and delinquency provides increasing reason to believe that measures of class are connected to crime and delinquency in interesting, albeit complicated, ways.

WHITE-COLLAR CRIME AND THE SOCIAL ORGANIZATION OF WORK

Not all white-collar crimes are committed by white-collar persons. For example, much embezzlement is committed by relatively low-status bank tellers (Daly, 1989). However, if it is true that white-collar crime is positively related to class position, it is also reasonable to ask why it should be so. The answer may lie in the power derived from ownership and authority positions in the occupational and organizational structures of modern corporations. These positions of power carry with them a freedom from control that may be criminogenic. That is, to have power is to be free from the kinds of constraints that may normally inhibit crime. As will be seen, the modern corporation facilitates this kind of freedom with the presumed goal of enhancing free enterprise and the unintended consequence of encouraging crime.

Crime and the Corporation

It is recognized that the organizational form of the corporation is crucial to understanding most white-collar crime (Ermann and Lundman, 1982; Hagan, 1982; Reiss, 1980). As Wheeler and Rothman (1982) succinctly note, the corporation "is for white-collar criminals what the gun or knife is for the common criminal—a tool to obtain money from victims." Of course, the importance of the corporation is not restricted to the world of crime. From the Industrial Revolution on, it has become increasingly apparent that "among the variety of interests that men have, those interests that have been successfully collected to create corporate actors are the interests that dominate the society" (Coleman, 1974). This reference to men in particular is not accidental, for corporate entities are disproportionately male in employment, ownership, and control. Our interest is in developing an understanding of the link between the power of the corporate form and the criminogenic freedom that this powerful structure generates.

The corporation itself is a "legal fiction," with, as H.L. Mencken aptly observed, "no pants to kick or soul to damn." That is, the law chooses to treat corporations as "**juristic persons**," making them formally liable to the same laws as "natural persons." Some of the most obvious faults in this legal analogy become clear when the impossibility of imprisoning or executing corporations is considered. However, there are more subtle differences between corporate and individual actors with equally significant consequences.

For example, the old legal saw tells us that the corporation has no conscience or soul. Stone (1975) describes the problem well:

> When individuals are placed in an organizational structure, some of the ordinary internalized restraints seem to lose their hold. And if we decide to look beyond the individual employees and find an organizational "mind" to work with, a "corporate conscience" distinct from the consciences of particular individuals, it is not readily apparent where we would begin—much less what we would be talking about.

Stone goes on to suggest some interesting ways in which the corporate conscience and corporate responsibility could be increased (see also Nagorski, 1989). However, the point is that these mechanisms, or others, have not been put in place. Corporate power in this sense remains unchecked, and it is in this sense criminogenic.

The problem is in part the absence of cultural beliefs to discourage corporate criminality (Geis, 1962). C. Wright Mills (1956) captured part of the problem in his observation that "it is better, so the image runs, to take one dime from each of ten million people at the point of a corporation than $100,000 from each of ten banks at the point of a gun." Nonetheless, there is some evidence that cultural climates vary across time and regimes. For example, Sally Simpson (1986), who studied antitrust violations in the United States between 1927 and 1981, found that such violations were more common during Republican than Democratic administrations. However, even when condemnatory beliefs about corporate crime have been strong, there have been too few controlling mechanisms in place to impose their controlling influence effectively.

Consider, for a moment, the internal structure of a typical modern corporation, as illustrated by Woodmansee's description of the General Electric Corporation (cited in Clinard and Yeager, 1980; see also Shearing et al., 1985). Note the complexity of this enterprise and its gender stratification:

> We begin by describing the way GE's employees are officially organized into separate layers of authority. The corporation is like a pyramid. The great majority of the company's workers form the base of the pyramid; they take orders coming down from above but do not give orders to anyone else. If you were hired by GE for one of these lowest level positions, you might find yourself working on an assembly line, installing a motor in a certain type of refrigerator. You would be in a group of five to 50 workers who all take orders from one supervisor, or foreman, or manager. Your supervisor is on the second step of the pyramid; she or he, and the other supervisors who specialize in this type of refrigerator, all take orders from a General Manager.

juristic person
The legal concept that corporations are liable to the same laws as natural persons. Treating corporations as individuals raises practical difficulties for legal enforcement and punishment.

There are about 180 of these General Managers at GE; each one heads a Department with one or two thousand employees. The General Manager of your Department, and the General Managers of the one or two other Departments which produce GE's other types of refrigerators, are in turn supervised by the Vice President/General Manager of the Refrigerator Division. This man (there are only men at this level and above) is one of the 50 men at GE responsible for heading GE's Divisions. He, and the heads of several other Divisions which produce major appliances, look up to the next step of the pyramid and see, towering above, the Vice President/Group Executive who heads the entire Major Appliance Group. While there are over 300,000 workers at the base of the pyramid, there are only ten men on this Group Executive level. Responsibility for overseeing all of GE's product lines is divided between the ten. At about the same level of authority in the company are the executives of GE's Corporate Staff; these men are concerned not with particular products but with general corporate matters such as accounting, planning, legal affairs, and relations with employees, with the public and with governments.

And now the four men at the top of the pyramid come into view; the three Vice Chairmen of the Board of Directors, and standing above them, GE's Chief Executive.... Usually, these four men confer alone, but once a month, 15 other men join them for a meeting. The 15 other members of the Board of Directors are not called up from the lower levels of the GE pyramid; they drift in sideways from the heights of neighboring pyramids. Thirteen of them are chairmen or presidents of other corporations, the fourteenth is a former corporate chairman, and the fifteenth is a university president. (Clinard and Yeager, 1980, 457–58)

Could the board of directors of the above corporation exercise the kind of control over its employees that individual actors are expected by law to exercise, for example, over their dependants? Stone (1975) points out that top officers and directors, theoretically, are liable to suit by the corporation itself (via a shareholders' action) if they allow a law violation to occur through negligence. However, the courts have not imposed a duty on directors to uncover corporate wrongdoing. This provides an incentive for senior managers and directors to remain uninformed about illegal activities.

Canadian law in this area will be tested in the case of YBM Magnex (see Box 15.4), a company that ostensibly sold a variety of products including industrial magnets and bicycles, primarily to Eastern European markets. Starting its Canadian life as a shell corporation on the Alberta Stock Exchange, YBM Magnex stock rose in value from 85 cents to $20 in less than three years. It was included as one of the stocks used in the prestigious Toronto Stock Exchange 300 index and had a total share value of about $1 billion. Several eminent Canadians served on its board of directors, including former Ontario premier David Peterson and First Marathon Securities vice-president Robert Mitchell. However, despite this face of respectability, the company had a very shady background. The company was controlled by Semion Mogilevich, one of Russia's most powerful organized criminals (Howlett, 2002). YBM Magnex had been investigated in Britain for a variety of offences, including money laundering. In Canada, the RCMP had been investigating the company since it was established in 1995 (Rubin, 1999). Stockholders' investments disappeared in May 1998 when the Ontario Securities Commission stopped trading in the company. Auditors had refused to accept the company's financial statements, and U.S. law enforcement officials had raided the company's Pennsylvania headquarters investigating charges of fraud and money laundering. Directors and auditors of the company are now being sued for $635 million and charged by the Ontario Securities Commission with withholding information from the public concerning the fact that the company was under investigation for its ties to organized crime. The results of this legal action should help clarify the responsibility of directors under Canadian law, but as of June 2003 the case had not yet been resolved.

How widespread is the use of "executive influence from afar" and "executive distancing and disengagement" in corporate criminality? Two intriguing studies (Baumhart, 1961; Brenner and Molander, 1977) suggest that the problem is large. The latter of these studies reports that the percentage of executives who indicate an inability to be honest in providing information to top management has nearly doubled since the earlier research, done in the 1950s. About half of those surveyed thought that their superiors frequently did not wish to know how results were obtained as long as the desired outcome was accomplished. Furthermore, the executives surveyed "frequently complained of superiors' pressure to support incorrect viewpoints, sign false documents, overlook superiors' wrongdoing, and do business with superiors' friends" (Brenner and Molander, 1977).

The recent bankruptcy of Britain's Barings Bank provides another example of **executive disengagement**. Barings Bank, which had been controlled by the same family since 1762, was brought down by the actions of a 28-year-old trader in their Singapore office. Nicholas Leeson lost almost $1 billion of the company's money on financial derivatives, which were essentially bets on the future performance of the Tokyo stock market. When the Tokyo market fell, Barings collapsed when it could not cover the losses. The size of this gamble was in violation of British banking laws. While bank officials were quick to blame Leeson for the entire affair, it is highly unlikely that senior bank officials did not at least tacitly approve of Leeson's trading activities. Several financial experts have suggested that the profits Leeson had previously made for Barings led bank officials to allow him to risk their shareholders' money by making illegal trades (Drohan, 1995).

The Criminogenic Market Structure

Corporate crime research suggests not only a growing freedom at the top of organizations from the need to know and accept responsibility for criminal activity below, but also a growing pressure from the top down that is itself criminogenic. Farberman (1975) has referred to such pressures in the automotive industry and in other highly concentrated corporate sectors as constituting a "**criminogenic market structure**." The crime-generating feature of these markets is their domination by a relatively small number of manufacturers who insist that their dealers sell in high volume at a small per-unit profit.

executive disengagement

The custom by which lower-level employees assume that executives are best left uninformed of certain decisions and actions of employees, or the assumption that executives cannot be legally expected to have complete control over their individual staff.

criminogenic market structure

An economic market that is structured in such a way that it tends to produce criminal behaviour.

Dealerships that fail to perform risk the loss of their franchises in an industry in which the alternatives are few. A result is high pressure to maximize sales and minimize service. More specifically, Farberman suggests that dealers in the car industry may be induced by the small profit margins on new cars to compensate through fraudulent warranty work and repair rackets. The connection between these findings is that the executives of the automotive industry can distance themselves from the criminal consequences of the "forcing model" (high volume/low per-unit profit) they impose. The result is an absence of control over repair and warranty frauds at the dealership level.

Farberman also points out that corporate concentration can be criminogenic in that it diminishes the corrective role competition can play in restraining criminal practices that increase the costs of production. Asch and Seneca (1969) conclude from their research that high concentration is in particular related to higher rates of crime in consumer-goods industries. This receives further support from Clinard and Yeager's (1980) finding that the oil, auto, and pharmaceutical industries appear to violate the law more frequently than do other industries. Particular types of crime, such as collusion and antitrust activity, may also be more common in highly concentrated industries (Coleman, 1987).

The scale of the crimes that access to corporate resources makes possible will now be considered. In an intriguing study, Wheeler and Rothman (1982) categorized white-collar offenders into three groups: those who committed offences alone or with affiliated others using neither an occupational nor an organizational role (individual offenders); those who committed offences alone or with affiliated others using an occupational role (occupational offenders); and those who committed offences in which both organization and occupation were ingredients (organizational offenders). The results of this study indicate in a variety of ways the enormous advantages accruing to those who use formal organizations in their crimes. For example, across a subset of four offences, the median "take" for individual offenders was $5279, for occupational offenders $17 106, and for organizational offenders $117 392. In a parallel Canadian study, Hagan and Parker (1985) reported that securities violators who make use of organizational resources commit crimes that involve larger numbers of victims and are broader in their geopolitical spread. Why the organizational edge? Wheeler and Rothman (1982) answer with an example:

> Represented by its president, a corporation entered into a factoring agreement with a leading ... commercial bank, presenting it with $1.2 million in false billings over the course of seven months; the company's statements were either inflated to reflect much more business than actually was being done, or were simply made up. Would the bank have done this for an individual? Whether we conclude that organizations are trusted more than individuals, or that they simply operate on a much larger scale, it is clear that the havoc caused when organizations are used outside the law far exceeds anything produced by unaffiliated actors.

Just as the organizational form has facilitated economic and technological development on a scale far beyond that achieved by individuals, so too has this

Criminal Misconduct: Alan Eagleson's Abuse of Power

In recent years, sentences of imprisonment have become more likely for high-status offenders. For example, Alan Eagleson, former head of the National Hockey League Players' Association, received an 18-month jail sentence after pleading guilty to multiple fraud offences. Eagleson was released on day parole after serving four months of his sentence and was on full parole after six months. Eagleson was also removed from the Order of Canada, thrown out of the Hockey Hall of Fame, and disbarred by the Law Society of Upper Canada. Some of Eagleson's offences are described by Jim Silver in a review of a book by Russ Conway, a U.S. journalist whose investigative work convinced the police to take on the case:

Russ Conway is a practitioner of the art, too little seen in Canada and especially among sportswriters, of muck-raking investigative journalism. And there's so much Eagleson muck to be raked. Eagleson wore at least four different hats while President of the National Hockey League Players Association [NHLPA]: union president, player agent, international hockey impresario, and close friend of NHL owners and management. As one former player said: "He wears so many hats I think even he gets screwed up sometimes."

Players complained about him for years, but Eagleson bullied and embarrassed any player with the temerity to ask questions about his conduct of union affairs, and put his own hand-picked, non-elected, yes-men on the union executive.

Disability Scams

[Eagleson's conduct] was criminal. For example, Eagleson ripped off players who suffered career-ending injuries.

The Jim Harrison case is revealing. Harrison's back was shot. He could scarcely walk, much less play. The Black Hawks jerked him around. He filed a grievance through Eagleson, head of the NHLPA and Harrison's agent. But Eagleson was also the agent for Chicago coach and general manager and long-time pal Bob Pulford, and Pulford was employed by Eagleson's yachting companion and Florida neighbour, Black Hawk owner Bill Wirtz. The grievance, as per the collective agreement negotiated by Eagleson, was heard by another pal, NHL President John Zeigler, "whose salary was paid by Wirtz and the other owners." The deck was stacked. Eagleson "cut a private deal with Pulford to the benefit of the Blackhawks and the detriment of his client." So much for Jim Harrison.

In another instance Eagleson convinced injured Boston Bruin player Mike Gillis to pay him, Eagleson, 15 percent of whatever was received from Gillis' disability insurance. Securing the claim, Eagleson intoned, would be tough. Yet Conway reveals that the meeting at which this deal was struck occurred *after* Eagleson had already been notified by the insurer that Gillis' claim had been approved. Eagleson was paid $41,250 for that scam.

Bobby Orr

The Bobby Orr story is also revealing. It was as agent of the great Boston defenceman that Eagleson first came to prominence, and he used his relationship with Orr to build a huge stable of players for whom he acted as agent. In 1976 Eagleson negotiated Orr's sale to Chicago, to Eagleson's close pal Bill Wirtz, even though Orr did not want to leave the Boston Bruins and Boston tried desperately to hold him. Boston even offered Orr an 18.5 percent ownership stake in the franchise—worth $16 million US by 1994. Eagleson never informed Orr of this offer, but instead lied to Orr that Boston did not want him. What kind of financial gain Eagleson made from this deal Conway does not know, though it likely was substantial. Orr clearly was the loser. When in 1980 he finally severed his ties with Eagleson, his agent and financial manager, Orr was effectively bankrupt—his taxes and legal and accounting bills exceeded his assets.

(continued)

Pension Scams

NHL veterans have been financially hurt by the pension scams and Conway brings the story up to the present. NHL pensions have been the worst in major professional sport. Eagleson touted himself as the savior of the players' pension plan. Money earned from international hockey tournaments organized by Eagleson was, the players and the public were repeatedly told, to go to the NHL players' pension fund, when in fact it appears those earnings were used merely to reduce the NHL's contribution. The owners benefited, not the players. Similarly, surpluses in the fund were being used to reduce the owners' contribution, with Eagleson's approval.

Lining His Pockets

As Conway reveals, this wasn't the half of it. Not only were profits from international hockey benefiting owners, rather than players, but also Eagleson himself was lining his pockets. He and his family and his associates and his companies apparently made millions in contracts associated with the tournaments, while "the Eagle" ran a sophisticated scheme involving the sale of rink-board advertising, hundreds of thousands of dollars in proceeds which he apparently salted away in Swiss bank accounts. All the while Eagleson was insisting to players and the public that he never earned a cent from international hockey.

Source: Jim Silver. (1996). "Review of Game Misconduct: Alan Eagleson and the Corruption of Hockey." *Canadian Dimension* 30 (4) (July–August).

form allowed criminal gains of a magnitude that men and women acting alone would fine hard to attain.

The structure of the modern corporation allows a power imbalance to prevail in which those individuals at the top experience a relative freedom, while those at the bottom often experience pressure applied from the top that encourages various kinds of white-collar crime. The point has also been made that the corporate form itself can be used effectively to perpetrate "bigger and better crimes" than can be achieved by individuals acting alone. Access to these corporate resources is a unique advantage of class positions involving ownership and authority in business organizations. It is in this sense that it can be said that in the world of the modern corporation, the social organization of work itself is criminogenic.

America's Accounting Scandals

While corporate crime has always been a major problem in the United States, the new millennium saw scandals that shocked even the most avid supporters of free enterprise. Several of America's largest corporations, including energy company Enron and the telecommunications company WorldCom, went bankrupt, stock markets crashed, and one of the world's largest accounting companies was forced out of business. What caused what one observer has called a "scandalous rot" (DeCloet, 2002)?

While each of the bankrupt companies had different problems, an overall explanation might start with the way in which corporate executives are paid. Many companies provide their senior executives with stock options that allow the executive to purchase shares in his or her company at a later date for a price that is guaranteed at the time the options are issued. This means that if the stock goes up in the future, the executive can buy it at the guaranteed price and keep the difference between the issue price and the value of the stock at the time it is purchased. If the stock goes down, the executive will not have to use the option, so will not lose money. The intent of stock options is to provide executives with an incentive to work hard and raise the company's value. This will ensure that the company's shareholders benefit from the company's growth.

While some executives took a long-term perspective and worked to build up the value of their companies, other executives took a short-term approach that proved disastrous for their shareholders. They used a variety of short-term measures to raise the stock price so they could make enormous profits on their stock options very quickly. For example, "Chainsaw Al" Dunlap (named for his willingness to reduce costs by firing employees) was the chief executive officer (CEO) of the household appliance company Sunbeam. Dunlap's aggressive methods included artificially inflating sales figures so the company's profits appeared higher than they actually were. Sunbeam eventually went bankrupt and Dunlap was fired and fined $15 million, which was only a share of the illegal gains he made from Sunbeam stock.

Dunlap was the not the last CEO of a major company to run into trouble because of his pursuit of millions of dollars. During the late 1990s, the stock market rose dramatically and CEOs became corporate superstars. Many paid themselves enormous sums of money, and pay levels for CEOs of large companies reached $50 to $100 million per year. This star system convinced executives that they deserved these high levels of pay even when their companies were losing money. The greed of senior executives led directly to two of the largest bankruptcies in American history: Enron and WorldCom.

The Collapse of Enron

How did those responsible for Enron cost their investors $63 billion? Enron was once a pipeline company that delivered natural gas. This business was very profitable, but to CEO Kenneth Lay and his senior executives it was a boring business that did not have the potential for quick growth in profits. They developed a business model that involved trading futures contracts that are essentially bets on the future prices of commodities such as natural gas, electricity, and pulp and paper. Initially, this new focus proved very profitable and the value of the stock climbed quickly until Enron was the seventh-largest company in the United States. Senior executives promised investors that the good times would continue. However, the company moved into riskier areas and at some stage the new business model broke down. To keep the company growing, Enron executives began to use illegal financial measures to make it appear as though profits were continuing to increase. Some of these complex measures involved the company selling its own assets to itself and showing the "profits" from this sale in its revenues. The company also tried to hide its debts by transferring them to outside "partnerships" that had been established by Enron.

Enron developed what can only be described as a culture of greed. Many senior Enron employees acted like children in a candy store and took massive personal profits from the financial schemes organized by the company. For example, several finance department employees invested $125 000 of their own funds in one of Enron's illegal financial transactions and made $30 million in only a few months (Butler, 2002). Executives were not content with the millions of dollars they had taken from the company. As the illegal schemes began to unravel and the company began to slide into bankruptcy, Enron paid $681 million to 140 top executives, including $67 million to CEO Kenneth Lay, who continued to encourage employees and members of the public to buy Enron stock even as he and his executives stripped the company of much of its remaining capital (Kranhold and Pacelle, 2002). Ultimately, creditors, stockholders, and other Enron employees suffered the loss of this money when the financial arrangements fell apart.

While Enron executives must take most of the blame for the company's demise, they had help from the managers of other large corporations. The Arthur Andersen accounting firm, one of the world's largest, allowed Enron's many lapses of legal and ethical standards to slip by its auditors in order to help it obtain lucrative consulting contracts with Enron. Many of Wall Street's largest banks and brokerage firms collaborated with Enron in order to profit from stock commissions, consulting contracts, and interest from loans.

WorldCom

The Enron debacle was quickly followed by an even larger bankruptcy. The failure of WorldCom, the largest long-distance telephone service provider in the United States, cost investors a massive $175 billion, as its share value dropped from $64.50 a share to only 83 cents (Kadlec, 2002). WorldCom, led by CEO Bernard Ebbers, a former Edmonton milkman, admitted it overstated earnings by $3.8 billion over a period of 15 months. That is, the company reported earning $3.8 billion more than it actually made. While the Enron fraud was very complex, WorldCom used a simple method of inflating its non-existent profits. It simply treated its everyday expenses (mainly payments to local phone companies for using their services to complete calls) as capital investments that could be written off over a period of several years. This made its profits look higher than they really were because it did not have to deduct these expenses from the money it took in from its customers. This would be like you pretending that you are paying your tuition over a period of four years instead of in the current academic year. This pretence could make your accounts look better than they really are, but eventually you are going to have to account for the missing money. In the case of WorldCom, that revelation led to a collapse in the company's stock.

A final footnote in this ongoing story is that Arthur Andersen, the global company that was responsible for auditing Enron, WorldCom, and several other companies accused of misleading accounting, was found guilty of a felony count of obstructing the Securities and Exchange Commission's investigation into Enron. Several Andersen employees had shredded documents and tried to persuade others to cover up the scandal. Following the verdict, the company announced that it was going out of business. It was victim of a corporate culture in which generating revenue for the company became a greater concern than protecting the public by doing its job competently.

WHITE-COLLAR CRIME AND LEGAL SANCTIONS

Given the distribution of freedom and pressure that has been identified within the structure of the modern corporation and the power this gives to those who run it, the question that recurs is: What does the law do to remedy the potential for abuse? This question raises issues of legal liability and the enforcement of law.

"We have arranged things," writes Christopher Stone (1975), "so that the people who call the shots do not have to bear the full risks." This, in a nutshell, is the consequence of the limited liabilities borne by modern corporate actors:

> Take, for example, a small corporation involved in shipping dynamite. The shareholders of such a company, who are typically also the managers, do not *want* their dynamite-laden truck to blow up. But if it does, they know that those injured cannot, except in rare cases, sue them as individuals to recover their full damages if the amount left in the corporations' bank account is inadequate to make full compensation.... What this means is that in deciding how much money to spend on safety devices, and whether or not to allow trucks to drive through major cities, the calculations are skewed toward higher risks than suggested by the "rational economic corporation/free market" model that is dreamily put forth in textbooks. If no accident results, the shareholders will reap the profits of skimping on safety measures. If a truck blows up, the underlying human interests will be shielded from fully bearing the harm that they have caused. And then, there is nothing to prevent the same men from setting up a new dynamite shipping corporation the next day; all it takes is the imagination to think up a new name, and some $50 in filing fees. (462–63)

It may be conceded that large corporations are not quite so free as the small corporation in the example to dissolve and reconstitute their operations. However, the separation of shareholder and management interests gives rise to a related problem of liability. Given that corporate officers gain their primary rewards through salaries, the effects of damage judgements are indirect and, judging from experience, limited.

These discussions raise the broader issue of how and why the law is used to control white-collar crime. It has already been seen that civil remedies are not very effective. We turn now to criminal sanctions. How does the state decide what kinds of upper-world indiscretions will be called criminal? The most interesting work that has been done on this issue in Canada involves the development of anticombines legislation. Given the powerful economic interests involved in forming the **monopolistic enterprises** this legislation presumably seeks to prevent, one might wonder how an **anticombines law** was ever passed in the first place. Goff and Reasons (1978) indicate that the initiative for the original legislation in 1899 "came not from the general populace but from small businessmen, who felt their firms were at the mercy of big business interests." However, more recently Smandych (1985) has noted that a "Royal Commission on Labour and Capital" created for the purpose of investigating industrial

monopolistic enterprise

Any corporation that controls all, or the majority, of the market for a particular product or service.

anticombines law

In order to protect the principle of competition, valued by all liberal, capitalistic societies, laws have been created to prevent and punish corporations that work together to reduce competition.

conditions in Canada interviewed and recorded testimony from numerous trade-union representatives and workers. This testimony, cited in the report of the commission in 1899, specifically sought legislation against monopolistic practices, and Smandych argues that "the possibility that worker demands for the elimination of combines went unnoticed by the government of the day is extremely doubtful."

Smandych goes on to conclude that "the first flourishing of Canadian anti-combines legislation was the product of an essential confrontation between labour and capital, and of the state's effort to find an acceptable solution." None of this is to say, as later noted, that this legislation was strong or effective. Quite the contrary, as Snider (1979) observes. Efforts over the years to strengthen the legislation with "proconsumer and procompetition" amendments regularly "were weakened or eliminated in the face of business opposition." Smandych, Snider, Goff, and Reasons are all agreed that this legislation has done less than it promised to reduce monopolistic practices and to punish those who promote them. In fact, many have argued that the laws are almost totally ineffective. Prosecutions are rarely successful, and when they are, the fines are so low that they do not act as an effective deterrent to anticompetitive behaviour. Not surprisingly, business has lobbied very strongly against changes to combines legislation.

Steven Box (1981) has noted another way in which the law favours corporate offenders:

> Some people benefit more than others from these laws.... By the criminal law's constructing *particular* definitions of murder, rape, robbery and assault other acts, which are in many ways very similar, are excluded, and these are just the acts more likely to be committed by more powerful individuals. Thus the criminal law defines only some types of killing as murder: it excludes, for example, deaths which result from acts of negligence such as employers' failure to maintain safe working conditions in factories and mines.... The criminal law includes only some types of property deprivation as robbery: it excludes, for example, the separation of consumers from part of their money that follows manufacturers' malpractices or advertisers' misrepresentations.... The criminal law defines only some types of violence as criminal assault: it excludes those forms of assault ... resulting from working in a polluted factory environment where the health risk was known to the employer but concealed from the employee. (48–49)

But what of the white-collar offenders who are held criminally liable and processed through the criminal justice system? Are they liable to as severe sanctioning as individual actors? Notions of "equality before the law" are perhaps nowhere more subjective in meaning than in their application to the sentencing of white-collar offenders (Hagan and Albonetti, 1982). This is reflected in at least two kinds of comments made by judges about the sentences they impose for white-collar crimes. It is reflected first in the suggestion that white-collar offenders experience sanctions in a different way from other kinds of offenders, and second in the assertion that different kinds of sanctions are appropriate in white-collar cases.

The view, common among judges, that white-collar offenders experience sanctions differently is well summarized in Mann et al.'s (1980) conclusions after interviewing a sample of judges who have tried such cases: "Most judges have a widespread belief that the suffering experienced by a white-collar person as a result of apprehension, public indictment and conviction, and the collateral disabilities incident to conviction—loss of job, professional licenses, and status in the community—completely satisfies the need to punish the individual." This belief persists in the face of findings from a recent study by Benson (1989, 474) that "although they commit the most serious offences, employers and managers are least likely to lose their jobs after conviction for a white-collar crime." The argument for white-collar leniency endures in the minds of judges and others: the defendant, having suffered enough from the acts of prosecution and conviction, does not require a severe sentence. However, the sentence must still provide a deterrent. Mann et al. (1980) conclude that most judges seek a compromise in resolving this dilemma. "The weekend sentence, the very short jail term, and the relatively frequent use of amended sentences (where a judge imposes a prison term and later reduces it) are evidence of this search for a compromise."

It is important to acknowledge the disputed role of fines in sentencing white-collar offenders. Posner (1980) asserts that "the white-collar criminal ... should be punished only by monetary penalties." His argument is that if fines are suitably large, they are an equally effective deterrent and cheaper to administer, and therefore socially preferable to imprisonment and other afflictive punishments. It has already been noted that corporate entities are liable to little else than fines. However, Mann et al. (1980) find judges to be sceptical of the effectiveness of fines. They report

> a conspicuous absence of responses by judges that a fine was the appropriate sanction to be imposed on a defendant.... Where fines were used in conjunction with another sentence it was generally the other sentence ... that was thought to have the intended deterrent effect. Where the fine was used alone, the idea that the commencement of the criminal process against the defendant was the punishment seemed to be more important in the judges' minds than the fine itself.

The sense that emerges is that judges are acutely aware of the issues of deterrence, disparity, and discrimination in the sentencing of white-collar offenders, and that they attempt to respond to these issues by fashioning sentences that combine sanctions in a compromise fashion. Consistent with this view, Hagan and Nagel (1982) found, in a sentencing study covering the period from 1963 to 1976 in the Southern District of New York, that judges attempted to compensate for the shorter prison terms given to white-collar offenders by adding probation or fines to their sentences. Similarly, fines were most frequently used in conjunction with prison and probation sentences. In any case, all these findings suggest that white-collar offenders are advantaged by the specific types and combination of legal sanctions that are imposed on them.

However, both in Canada and the United States, there is some evidence that the mid-1970s brought a new and somewhat harsher attitude toward white-collar crime. Katz (1980) speaks of a "social movement against white-collar crime" that began in the United States in the late 1960s, and the evolution of public opinion documents an increasing concern with the occurrence of such crimes (Cullen et al., 1982; Schrager and Short, 1978). This new concern seems at least in part to have been a response to incidents such as the American experience with Watergate and the Canadian experience with Harbourgate. It was illustrated by the "proactive" prosecutorial policies of several U.S. attorneys (Hagan and Nagel, 1982) and in the increased prosecution of large-scale securities violations in Ontario (Hagan and Parker, 1985). In 1987 the Canadian government replaced the Environmental Contaminants Act with new legislation that provides for fines of up to $1 million per day and jail terms of up to five years for guilty executives. Further, the government of Ontario has increased the fine for insider trading of securities from $25 000 to $1 million, and it has increased the possible jail term from one to two years.

So, there *appears* to be a move toward tougher legal sanctions for white-collar offences. Of course, charges must be laid before sanctions can be imposed, and the power of corporations and of persons in high social-class positions makes the decision to prosecute problematic (see Benson et al., 1988). Wheeler et al. (1982) have sought to demonstrate that policies like those described above have led to the more severe sentencing of high-status white-collar offenders. Hagan and Palloni (1983) concur in reporting an increased use of imprisonment with white-collar offenders after Watergate, but they also indicate that the length of these prison sentences was unusually short. The Canadian study of the enforcement of securities laws in Ontario (Hagan and Parker, 1985) reveals a similar pattern of trade-offs in the severity with which white-collar offenders are treated. Overall, treatment of white-collar offenders seems to have been lenient in the past, and despite some examples of harsher sentences, there is no unambiguous evidence that this situation has changed markedly. Even where white-collar offenders have received prison sentences, they typically obtain parole very early in their terms.

There is a possibility that the massive losses due to the failures of companies such as Enron and WorldCom will lead to harsher treatment of corporate criminals. These crimes led to a serious loss of confidence in the stock market— why would someone want to invest money in companies whose earnings reports could not be trusted? This had a major impact on the economy as investors moved their money out of the stock market. The scandals were so pervasive that it became obvious that major changes were needed in regulation and corporate governance, and governments in the United States have become more involved in regulating corporations and making their laws tougher. They have also put more resources into investigating and prosecuting corporate crime. Many senior executives have been publicly arrested and taken into custody in front of the media in so-called "perp walks," designed to show the public that politicians have acted. Several of the lower-level executives charged in these scandals have received jail sentences, but none of the higher level officials had come to trial by the summer of 2003.

Even if sanctions are becoming tougher, governments have helped to create an environment conducive to white-collar crime through weak legislation and lax enforcement. You have already seen how Canada's ineffective competitions legislation has allowed anticompetitive business practices to flourish. An even more dramatic example is the wave of failures in the savings and loan business in the United States. A major reason for these failures was the strong belief of President Reagan and his officials that free enterprise worked best if business was left alone by government. Accordingly, they dismantled many of the agencies and regulations that controlled the industry. This move was, of course, strongly encouraged by businesspeople who ultimately benefited by the government's mistake. The result was a wave of criminal activity in the savings and loan industry. According to the government's General Accounting Office, bailing out these institutions will ultimately cost the American taxpayer between $325 and $500 billion (Pontell and Calavita, 1993). Although not all the losses were due to criminal activity, crime was a major contributor to these massive financial failures. Similarly, regulatory failures were partly responsible for the billions of dollars lost to corporate crime in the late 1990s and early 2000s.

OCCUPATIONAL CRIME

In the rest of this chapter you will learn about crimes that are committed by individuals who violate the law in the course of practising a legitimate occupation. As with corporate crime, at the heart of much occupational crime is a violation of positions of trust (Shapiro, 1990).

Unprofessional Conduct and Malpractice

Historically we have known little about unprofessional conduct and malpractice among groups such as lawyers and doctors because most of it has been dealt with privately by the governing bodies of professional associations. However, in recent years society has become less tolerant of professional deviance. Complainants have become more vocal and more violations have come to the attention of the public. Governments have also been more willing to prosecute in cases that involve violations of the criminal law.

Every occupation includes people who are willing to violate legal or ethical codes for their own benefit. However, the problem is made worse when those responsible for regulating the conduct of individual practitioners fail to do their job. The examples of sexual abuse by members of the clergy and malpractice by doctors illustrate how the failure by church and medical authorities to respond to complaints against members of their professions has led to much greater harm being done.

Perhaps the most widely publicized cases of unprofessional conduct over the past decade have involved sexual abuse by members of the clergy. In Canada, the Anglican Church has been named as a co-defendant in over 1200 complaints from former students of Indian residential schools, and several Catholic priests have been convicted of sexual assault charges in which the victims were former residential school students. Aboriginal children who attended residential schools have not been the only victims of abuse. The first major case to come to the attention of the Canadian public involved the Mount Cashel Orphanage in St. John's, Newfoundland, which was run by members of the Christian Brothers order. Abuse at the orphanage was hidden for many years. In 1975 a police investigation heard testimony such as this statement from a former resident:

> I am 11 years old.... I have been at Mount Cashel Orphanage for about five years. I am happy at the orphanage except for Brother Burke, Brother Ralph and Brother English. I don't like Brother Burke because he beats me across my bare backside with a stick about three days ago Brother Burke took me into a closet and made me pull down my pants he hit me five or six times across my backside with a stick. He beat me because I threw a after shave tin into the garbage and it made a noise and Brother Burke was watching T.V. Both Brother Ralph and Brother English on seven or eight times have caught a hold of me and have felt my legs and felt my bird. Sometimes this has happened when I have been in bed. Brother Ralph would sit down on the bed and feel my bird inside my pyjama pants. Most times Brother English would feel my bird when I was in the dining Hall he would do it sometimes when I was in bed. (Law Commission of Canada, 2000, 28)

While the police who conducted this investigation recommended laying charges against members of the Christian Brothers, the chief of the Royal Newfoundland Constabulary ordered them to change the report and refused to allow charges. As a result, no further action was taken until a Royal Commission was established in 1989 following a series of public complaints from former residents of the orphanage. The commission found that senior Catholic Church officials who knew about the abuse covered up accusations of sexual and physical abuse. The commission also concluded that the police chief and a provincial deputy minister also covered up the abuse. Following the Royal Commission, 15 members of the Christian Brothers were charged and both the Newfoundland government and the Christian Brothers order have been forced to make multimillion-dollar payments to abuse victims.

The failure of church officials in Newfoundland to deal with abusive clergy is by no means unique. Former Boston Cardinal Bernard Law resigned his post in 2002 after facing criticism that he had failed to act in many cases of sexual misconduct by priests. Not only did he fail to take action, but he covered up many instances of misconduct and reassigned several priests who had been accused of abusing children to positions where they would continue to work with children. A number of these priests reoffended, including Father John Geoghan, who has been accused of fondling or raping 150 children. Geoghan received a sentence of nine to ten years for one case, and by 2002 the Catholic Church had paid out over $10 million in settlements with 86 victims. Geoghan had been moved to a number of parishes in the Boston area in response to complaints, but the Church otherwise took no action until after the case had received wide publicity.

Medical doctors have been accused of sexual misconduct with patients as well as other violations, ranging from false billing to ethical lapses in the treatment of patients. Perhaps the most serious violations by doctors involve mal-

Survivors Network of Those
Abused by Priests
www.survivorsnetwork.org

practice. Most doctors are competent professionals, but accusations of mal-practice are not uncommon. For example, in 2001, patients began 1308 legal actions against physicians, although typically only about one-third of these actions are successful (Canadian Medical Protective Association, 2002). Examples of cases that have resulted in action against doctors include one Manitoba doctor who was sanctioned for sewing beads into the stitches of an Aboriginal woman, and an American doctor who was convicted of assault for carving his initials into a patient (Henderson, 2000). In one rather bizarre case, a South Carolina doctor was fined and reprimanded for using an amputated foot as bait in his crab trap (*Vancouver Sun*, 2000).

One tragic case of malpractice involved a Winnipeg surgeon who special-ized in pediatric cardiac surgery. In 1994, 12 young children died while under-going surgery at the Health Sciences Centre. A judicial inquiry into the case found that at least five of the deaths were probably preventable (Sinclair, 2000). The inquiry determined that the surgeon was at fault; but so was the hospital, which failed to ensure that the surgeon was qualified, and so were his supervi-sors, who failed to take action even when there were complaints about his per-formance. Part of the problem in this case was a culture of secrecy surrounding the work of the doctor. Parents had great difficulty getting any information about the pediatric cardiac surgery program, and nurses who complained about the program were ignored. While no charges were laid as a result of this inquiry, the doctor is no longer doing cardiac surgery and Manitoba now sends pediatric cardiac cases to Alberta, where the surgical failure rate is extremely low.

The failure by professional licensing and regulatory bodies to hold their members accountable has seriously harmed clients and patients. For example, gynaecologist and obstetrician Dr. Richard Neale lost his surgical privileges in British Columbia after a series of complaints. However, rather than being removed from the profession, he was allowed to retrain for six months and then to return to his surgical duties. In 1981 an Ontario patient died as a result of Dr. Neale's incompetence, but he continued to operate and to injure patients until he was finally banned from practice in 1985 as a result of the 1981 case. Leaving Canada, he continued to practise in England, where he had a complica-tion rate five times higher than that of his colleagues (Wente, 2000). Even though British authorities had been warned about Neale, they did not remove him from practice until 2000. Following his removal from practice, he was the subject of more than 100 complaints from women in England and another 60 in Canada.

Betrayal of trust can occur in many professions. In 2003, *The New York Times* reported that Jayson Blair, one of its reporters, had plagiarized and fabricated much of the information in dozens of stories he had written. His "eyewitness" reports from distant states were actually written in his New York apartment. The government was considering laying fraud charges against Blair. More serious were the crimes of Robert Courtney, a Kansas City pharmacist who received 30 years in prison for diluting medicine used for cancer chemotherapy. This meant that hundreds of patients did not receive the required doses of their med-ication. One test showed that a prescription contained only 1 percent of the proper dose of medication. Courtney profited by selling the diluted medicine for the normal price and selling the rest to other customers. Many of the patients died, though it will never be clear whether their cancer would have killed them even if they had received the proper medication.

Investment and Securities Fraud

Many Canadians rely on financial advisors to help them prepare for their retirement. In most cases, this is a good idea, but unfortunately not all advisors can be trusted. For example, Patrick Kinlin recently received a five-year prison sentence after pleading guilty to 54 counts of fraud for defrauding a number of Ontario residents, many of them senior citizens, of $12.5 million. He was very close to these victims, one of whom was his own aunt; he attended family weddings with them and frequently bought them gifts. However, instead of investing his clients' money, he was spending it on his own lavish lifestyle. It is unlikely that any of the victims will receive compensation, as Kinlin has declared bankruptcy (Gadd, 2000). In another case, a Montreal land developer committed suicide prior to his trial on charges of stealing $100 million from two Quebec religious orders of nuns. Jean-Alain Bisaillon used the money, which the nuns had invested to pay for their retirements, to pay for fancy hotels, private jets, jewellery, and a hunting lodge. A lawyer who worked with Bisaillon was sentenced to five years in prison for his role in the case.

Another type of securities fraud is insider trading. Insider trading occurs when someone, usually an owner or employee of the company, receives information about the company that is not available to the general public. It is unlawful to buy or sell stock using this information because this would give the insider an advantage over other investors. In 2000, Glen Harvey, former president of Alberta-based Golden Rule Resources, was sentenced to one year in jail and fined $3.95 million for trading $4 million worth of company stock while withholding assay results showing that the company had almost no gold on one of its properties. When the news was finally released, the company shares dropped by over half. Harper was only the second person to be sentenced to jail in Canada for insider trading (Canadian Press, 2000); successful prosecutions for this offence are rare.

A third type of investment fraud is the "pump and dump." In this scam, stock promoters take a worthless company, invent a story about the company, then tell that story in order to get people to buy the stock. If they are successful, the stock price will rise and the promoters will sell their shares for a profit and other investors will be left only with worthless shares. The story of Bre-X, the most expensive stock fraud in Canadian history, is described in Box 16.3.

Internet Fraud

White-collar criminals have never been slow to adopt new technologies. As the Internet becomes more prevalent and as more people use it to conduct economic transactions, Internet crime will become more common. Some individuals have found it profitable to advertise on Internet auction sites such as eBay, to collect cheques from purchasers, and then to fail to deliver the promised article. Others have used spam e-mail to get people to order products such as Norton Anti-Virus. Some of these spam advertisers deliver a pirated copy of the

Bre-X: The Anatomy of a Stock Fraud

The speculative segment of the Canadian stock market has had a very bad reputation. *Forbes* magazine once called Vancouver the "scam capital of the world" because of the fraudulent stocks that were sold on the Vancouver Stock Exchange. Governments have not been willing to regulate the activities of some of the more aggressive stock promoters. Perhaps, then, it is fitting that Canada was the home of one of the world's largest stock swindles.

According to the autopsy report that marked the end of one of history's largest frauds: "Testimonies of witnesses and existing evidence indicate that victim Michael Antonius [*sic*] de Guzman did not fall by accident but that he deliberately ended his life by dropping himself from the helicopter" (Wells, 1998, 29). Michael de Guzman was the chief geologist of Bre-X, a Canadian gold mining company that claimed to have discovered one of the world's largest gold mines in Indonesia. Shortly after de Guzman's death, assay reports revealed that there was no gold and that the Bre-X property was worthless. Investors collectively lost $6 billion when the market for Bre-X stock collapsed.

Mines have been "salted" for hundreds of years. Owners of a worthless property could attract investors by scattering gold at the mine site or by adding it to rock samples after they had been collected. Despite this long history of fraud and deception, investors around the world fell for the story of Bre-X. Many of these investors lost their life savings, and at least one killed himself after Bre-X stock collapsed.

Bre-X was built on a flimsy structure of lies. However, the greed of those who hoped to make a fortune on the company's stock led many to ignore the risks and warning signs and to believe the story spun by the Bre-X principals and by their supporters in the financial world. Jennifer Wells describes the press release by company president David Walsh, a man whose career as a stock promoter had been, up until Bre-X, a disaster:

The Walsh press release described the prospect as a "deposit," which it was not, the presumed gold resource as "reserves," which they were not, and said that drilling on the property by the previous tenant had yielded numerous intersections of more than two grams of gold per tonne, which was a lie. It also projected the potential of the property at 20 million tonnes at more than 2 grams per tonne of gold, which was absurd. (1998, 122)

In his attempt to raise exploration money, Walsh was essentially announcing that he had a producing gold mine, even though the company had not yet begun to explore the property.

After initial samples from the property showed no signs of gold, somebody, most likely de Guzman, began salting the samples. Not surprisingly, these samples were more successful, and Bre-X officials used the results to increase regularly their estimates of the amount of gold on the property. As the mythical gold reserves increased, the stock began to soar. Shares that once sold for six cents per share were soon worth hundreds of dollars.

In addition to the problems with the mine, Bre-X also had to contend with the corrupt Indonesian government, which eventually took nearly half of the project. Investors did not panic, however, because company officials simply doubled their estimates of the amount of gold. Investors were comfortable that they had not really lost anything even though over half their investment had been assigned to the Indonesians and to a large mining company selected by the Indonesian government (Wells, 1998).

The involvement of this company, Freeport McMoRan, spelled the beginning of the end for Bre-X and its investors. When Freeport carried out its own testing program, assay results showed there was no gold on the Bre-X property. The last nail was hammered into the Bre-X coffin by Graham Farquharson, an independent analyst whose report concluded:

(continued)

The magnitude of the tampering with core samples that we believe has occurred and resulting falsification of assay values at Busang, is of a scale and over a period of time and with a precision that, to our knowledge, is without precedent in the history of mining anywhere in the world. (Wells, 1998, 368)

It is highly unlikely that anyone will ever be punished for the Bre-X fiasco. De Guzman committed suicide and David Walsh died of natural causes in 1998. Lawsuits from unhappy investors will likely continue for a decade, but the company is bankrupt and nobody associated with Bre-X has the resources to replace the billions of dollars lost by investors.

software that cannot be registered or updated; others simply use the customer's credit card number to order other goods. Other entrepreneurial criminals swindle funds through phony investment schemes or sell phony products. An innovative former community college student found another way to use the Internet to commit fraud. Mark Jakob put out a false press release over the Internet about alleged problems at Emulex Corporation. The stock immediately dropped by about 60 percent. Jakob had sold the stock short (a way of "betting" that the stock would go down) and made a profit of over $350 000 when it dropped after his press release. Although the stock eventually regained its value, investors who sold as it was declining lost a total of $110 million. Jakob received a jail sentence of 44 months and was forced to return the money he had made on the transaction (U.S. Securities and Exchange Commission, 2001).

Another Internet fraud victimized Cryptologic, a Canadian firm that develops software for Internet gambling. In 2001, a computer hacker broke into the company's servers and altered Cryptologic's programs for online slot machines and craps games at two Web casinos to ensure that players would always win. As a result, several online gamblers made a total of $1.9 million.

Tax Fraud

The Auditor General of Canada estimated that the amount of money lost to tax cheats in 1997 was $12 billion (Auditor General of Canada, 1999), a sum greater than the budget of the Department of National Defence. The income tax system in Canada is one that requires all taxpayers to report their incomes honestly. However, they clearly do not do so, and there is evidence that in some occupations, the rate of noncompliance is as high as 90 percent (Gabor, 1994).

How do so many people avoid taxes? People who are working at jobs where all their income is paid by an employer have little opportunity to avoid tax because the employer deducts the tax and reports salary information to the government. However, a large segment of the working population have jobs that enable them to hide income. Many of you have likely worked as servers in the restaurant industry or have friends who work in this field. Since much of the income of servers comes from tips, the employer usually does not keep a record of this income, so many servers do not pay tax on this portion of their earnings. Another major source of under-payment is the construction industry. Unscrupulous contractors will offer customers a reduced price if the customer will pay them in cash so they will not have records of income that could be uncovered through an audit. These workers are part of what is called the "underground economy," whose size in 1997 was estimated at $38 billion. Another important part of the underground economy is buying smuggled goods, particularly cigarettes and alcohol, in order to avoid Canadian taxes.

Surveys suggest that many people would be willing to cheat on their taxes and do not strongly disapprove of others who commit this offence (Gabor, 1994). People often feel that tax fraud is justifiable because of their view that taxes are too high and governments are just taking money that rightfully belongs to the taxpayer. Many Canadians were particularly upset when the GST was implemented, and there is some evidence that people in businesses such as contracting turned to the underground economy as a way of avoiding the GST.

Political Corruption

Compared with many other countries, Canada is blessed with honest politicians. However, over the years there have been a number of major scandals that show we are not immune to political corruption. In 1873, just six years after Confederation, the government of John A. Macdonald was forced to resign over allegations of bribery over the selection of a contractor to build and to operate the Canadian Pacific Railway. Perhaps the most corrupt political regime in Canada was that of Maurice Duplessis, who was the premier of Quebec for most of the period between 1936 and 1959. He created a powerful political machine that routinely violated election rules and violated many of Quebecers' basic rights, such as the right to freedom of political expression. In addition, his supporters used inside information to make money on the stock market and accepted financial kickbacks from people who wanted to do business with the Quebec government (Corrado, 1996).

In more recent years, members of two Conservative governments have been accused of widespread political corruption. Raymond Corrado (1996) has documented many of the corrupt activities engaged in by members of Brian Mulroney's government between 1984 and 1993. Mulroney's use of patronage was widespread, as political supporters were given government jobs and contracts, often without any competitions. Although this practice is not illegal, it set the tone for other misconduct. Several of his cabinet ministers and MPs were forced to resign after being charged with bribery and influence peddling and many other Conservative Party officials were prosecuted for similar offences in connection with party fundraising activities. There were also many allegations that the government interfered with the judicial process in an attempt to cover up some of these illegal activities. Dissatisfaction with the ethical standards of Prime Minister Mulroney and his colleagues was one reason why the federal Conservative Party was almost wiped out in the 1993 election.

The Saskatchewan government of Premier Grant Devine had an even worse record for corruption. Many members of Devine's government were convicted of fraud involving their communications expenses. Some of this money, which was supposed to be used for things like stamps, notices to constituents, and advertising, was diverted to numbered companies and used for personal expenses, including holidays. The consequences of this scheme were disastrous for the party. Twenty politicians and party members were charged and many received jail sentences, including Senator Eric Berntson, the former deputy premier. Another committed suicide rather than face charges. The Conservative Party dropped its name and became the Saskatchewan Party to try to erase some of the stigma it had acquired.

Blue-Collar Crime

The concept of white-collar crime also fits many people who wear blue collars. Because of this, some have suggested that the term *occupational crime* may be a better one to use. Many tradespeople defraud the government by doing work "off the books" to avoid provincial sales tax and the GST. Some blue-collar businesses have very bad records of consumer fraud. For example, Robert Sikorsky (1990) documented an appalling degree of misconduct in the automobile repair business. Travelling across Canada, he visited 152 repair shops. Before each visit, he disconnected the idle air control in his car, triggering a warning light on the instrument panel. The repair was obvious and very simple—reinsert the connector. Over half the shops Sikorsky visited performed unnecessary work, overcharged him for work that was done, or lied about the work that had been done. In one case he was presented with an estimate of $570. A similar study was conducted by David Menzies (2000). In this case a mechanic disabled one of the sparkplugs on a car that was otherwise in good working order. In each case Menzies requested and paid for an engine diagnosis that ranged in price from $69 to $103, so there was ample information available to do the repair that should have cost about $20. Menzies visited only four Toronto repair shops, but his study reinforced Sikorsky's findings. Only one shop, a Honda dealership, repaired the problem without recommending any further work. Of the other three, Goodyear estimated the repair would cost $234, Speedy Auto Service estimated $300, and Canadian Tire estimated $648 would be required to return the car to working order.

Employee Fraud

Corporations are also often the victims of crime. A 2001 survey sponsored by the accounting company Ernst & Young found that about 25 percent of the Canadian workforce reported either having committed fraud against their employer or witnessing someone committing fraud during the previous year. Given these numbers, it is not surprising that an earlier survey of employers found that 80 percent reported having been victimized by employee fraud (Canadian Broadcasting Corporation, 2001). Examples of frauds reported to Ernst & Young include taking kickbacks from suppliers in exchange for contracts, creating phony invoices and collecting the money, stealing company property, and stealing cash from the company. Canadian retailers estimate that in 2001 they lost $1 billion to employee theft, was almost as much as their losses from shoplifting and other types of customer theft. To put this figure in perspective, the Retail Council of Canada reported that in 2002, losses due to robberies were $5.6 million and losses from credit card fraud were $204 million (2002). Corporations of all sizes are victimized, but often the toll has been greatest on small companies. For example, there have been reports of many small restaurants going out of business because of theft of money and food by staff. Lisa Leduc interviewed Ottawa restaurant employees about ways of "scamming" their employers. One of the interviewees described some of these methods:

> A manager would bring in his friends, a table of, let's say, eight, and [they would have] wings and beer, and he would go into the cooler where the beer was and grab it when the bartender wouldn't even notice, and [there would be] free dinner and beer for this person's friends.... Also, people weren't punching in drinks and [were] pocketing the money. Cooks [were] taking food home, all staff [were] taking dishes and cutlery. (Quoted in Gabor, 1994, 78–79)

In recent years technology and changes in financial practices have made larger corporations more vulnerable to the actions of individual employees. Earlier in this chapter you read about the illegal trades by Nicholas Leeson that drove Barings Bank into bankruptcy. Since the Leeson case, there have been several others where an individual trader has done significant harm to his company. Toronto's Stephen Duthie lost $182 million through unauthorized trading that was essentially gambling with his company's money. Duthie would have received a huge bonus if his gamble had succeeded in making large profits for his company. However, the trades lost money, and Duthie's employer, Phoenix Trading and Research, was forced to close. These cases have become so common that the term "rogue trader" has been invented to describe the actions of people like Leeson and Duthie.

SUMMARY

- The study of white-collar crime has altered our view of some of the major issues in criminology. Most importantly, it has demonstrated that the relationship between class and crime is more complicated than early criminologists had believed. Our theories of crime must account for the crimes of the privileged as well as for the crimes of the poor.

- Even when they come to the attention of the authorities, white-collar crimes are often not reported in official crime statistics because they are dealt with under quasi-criminal statutes.

- Corporations are instruments that enable people to commit crimes that are vast in scope. The financial and physical costs of corporate crimes are very high.

- The structure of the modern corporation provides managers with a great deal of freedom from control. This has the unintended consequence of encouraging crime. In some industries, high-level managers demand such unreasonably high levels of profit that their subordinates feel pressured to break the law.

- While corporations are subject to legal regulation, the laws that govern them are weak. Even when punishment is administered, it is often so light that it does not act as a deterrent but is an accepted cost of doing business.

- There is some evidence that penalties for white-collar offenders are increasing.
- One of the major contributions to many types of occupational crime is the failure of professional organizations to adequately control the behaviour of their members. Another is the fact that many people do not strongly condemn crimes such as tax fraud.

QUESTIONS FOR CRITICAL THINKING

1. The argument is made in this chapter that the structure of the corporation facilitates crime. What changes could be made in the organization and operation of corporations that would increase corporate responsibility?
2. Why do you think the government has refused to implement laws that would hold corporate officials responsible for their actions in cases like the Westray mine explosion?
3. In previous chapters of this text, you have studied a number of theories of criminal behaviour. Select one of these theories and assess how well it explains white-collar and corporate crime.
4. Some judges give light sentences to white-collar offenders because they feel that these offenders have already suffered from the publicity surrounding their conviction and because their employment prospects have suffered. Do you feel that these are appropriate sentencing criteria?
5. Can you think of three different actions that might be taken by governments and/or corporations to reduce the amount of white-collar and corporate crime in Canada?

NET WORK

There are several websites dealing with fraud. Two of the best are **www.scambusters.com** and **www.fraud.org**.

1. Go to these websites and briefly describe three different types of fraud. How can each of these frauds best be prevented?
2. How have the white-collar criminals who carry out these frauds adapted to new communications technology?

KEY TERMS

anticombines law
criminogenic market structure
executive disengagement
juristic person

monopolistic enterprise
occupational crime
organizational crime
white-collar crime

SUGGESTED READING

Coleman, J.W. (2002). *The Criminal Elite: Understanding White Collar Crime* (5th ed.). New York: St. Martin's Press. Coleman focuses on the "culture of competition" as well as inequities of class and power to explain and suggest remedies for white-collar crime.

Ermann, M. David, and Richard Lundman. (1978). *Corporate and Governmental Deviance: Problems of Organizational Behavior in Contemporary Society*. New York: Oxford University Press. A collection of readings that combines classic papers by James Coleman, Albert Reiss, Edwin Sutherland, Gilbert Geis, Marshall Clinard, and Richard Quinney with more recent research and analysis.

———. (1982). *Corporate Deviance*. New York: Holt, Rinehart and Winston. This book provides a conceptual framework for the study of corporate deviance, a typology of corporate deviance, and a discussion of efforts to control corporate deviance.

Glasbeek, Harry. (2002). *Wealth by Stealth*. Toronto: Between the Lines. Glasbeek provides a lawyer's perspective on corporate crime. The book shows how corporations are criminogenic organizations that protect owners from legal sanctions. It also provides some suggestions for reforming the law to make corporations more accountable.

Goff, Colin, and Charles Reasons. (1978). *Corporate Crime in Canada*. Toronto: Prentice Hall. The first comprehensive treatment of the development of anticombines legislation in Canada, set in the broader context of issues surrounding corporate crime and criminological theory.

Reasons, C., L. Ross, and C. Paterson. (1981). *Assault on the Worker: Occupational Health and Safety in Canada*. Toronto: Butterworths. This book provides a critical analysis of the complicated issues surrounding death and injury in the workplace, with a particular emphasis on the Canadian experience.

Reiman, Jeffrey. (2000). *The Rich Get Richer and the Poor Get Prison: Ideology, Class and Criminal Justice* (6th ed.). Boston: Allyn and Bacon. An inquiry into the failure of the American criminal justice system—its causes, mechanisms, and moral implications. The causes as well as the consequences of white-collar crime are a part of this story.

Shover, Neal, and John Paul Wright. (2001). *Crimes of Privilege: Readings in White-Collar Crime*. New York: Oxford University Press. A reader incorporating some of the classic articles on white-collar crime as well as a number of recent articles that describe some of the famous scandals of the 1990s. The book applies the rational-choice perspective to white-collar crime.

Snider, Laureen. (1993). *Bad Business: Corporate Crime in Canada*. Scarborough: Nelson. A very thorough review of corporate crime theory and research in Canada. The book has a strong focus on issues concerning the social and legal control of corporate crime.

Sutherland, Edwin. (1984). *White Collar Crime: The Uncut Version*. New Haven, Conn.: Yale University Press. The original and still classic study of white-collar crime, including sections of the original manuscript that were originally suppressed.

BIBLIOGRAPHY

Akers, Ronald. (1973). *Deviant Behavior: A Social Learning Approach*. Belmont: Wadsworth.

Asch, P., and J.J. Seneca. (1969). "Is Collusion Profitable?" *Review of Economics and Statistics* 58:1–12.

Auditor General of Canada. (1999). "The Underground Economy Initiative." *Report of the Auditor General of Canada*. Ottawa: Office of the Auditor General of Canada.

Baumhart, Raymond. (1961). "How Ethical Are Businessmen?" *Harvard Business Review* 39:5–176.

Benson, M.L. (1989). "The Influence of Class Position on the Formal and Informal Sanctioning of White-Collar Offenders." *Sociological Quarterly* 30:465–79.

Benson, M.L., W.J. Maakestad, F.T. Cullen, and G. Geis. (1988). "District Attorneys and Corporate Crime: Surveying the Prosecutorial Gatekeepers." *Criminology* 26:505–18.

Box, Steven. (1981). *Deviance, Reality and Society* (2nd ed.). Toronto: Holt, Rinehart and Winston.

Brenner, S.S., and E.A. Molander. (1977). "Is the Ethics of Business Changing?" *Harvard Business Review* 55:57–71.

Butler, Steve. (2002). "Colossal Enron Collapse a Good Thing for the Rest of Us." *Winnipeg Free Press* (February 22), p. A15.

Canadian Broadcasting Corporation. (2001). "Study Shows Employee Fraud Prevalent in Workplace." http://cbc.ca/cgi-bin/templates/print.cgi?/news/2001/01/08/workplace_fraud010108. Accessed January 9, 2001.

Canadian Medical Protective Association. (2002). *2001 Annual Report.* Ottawa: Canadian Medical Protective Association.

Canadian Press. (2000). "CEO Jailed for Insider Trading." *Winnipeg Free Press* (September 19): B8.

Casey, John. (1985). "Corporate Crime and the State: Canada in the 1980s." In Thomas Fleming (ed.), *The New Criminologies in Canada* (pp. 100–101). Toronto: Oxford University Press.

Clinard, Marshall. (1952). *The Black Market: A Study of White Collar Crime.* New York: Holt, Rinehart and Winston.

Clinard, Marshall, and Peter Yeager. (1980). *Corporate Crime.* New York: Free Press.

Coleman, James. (1974). *Power and the Structure of Society.* New York: W.W. Norton.

———. (1985). *The Criminal Elite.* New York: St. Martin's Press.

———. (1987). "Toward an Integrated Theory of White-Collar Crime." *American Journal of Sociology* 93:406–39.

Corrado, Raymond. (1996). "Political Crime in Canada." In Rick Linden (ed.), *Criminology: A Canadian Perspective* (3rd ed.) (pp. 459–93). Toronto: Harcourt Brace.

Cullen, Francis, Martha Larson, and Richard Mathers. (1985). "Having Money and Delinquency Involvement: The Neglect of Power in Delinquency Theory." *Criminal Justice and Behavior* 12(2):171–92.

Cullen, Francis, Bruce Link, and Craig Polanzi. (1982). "The Seriousness of Crime Revisited: Have Attitudes Toward White Collar Crime Changed?" *Criminology* 20:83–102.

Daly, Kathleen. (1989). "Gender and Varieties of White-Collar Crime." *Criminology* 27:769–93.

DeCloet, Derek. (2002). "Deceit Began This Scandalous Rot." *National Post* (July 11).

Drohan, Madelaine. (1995). "Barings Was Warned of Risk." *The Globe and Mail* (March 6): A1.

Ermann, M. David, and Richard Lundman. (1982). *Corporate Deviance.* New York: Holt, Rinehart and Winston.

Fantel, Hans. (1989). "Tape-Copying Decks Improve Their Act." *New York Times* (July 9), p. 27.

Farberman, Harvey. (1975). "A Criminogenic Market Structure: The Automobile Industry." *Sociological Quarterly* 16:438–57.

Gabor, Thomas. (1994). *Everybody Does It.* Toronto: University of Toronto Press.

Gadd, Jane. (2000). "Fraud Artist Jailed for Bilking Seniors." *The Globe and Mail* (January 11): A1, A8.

Geis, Gilbert. (1962). "Toward a Delineation of White-Collar Offenses." *Sociological Inquiry* 32:160–71.

———. (1984). "White Collar Crime and Corporate Crime." In Robert F. Meier (ed.), *Major Forms of Crime.* Beverly Hills: Sage.

Geis, Gilbert, and Robert Meier. (1977). *White Collar Crime.* New York: Wiley.

Glasbeek, Harry, and Eric Tucker. (1994). "Corporate Crime and the Westray Tragedy." *Canadian Dimension* (January–February):11–14.

Goff, Colin, and Charles Reasons. (1978). *Corporate Crime in Canada.* Scarborough: Prentice Hall.

Greenwood, Peter. (1982). *Selective Incapacitation.* Santa Monica, Calif.: Rand.

Hagan, John. (1982). "The Corporate Advantage: The Involvement of Individual and Organizational Victims in the Criminal Justice Process." *Social Forces* 60 (4):993–1022.

Hagan, John, and Celesta Albonetti. (1982). "Race, Class and the Perception of Criminal Injustice in America." *American Journal of Sociology* 88:329–55.

Hagan, John, A.R. Gillis, and John Simpson. (1985). "The Class Structure of Gender and Delinquency: Toward a Power-Control Theory of Common Delinquent Behavior." *American Journal of Sociology* 90:1151–78.

Hagan, John, and Fiona Kay. (1990). "Gender and Delinquency in White-Collar Families: A Power-Control Perspective." *Crime and Delinquency* 36(3):391–407.

Hagan, John, and Ilene Nagel. (1982). "White Collar Crime, White Collar Time: The Sentencing of White Collar Criminals in the Southern District of New York." *American Criminal Law Review* 20(2):259–301.

Hagan, John, and Alberto Palloni. (1983). "The Sentencing of White Collar Offenders Before and After Watergate." Paper presented at the American Sociological Association Meetings, Detroit.

Hagan, John, and Patricia Parker. (1985). "White Collar Crime and Punishment: The Class Structure and Legal Sanctioning of Securities Violations." *American Sociological Review* 50(3):302–16.

Hartung, Frank E. (1950). "White Collar Offenses in the Wholesale Meat Industry in Detroit." *American Journal of Sociology* 56:25–34.

Henderson, Tanya. (2000). "Delivered and Signed." http://abcnews.go.com/onair/2020/2020_000428_zorro_feature.html. Accessed May 12, 2003.

Howlett, Karen. (2002). "The Two Faces of YBM Magnex." *The Globe and Mail* (December 29): B13.

Kadlec, Daniel. (2002). "WorldCon." *Time* (July 8):15–20.

Katz, Jack. (1980). "The Movement against White-Collar Crime." In Egon Bittner and Sheldon Messinger (eds.), *Criminology Review Yearbook*, Vol. 2. Beverly Hills: Sage.

Kranhold, Kathryn, and Mitchell Pacelle. (2002). "Enron Paid Top Managers $681 Million, Even as Stock Slid." *The Wall Street Journal* (June 17): B1, B4.

Law Commission of Canada. (2000). *Restoring Dignity: Responding to Child Abuse in Canadian Institutions.* Ottawa: Law Commission of Canada.

Lewis, Peter. (1989). "Cracking Down on Computer Pirates." *New York Times* (July 9):10.

Mann, Kenneth, Stanton Wheeler, and Austin Sarat. (1980). "Sentencing the White Collar Offender." *American Criminal Law Review* 17(4):479.

McIntyre, Mike. (2001). "Deaths Cost Firms Dearly." *Winnipeg Free Press* (March 3):A1, A4.

Menzies, David. (2000). "Looking for Mr. Goodwrench." *National Post* (September 23).

Mills, C. Wright. (1956). *The Power Elite.* New York: Oxford University Press.

Nagorski, Zygmunt. (1989). "Yes, Socrates, Ethics Can Be Taught." *New York Times* (February 12):F2.

Pontell, Henry N., and Kitty Calavita. (1993). "The Savings and Loan Industry." In Michael Tonry and Albert J. Reiss (eds.), *Beyond the Law: Crime in Complex Organizations* (pp. 203–46). Chicago: University of Chicago Press.

Posner, Richard A. (1980). "Optimal Sentences for White Collar Criminals." *American Criminal Law Review:* 409–18.

Reasons, Charles, and Duncan Chappell. (1985). "Crooked Lawyers: Towards a Political Economy of Deviance in the Profession." In Thomas Fleming (ed.), *The New Criminologies in Canada.* (pp. 206–22). Toronto: Oxford University Press.

Reasons, C., L. Ross, and C. Paterson. (1981). *Assault on the Worker: Occupational Health and Safety in Canada.* Toronto: Butterworths.

Reiss, Albert. (1980). *Data Sources on White Collar Law Breaking.* Washington: National Institute of Justice.

Retail Council of Canada. (2002). *2001 Canadian Retail Security Report.* Toronto: Retail Council of Canada.

Richard, Justice K. Peter. (1997). *The Westray Story: A Predictable Path to Disaster,* Executive Summary. Halifax: Government of Nova Scotia.

Ross, E.A. (1907). *Sin and Society.* Boston: Houghton Mifflin.

Rubin, Sandra. (1999). "RCMP Investigated YBM in Early 1995." *The Financial Post* (January 9).

Schrager, Laura, and James F. Short. (1978). "Toward a Sociology of Organizational Crime." *Social Problems* 25(4):407–19.

Shapiro, Susan P. (1990). "Collaring the Crime, Not the Criminal: Reconsidering the Concept of White-Collar Crime." *American Sociological Review* 55:346–65.

Shearing, Clifford, Susan Addario, and Phillip Stenning. (1985). "Why Organizational Charts Cannot Be Trusted: Rehabilitating Realism in Sociology." Paper presented at a Symposium on Qualitative Research: Ethnographic/Interactionist Perspectives. University of Waterloo (May 15–17).

Sikorsky, Robert. (1990). "Highway Robbery: Canada's Auto Repair Scandal." *Reader's Digest* (February):55–63.

Silver, Jim. (1996). "Review of *Game Misconduct: Alan Eagleson and the Corruption of Hockey.*" *Canadian Dimension* 30(4) (July–August).

Simpson, Sally. (1986). "The Depression of Antitrust: Testing a Multilevel, Longitudinal Model of Profit-Squeeze." *American Sociological Review* 51:859–75.

Sinclair, Judge Murray. (2000). *The Report of the Manitoba Pediatric Surgery Inquest.* Winnipeg: Provincial Court of Manitoba. www.pediatriccardiacinquest.mb.ca. Accessed May 12, 2003.

Smandych, Russell. (1985). "Marxism and the Creation of Law: Re-Examining the Origins of Canadian Anti-Combines Legislation, 1890–1910." In Thomas Fleming (ed.), *The New Criminologies* (pp. 87–99). Toronto: Oxford University Press.

Snider, Laureen. (1979). "Revising the Combines Investigation Act: A Study in Corporate Power." In Paul J. Brantingham and Jack M. Kress (eds.), *Structure, Law and Power: Essays in the Sociology of Law* (pp. 105–19). Beverly Hills: Sage.

———. (1988). "Commercial Crime." In Vincent F. Sacco (ed.), *Conformity and Control in Canadian Society* (pp. 231–83). Scarborough: Prentice Hall.

Stone, Christopher. (1975). *Where the Law Ends: The Social Control of Corporate Behavior.* New York: Harper and Row.

Sutherland, Edwin. (1940). "White Collar Criminality." *American Sociological Review* 5:1–12.

———. (1945). "Is 'White Collar Crime' Crime? *American Sociological Review* 10:132–39.

Swartz, Joel. (1978). "Silent Killers at Work." In M. David Ermann and Richard Lundman (eds.), *Corporate and Governmental Deviance* (pp. 114–28). New York: Oxford University Press.

Tappan, Paul. (1947). "Who Is the Criminal?" *American Sociological Review* 12:96–102.

Tittle, Charles, W.J. Villemez, and Douglas Smith. (1978). "The Myth of Social Class and Criminality: An Empirical Assessment of the Empirical Evidence." *American Sociological Review* 47:505–18.

U.S. Securities and Exchange Commission. (2001). *Securities and Exchange Commission v. Mark S. Jakob.* www.sec.gov/litigation/litreleases/lr17094.htm. Accessed May 12, 2003.

Vancouver Sun. (2000). "Doctor Baited Crab Trap with Human Foot." (August 9): A3.

Weisburd, David, Elin Waring, and Stanton Wheeler. (1990). "Class, Status and the Punishment of White-Collar Criminals." *Law and Social Inquiry* 15(2):223–46.

Wells, Jennifer. (1998). *Fever: The Dark Mystery of the Bre-X Gold Rush.* Toronto: Viking.

Wente, Margaret. (2000). "Dr. Bloody and Mr. Whizzo." *The Globe and Mail* (July 25): A17.

Wheeler, Stanton, and Michael Rothman. (1982). "The Organization as Weapon in White Collar Crime." *Michigan Law Review* 80(7):1403–26.

Wheeler, Stanton, David Weisburd, and Nancy Bode. (1982). "Sentencing the White Collar Offender: Rhetoric and Reality." *American Sociological Review* 47:641–59.

Wolfgang, Marvin. (1972). *Delinquency in a Birth Cohort.* Chicago: University of Chicago Press.

Glossary

acephalous society

Literally "headless," meaning that the society is without any formalized or institutionalized system of power and authority. Collective decisions are made in a variety of ways, including informal community gatherings, that will change according to circumstances.

actus reus

All of the elements contained in the definition of a criminal offence—other than the mental elements (***mens rea***).

administrative record

Collection of information about individual cases, such as statistics concerning what is common among individual cases. An administrative record contains information that can be the basis of statistics, provided that clear procedures are developed for handling the data and generating statistical descriptions.

anomie

A concept developed by Émile Durkheim (1858–1917) to describe an absence of clear societal norms and values. Individuals lack a sense of social regulation: people feel unguided in the choices they have to make. American sociologist Robert Merton (1910–) used the term more narrowly to refer to a situation in which people's goals—what they wanted to achieve—were beyond their means. Their commitment to the goal was so strong that they would adopt deviant means to achieve it.

anticombines law

In order to protect the principle of competition, valued by all liberal, capitalistic societies, laws have been created to prevent and punish corporations that work together to reduce competition.

Antisocial Personality Disorder

A personality disorder that involves disregard for the rights of others, as well as impulsive, irresponsible, and aggressive behaviour.

assumption of discriminating traits

The view that offenders are distinguished from nonoffenders by, for example, their high levels of impulsiveness and aggression.

assumption of offender deficit

The view that offenders who break the law have some psychological deficit that distinguishes them from normal law-abiding citizens.

atavism

Cesare Lombroso (1836–1909) believed that some criminals were born criminals; they were atavistic. This suggested that they were throwbacks to an earlier stage of human evolution and that this limited evolutionary development meant that they were morally inferior. This inferiority could be identified through a series of physical **stigmata**.

attachment

The degree to which an individual has affective ties to other persons. One of the social bonds in Hirschi's theory.

autonomic reactivity

A measurement of the extent to which an individual's physical organism reacts to external stimuli.

belief

The degree to which an individual believes in conventional values, morality, and the legitimacy of law. One of the social bonds in Hirschi's theory.

bourgeois class

The term bourgeois class, or bourgeoisie, was used by Marx to refer to the capitalist or ruling class in modern societies.

Canadian Centre for Justice Statistics

A division of Statistics Canada, formed in 1981, with a mandate to collect national data on crime and justice.

career

In common use, this refers to the sequence of stages through which people in a particular occupational sector move during the course of their employment. It has also been applied to analyzing the various stages of an individual's involvement with criminal activity.

career contingency

An unintented event, process, or situation that occurs by chance.

career criminal

An individual with a long criminal history who organizes many aspects of his or her life around criminality. These individuals tend to commit a large portion of the total amount of crime in a community.

career criminality

Where commission of criminal acts becomes a central aspect of a person's social behaviour. Career criminality is associated with an individual's exposure to deviant subcultures.

Charter—Charter of Rights and Freedoms

Part of the Constitution Act of 1982, the Charter came into effect in April 1982. The Charter provides protection for a wide range of individual rights typical of liberal democracies that until this time were protected by common law rather than constitutional guarantee. As a part of the Constitution of Canada, the Charter cannot be changed without the consent of both Parliament and provincial legislatures. The Charter includes provisions to protect freedoms of speech, conscience, and religion; protection against unreasonable search and seizure; rights to due legal process; and mobility and minority language rights.

Chicago School

Refers to the main themes in research and theoretical ideas that emerged from the University of Chicago in the first half of the 20th century. In criminology, the Chicago School focused on the socio-cultural causes of urban crime and on crime prevention.

class conflict theory

Laws are passed by members of the ruling class in order to maintain their privileged position by keeping the common people under control.

classical conditioning

A basic form of learning whereby a neutral stimulus is paired with another stimulus that naturally elicits a certain response; the neutral stimulus comes to elicit the same response as the stimulus that automatically elicits the response.

Classical School

Considered to be the first formal school of criminology, Classical criminology is associated with 18th- and early 19th-century reforms to the administration of justice and the prison system. Associated with authors such as Cesare Beccaria (1738–1794), Jeremy Bentham (1748–1832), Samuel Romilly (1757–1818), and others, this school brought the emerging philosophy of liberalism and utilitarianism to the justice system, advocating principles of rights, fairness, and due process in place of retribution, arbitrariness, and brutality.

collective solidarity

Similar in meaning to Émile Durkheim's term mechanical solidarity, this refers to a state of social bonding or interdependency that rests on similarity of beliefs and values, shared activities, and ties of kinship and cooperation among members of a community.

commitment

The degree to which an individual pursues conventional goals. One of the social bonds in Hirschi's theory.

common law

The common law tradition found in English Canada derives from feudal England, where it had become the practice for the king to resolve disputes in accordance with local custom. Customs that were recognized throughout the country were called common custom, and decisions made by the king and by subsequent courts set up to settle disputes became known as common law. Common law is considered a source of law. *Also*, the body of judge-made laws that has evolved in areas not covered by legislation.

community psychology

A perspective that analyzes social problems, including crime, as largely a product of organizational and institutional characteristics of society. It is closely related to sociology.

conduct norms

Specifications of proper and appropriate behaviour generally supported and shared by members of a group. Societies contain different groups whose norms of conduct are to some extent divergent.

conflict perspective

Sociological perspectives that focus on the inherent divisions of societies based on social inequality and the way these social divisions give rise to different and competing interests. The central assumption is that social structures and cultural ideas tend to reflect the interests of only some members of society rather than society as a whole. This contrasts with consensus or functionalist perspectives that assume a foundation of common interest among all members of society. Marxism and feminism are examples of conflict perspectives.

consensual crime

Any crime in which the "victim" is a willing participant (drug use, prostitution, etc.).

consensus perspective

Also known as functionalism, the foundation of this perspective is the assumption that societies have an inherent tendency to maintain themselves in a state of relative equilibrium through the mutually adaptive and supportive interaction of their principal institutions. The approach also assumes that effective maintenance of a particular form of society is in the common interest of all its members.

consensus theory

Laws represent the agreement of most of the people in society that certain acts should be prohibited by the criminal law.

conservative approach

An approach that understands "difference" between men and women as biologically based sex differences. Women are viewed as "naturally" inferior or unequal to men.

conspiracy

An agreement by two or more persons to commit a criminal offence.

continuance commitment

Adherence to a criminal or other identity arising from the unattractiveness or unavailability of alternative lifestyles.

conventional crime

Those traditional, illegal behaviours that most people think of as crime. Nonconventional crime may be organized crime, white-collar crime, political crime, etc.

correlate

Any variable that is related to another variable. Age and sex are the two strongest correlates of crime.

correlation

A relationship that exists when two or more variables are associated.

counselling

Procuring, soliciting, or inciting another person to commit a crime.

counting procedure

In any statistical system, there must be consensus on how to count units and data elements. This is not as easy an issue as it appears. For example, if an offender goes on a break-and-enter spree and steals from a half dozen houses, is this to be counted as one incident or six?

crime

Conduct that is prohibited by law and that is subject to a penal sanction (such as imprisonment or a fine).

crime rate

When studying crime, if a researcher wishes to compare the amount of crime over time or between communities of different sizes, it is not enough to just do a gross count of the amount of crime. To get around the problems involved with this, criminologists calculate crime rates (or rates of incarceration, conviction, or recidivism). This is done by dividing the amount of crime by the population size and multiplying by 100 000. This produces the standard rate per 100 000, but occasionally it is useful to calculate a rate per million or some other figure.

criminal attempt
A criminal attempt occurs when an individual does—or omits to do—anything for the purpose of carrying out a previously formed intention to commit a crime. The conduct in question must constitute a substantial step toward the completion of the crime that is intended.

criminal definition
Refers to the fact that crime is socially defined and that this definition will vary from society to society.

criminal identity
This social category is imposed by the community and correctly or incorrectly defines an individual as a particular type of criminal. The identity will pervasively shape his or her social interactions with others. It is similar in concept to **master status**.

criminal law
A body of jurisprudence that includes the definition of various crimes, the specification of various penalties, a set of general principles concerning criminal responsibility, and a series of defences to a criminal charge.

criminal procedure
A body of legislation that specifies the procedures to be followed in the prosecution of a criminal case and defines the nature and scope of the powers of criminal justice officials.

criminogenic market structure
An economic market that is structured in such a way that it tends to produce criminal behaviour.

criminology
The body of knowledge regarding crime as a social phenomenon. It includes the processes of making laws, of breaking laws, and of reacting to the breaking of laws. Its objective is the development of a body of general and verified principles and of other types of knowledge regarding this process of law, crime, and treatment.

cross-sectional investigation
A study, survey, or measurement of a phenomenon or a population taken at one point in time. For example, a census survey is cross-sectional.

cultural construction
A perspective on a subject that is shaped by cultural assumptions rather than having a natural or objective basis. For example, concepts of masculine and feminine suggest how men and women should behave, but very few of these gender differences are determined by biological sex.

cultural explanation
An explanation for crime that is phrased in terms of the culture of the subgroup or the culture of that nation.

culturally prescribed aspiration
A rejection of the notion that aspirations are entirely self-created; rather, they are defined by culture and transmitted by other members of the society.

dark figure of crime
The amount of crime that is unreported or unknown. The total amount of crime in a community consists of crimes that are known or recorded and the dark figure of crime. Criminologists have used differing methods (such as victimization surveys) to try to decrease the amount of unknown or unrecorded crime.

data element
What, specifically, is to be collected. Operational issues may require more detail than the statistical system does. Also, statistical needs may require that operational agencies collect data that they do not need (or do not think that they need) for operational purposes. In any statistical system, there must be detailed agreements on exactly what is to be collected.

deterrence
As used in criminal justice, it refers to crime prevention achieved through the fear of punishment.

developmental crime prevention
An approach to crime prevention that focuses on reducing the number of **motivated offenders** by changing the social environment. Examples include preschool education programs and effective parenting training; also called crime prevention through social development.

differential association
Developed by Edwin Sutherland in the 1930s, this theory argues that crime, like any social behaviour, is learned in association with others. If individuals regularly associate with criminals and are relatively isolated from law-abiding citizens, they are more likely to engage in crime themselves. They learn the specific skills needed to commit crime and the ideas that justify and normalize crime.

diffuseness of roles
A characteristic of relatively simple societies in which people encounter one another in a variety of overlapping roles—there is little occupational specialization and no clear separation of private and public spheres of life. People are continuously reminded of their extensive bonds with others.

dizygotic twins
Commonly known as fraternal twins, they are from two fertilized eggs; consequently they share no more genetic material than any other siblings and may be of different sexes.

drift
A psychological state of weak normative attachment to either deviant or conventional ways.

duress
Duress may be a defence to a criminal charge when the accused was forced to commit a crime as a consequence of threats of death or serious bodily harm made by another person.

ecological fallacy
A research error made when data or information is gathered at a group level (the unemployment rate of various communities or neighbourhoods) and then conclusions are drawn about individuals (the unemployed person). Areas with high unemployment may have high crime rates, but this does not tell us that those crimes are necessarily committed by unemployed persons.

economic determinism
The theory that all the main features of a society, including its cultural ideas and social organization, are chiefly shaped by its form of economic organization.

effective guardianship
An aspect of the **routine activities approach** to understanding crime victimiza-

tion that argues that three key factors are required for crime to happen: a motivated offender, a suitable target, and ineffective guardianship of that target. Effective guardianship would include having locks on bikes, security lights in the backyard, or putting goods in the trunk of the car. Measures like this should reduce the risk of being victimized.

ego

A psychoanalytical term that denotes the rational part of the personality. It mediates between the **id** and the **superego** and is responsible for dealing with reality and making decisions.

electrodermal response

Electrical activity of the sweat glands in the skin. Tests of electrodermal activity have indicated correlation between skin conductivity and tendency to delinquency, aggressiveness, and recidivism.

empirical evidence

Evidence that can be observed through the senses. That is, it can be seen, touched, heard, smelled, tasted, and, to some extent, measured. This is the only form of evidence acceptable to science.

ethnic group

A group of individuals having a distinct subculture in common. An ethnic group differs from a race because it implies that values, norms, behaviour, and language, not necessarily physical appearance, are the important distinguishing characteristics.

ethnomethodology

A sociological theory developed by Harold Garfinkel. Roughly translated, the term means the study of people's practices or methods. The perspective does not see the social world as an objective reality but as something that people must build and rebuild constantly in their thoughts and actions. Ethnomethodologists try to uncover the methods and practices that are used by people as they create the taken-for-granted world.

etiological factor

A factor that encourages or causes a particular outcome. For example, addiction to hard drugs is a factor that can lead people into prostitution or criminal behaviour; being

raised in a violent home is a factor that can lead to violent behaviour or being victimized by violence.

executive disengagement

The custom by which lower-level employees assume that executives are best left uninformed of certain decisions and actions of employees, or the assumption that executives cannot be legally expected to have complete control over their individual staff.

extraversion

A personality characteristic associated with sociability, impulsiveness, and aggression.

false positive

When trying to identify dangerous offenders (or other things as well), researchers often make mistakes. One of these mistakes is known as a false positive. The error is identifying someone as dangerous (and possibly keeping them incarcerated or denying them parole) when they are not dangerous.

feminist approach

Understands "difference" between men and women as structurally produced by inequalities of class, race, and gender that condition and constrain women's lives.

feudalism

A system of economic and social organization found historically in several areas of the world including Japan and other parts of Asia and many countries of eastern and western Europe. In western Europe, feudalism was at its height between about 1000 and 1500. The usual economic foundation of the system was the feudal manor, an agricultural organization that included a central farm owned by the landlord and small land holdings for a class of bonded farm labourers (serfs). The serfs were required to work the central manorial farm and to provide the lord with produce and money payments in return for their right to use the land. The system gradually declined as cities and towns grew and power became centralized in nation-states under monarchies.

free trade zone

A specially designated geographical area within a nation that is exempt from the regulations and taxation normally imposed on business. These zones are intended to facilitate cross-border production and

trade. Examples of these zones are found along the United States–Mexico border, where they are referred to as *maquilladora*.

Gemeinschaft

A German word, translated as "community," used by sociologist Ferdinand Tönnies (1855–1936) to define an **ideal type** or model of a society in which social bonds are personal and direct and there are strong shared values and beliefs. Characteristic of small-scale, localized societies, it is in contrast to *Gesellschaft*, which refers to complex, impersonal societies.

gender-ratio problem

Poses the question of why are there sex differences in rates of arrest and types of criminal activity between men and women.

generalizability problem

Raises the issue of whether mainstream theories of crime—which have largely been developed with men in mind—can be made to "fit" women.

Gesellschaft

A German word, translated as "society-association," used by Ferdinand Tönnies (1855–1936) to refer to an **ideal type** or model of a society in which social bonds are primarily impersonal, instrumental, and narrow. Characteristic of large-scale, complex societies, with a strict division between private and public spheres of life, it contrasts to the community-oriented life of the *Gemeinschaft*.

gross counts of crime

A count of the total amount of crime in a given community, making no distinction between crime categories.

human capital

The talents and capabilities that individuals contribute to the process of production. Companies, governments, and individuals can invest in this capital, just as they can invest in technology and buildings or in finances.

human rights

The minimum conditions required for a person to live a dignified life. Among the rights set out by the Universal Declaration of Human Rights are the right to life, liberty, and security of the person; the right to be free of torture and other forms of cruel and degrading punishment; the right to equality before the law; and the right to the basic necessities of life.

hunting and gathering society

Probably the earliest form of human society that still persists in remote regions of the world, to some extent. These societies have an economic base that rests on the use of the naturally occurring animal and plant resources of the environment. They do not practise agriculture or raise animals.

id

A psychoanalytical term that denotes the most inaccessible and primitive part of the mind. It is a reservoir of biological urges that strive continually for gratification. The **ego** mediates between the id and the **superego**.

ideal type

An abstract model of a classic, pure form of social phenomenon. It is a model concept and does not necessarily exist in exact form in reality. An example is Ferdinand Tönnies's (1855–1936) dichotomy **Gemeinschaft** and **Gesellschaft**.

ideology

A linked set of ideas and beliefs that act to uphold and justify an existing or desired situation in society. Ideologies offer explanations and justifications of features of society such as the distribution of wealth, status, and power.

incapacitation

The policy of locking offenders in jail to prevent them from repeating their crimes.

inchoate crime

A criminal offence that is committed when the accused person seeks to bring about the commission of a particular crime but is not successful in doing so. The three inchoate offences in the Criminal Code are attempt, conspiracy, and counselling.

incidence

Incidence tells us the frequency of new occurrences of some event during a particular time period. For example, there were 554 criminal homicides in Canada in 2001.

independent variable

A presumed cause of a dependent variable. If unemployment is thought to cause crime rates to increase, unemployment is the independent variable, and crime rates the dependent variable.

individual pathology

A term used to refer to biological or psychological explanations of criminal or deviant behaviour by individuals. The assumption is that the deviant behaviour of individuals can be at least partly explained by some physical or psychological trait that makes them different from normal law-abiding citizens.

individualistic

A theory that focuses on explaining the behaviour of individuals and using factors or features of the individual in explaining this behaviour.

instrumentalist Marxism

A perspective that stresses the intimate connection between the state, its organization, and personnel and the capitalist class as the key influence on the state's role in society.

intoxication

Intoxication caused by alcohol and/or other drugs may be a defence if it prevents the accused from forming the intent required for a specific intent offence, such as murder or robbery.

involvement

The degree to which an individual is active in conventional activities. One of the social bonds in Hirschi's theory.

juristic person

The legal concept that corporations are liable to the same laws as natural persons. Treating corporations as individuals raises practical difficulties for legal enforcement and punishment.

labelling

According to labelling theory, deviance is not a quality of the act but of the label that others attach to the act. This raises the question of who applies the label and who is labelled. The application of a label and the response of others to the label may result in a person becoming committed to a deviant identity.

legal definition of crime

Crime is an act that violates the criminal law and is punishable with jail terms, fines, and other sanctions.

levels of aggregation

This refers to how data are to be combined. Do we want city-level, provincial, or national data? Among other things, data aggregation requires common rules, allowing confidence in the **reliability** and **validity** of the measures used.

liberal approach

Distinguishes sex (biological) from gender (cultural) and sees differences between men and women as resulting from gender roles and socialization patterns.

lifestyle/exposure theory

A theory of victimization that acknowledges that not everyone has the same lifestyle and that some lifestyles expose people to more risks than others do. If you go to bed early, you are less at risk of robbery or assault than if you like to visit the bars several nights a week. Similar to **routine activities approach**.

longitudinal study

This measures relationships between variables over a period of time. For example, one might follow a group of males from birth to age 30 to measure their involvement with the criminal justice system over time.

Mafia

A term originally used to identify a specific Sicilian crime group, it is now commonly used to identify any ethnic or regionally based crime organization.

master status

A status that overrides all others in perceived importance. Whatever other personal or social qualities individuals possess, they are judged primarily by this one attribute. Criminal is an example of a master status that determines the community's identification of an individual.

maturational reform

The observation that involvement in crime tends to decrease as people age.

mens rea

Criminal intent. The mental elements (other than voluntariness) contained in the definition of a criminal offence.

methodology

The study or critique of methods. There are many philosophical issues about the use of a particular method or about positivism or measurement itself.

middle-class measuring rod

A phrase suggesting that children and young people from the lower class often find themselves in situations in which they are measured against middle-class standards.

mistake of fact

Mistake of fact may be a defence where the accused person acts under the influence of an honest mistake in relation to any of the elements of the *actus reus* of the offence charged.

mode of production

The dominant form of social and technical organization of economic production in a society. Historically, a variety of modes of production can be distinguished based on both technology and the structure of social relationships.

modelling

A form of learning that occurs as a result of watching and imitating others.

monopolistic enterprise

Any corporation that controls all, or the majority, of the market for a particular product or service.

monozygotic twins

Commonly known as identical twins, they are from a single egg that has divided after fertilization to create two embryos; consequently, they share exactly the same genetic material and are of the same sex.

moral development theory

Refers generally to theories of individual psychology that investigate how moral reasoning emerges in the individual and develops as the individual matures.

moral entrepreneur

Someone who is engaged in the process of defining new rules and laws or who advocates stricter enforcement of existing laws. Often such entrepreneurs will have some financial or organizational interest in particular definitions or applications of law.

moral rhetoric

In the study of crime, this is the set of claims and assertions that deviants make to justify their deviant behaviour. The moral rhetoric of a group is an important component of socialization into a deviant identity.

motivated offender

A person who is ready to engage in some type of crime.

mutual conversion

A phrase suggesting that conversion to deviance (and perhaps to other lifestyles) is not a solitary activity but is achieved through a process of interaction with others.

NCRMD

The special verdict of "not criminally responsible on account of mental disorder." In order to be found NCRMD, it must be proved on the balance of probabilities that, because of mental disorder, the accused lacked the capacity to appreciate the nature and quality of the act or omission in question or of knowing that it would be considered morally wrong by the average Canadian.

necessity

Necessity may be a defence to a criminal charge when the accused person commits the lesser evil of a crime in order to avoid the occurrence of a greater evil.

norms

Established rules of behaviour or standards of conduct.

objective *mens rea*

The *mens rea* elements of a criminal offence are considered to be objective if they are based on a determination of whether a reasonable person, in the same circumstances and with the same knowledge as the accused, would have appreciated the risk involved in the accused's conduct and would have taken steps to avoid the commission of the *actus reus* elements of the crime in question.

occupational crime

Refers to individuals who violate the law in the course of practising a legitimate occupation.

operant conditioning

The basic process by which an individual's behaviour is shaped by reinforcement or by punishment.

operationally defined

To define some concept of study in such a way that it can be observed and measured. For example, well-being might be measured by asking people to rate their overall satisfaction with their lifestyle, or antisocial behaviour might be measured by frequency of arrest or criminal prosecution.

opportunity structure

Opportunity is shaped by the way the society or an institution is organized or structured.

organizational crime

White-collar crime committed with the support and encouragement of a formal organization and intended at least in part to advance the goals of that organization.

over-representation

A group that has a number of its members in some condition in greater numbers than their population would suggest. If a group makes up 20 percent of the population, then a researcher might predict, other things being equal, that they would represent 20 percent of offenders.

paramount chieftainship

A political system similar to a kingdom that brings together a number of partly autonomous villages or communities under the hierarchical rule of a grand chief.

party to a crime

The Criminal Code specifies that one is a party to—and liable to conviction of—a criminal offence if one actually commits it; aids and/or abets it; becomes a party to it by virtue of having formed a common intention with others to commit a crime; or counsels the commission of an offence that is actually committed by another person.

patriarchy

A system of male domination that includes both a structure and an ideology that privileges men over women. For example, men exercise control over women both overtly by objectifying women's bodies in pornography and covertly in the form of a "monogamous heterosexuality" that legitimates male control over women and children and reinforces the ideology that women are dependent on men for both their economic and sexual needs.

population

All members of a given class or set. For example, adult Canadians, teenagers, Canadian inmates, or criminal offenders can each be thought of as populations. Populations are difficult to study because we cannot find all the members (heroin addicts) or because of the expense (teenagers). Social scientists avoid this problem by gathering a **sample** from the population and then generalizing from the sample to the population.

Positive School

The first scientific school consisting of the Italian criminologists Cesare Lombroso (1836–1909), Raffaelo Garofalo (1852–1934), and Enrico Ferri (1856–1929). They supported the assumptions of positivism and argued that criminality is determined—the effect in a cause–effect sequence—and that the mandate of criminology should be to search for these causes. It was believed that with the exception of those deemed to be born criminals, the discovery of the causes of crime would allow for effective treatment.

primary deviation

Where the individual commits deviant acts but does not adopt a primary self-identity as a deviant.

provocation

Provocation may be a partial defence to a charge of murder (if successful, it reduces the offence from murder to manslaughter). The required elements of provocation are (i) that the accused responded to a wrongful act or insult that was of such a nature that an ordinary person would have been likely to lose the power of self-control and (ii) that the accused acted "on the sudden and before there was time for his (or her) passion to cool."

psychopath

Psychopathy is typically classified under personality disorder. Psychopaths tend to be lacking in conscience, are unable to form emotional attachments (even to friends or family), are quite impulsive, and are only self-interested.

radical feminism

A perspective that sees women's social situation as chiefly shaped by male dominance (i.e., patriarchy) rather than by the capitalist class structure of society. Within criminology, radical feminists focus on documenting and analyzing ways in which the content of law and practices of law enforcement have served to entrench and strengthen male dominance in society.

reaction formation

In Freudian terms, it is an adaptation in which the **ego** unconsciously develops attitudes and interests the direct opposite of those in the **id** striving for expression. In Albert Cohen's theory, lower-class children who cannot succeed when measured by middle-class criteria collectively reverse these values and obtain status by doing the opposite.

recidivism

Where an individual commits new criminal offences after having been sentenced for previous crimes. Although difficult to measure, the rate of recidivism is a basic tool in evaluating the effectiveness of various corrections programs.

regulatory offences

Regulatory offences arise under legislation (either federal, provincial, or territorial) that regulates inherently legitimate activities connected with trade, commerce, and industry or with everyday living (driving, fishing, etc.). These offences are not considered to be serious in nature and usually carry only a relatively minor penalty upon conviction.

relative deprivation

Relative deprivation and absolute deprivation are often contrasted. Absolute deprivation refers to the inability to sustain oneself physically and materially. However, in relative terms, deprivation is not judged against some absolute standard of sustainability but against deprivation in relation to others around you. You may have sufficient money to meet your needs and even meet them adequately, but you may feel relatively deprived because others around you have more.

reliability

Identifies one of the standards (another being **validity**) against which the tools used to measure concepts are judged. Reliability refers to consistency of results over time. If a bathroom scale is used to measure the concept of weight, one must ask: Is this tool (the bathroom scale) reliable? Does it provide consistent results? Notice that the bathroom scale or any other measure may be reliable and yet be inaccurate.

restorative justice

A system of justice that tries to reconcile victims and offenders and to reintegrate offenders into their communities.

role convergence

One explanation for the rising crime rate among women has been that their roles have become similar to (converged with) those of men.

routine activities approach

Similar to the **lifestyle/exposure theory**, this approach assumes that crimes are the expected outcomes of routine activities and changing social patterns. For example, those with more property can expect to be the victims of property crime more often than those with less property. Young people who like to hang out in the evenings are more likely to be victims than are those who go to organized activities or remain at home to study.

sample

A group of elements (people, offenders, inmates) selected in a systematic manner from the population of interest.

secondary deviation

Occurs when an individual accepts the label of deviant. This results in the adoption of a deviant self-identity that confirms and stabilizes the deviant lifestyle.

selective incapacitation

A philosophy of incarceration that argues that some offenders might have to be incarcerated not for what they have done, but to prevent future harm to the community. This depends on the community's ability to identify those who might re-offend. Some also argue that it is unfair to punish people for what they might do rather than for what they have done. Selective incapacitation is provided for under dangerous offender legislation.

self-defence

The Criminal Code permits the use of force in self-defence in certain circumstances where the individual concerned becomes the object of an unlawful assault. Where the individual acted in self-defence without intending to inflict death or grievous bodily harm on the assailant, it must be shown that no more force was used than was necessary in the circumstances. Where the individual concerned inflicted death or grievous bodily harm, then it must be shown that he or she acted under a reasonable apprehension of death or grievous bodily harm and under a reasonable belief that he or she had no alternative but to employ lethal force.

self-degrading commitment

Commitment leading to a poorer opinion of oneself.

self-enhancing commitment

Commitment leading to a better opinion of oneself.

self-report study

A method for measuring crime involving the distribution of a detailed questionnaire to a sample of people, asking them whether they have committed a crime in a particular period of time. This has been a good method for criminologists to determine the social characteristics of offenders.

seriousness rule

If there are multiple crimes committed in one incident, only the most serious crime is counted.

sexism

Attributing to women socially undesirable characteristics that are assumed to be intrinsic characteristics of that sex.

situational crime prevention

Premised on the belief that most crime is opportunistic rather than being the outcome of those driven to commit a crime no matter what the circumstances. This form of prevention attempts to reduce the opportunities for crime rather than just relying on the police after the crime has occurred. An example is

the exact fare system used on buses, which removes the opportunity to rob the driver.

social bond

The degree to which an individual has ties to his or her society. In Hirschi's theory, social bonds include **attachment**, **commitment**, **involvement**, and **belief**.

social control theory

The theory that people do not become criminal because they do not want to jeopardize their bonds to conventional society.

social disorganization theory

The theory that crime and other deviant behaviour is most likely to occur where social institutions are not able to direct and control groups of individuals.

social intervention program

Activity by governments, social agencies, and volunteers designed to change and improve the social situation of individuals, groups, and communities; strengthen social bonds; and encourage internalization of social control.

social structure

The patterned and relatively stable arrangement of roles and statuses found within societies and social institutions. The idea of social structure points out the way in which societies, and institutions within them, exhibit predictable patterns of organization, activity, and social interaction.

socialist feminism

A perspective that views women's social situation as being shaped by both patriarchal gender relations and the class structure of capitalism.

socialization

The interactive process whereby individuals come to learn and internalize the culture of their society or group.

sovereignty

The authority possessed by the governing individual or institution of a society. Sovereign authority is distinct in that it is unrestricted by legal regulation since the sovereign authority is itself the source of all law.

state

As defined by Max Weber (1864–1920), the state is an institution that claims the exclusive right to the legitimate exercise of force in a given territory through the use of police to enforce laws or the army to maintain civil stability. While there have been stateless societies, most complex societies have state systems of formal government and administrative bureaucracies.

Statistical School

Associated with early social scientists such as Adolphe Quetelet (1795–1874) and André-Michel Guerry (1802–1866), who began to explore the structure of emerging European societies with the assistance of statistical methods. While their early use of statistics is important, they also developed a **structural explanation** of crime and other social problems.

statistically significant

When researchers study differences within or between groups, they need a technique to determine if these differences would have occurred by chance. Various statistical techniques can determine this, and if it is unlikely that the differences could have occurred by chance, it is called a statistically significant difference. Usually, a .05 level of significance is used (there are five chances of 100 trials that this difference would occur by chance), but other levels can be used.

stigma

As used by Erving Goffman (1922–1982), a characteristic of an individual that is given a negative evaluation by others and thus distorts and discredits the public identity of the person. For example, a prison record may become a stigmatized attribute. The stigma may lead to the adoption of a self-identity that incorporates the negative social evaluation.

stigmata

Physical signs of some special moral position. Cesare Lombroso (1836–1909) used the term to refer to physical signs of the state of **atavism** (a morally and evolutionary inferior person).

strain theory

The proposition that people feel strain when they are exposed to cultural goals that they are unable to obtain because they do not have access to culturally approved means of achieving those goals.

stratification

A social division of individuals into various hierarchies of wealth, status, and power. There is disagreement about how to describe stratification systems; some sociologists favour the concept of class and others discuss status differentiations.

structural explanation

An explanation for crime that focuses on **social structure** (usually this refers to inequality, poverty, or power differentials). For example, the patriarchal structure of the family might help explain the abuse of women and children within the family.

structuralist Marxism

The view that the state in a capitalist society is set in a context in which its actions will be determined by the necessities of the reproduction and accumulation of capital. The state serves the social order, or structure, within which it is located.

subculture

A group of people who share a distinctive set of cultural beliefs and behaviours that differs in some significant way from that of the larger society.

subjective *mens rea*

The ***mens rea*** elements of a criminal offence are considered to be subjective if they are based on a determination of "what actually went on in the accused person's mind." The forms of subjective *mens rea* are intention and knowledge; recklessness; and wilful blindness.

superego

A psychoanalytical term that denotes the ethical and moral dimensions of personality; an individual's conscience. The **ego** mediates between the superego and the **id**.

surplus

The excess of production over the human and material resources used up in the process of production. In simple societies, there was often little if any surplus since the production from hunting and gathering was entirely used up in subsistence. With the

development of animal herding and settled agriculture, production exceeds immediate subsistence needs, and social inequality and class division become possible when particular individuals or groups are able to take control of this surplus.

symbolic communications

All communication with others is symbolic and involves the use of language, sound, bodily gesture, and expression.

symbolic interactionism

A sociological perspective that focuses on the dynamics of how people interpret social situations and negotiate their meaning with others. It differs from more structurally focused perspectives in seeing individuals as actively creating the social world rather than just acting within the constraints of culture and **social structure**.

target suitability

Because of their vulnerability, some potential crime targets are more attractive than others. A home that is unlit, has shrubs blocking a view of the front door, and has no alarm system will be seen as a more suitable target than a well-protected home.

theory

All sciences use theory as a tool to explain. It is useful to think of theory as a conceptual model of some aspect of life. We may have a theory of mate selection, of the emergence of capitalist societies, of criminal behaviour, or of the content of dreams. In each case, the theory consists of a set of concepts and their nominal definition or assertions about the relationships between these concepts, assumptions, and knowledge claims.

token economy

A behaviour therapy procedure based on operant learning principles. Individuals are rewarded (reinforced) for positive or appropriate behaviour and are disciplined (punished) for negative or inappropriate behaviour.

transnational corporation

A corporation that has sales and production in many different nations. As a result of their multinational reach, these corporations are often thought to be beyond the political control of any individual nation-states.

Triads

These Chinese groups came into existence in the 17th century as resistance fighters against the Manchu invaders. They eventually developed into crime groups.

tribalism

Where social bonds are based primarily on people's real or assumed common descent from an ancestor or group of ancestors, and this shared identification distinguishes the group from outsiders. In such societies, all social relationships tend to be direct and quasi-familial.

"true crime"

A "true crime" occurs when an individual engages in conduct that is not only prohibited but also constitutes a serious breach of community values: as such, it is perceived by Canadians as being inherently wrong and deserving of punishment. Only the Parliament of Canada, using its criminal law power under the Constitution Act, 1867, may enact a "true crime."

Tudor

Refers to the period of English history from 1485 to 1603, when the nation's monarchs were descended from Owen Tudor and Catherine (1401–1437), widow of Henry V.

Uniform Crime Reports (UCR)

Since 1961, Canada has had a Uniform Crime Reporting system developed by Statistics Canada and the Canadian Association of Chiefs of Police. This system is designed to provide a measure of reliability for crime statistics through providing police agencies with a standardized set of procedures for collecting and reporting crime information.

validity

The extent to which a tool or instrument (questionnaire, experiment) actually measures the concept the researcher claims to be interested in and not something else. For example, measuring people's feet to learn about the concept of intelligence, on the surface at least, does not seem valid.

value

A collective idea about what is right or wrong, good or bad, and desirable or undesirable in a particular culture.

victimization survey

A survey of a random **sample** of the population in which people are asked to recall and describe their own experience of being a victim of crime.

violent predator

An offender who has a very high rate of offending for serious and violent crimes.

Volstead Act

Passed by the United States Congress on October 28, 1919, this legislation prohibited the manufacture and sale of alcohol in the United States. Since a ready market existed for this prohibited good, organized crime in America gained a ready foothold.

white-collar crime

Crime that is committed by middle- and upper-class people in the course of their legitimate business activities. This concept has had changing definitions. As used by Edwin Sutherland in 1940, the concept referred to corporate behaviour that caused social harm and for which there was a legal sanction. This sanction need not be criminal; it could be regulatory. Since that time, criminologists have also included the illegal actions of executives or employees who commit crimes against their employer or use organizational resources to gain personal benefit.

Index